MW00770447

ALSO BY KEVIN BAKER

Nonfiction

The Fall of a Great American City: New York and the Urban Crisis of Affluence

America the Ingenious: How a Nation of Dreamers, Immigrants, and Tinkerers Changed the World

Becoming Mr. October, by Reggie Jackson, as told to Kevin Baker

America: The Story of Us

The American Century, by Harold Evans, with Gail Buckland and Kevin Baker

Fiction

The Big Crowd

Luna Park, with Danijel Zezelj

Strivers Row

Paradise Alley

Dreamland

Sometimes You See It Coming

THE NEW YORK GAME

THE NEW YORK GAME

Baseball and the Rise of a New City

KEVIN BAKER

ALFRED A. KNOPF
New York
2024

THIS IS A BORZOI BOOK
PUBLISHED BY ALFRED A. KNOPF

www.aaknopf.com

Knopf, Borzoi Books, and the colophon are registered trademarks of Penguin Random House LLC.

Library of Congress Cataloging-in-Publication Data
Names: Baker, Kevin, 1958– author.
Title: The New York game : baseball and the rise of a new city / Kevin Baker.
Description: First edition. | New York : Alfred A. Knopf, [2024] |
Includes bibliographical references and index.
Identifiers: LCCN 2023028054 (print) | LCCN 2023028055 (ebook) |
ISBN 9780375421839 (hardcover) | ISBN 9780593537893 (ebook)
Subjects: LCSH: Baseball—New York (State)—New York—History—20th century. | Baseball players—New York (State)—New York—History—20th century. | New York (N.Y.)—History—20th century. | New York (N.Y.)—Social life and customs—20th century.
Classification: LCC GV875.N72 B35 2024 (print) | LCC GV875.N72 (ebook) |
DDC 796.35709747—dc23/eng/20230828
LC record available at https://lccn.loc.gov/2023028054
LC ebook record available at https://lccn.loc.gov/2023028055

Front-of-jacket image: Babe Ruth in exhibition Yankee-Dodger game at Ebbets Field, April 10, 1927. Bettmann/Getty Images
Jacket design by John Gall

Manufactured in the United States of America
Published March 5, 2024
Reprinted Three Times
Fifth Printing, December 2024

To my father, Kenneth Baker, with whom I always got along best at the ballpark, and to my uncle Bruce Baker, who took me to see Willie Mays. Both fans of the old breed, Giants rooters from the Irish Bronx.

To my wife, Ellen Abrams, who wanted to see this book finished even more than I did. With love.

And to Abadi Leynse, who loves the game today and who I hope finds as much joy and gratification in it as I have.

Contents

PART ONE
Origins

PART TWO
The Inside Game, 1901–1919

PART THREE
The Babe in Nighttown, 1920–1929

PART FOUR
The Virtuous City: New York in the Great Depression, 1929–1939

PART FIVE
Singing in the Dark: The City in Time of War, 1939–1945

PART ONE

ORIGINS

Some boy too far from town to learn baseball,
Whose only play was what he found himself.

—Robert Frost, "Birches"

1

City Game

It was always a city game, baseball.

For all the efforts to slap a pastoral gloss on the sport, for all the attempts to make it about little boys playing in a cow pasture, only someone unfamiliar with the isolation of American farm life could truly believe that baseball came of age in the country. One of the countless names of the game gives it away. It was called town ball because it was played on those days when everybody came into town for church or market, because town was the only place where enough men or boys could be assembled for a full nine.

What we think of as baseball today is really an urban game. More precisely, it is "the New York game." That's what modern baseball was first called, and where it was first played. New York is where its rules were perfected, and where we first kept score. New York was where the curveball was devised, and the bunt, and the stolen base, and where the home run came into its own. New York was where admission was first charged to see a game, and where the very first all-star game was played, and the first "world championship."

It was in New York, too, where the game's color line was finally broken, and where the reserve clause was made law, and where a players' league was conceived, and died, and where the first modern free agent was signed. It was here that the sport's—or *any* sport's—first true superstar emerged, and where the first true baseball stadiums were built. Where sportswriting came into its own, where the first great radio broadcasters plied their trade, and where the first game was televised. It was in New York that the only perfect game in World Series history was pitched, where an expansion team won a World Series for the first time, where fourteen World Series were played exclusively within the city limits (fifteen, if you count the nineteenth century), and where the World Series was fixed by gamblers.

New York was where the Babe and the Iron Horse, and Joltin' Joe and the Say Hey Kid, and the Mick, and the Duke, and the Big Chief and the Big Six and the Big Cat, and Wee Willie and the Little Napoleon and Pee Wee, and Doctor K and Tom Terrific and Happy Jack and Twinkletoes, and Mr. October and Mr. November, and Sal the Barber and the Curveless Wonder, and Ducky-Wucky and King Kong, and the Lively Turtle and Death to Flying Things, and Poosh 'Em Up and Old Reliable and Marvelous Marvin, and the Fordham Flash and Grandma, and the Mahatma, and Mex and Donnie Baseball, and the Polar Bear and the Judge, and the Chairman of the Board, all came to play the game.

Baseball is a game that grew up inextricably linked to the pace, and the customs, and the demands of New York. It was shaped by the challenges and the possibilities the city had to offer, by its inventiveness and its ambitions, its grandiosity and its corruption. For the last two centuries, the game's trajectory has followed the city's many rises and declines, its booms and its busts, its follies and its tragedies.

This is the story of that city and its game. It is, as well, a fan's story. It is not devoid of statistics, for the numbers are as inextricably wrapped up with baseball as they are with all of American life, but those looking for another exercise in sabermetrics should look elsewhere. It is not a sociological study, other than in what I have learned and observed from spending my whole adult life in the city and watching baseball since I was eight years old. It is a story of the games and the heroes, though any attempt to tell the tale of all the great games and the great heroes would overwhelm any book, as it nearly overwhelmed this one. It is, first and foremost, I would hope, the story of all those who lived the game and the city. Of those who tried and fell short, who had bad luck, who had bad intentions or bad habits. Of those who contributed something important, however minor it might have seemed at the time. Of those who wrote of the game and described it, their words devoured by boys in their bedrooms during the winter months, or fluttering out over the airwaves on a sweltering summer night, the sound of the crowd rising and falling behind their voices like the swell and recession of the waves on a beach.

Not long ago, there was a heated dispute between Bill James, the iconoclastic writer and researcher whose work has done so much to change how we look at the game, and the major-league players' union over just whom the game belonged to: those who watch it or those who play it at the very highest level. It was a silly debate because the answer is both, of course. Without players and fans there could no more be baseball than there could be theater without actors or theatergoers. The game endures, this ineffable, silly thing, to which too much attention is paid; this uneasy, wobbly, wonderful contraption which is always threatening to blow itself up, and which in this manner is never more like the city from whence it sprang.

"The history of baseball is a lie from beginning to end, from its creation myth to its rosy models of commerce, community, and fair play," the irrepressible John Thorn tells us in *Baseball in the Garden of Eden.* The lie begins with where and how it was founded.

It is not the intention here to decide the eternal debate over exactly when and where the very first contest involving a bat and a ball took place. Claimants range from Prague to Pittsfield, and just about every burg in between. As David Block makes clear in *Baseball Before We Knew It,* mankind was probably playing some sort of bat-and-ball game from the moment we first came off the savanna.

Ancient hieroglyphics depict Egyptians with bats playing at something called *seker-hemat* around 2500 BC. Berbers in the 1930s were observed playing *ta kurt om el mahag,* or "the ball of the pilgrim's mother"—a game one historian theorized was brought to North Africa in the fifth century AD by the Vandals, who were credited in turn with inventing the ancient northern European game of "longball." Medieval Normans played *grande thèque,* while their French cousins played *la balle empoisonée,* the Germans had *Schlagball,* and the Finns played *pesapällo.*

Countless other bat-and-ball games evolved under any number of different rules and different names in England. There was hand-in and hand-out, and wicket and cricket, and the notorious rounders. There was prisoner's base, or just "base"; there was tip-cat and one-old-cat; there was feeder, and squares, and northern spell; there was stool-ball, and stobball or stow-ball, and trap ball, and tut-ball;

and there was goal ball, barn ball, sting ball, soak ball, stickball, and burn ball; and round-ball and town ball, and finally—baseball (or base-ball, or base ball).

The whole welter of English and continental games followed the colonists over to America. Hired Polish laborers were playing "long ball" in the Jamestown settlement by 1609. On Christmas Day 1621, Governor William Bradford of Plymouth Colony was enraged to find some of his fellow Pilgrims "frolicking in ye street, at play openly; some at pitching ye barr, some at stoole ball and shuch-like sport." At Valley Forge, George Washington was recorded as having taken part in a game of "wicket," while Lewis and Clark tried to teach a form of "base" to the Nez Perce, and small boys wrote later of watching a grown Abe Lincoln join in their games of town ball: "how long were his strides, and how his coat-tails stuck out behind, and how we tried to hit him with the ball, as he ran the bases. He entered into the spirit of play as completely as any of us, and we invariably hailed his coming with delight."

The one thing that is clear is that Abner Doubleday had nothing to do with it. This was widely acknowledged even at the time the myth was first propagated, by the Special Base Ball Commission, handpicked by Albert Spalding in 1905. Spalding, one of the game's earliest stars turned team owner and sporting goods magnate, was eager to refute the thesis of his friend Henry Chadwick that baseball had evolved from the English girls' game of rounders. Certain that such antecedents would not serve for the pastime of a young, proud nation just emerging on the world stage, Spalding's commission seized instead upon the weakest reed imaginable. This was a letter sent by an aged western crank named Abner Graves who would murder his wife in a fit of senile paranoia a few years later. Graves swore that he had seen Doubleday lay out the whole game one afternoon in 1839 along the banks of the Glimmerglass, in Cooperstown, New York, and that was good enough for the chairman of Spalding's commission, A. G. Mills.

Abner Doubleday was the Forrest Gump of the nineteenth century, a soldier, mystic, and bibliophile with an uncanny ability for being on hand when anything of interest was going on. The first shot of the Civil War, a Confederate cannon blast at Fort Sumter, "penetrated the masonry and burst very near my head," he later recalled, and in turn he "aimed the first gun on our side in reply to the attack." He would rise to the rank of major general, sustain two serious wounds, hold the Union line on the first day of Gettysburg, and take the train with President Lincoln back there a few months later, when the president gave his Gettysburg Address. He read Sanskrit, corresponded with Ralph Waldo Emerson, commanded an all-Black regiment of troops, attended séances at the White House with Mary Todd Lincoln, obtained the first charter for San Francisco's cable cars, and served as president of Madame Blavatsky's Theosophical Society. But he did *not* invent baseball.

Nobody really thought he did, even on Spalding's commission. A. G. Mills had been friends with Doubleday for twenty years, including a period *when Mills was president of the National League.* A fellow Civil War officer, Mills had arranged Doubleday's funeral and his burial at Arlington Cemetery. Yet for as long and as well as he knew him, Mills admitted, he never heard his friend so much as mention baseball. In a brief autobiographical sketch, Doubleday himself wrote, "In my outdoor sports, I was addicted to"—drumroll, please—"topographical work."

Just why anyone took Graves's claim seriously in the first place is something of a mystery. John Thorn speculates that this might have come about thanks to feuding factions of Theosophists, who for a time included Spalding. If true, it's hilarious. Theosophy was an early gobbledygook of new age religion, occultism, and spiritualism. It's as if a group of feuding Scientologists hatched a plot to have L. Ron Hubbard replace Dr. Naismith as the inventor of basketball.

Confronted by reporters years later, Mills *fumfahed* that his commission had only concluded "that the first baseball diamond was laid out in Cooperstown." This was one lie on top of another. In the same answer, though, Mills revealed another reason for his commission's determined gullibility. That is, the need to move the national game out of the clutches of the dirty, immigrant city: "I submit to you gentlemen, that if our search had been for a typical American village, a village that could best stand as a counterpart of all villages where baseball might have been originated and developed—Cooperstown would best fit the bill."

And so it would. Though of all the great stars and the makers and shakers of the game that it honors, not even the charming Baseball Hall of Fame that would arise in that charming American village has ever had the temerity to admit Abner Doubleday.

So where *did* baseball come from?

By the 1950s, an alternative foundation myth had been set in place. That is, how a lanky, twenty-five-year-old Manhattan shipping clerk named Alexander Joy Cartwright insisted that his fellow ballplayers organize themselves into the New York Knickerbockers Base Ball Club. One fine day in 1846, they took the steam ferry over to the Elysian Fields, a park just across the Hudson from Manhattan in Hoboken, New Jersey, to play the mysterious "New York Base Ball Club" in the very first game of "real" baseball—and lost, 23–1.

Cartwright would next embark on a career as the "Johnny Appleseed" of baseball, leaving on a long trek to the California goldfields and then on to Hawaii. Wherever he went, he would teach the game, carrying along an original Knickerbockers ball that survives to this day. The Cartwright saga was given much play during one of baseball's many centennials in 1969, including a colorful feature in *Sports Illustrated,* complete with map and excerpts from a Cartwright diary.

Alas, this too falls apart on closer examination, being largely the product of multiple forgeries and an extended lobbying effort by Cartwright's son (which did get *his* father into Cooperstown). But it was always less than convincing. The giveaway is that thumping defeat. If the Knickerbockers invented the damned game, how did they manage to lose the first one so badly?

The truth, of course, is that they weren't the first. The Knickerbockers, as Thorn puts it, "were consolidators rather than innovators," combining and formalizing rules that others were already playing by. At least five other baseball clubs existed before them in what is now New York City—the Gotham, or Washington club, the New York, the Eagle, the Magnolia, and the Brooklyn club—and several of the Knicks had previously belonged to one or more of them. The Gotham club, founded in 1837, claimed to be first—at the time, the term "Washington" was regularly used to designate the "first," or the "premier"—but we can't be sure of this.

There was a prohibition against ball playing in the city that dates all the way back to 1656, when old New York used to be New Amsterdam, though we don't know just what sort of ball this was referring to. As early as 1805, two clubs from Columbia College, the Gymnastics and the Sons of Diagoras, were playing some form of bat-and-ball game, next to Tyler's "pleasure garden" at what is now the corner of Spring and Hudson Streets. The earliest evidence of club play is a letter that appeared in several of the city's eight daily papers on April 25, 1823. Signed only "A SPECTATOR," it advised,

> I was last Saturday much pleased in witnessing a company of active young men playing the manly athletic game of "base ball" at the Retreat in Broadway (Jones'). I am informed that they are an organized association, and that a very interesting game will be played on Saturday next at the above place, to commence at half past 3 o'clock, P.M. Any person fond of witnessing this game may avail himself of seeing it played with consummate skill and wonderful dexterity. It is surprising, and to be regretted that the young men of our city do not engage more in this manual sport; it is innocent amusement, and healthy exercise, attended with but little expense, and has no demoralizing tendency.

Most New Yorkers surely saw this notice for what it was: an advertisement for Jones's Retreat, a tavern on Broadway between Eighth Street and Washington Place. And invocations of moral rectitude and healthy exercise became running themes in the game's development.

Respectable grown men in the still puritanical America of the early nineteenth century didn't just *play games.* Hence all that stuff about "innocent amusement, and healthy exercise," which recurs again and again in defensive, firsthand accounts from the game's early players. Baseball was sold as a necessary relief from the crushing cares and woes of business.

In fact, the early, amateur ballplayers of New York were some of the least worked men in America. They were mostly "merchants, lawyers, Union Bank clerks, insurance clerks and others who were at liberty after 3 o'clock in the afternoon," as the sport's very first shortstop, Dr. Daniel Lucius "Doc" Adams, would recall. In an early daguerreotype, the Knickerbockers look like a conclave of sporty Mennonites out on a toot, with their beards, jackets, vests, bow ties, and broad-rimmed hats—outfits that included parts of their basic uniform on the playing field.

The Knickerbockers and the other early clubs really were *clubs,* preferring to play among themselves, which was why so many of their meetings took place near taverns, hotel dining rooms, and pleasure gardens ("pleasure" standing in, as it so often does, for "beer"). These were social occasions, all the fresh air and other healthful effects of the ball playing at least partly undone by the chowders, champagne suppers, and innumerable cigars and gin punches that followed. But for all their fun and their "exercise," New York's baseballists found themselves increasingly confronted by a question that has obsessed the city's ball clubs to this day: Where were they to play?

The tavern yards and vacant lots where New York ballplayers gathered were being rapidly filled in by the ever-expanding city. The clubs tried moving uptown as well, gathering at the margins of Madison Square—then a parade grounds—in the early 1840s and a field in Murray Hill, at Twenty-Seventh Street and Fourth Avenue. But both these sites were soon appropriated by railroad tracks and depots.

There were some alternatives, much farther uptown, in what would become Harlem and Yorkville. But just to get to such sites was a major, hours-long affair for most New Yorkers. The rest of upper Manhattan was a tangle of farms, squatter villages, small towns, rock-strewn hillocks, woods, and swamps, with hardly a spot for a presentable field to be found.

The city, it seemed, was growing too fast for baseball.

2

The Whirlpool and the Volcano

New York by the mid-nineteenth century had already claimed its title as "the Empire City of the West."

It was the city that made everything, sold everything, moved everything, *thought* of everything. Long the center of the country's shipping industry, New York had surpassed Philadelphia to become the nation's most populous city and its financial center and had stolen the publishing industry from Boston. At the end of the Civil War, New York's stockyards were slaughtering more animals than Chicago's, and its ninety thousand factory workers made it far and away the country's greatest industrial city, churning out steamships and furniture, refined sugar and shoes, chemicals and finished clothing.

"Everything in the city is in motion; everywhere the shops resound with the noise of workers," a visiting Frenchman remarked in 1801. Mark Twain would decry Manhattan a few decades later as a place where "every man seems to feel that he has got the duties of two lifetimes to accomplish in one, and so he rushes, rushes, rushes, and never has time to be companionable—never has any time at his disposal to fool away on matters which do not involve dollars and duty and business."

New York was a city of wonders—and a wonder to be seen, already a tourist town by the 1850s. Visitors could stay at any of the nineteen first-class hotels to be found on Broadway alone, with their dazzling new luxuries, including hot-and-cold running water, elevators, and "sky lobbies." They could eat at grand new restaurants such as Delmonico's, shop the Ladies' Mile with its fabulous department store palaces, A. T. Stewart, Brooks Brothers, Lord & Taylor, Tiffany, B. Altman, Macy's. Tourists and residents alike marveled at its ceaseless energy, its vitality, its bustle. Walt Whitman, already the city's most perceptive (and sympathetic) chronicler, agreed that it was a "noisy, roaring, rumbling, tumbling, bustling, stormy, turbulent" city, "amid the universal clatter, the incessant din of business, the all swallowing vortex of the great money whirlpool."

"Whirlpool" and "vortex" would stick, becoming common descriptions of New York in the nineteenth century. The city seemed to draw everything to it. It advanced in brilliant, unsentimental coups that its financiers and merchants then ruthlessly exploited. "Organize, commercialize, monopolize" might have been its operating motto.

In the first years of the republic, thanks to Alexander Hamilton, New York had traded the capital for the capital, giving up the federal government but trading the government debt on Wall Street. It dominated American shipping once the Black Ball Line announced that its vessels would leave on a set schedule. Its dynamic mayor, DeWitt Clinton, would not only impose the grid system of streets on Manhattan but push through the Erie Canal, connecting New York to the abundance of the American heartland.

In just so many strokes the city had, in the words of the historian Mike Wallace, "adroitly inserted itself between three of the most dynamic regions of the early nineteenth-century global economy—England's manufacturing Midlands, the cotton-producing slave South, and the agricultural Midwest."

By 1835, one-third of all the goods America exported went out through New York Harbor, and two-thirds of its imports came in the same way. By 1868, no fewer than thirty thousand ships a year were tying up at the acres of docks along the East River and the Hudson and Brooklyn's Red Hook waterfront. By 1851, the nation's original robber baron, "Commodore" Cornelius Vanderbilt—a semiliterate but immensely shrewd Staten Island farm boy who got his start at the age of sixteen, ferrying travelers across the harbor—had consolidated a gaggle of early railroad lines into the New York Central, pushed it out along the Great Lakes to Chicago and Detroit, then anchored it to midtown Manhattan with "the almightiest train shed in the world" on Forty-Second Street.

The Commodore's Grand Central Depot was capable of holding a hundred trains and fifteen thousand people, its vast waiting room lit by gigantic gas chandeliers. To keep waiting passengers from being asphyxiated by train smoke, Vanderbilt's engineers employed the "fly-switch" method of pulling into the station. The locomotive would speed up and uncouple itself from the rest of the train as it approached the station, then scuttle onto a side track. With phenomenal skill and timing, the brakemen would then let the remaining, engineless cars roll safely to the platform. Visitors coasted into the city as if by magic—another marvel of utility turned into entertainment.

New York outwitted and outdared its rivals, defying every attempt by other cities or regions to rein in its dominance. This was the triumph of the Big City, the capital of everything, always grander and more glorious, higher and richer and bigger and better.

Yet the whirlpool drew all to New York, the clever and the conniving, the rich and the poor, along with a host of mounting social problems. Always, the grand accomplishments of the Big City would be threatened by its callous neglect of the Little City, the place where working-class New Yorkers labored and rose—or fell and died. Another common nickname for the city by the mid-nineteenth century was the Volcano. To many, it seemed that New York was destined for a catastrophic eruption, thanks to the terrible disparities between how its people lived.

By 1860 there were at least 800,000 individuals clustered in the lower precincts of Manhattan, and maybe as many as a million all told, scattered throughout the island. They were pushing the limits of existence for a horse-drawn city. More than fifteen thousand vehicles a day clattered down lower Broadway, their iron-rimmed wheels making an infernal racket along the paving stones. By the end of the Civil War, thirty-five million passengers a year were riding the city's horse-drawn trolleys and streetcars, so badly maintained that they were commonly referred to as "hog-pens on wheels." Simply removing the waste generated by the 120,000 horses this traffic required was a herculean task. Each day, an estimated 500,000 pounds of manure and 45,000 gallons of urine had to be scraped from the city's streets. The horses themselves, maltreated and overworked, died at a rate of fifteen thousand a year, rotting in the streets for days while street children pulled the hairs from their tails to tie rings around their fingers.

The animals fared no worse than many of New York's human inhabitants. The city was the main portal for the greatest voluntary—or at least semi-voluntary—human migration in world history to that point. From 1845 to 1860, some 250,000 refugees fleeing the famine in Ireland settled permanently in New York, most of them destitute and uneducated, many speaking only Gaelic, nearly all of them Roman Catholics. They were joined by another 75,000 Germans fleeing a failed revolution, enough to make New York the third-largest German-speaking city in the world. Overnight, they transformed what had been an overwhelmingly Protestant, Anglo-American town into a polyglot metropolis.

Most of the new immigrants lived in bumptious, notorious neighborhoods such as the Five Points. By 1880, the population density in some of Manhattan's lower wards exceeded 275,000 people per square mile—more crowded than most of Dickensian London. Conditions were appalling. By the 1850s, tenants routinely lived five or six to a 225-square-foot apartment in the new tenements, foul, lightless buildings whose owners often refused to hook them up to the city's new water mains. Toilets were crude privies, stuck between the tenements and the even less inviting *back* tenements. These outhouses overflowed frequently, contributing to epidemics that swept through the city on a regular basis. In New York, the rich and the wellborn routinely perished from diseases of the poor. Horace Greeley's young son died of cholera, Teddy Roosevelt's mother from typhus, thirty years later. By 1856, New York's annual death rate *exceeded* its birthrate, its population increasing only by dint of the immigrant masses that kept pouring in through Castle Garden.

The constant, sweeping changes and the frenetic pace of them often induced a feeling of incipient anarchy. This was a city of sulfur and blood. Where pigs ran loose in the streets, knocking over pedestrians and pulling food from their hands, where butchers tossed so much offal down the public drains that little boys sailed paper boats on the pools of blood that bubbled up constantly from the sewers. Stagecoach drivers cursed and whipped at one another along the avenues, while the commuter steamboats raced and collided and occasionally exploded out on the Hudson. At fires, the all-volunteer companies fought each other for control of the hydrants in epic brawls; one such feud ended only after a company fired a loaded mortar at its rival's firehouse. The city's streets were full of prostitutes, or nightwalkers, as they were called, and abandoned children, or "street Arabs," as the newspapers dubbed them.

The murderousness of this New York has often been wildly overstated. In the days before readily available firearms, its homicide rate was still below that of the city today. But a sense of lurking menace persisted. Periodically the Volcano did erupt, in spurts of rage that often had their comic or ludicrous sides but provided terrifying indications of what the fire next time might bring. There was the Doctors' Riot, the Flour Riot, the Orange Riot, the Dead Rabbits Riot. In the Police Riot, officers from two competing police forces—one appointed by the mayor, the other by the state legislature—slugged it out on the steps of city hall. The Shakespeare Riots started as a rivalry between two popular actors of the day; before it was over, thirty-four people were lying dead in Astor Place.

The capper was the Draft Riots, a revolt against the military draft at the height of the Civil War that became a class rebellion, then a shameful, white-on-Black race riot, a five-day orgy of looting, burning, and savage lynchings. African Americans were perhaps 1 percent of the city's population, and Black men had repeatedly petitioned the state government to be allowed to go fight in the South. Nevertheless, they became a leading object of the mob's fury, blamed for the war and falsely accused of taking jobs from those who were doing the fighting. Belligerent, drunken white men and even women stormed the city's armory and its leading newspaper, torched police stations and the Colored Orphan Asylum, and set up barricades in the streets before finally being put down by federal troops. By the time it was all over, perhaps as many as five hundred New Yorkers were dead, to this day the worst confirmed toll of any civil disturbance in our history.

It was more a revolution than a riot, as one observer remarked—the new, immigrant America's final warning that attention must be paid. Runaway corruption; unspeakable vice; riots and gang violence; demoralizing poverty, neglect, mounting filth and disease and disorder—clearly, something needed to be done if the city was not to spin out of control.

Many looked to the immediate symptom, the physical state of the city. DeWitt Clinton's ambitious grid system stretched the whole length of the island but allocated almost nothing for park space. Its planners themselves acknowledged "that so few vacant spaces have been left, and those so small, for the benefit of fresh air and consequent preservation of health," but noted that in compensation "those large arms of the sea which embrace Manhattan Island render its situation, in regard to health and pleasure . . . peculiarly felicitous."

The large arms of sea around Manhattan, stuffed with the refuse from untold ships, factories, and charnel houses, were indeed peculiar but hardly felicitous. In between, New York remained a city of squat brick tenements and houses, four or five stories high. The elevated railroads that began to rise along the avenues after the Civil War provided relief from the congestion on the street, but only added a roaring, screeching horror next to the window, dripping oil and burning cinders on anyone traversing the now dappled sidewalks down below.

Those wishing relief from the city's racket and bustle resorted to the splendid new public cemeteries, such as Brooklyn's Green-Wood, but these were thought to leak unhealthful, even deadly "miasmas" up from their graves. Visionary reformers pushed through Manhattan's Central Park, the "big art work of the Republic," the largest public space in the United States and the start of a long string of stunning new green spaces from the landscape architects Frederick Law Olmsted and Calvert Vaux.

Yet Central Park was intended very specifically to be a means of reform and edification. Its purposes were both practical and moral. Visitors would be morally uplifted by the great cultural institutions intended for the park's margins, by the exquisitely planned, pastoral vistas that every hedge and tree and rock contributed to, and most of all by the opportunity to learn from watching their betters at leisure. Central Park was, in Olmsted's words, supposed to provide "places and times for re-unions [where] the rich and poor, the cultivated and the self-made, shall be attracted together and encouraged to assimilate."

But on whose terms?

Those few poor able to make it up to the park were immediately confronted with a list of rules telling them what *not* to do. Restrictions included no walking on the grass, no "group picnics," and no "strenuous activity." Although Olmsted had originally designated a ten-acre playground by the Sheep Meadow as "the Ball Ground," ball playing was completely forbidden when Central Park opened in 1857. The rule was eased after nine years of remonstrations, to allow schoolboys to play on three designated days a week, *if* they could produce a note from their principal and a certificate of good attendance.

Certainly there was no ball playing even contemplated by grown men, much less Broadway actors. Nothing like that would be allowed until the 1920s. While the rich were allotted drives and transverses for *their* favorite outdoor pastimes, riding and carriaging, no favor was shown to anyone else.

Traveling hours just to watch the rich cavort? This was not what most New Yorkers thought of as fun. Especially when it was so much easier just to go to Jersey.

The Elysian Fields had been opened in 1824 by John Stevens, one of those gratingly productive polymaths the nineteenth century seemed to turn out by the bushel. An inventor, engineer, lawyer, and businessman, Stevens had also served as a captain in the Continental army and snatched up seven hundred acres of land in Hoboken after it was confiscated from a prominent Tory. Hoping to develop most of this, he sought to draw prospective buyers from New York with a riverfront amusement park. The Elysian Fields offered almost every entertainment imaginable: plays and concerts, dancing and skating, landscaped gardens, a deer park and a "buffalo hunt," tenpin bowling, a miniature railway, a wax museum, "a drinking spa," hotels and taverns, parades and fireworks, primitive carnival rides, fishing, boxing, wrestling, horse racing, lumberjack contests, and, eventually, baseball.

None of this could be called fun, of course. Stevens promoted his park, too, as a place of "health and recreation" and "pure air," where one might escape "the dust, noise, and bad smells of the city." Like so many generations of ballpark proprietors to come, he even lobbied for the city authorities to subsidize his enterprise as a civic good.

New York's elected officials were too busy stealing directly for themselves to consider handouts to the owners of ballparks, particularly ones in New Jersey. But even without a subsidy, by the 1830s twenty thousand Manhattanites a day were ferrying over to Hoboken on summer weekends. They sailed over on a John Stevens–invented steamboat, to ride on a Stevens-invented train, and play in the Stevens-built park. By the 1840s, though, the resort had begun to decline. Muggings, robberies, knifings, brawls, and rapes abounded. A beautiful shopgirl was murdered in its lovers' lane, a crime so lurid and infamous it inspired an Edgar Allan Poe mystery. The Elysian Fields became a place of gamblers and gang *b'hoys,* loitering in low dives and rancid hotels that, in the words of one visitor, "blasted the senses . . . by reeking forth fumes of whiskey and tobacco."

Central Park, it wasn't. But none of this deterred ballplayers from making their way over—at least in part because they were already quite used to this rough-and-tumble milieu back in New York. The game was not played exclusively by lawyers and clerks and aspiring gentlemen. John Thorn would manage to exhume the records of the Magnolia Ball Club, which had apparently been quite consciously buried deep beneath the pastoral baseball legend. The Magnolia, Thorn discovered, was "a ball club composed not of white-collar sorts with shorter workdays and gentlemanly airs but sporting-life characters, from ward heelers to billiard-room operators and bigamists." They "included shoulder hitters and fire laddies, Bowery Boys and ward heelers, Nativists and anti-Masons, brothel owners and saloonkeepers, sporting men and subterraneans. . . . Baseball was *their* game, too."

These were the other gentlemen of New York who might find their afternoons free for a game of ball. They drank grog and beer at their postgame banquets, rather than claret and champagne, and they marked the start of New York baseball's intimate involvement with local politics, a connection that would both hobble and facilitate the game's progress, right up to the present day.

The Magnolia was playing ball at the Elysian Fields as early as 1843. The New York Club, for one, might have made it to Hoboken even earlier, and others soon followed. The Knickerbockers played their first match in Hoboken on October 6, 1845, another intramural game. And on the cold, windy afternoon of October 21, 1845, the New York Ball Club played the first *known* interclub game, drubbing the Brooklyn Ball Club, 24–4, in four innings. The two clubs would go on to play again on October 24, back in Brooklyn, with New York winning, 37–19, to claim the first, informal baseball championship.

By 1855, the Knickerbocker, the Eagle, and the Empire clubs were all playing regularly at the Elysian Fields, and by the Civil War there were eight clubs there, occupying five acres of baseball and cricket fields. Several of these teams built themselves clubhouses, and the Knickerbockers kept a room in the Colonnade Hotel. By 1856, matches between the top clubs—still a rarity—were drawing as many as eight thousand spectators.

What this meant was men of all different classes playing each other—and playing even in the most turbulent, working-class surroundings. Ironically, it was the baseball fields of Hoboken that were bringing about the "consolidation," the coming together of rich and poor, immigrants and "native Americans" (as American-born whites were then called), that the city's reformers had hoped to accomplish in Central Park. It was baseball, played next to bawdy houses and "drinking spas," that had a more democratizing—and assimilating—effect than watching toffs trot by in their carriages. The ball field was established as a public space where, for better and for worse, men and boys could go and act out—the start of another long tradition in New York, one that more than once threatened to overwhelm the sport on the field.

3

"The Snap, Go, Fling"

Why were they drawn to baseball? For starters, it was pretty much the only game in town.

It was not quite true, as an English visitor sneered, that "the Alpha and Omega of sport in the United States" was "to roll balls in a ten pin alley by gaslight or to drive a fast trotting horse in a light wagon along a very bad and dusty road"—but it was close. The only major, professional sports in the United States by the mid-nineteenth century were horse racing, always a rich man's game, and bare-knuckle prizefighting, a gory, corrupt spectacle that was banned in many places.

Aside from the sport of kings and the sweet science, outdoor pastimes might include the occasional foot race, lawn bowling or tennis, rowing and sailing, and target shooting—though most of these activities, too, were restricted to the well-off.

For the urban poor, the choices were dismal. According to Luc

Sante, "the premier betting sport of the nineteenth century" in New York was rat baiting, in which men bet on how long it would take a trained "rat terrier" to kill a "century" of rats. (The record was eleven minutes, thirty seconds.) Organized dogfights, cockfights, and other forms of animal torture proliferated. Even bearbaiting had once been popular in New York, though, as Sante notes, "that sport gradually dissipated as the number of available bears decreased, although matches continued to be held up to the Civil War, notably in McLaughlin's bear pit at First Avenue and Tenth Street."

Those men *not* so drunk at the end of an evening that they felt like falling into a dark hole filled with criminals and the stench of thousands of dead rats were continually searching out other manly associations. They joined militia companies, political clubhouses, workingmen's associations, guilds, even society libraries—anywhere they could band together against the terrors and anonymity of life in the city.

Another venue was the city's many volunteer fire companies. These served as intricate social organizations from which arose many of the city's first political factions—and its baseball teams. The Knickerbockers were derived in part from a fire company of the same name. Much of the Magnolia's roster belonged to the same fire company. Boss Tweed got his start with the Americus Fire Company, down on the Lower East Side, which would lend its tiger head symbol to Tammany Hall and its nickname, Big Six, to the city's first baseball superstar. Tweed would also become the major, behind-the-scenes sponsor of the New York Mutuals, drawn from the Mutual Hook and Ladder Company No. 1.

In the streets of New York, firefighting presaged all of the spectacle and the fetishes of modern, professional sports. Each volunteer company had detailed histories of their service carefully recorded by company clerks, wore distinctive uniforms, and elected a hierarchy of captains and assistant captains. "Fire laddies" tended to be the biggest, boldest, most athletic young men in their wards. They were worshipped by local boys, who vied to be runners for the companies and pooled their pennies to buy special suspender buckles and wagon fixtures for their heroes. The companies all had their own colorful bramble of nicknames: the Old Honey Bee, the Boots Out the Window company, the Dashing Half-Hundred, the Live Oak, the

Old Turk, the Singing Engine, Ye Old Silver Nine. (One company, known as the Quills, was made up solely of clerks and was famous for the fastidious minutes of its meetings.) While fires blazed, company stewards walked among the men like hot dog vendors, handing out food and brandy, singing at them, "Eat some more cheese and a good slice of ham / And wash it well down with another good dram," while "fire tenors" would come out to further entertain the onlookers with their favorite tunes.

The game of baseball offered an entertainment that was not as dramatic as a fire, but one that moved with the pace of the city, the nation, the time. Whitman called it "America's game; it has the snap, go, fling of the American atmosphere; it belongs as much to our institutions, fits into them as significantly as our Constitution's laws; it is just as important in the sum total of our historic life." To Mark Twain it was "the very symbol, the outward and visible expression of the drive and push and rush and struggle of the raging, tearing, booming nineteenth century."

Strange as this may sound today, when baseball is generally derided for proceeding at a glacier's gallop, the game *did* move quickly, as yet unburdened by commercials, and endless pitching changes, and batting-glove adjustments. Unlike cricket, baseball didn't require a pristinely rolled playing field. Much like the premier urban game of today, basketball, players needed relatively little equipment and virtually no money to take part.

"In baseball," exulted Henry Chadwick, "all is lightning; every action is swift as a seabird's flight."

By the Civil War, it was New York City's version of baseball that had become the national game, all but extinguishing every other form of bat-and-ball game in the Northeast. The war would spread it around the country, establishing its dominance everywhere.

Why was this? What exactly was the New York game, and what distinguished it from everything else?

Here the Knickerbockers made their seminal contribution, in consolidating, formalizing, and studiously jotting down what other ball clubs around the city had already improvised. The "Knickerbocker Rules" decreed the following: The infield was to be shaped like a diamond, with four bases, including home plate. No physical interference with fielders by base runners was allowed. The ball was to be pitched underhand to a batter at the plate, a fixed number of players were allowed on the field at any one time, and they were to take regular turns at bat, in an established order. Batters were out if they missed three (swinging) strikes, but only if the catcher held on to the last one—an ancient rule that would devastate all of Brooklyn almost a century later. There were three outs to an inning, and batters were retired by striking out, by being tagged or forced at a base, or by a ball caught on the fly or the first bounce—*not* by a fielder hitting them with a thrown ball. Fair and foul territory were clearly distinguished, and players could not reach base on a foul ball. The umpire's decisions would stand. And there was a balk rule, although no one understood it even then.

Over the years to come, the Knickerbocker Rules would be modified repeatedly. The ball-and-strike regulations would change several times, and the distance between home plate and the pitcher's mound would shrink, then lengthen, before settling in at sixty feet, six inches. The "first bounce" rule was eliminated (1865), and sidearm (1883) and then overhand (1884) pitching would be allowed. Major revisions would come with the first two conventions of the National Association of Base Ball Players (NABBP), held at Smith's Hotel in Manhattan, which set the basepaths at ninety feet, the length of the game at nine innings—as opposed to when one team scored twenty-one "aces," or runs. The number of men on the field was also fixed at nine, giving baseball its seemingly mystical concatenation of nines and threes.

By the Civil War, almost every region still had its own favorite variations of bat and ball. Some were already fading fast, such as "wicket," the form of English "country cricket" that was favored in Connecticut and that George Washington had played at Valley Forge. It would soon vanish almost entirely—leaving only the vestigial dirt path from mound to plate that would also come to play its own strange part in the epic of New York baseball.

The New York game's main competitors were Philadelphia town ball and the Massachusetts game. The field for the Philly game was arranged around a circle of four stakes, twenty feet apart, along with a fifth stake in the middle serving as a sort of substitute pitcher's mound. Batters used either a small, rounded bat called a "delill," which they swung with one hand, or a larger, flat-sided, cricket-style bat. Teams played either eleven innings with one out an inning or a two-inning game in which the entire side (all eleven men) had to be retired before the inning was over. Scores tended to be very high, with teams routinely plating more than seventy-five runs.

The Massachusetts game was something else again. It was played not on a diamond or a circle but a square. There were four bases, one at each corner, set sixty feet apart from each other, and that same fifth stake or base serving for a pitcher's mound. The ball was pitched overhand, from a distance of thirty to thirty-five feet. There could be seven to fourteen players a side, though the usual number was eleven, and just one out an inning. But the big differences were these: runners were retired by being hit with a thrown ball, and there was no foul territory or even rules that the runners had to stay within the baselines.

There is the promise of a certain wonderfully daft anarchy embedded in these rules or anti-rules, a sort of baseball combined with dodgeball. Batters could theoretically hit the ball *behind* them, or race all over the field trying to avoid a throw.

John Thorn jibes that "the Massachusetts game of baseball was in many ways the superior version, for both players and spectators." It demanded a superior athleticism to the "prissy New York game," which was designed "for unathletic clerks to play." The latter prevailed, he speculates, only "through superior press agentry."

"It did not matter that the Massachusetts game more accurately reflected American reality, who we were in the 1850s," contends Thorn. "The genteel New York game represented who we wished to become."

A greater problem would be building a stadium large enough to accommodate this three-ring circus. Nor were the players of the Massachusetts game quite as manly and rugged as Thorn implies. Players were hit or "soaked" with a light rubber ball that could not be hurled more than two hundred feet. The Knickerbockers had started play with a similar ball, but it had begun to wear out Doc Adams, the first shortstop, who had to constantly run out from his position to field relays.

While it can't be said that there was any one father of baseball, the best claim to paternity is held by Adams. Son of an outspoken abolitionist, graduate of Yale and Harvard, he was a general practitioner who spent much time treating the poor at the New York Dispensaries and who considered his marriage "the crowning achievement of my life." Universally well regarded, he was named "the Nestor of Ball Players" when he finally resigned from the Knickerbockers.

It was Adams—not Doubleday, not Cartwright, not Henry Chadwick—who was the single most important individual in the development of the modern game. It was Adams who was elected president of the Knickerbockers and president of the convention of ballplayers who would consolidate "the Knickerbocker Rules." And it was Doc Adams who was in charge of making baseballs and bats for all the clubs in Manhattan at that time. The good doctor happened upon a "Scotch saddler" who showed him how to put together, in his description, "three or four ounces of rubber cuttings, wound with yarn and then covered with the leather [horsehide]."

This made for something still much softer than a modern baseball. But it was not a ball with which you could easily soak a runner—not without risking a serious injury or starting a brawl. "Hardball" sounded the death knell, as Thorn astutely notes, of the fascinating "running/fielding" game that was the Massachusetts version, in favor of the "pitcher/hitter" game we know today. But it is this very confrontation of the pitcher and the hitter that makes baseball unique—that makes it an individual competition *within* a larger team game.

Far from mandating the triumph of a *less* athletic game, Adams's brilliant innovation was the first step toward the modern fastball, a weapon that could be hurled toward one's head—or batted back—with truly lethal force. Only the very best athletes would be able to throw it, field it, hit it, *dodge* it. It also brought the faintest whiff of death into the game, the consequence if you failed to handle the hardball. This would become all too real a threat on a New York ball field.

4

"One or More Colored Persons"

By the start of the Civil War there were an estimated 50 clubs in New York and Brooklyn alone, along with another 60 youth, or "feeder," clubs. The sport had become almost a mania in New Jersey, where there were 130 adult clubs, including 42 in Jersey City and 36 in Newark.

The players dressed themselves in elaborate new uniforms, modeled after the militia companies of the time, complete with trimmed pants, and shirts, and caps. They comprised all classes and professions. There were teams composed solely of shipbuilders, firefighters, actors, postal clerks, bank clerks, ferrymen, newspaper reporters and printers' devils, government bureaucrats, and ministers. There were the Manhattans, a club made up of policemen; and the Phantoms, who were bartenders; and the Pocahontas Club, who were all milkmen (Pocahontas being a sort of secular American saint in the common white imagination). There were the Metropolitans, who were schoolteachers; and the Columbia Club of Orange, New Jersey, who were hatters; and the Aesculapians of Brooklyn, who consisted entirely of eye doctors.

Teams such as the Knickerbockers tried hard for a time to maintain the genteel, white-collar cast of their games. The club fined its own players fifty cents for disobeying the captain, twenty-five cents for arguing with the umpire, six cents for profanity. Women were invited to attend games, in the fond hope that they would maintain baseball's respectability. In 1867, the Knickerbockers even held baseball's first "ladies' day" promotion, a tradition that would continue for more than a century. The growing rowdiness of the sport, both on the field and in the stands, was commonly blamed on Irish and German immigrants.

"The emerging baseball fiction of the day, written mainly by

Northeastern Victorian literati for a respectable middle-class audience, featured proper Brahmin heroes and suitably coarse Irish antagonists described as gang members, 'blackguards,' and 'brutes,'" notes historian Robert F. Burk.

Yet the runaway popularity of baseball swept it inevitably toward professionalism. Big crowds meant gambling—an obsession among American men at the time—and gambling meant money, and once money was on the line, clubs would look for the best players, regardless of their "breeding" or their background. The older Anglo clubs attempted, ironically, to preserve their amateurism by erecting walls of money against interlopers. The NABBP charged a $5 initiation fee, passed a code of conduct, and banned gambling, the jumping by players from one club to another, and even the Knickerbockers' beloved postgame banquets. Here already, four years before the Civil War, were the same points of contention that would bedevil the game for years to come: just compensation, freedom of contract, gambling, and the use of dubious substances.

The NABBP would fail utterly in dealing with all of these issues. It would do even worse in dealing with another subject that would bedevil baseball for many decades to come—just as it had always bedeviled America.

Irish and German immigrants might be grudgingly allowed into baseball, even occasional Jews and Italians and Native Americans. Yet the need to find more professional talent did not extend to another group who had been there from the beginning of the New York game, just as they were there almost from the beginning of the city. As early as 1840, a Black newspaper, *The Colored American,* was mentioning "lads" of color playing in the same Madison Square Garden area where white players convened. Black clubs such as the Unknown of Weeksville, the Henson of Jamaica, the Monitor of Brooklyn, and the Uniques and the Union, both of Williamsburg, were soon in action, and the first confirmed game between two Black teams in what is now New York City took place in what was then the independent town of Jamaica, on November 15, 1859. (The Henson Base Ball Club topped the Unknowns in a pitchers' duel, 54–43.) Black clubs were organized throughout the Northeast, including an early Washington,

D.C., squad, the Alerts, whose players included a young government clerk named Frederick Douglass, Jr., son of Frederick Douglass, the great abolitionist leader.

Yet no Black club was invited to convene with the National Association of Base Ball Players. No doubt, this reflected in part the NABBP's eagerness throughout its existence to recruit white southern clubs (which could not have been less interested in joining). But there was plenty of racism up north, too. Even raising the question of including Black clubs was thought to risk a "rupture" and a dangerous "division of feeling"—though in fact there appeared to be sadly little "division of feeling" on this issue among the white clubs.

The issue was finally forced by a bunch of out-of-towners. The Pythians of Philadelphia were a leading Black club, one with impeccable credentials. The team was organized and led by a pair of Black school principals, Octavius Valentine Catto and Jacob C. White, Jr. Both men were scholars in mathematics, teachers, and tutors. Both had also been born free and were activists fighting for abolition and equal rights. White was a successful businessman as well; Catto had served as a major during the Civil War and helped to raise eleven regiments of Black troops.

They also played baseball. Catto, a hard-hitting infielder, led the Pythians on the field, while White was the club secretary. They occasionally played white ball clubs in Philly as well as Black ones and shared a field with the original Philadelphia Athletics, who supported the idea of integrated baseball. In 1867, Catto and White put the NABBP to the test, by formally applying for membership at the association's winter meeting. They were denied entrance, the Pythians, by the NABBP's three-man Nominating Committee, which claimed that as far as it knew, no clubs in the association "are composed of persons of color, or any portion of them," and that "based upon this view . . . they unanimously report against the admission of any club which may be composed of one or more colored persons."

The New York State Base Ball Association would also rule out Black players in 1870—at the same meeting in which it readmitted two of Boss Tweed's Mutual players, expelled for fixing games, as members in good standing. Instead, Blacks were advised "to organize a National Association of their own."

The following year, Octavius Catto, just thirty-two, was murdered during a contentious Philadelphia election, shot dead on the street for trying to vote by one Frank Kelly, an Irish tough from the city's Democratic political machine. Kelly would be acquitted. Catto would be honored with a statue in front of Philadelphia's city hall—146 years later.

5

The Professionals

The drive toward professionalism—at least for white players—would go on. Within a year of its founding, the Knickerbockers had recruited a paid "ringer," a young English immigrant jeweler and pitching star named Harry Wright who would revolutionize the game.

Wright, already a professional cricketeer, saw nothing wrong with accepting money for spending his valuable time on a ball field. Why should he? The same year of Wright's baseball debut, 1858, marked the first time an admission fee was levied to see a baseball game. The proprietors of the Fashion Race Course, out on Long Island—very near the site of the Mets' home park in Flushing—put together what was the first all-star game in history, a series of three matches over the course of the summer between all-star teams from New York and Brooklyn.

The promoters charged fifty cents a head. This was a considerable sum for the day—perhaps as much as $92 in today's currency, when figured as a percentage of the wages of an unskilled laborer. Nevertheless, they got their money. For each game, packed special trains brought capacity crowds of four thousand "kranks," as fans were then called, out from the two cities to see the New Yorkers capture two out of three. The all-star games were so popular they soon became a regular event, the "Silver Ball" championships, played for a rather sinister trophy of a hand holding an inscribed silver baseball.

Once money was being collected at the gate, the players wanted a piece of the action, and they got it. By the late 1860s, players in the New York area might well have been averaging $600–$900 a season, including $1,000–$2,500 for top stars—all at a time when even clerks and skilled laborers rarely made more than $500 a year. This meant players were making somewhere between $50,000 and $200,000 in today's terms, which created a frenzy among kranks and the new "sportswriters," just as it always would when ballplayers were revealed to be playing for more than the love of the game.

Henry Chadwick, "Father Baseball," an austere, disputatious writer for several metropolitan papers, decried a host of new, "evil influences" upon baseball, which he saw chiefly as gamblers, "rough[s]," and "foul-mouthed, blaspheming 'sport[s].'" "Revolvers"—players who switched teams for the promise of more money—were especially reviled. And in 1868, Old Pete O'Brien, a veteran baseballist on the Brooklyn Atlantics, set what might have been the official record for Earliest Lamentation for Some Bygone Era of Baseball:

> Somehow or other they don't play ball nowadays as they used to some eight or ten years ago. I don't mean to say that they don't play it as well. . . . But I mean that they don't play with the same kind of feelings or for the same objects they used to. . . . It appears to me that ball matches have come to be controlled by different parties and for different purposes than those that prevailed in 1858 or 1859.

Ah, for the halcyon days of 1858! But Father Baseball and Old Pete had a point. Professionalism and especially gambling *were* threatening to make a farce of the game. "Hippodroming," or fixing games, was rife, with the worst abuses, unsurprisingly, perpetrated by various elements of Tammany Hall, New York's burgeoning political machine. John "Old Smoke" Morrissey, the boxer, gang leader, and Tammany sachem who would soon make Saratoga into a gamblers' paradise, was said to use the players on his Troy Haymakers team "like loaded dice and marked cards."

Boss Tweed ran his own club, the New York Mutuals, who were reputed to have a payroll of $38,000—all of it supplied by taxpayers, in the form of no-show jobs in the city's Street and Coroner's departments. In 1865, three of Tweed's Mutuals were accused of "laying down" in a game against the Brooklyn Eckfords. One of them was banned for life, and the Mutuals were summarily booted out of the NABBP, only to have Tweed "persuade" the association to reinstate both player and team.

Yet money, legitimate or not, was also making the game better. John Thorn credits gamblers with bringing the big money into the game, and "money," for Thorn, "was not the snake in the garden, spoiling a pastoral, amateur idyll, but instead the stimulus to creativity and excellence."

Much like everything else in New York, baseball would now advance in brilliant improvisations. The bunt was invented by one Tom Barlow of the Atlantics, inspiring some players to use specially flattened bats. Harry Wright invented the (underhand) off-speed pitch, or "dewdrop." And on October 7, 1867, an eighteen-year-old hurler for the Brooklyn Excelsiors named William Arthur "Candy" Cummings tried out a pitch he had been practicing for years in a match against the Harvard varsity up at Cambridge. With just "a sharp twist with the middle finger," he gave the ball "a swift rotary motion." (In keeping with the pastoral traditions of the game, he claimed to have developed his new pitch zipping clamshells across the Gowanus Creek.)

Cummings had discovered the curveball, a sensation so profound that "a surge of joy flooded over me that I shall never forget"—a joy that must have been tempered by the fact that he lost the game, 18–6. It was wasted altogether on Harvard's president, Charles Eliot, who, referring to a pitcher for the Crimson's nine a few years later, huffed, "I understand that a curve ball is thrown with a deliberate purpose to deceive. Surely this is not an ability we should want to foster at Harvard."

Here was the birth of what would become another perennial baseball debate. The argument over what was cheating and what was not would continue all the way down to the age of steroids. Officially, throwing a curveball was illegal in 1867. So, later, was the custom of the catcher blocking the plate, or the phantom double play, or any number of the improvisations that the Johnny Everses, the John

McGraws, the Billy Martins, and so many others would contrive on the fly (and so often in New York). This constant testing of the rules would become an essential part of the game in and of itself.

Yet Cummings was not the first New York star to push the boundaries of the sport. In 1859, another eighteen-year-old—then as now, baseball genius ran young—named James Creighton had already unveiled the first novelty pitch. Hurling for the Brooklyn Niagaras, Creighton managed to snap his wrist in a way that batters could not detect but that sent the ball spinning dizzily toward the plate, and sometimes rising as high as the hitter's neck.

Why this was not considered a curveball, too, is unrecorded. It sounds almost like another unhittable pitch of later years, Mariano Rivera's fabled cutter. But whatever it was, Creighton found he could get just about anybody out by alternating these "speedballs" with his off-speed "dewdrops," leaving batters to lurch futilely about the plate. Changing speeds? Mixing up fastballs and breaking pitches? Officially, this was cheating, too. After all, the pitcher was there to *let* the batter hit the ball, and thereby produce all the action. Henry Chadwick would still be insisting a decade later that "the true estimate of good pitching, is based on the chances offered fielders for outs. Striking out [hitters] simply shows inferior batting, not superior pitching. . . . [A pitcher] would be more effective were he to depend less on mere speed."

All of Chadwick's protests were in vain. A teenager had stood the game on its head with one pitch. The question that still lingers is why he was allowed to do it. Creighton's opponents, after all, could simply have refused to hit all these unpredictable pitches that were decidedly *not* thrown where they wanted them, and that would have been the end of it. But they didn't. Batters took up the challenge out of professional pride, or a desire to smash the ball back in the snot-nosed kid's face, or simply because people liked seeing the new pitches.

Creighton proved to be as precocious about marketing himself as he was at playing the game. He turned revolver, jumping from the Niagaras to the Brooklyn Stars, then to the Excelsiors in return for more money or the promise of a better job in the offseason. In the uneasy summer of 1860, he led the Excelsiors up through New York and into Canada, then down through Pennsylvania, Delaware, and Maryland on one of the earliest "barnstorming" tours. Crowds flocked to see him, and teams in the small towns they passed through renamed themselves the Creightons. The object of their adoration lived up to all the ballyhoo. Not only could no one hit him; no one could get him out. During the entire 1862 season, Creighton was retired at the plate only *four* times.

He would become the archetype for a legend, this boy. He was the first "natural," somehow able to master this most frustrating game right from the beginning. How he did it was something of a mystery, too, trick pitch or no. In a surviving tintype, he is staring manfully into the distance, his right arm holding a ball cocked back behind him, right foot hooked in front of the left. Unlike other pitchers, who at the time were still getting a running start before they let the ball go—something that implies they were, at least, doing their best to get the batter out, Father Baseball be damned—Jim Creighton took only one step forward with that left foot, the right one still in place, before releasing the ball.

In his youth and his determination, and with the "Brooklyn-style" cap—the modern baseball cap that the Excelsiors had debuted—Creighton looks like so many of the young men of the moment, posing in their new uniforms for the inferno to come. It is a testament to baseball's appeal that he could remain such a sensation in the midst of the bloodiest war the nation has ever known, though he himself would not survive it. On October 14, 1862, at the end of his greatest season, Jim Creighton smashed one more home run for the Excelsiors against a Bronx team, the Unions of Morrisania. But after crossing home plate, he collapsed, gripping his side. Creighton thought that his belt had broken; instead, it was claimed that his swing had somehow ruptured his bladder. More likely, he had suffered a ruptured inguinal hernia, but whatever the cause, after four days of agonizing pain, Creighton was dead at age twenty-one. He would be buried in Green-Wood Cemetery, with a granite obelisk and a marble baseball to mark his resting place, and the fresh graves of many other young men close by.

The game's proprietors put it about that he had died while playing cricket, not baseball—a debate that has continued in some circles to this day (along with questions about whether his last at bat really was so dramatic). But whatever the legends, the fact was that James Creighton would be the first in a long line of New York ballplayers who would meet tragic, untimely ends, and in a weird twist his last home run almost uncannily prefigured the ending of the movie version of *The Natural*—the tragic hero, his life jeopardized by even one more swing, his abdomen bleeding as he slowly rounds the bases. It would prove to be an irresistible theme, this intrusion of death into a game of young men, told again and again in works as diverse and iconic as *The Pride of the Yankees,* Mark Harris's *Bang the Drum Slowly,* Eric Rolfe Greenberg's *Celebrant,* and Robert Coover's *Universal Baseball Association, Inc., J. Henry Waugh, Prop.* It would carve a place in the culture (often abused) for baseball as metaphor, baseball as embodying the sudden swings and pitfalls of American life in a way that no other sport would quite manage.

6

Making the Welkin Ring

James Creighton had brought romance to the professional game, still thought to be low, base, corrupted by its very nature. The revolvers were heroes now, and here to stay. But money, as it would soon develop, threatened something much more important than the integrity of the game. It threatened the baseball supremacy of New York. By the late 1860s and early 1870s, most of the leading baseballists—particularly the captains of the top clubs—still were either New York natives or English immigrants who lived in the city. With the city's trademark narcissism, its kranks and sportswriters had come to believe that the Silver Ball all-star matches between Brooklyn and New York decided the "world championship."

Yet with an estimated two thousand clubs throughout the United States, the balance of power was beginning to shift, moving westward with the population center of the nation. The good burghers of Cincinnati decided to hurry things along. They formed a joint-stock venture, endowing their hometown Cincinnati Red Stockings with a $10,000 payroll and making them the first avowedly professional baseball team in history. More boldly still, they spent perhaps as much as $2,000 of this money to hire thirty-four-year-old Harry Wright, the former jeweler and cricketeer turned Knickerbocker, as their manager.

It was a shrewd investment. Wright was an assiduous student of the game, the progenitor of today's statistics-driven managers. He kept his own detailed box scores and studied them so intensely that supposedly he later lost his sight for a year. No aspect of the game seemed to escape his attention. He used hand signals and invented the practice of having fielders back up a play. He was a paragon of virtue both on and off the field, "the best captain in the world" and "tutor and moral advisor of his players," whom he constantly urged to eat right, stay in training, and refrain from using tobacco or alcohol. Despite this, he appears to have been beloved by his team. The harshest admonition Harry Wright ever used—"You need a little ginger"—was reputedly enough to fill them with shame and get them hustling again.

More important, Wright was a conduit to the brightest young stars in and around New York—including one in his own family. His younger brother George was a mustachioed, wall-eyed engraver and shortstop, with a grin so toothsome it was later said to outshine Teddy Roosevelt's. He was just twenty-two but already acknowledged as the best ballplayer alive. For another $1,400–$1,800 of the investors' money, George was persuaded to sign on with the Red Stockings. A further $1,100 brought in Asahel "Count" Brainard from Albany, a "scientific" pitcher who had played the field behind Creighton with the Excelsiors and specialized in changing speeds. A host of other young stars followed, most of them from the New York area, all of them paid at least $600. Only one player on the roster was actually from Cincinnati.

In the summer of 1869, the Red Stockings went out to take on the world for the pride of the Queen City (or Porkopolis, as Cincinnati was more commonly called). They traveled by Pullman car, charged fifty cents admission, and drew big crowds everywhere. They were, it seems, as much a vaudeville act or a circus as a ball team. After detraining, they would pile into a wagon or omnibus and ride to the park, festooned in their full beards, moustaches, and/or sideburns, wearing their flashy uniforms and singing the team song:

We are a band of baseball players
From Cincinnati city.
We come to toss the ball around
And sing to you our ditty.
And if you listen to the song
We are about to sing
We'll tell you all about baseball
And make the welkin ring.
The ladies want to know
Who are those gallant men.
In Stockings Red, they'd like to know.

Whereupon each of the Red Stockings would step forward in turn and introduce himself, *still* in song and verse.

After this remarkable performance, the Cincinnati squad would get down to business. It soon became evident that no one else could ring that welkin quite the way they could. They pummeled the local talent by scores of 86–8, 65–1, and 103–8. The established, big-city eastern teams fared better, but still lost. The Red Stockings reeled off three wins against the best Philadelphia had to offer, then two more in Washington, after which they were received by President Grant.

The Cincinnati club was, as one awed observer commented, a "nicely adjusted machine"—the very first Big Red Machine. In an irony fans throughout America would come to relish, the nation's baseball powerhouse had been put together by drawing the best players *from* New York and *to* a smaller, upstart city. There would be no more of the smug "national championships" played between nines from New York and Brooklyn. The city's teams would have to put up or shut up, starting with a showdown between Cincinnati and the New York Mutuals.

New York was predictably unimpressed. Local gamblers made the home team a narrow favorite, and on June 15, 1869, a huge crowd poured out to Ridgewood Park, in present-day Queens, eager to see the outlanders get their comeuppance. They jeered and taunted the visitors so severely that John Morrissey, prince of gamblers, wondered aloud if the Red Stockings would rattle. Assured by a Cincinnati sportswriter that they would not, he put down a large bet on the visitors.

His confidence was rewarded. Asa Brainard shut down the Mutuals with his "scientific pitching," if only by the more prosaic score of 4–2. News of the victory stunned New York and set off a wild celebration in the streets of Cincinnati. The jubilant Red Stockings' management extended their tour for months, and the team remained undefeated, going 65-0-1. George Wright hit .519 on the tour, belting fifty-nine home runs, scoring 339 runs, and winning acclaim as "the beau ideal of a shortstop." Harry Wright, pitching and playing centerfield, blasted seven home runs in a single game. The following April the Red Stockings took up where they had left off, running their undefeated streak to 130 consecutive games. They appeared as unbeatable as ever, the undisputed kings of baseball. In desperation, New Yorkers turned to Brooklyn.

Across the East River, a bevy of new teams—the Atlantics, Excelsiors, Eckfords, and Putnams—had surpassed the old Brooklyn Club, and others were nearly as good. They played wherever they could, on the Capitoline Grounds and at Wheat Hall, and as early as 1856 a local newspaper bragged, "Verily, Brooklyn is fast earning the title of the 'City of Baseball Clubs' as well as the 'City of Churches.'"

It was a sorely needed balm to civic pride. Brooklyn had been expanding in every way throughout the nineteenth century, its rate of growth outpacing even Manhattan's. In 1820, there were only seven houses along the whole of Brooklyn Heights, and most of Kings County remained so many more acres of Long Island farmland. By 1870, Brooklyn had a population of nearly 420,000, making it the third-largest city in America. Prospect Park—which Olmsted considered his true masterpiece—had already been built, along with 352 of the town's famous churches. More parks, theaters, schools and colleges, hotels, department stores, and newspapers were springing up every day, and a bold new museum was already in the works, designed to dwarf Manhattan's Metropolitan Museum of Art.

Yet Brooklyn was also the nation's first great commuter suburb. More than 50 million people a year crossed the East River on fourteen different ferries, some 150,000 of them every working day. A pair of massive, 276-foot towers—the tallest structures on the continent—had already begun to rise on either side of the river, but proud as they were of the bridge that would bear their city's name, Brooklynites had to fund the lion's share of it and were inevitably overshadowed by their flashier sister city across the river.

"Brooklyn works for New York, and is paid off like a shop-girl on Saturday nights," sneered the journalist Julian Ralph.

What's more, New York's big-city turbulence was no longer restrained to the other side of the East River. "With this increase in size, the decay, noise, and fast lifestyle so many had fled Manhattan to avoid followed them across the river," Kenneth T. Jackson would write in his history of suburbia, *Crabgrass Frontier.*

By 1855, nearly 47 percent of all Brooklyn residents were foreign-born, most of them from Ireland. The city had five hundred factories by 1865; fifteen years later, it had more than *five thousand.* Many of these were enormous industrial-age concerns, employing hundreds of workers. There was now a huge bookbinding and printing enterprise near the Navy Yard, breweries in Williamsburg, chemical works in Bushwick, oil refineries in Greenpoint, vast grain silos and sugar refineries along the Red Hook docks; garment factories, metalworks, and food processing plants were everywhere.

Brooklyn had become a workingman's town, and this would influence the baseball played there as well. Brooklyn teams were distinctly more blue collar, more ethnic than their Manhattan rivals. So were their fans. In 1860, the decisive game in a "national championship" match—between Jim Creighton's "effete" Brooklyn Excelsiors and the working-class Brooklyn Atlantics—ended when the taunts of the Atlantics' "Irish" kranks and gamblers became so menacing that the Excelsiors, who were winning the game, walked off the Putnam grounds and refused to ever play the Atlantics again.

This didn't stop the Atlantics from happily claiming the crown as the best ball team in existence. They won more alleged national titles in 1864 and 1865, and by 1870 they looked to be the only team in sight capable of playing with Cincinnati.

In mid-June, the Red Stockings returned east for a showdown with the Atlantics. The East River ferries and the horse cars bulged with fans again, making their way this time to the Capitoline Grounds, located between Putnam and Nostrand Avenues, in the heart of what is now Bedford-Stuyvesant. By the first pitch an estimated twenty thousand were on hand, with still more teetering from nearby tree limbs or on the tops of the grandstand fences. They provided the visitors with a hearty Brooklyn greeting, *The New York Times* railing the next day about "the miserable partisan character of the assemblage which was the most discreditable gathering we have seen on the Capitoline Grounds for many years."

Discreditable or not, what they took part in was the first epic contest in the history of Brooklyn baseball. Cool as ever, the Red Stockings ignored the abuse from the looming spectators just behind the ropes strung along the outfield and the baselines, and jumped out to a quick three-run lead. It looked as if Cincinnati's winning streak would go on forever.

But as the hot, sunny afternoon continued, the Atlantics' starter, George "the Charmer" Zettlein (known also as the Lively Turtle), kept the game close, the Red Stockings—perhaps rattled a little after all by the menacing mobs just beyond the playing field—made some uncharacteristic errors, and Brooklyn rallied. At the end of nine innings the game was even, 5–5, and the Brooklyn nine was willing to take the tie and go home. But Harry Wright, virtuous as ever, insisted on extra innings. The Red Stockings scored two more runs in the top of the eleventh, and it look as though that were that. But in the bottom of the inning, a run-scoring triple by Brooklyn's first baseman, "Old Reliable" Joe Start—that is to say, a fly ball aided by an Atlantics fan jumping on the back of the Cincinnati left fielder—sparked another rally. (The fan was arrested, but the play was allowed to stand.) The Atlantic captain, Bob "Death to Flying Things" Ferguson—believe it or not, only one of two players on the team with that nickname—singled in Start, then scored the winning run on another error.

The Brooklyn fans went mad, swarming the field, ringing cowbells, and carrying their heroes off on their shoulders, and the match was immediately dubbed "the Most Exciting Game on Record." Harry Wright, true to form, marched resolutely to the nearest telegraph office and sent the following wire back to Ohio: 'TO THE CINCINNATI COMMERCIAL. JUNE 14. ATLANTICS 8, CINCINNATI 7. THE FINEST GAME EVER PLAYED. OUR BOYS DID NOBLY, BUT FORTUNE WAS AGAINST US. THOUGH BEATEN, NOT DISGRACED."

The Cincinnati fans saw it differently. Once the Red Stockings had surrendered their aura of invincibility, they lost all interest in the team, in what remains to this day an unsurpassed display of front running. (Even some Yankees fans would settle for a record of 130-1.) Wright packed up his bat and ball, his brother, and most of his other stars and took them up to Boston, where they soon established a new dynasty under the same team name of "Red Stockings."

7

A League

The consequences of Cincinnati's barnstorming would outlive the team itself. In their three seasons on the road, the Red Stockings had drawn 179,000 fans, and established businessmen of all sorts pondered how to fully exploit this latest, marvelous American industry. What they came up with was an audacious, rationalized, and quite likely illegal system typical of American capitalism of the time: a cartel, designed to extend its reach as far as possible across the country, minimize costs, and place all the power and the capital in the hands of management.

That is to say, a *league.*

At the end of 1870, the ineffectual old National Association of Base Ball Players, meeting at Collier's Café at Thirteenth Street and Broadway in Manhattan, effectively dissolved itself and reformed as the National Association of *Professional* Base Ball Players. The new National Association would be limited to nine teams, who would schedule and play a set number of games against each other. At the end of the season, the team with the best record would be declared the league champion.

Today, nearly a century and a half later, we take it for granted that professional sports will be organized around leagues, divisions, conferences. But there was no per se reason why this should be—why professional baseball shouldn't have continued to revolve around barnstorming tours and occasional test matches or tournaments much like, say, cricket or boxing or professional wrestling. In 1871, formal, professional leagues existed nowhere in America—nowhere anyplace else in the world.

The league system was another profound innovation, and it would provide baseball with both a workable structure and, eventually, one of its greatest glories, that of the long season. It would, for a start, define the whole psychology of the sport, the way in which ballplayers and managers learned to approach the game—and one that all too many fans and owners could never learn to accept. Baseball was not football, with emotions pushed to near-hysterical heights on a weekly basis. It would be a game played every day, and only the contained, the level, and the even-tempered would last, never *too* elated by victory or too despondent in defeat.

More important, the long season would become a vital part of the game's place in our collective memory. Baseball's day-to-day rhythms would frame and color the quotidian transit of our lives, and thus generate an unparalleled sense of nostalgia. Forever after, fans would remember where they were not only during some big game or critical inning but also during an entire season, a time in their lives. Running down a Brooklyn street, listening to the voice of Red Barber emanating from the radio through every window. Listening on a transistor on the beach, watching the scores go up in the big betting parlor window boards in Times Square. Talking the game over on summer porches in the encroaching twilight, going down to the corner drugstore to get the early edition and check out the ball scores. Watching each night on the flickering screen above the bar, following the feed on one's laptop. All of these memories sound like clichés because they are so universal and so deeply ingrained.

"Endless Red Sox thoughts on beaches, and in cabs, and while watching movies with Anthony Quinn in them," the radio host Jonathan Schwartz would remember of following his team through the fateful summer of 1978.

"Far from any ballpark, and without a television set, I went to bed early on most nights and lay there semi-comatose, stunned by another day of sunshine and salt air but kept awake, or almost awake, by the murmurous running thread of Bosox baseball from my bedside table," the game's great chronicler for *The New Yorker,* Roger Angell wrote of the same team, in the same season.

Who can reckon the quiet ecstasies passed by the less articulate among us, living our own special summers? Or summers that were not really special at all, following teams that did little or nothing, the endless, toddling summers of Washington Senators or Philadelphia Phillies? Stealing what little victories there were to be had: that rookie who pitched the shutout, or the outfielder who homered in his very first game, or that series so unexpectedly swept from the champs. The games go on and on, one season merging into another, both as startling and as blessedly mundane as the rest of our lives, with the pattern recognizable only after the fact.

8

"Lies, Damned Lies, and . . ."

Like so much of what we have come to treasure about baseball, the long season came about not because of any romantic tendencies on the part of the game's owners but for the most hardheaded of reasons. *Organize, commercialize, monopolize.* Like the cartels then blossoming in all American industries, a baseball league was supposed to rationalize everything, strictly define the difference between "major league" and the bushers, provide rules and predictable numbers of games, and thereby profit. Baseball would become not only professional but increasingly professional*ized,* its strategies sharpened, its rules refined, the very measures of the game constantly improved. It was a philosophy of refinement that would eventually, many years later, take the sport to where many of its most devoted fans did not want it to go.

Leading the way was Henry Chadwick, who tested baseball's laws each season in a preseason game at the Capitoline Grounds that he umpired himself. High-strung, combative, and eccentric, Chadwick claimed to be too nervous to umpire more meaningful contests. Everything about the game he loved brought him close to a state of religious torment. Born in England, Chadwick had moved to Brooklyn with his parents when he was twelve years old. He was a young sportswriter (and leading cricketer) in 1856, when he came across a baseball match between the Eagle and the Gotham teams at the Elysian Fields. The game enthralled him, and soon he was promoting it tirelessly in the many New York dailies he worked for and then the immensely popular *Beadle's Dime Base-Ball Player* and *Spalding's Base Ball Guide,* which he edited successively over a period of fifty years.

He was, as Bill James called him, "an intelligent, organized man" and "the first of that type to take the game seriously enough to get as much as he could to the public."

A true Victorian, Chadwick viewed the sport as both a moral calling and another industrial puzzle to be solved. No press-box hack, he was a devoted pianist and songwriter who also covered chess, billiards, yachting, theater, and, for a short time, the Civil War. His father had been a radical intellectual; his much older half brother, Edwin Chadwick, had won worldwide acclaim and a knighthood for his long work as England's "sanitary philosopher," the great reformer of its health laws and poor relief. For Henry, if he was going to devote himself to baseball, the game must possess uplift, meaning, and maximum efficiency.

"The saloon and brothel are the evils of the base ball world at the present day," Chadwick would typically proclaim in 1889. His priggishness and pontificating got on the nerves of his fellow sportswriters, one of whom described him in action: "[He] flouts himself down on a small stool in the way of the players and umpires—pulls out a large score book and several pencils, and throws a disdainful look towards the other members of the press, as much as to say, 'Do you know who I am? Why I am the 'What is it!' author of base ball and cricket, and the only writer on these subjects.' The conceit of this fellow runs away with his brains and we must have compassion on him."

Chadwick would, nevertheless, set the basic attitudes in the press box for decades to come. Ballplayers interested in forming a players' union he considered guilty of terrorism. He disdained anything "flashy," not only the strikeout, but also the home run, which he belittled as "the easiest hit . . . which the veriest novice at bat can make" but which then required "a good half-hour's rest to recuperate" from: "How much more effective is it, in the saving of strength, to earn single bases by hits."

To back his theories, Chadwick devised what would become another building block of the game. Statistics were already a national obsession. As early as 1830, an English visitor remarked that Americans were a "guessing, reckoning, and calculating people." Stock quotes, fishing hauls, and commodity prices filled countless columns of newspaper. Statistical periodicals and manuals abounded in every new business.

This was an entirely natural development for a people faced with what they saw as a new and seemingly infinite continent. It was reflected in the baseball field of the New York game, which was also theoretically infinite and made navigable only by strict division of territory into "fair" and "foul." Statistics were the tool of rational inquiry, the concession that what you thought you knew—or even what you saw—might not be right. American businessmen became obsessed with Frederick Taylor's thoughts on time management and industrial efficiency. Liberal social reformers such as Florence Kelley and Louis Brandeis used statistics to pick apart grand, utopian theories about laissez-faire capitalism. Henry Chadwick's older brother used stats to measure the cleanliness of so great and messy an amalgamation as nineteenth-century London and bring it to health.

Baseball, broken down into countless discrete, individual pitches and plays could be dissected like no other game. Statistics would become an integral part of the sport, subject to as much commentary upon commentary as the Talmud.

Chadwick's Ur-statistics predictably favored team play and consistency over spectacle: "We are frequently surprised to find that the modest but efficient worker, who has played earnestly and steadily through the season . . . has come in, at the close of the race, the real victor." He was not really surprised at all, but like most of us clung to those stats that supported his own worldview. In this sense, Father Baseball might also be considered the father of the *mis*measurement of the game, with his emphasis on batting average, which he practically invented, over the home run, and his obliviousness to what today's legions of sabermetricians have shown to be much more telling statistics, such as on-base percentage and slugging average.

But Chadwick's preoccupation with statistics did leave us with two wonderful gifts. The first was his system of keeping score, that all-American pastime. Scorekeeping in general would undergo many changes over the years, but Chadwick's bold, distinctive *K* to indicate a "strikeout"—a word he coined—remains. The second was the box score—"the mortar of which baseball is held together," according to Branch Rickey; for Roger Angell, "one of my favorite urban flowers . . . a precisely etched miniature of the sport itself." Chadwick's first appeared in the *New York Clipper* in 1859, reporting an upset in South Brooklyn by the Stars over the powerhouse Excelsiors.

Box scores in one form or another had been appearing in newspapers since at least 1845, when one popped up in New York *Morning News* articles reporting on the first championship series between the New York and the Brooklyn clubs. But these were only rudimentary lists of outs made and runs scored. It was Chadwick who added hits, putouts, assists, errors—all designed, in the description of baseball historian Jules Tygiel, to make of each game "a series of mini-morality plays." For Chadwick, it was just that, with errors handed out freely and hits hard-won.

9

Drawing the Color Line

After the bitter rejection endured by Octavius Catto and the Pythians of Philadelphia in their effort to join the NABBP, Black ballplayers had tried to take the white advice that they "organize a National Association of their own."

Easier said than done. The ten-team Southern League of Colored Base Ballists debuted in 1886, but quickly folded. The following year, African Americans in the North formed the National Colored Base Ball League, or League of Colored Base Ball Clubs, with the New

York Gorhams defeating the Pittsburgh Keystones, 11–8, in the league opener on May 6, 1887. But this eight-team circuit lasted only a week. The African American community, poor, despised, and relentlessly persecuted by whites in the atmosphere of runaway racism that marked the end of Reconstruction, simply could not spare the capital to support a baseball league of its own.

Instead, they were forced to settle for barnstorming tours or, occasionally, a chance to play in white minor leagues. Probably the best Black professional club in the New York area was the New York Cuban Giants. They were founded by Frank P. Thompson, headwaiter of the Argyle Hotel out in Babylon, Long Island, who merged four earlier Black clubs—the original hotel team, known variously as the Argyle Athletics and the Babylon Black Panthers, the Manhattans, the Orions, and the Keystones—into a single all-star team in the summer of 1885. The Cuban Giants were not, in fact, Cubans. This fig leaf was necessary to appease white crowds. Observers reported that the Giants even babbled nonsense to each other on the field, hoping to foster the idea that they were really speaking Spanish. The whole act was the start of an extended hope on the part of Black players that somehow they might be able to make it into the big leagues as Hispanics, or maybe Indians—anything other than what they were: the only people banned from the national game.

It proved a vain hope. The playing waiters took the unofficial title of "Colored Champions" in 1887 and 1888, after they defeated the Big Gorhams, in a silver ball game. They regularly played white semiprofessional, college, and major-league teams and lost a match to the Detroit Wolves—the white World Series champions at the time—by only 6–4. Weirdly, sadly, the Cuban Giants and the Big Gorhams even rented themselves out to play for different cities in white minor leagues. The Cuban Giants represented Trenton, New Jersey, and York, Pennsylvania, in the Middle States League in 1889 and 1890, respectively, and played for Ansonia in the Connecticut State League in 1891. The Big Gorhams played for Easton in the Middle States League in 1889 and reportedly put together a 100-4 record in 1891.

Nevertheless, the Big Gorhams went belly-up at the end of that halcyon season. The plight of Black ballplayers reflected that of African Americans everywhere during the hate-filled, rapidly segregating days of post-Reconstruction America. They played where they could, often excluded from "white" ball fields. An early site Black Brooklyn clubs had to use was the "Yukaton Skating Pond." Little money ended up in the hands of the players; the Cuban Giants, the most financially successful Black ball club of the era, usually made all of $12–$18 a game.

A few dozen brave souls persisted in trying to force their way into white baseball, especially after the National Association came apart in 1875 and its successor, the National League (NL), was formed without any *formal* color line. These men were literally risking their lives during a time when lynching was constant and unpunished. Full equality was out of the question; even the best Black players were paid $100 less than their worst white teammates. Everywhere, African Americans were met with a cascade of vitriol from the stands, from opponents, from teammates, and even from umpires. An International League arbiter announced publicly that he would always rule against a Black player. The catcher Moses Fleetwood Walker found that his own pitcher, Tony Mullane, wouldn't take his signals when Walker joined the big-league Toledo Blue Stockings. Robert Higgins, a Black rookie pitcher for the minor-league Syracuse Stars, was greeted with chants of "Kill the n——r!" from the fans. Three southern teammates deliberately tried to lose games Higgins pitched; in one, they made enough errors to surrender twenty-one unearned runs. Two of them refused to even pose in the same team picture with Higgins. "I am a Southerner by birth, and I tell you I would rather have my heart cut out before I would consent to have my picture in the group," one of them informed him.

Still, an estimated fifty-five Black players managed to take the field in twenty different white professional leagues—including the big leagues—from 1883 to 1898. Many proved themselves at least the equal to their white teammates—to no avail. The Cuban Giants' star pitcher, George Washington Stovey, dominated the Eastern League during the two seasons he was allowed to play there, winning thirty and thirty-four games. This earned him neither a raise nor a promotion, only a release and a return to the Cuban Giants. John W. Jackson, a.k.a. Bud Fowler, the very first professional Black player, starred in several white leagues, mostly at second base. The son of a barber in Cooperstown, New York, Fowler stuck it out for ten seasons in the white leagues—a record for a Black player that would be unmatched until Jackie Robinson—before moving on to the Cuban Giants as well, then back to his old hometown, the designated sacred ground of baseball. He died there of anemia, in abject poverty, after friends could not even organize a benefit game for him.

Ulysses F. "Frank" Grant was probably the leading Black player of the era, a steady .300 hitter with power who could also run and play second base as well as anyone in the white major leagues. Playing for the Buffalo Bisons in the International League, one step away from the majors, he endured it all: the chants of "Kill the n——r," the attempts to pass him off as a "Spaniard," the kicks and spikings from opposing base runners that became so insistent Grant eventually took to wearing a pair of wooden shin guards. Even this availed him little. A rare sympathetic white opponent, Ned Williamson, remembered that other whites "made a cabal against this man [Grant] and incidentally introduced a new feature into the game. . . . They filed their spikes and the first man at second generally split the wooden half cylinders [Grant was wearing]. The colored man seldom lasted beyond the fifth inning, as the base-runners became more expert."

Grant's teammates were more willing than Robert Higgins's to pose with him in the team picture, but the resulting photograph is revealing. In a composition that is the epitome of brotherly diamond devotion, nearly all of the fifteen players depicted are touching each other—a common masculine sign of affection at the time: a hand on a shoulder or an arm. Only Grant sits alone, hands to himself, neither touching nor touched by anyone around him.

During his three seasons with Buffalo, Grant hit .344, .353, and .346 and led the league in home runs twice and stolen bases once. His reward, at the end of the 1888 season, was to be informed that the International League would no longer tolerate Black players. The major leagues had already reached a "gentleman's agreement" to the same effect. The "gentleman" in question was Cap Anson, one of the most venerated players in the game, who yelled out, "Get that n——r off the field!" when he first spotted Fleet Walker before an exhibition against Toledo.

Anson seems to have been an obsessive racist even for his day, one who bragged of keeping "a little darkey . . . a little coon" that he hauled around with his team on road trips, to be entertained by his singing and dancing. Cap did not even play in the same league as Walker, but he was fixated on driving Fleet and his teammate and brother, Welday Walker, out of the game, publicly calling them a pair of "chocolate-covered coons."

The Walkers would be the last African Americans to play major-league baseball until Jackie Robinson, sixty years later. The experience was galling for both brothers, college men whose father was a doctor. After being forced out of baseball, Welday would become a businessman and Fleet would become an inventor with four patents to his name, but they still found no acceptance in white society. Civil rights activists, they wrote and published a pamphlet titled *Our Home Colony: A Treatise on the Past, Present, and Future of the Negro Race in America,* that urged Black people to return to Africa, since they could expect "nothing . . . but failure and disappointment in America."

Frank Grant would also be banished back to the Cuban Giants, then spend the last thirty-six years of his life working as a waiter. Cap Anson, on the other hand, became one of the very first players inducted into the Hall of Fame, and when he fell on hard times in his later years, the National League owners volunteered to give him a pension.

One player from another ethnic group that white America remained ambivalent about also made it to the major leagues during this period. Esteban "Steve" Bellán, an actual Cuban who had been educated at Fordham's Rose Hill prep school, played the infield and outfield for three years on the Troy Haymakers and then the New York Mutuals of the National Association. Bellán was one of a group of Cuban students who picked up the game at American schools and colleges, and he would return to play for Club Habana in his native Cuba. In 1878, he founded that country's first professional league, which would last until another former ballplayer, Fidel Castro, shut it down in 1961. A spark had been struck. As early as 1879, American players had begun touring and playing winter ball for Cuban clubs. The game would soon take off across the Caribbean.

10

"We Are the People!"

Racial discrimination didn't much bother the owners of the first major leagues. They were more concerned with why their new cartel was not proving to be the cash cow they had figured it to be. Attendance for the entire National Association never reached 400,000 in a season, and within five years professional sports' first league had folded.

One big problem was the fact that the franchises were largely self-selecting. The nine original National Association teams did not include many of the leading population centers in the United States, or hotbeds of baseball such as Cincinnati and Brooklyn. The sole original entry from the New York area, Boss Tweed's Mutuals, finished a dismal 16-17 in 1871—a bad year capped by the fact that Tweed himself was packed off to the Ludlow Street jail in October, for Homeric acts of malfeasance. Brooklyn joined the league in 1872 with both the Atlantics and the Eckfords, but the latter dropped out after one season and the Atlantics floundered, going 2-42 in 1875 and managing the remarkable feat of finishing more games out of first place—51½—than they had played.

Baseball regrouped, forming the National League of Professional Base Ball Clubs on February 2, 1876, once again in New York. This time, all clubs were charged an annual $100 fee to participate, and franchises were (supposedly) limited to cities with populations of at least seventy-five thousand. They did not include New York, with Tweed's old "Mutes" having folded after the 1876 season. From 1877 to 1883, there was not a single major-league franchise representing either New York or Brooklyn, the nadir of the professional game in the city. (In 1877, the NL's Hartford Dark Blues played their home games at Brooklyn's old Union Grounds, between Rutledge Street and Lynch Street, Harrison and Marcy Avenues in Williamsburg. But adding insult to injury, the team held fast to the name Hartford and the idea that they were representing the Connecticut capital—which would not crack the seventy-five-thousand population mark until the turn of the century.)

Relief came from a pair of sportsmen and impresarios. John B. Day was a wealthy young tobacco dealer from Connecticut with an in at Tammany Hall, but he liked to consider himself first and foremost a ballplayer, pitching for amateur squads from New Jersey. Jim "Smiling Jeems" Mutrie was a first baseman from Chelsea, Massachusetts, who liked to think of himself as a manager. Together, they would bring the New York game back to its birthplace.

Mutrie was the more flamboyant of the two men, as his other nickname, Truthful James, might imply. He boasted an extravagant handlebar moustache and wore a stovepipe hat, tails, and tux whenever possible, including to the ballpark. It was Mutrie who took on what had been the leading challenge to New York ball clubs ever since the Knickerbockers had lost their lot on Madison Avenue, and would continue to be their biggest obstacle for decades to come: finding a decent place to play.

Searching around Manhattan's sparsely populated upper reaches for a venue, Mutrie came across a large, open field off the northeastern tip of Central Park, encompassing four square blocks between 110th and 112th Streets and what was then Fifth and Sixth Avenues. The site had a special history. It was where James Gordon Bennett Jr., the flamboyant publisher of *The New York Herald,* indulged one of his favorite hobbies, polo. But neither Bennett nor anyone else had played polo there since 1877, when the publisher had ruined both his engagement and his tenuous standing in New York society by showing up blind drunk at a party hosted by his fiancée, Miss Caroline May, and urinating into the fireplace. Following this performance Bennett fled to Europe, where he would largely remain for the rest of his life. His old polo club had been casting about for tenants ever since.

All Mutrie needed now was a moneyman. He found one after a game in which his semipro team walloped Day the tobacco dealer's team and drove the merchant-pitcher from the mound. There were no hard feelings, and the two men soon set about signing leading players, primarily from Brooklyn and from a recently dissolved minor-league team with the irresistible name the Rochester Hop Bitters. The

Hop Bitters became "the Metropolitan," as Mutrie and Day regally intended to style their team, sans the final *s.* Day's bankroll made it all possible, but even more important were his political connections.

Baseball, like everything else in New York, came down to that double-headed hydra: real estate and politics. Without a field, there could be no ball, and without a friend at Tammany Hall there could be no field.

It is still a commonplace for political analysts to refer to modern political organizations as "machines." But the truth is that no political organization in the United States today is any more than a shadow of what urban political machines were before the 1930s, and the greatest machine of all held court at Tammany Hall, then housed down on East Fourteenth Street. By the 1880s, Tammany was coming into its own as an organization, collecting payments and doling out favors and contracts with machinelike efficiency. Its power rested ultimately on the city's new immigrants and America's neglect of them. They went to Tammany for help in getting all the basic necessities of life, for jobs and bail money and shoes, and for the famous turkey at Christmas.

In return, Tammany asked for their votes. These it used to wield power over everything in the public realm—street paving, garbage collecting, policing, firefighting, building inspection—and thus put itself in a position to *provide* the jobs and the turkeys and the favors. The machine's reach extended everywhere. It controlled the city's roisterous street gangs—useful for intimidating "reform" voters and throwing ballot boxes in the river at election time—and extracted tribute from all of the city's known gamblers, whoremasters, and contractors. The machine was inherently conservative. Tammany might have been the only institution in the city at the time that consistently cared for the poor, but it needed them to stay poor. The machine favored business, from which it could also extort money, and suppressed unions, which were a potential rival. It ran the largest city in America along the lines of an Irish village, which is not surprising, considering where nearly all of Tammany's sachems traced their lineage to.

In Tammany's New York, anything might be granted as a privilege, but nothing as a right. Another of the clubhouse's many powers was control of land use. This meant that, again and again, the destinies of one baseball franchise after another would be decided by their success or failure at wheedling *land,* that age-old Irish obsession, out from under the control of the machine and its successors.

John B. Day got off easy. Thanks to his connections, Day was able to fend off threats to extend the Manhattan street grid through the middle of his new ball field, mostly by handing out free season tickets to the Board of Aldermen. Up went the first "Polo Grounds," a two-story wooden grandstand and bleachers—an ordinary, low-minor-league or college ballpark by today's standards, but as large and lavish a major-league stadium as existed at the time. There, on September 29, 1880, the Mets (or Met) played their first game, defeating the Washington Nationals, 8–3, behind Hugh Ignatius "One Arm" Daily. (One Arm Daily, who had lost his left hand in a shooting accident, would, appropriately enough, go on to become the first major-league pitcher to throw back-to-back one-hitters.)

That first season, the Metropolitan(s) played sixty games against National League teams, but they remained an unaffiliated minor-league club until 1883, when Day received an offer to join the new American Association (AA), the raucous new "Beer & Whiskey" circuit. He decided to mull it over for a season. In the interim, two teams in the National League went belly-up—one of them the Troy Trojans, who had been reduced to playing their games on an island in the Hudson before all of twelve fans. Now it was expected that the Metropolitans would turn down the American Association and take up residence in the NL.

Instead, Day pulled off as bold a coup as has ever been executed by a New York baseball owner, Jacob Ruppert, Walter O'Malley, George Steinbrenner, and Fred Wilpon included. Belatedly accepting the offer to place his Metropolitans in the American Association, Day then turned around and joined the National League as well. He signed most of Troy's roster, distributed its best players to his brand-new National League franchise—which he dubbed simply the New-Yorks, or Gothams—and handed the rest over to the Metropolitans.

New York was suddenly back in the big time with not one but two teams, and they were owned by the same man.

Day had also come up with a scheme to have both teams play not only in Manhattan but in the same park at the same time. While the NL Gothams took over the finished diamond in the south*east* corner of the Polo Grounds, Day went about installing the AA Metropolitans in the south*west* corner, hastily throwing up a new set of grandstands and bleachers there. He had an immediate success at the box office, with a crowd of more than fifteen thousand, including the former president Grant, mobbing the southeast field to see the Gothams play and win their home opener. (Unlikely as it may sound, it would *not* be the last time two different teams in two different leagues occupied one field called the Polo Grounds.)

The crowds kept coming. Day proved himself a tireless promoter, staging such stunts as having the heavyweight boxing champion John L. Sullivan pitch an exhibition game for the Metropolitans. But problems with his ballpark arrangement soon became apparent. The Mets' corner of the Polo Grounds was in awful condition, the diamond leveled off in part with "landfill" that proved to be raw garbage. The resourceful Day found his American Association entry their own "Metropolitan Park" the next season, located between 107th and 109th Streets along the East River. It seemed on paper like a great location, a scenic waterfront stadium with ready access from both the Second and the Third Avenue elevated lines and the Harlem Steamboat Company. Yet Day turned out to have an unerring nose for garbage. Metropolitan Park was also built over an old city dump, and just across the river from Astoria factories that pumped "foul smoke" into the faces of the fans. According to the New York *World,* the park was "decidedly unpleasant to the olfactory organs," and the Mets' pitcher John H. "Jack" Lynch claimed that a player might "go down for a grounder, and come up with six months of malaria."

The Mets were allowed to return to the Polo Grounds, at least on those days when the Gothams weren't playing at home. Plainly, Day considered them a poor stepchild to his National League investment. The team was run on such a limited budget that it resorted to stealing bats from opposing teams when they weren't looking.

Nonetheless, the nineteenth-century Mets would display the true underdog spirit of their later namesakes. They outstripped their cross-field rivals in 1884, running away with the American Association flag while the Gothams finished far out of contention. This Metropolitan squad was led by the likes of the shortstop Candy Nelson, who doubled the league record for walks, and the mammoth, 250-pound first baseman Dave "Jumbo" Orr, who led the league in hits and batting and who would go on to compile a lifetime slugging percentage of over .500 before suffering a paralytic stroke at the height of his career.

On the mound, Jack Lynch and the future Hall of Famer Sir Timothy Keefe racked up thirty-seven wins apiece. Keefe was a sensitive, gentlemanly soul who had been forbidden to play baseball as a boy by his father, liked to design his team's uniforms, and would later suffer a nervous breakdown after beaning a batter. A control artist, he might have been the first pitcher to learn how to change the speed of his pitches without changing his arm motion, and over the 1883 and 1884 seasons he and Lynch would pitch in all but one of the Metropolitans' 209 league games, running up a combined record of 128-74, with 206 complete games. (Few pitchers were as good, but most were expected to pitch as often, their endurance made possible by the fact that rule changes in the 1880s not only provided for a "dead" ball that was difficult to hit very far but also moved the mound to within fifty feet of home plate.)

After the 1884 season, Mutrie baited the National League champion Providence Grays into meeting the American Association Mets in the first officially sanctioned "World's Series." The Metropolitans lost all three games, but they had still had an outstanding season for a team that was forced to play on top of not one but two garbage dumps. Contemplating the unexpected results of his dual ownership, the grit and determination of his spunky, underdog Mets, and the failure of the Gothams, Day transferred the manager, Mutrie, Keefe, and the star third baseman Dude Esterbrook over to his National League franchise.

It would not be the last time that a New York team benefited by callously stripping another franchise's roster. The valiant Metropolitans sank to seventh place. After the 1885 season, Day ended his little experiment in dual ownership altogether, a sad fate for the Mets, but one that ensured that a major-league team would play in every borough in the (future) city of New York. Day fobbed the team off on one Erastus Wiman, who ran both the Staten Island Ferry and a primitive amusement park in Richmond County. Wiman plunked the Mets down in the middle of his park, on the grounds of the old St. George Cricket Club, and included the price of admission in his round-trip ferry ticket for fans coming over from Manhattan.

Yet Erastus Wiman, in that spring and summer of 1886, could offer his patrons something even better. From his ferry, and from the top rows of his Staten Island ballpark, fans could watch the workmen as they went about raising the Statue of Liberty on Bedloe's Island. Alas, even Lady Liberty did not prove to be enough of an attraction, and at the end of the 1887 campaign, after just two seasons on Staten Island, the original Mets quietly folded.

Day, meanwhile, set about consolidating his dream team, the first in a long line of New York owners chasing the chimera of perfection that baseball dangles before us. On the mound for the Gothams, Sir Timothy Keefe was joined by his fellow, future three-hundred-game winner, Mickey Welch, a five-foot-eight finesse pitcher who would complete his first 105 starts, and once struck out the first nine batters he faced, a record still unbroken in major-league ball today. In 1885, Keefe and Welch went 32-13 and 44-11, respectively, and finished 1-2 in the league with ERAs of 1.58 and 1.66. There were more future Hall of Famers in the infield, and at catcher with Buck Ewing, a power-hitting, hard-throwing receiver who was considered by many the best all-around player of the nineteenth century. Patrolling the outfield was the wonderfully matched combination of Silent Mike Tiernan and Orator Jim O'Rourke.

"Words of great length and thunderous sound simply flowed out of his mouth," one newspaper obituary would eulogize Orator Jim.

The most significant Gotham, though, would prove to be John Montgomery Ward, who looked every inch the team captain he was: a trim, handsome man who often posed for pictures with his muscular arms flexed in front of him. Breaking into the major leagues while still a 140-pound, jug-eared, eighteen-year-old hurler for the NL's Providence Grays, Ward pitched a perfect game in his first season. He ran up the highest single-season total of strikeouts in the 1870s, had won 164 games by the time he was twenty-four, and allowed fewer base runners per game than any man who has ever pitched in the majors.

When his arm went bad, Johnnie Ward (although often called Monte by baseball historians, Ward hated anything to do with his middle name, which he considered effeminate) converted himself into a base-stealing, hard-hitting infielder. Arriving in New York, Ward truly came into his own, taking one Broadway diva for his wife and another for his mistress, while still finding time to earn both political science and law degrees from Columbia University. (Yet another testament to what could be accomplished before the advent of television.) By the time he was thirty years old, Ward spoke five languages and was a practicing attorney, his courtroom style described as "shrewd, quick-witted and humorous; smiling and sarcastic."

Monte Ward was, as well, a natural leader, later described by Bill James as "the smartest, most alert player of his time"—smart enough to recognize, as he wrote in an article shortly after his retirement, that professional baseball "is not a Summer snap, but a business in which capital is invested. A player is not a sporting man. He is hired to do certain work, and do it as well as he possibly can." As much as any of his fellow ballplayers, Ward chafed under the reserve clause system by which baseball's owners kept most players in permanent thrall to themselves, and yearned to overturn it. More than any other, he possessed both the will and the ability to do something about it.

Life on the Gothams at least was a benevolent dictatorship. Day showered his stars with money. The payroll was a record $40,000, four times what the Cincinnati magnates had paid their original Red Stockings just fifteen years earlier and enough to have newspapers dub the franchise "the Gilt-Edged Team." They were an imposing squad: big, powerful men dressed in the hip black "funeral" uniforms that Keefe had designed for them, and the manager, Mutrie, began to refer to them as "my giants." The name stuck, and New York's first great team was born.

The Giants have largely faded from New Yorkers' collective memory now, a footnote to the charisma of all those postwar Dodgers teams, remembered mostly for Bobby Thomson and for Willie Mays, when they are remembered at all. Yet it was the Giants who dominated the city's sporting world from their inception to the rise of the Yankees in the early 1920s, and even after that they remained a far more popular and successful team than the Dodgers for another twenty years.

Many of the nineteenth-century Giants lived at the Broadway Central Hotel, near Washington Square, then the largest hotel in the world. On game days, the team would drive up to the Polo Grounds in open carriages, while their fans lined the streets to cheer. Once at the ballpark, Truthful James Mutrie would exhort the kranks, strutting around the grounds in his top hat and tails, shouting to the crowd, "Who are the people?" The fans would roar back, "We are the people! The Giant fans are the people!"

In fact, many of those in attendance were stars themselves, the biggest stage names in New York. They flocked to the Polo Grounds the way celebrities fill boxes at Yankee Stadium and courtside seats at Madison Square Garden today, before hastening back down to the theater district, then located around Fourteenth Street, for the evening's performance. They usually got their money's worth. Keefe and Welch propelled the club to a pennant in 1888, and in the World Series they breezed past Chris Von der Ahe's St. Louis Browns, considered by many the greatest team of the nineteenth century. Keefe won all four starts in the ten-game series, surrendering only two earned runs in thirty-five innings, while Johnnie Ward hit .379 and stole six bases.

In the fifth game, the Giants took a 6–4, darkness-shortened victory that would prove the last game ever played at the (real) old Polo Grounds. Later that year, the city finally succeeded in driving 111th Street through James Gordon Bennett Jr.'s former playground. Forced to search for a new park, Day took his Giants out to Jersey City for a couple of games to start the 1889 season, then over to the St. George Cricket Grounds on Staten Island, where his old foundling, the Metropolitans, had gone to die. The Cricket Grounds had been used for outdoor theater the year before, leaving it mostly devoid of grass, and stage scaffolding remained on part of the field. Heavy rains left the outfield so waterlogged that the Giants were forced to lay down wooden planks for their outfielders to clatter across in pursuit of fly balls. Picture a world-champion major-league team today trying to play in the pond behind Central Park's Delacorte Theater.

Yet Day retained his knack for sniffing out the most noxious, marginal fringes of the metropolis for his ball teams. Now his nose led him from a grassless swamp in Staten Island to a part of Manhattan that had been underwater just fifteen years earlier.

Coogan's Hollow, named for James J. Coogan, another politically connected businessman, was actually two lots of land, each of them running along Eighth Avenue below the 155th Street viaduct. Until 1874 it had literally been under the East River, but like so much of Manhattan the wonders of landfill had raised it from the depths. Christened Manhattan Field, it was rented out from time to time, but largely unimproved from its submerged days. It was such a large area that Day decided he only had to lease the southern lot. It was a choice that would cost him everything.

No doubt it was made in haste. Day spotted the site for his new park on June 21, 1889; he had it up and open for business by July 8, and called—the Polo Grounds. In the course of those seventeen days he not only purchased the field but also hired a leading ballpark architect, graded the property, and frugally hauled up the grandstand of the original Polo Grounds for its lumber. Some ten thousand fans made the trip uptown for the first game. The crowd included the actor DeWolf Hopper, already famous for his dramatic stage recitals of "Casey at the Bat" and who in true thespian fashion let out "a blood-curdling war whoop" as he entered the park. Less fortunate fans started a new tradition by crowding Coogan's Bluff, or "Dead-Head Hill," a rocky promontory high above the new Polo Grounds. There they would become a fixture in newspaper photos over the next few decades, pacing or sitting; forlorn-looking men in dark suits and dark bowlers, a flock of envious crows overlooking the festivities.

Settling into their new digs, the Giants went on a tear, getting another fifty-five wins from Keefe and Welch, both in their last, great season. (On September 10, Welch struck out in a new role, as the first pinch hitter allowed under major-league rules. Yes, the first pinch hitter was a pitcher.) The Giants squeaked past a rising young Boston Beaneaters team on the last day of the season and made it back to the postseason, where, for the first and only time in their existence, they would play the World Series against the Brooklyn Dodgers.

11

"Work of the Sneaky Order"

Technically speaking, the Giants would actually be playing the Brooklyn Bridegrooms, as they were known at the moment. Brooklyn was happy to call them anything. The city had suffered an even longer hiatus from the majors than New York had. Ever since the departure of the inscrutable "Brooklyn Hartfords" after the 1877 season, the city had been without a big-league team and almost bereft of professional baseball altogether.

Late in 1882, George Taylor, James Gordon Bennett Jr.'s editor at the *Herald,* set out to do something about this. Taylor formed the Brooklyn Base Ball Association with the help of two partners he had recruited, his lawyer, John Brine, and Brine's office partner, a realtor named Charles Byrne. Byrne would be the real power in this triumvirate, since most of the money for the venture was provided by a silent partner, one Joseph Doyle, who was both Byrne's brother-in-law and the proprietor of a gambling den in Manhattan. Also hired on was an ambitious young Brooklyn printer named Charles Hercules Ebbets, to print scorecards, keep the books, and sell tickets.

Before they could set up shop, though, this unlikely crew had to go through the usual, tortured search for a place to play. They settled on a space known as the Washington skating pond, near the Gowanus Canal, between Third and Fifth Streets, and Fourth and Fifth Avenues. Crews worked throughout the winter of 1882–83 to grade the property and build a $30,000 grandstand, with dressing rooms and a bar under the seats. The famous "old stone house at Gowanus," where three hundred Marylanders died saving Washington's army during the Battle of Brooklyn in 1776, was converted into a clubhouse, according to some accounts. The new owners spared no expense, lavishing so much money on the park that Doyle had to bring in a fellow gambler, one Ferdinand Abell, from Narragansett, Rhode Island, to lay off the costs.

To find ballplayers, the Brooklyn Base Ball Association put an ad in the papers seeking men with "integrity of character," "a clear record for temperate habits," "intelligence," and not "corner-lot roughs who happen to possess some skill as players but whose habits and ways make them unfit for thorough teamwork."

Bold words for a club financed by gamblers. But Byrne and company immediately received forty applications and were able to field a squad that spring, joining the minor-league Interstate Association and playing against teams such as the Active of Reading, the Anthracite of Pottsville, the Merritt of Camden, and the Quickstep of Wilmington, Delaware. One wonders why this circuit was not renamed the Death to Plural Names League, though the Brooklyn squad was unimaginatively dubbed the Grays, after the color of their—and pretty much everyone else's—uniforms.

After dropping their very first game on the road, the Grays won their home opener against Harrisburg, 7–1, on May 9, 1883. Because Washington Park was still not ready, the game had to be played, free of charge before some two thousand kranks, on the Parade Ground of Prospect Park—the one and only professional game ever played there. Three days later, the Grays pounded Trenton, 13–6, before a crowd of more than six thousand at the official grand opening of their new park.

Yet the big story in Brooklyn that month was not the return of baseball. On May 24, "the Eighth Wonder of the World," the Brooklyn Bridge, fourteen years in the making, was opened in a grand ceremony that featured fireworks, parades, and a speech by President Chester Alan Arthur. The bridge was a marvel of technology and design, the longest suspension bridge in the world at the time, the five lanes along its platform able to accommodate wagons, carriages, trains, and pedestrians.

Brooklyn had paid for the bridge, had lent the span its name, its genius, and its aspirations for the future. And yet it would also spell the beginning of the end of its independence. The bridge would connect it to New York as never before, making it easier than ever to commute. It would put out of business all the ferry lines across the East River—the crossings on which Walt Whitman had marveled at the streams of humanity all around him. Whitman had celebrated a Brooklyn full of rural fields, in which men and boys played pickup games of baseball. Now it was a denser, harder, more complex place, choked with all the opportunities, the grandeur, and the squalor of an industrial-age city.

Yet if its independence had begun to seep away, Brooklyn was back in the big leagues. After taking the Interstate flag, the Grays were admitted into the American Association in 1884, then bought the player contracts of John Day's discarded Metropolitans. By this time, they were no longer the Grays so much as the Trolley Dodgers, a derisive name New Yorkers flung at all Brooklynites, due to the maze of trolley lines that crossed their city. Thus, the old Mets became the new Dodgers.

Brooklyn's first few years in the American Association were disappointing, but before the 1889 season began, several of the Dodgers' leading stars got married, and it was put about that the newlyweds were refraining from sex down the stretch run—an idea so titillating that the fans temporarily rechristened the club the Bridegrooms. Whatever the reason, Brooklyn was able to dethrone the champion Browns by two games and advance to what would have been the very first Subway Series against the Giants—save for the fact that the subway would not be built for another fifteen years.

The Bridegrooms were the clear underdogs going into the—Streetcar? Omnibus? Carriage?—Series. They were a quietly efficient, solid team, but one lacking most of the Giants' panache or their power. Their best player was the pitcher Parisian Bob Caruthers, who was so named because he had once negotiated a large salary increase for himself while vacationing in the French capital. In 1889, Parisian Bob led the American Association with forty wins and seven shutouts, but by the World Series he and every other Brooklyn hurler seemed to be pitched out, and they were hammered early and often by the Giants.

The series in general was marred by bickering and disputed decisions. The Bridegrooms took three of the first four games, mostly by eking out a narrow lead, then deliberately stalling until the game had to be called for darkness. Their tactics enraged the Giants and their fans.

"We have played like men, but the Brooklyns have disported themselves like schoolboys. Their work throughout has been of the sneaky order," accused the New York star Buck Ewing.

All tactics of the sneaky order aside, the Giants took the last five games of the series as Johnnie Ward led the team with a .417 average, drove in seven runs, and stole ten bases. But it was only after the series that Ward truly amazed the sporting world.

12

Strike!

At the conclusion of the 1889 season, professional baseball seemed to be solidly reestablished in New York and Brooklyn. The professional game in general had never looked more stable or more prosperous. But to a baseball owner, things can never be prosperous enough.

The major leagues remain to this day the most complete and enduring cartel in American history. A cartel directed against not only potential business rivals but also the customers, whom they charge ever-higher prices; the general public, whom they constantly lobby for subsidies; and their own employees, whose compensation, or even right to have anything to say about their compensation, baseball's owners still contest.

As early as the 1870s, owners had tried to contain their payroll costs by adopting salary caps, but they proved unable to abide by their own rules. Instead, they granted themselves an insuperable advantage in any and all contract negotiations by adopting the "reserve clause," originally just for star players but eventually for all players on all rosters.

The two, supposedly rival leagues even agreed to honor each other's reserve clauses. Contrary to everything in both the U.S. Constitution and established labor law, baseball players alone, among all the workers in America, would be deprived of the right to sell their services in the marketplace. Instead, they were "owned" in perpetuity by their teams, who could decide to offer them a new contract, or fire them, or trade or sell them to another team. If they wanted more money, or they wanted to live in a different city, or they hated their manager, that was too bad. They could play for the franchise that owned them, or they could take up another line of work.

"Players have been bought, sold and exchanged as though they were sheep instead of American citizens," John Montgomery Ward protested in an 1887 magazine article titled "Is the Ballplayer a Chattel?" that compared the reserve clause to the Fugitive Slave Act.

Yet then as now, few if any kranks or sportswriters thought of men who got to play baseball for a living as slaves. If Ward were going to do something about the reserve clause, he would have to do more than take his case to the public. He would have to organize.

Working with the utmost secrecy, Ward recruited the top stars in the game. On October 22, 1885, they announced the formation of the very first players' union, the Brotherhood of Professional Base Ball Players. (Ward also wanted to open the brotherhood to Black ballplayers, but was stopped by a faction led, of course, by Chicago's Cap Anson.)

Caught flat-footed, the baseball owners officially recognized the brotherhood and agreed to some limits on the reserve clause and to give players a say in how they would be treated and disciplined. It was more than any baseball union would accomplish for another eighty years. But the peace was an illusion. The owners waited until Albert Spalding took Ward and the other leading lights of the brotherhood on a round-the-world, barnstorming junket. While the American all-stars played ball under the nose of the Sphinx and the shadow of the new Eiffel Tower, the National League owners met and threw out their previous agreement with the players. They replaced it with a "classification" system under which all ballplayers would fall into one of five categories and be paid accordingly—no less than $1,500, no more than $2,500. There was no appeal; the National League owners refused to even meet with the brotherhood until the 1889 season was over.

It was a clear attempt to break the union. On October 29, five days after leading his Giants to their World Series triumph, Ward responded with a countercoup, a grand vision he had been formulating for some time: the players would start a league of their own. Each team would be run by a board that included both players and investors, or "contributors," with the moneymen to get the first $10,000 in profits made by each club, the next $10,000 to go to the players, and any profit after that to be divvied up evenly. No players could be traded or sold without their consent. None could be released without the consent of their fellow players. The hated reserve clause and the salary cap would be eliminated, but to ensure stability for the contributors, all of the players would sign three-year contracts to start with. Gate receipts would be split evenly among all the teams, and the league would be administered by a "senate" of eight investors and eight players.

It was a remarkable plan. Even the Players' League equipment contract was given over to a new sporting goods firm co-owned by Tim Keefe—the idea being to further drain the NL of cash by breaking owner Al Spalding's monopoly on major-league balls and bats. The formation of the Players' League was announced on November 6, 1889, at the Fifth Avenue Hotel, a swank establishment near Madison Square, the site of so much early New York baseball. It set off a dizzying game of musical chairs, until it was hard to tell the local teams without a scorecard.

Charles Byrne moved first and took his Brooklyn Bridegrooms from the tottering American Association over to the financially more secure National League. The American Association tried to fill the gap by creating a new team, the Brooklyn Gladiators. John Ward jumped the East River to found the Players' League's Brooklyn Wonders franchise, with himself installed as the club's manager and shortstop. Back in Manhattan, a local tobacco magnate, Edward McAlpin, and his partner, the stockbroker Edward B. Talcott, set up the Players' League's *own* New York Giants team. They also snatched up the northern half of Manhattan Field, right alongside the Polo Grounds, and christened their new field Brotherhood Park.

When the music stopped, New York and Brooklyn had not two but *five* major-league teams between them—more professional baseball teams than would ever play again at one time within the confines of what is today New York City. The Brooklyn Gladiators were the first to lose out in this battle royal. A largely anonymous team, moving from field to field, they compiled a miserable 26-73 record. One of the losses included a game they had been leading but were forced to forfeit to the Columbus Solons when they ran out of baseballs. Before the end of August, the Gladiators had fallen on their sword. Johnnie Ward's Wonders finished second in the Players' League, probably outdrew the National League Bridegrooms at the gate, but still lost money. The Bridegrooms fared best on the field, winning the depleted National League along with two-thirds of their games, but struggled at the box office.

Back in New York, the season was even weirder, with two different "New York Giants" teams playing cheek by jowl, often on the same day, on neighboring lots up at Manhattan Field. Forced to scramble for replacement players, John Day's National League Giants managed to acquire a hard-throwing teenager named Amos Rusie, "the Hoosier Thunderbolt," who would become probably the greatest New York ballplayer nobody today has ever heard of. A strapping, hot-tempered farm boy from Indiana, Rusie stood six feet one and 200 pounds in a day when pitchers averaged five ten and 170. He threw a biting curve and a changeup that played havoc with batters. But most of all, there was his fastball—one of the first great fastballs, the power pitch that would capture the imagination of baseball fans nearly as much as the home run. It was said that Rusie's speed was what forced the big leagues to move the distance from the pitcher's mound to home plate back from fifty feet to sixty feet, six inches, once and for all. It was said that Rusie threw so hard that his first major-league catcher, Dick Buckley, lined his primitive catcher's mitt with lead. The fact that the Hoosier Thunderbolt could not always control the pitch, that he was wilder than any leading pitcher to date, did not detract from his effectiveness.

Rusie's first summer in New York often seemed like a game of catch between himself and the catcher as he walked 289 batters and fanned 341. His best game of the season served to illustrate not only his talent but also the ludicrous position his team was in. On May 12, 1890, still shy of his nineteenth birthday, Rusie hooked up in a duel with the Boston Beaneaters' own phenom, Kid Nichols, a twenty-year-old rookie but already one of the best pitchers in the majors. The two young hurlers traded goose eggs deep into the afternoon, mowing down hitter after hitter, and for a little while the years seemed to slip away and the game reverted to its essence, just a couple of talented kids trying to throw the ball past anyone who dared to stand up against them, without regard to labor wars or industrial cartels.

Word of this pitching duel for the ages quickly spread over to Brotherhood Park, where the Players' League doppelgängers of Boston and New York were performing in front of a crowd that was more than twice as large. As the innings went by, the fans began to slide over to the top of the right-field bleachers of Brotherhood Park, where they could see into the Polo Grounds, gleefully enjoying that ultimate New York deal, two games for the price of one.

In the top of the thirteenth inning, Nichols struck out Rusie—under what were the official rules until the 1940s, the Giants could and did choose to hit first in their own ballpark—then laid one in a little too fat to Silent Mike Tiernan, who drove a prodigious shot to centerfield that not only cleared the Polo Grounds wall but landed in the alleyway between the two parks. The crowd in both parks went wild.

"And why not?" asked *The New York Times.* "Tiernan had done what few people ever believed could be accomplished. The ball struck the fence of Brotherhood Park." Rusie put the Beaneaters down again in the bottom of the thirteenth for a stirring 1–0 victory.

It was not enough to save John B. Day. His Giants were outplayed and outdrawn by the brotherhood, and at the end of the season he was forced to sell out to his club's minority owner. Had Day only thought to buy up the rest of Manhattan Field, he might have deprived his rivals of a place to play and won the battle for New York. Instead, he ended up living off token jobs around the National League offices, dying in poverty in 1925.

Yet if the Players' League won the battle for Manhattan, it would lose the war. The brotherhood had all but wrecked the American Association, had outdrawn the National League, and had even won a pair of court decisions that invalidated the hated reserve clause—the greatest legal victories the players would ever win against this device that so clearly violated every aspect of American law and custom but somehow proved so hard for justices to outlaw.

All of this would count for nothing against the wiles of Albert Spalding, who led his fellow National League owners in cleverly exaggerating their gate receipts and cash reserves, and so gnawed away at the confidence of the Players' League's "contributors."

"If either party ever furnished to the press one truthful statement, a monument should be erected to his memory. . . . We had been playing two games—baseball and bluff," Spalding later crowed.

It was the bluff that prevailed. The Players' League had sustained serious financial losses, forgoing two major streams of revenue by refusing to play on Sundays or to allow the sale of alcohol. The contributors sold out for the cash payoffs or the part ownerships Spalding offered them in National League teams, and by October 20, 1890, just days after the end of its first and only season, the Players' League was dead.

John Ward railed at first against the "stupidity, avarice, and treachery" of his investors. But he soon calmed down and joined Albert Spalding at a wake held for the Players' League at "Uncle" Nick Engel's Home Plate Saloon, at 16 West Twenty-Seventh Street in Manhattan. The Home Plate, as the baseball historian Don Jensen notes, laid a fair claim to being America's very first sports bar. But it was something more, much more than how we think of such establishments today, franchised drones or dilapidated, faux Irish pubs with the word "Blarney" in their names, and rows of dull-eyed faces staring dutifully up at the TV sets above the bar. In those pre-electronic days, a sports bar was where you went to see the sports, not the games; manly reserves where the stars of other pastimes came to mingle with the athletes. Mark Twain and Maurice Barrymore, patriarch of the theatrical clan, were regulars at Uncle Nick's, along with countless swells and society toffs, theatrical producers, press agents, boxing champs, bicycle racers, and assorted New York Giants.

"Engel's Home Plate sat on an entertainment fault line," Jensen notes, and it was one that said a great deal about the city.

Just opened to the east was Stanford White's diaphanous new Madison Square Garden, surmounted by Augustus Saint-Gaudens's golden statue of a naked Diana, the huntress, with bow in hand. New York's ever-peregrinating theater district had come to roost nearby, and the hit makers of Tin Pan Alley had followed, filling West Twenty-Eighth Street with the torture of decrepit pianos. Hither and yon were scattered the most brilliant hotels and women's shops of the "Ladies' Mile" and assorted other entertainments (including a wax museum that held a cast of Johnnie Ward's famous actress wife, Helen Dauvray). And just a few yards away could be found all the most openly depraved bars and brothels of the Tenderloin, Manhattan's brazen red-light district.

It was a stupefying intersection of New York as it approached the turn of the century. Gaudy with talent and genius, jeweled and (literally) electrified, dripping with wealth, and begrimed and corrupted beyond belief. Nick's stood as an odd middle ground in this carnival of pleasures, Janus-faced, full of the latest celebrities but infused with a touch of the old New York. Uncle Nick claimed to have been an umpire, but mostly he'd made his way as a restaurateur, renowned for his chowders and steaks. He had learned his trade under Uncle Billy Miller in an ancient cave by the Lower East Side waterfront known as Shannon's Corner, from whence Nick had brought the barbaric ritual of the beefsteak: slabs of hickory-broiled beef, smeared with butter and eaten *solely by hand*—no utensils allowed—and washed down with countless mugs of ale. It was a feast for carnivores, the bright-toothed movers and shakers of the world's most ambitious city, who would drape smocks over their fine suits and employ towels for napkins before digging in. It would become a city tradition—one often indulged in, unsurprisingly, by that later shanghaier of the Dodgers, Walter O'Malley.

But that was far in the future. Now, near the end of that fall afternoon in 1890, Ward raised his glass for a last toast: "The League is dead, long live the League."

It was the end of a dream—a dream that the players themselves might own the game and play it as they wished. This was all right for Ward, who was allowed to return to the consolidated Brooklyn National League team as its manager and shortstop. Other members of the brotherhood, who were not blessed with his college degrees or his star magnitude, did not fare as well. Many were released, some were blacklisted, and salaries were driven down to an average of $2,000 by the end of the 1890s.

Spalding's National League, so close to ruin, ended up as the only one left on the field. After the 1891 season, the American Association folded, too, with its four most successful franchises allowed into the NL. The National League owners now formed a twelve-team cartel and controlled every minor league in the country. But the sort of unchallenged, monopoly capitalism that Spalding extolled, a system that seemed triumphant everywhere in America by the last decade of the nineteenth century, was about to be severely roiled again. Baseball would not be immune to the consequences.

13

Consolidation

"Like everything else American it came with a rush," John Montgomery Ward wrote about the onset of professional baseball.

By the last decade of the nineteenth century the game was firmly established in the national psyche, the country's only major professional team sport. People of all sorts played baseball everywhere, on every level, at school and in the sandlots, in college, on hundreds of minor-league and thousands of semipro or industrial teams. The game's traditions and rituals, its lexicon, and even the fervor of its fans were all staples of American popular culture. The first hit baseball song, "Slide, Kelly, Slide," would sweep the country in 1892. DeWolf Hopper's recitation of "Casey at the Bat" was already mesmerizing Broadway audiences.

"I believe that baseball is a homeopathic cure for lunacy," a Dr. S. B. Talcott, superintendent of New York's State Lunatic Asylum, told the press. "It is a kind of craze in itself, and it gives the lunatics a new kind of crazing to relieve them of the malady which afflicts their minds."

Baseball was now clearly recognizable as the same game that we know it to be today. After years of fiddling, the basic rules had been largely settled. Three strikes and you're out, four balls and you take your base; the pitcher's mound was sixty feet, six inches from home plate, the bases ninety feet apart. Foul balls did not yet count as strikes, but that would change with the century. The equipment was much the same. Catchers wore masks, chest protectors, and other armor. Bats were round, if bigger and cruder than they are today. All but two players wore gloves, which were much smaller and thinner than they are now and were left on the field while their owners were batting (a custom that would continue through the 1940s).

Players' uniforms still looked quaint, with baggy knickers and high stockings, long-sleeved shirts that laced at the top, and boxy caps. Ballparks were still rudimentary structures, with wooden grandstands and bleachers that never extended past the baselines—the outfields still left vast, open, and theoretically infinite. Those early parks were throwaway things. They burned like summer barns, replaced every few seasons.

All players now practiced relays from the outfield, the bunt, the hit-and-run, the steal and double steal. Each club now carried four dependable pitchers, who threw any number of overhand pitches, including the "inshoot," the "drop," and the "jump ball." And as their profession became increasingly complicated and specialized, more and more of them were flops at the plate. There were already proposals that a "designated hitter" be substituted for the pitcher on his last at bat.

The question of ethnicity had been settled for the next five decades, as it had been in the United States as a whole. African Americans were out, relegated to their own diamonds, when they could secure them. Everybody else was allowed in, at least to some extent. In the 1890s, nearly a third of all ballplayers could claim German ancestry. About one in five were Irish, including a disproportionate number of the best players in the game. There were even eleven known Jewish ballplayers. This inclusiveness (for white people, anyway) was necessary in cities such as New York, which was nearly three-quarters foreign-born by the 1890s. The Polo Grounds' bleachers were dubbed Burkeville, in reference to the raucous Irish fans who flocked there—a relatively mild form of prejudice in a society that found much of its amusement in ethnic humor.

Baseball was still very much a man's game. Aside from the players' wives, the occasional actress, or other visiting celebrities, ballpark crowds were almost exclusively male. Pictures of the time show the men hunched forward on their wooden benches in bleak, industrial-age uniformity, row after row of black suits and black bowler hats (straw boaters, at the height of the summer).

The game was also rowdier than ever in the 1890s. The sport was rife with gambling, brawling, and drunkenness, on and off the field. It had become standard to set a keg of beer—known as a German Disturber—out on the field by third base. Any runner who made it that far would be allowed to draw a dipperful. Umpires were regularly bombarded with pop bottles, eggs, beer bottles, beer steins, and any other object that might conceivably hold beer, and bodily assaulted by fans and even dogs. Two were actually killed in the minor leagues, and the toughest ump in the majors, the immortal Bob "Death to Flying Things" Ferguson, once broke a player's arm with a bat to escape an encroaching mob. Spiking and bodily blocking base runners was commonplace, and fights broke out on a daily basis.

Ballplayers were "worthless, dissipated gladiators; not much above the professional pugilist in morality and respectability," huffed *The New York Times,* which accused them of spending their free time "in those quiet retreats connected with bars, and rat pits, where sporting men of the metropolis meet for social improvement and unpremeditated pugilism."

More pressing problems were also at hand. From 1893 to 1897, the United States was hit with the second-worst depression in its history, an awful nationwide slump that shook the nation's very faith in its destiny. While not as extended as the Great Depression of the 1930s, the economic downturn of the 1890s was nearly as terrible, with 20 percent unemployment at its nadir. This at a time when no regular system of public relief existed at any level of government.

In New York, the threat of mass starvation became so dire that many wealthy individuals, led by the city's newspapers, began to organize efforts to distribute bread and coal. During the hard winter of 1894, the yeast manufacturer Louis Fleischmann set up the first known breadline at his Model Vienna Bakery, next to Grace Church down on lower Broadway, distributing a third of a loaf of bread to anyone who wanted it. Hundreds stood in line all night in a blizzard to get it, their desperation immortalized by Stephen Crane in his story "The Men in the Storm."

Fleischmann's generosity was immediately denounced by Governor Roswell P. Flower, a Wall Street banker, as promoting "corruption, socialism, and anarchy." Such laissez-faire fervor only drove the poor all the more quickly into the arms of Tammany Hall, the one source of relief remaining. Big Tim Sullivan, the new district leader on the Lower East Side, responded with the first of his free Christmas dinners, serving turkey, ham, beer, all the fixings, and dessert to five thousand destitute individuals at his Comanche Clubhouse, while vaudeville stars sang for the entertainment of the destitute. Small wonder that Tammany, despite a record of unprecedented corruption throughout the decade, stormed back into power in 1897. The beleaguered immigrant masses of Manhattan tied brooms to their stoops to symbolize a sweep for the machine, and sang, "Well, well, well, Reform has gone to Hell!"

Baseball was late to feel the effects of the 1890s depression, but attendance stagnated after 1895, then declined sharply. The National League, officially retitled the National League and American Association of Professional Base Ball Clubs, was just as unwieldy as its new moniker. Twelve teams in a league meant that clubs routinely finished fifty to sixty games out of first place. Worst of all, the league's rules allowed owners to acquire partial and even controlling interests in other clubs, an idea fraught with the potential for disaster. This would bring the National League a bold, new competitor and dramatically change the fortunes of baseball in the city once again.

The two dominant teams of the 1890s were the Boston Beaneaters and the Baltimore Orioles. The Beaneaters were stacked with some of the most graceful and beloved players of their age, the beau ideal of the baseball world. The Orioles were just as talented, but preferred to regard themselves as the constant underdog: the gritty, blue-collar representatives of a tough, blue-collar city. Their play seemed to match the urgency and turmoil of the time. Under Manager Foxy Ned Hanlon, the Orioles honed the "inside game" of baseball to perfection and added any number of new twists—not all of them legal or especially savory.

"They were mean, vicious, ready at any time to maim a rival player or an umpire if it helped their cause," wrote the umpire and later National League president John Heydler of the Orioles. "The things they would say to an umpire were unbelievably vile, and they broke the spirits of some very fine men."

The Sporting News accused Baltimore of "playing the dirtiest ball ever seen in the country." Certainly it was the most physical. The Orioles assaulted other teams constantly, with their spikes, fists, legs, bats, and an unending stream of obscenities. Playing at a time when only one umpire worked most games, they took shortcuts going from first to third, hid baseballs in the high grass of the outfield, tripped and kicked opposing players, and grabbed hold of their belts to slow them down.

The mind behind all this creative anarchy was Hanlon's. Hanlon was a hands-on manager—so hands-on that the Baltimore owner, Harry Von der Horst, took for a time to wearing a button that read simply, "Ask Hanlon." He became the first manager to hire a full-time groundskeeper, directing him to groom the field to help his team's running game. A rough-edged man—and, like so many successful managers, a mediocre player—he liked to force the action.

He was also the progenitor of a great dynasty—or rather, several great dynasties. As Bill James has pointed out, "most major league managers today can be traced back to Ned Hanlon" through the players he managed on the Orioles or on other teams before and after. These would include John McGraw, Connie Mack, Miller Huggins, Wilbert Robinson, Hughie Jennings, Hans Lobert, Joe Kelley, and Fielder Jones. In their ranks were several of the greatest managers in the history of the game, and their influence would extend to one generation after another, to Ty Cobb and Donie Bush, Pie Traynor and Frankie Frisch, Billy Southworth and Leo Durocher and Mel Ott, Bill Rigney and Eddie Lopat, Bobby Bragan and Al López, Earl Weaver and Joe Altobelli, Felipe Alou and Don Baylor, Mike Hargrove and Tony La Russa. Most directly—and most important for New York baseball—it was Hanlon who nurtured and channeled the considerable baseball instincts of a teenage McGraw, and McGraw who begat Casey Stengel, Stengel who begat Billy Martin, Martin who begat Lou Piniella.

At the end of the decade, Hanlon would make another lasting contribution to New York baseball. A Connecticut boy who had developed a deep love for Baltimore, Foxy Ned was objective enough to note that his aging team was flopping at the gate, despite all of its success on the field. The terrible depression of the 1890s was over, but many fans' discretionary income was exhausted, and the Spanish-American War "wrecked the game for months," according to the *Reach Guide,* monopolizing public interest and drawing away thousands of young men as they rushed to volunteer. The Orioles' attendance dropped from more than 273,000 to just 123,416 in 1898. Hanlon looked around for a way out. He thought he saw it in Brooklyn.

The 1890s had been a disappointing era in New York baseball. Twenty-three-year-old Amos Rusie put together his greatest season in 1894, going 36-13, leading the league in strikeouts, shutouts, and ERA, and carrying the Giants to second place and a four-game sweep of the Orioles in the Temple Cup—the National League's shabby, substitute World Series between the teams that had finished first and second during the regular season. Rusie compiled one of the great playoff performances in major-league history, giving up just one earned run in two complete-game victories and hitting .429. (The only other pitcher the Giants used, one Jouett Meekin, was nearly as good, surrendering only three earned runs in *his* two complete-game victories and hitting .556.) But aside from that banner year the Giants floundered under the management of their latest Tammany owner, Andrew Freedman.

Brooklyn fared even worse, the team bouncing up and down the standings between third and tenth and wandering about the city. In 1891, the Bridegrooms moved into the Brooklyn Wonders' old Eastern Park, out on Eastern Parkway by Belmont Avenue. By 1898 they had returned to a brand-new Washington Park, diagonally across Fourth Avenue and Third Street from the old one, but the team was bad, and attendance fell by nearly 100,000.

Hanlon, as usual, saw his opportunity. In the winter of 1899, he purchased 10 percent of the Dodgers and got Von der Horst to pick up another 40 percent. Hanlon and Von der Horst then sold 40 percent of the Orioles to Ferdinand Abell, the Rhode Island gambler who now controlled the Brooklyn team, and another 10 percent to Abell's young partner, the former scorecard printer and ticket taker, Charles Ebbets, who had gone on to become an architectural draftsman and designer and win election to the New York State Assembly and the Brooklyn City Council. (Charlie had even managed the team for a dismal 110 games in 1898.)

The four men were now joint owners of *both* the Baltimore and the Brooklyn clubs. Unworkable as this may sound, it was not an uncommon arrangement. Cincinnati's owner, John T. Brush, owned shares in the Giants, as did Boston's owner, Arthur Soden. Barney Dreyfuss owned both the Louisville and the Pittsburgh franchises, while the brothers Frank and Stanley Robison jointly owned Cleveland and St. Louis. It was all perfectly legal under the new National League rules—and perfectly absurd. The Robisons moved all of the Cleveland Spiders' best players to St. Louis in 1899, leaving a shell of a team behind to finish with an all-time worst, 20-134 record. The following winter, Dreyfuss moved all of *his* best players to Pittsburgh, ending major-league ball in Louisville.

Hanlon now pulled a similar coup, taking his Baltimore stars, Jennings, Kelley, and Wee Willie Keeler, with him to Brooklyn. The revitalized Bridegrooms romped to pennants in 1899 and 1900, and Brooklyn fans returned to the ballpark in droves, giddily redubbing the team the Superbas, after a popular vaudeville troop known as Hanlon's Superbas. The desiccated Baltimore club disbanded, and Hanlon and Ebbets moved the rest of its players up to Brooklyn, or peddled them off for cash as the National League shrank back down to a more manageable eight clubs.

Few doubted that consolidation was necessary, but it was carried out in such a crude and peremptory manner that everyone was now as disgusted by the owners as they had been by the supposedly greedy players. *Sporting Life* railed against their "gross individual and collective mismanagement, their fierce factional fights, their cynical disregard of decency and honor, their open spoliation of each other, their deliberate alienation of press and public, their flagrant disloyalty to friends and supporters, and their tyrannical treatment of their players." The cartel was out of control.

At nearly the same moment, another sort of consolidation would alter Brooklyn forever, even as it celebrated its return to the top of the baseball world. On the last night of 1897, 100,000 New Yorkers marched through a freezing rain from Manhattan's Union Square to city hall—a vast tide of black umbrellas, surrounding an undulating line of marching bands, militia companies, choral societies, and illuminated floats. City hall itself was incandescent, lit by electricity, the latest and greatest of the century's many marvels. There, as the rain turned to snow and the last seconds of the old year ticked away, a battery of cannons roared a hundred-gun salute. The whistles of all the tugboats and ferries filling New York's harbor shrieked, and a spectacular fireworks display split the sky.

It was, according to the *New-York Tribune,* "the biggest, noisiest, and most hilarious New Year's Eve celebration that Manhattan Island had ever known." As the noise from the guns and the aerial "bombs" died away, the tipsy crowd broke into "Auld Lang Syne." Three thousand miles away, clear across the American continent, the mayor of San Francisco pushed a button that sent an electrical charge pulsing to the city hall flagstaff, where it unfurled New York City's new blue, white, and orange banner—the flag of the New York we all know today. Not far away, across the East River, a small gathering outside Brooklyn's city hall grieved in silence, and the windows of nearby shops and houses were hung with black crepe paper.

Greater New York—consolidated, five-borough New York City—was born. Brooklyn—independent Brooklyn, the fourth-largest city in the United States—was no more, reduced to just one more borough.

Consolidation was the end of a thirty-year fight, one designed to increase government efficiency, promote business, and contain the power of both Tammany Hall and the robber barons by joining Manhattan to all the dozens of rural and suburban municipalities that surrounded it in the Bronx, Queens, Staten Island, and Brooklyn.

It was a close-run thing. Before consolidation, Brooklyn was physically a bigger city than New York, had been outpacing it in population growth over most of the century, and was fast overtaking it in manufacturing and shipping. There were more than 900,000 souls in the City of Churches. Every year, four thousand ships unloaded their cargoes in Brooklyn, their tonnage challenging that deposited on New York's piers. Enormous mills in Red Hook refined half the sugar used in America; plants in Williamsburg and Long Island City refined nearly all the oil used on the Eastern Seaboard; gigantic grain silos along the docks served as the area's breadbasket. Who needed Manhattan?

Yet Manhattan's tax base dwarfed that of its sister city, which was heavily in debt and nearing the limit of its ability to issue bonds.

And Brooklyn was running out of water. Unlike Manhattan, which had purchased an enormous watershed upstate and had just completed the New Croton Aqueduct, Brooklyn had failed to secure the likeliest source of new water for itself, out in Suffolk County. In the end, Brooklyn was cowed into consolidation, though only by 277 votes out of the 129,211 cast in the city, in a referendum to determine whether it should merge with the new New York. The great union would indeed lead to many economies of scale and facilitate New York City's ability to go forward as a single colossus. But it would not curb political corruption or corporate power, and the fear would soon arise that the city was *too* big, that it had, at last, become wholly ungovernable.

All that lay ahead. For now, New York City had once again, with a single, brilliant stroke, put itself far ahead of its rivals. At 327 square miles and 3.5 million people, the consolidated city was more than twice the size of Chicago. It was bigger than all the great capitals of Europe save for London, and every new boatload of immigrants assured that London, too, would soon be overtaken. The imperial city was born.

"What London is to the Continent, what Rome in its imperial day was to the Empire," a Wall Street financier would proclaim a few years after consolidation, "New York is to the immense domain of the American republic, a natural stage . . . for the great drama of civilization on this Continent."

It was, as well, about to become center stage again for the national pastime, thanks to all of the chaos that Ned Hanlon had put in motion. Before long, a rough new beast would be on his way up from Baltimore to take control of the Superbas' leading rival, while a pure-hearted crusader brought a whole new venture to the city, and Hanlon himself was overthrown by a humble scorecard printer. The fun had just begun.

PART TWO

THE INSIDE GAME

1901–1919

The city was one long banner of light that sparkled and scintillated in the crisp night air, paling even to insignificance a moon of harvest splendor. There were electric wonders for all to gape at, tall buildings enough to send their shafts of molten splendor where all might see, and searchlights enough to streak the sky wherever crowds were gathered.

—*The New York Times*

14

"Scholastic Contests"

On March 8, 1900, goodness and decency arrived in New York in the form of an egg-shaped thirty-six-year-old president of an obscure minor league somewhere out west. He had come to sell the annual National League meeting on his idea of forming a second major league, and he was about as welcome as an evangelist at a convocation of the College of Cardinals. The NL magnates let him cool his heels in the hall while they lopped four franchises from their own bloated league. Then they adjourned and went home without ever having set eyes on the intruder.

This was a mistake. To be sure, Ban Johnson might have *seemed* like a walking cartoon character: almost three hundred pounds, bulbous, bibulous, fusty, hot-tempered, maudlin, dictatorial, and tediously self-important, he lived in a perpetual veil of humidity, with tears constantly streaming down his face or clouds of steam pouring out of his ears.

"Ban Johnson never missed an opportunity to make a speech," a sportswriter of the period recalled. "It was always the same speech: all about how he and he alone had made baseball a gentleman's sport, and it must be kept forever clean because sportsmanship spoke from the heart of America and he lay down his life to save our beloved nation, at which he would begin to cry."

Yet Johnson was also a man with a plan and the chops to make it work. A college ballplayer and law student turned sportswriter, he had befriended a shrewd old first baseman named Charles Comiskey. Together, they took over the woebegone Western League, turned it into the best-run circuit in baseball, and rechristened it the American League (AL).

Nothing would deter him. Within eight days of the NL owners' snub, Johnson had returned to Chicago and declared his baby a full-grown major league anyway. Over the next two years he went head-to-head against the Nationals, moving American League clubs into Boston, Philadelphia, Chicago, and St. Louis, along with two of the towns the NL had just abandoned, Baltimore and Washington. He chose club owners with deep pockets, offered lucrative contracts to draw the best and most popular players away from NL teams, and then placed them on AL squads right across town. Wherever his new league pushed its way in, they offered a welcome respite from what had become the nearly nonstop drinking and brawling of a National League ballpark, both on the field and off.

"My determination was to pattern baseball in this new league along the lines of scholastic contests," Johnson would claim, "to make ability and brains and clean, honorable play, not the swinging of clenched fists, coarse oaths, riots or assaults upon the umpires, decide the issue."

By 1903, Johnson had lured 111 players over from the National League, including many of the biggest stars in the game. But one major hurdle remained. Johnson knew he had to break into New York, if the American League was going to be seen as a true major league. Doing so would test all of his high principles, and at times his sanity.

New York at the beginning of the twentieth century stood on the brink of a stunning metamorphosis. Where luck, pluck, vision, and a rare instinct for the jugular had made it the greatest city in America, the need to simply keep it moving would transform it. New York would burst its bonds, exploding upward and outward, and even deep into the granite bedrock below, coiling great tentacles across the rivers that had once contained it, binding all that surrounded it to its Manhattan core. For the first time, the city would come to rival the great European capitals in its public architecture, its culture, its population. Soon it would begin to move beyond them.

The first years of the new century witnessed a building spree in the city unparalleled in human history. The construction of the original Pennsylvania Station and the current Grand Central; the Williamsburg, Manhattan, and Queensboro Bridges; the Hell Gate rail bridge with its elegant arch; the first lines of the New York City Subway system; the fourteen miles of the "tubes" (later PATH) train tunnels to New Jersey; the Steinway trolley tunnels under the East River (that would later be filled with No. 7 trains carrying happy Mets fans to Shea Stadium); the Pennsylvania Rail tunnel that slithered beneath the Hudson and connected with a new East River tunnel to Long Island, thereby truly spanning the width of the country by rail for the first time—all this was constructed in New York between 1900 and 1917.

The city began to reach fantastic heights. Manhattan office buildings had edged up to ten stories and beyond by the 1890s, but now they simply took off into the heavens. One after another claimed its place as the tallest structure in not only the city but also the world—most for no more than a few months before being replaced by something even bigger, grander. By 1902, there were already sixty-six skyscrapers in lower Manhattan and more would soon follow, designed by the greatest architects in the nation and ornamented with wonderful frippery: Cass Gilbert's sixty-story Woolworth Building, the "Cathedral of Commerce," with its gleaming white terra-cotta skin and its gorgeous Beaux Arts interiors. The colossal Metropolitan Life Tower at Madison Square, breaking the fifty-story mark with a clock face bigger than Big Ben's and a search beam that broadcast the weather to ships out at sea. Daniel H. Burnham's Flatiron Building, plowing into Madison Square—and modernity—in the words of Alfred Stieglitz, "like the bow of a monster ocean liner." The vertical city was born.

Yet the most spectacular edifices of all were not skyscrapers. Nor were they the Andrew Carnegie–donated theater on Fifty-Seventh Street that gave New York a world-class concert hall for the first time, or the handsome new campuses for Columbia, and City College, and New York University sprawling out over acres of upper Manhattan and the Bronx; or St. John the Divine's, the largest Gothic cathedral in the world, towering above Morningside Heights. Nor were they William Kendall's formidable new General Post Office at Thirty-Fourth and Eighth, with its block-long row of Corinthian columns, nor even the stunning new edifices housing the American Museum of Natural History, the Metropolitan Museum of Art, the Brooklyn Museum.

They were *train stations*—two of the greatest structures in history, built less than ten years and a few blocks apart in the same city. The new Beaux Arts Grand Central Terminal, lavished with statues of

Minerva, Mercury, and Hercules (and old Commodore Vanderbilt), its soaring, 125-foot ceiling adorned with a gorgeous blue map of the zodiac. And across town, Charles McKim's Pennsylvania Station, a symphony in steel and honey marble; large enough, in the novelist Thomas Wolfe's phrase, "to hold the sound of time," yet still a structure of measureless beauty.

When it opened for business on September 8, 1910, Penn Station was immediately recognized as one of the premier public spaces in the world. Here was something that was neither king nor cathedral, but a fitting icon of the melting-pot republic. A monument to speed, to mobility, to commerce and conquest and democracy that many of the same free citizens who had built it marched through every day. It would epitomize New Yorkers' sense of dominance and sophistication in the new century, and its loss would signal an incalculable fall from grace.

Each one of these achievements was a monumental endeavor in its own right. Each spurred on trade, ingenuity, immigration, and assimilation. Each required armies of laborers, skilled craftsmen, managers, and engineers, along with prodigious helpings of capital and more of the marvelous innovation that had always characterized the city. To build the sixteen miles of the Pennsylvania Rail tunnels, an international team of engineers devised two-hundred-ton iron cylinders, or shields. Behind them, crews of sandhogs worked doggedly toward each other beneath the Hudson River with such precision that after three years of their continuous digging, "the shields met, coming together rim to rim," in the historian Lorraine Diehl's description, "like two gargantuan tumblers."

The three new East River bridges never matched the Brooklyn Bridge in either beauty or the popular imagination, but each of them was even longer, each built with its own new design, and each completed in half the time or less that the Roeblings' masterpiece was, showcasing an exponential gain in knowledge and expertise over the intervening twenty years. All these marvelous new means and ways of transportation deftly intersected and entwined. Trolley cars, subways, and elevated railroads all met at the new Grand Central, where a system of traffic ramps would soon raise the street so that the ever-increasing flow of automobiles would move right on *through* the colossal structure—motion transecting motion, wheels within wheels.

—

New York, beyond all other places, had assembled the elements necessary for a mass entertainment culture. Thanks to the limitless heights of steel-frame construction, people could be gathered as never before. All the spectacular new bridges and tunnels and train stations meant that millions more could be assembled (and dispersed) in record time, whisked back and forth between work, pleasure, and their neighborhoods in the city or its suburbs.

And all of it was driven, all of it was illuminated, by the most spectacular new discovery of all. As David Nasaw wrote in *Going Out: The Rise and Fall of Public Amusements,* "Incandescent lighting transformed the city from a dark and treacherous netherworld into a glittering multicolored wonderland." New York had surpassed even Paris as the city of light. From the moment Edison's first primitive, direct-current station opened on Pearl Street in 1882, electricity transfigured the city. It was electricity that powered the skyscrapers' safety elevators and all the underground and underwater trains; electricity that ran the projectors that spewed forth the new century's boldest new art. The new light could seem terrifying, even surreal. "Squares and squares of flame set out and cut into the ether," as Ezra Pound wrote, pondering the night skyline. But where the murky gaslight of the nineteenth century had fed only the lurid imagination, exaggerating the terrors of the city, the dazzling light of electricity made people want to linger after work around the downtown theaters and restaurants, the dance halls and saloons.

It was the light that would usher in entire new entertainment districts, like nothing else ever quite seen before. One of them was Coney Island, out along the farthest shores of Brooklyn, where three stupendous "amusement parks"—another new concept—would shine with enough electrical power to light a city of half a million people, the power plants themselves a leading attraction.

Another was right in the heart of Manhattan, in what had been Longacre Square. When *The New York Times* opened its skyscraper there in 1904, the redubbed Times Square was already filling with theaters and dance halls, nickelodeons and motion picture palaces, rooftop cabarets, grand hotels, casinos, and lobster palaces. Here was the ultimate synergy of the new century: a transportation hub, anchored by a skyscraper housing a newspaper, and all of it lit to the skies with electricity. It was the start of the city's relentless, century-long transition from a hub of industry to one of diversion.

"The center of the classical city was the forum and the agora," points out historian William Taylor. "Times Square, located at a major transportation hub, was neither. . . . Times Square's very centrality meant that whatever took place was immediately in the national spotlight."

The spotlight was quite literal. The Times Tower, 375 feet high, "was said to be visible from eight miles away," according to journalist James Traub, "an 'X' that marked the center from which the great, glowing city radiated." The first electric sign had already appeared on Broadway in 1897, and by 1906 the Knickerbocker Theatre was advertising its production of *The Red Mill* with a windmill composed entirely of lightbulbs, the arms of which actually seemed to turn. By 1913, there were more than a million lights illuminating what was now known as the Great White Way. They announced a city that held more theaters than any other town on earth, with a total capacity of nearly two million seats.

Who filled them? A whole new class of Americans. In the half a century between 1870 and 1920, the number of white-collar workers—clerks, managers, assistant managers, salesmen, saleswomen, stenographers, typists (or "typewriters," as the men and women who operated the machines were then called)—increased by nearly 500 percent, to 11 percent of the total workforce. Their hours were shorter than those of the vast majority of Americans still toiling in factories or fields, they had more spending cash, and an unprecedented number of them were single men and women, living alone in the city.

They needed something to do. What they got was "the show business"—a professionalized, regularized array of entertainments. Many of these were new, including the amusement parks and the live theater of vaudeville. Phonograph and kinetoscope parlors, outfitted with fronds and carpets, where people could pay a nickel to stick an ear into a "listening tube" or peer through a peephole at a couple minutes' worth of a flickering, *moving* image.

An incredible amount of the content for these new venues was produced in or around New York. Music publishers and songwriters ensconced themselves in Tin Pan Alley—which, like everything else, had moved up to Times Square. The first real movie studio in the country opened in Flatbush, while Edison churned out motion pictures in the Bronx, and others did the same in Flushing, and Astoria, and Fort Lee. Before long, Mary Pickford would be gesticulating across a rooftop on West Twenty-Sixth Street in Chelsea, another production hub.

All of these entertainments were defined by their appeal to this new middle class. They offered affordable, popular, changeable entertainments, in ostentatiously respectable, "decent" areas, located at the crux of busy shopping and business districts. Ladies were welcome. Rowdies were ejected. Drinking and smoking were largely forbidden, or at least segregated (as was anyone of color). Best of all, it was cheap. The 10-20-30 theaters were so named for the prices they charged for their melodramas (in pennies). Vaudeville—from *voix de ville,* or "voice of the city"—cost between 25 cents and $1.50 for the top boxes. In return, it offered a vast array of constantly changing diversions, including singers, dancers, comedians, jugglers, acrobats, minstrels, performing animals, freaks, and celebrities.

"It may be a kind of lunch-counter art," playwright Edwin Milton Royle wrote in *Scribner's* in 1899, "but then art is so vague and lunch is so real."

This was the entertainment trend that Ban Johnson, as canny as he was impossible, had hooked into—and one that the dominant National League had been bizarrely reluctant to embrace. What Johnson understood was that baseball was ideally made for the new, mass entertainment. It could not, of course, be played over and over again in endless reels or repeat bills. But it was episodic and discrete, with every contest adding to the ongoing narrative of the pennant race. It remained a swift, snappy game. In 1919, the New York Giants would play the fastest major-league game ever recorded, needing just fifty-one minutes to dispatch the Phillies at the Polo Grounds; in 1926, the Yankees would require only two hours and seven minutes to drop a *doubleheader* to the St. Louis Browns.

Yet at the start of the new century, there was still a rough primitivism about the sport. The baseball park remained a droopy, wooden, seedy place, highly susceptible to fire, a favorite haunt of gamblers and voluble drunks. Few ladies made an appearance, even on Ladies' Day. It was common for teams to have a batboy or "mascot" who might be a little person, or even a mentally disabled individual.

At a time when the owners of other entertainment industries were concentrating on volume and one low price, baseball was going in the opposite direction. Major- and even high-minor-league games cost more than most popular theaters, and increasingly fans were separated into rows of box seats, grandstands, and those plain, uncovered benches in the distant outfield where they would be "bleached" by the sun. It was clear whose business was most valued. Starting times were generally geared to the convenience of the box-seat holders, as with the Polo Grounds' three thirty or four o'clock first pitch, designed for Wall Street fans who would hop an express train uptown after their three o'clock, "bankers' hours," quitting time.

Of all the new mass entertainments, baseball was almost alone in failing to exploit the greatest wonder of the age. There was scarcely a thought of utilizing electricity to play night games. For that matter, baseball owners still preferred to regard their employees as, say, interchangeable mill hands or coal miners, rather than Broadway performers. They chafed at the emergence of stars and remained unwilling to offer the players either a good wage or any freedom—conditions that would, before the era was over, come to threaten the integrity of the sport.

Like everything else in American life, baseball professed to being thoroughly democratic, played by men from all classes and walks of life, in parks where the very richest and the very poorest sat within a few yards of each other. It was true that the makeup of its players had become more ethnically heterogeneous than ever before, and that a startling one-quarter of all major leaguers had at least some college education by the end of the 1910s—many times the percentage of the general public who had attained that level. Commentators celebrated this sort of egalitarianism, but all African Americans and all but an incidental Latin player or two were still excluded from the game. Even the presence of all those college boys still spoke mostly to how much baseball remained a game for the distinct minority of Americans with ample leisure time.

True equality in baseball existed more in the breach than in the practice—much as it did everywhere else in the United States. For all the ballparks and the vaudeville houses, the lobster palaces and the amusement parks, the sardine cans of its subway, and the crowded elevators of its new towers—for all that, even in New York, democracy was a very limited business.

More than half of the city's population still lived (and often worked) in tenements by 1900, most of them toiling endlessly at jobs that wore away body and soul. They lacked the time or the discretionary income to dawdle at vaudeville houses or nickelodeons, much less afternoon baseball games. Conversely, by 1892, some eighteen hundred millionaires—nearly half of all those in the United States—lived in either New York City or its suburbs. Unhindered by an income tax, they retained the wealth to turn Manhattan's Fifth Avenue into their own private fantasia—two full miles of turreted, marble castles, built nearly one against the other.

"Never . . . has civilization beheld greater lavishness than that which our metropolitan plutocracy displays," the scholar Edgar Saltus wrote at the time. "More ornate than the swirl of London and more resplendent than that of Paris, only royalty can vie with it, and not always with success. There is many a palace in Europe that would hide its diminished roof beside the sheer luxury of Fifth Avenue homes."

Power, in this wildly unequal city, remained an inside game, wielded in boardrooms and barrooms, mansions and clubhouses. Enabling all the robber barons were the city's professional politicians, now more efficiently organized than ever and a good deal more subtle. Despite the hopes that a bigger, consolidated New York would contain and diffuse the power of the machine, it was still Tammany that made sure that business went on unimpeded by the likes of labor unions or pesky regulations about unsafe working conditions and unsanitary housing. It was still Tammany that the immigrants depended upon, still Tammany that, more than ever, held the reins of organized crime—mobilizing street gangs to control the ballot box during elections; "taxing" for its own coffers the ill-gotten gains of countless brothels, casinos, clip joints, and blind pigs. Beneath the bright lights and the gaudy new emporiums offering respectable entertainment to the new middle class, even Times Square was honeycombed with brothels and casinos.

It was Tammany, too, that controlled all the city's games, legal and not: dice and cards; horse racing and boxing; the glowing amusement parks out on Coney Island and the flickering movies in a hundred "parlors"—and baseball, too.

15

"Truxton Against the World!"

No one was better positioned to play the political inside game than Andrew Freedman, the owner of the New York Giants at the turn of the century. He has been called "perhaps the most hated team owner in baseball history," a man of "arbitrary disposition, a violent temper, and an ungovernable tongue." Bill James describes him as "George Steinbrenner on Quaaludes, with a touch of Al Capone," and "a thug who skated on thin ice above an ocean of lunacy." He had, as the New York *World* pointed out, "an astonishing ability for making enemies."

In the eight years he controlled the Giants, Freedman changed managers sixteen times, often firing and then rehiring the same men. Nor were his managers his only targets. Freedman launched as many as twenty libel suits in a single year, and—shades of James Dolan—banned sportswriters who criticized him from the Polo Grounds. Once, in a barroom fury, he tried to beat up the disabled John T. Brush, a man with whom he had been partners for years and to whom he would eventually sell the Giants.

Like Steinbrenner, Freedman seemed the personification of big-city arrogance, always in the newspapers special pleading for himself and his team. At various times he demanded the firing of the league president, the right to pick his own umpires, and even territorial rights to Brooklyn, after the borough was incorporated into Greater New York. He refused to contribute to the buyout fund of the four teams the NL disbanded in 1899, but insisted on getting first crack at their players. Next he pushed for making the league into a single syndicate—with much of its best talent to be reallocated to his Giants. He was notoriously cheap and dictatorial with the players he did acquire, selling and trading them if they failed to treat him with the respect he demanded. They hated him in turn, and his teams mostly dawdled in the second division.

Why Freedman should have been so irascible is unclear. A handsome bachelor who studied law at City College before making millions in real estate, he had everything going for him. He was a fixture on Tammany's powerful policy board and finance committee and later treasurer of the national Democratic Party. Wealth, good looks, political connections, and a ball team. What more could a man want?

It was said that an early, failed engagement had permanently soured Freedman and left him a lifelong bachelor. Or perhaps it was the insecurity he felt when his successful parents lost all their money during his childhood. At least some of Freedman's disposition no doubt stemmed from the abuse he had to take about his background, even in modern, democratic New York. Freedman was a rare Jewish owner in the game at a time when anti-Semitism was both rife and accepted, and neither fans nor players nor sportswriters—nor Freedman's fellow owners—ever let him forget where he came from. In 1898, the former Giant James "Ducky" Holmes, a notorious troublemaker being taunted as a "lobster" by the fans on his return to New York with the Orioles, responded loudly, "Well, I'm glad I don't have to work for no sheeny anymore." Enraged, Freedman vaulted from the owner's box with a phalanx of his private cops and made for Holmes, who was saved only by his Oriole teammates, defending him with their bats.

Ducky was initially suspended for the rest of the season, but the penalty brought an outcry. *The Sporting News,* fast emerging as "the Bible of baseball," and a grossly anti-Semitic publication at the time, sniffed that "insulting the Hebrew race" was "a trifling offense" and Holmes's suspension a "perversion of justice." It was quickly shortened to ten days—a calculated insult to Freedman by his fellow magnates.

No doubt, most of them would have been glad to get rid of the Giants' owner altogether, but this was impossible. For along with his other political offices, Andrew Freedman was a board member of the new Interborough Rapid Transit Company (IRT), in charge of deciding where the city's long-awaited subway system would run. This positioned him perfectly to make millions off the changing nature of life in Manhattan and to fend off a new threat to his fellow owners.

From 1904 to 1912 alone, four thousand new apartment buildings, each with a hundred tenants or more, went up in Manhattan. They housed many of those new, single white-collar workers flooding into the city—not to mention ballplayers themselves. Most of the new apartment houses went up in what were then still the bucolic reaches of the Upper West Side, served by the elevated rails and by the new subway lines. Andrew Freedman, knowing where the subway would go, scooped up the best sites for apartment houses like so many one-hop grounders. Then he compounded his winnings by serving on the boards of leading construction companies.

More important for his fellow National League owners, Freedman could also *keep* any unwanted structure—such as a ballpark—from going up in Manhattan, by threatening to run a street through it or to erect a transportation facility on the site. It was the same Tammany trump card that the clubhouse boys had used to solicit free passes to the original Polo Grounds. Now Freedman would play it again, but for much bigger stakes. In turn, Ban Johnson and the Forces of Virtue would employ the most unlikely weapon available to them.

If there was one individual who most thoroughly embodied everything about the game that Johnson professed to hate—rowdyism, gambling, dirty play, profanity, and outright assaults upon the umpires—it was John Joseph McGraw.

Born in 1873 in the little town of Truxton, New York, McGraw was eleven years old when his world fell apart. John's mother, brother, two sisters, and a half sister died within days of each other during a diphtheria epidemic. His father, bereft and unable to manage the five remaining McGraws, began to knock John around. When the boy was twelve, he beat him so badly for the crime of breaking a window while playing baseball that John ran away to live with a kindly widow across the street.

There he remained for the rest of his childhood, if one could call it that. McGraw left school and found work as a "butcher boy" on the railroad, selling periodicals and snacks to the passengers to the end of the line, then fitting in a game of ball while waiting out the layover for the trip back. At sixteen, he signed a professional contract with Olean of the New York–Penn League. In his very first game he had a single—and committed eight errors in ten chances at third base. By the following August, though, he'd caught on with the old Baltimore Orioles, informing all who would listen, "You can tell [Baltimore manager Bill] Barnie I'm as good as they come." In his first game McGraw made a run-scoring error but singled and scored what proved to be the winning run. He told the press afterward, "It's nice. Just give me a little time and I have got 'em skinned to death."

He was right. John McGraw would go on to compile the third-best career on-base percentage in major-league history. When it comes to getting on base, the primary aim in baseball, there is Ted Williams, Babe Ruth, and McGraw. He would also stand up to anyone, on or off a ball field. The dean of sportswriters, Grantland Rice, wrote that "McGraw's very walk across the field in a hostile town was a challenge to the multitude." He fought all comers and almost always lost. McGraw was, in Damon Runyon's description, "a café gladiator," even punched out once during a naked fistfight in the showers by the cheerful, elfin Wee Willie Keeler.

He played as if possessed by the furies. In his most notorious moment on a ball field, his 1894 brawl with Boston's Tommy Tucker escalated into a melee that swept up both teams and much of the crowd, culminating in a fire that consumed the old South End Grounds, along with 170 neighboring buildings. Even the Yankees never burned down Fenway Park.

"He has the vilest tongue of any ball-player," one sportswriter wrote. "He adopts every low and contemptible method that his erratic brain can conceive to win a play by a dirty trick." Anyone on the ball field was fair game for his tongue, his fists, or his feet—especially umpires. He believed in using "judicious kicking" on the umps, insisting once that "good kickers" could gain their team fifty runs a year.

Supposedly it was all about winning. "The only road to popularity is to win. The man who loses gracefully loses easily. Sportsmanship and easygoing methods are all right, but it is the prospect of a hot fight that brings out the crowds," McGraw would insist.

Yet the evidence suggests that McGraw often really was out of control on the field. Christy Mathewson would describe his antics as a manager while in the third-base coaching box, from where he sometimes liked to survey the field, complete with mitt on hand: "McGraw leaps in the air, kicks his heels together, claps his mitt, shouts at the umpire, runs in and pats the next batter on the back, and says something to the pitcher."

Again and again, his sense of being wronged shone through. He protested vociferously whenever he was punished for even his most flagrant transgressions, insisting that umpires, league presidents, and opposing owners all had it in for him and his team. There was always present the abused boy who had been forced to go out in the world and fend for himself from the age of twelve. Embarrassed by his lack of formal education, he hated his prevailing nickname, Muggsy, because it was inspired by an unlettered character in the funny pages. He spent the winters of his first few years in professional ball studying at Allegany (later St. Bonaventure) College in upstate New York, paying his tuition by coaching the baseball team (and one year, even the college's first football team, though he knew nothing about the sport). Before he was through, he would become probably the only manager in the history of the game to be given a complete set of Shakespeare by a grateful team.

Still the chip remained. McGraw would own a series of terriers, each of which he named after his old hometown and each of whom he would greet at the end of the day with the cry "It's Truxton against the world!"

Off the field, McGraw could be very different, "the kindliest, most generous and most sympathetic of men." He was renowned as an easy touch for old teammates down on their luck. His second wife wrote that he liked to simply sit and watch her close family interact. He had what she described as "a sort of gnawing hunger" to belong.

By 1899, McGraw seemed to find a new home in Baltimore. Revered by the fans, he and his best friend on the Orioles—the jocular, rotund, moustachioed catcher, Wilbert Robinson—bought a bar across the street from the ballpark, complete with billiard tables and a bowling alley, and dubbed it the Diamond Café. It was hugely profitable and enabled McGraw to marry a quiet local girl named Minnie Doyle, whom he adored. Still just twenty-six, he was appointed manager when Ned Hanlon pulled his coup, taking Baltimore's best players with him to Brooklyn, and Muggsy showed immediately what he could do in the dugout. Serving not only as field manager but also as the ball club's general manager and chief scout, he kept his team hustling and winning. He seemed to love the job, joking and even playing pranks on his players.

Then, at the end of August, it all came apart—again. Minnie died of a ruptured appendix. Staggered by yet another sudden death in his young life, unable to sleep, McGraw still managed to bring his team in fourth, only to discover that winter that he no longer had a team. The same National League meeting that had snubbed Ban Johnson decided to eliminate Baltimore for the 1900 season and transfer McGraw's contract to St. Louis. McGraw swore at first that he would stay on in Baltimore—"I am going to stay here if I have to play on a town lot"—but went to St. Louis and did well, once the owner promised to release him at the end of the season.

He was looking for something more. McGraw was still a young man, but his frenetic style of play had taken its toll. Only five feet seven with a playing weight that rarely exceeded 130 pounds, by midseason his body would be "worn to a shred." All his life he was vulnerable to illness and injury, losing most of one season to malaria, another to typhoid. Even as a manager he suffered a nearly fatal hemorrhage when struck by a stray ball that gave him his trademark flattened nose; later he nearly lost a finger to infection. By 1900, his legs were hobbled by repeated spikings and other injuries, and he was looking to move up in the baseball world.

He thought he had found his chance in the American League. That November, Ban Johnson gave McGraw and his buddy Robinson exclusive rights to form a new Baltimore franchise in the AL. The three men celebrated with a dinner of champagne and pheasant. It was the high point of their relationship. Almost from the start, Johnson was appalled by McGraw's rowdy, unscrupulous tactics. Worse yet, he became suspicious that Muggsy was trying to jump the new Orioles back to the National League.

He was right.

Andrew Freedman had stymied Johnson's initial efforts in New York just as his fellow National League owners hoped he would. He and his Tammany pals leased or optioned every possible site for a ballpark from the bottom of Manhattan up to 155th Street, then turned it into a public park or ran a street or a streetcar line through it.

Johnson countered with McGraw, sending the Orioles manager on clandestine trips to New York all through 1901 and into the following year, trying to sniff out some way to get the American League into the city even as relations between the two men deteriorated. Things came to a head in another out-of-control McGraw tantrum on May 1, 1902. Umpire Jack Sheridan watched Boston's Bill Dinneen hit McGraw five different times without letting him take his base, insisting that Muggsy had not tried to get out of the way of the ball. After being plunked for the fifth time, McGraw simply sat down in the batter's box and refused to move until Sheridan ejected him. When the game ended a few minutes later, the fans rushed the field, nearly mobbing the umpire. Johnson hit McGraw with another five-day suspension, and rumors flew that something was up.

"Certainly it looked as if Johnson had instructed his arbiters to take no abuse from McGraw, and some observers even suspected that Johnson was trying to run him out of the American League," wrote McGraw's biographer Charles Alexander. "Others thought McGraw was actually inviting Johnson to run him out of the League—and into the eager embrace of Andrew Freedman in New York."

McGraw, it turned out, had been secretly meeting with the Giants' owner for many months, convinced, as he later wrote, that Johnson was planning "to ditch me at the end of the 1902 season. So I acted fast. . . . Someone would be left holding the bag, and I made up my mind it wouldn't be me." Now he used his suspension to meet with Freedman one more time and set his plans.

First, McGraw managed to get himself ejected from a game once again—and again refused to leave the field. Johnson backed the umpire, telling the press he was glad the arbiter "maintained his position and humiliated McGraw." Muggsy responded, "No man likes to be ordered off the earth like a dog in the presence of his friends. Ballplayers are not a lot of cattle to have the whip cracked over them." A few days later, he sold his stock in the Orioles to the other team directors for $6,500, then asked for and received his release as player and manager. That same night he signed a contract with Freedman's

Giants for $11,000 a year, for four years, then the highest salary of any manager or player in the game.

The man who had sworn to stick by Baltimore if he had to play on a town lot now called New York "the cornerstone of baseball" and sneered that "Czar Johnson['s]" American League "is a loser and has been from the start." Muggsy did promise, "I will certainly not draw on the Baltimore team for players." It was a pledge that lasted less than ten days. Freedman bought a controlling interest in the Orioles and released the team's leading stars. McGraw and his new wife escorted them personally to Baltimore's Penn Station, from whence they embarked for New York to sign lavish contracts with the Giants.

It was a stunning coup. For the second time in just three years, Baltimore had seen its beloved Orioles stripped of its best players, who were then carted off to play in New York. This time, Baltimore was left without enough men to even field a team and was forced to forfeit its next game.

"Loyalty and gratitude are words without any meaning to ballplayers and especially to McGraw," inveighed a writer for the Baltimore *Sun. The Sporting News* compared McGraw to a terrorist and wailed, "He was and is in the game for loot."

Baltimore would not make it back to the big leagues for another fifty years. The boy from Truxton had pulled off the classic heartless, big-city move, the sort of maneuver that over the years taught sports fans around the country to hate New York. Not only did Johnson appear to be permanently shut out of New York, but his new league tottered on the edge of chaos.

16

The Christian Gentleman

The Giants were stumbling along with a record of 23-50 when McGraw took the reins, and he would not be able to budge them from the cellar before the season ended—a failure that would make John McGraw, perhaps the greatest manager who ever was, the only man ever to manage the last-place team in each major league in the same year. Yet the bugs—as fans were now called—who came to see his first game in New York on July 19, 1902, noticed an immediate difference in their Giants. Watching the home team whip through their pregame warm-ups with unaccustomed zeal, one of them yelled out, "They're awake!"

So they were. That September, the mercurial Freedman did McGraw one last favor. He sold his interest in the Giants to John T. Brush for $150,000 and devoted the last fourteen years of his life to his political duties and one last building project: a block-long, three-story, Italian Renaissance palace along the Grand Concourse in the Bronx—just a few blocks from where Yankee Stadium would rise—where "gentlefolk, people of culture and former wealth, who had once been in good circumstances, but who, by reasons of adverse fortune, had become poor, could live in the comfort to which they had been accustomed."

Freedman would leave a whopping $7 million for the establishment of his "ex–rich man's poorhouse," complete with manicured grounds, a library, and a ballroom. But when it finally opened in 1924, not enough impoverished millionaires could be found, and the rooms had to be filled with the likes of more middle-class "jewelers, dressmakers, nurses, teachers." Nonetheless, all were required to dress for dinner every night.

Brush, the Giants' new owner, was "the Hoosier Wanamaker," a department store magnate, much of whose adult life was spent in agonizing pain from locomotor ataxia, a wasting disease of the nervous system that is often caused by syphilis and that gave him a sinister air to many, especially sportswriters. A critic in *The Sporting News* claimed that "chicanery is the ozone which keeps his old frame from snapping, and dark-lantern methods the food which vitalizes his bodily tissues." But Brush was often generous to his players and deeply loyal to McGraw throughout his ten years of ownership. Asked upon his purchase of the Giants if the stubby manager would be retained, he replied simply, "He's a fixture." John McGraw was just twenty-nine years old.

Amid all of his schemes, Muggsy had also found time to marry an "infinitely patient" nineteen-year-old Catholic girl from Baltimore named Blanche Sindall, a woman who would love him and, for once, outlive him. The boy from Truxton had found a home at last, and he would make the most of it. In the course of his twenty-nine full seasons as manager, Mickey Face's Giants would finish out of the first division exactly once, winning three World Series and ten pennants and placing second ten more times—an unmatched record of success. McGraw was, as baseball historian Steven Goldman wrote, "the father of all baseball managers, and all football coaches too . . . the master, 'the czar,' as he put it, of the New York Giants, the proudest team in professional baseball." Like a football coach, he wanted total control of his team, going so far as to call every single pitch that was thrown to Babe Ruth in the 1922 World Series. Throughout his career he would serve as his own general manager, sometimes leaving the Giants for weeks at a time to go scour the sandlots for fresh talent.

"I think we can win it all, if my brain holds out," he always maintained, and told his ballplayers, "Do what I tell you, and I'll take the blame for mistakes." In this sense, like Joe Torre many years later, he would prove the perfect manager for New York, providing cover for his team from the city's vast and often hostile tribe of sportswriters.

"All I want to know is that they are honestly trying to do what I tell them," he said of his players. "If they haven't the ability it is my fault if I keep them." He never punished them for physical mistakes: "I wouldn't have a man on my team who doesn't make errors. It shows he doesn't go after the ball."

Mental errors—or, God forbid, disobedience—were another matter. On at least two occasions, McGraw fined players who hit game-winning home runs. Both had been ordered to bunt. Chastisement might turn into tirades that turned into fistfights, and he always worked his men hard. McGraw had the first, primitive spring training complex constructed in little Marlin, Texas, where he hoped his men would be isolated from the usual diversions of ballplayers. Each day, they walked the two miles from the hotel to the complex and back along the railroad tracks. At the same time, McGraw saw to it that they were better cared for than any other players in the game, putting his Giants up in first-rate hotels throughout the regular season. They generally loved him in return.

"I liked him, and I liked playing for him," conceded Al Bridwell in Lawrence S. Ritter's oral history of the early game, *The Glory of Their Times*—even though Bridwell had once knocked McGraw down the dugout steps with a punch after a particularly vituperative harangue from the manager. Even Frankie Frisch, a frequent whipping boy Muggsy dealt to the Cardinals, confessed, "I always thought McGraw was sort of on the genius side." Rogers Hornsby, the great, bad-tempered slugger Frisch was traded for, maintained, "When you train under most managers, you merely get yourself in good physical condition. When you train under McGraw, you learn baseball."

McGraw knew ballplayers. Where his predecessor on the Giants experimented with Christy Mathewson at first base, Muggsy immediately put Matty back on the mound and left him there. He did just the reverse with his eventual successor as manager, Bill Terry. He saw that Roger Bresnahan was a catcher. He recognized the talent in Mel Ott when Ott was a seventeen-year-old rookie, keeping him on the Giants and moving him from catcher to the outfield. He went so far as to redesign his Giants' uniforms, taking off the collars that players had worn since the earliest days of the New York game and dressing them—once again—all in black because he had "heard army officers say that the snappiest dressed outfit is usually made up of the best fighters."

"It was an important part of McGraw's great capacity for leadership," journalist Heywood Broun would write, "that he could take kids out of the coal mines and out of the wheat fields and make them walk and chatter and play ball with the look of eagles."

This was a more important skill than it might seem today, back in an age when a player could move from the bushes to the majors with startling rapidity. One George "Specs" Toporcer actually went from the Manhattan sandlots to the majors without spending a day playing high school, college, or minor-league ball. Yet there was another, less heartwarming side to guiding a ball club in the early years of the twentieth century, as Steven Goldman points out: "Just as often, though, it wasn't coalminer kids who McGraw was trying to turn into eagles but hard-core alcoholics, gamblers, and thieves." McGraw was always confident he could do it, to the point where it became an axiom: "If you have a bad actor, trade him to McGraw." This was true of players who were considered slackers, or locker-room lawyers, such as Emil "Irish" Meusel, or out-of-control drunks, such as Turkey Mike Donlin, a lifetime .333 hitter who might do anything when on a bender, including pulling a pistol on a crowded train, or going to a theater and belting a popular actress in the face.

Arthur "Bugs" Raymond, was a spitballing alcoholic of whom it was said he need only *breathe* on the ball to make it wobble. Raymond was so desperate a drinker that he was suspected of stealing the tip money from tables in the team's spring training hotel, in order to get the cash for more booze. Once, when McGraw sent him out to the Polo Grounds' remote bullpen to warm up, he kept on going, all the way out to a saloon across Eighth Avenue, where he downed enough whiskey to blow the game wide open when he did come in. McGraw tried to reform him through every method he knew, sending Raymond to a sanatorium, sending his paycheck straight to his wife, finally trying to give him an admonitory beating—something at which, as usual, Muggsy failed miserably.

There was another category of McGraw's special cases, too. These were men accused of "laying down," a broad term that would cause some confusion. A player who "laid down" early in the twentieth century might be one who was simply lazy or accused of not hustling, or he could be engaged in something considerably worse. Again and again, McGraw would hire on men whose careers were shadowed by accusations of deliberately throwing ball games. His hubris in thinking he could turn even these hard cases around would come to smear the edges of his legacy and threaten his tenure in the game.

—

On the field, McGraw innovated constantly, flashing signs from the bench by blowing his nose, or using the sign language all his Giants learned when the deaf pitcher Luther "Dummy" Taylor was on the team. Strategically, he understood any kind of baseball, conducting some of the early experiments in employing a full-time relief pitcher and adjusting in the 1920s to the style of Ruthian "lively ball" that he hated.

Yet it was the scrappy, low-scoring "dead-ball" era that was best wedded to McGraw's temperament and his desire for control—a time when a manager could have the greatest effect on one low-scoring game after another. With foul balls now counted as strikes, and the old, smaller home plate replaced by the current, much more visible, five-sided version, baseball was, once again, a pitcher's game. Doctored balls were legal and widely employed, with no more than three or four balls used in a game; ushers retrieved fouls from fans whenever they could and threw them back into play. By the end of most games pitchers were heaving a soft gray wobbly mass to the plate. The four o'clock start at the Polo Grounds ensured that in the early and later weeks of the season the Giants were always playing in the twilight hour in an age before stadium lights, that gray ball less and less visible with each inning.

Hitters routinely used huge, oversized bats by today's standards, as much as forty-seven to forty-eight ounces, and they usually choked up, just hoping to make contact. McGraw would bunt when he thought it necessary but much preferred the hit-and-run, reasoning, "What's the use of having hitters, if they can't advance the base runner in that way?" He understood that hitting the ball anywhere increased a batter's chances of reaching base in an era of tiny gloves and rock-strewn infields. He loved to run. From 1903, his first full season in New York, through 1919 and the end of the dead-ball era, his Giants never swiped fewer than 130 bases in a season, and fell below 200 thefts only five times.

And by 1904, after just a season and a half at the helm in New York, he was sure that he had the ball club he wanted.

"I have the strongest team I've ever led into a pennant race," McGraw announced. "I ought to come in first."

As usual, he was right. The Giants won what was then a major-league record 106 games, finishing 13 games ahead of the Cubs. They won as a team—McGraw's team. The Giants led the league in nearly every offensive category, yet did not boast a single full-time player who played the entire season in New York and hit .300. They also led the league in fielding and stole 283 bases.

There were outstanding everyday players on the roster, such as Donlin and Bresnahan, "the Duke of Tralee," a feisty, Irish-born receiver who was the best catcher of his era and who served as a sort of projection of McGraw on the field. Like McGraw, Bresnahan was short, smart, and foulmouthed, a merciless baiter of umpires swift enough to bat leadoff and steal as many as thirty-four bases in a season. Muggsy called him "the greatest catcher I ever saw," although even he bemoaned Bresnahan's temper. When the Duke wasn't getting thrown out of games or suspended for his constant harassment of the umpires, he was busy improving his protection, devising the first workable set of shin guards, attaching leather shock absorbers to his mask, using a primitive batting helmet that resembled an old-fashioned, leather football helmet.

The biggest stars on the Giants were the pitchers, just as they were on most teams of the time. McGraw got twenty-seven wins from Luther Taylor, who could neither hear nor speak and who, like all such players in the major leagues—there were three on McGraw's teams alone—was called Dummy for being "deaf and dumb." (Taylor, a cutup, insisted on going to see vaudeville with teammates and making them sign the jokes for him.) He got another thirty-five wins from "Iron Man" Joe McGinnity, a tough, bull-chested hurler who worked as his own bouncer in the saloon he owned, raged openly on the mound when his fielders booted balls behind him, and once spat in the eye of a rookie umpire to welcome him to the big leagues. A quick-pitch artist who attributed his amazing endurance to the way he altered his pitching style, going back and forth between over-hand, underhand, and sidearm deliveries, McGinnity *averaged* 344 innings a year during his major-league career. His trademark was starting—and winning—both games of a doubleheader, something he did three times in the month of August 1903 alone. That year he threw 434 innings—more than *two* full seasons by a top starting pitcher today.

—

Yet there was one Giant who clearly stood above the rest—one man who captured the hearts of the fans and above all the heart of his manager. He would become the greatest star in the history of the sport, at least before the game changed entirely, and one of its greatest tragedies.

Christy Mathewson looked every bit the part of a storybook sports hero. Six feet two, broad shouldered, blond, blue-eyed, and handsome as a Broadway idol, he was compared almost from the beginning to the fictional dime-novel hero Frank Merriwell. Like Merriwell, Mathewson exemplified a leading ideal of the time, that of "rugged Christianity," or the idea that a man could be good but still be a man. Well mannered, well spoken, he was the son of a "gentleman farmer" from the definitely fictional-sounding town of Factoryville, Pennsylvania. He had seriously considered going to work in forestry, or as a Presbyterian minister, and he promised his mother he would never pitch on Sunday.

Early in his career, Mathewson—or Matty, as everyone called him—was given to mouthing such pieties as "A man who would cheat on his wife would also cheat in baseball. . . . Would such cheaters also betray their country?" His wife, Jane—a former Sunday school teacher—tended to protest a little too much that her husband was "a good man, very good" but no "goody-goody." Sportswriters liked to refer to him as "the Christian gentleman" and raved about his refinement, his manners, his every accomplishment, real and trivial, right down to how he read Victor Hugo and was the checkers champion in six states.

"Christy Mathewson," gushed Grantland Rice, "is the only man I ever met who in spirit and inspiration is greater than his game."

Like Merriwell, he was a college man, an A student at Bucknell, where his courses included chemistry, philosophy, Latin, literature, and the classics. He sang in the glee club, acted in student theatricals, wrote poetry, and was elected class president. He was the pitcher on the baseball team, the center on the basketball team, the fullback on the football team, where Walter Camp, "the Father of American Football," called him "the greatest drop-kicker in intercollegiate competition" after he booted a forty-eight-yard field goal through the uprights against Army.

Unlike Merriwell, Mathewson left school before his senior year and took his chances in the big, bad city. Mathewson joined the Giants just weeks short of the twentieth birthday in his star-strewn life—and fell flat on his face. The young pitcher was strafed by major-league hitters, losing all three of his decisions. For the first and only time in his life, Matty even seemed to lose his composure, letting base runners steal third on him. The impatient Andrew Freedman shipped the busher to the minors, and the Giants nearly lost him for good when Connie Mack offered him $50 to sign with his new American League Philadelphia Athletics team—thereby raising one of those what-if scenarios that all who follow the game are so addicted to. Mack's teams in the years to come would have been all but unbeatable, with Mathewson added to a staff that included Chief Bender, Rube Waddell, Eddie Plank, and Jack Coombs.

Instead, Cincinnati claimed Matty off the Giants' roster for $100, then dealt him back to New York for Amos Rusie, the old "Hoosier Thunderbolt," who was actually still only thirty but who had not pitched for three years, thanks to his running battles with Freedman. Mathewson agreed to return to the Giants when Freedman said he would repay Mr. Mack his $50 signing bonus, which he did not.

Given a second chance in New York, Matty excelled immediately, winning twenty games, although he was such a good hitter that he was tried at first, shortstop, and the outfield. McGraw ended this little experiment when he came up from Baltimore, calling the idea of putting Mathewson at first or anywhere else "sheer insanity."

It's inevitable, perhaps, that we think of McGraw and Mathewson as enjoying a father-son relationship, but in fact the manager was only seven years older than his ace. Matty and Muggsy's respect for each other was immediate and unshakable, founded on the intelligence with which they both approached the game. The very first spring they were together, McGraw told his wife that Mathewson "looks like he can pitch with his head as well as his arm," the highest compliment he could offer a player. Even their wives hit it off immediately—so much so that the two couples shared an apartment at Columbus and Eighty-Fifth Street, with Mathewson paying for the food and McGraw for the gas and rent.

As Mathewson's biographer Frank Deford would marvel, "Did ever any other manager and star player in any sport room together with their wives?" The setup seemed like a prescription for disaster, and yet the two couples only drew closer—the refined, college-educated, Protestant, Anglo, Republican Mathewsons living with the rough-edged, self-made, Catholic, Irish, Democratic McGraws. Here, it seemed, was the fulfillment of the democratic ideal that America, and New York, so constantly promised but so rarely delivered.

It is easy enough to understand the attraction on McGraw's part at least. Matty had what was considered a good but not a dominating fastball for the era and an outstanding "drop curve." Where he thrived was in that pitching with his mind. He changed speeds and locations constantly, mixing in the occasional "rise ball" or spitter. His control was unparalleled. One hitter claimed that "he could throw a ball into a tin cup at pitching range," and Mathewson once went sixty-eight consecutive innings without walking a batter. John Tortes "Chief" Meyers, his longtime batterymate, asserted, "I don't think he ever walked a man in his life because of wildness. The only time he might walk a man was because he was pitching too fine to him, not letting him have a good ball to hit."

Matty led the league in strikeouts five times and ran up more than twenty-five hundred in his career, but he preferred letting batters hit 'em where they *were*—the now lost art of "pitching to contact." It was common for him to toss a complete game with just seventy-five to eighty pitches—an invaluable habit at a time when hurlers were commonly expected to work every two to three days. He remembered hitters, too, a trait Meyers associated with the same brains that made Mathewson able to play a dozen checkers matches simultaneously with his eyes blindfolded.

"Actually that's what made him a great pitcher," claimed Meyers, himself a Dartmouth man. "His wonderful retentive memory. Any time you hit a ball off him, you never had another pitch in that spot again."

Yet like many great pitchers, Christy Mathewson had a little something more, a special pitch that intimidated batters just with the fear that he might throw it. Mathewson himself called it his "freak pitch" or a "fall-away," but it soon acquired the romantic name of the "fade-away." To throw it, he gripped the ball the same as he did his curve but twisted it "off [his] thumb, with a peculiar snap of the wrist," so that his palm was face up at the end of his delivery. It has been compared to a screwball, and—much like James Creighton's legendary pitch—its effect was akin to that of Mariano Rivera's famed cutter. The ball broke sharp but in the opposite direction of a curve, moving *in* on right-handed hitters and *away* from lefties. The fadeaway put a tremendous, "unnatural" torque on his arm, enough so that Matty was smart enough not to throw it more than a dozen times a game, usually when he was "pitching in a pinch," as he liked to call it. As such it was all the more effective, a devastating out pitch that could also be used as a decoy, freezing the batter for his sharp-breaking curve, or a fastball with plenty of movement.

The fadeaway cemented the legend of Matty the pitcher. But his superstar status rested on more than just his ability on the mound. For all his Christian humility, he was a natural showman, making what was no doubt the most dramatic entrance by any pitcher in New York, at least until the great Rivera's. Mathewson stepped onto the field like a caped knight, wearing a long, linen duster of the type popular with early motorists. He would wait until about ten minutes before the game, then start to walk in from the Polo Grounds' clubhouse, located beyond the outfield. There was no canned music, no organ playing. Just a lone figure, moving across the outfield grass, and with every stride he took toward the mound, the fans grew louder, whistling and clapping and stomping on the wooden bleachers.

The bugs adored him. They dubbed him the Big Six, a moniker first used in print by the sportswriter Sam Newhall Crane, and one resonant with New York history. It has been variously attributed to a popular motorcar of the time, or a union local, but it most likely referred to the legendary fire wagon captained by Boss Tweed. Frank Deford would question why, "if Matty was a flamethrower, would you name him after an anti-flamethrower"? But in New York the name meant *power.* The power of the Big Six engine itself, the biggest and mightiest fire engine in the city, in its time—and the power of Tammany Hall, the indomitable political machine that Tweed would come to lead.

Mathewson was the first ballplayer to reap major money from endorsements. Fans flocked to see him on the vaudeville circuit and in the one-reel films he made in the offseason. They snapped up any of the countless items he lent his name and image to: insurance, stocks, sweaters, razors, an early board baseball game, Coca-Cola ("proof of its wholesomeness!"), Tuxedo pipe tobacco ("what I call good, honest, companionable tobacco"). Ghostwriters helped him pen a play, and even his own series of boys' baseball novels. (Though Matty himself was no slouch with a pen. It was he who coined the phrase "the old college try" during one of his post-pitching excursions into sportswriting.)

He seemed, as well, the very paragon of the new decency that Ban Johnson and others were trying so hard to inflict upon baseball. Mathewson's mother, Minerva, a devoted member of the Woman's Christian Temperance Union, saw divine intervention in his unprecedented influence. The Episcopal Cathedral of St. John the Divine—that largest Gothic cathedral in the world, now rising over Morningside Heights—agreed, immortalizing Matty as a figure in a stained-glass window that celebrated sport. Mathewson himself told reporters, "I feel strongly that it is my duty to show youth the good, clean, honest values that I was taught by my mother. That, really, is all I can do."

That, really, was a bit much for Matty's fellow ballplayers. Considered aloof and conceited when he first broke in, he was ridiculed as "Sis" for his high voice, or "Old Gumboots" for his slightly knock-kneed stride. A teammate on one of his first Giants teams wrote home, "Hardly anyone on the team speaks to Mathewson. He deserves it. He is a pinhead and a conceited fellow who has made himself unpopular." Yet within a very short time Matty was one of the most popular players in the Giants' clubhouse. If he was never quite one of the guys, he was soon a respected, even beloved team leader.

"How we loved to play for him!" remembered Meyers, many years later. "We'd break our necks for that guy."

What brought about this change? In part it was that old college attitude. According to Meyers, "If you made an error behind him, or anything of the sort, he'd never get mad or sulk. He'd come over and pat you on the back." In part it was his generosity. In an age when veterans routinely savaged rookies in the Darwinian fight to retain their jobs, Matty spent hours working with the young pitchers every spring training, helping them any way he could.

Yet it wasn't just through a sense of noblesse oblige that Matty won his teammates over. Laughing Larry Doyle, the Giants' hard-nosed second baseman, remembered, "He'd gamble, play cards, curse now and then and take a drink now and then." Rube Marquard, another star pitcher and roommate, claimed, "If you had a dollar in your pocket, he would never be satisfied until he got that dollar from you." Once the Christian gentleman supposedly threw a $1,000 bill on the floor and told his teammates, "Fade that if you dare!" He would take all the action he could get, gambling at chess, checkers, dice, poker, gin, bridge, sometimes losing as much as $700 to $800 in a night to his fellow Giants.

Mathewson's pastime spoke to the pervasiveness of gambling in male society—in baseball—at the time. But it also implies a shrewd, conscious effort to knock down the walls between himself and his teammates. Notoriously tightfisted most of the time, Matty might have used gambling as a way to spread the wealth around to his less compensated colleagues without patronizing them—the equivalent of a pro quarterback buying his linemen expensive dinners today.

Over and over again, finding a way to be the big man—to be a magnet to the fans, the sportswriters, the sponsors—without provoking the jealousy and suspicion of teammates would prove to be the greatest challenge to superstardom in New York. It was a trick that would be mastered by very different men in very different ways, from Babe Ruth to Joe DiMaggio, Willie Mays to Derek Jeter, leaving them revered figures in their own clubhouses. For those who never found a way—for the likes of, say, a Reggie Jackson or an Alex Rodriguez—it would be a worrisome burden, an unnecessary distraction even when they played brilliantly.

That Mathewson found a solution shouldn't be too surprising. The man ran deep, often unexpectedly so. Grantland Rice related in his memoir, *The Tumult and the Shouting,* that Matty once confided in him the value of a good alibi to an athlete.

"An alibi is sound and needed in all competition," he told Rice with startling frankness. "I mean in the high-up brackets. One of the foundations of success in sport is confidence in yourself. You can't afford to admit that any opponent is better than you are. So, if you lose to him there must be a reason—a bad break. You must have an alibi to show why you lost. If you haven't one, you must fake one. Your self-confidence must be maintained."

Who knew? Deep down inside, where no one else could see, Frank Merriwell was also Ring Lardner's "Alibi Ike." Mathewson's machinations might have extended to his gambling and his brawling. During the first month of the 1905 season, he erased any remaining doubt that he was one of the boys when a fistfight broke out down in Philadelphia. McGraw's team stormed the field behind their manager, setting off a wild, running brawl. When an adolescent lemonade seller ventured over to yell something near the Giants' dugout, Mathewson knocked him down with a punch, splitting open the boy's lip and loosening several of his teeth. The cry went out that even virtuous young Matty had fallen prey to "McGrawism."

Mathewson offered no apology or even explanation. The Giants were on a tear, picking up right where they had left off after their dominant 1904 season. Much as his pupil Casey Stengel did after him, McGraw drove his team hardest when it was winning, keeping himself in a perpetual frenzy. A week after the Philly brawl, he "twisted the nose" of the New York *Evening World* reporter Allen Sangree in a hotel lobby. A couple weeks later, after being ejected from a game at the Polo Grounds, he went up into the grandstand and led the fans there in taunting the Pittsburgh Pirates owner, Barney Dreyfuss, bawling at the top of his lungs that Dreyfuss didn't pay his gambling debts and greased the umps. When the league president, Harry Pulliam, phoned to chastise him, McGraw called him "Dreyfuss's employee" and went to court to get an injunction against any fine or suspension.

Back in Philadelphia on their next trip, the Giants loaded up their carriages with their own rocks and threw them right back at the Phillies' fans. In Pittsburgh, McGraw protested a call so vociferously that the umps forfeited the game to the Pirates, provoking another stoning from the stands, and Mickey Face and his players ended up holding off a crowd of eighteen thousand with their bats. This was a virtuoso performance, even for McGraw, and it worked brilliantly. The Giants won 105 games, only one less than in 1904, and prepared to face off in the second World Series ever played, against Connie Mack's Philadelphia Athletics.

This would be Christy Mathewson's greatest performance, coming awfully early in a career where the Big Six had already done any number of things seemingly impossible to top, winning thirty games in 1903, thirty-three in 1904, and thirty-one more in 1905. Ball fans everywhere eagerly awaited his matchup against Rube Waddell, the dominant pitcher in the American League. Unlike Matty, Waddell was a big, fireballing lefty, with the best curve in the majors. He had gone 27-10 in 1905, leading the AL with a 1.48 ERA and 287 strikeouts. The year before, he had struck out 349 batters, a major-league record that would last until Sandy Koufax.

Yet where Matty was a matinee idol, Rube's looks were irretrievably comic, with his googly eyes, a big nose, and a jutting chin. The funny face reflected a strangely childlike interior. He was known to run off the mound to chase a passing fire engine and delayed games he was scheduled to pitch while he played marbles with children outside the ballpark. He liked to stop into a saloon on his way to or from the park, and sometimes ended up tending bar. Sportswriters took to dubbing him the Sousepaw. Opposing managers distracted him by dangling rubber snakes and shiny toys from the coaches' boxes.

Was Rube mentally disabled in some way? It is impossible to say, but he was capable of staying with the Big Six on a ball field. Then, late in September, it was announced that Waddell had hurt his arm by falling in the team sleeping car. Rumors flew that Rube had been taken advantage of by gamblers, bribed or threatened into faking an arm injury. Connie Mack vehemently denied this, but the great matchup was off. The ugly duckling had left the field, and baseball's beau ideal would have it all to himself.

Matty did not disappoint, putting on the greatest display of pitching ever seen in a World Series *to this day.* In the span of five days, he threw three shutouts, two of them on the road. In twenty-seven innings, he allowed only fourteen hits—four doubles and ten singles—struck out eighteen, and walked just one batter. The A's got just one man as far as third base in the games he pitched. In the fifth and last game of the series, Mathewson retired the last ten men in a row, seven of them by groundouts, while McGraw hooted and hollered gleefully from the sidelines, taunting the A's Indian starter, Charles Albert "Chief" Bender, "It'll be off the warpath for you today, Chief!"

When it was over, the twenty-five thousand fans in attendance rushed the field, while Mathewson and his teammates raced back to their clubhouse. Some tossed their gloves and caps to the bugs, while Larry Doyle told the writers, "It's great to be young and a Giant."

Matty, that natural actor, and his batterymate Bresnahan appeared last, unfurling a big banner that read THE GIANTS WORLD'S CHAMPIONS 1905. The crowd went even wilder. Matty waited for the cheering to die down, then told them, "Gentlemen, I want to thank you for your kindness, but you must remember there were eight other members of the team who worked for our success just as much as I did."

It was the perfect, aw-shucks, Jeter-y thing to say, rugged Christianity in action. It was, as well, a very good day for his close friend and housemate, John McGraw. Muggsy had been in fine spirits through the World Series, happy to win another round in his endless feud with Ban Johnson, and as he took further bows from the balcony of the Giants' clubhouse, he seemed content for one of the very few moments in his contentious life. His 1905 squad was, McGraw would later decide, the best and the smartest one he had ever managed. Over the past two seasons, his Giants teams had won a total of 211 games. No one had ever done anything quite like that, and a month after the series ended, Brush rewarded him with a new three-year contract at $15,000 a year.

McGraw had also won $400 betting on his team in the series, and he put some of his new money to work by opening up a fifteen-table pool hall in Herald Square, with a jockey, Tod Sloan, and a gambler, Jack Doyle, as partners. No one so much as batted an eye about either a manager in the World Series betting on his own team or his opening up a billiards parlor with a known gambler—not even at a time when running a pool hall mandated regular payoffs to the NYPD.

That winter, too, the McGraws reluctantly moved out of their cozy household with the Mathewsons on Eighty-Fifth Street and Columbus, and into residence at the Washington Inn, a nice hotel at 155th Street and Amsterdam and an easy walk to the Polo Grounds. Mac missed Matty's company, but he would be consoled by the presence at the Washington of another young, gifted player who also knew the inside game of baseball forward and backward, even if he did play for another team. His name was Hal Chase, soon to become the most nefarious ballplayer in the history of the game, and his association would come to have dire consequences, ones that came close to ruining both McGraw and the game he loved so much.

17

The Bad Guys Come to Town

Ban Johnson was nothing if not persistent. Despite the razzle McGraw had pulled on him, his new American League outdrew the Senior Circuit (as sportswriters would forever after call the National League) by more than half a million fans in 1902. Johnson had at last got the NL's attention, and its owners signed a new "National Agreement" with the AL, giving Johnson de facto control of a three-man commission appointed to preside over the game—and the right to move the Baltimore AL franchise to Manhattan.

When that was done, major-league baseball would be locked in place for the next fifty years, sixteen teams in eleven cities, an unmatched period of stability in any professional American sport.

The National League might have conceded to Johnson, but Tammany Hall had not. The AL president still needed a ball field for his New York team. After extended stonewalling, Johnson finally gave in. On March 11, 1903, he awarded the new franchise to a murky syndicate of "businessmen" that had somehow secured the lease on a piece of land from 165th to 168th Street, and between what was then Eleventh Avenue and Broadway. Appropriately, the area would be rented from the New York Institute for the Blind, for Ban Johnson would be required to turn at least one unseeing eye to the deal. The syndicate Johnson had given his blessing to—for a low, low price of just $18,000—had a plausible front man, a coal supplier named Joseph Gordon who had been the city's deputy superintendent of buildings and had owned a small percentage of the Giants. But right behind Gordon, as even Johnson must have realized, was the machine at its ugliest.

One of Gordon's minority partners was Tom Foley, son-in-law of the Tammany boss "Silent Charlie" Murphy. Foley was fast emerging as a power in his own right, operating from the saloon he ran across from the Manhattan Criminal Courthouse and the Tombs prison. Next door was a lucrative real estate and bail bond business, where Foley was partners with a bright young gambler and bankroller for the mob—another Tammany protégé named Arnold Rothstein.

The two principal owners were even worse. Frank Farrell looked like skulduggery walking, with his pulled-down bowler and baggy suits, his slitted eyes and turned-down moustache. Known as the Poolroom King, Farrell was, in the historian David Pietrusza's estimate, "perhaps the most successful operator of gambling establishments in the country before the rise of Las Vegas after World War II." Originally a liquor dealer, by the time he bought into major-league baseball, Farrell owned two racetracks and an estimated total of three hundred pool halls and gambling parlors around the country. In partnership with the Tammany sachem Big Tim Sullivan and others, he was believed to control two-thirds of all gambling in New York, for an annual take of $3 million—perhaps as much as $7 billion in today's money.

Farrell's headquarters was the fabulous House with the Bronze Door casino, down on West Thirty-Third Street in the old Tenderloin, where high rollers such as Diamond Jim Brady lost and won fantastic sums. Its interior had been designed by no less than Stanford White, who for the whopping fee of $100,000 had filled the place with lush velvet carpeting and Persian rugs and covered the floors of the roulette room with hand-painted frescoes. Ten Venetian artisans were imported to work for two years, carving allegorical figures into a second-floor banister. The casino's name came from its massive front door, which Farrell had also imported from a Venice wine cellar for $20,000 but which had a very practical role to play. When reformers finally goaded police into raiding the joint in 1901, the cops needed blowtorches to force their way in. By the time they did, Farrell had escorted Brady and other celebrity guests through a back passage and over an adjoining rooftop to freedom.

Farrell's co-owner was even more flamboyant. Big Bill Devery was a huge, habitually drunk, walrus-like individual with a fifty-seven-inch waist and a white handlebar moustache. He had started out as a bartender, before paying $200 to the machine to become a beat cop on the Lower East Side. Like the rest of the force, he worked—and bribed—his way up the ranks, making lieutenant ($1,400) and then captain ($14,000) in the prized Tenderloin, which was where he had met Farrell.

There were plenty of crooked cops in New York—just none so brazen. Devery's motto on the street was "Hear, see, and say nothin', eat, drink, and pay nothin'," and he followed this dictum with a religious dedication. Hauled up before the Lexow Committee investigating police corruption, Devery insisted, "Touchin' and appertainin' to that matter I disremember." He described himself as undoubtedly the most pacific policeman in the history of New York City. "I just stand there and breathe the fresh air," talking to everyone, he claimed, "from the meekest to the highest, no matter who came along." Incredibly, Devery not only survived this interrogation but was made chief of police.

"He was no more fit to be chief of police than the fish man was to be director of the Aquarium," wrote the muckraker Lincoln Steffens, "but as a character, as a work of art, he was a masterpiece."

By 1901, Devery had turned his opportunities for graft into an estimated $600,000 to $1 million in Manhattan real estate. The district attorney candidate William Travers Jerome denounced him as "the head of the city's pimps, procurers, and madams," and the state legislature abolished the post of chief of police in an effort to get rid of him. Feeling underappreciated, Devery ran for mayor in 1903 against Murphy's favored candidate, on the novel slogan "You can trust a thief, but you can't trust a liar." A brass band followed him everywhere, banging out his campaign tune, "I'm for Mr. Dev-ery / Ev-ery, ev-ery time!"

Crushed in the Democratic caucuses, Devery responded by publicly listing every pool hall, whorehouse, and gambling dive that Silent Charlie Murphy had an interest in. This was skating on very thin ice indeed, and both Devery and Farrell seem to have realized it. The two men decided it was time to divest themselves of their more obvious gambling interests and become respectable baseball owners, an arrangement that served to pacify everyone, at least for the time being.

All they needed now was a ballpark—one that had to be constructed in less than two months, in time for opening day. This elicited one more Tammany stickup. The American League forked over $275,000 to farm the work out to yet another minority owner of the team, Thomas McAvoy, a police inspector and leader of the assembly district where the new park would rise whose sole claim to morality was that he would not take "whore money." Apparently Ban Johnson's money was acceptable. What it bought was a ramshackle, wooden grandstand, twenty rows deep and seating 4,186 fans willing to put up a dollar apiece, flanked by 5,000 bleacher seats at fifty cents each, and another 2,500 outfield bleacher seats for two bits. Said outfield was, in any case, rather amorphous. American League Park, as it was officially called—Hilltop Park, or the Rockpile, as it was soon dubbed—stretched 365 feet to left field, 400 feet to right, and an endless 542 feet to dead center.

Today, if one stands where home plate supposedly was—now on the grounds of the New York–Presbyterian Columbia University Irving Medical Center—it is impossible to understand just how anyone could have played ball there. Unless the landscaping was changed dramatically, batters would have been standing on the side of a hill. The baseball historian Glenn Stout describes the field as a "barren, rocky outcrop . . . dotted with massive boulders and dead trees and cleaved by deep gullies. A fetid pond ran the length of the eastern side."

McAvoy's contractors dealt with this mainly by dumping tons of landfill into the site. Most of it sank. By opening day, April 30, 1903, there was grass only in the infield, and the sun reflected so brightly off the baked earth and rocks that fans complained they were blinded by the glare. There was no clubhouse yet, and both teams had to change in a nearby hotel. Neither the roof nor the bleachers were finished, and thousands of fans were forced to stand behind a rope in the outfield. The pond had been transformed into a gaping crater in right field that would charitably be referred to as a "hollow." Farrell and Devery had it roped off and declared ground-rule double territory. Later, the team would try such ingenious devices as covering it with wooden planks or having fans stand in it.

Still, an overflow crowd of 16,243 filled the outfield and some 5,000 temporary folding chairs in the grandstand. Commencing what would become an endless Yankees tradition of using puerile displays of patriotism to cover up other shortcomings, every fan was given a little American flag. Mr. Devery's band played, and Ban Johnson threw out the first ball. New York had got off to a slow start on the road, losing its first game, 3–1, before witty Washington fans who mocked the team as "New York's Finest." But back in their new home, Jack Chesbro—a star National League pitcher Johnson had lured away from the Pittsburgh Pirates—returned the favor, topping the Senators, 6–2.

Optimism ran amok. The player-manager Clark "the Old Fox" Griffith, a part-time vaudevillian, promised to work his team hard and told reporters that "we expect to be in the chase from the jump and can be counted on to finish in the first division." Johnson had seeded the team with stars drawn from both his National League acquisitions and other AL teams, including the great Orioles outfielder (and McGraw's former sparring partner), Wee Willie Keeler, and later Kid Elberfeld, a.k.a. the Tabasco Kid, a five-foot-five bundle of frequently misdirected energy who liked to attract waiters' attention by throwing plates against the wall, poured whiskey into the numerous spike wounds on his legs, and had an unfortunate habit of physically attacking umpires in critical games.

Right from the beginning, the team that would become the Yankees was loaded with pricey, veteran stars from around baseball and expected to run the table. It didn't work out that way. Forced on an early, twenty-four-day road trip so McAvoy's carpenters could finish their park, the team slumped badly and finished a distant fourth.

Johnson remained determined to make his New York team a champion, maneuvering to add still more stars to its roster over the winter. But again in 1904, the New Yorkers stumbled out of the gate while the champion Boston Pilgrims—also known as the Somersets and occasionally the Red Stockings—got off to another fast start. Johnson would not give up, forcing yet another trade, this one involving the Boston centerfielder Patsy Dougherty, a swift base runner who had led the American League in hits and runs scored in 1903.

There had been bitterness between Boston and New York almost from the very beginning of their coexistence in the American League, caused by a collision at first in 1903 between New York's Dave Fultz and the Boston pitcher George Winter. Now Dougherty was peddled off to New York in exchange for a .211-hitting, rookie infielder named Bob Unglaub who at the time was too sick even to play. ("Sick" most likely being a euphemism, because poor Unglaub would alternate during most of his career between bouts of dipsomania and drum thumping for the Salvation Army.) Never before had a league president in a major American sport so blatantly tried to influence a pennant race. But at last it seemed that all of Johnson's manipulations were paying off. The New York team finally began to win consistently, and the fans started to brave the rugged terrain of Hilltop Park.

There, the first challenge they faced was what to call their team. The most popular nickname through its first year of existence was the Highlanders, a play on both where the park was situated, high atop Washington Heights, and on the Scottish origins of its alleged owner, Joseph Gordon. Other favorites in this vein included "Hilltoppers," and "Kilties," while some went with "Americans," "Invaders," and the "Greater New Yorks."

By 1904 another name was being popularized by Hearst's *New York Evening Journal.* This was the "Yankees," and its origin is somewhat mysterious. If anything, New York's rival in Boston should have laid claim to the appellation. It seems to have been inspired either as a derivation of "Americans" or by the fact that the team played to the north of the Giants in Manhattan. Whatever the case, it was soon a favorite of headline writers and typesetters, who seized the chance to shorten the name to "Yanks" (and thereby robbed their descendants of the chance to run endless variations of HIGHS HIT NEW LOW headlines).

A couple of other permanent aspects of the team would presently be added as well. Contrary to popular rumor, the Yankees did *not* start wearing pinstripes to make Babe Ruth look slimmer, or because they were long associated with bankers. They were actually just aping the most successful teams of their day—first the Cubs, who started wearing them in 1907, then the Giants, who donned them in 1911. In 1912, the Yankees followed suit, wearing black pinstripes on a white home uniform. They forswore the stripes after that season—maybe because the club finished dead last—then donned them again, for good, in 1915.

The famous, interlocking "NY" made its first appearance in 1905, the only positive contribution Big Bill Devery made to the team. It had been designed by that quintessentially New York firm, Tiffany, as part of a medal awarded to Officer John McDowell. McDowell had won the medal for his actions on the evening of January 8, 1877, when he supposedly interrupted a group of thieves trying to make off with $120 worth of cigars from Courtney's Liquor Store on Seventh Avenue, in Hell's Kitchen. After McDowell clipped one of the thieves with his nightstick, the burglar opened fire, grazing McDowell's head with a bullet. Seriously injured, McDowell nonetheless wrestled the thief to the ground and held him until help arrived. Or so the story ran. Ugly rumors had it that Officer McDowell had in fact been following the usual practice of patrolmen on cold, wintry New York nights and had let himself into Courtney's to snooze for a while, only to have the burglars tumble down on his head through the ceiling, interrupting his winter's nap. Yankee-haters will not be surprised.

From their very first pennant race, then, the Yankees were the Yankees. By any name—and in any uniform—they looked formidable. At the plate, they were led by the raging Elberfeld and by his mirror opposite. Wee Willie Keeler, as his name implies, was a small, nimble player and remembered chiefly for saying, "Keep your eye on the ball and hit 'em where they ain't." The son of a Brooklyn trolley switchman who had "Americanized" his name from "Kelleher," Keeler had left high school after his freshman year to start playing semipro ball. He was the epitome of a slap hitter, his game perfectly geared to the dead-ball, contact hitting game that baseball was at the turn of the century. He choked up on the bat and excelled at the hit-and-run and punching the ball just over the infielders' heads. He hit 206 singles in the 1898 season alone, a record that stood until it was broken by Ichiro in 2004, batted as high as .424, and stole 495 bases in his career. He could fly down the line and was such an adept bunter that it was said they changed the rule to make a two-strike foul bunt a strike, in order to keep Wee Willie from running up interminable at bats.

The Highlanders were his third New York team, after stints with both the Giants and the Dodgers. Keeler was in decline but not very noticeably so, valiantly patrolling the Highlanders' Rabelaisian outfield while hitting .343. Chatty and likable, he seems to have been a paragon of good humor in an era of stormy if not deranged baseball personalities, humming and whistling continuously. Though a lifelong bachelor, he loved kids, and during breaks in the action he would go over to Hilltop Park's low, wooden bleacher fence and talk to them about what they were watching, explaining the inside game. At the same time, the little man was plenty tough, having once made a leaping, barehanded grab of a line drive that carried him into a barbed-wire fence lining the stands. There he stuck, until his teammates could disentangle him. Once he was freed and had his arm bandaged, he kept playing, even though his team was hopelessly behind.

Great as Keeler was, the player driving the Yankees in 1904 was the pitcher Happy Jack Chesbro. A beefy, right-handed, and famously dour hurler from the Berkshires (the "Happy" tag was a typically ironic nickname of the era), Chesbro was already established as a star. But as the 1904 season unwound, it became clear to Happy Jack—and to the league—that he had lost a foot off his fastball. Casting about for a remedy, he remembered the spitball he had seen one Elmer Stricklett throw in spring training.

"I said to myself," he would later remember, "Mr. Chesbro, that is something you must learn."

The spitter was still legal at the time. Thrown with a stiff wrist, it came out of the pitcher's hand looking like a straight fastball, only to dip sharply downward as the air did its work on the saliva, or whatever other substance—hair oil, skin balm, tobaccy juice, chewing gum, assorted gunk—was attached. But it still mattered who threw it.

Chesbro would become the maestro of the spitter. He threw it as he would a curveball, from a three-quarters motion, and exercised remarkable control over the pitch. He could make his spitball dip anywhere from two inches to a foot and a half, in whatever direction he chose. In the first game he threw it, Jack breezed happily to a 10–1 win. After that he kept winning, and winning, as nobody ever quite would again: fourteen complete-game victories in a row through July 4, in which he surrendered a total of only twelve earned runs. He had twenty wins by July 16, then thirty by September 3, with a whole month left to go in the season. From July 14 on, he later reported, he threw almost nothing but spitballs, and he noticed that an ache in his arm grew steadily worse, and never did go away. But no matter how sore his shoulder was, it didn't diminish the way the ball moved, dropping suddenly down and away, like a particularly devilish slider.

On August 5, 1904, Chesbro's teammate Al Orth, possessor of the marvelous nickname the Curveless Wonder, flatlined his way to a 5–0 shutout of the Cleveland Napoleons. For the first time in their existence, the New York Yankees were in first place. Meanwhile, McGraw's Giants were running away with the National League, and New York was giddy with the idea of a Subway Series—even as the city's first underground train lines inched their way toward completion.

Still, the Yankees could not put Boston away, and Orth hurt his arm. Clark Griffith went to a two-man rotation, alternating Chesbro and Jack Powell, who threw nearly four hundred innings himself. Both pitched well, but on October 7, Boston still led in the standings with a record of 92-57, to the Yankees' 90-56. Any hope of a New York world championship was off now, McGraw and John Brush having refused to risk the Giants' New York supremacy on one series with a bunch of upstart bushers. But the pennant was still up for grabs. Under the rather arbitrary rules of the time, there was no talk of the Highlanders making up those extra three contests. Instead, the race would come down to a five-game series against Boston in New York, beginning with a single game that Friday and followed by doubleheaders on Saturday and Monday.

Or at least the games were *supposed* to be in New York. Months earlier, Farrell and Devery had rented out Hilltop Park for a Columbia-Williams college football game on Saturday, without a thought of how it might affect their team. Now, after the Friday game, the Highlanders would have to take the train up to Boston and play a Saturday twin bill *there,* before returning to New York for the Monday doubleheader.

At least the Yankees still had Chesbro. He shut down Boston on four hits in the series opener for his forty-first win, and after the final out the ten thousand New York fans on hand carried him off the field on their shoulders. The Yankees were back in first by half a game with four to play, and Manager Clark Griffith crowed to the press, "We've got Boston on the run." Everyone was now supposed to get on the train for South Station—except for Chesbro, who would stay in New York and prepare for the season-ending doubleheader on Monday. Instead, Happy Jack met Griffith on the train platform and demanded to be taken along after all.

"Do you want to win the pennant or not?" he asked his manager. "I'll pitch and I'll win."

Silently, the Old Fox waved him on to the train. It was a fatal surrender to sentiment. On Saturday, thirty thousand raucous fans—one-tenth of the city of Boston at the time—turned out to watch the Pilgrims hammer Chesbro, 13–2, in the opener of the doubleheader. In the second game, which started as soon as the first was over, Cy Young pitched Boston to a 1–0 victory in a contest shortened to seven innings by darkness, the only run scoring on an error. (At least Columbia had topped the Williams Ephs, 11–0.)

Boston returned to New York needing to win only one of two games to clinch the pennant—the exact same position the team would find itself in again, forty-five years later, over the long skein of the seasons. Another thirty thousand fans overran Hilltop Park, spilling into the endless wastes of the Rockpile's outfield. Griffith went with Chesbro in the first game—his third start in four days. His ace was undaunted, telling his manager the day before, "I'll trim 'em on Monday if it costs an arm."

Everything pointed to a heroic afternoon. When Happy Jack stepped to the plate for the first time, a group of boosters from his hometown of North Adams, Massachusetts, swarmed onto the field, hugged him, and presented him with a sealskin coat and matching cap, in commemoration of his magnificent season. It was one more indication of how informal and unpretentious the sport still was, this interruption of the decisive game of a pennant race to give a player gifts. Baseball was a business, but it was also not so far removed from its rough beginnings on the sidewalks and back lots of New York.

No one seemed to mind the bugs' enthusiasm. Chesbro responded to his tribute by hitting a triple over "Keeler's Hollow," the big hole in right field, and in the fifth Chesbro lashed his second hit of the game, an infield single off Dinneen's pitching hand, to give the Yankees a 2–0 lead. It seemed as if Chesbro could do anything. But in the seventh, Boston tied the score on three Yankee errors, and Happy Jack was obviously running out of steam. The Old Fox decided to keep him in. It was the same decision that managers would face again and again in crucial, late-season games on the playing fields of New York through the century ahead. Always the decision would be to stay with the ace, the known quantity. And always, it would be wrong.

Chesbro managed to stagger through the eighth, giving up three hits but no runs. Unfazed, Griffith sent his ace back out for the ninth. The park rocked with cheers, the New York fans trying to will Chesbro through his 455th inning of work since the season began. He almost made it. Yet another Yankees error put the go-ahead run on third with two out, but Chesbro got two strikes on Boston's shortstop Freddy Parent. He then threw one spitball too many, a pitch that rose from the moment it left his hand and never did cut down toward the ground. It sailed "ten feet over Parent's head," according to one newspaper account (others claimed that catcher Red Kleinow was just slow to react). Whatever the case, the doctored ball flew over everything, not stopping until it hit the backstop, seventy-five feet behind home plate. A wild pitch.

Lou Criger ran in with the go-ahead run, and the Yankees seemed undone. Chesbro turned away and wiped his face. Griffith, in a less than magisterial display of leadership, "fell prostrate in front of the Yankee bench and buried his face in the dirt." The park went silent, save for Boston's "Royal Rooters," a contingent of voluble fans organized in a saloon near the Pilgrims' home field, who serenaded the New Yorkers with derisive songs and chants.

Chesbro, still on the mound, gave up a single to Parent before finally getting the elusive third out. Then he walked back to the bench and "cried like a baby," unable even to watch as the Yankees batted in the bottom of the ninth. His teammates worked a pair of walks off the tiring Dinneen, but Patsy Dougherty—the very player stolen from Boston as part of Johnson's blatant New York favoritism—went down swinging on a 2-2 count. The race was over—though the two teams still played out the second game of the doubleheader, with the Yankees winning the meaningless game, 1–0, in ten innings. In 1904, when you were promised a doubleheader, you got a doubleheader.

"Can you imagine someone grabbing you by the throat, tearing your heart out by the roots and leaving you to die, suffering the tortures of the damned?" Clark Griffith was quoted as saying after the game.

PENNANT LOST BY WILD PITCH, was the way the newspaper headlines played it. Jack Chesbro would become the first of a long parade of New York players unfairly tagged as goats for late-season calamities. For years after his retirement, enterprising sportswriters would beat a trail up to Chesbro's North Adams farm, where he would have to tell the tale once again of how he "blew" the pennant by delivering that wild pitch "with too much force."

It was rubbish. Jack Chesbro in 1904 was worked harder than all but one other pitcher would ever be after 1900, and he responded by completing forty-eight games and winning forty-one—a single-season record that will stand forever, barring some unimaginable change in how the game is played. He compiled an ERA of 1.82 and allowed less than one runner an inning to reach base. Along the way, he beat five future Hall of Fame pitchers and received precious little support; the Yankees scored more than five runs in only thirteen of his starts, and he lost all but one game in which he gave up as many as four runs. In the pennant-deciding game Chesbro had "blown," he gave up only three unearned runs, and even hit a triple and a single. It is impossible to assume that the Yankees would have won if he had not cut loose with that wild pitch, and even if they had, they still would have had to win the second game of the doubleheader—with Boston presumably playing harder than they had. For the fans and the writers, none of this meant a thing.

"It's an old, old story," Happy Jack said years later. "In all New York I don't believe there was a more sorrowful individual."

18

Subterraneans

So there would be no Subway Series, but the subway came anyway. Just after 2:30 p.m. on Thursday, October 27, 1904, Mayor George B. McClellan Jr., son of the famous Civil War flop, walked down to the first station of the Interborough Rapid Transit System, built just below city hall. There he started the motor of the city's first subway train and began to guide it uptown by a silver commemorative throttle provided for the occasion.

McClellan, just thirty-eight, was a handsome, cold-eyed Tammany figurehead who had studied Italian art and history in college and was fluent in Italian, German, and French. (He liked nothing better than to venture into some ethnic neighborhood where a plant in the crowd would yell out, "Speak to us in our own language!"—at which he would give forth with a "spontaneous" speech in the desired tongue.) When the motorman tried to take the throttle back from him, the mayor told him, "I'm running this train!" and on he went, driving the original four-car, olive-colored subway train in his silk hat and frock coat.

Beside him, Frank Hedley, general manager of the new system, was apoplectic, repeatedly urging the mayor, "Slower here, slower! Easy!" McClellan only leaned harder on the throttle. There was one awkward moment when the mayor accidentally hit the emergency brake, sending his passengers—bankers and college presidents, bishops and congressmen—tumbling out of their rattan seats. Soon, though, he was back on course, driving the train on up to Grand Central, then over to Times Square and up the West Side. He drove past cheering crowds who lined the surrounding hills to watch it burst out of a tunnel and over the viaduct across Manhattan Valley, all the way to the line's temporary terminus, at the 145th Street stop. Only there did a satisfied McClellan give over the controls, lighting up a victory cigar and going back to crow over his performance with his bruised guests.

When the subway opened to the general public at seven that evening, an estimated 110,000 people swarmed underground. There, many of them rode the trains free for the rest of the night, singing lustily. Others made a whole evening of it, getting dressed up and going out to dinner to celebrate. The city was "subway mad," as the transit historian Clifton Hood records, with people having already held "subway parties" all over town for weeks. Buildings were festooned with bunting and flags, while on the big day New Yorkers blasted horns and sirens, rang church bells, fired off guns. The following Sunday—the one day of the week most New Yorkers had off—*one million* people tried to ride the subway, nearly three times the capacity of the system at the time.

"Doing the subway," as it was called, would remain a tourist treat for years, and the system became the subject of songs, nickelodeon reels, and a popular dance number called the Subway Express Two-Step. Riders marveled at stations that were little jewel boxes of craftsmanship, the ticket booths made of polished oak with bronze fittings;

the leaded glass skylights and chandeliers; the ornate, iron-and-glass entrances. The tiled walls with the intricate mosaic work spelling out each stop's name and street number; the bas-relief panels for each station: Robert Fulton's first steamboat at the Fulton Street stop, the *Santa Maria* at Columbus Circle, a beaver at Astor Place, in honor of that old fur trader, John Jacob Astor. They were enraged when the privately owned Interborough Rapid Transit Company started hammering up tin advertising signs on the pristine walls. After the outcry was joined by everyone from realtors' associations to the Municipal Art Society, the city sued to have them removed. (They were not.)

The enthusiasm was understandable. The new subterranean trains must have seemed astonishingly fast. Express trains reached speeds of forty miles an hour—the swiftest urban rail system in the world, moving at three times the speed of the city's elevated trains, six times that of its streetcars. New York had suddenly accelerated again. And yet the subway was more than just a way to get around. It was, as the city's great chronicler, Pete Hamill, would point out, one of the great, binding forces in New York life. New Yorkers of nearly all stripes used the subway, and always would. By 1914, the average New Yorker was taking 343 subway trips a year; by 2019, some 54 percent of city residents still used it to commute to work and back—numbers that remain unmatched anywhere else in the United States.

The dark tunnels in the earth had turned out to be the greatest building feat of all, more vital than all the tall, well-lit buildings or the spectacular bridges and train stations, with a replacement value recently estimated at nearly $300 billion.

"Without the subway, New York might very well have turned out to be Bridgeport," wrote the historian Kenneth T. Jackson.

By 1910, one-sixth of all New Yorkers still lived below Fourteenth Street, on a mere one eighty-second of the city's land. The population of the Lower East Side alone was seven hundred per acre, and Jackson estimates that "with no cheap and efficient way to disperse the immigrant tide, Gotham might ultimately have crammed 15 million people into its overcrowded neighborhoods." More likely, today New York "would be a typical big Northeastern or Midwestern city," where "vast highways" would have emptied out the urban core and halved its population.

Instead, thanks to the subway, the population of Manhattan above

125th Street increased by 265 percent from 1905 to 1920 alone, to 323,800 people. Soon, express trains were rushing crowds of brokers up from Wall Street to the Polo Grounds in as little as fifteen minutes. By 1905, the IRT had reached the northernmost tip of Manhattan Island, and that July a new station opened outside Hilltop Park, enabling fans to reach the stadium directly for the first time. The Yankees' attendance reached twenty-two thousand for a doubleheader against the Browns a month later. The future looked limitless.

In fact, the Yankees had already reached the zenith of their stay in Washington Heights. They made it to within three games of first in 1906, finished a remote second to the Athletics in 1910, but otherwise spent most of the next ten years bumbling around in the second division. Griffith, "the Old Fox," debarked to Washington, where he bought the Senators. Farrell and Devery lost patience and began selling off players. The Highlanders were soon the only American League team to be consistently outdrawn in the same city by a National League competitor, and even their onetime guardian angel, Ban Johnson, lost interest in their fortunes.

Soon, the Highlanders' only remaining attraction would be John McGraw's new neighbor.

19

"The Man with the Corkscrew Brain"

Right from the beginning, there was something slippery about the man. Any number of his contemporaries tried to pin him down—McGraw, Mathewson, Damon Runyon, Judge Kenesaw Mountain Landis. All failed. Bill James maintains, only half jokingly, that Hal Chase was altogether a creation of fiction: "There is some evidence to say that he appeared in the flesh, but I lean more toward the invention theory."

Indeed. The story of Prince Hal Chase, "the man with the corkscrew brain," is so outlandish that one could be forgiven for thinking it altogether fictitious. Officially, he was a six-foot tall, ruggedly built, redheaded southpaw, with big ears, an easy grin, and looks good enough to make him a lifelong ladies' man. Though others described him as sinister and pockmarked after mid-career bouts with smallpox and malaria, a bitter, ruined man, whose corruption was reflected in his face.

Which was it? Who knows? That was the thing about Hal Chase.

It seems most safe to say that Chase existed as some hazy mirror image of Christy Mathewson, baseball's beau ideal—the proverbial evil twin. And in the end, their fates would become bitterly intertwined.

Like Mathewson, Hal Chase was a college man, out of Santa Clara, in his native California. Or so it was believed. Certainly he played baseball for Santa Clara; there just is no record that he ever set foot in a classroom there. Like Mathewson, he was adept at almost anything physical that he put his hand to. He rode and hunted and played pool so well that he once ran sixty-five straight balls off Willie Hoppe, winning $2,000 and Hoppe's trademark ivory-inlaid pool cue. He gave the stick back to the pool legend, along with $100 and a characteristic piece of advice: "Don't get attached to people or things."

Words to live by. And sure enough, Hal was a lousy husband to two wives, a worse father to his only son. Sooner or later, he alienated almost everyone he ever knew, no doubt one reason why he was always in such a hurry to move on.

"He was a good-time Charley, then a troublemaker, and then a crook," wrote his biographers Donald Dewey and Nicholas Acocella. "He dazzled everybody, hoodwinked everybody, then disgusted everybody."

Like Mathewson, Hal Chase had a taste for the sporting life. He gambled on everything, especially pool and cards, where he cheated. Gabby Street, a teammate, recalled standing behind him while Chase was playing for a big poker pot and watching a fourth king mysteriously materialize in his hand. He might not have been able to help himself. Several players described him as a kleptomaniac. Harry Hooper said he took "a perverse pride in stealing cigars and other small items" from the lockers of his teammates, while Hippo Vaughn, another Chase roommate, confirmed, "No stranger man ever came my way. Chase couldn't pass a vending stand without lifting something—whether a newspaper, candy bar, apple, or bag of peanuts. It was a compulsion with him."

Like Mathewson, no one doubted his ability on a ball field. Chase was a .291 batter over the course of his fifteen-year career. He had enough pop to lead the outlaw Federal League in home runs—albeit in a bandbox in Buffalo—and won a batting title with Cincinnati. He had enough speed to swipe 363 bases before he was through, and Babe Ruth would claim that "aside from Ty Cobb, he was the best baserunner I ever saw."

Yet most of all, Hal Chase was celebrated for his fielding. For decades to come, long after he had retired and been discredited, baseball men of all stripes named him the greatest first baseman in the history of the game because of his ability in the field. Ruth—or more likely a sportswriter ghost—picked him over Lou Gehrig because "Prince Hal was the greatest fielding first baseman that ever played. He was worth the price of admission just to watch him dance around first base and pick those wild throws out of the dirt." Before his rookie season was half over, Joe Vila was writing in *The Sporting News* that "Chase today is the greatest first baseman in America." Dirty Jack Doyle, his teammate on the Yankees the same year, readily declared that Chase was "the best I ever saw in my life," while *Sporting Life* judged that "a more brilliant ball player never broke into base ball."

What turned so many heads? As with all great fielders it was something almost indefinable, physical but also instinctual. The sportswriter Joe Williams thought that "no other player ever had quicker reflexes." An opponent remembered, "His uncanny foresight in smelling out a play defied imagination. He was always at least one jump ahead of the batter. Invariably he outguessed the batter. He always played exactly where he should have been playing."

Prince Hal's quickness was critical, in an era when the first baseman was a much more important fielder than he is today. He was adept at the 3-6-3 double play, making a perfect throw to second, then beating the batter back to first. His range was amazing. He would play deep enough in the hole to steal sure base hits, throwing the hitter out at first. He would also cut in front of the pitcher to scoop up a bunt and nail a lead runner trying to go from second to third, or he might venture all the way over to the third baseline and throw back to first. He was known to grab a bunt or a chopper and start a double play by tagging out the hitter, and only then throwing to third. He was known to complete an unassisted double play by grabbing a bunt, tagging out the bunter, then beating the runner coming home on a suicide squeeze. Occasionally he caught foul pops *behind* the catcher. He could play second base credibly, even as a lefty.

The man was an artist on the diamond. But, also right from the beginning, there was something missing. Somehow, the air seemed to go out of ball teams when Hal Chase joined them. Fights broke out, controversies simmered, charges and countercharges abounded. There was, at the core, something false about Hal Chase, and just like Christy Mathewson's class, it showed through at once.

Almost from the start of his time in the majors, he was accused of fixing games. Opposing players would taunt him as he ran out on the field: "Hey, Hal, what are the odds today?" As early as 1906, Kid Elberfeld was accusing him of "not having enough fight" during the Yankees' failed stretch drive. Late in the 1910 season, when the Yankees finished second, the manager George Stallings claimed that Chase had cost the team games "either through carelessness or willful indifference." In 1913, yet another manager, the venerable Frank Chance, told sportswriters that Chase was purposely missing balls at first: "They weren't wild throws; they were only made to look that way. He's been doing that right along. He's throwing games on me!"

It was the same everywhere he went. The pitcher Jimmy Ring, a teammate in Cincinnati, claimed Chase offered him $50 to throw a game to the Phillies in 1917. Pol Perritt, another pitcher, claimed he made a similar offer to him to throw a game to the Giants a year later. Fans who had loved his flashy play in the field began to boo him, accusing him of "laying down" and "not putting enough ginger into his play."

And yet nothing ever stuck. With all of the accusations that hounded him throughout his time in baseball, the most remarkable thing about Hal Chase was how he managed to escape retribution.

Partly the problem was one of how easy it is to cheat in baseball, where the margin of success or failure is so thin. Sure, Hal made a major-league record 285 errors at first base, but this was an era when rock-strewn fields, small gloves, and unforgiving scorekeepers hiked error totals everywhere. A first sacker who played the way Chase did, roaming all over the infield, getting to many balls that lesser players could not have reached, was bound to make more errors. Still more of his fumbles must be attributed to sheer exhaustion. Herein lies one of the problems with the constant accusation from Chase's time of "laying down." It could refer both to a player who was tanking games *and* to one who was seen as not hustling enough, for whatever reason.

Hal Chase seems to have burned the candle at both ends and in the middle, spending his nights carousing, romancing, hustling in any barroom or brothel or pool hall he could find. He also played baseball almost obsessively. With New York's blue laws still prohibiting Sunday ball, Chase would go across the river and dig up semipro games in northern New Jersey for a few extra dollars—as if the major-league schedules of the day weren't grueling enough.

In the middle of the 1906 pennant race, during his team's one day off in a stretch of five consecutive doubleheaders, Chase skipped over to play a Sunday twin bill for an Elizabeth, New Jersey, team. (New York went 10-0 in those games, and Chase hit .415.) In the offseason, he played regularly for semipro and college teams back in California. Major-league teams of the time played constant exhibitions during their "off days," meaning that a big leaguer might play as many as two hundred games over the course of a season in his enervating woolen uniform. Who could blame a man for not necessarily giving his all, every time out?

Another reason why Chase got away with whatever he got away with was some sort of unfathomable charm—or at least an unparalleled ability to feign innocence. In a grotesque incident during the 1907 season, Chase's fiancée and the young wife of the Yankees' trainer were caught trying to burn the fetus from the trainer's wife's secret abortion; a dog, it seems, kept pulling the body out of the fire. Both women were arrested, and in the course of the investigation it soon became clear that Chase and his fiancée were living, as the phrase used to go, *in sin.* Two more damning strikes—association with an abortion and "shacking up" with a young woman—are hard to imagine. But somehow the whole incident was hushed up, the women released, Chase soon right back with the team.

"He was the sharpie, the wiseguy, and the angler. He knew everybody, everybody knew him," wrote Dewey and Acocella. "He was Mr. Charm and Mister-One-for-the-House-on-Me."

It began to seem as though Hal Chase could head fake a locomotive. After a quarrel with Elberfeld, by then his manager, in 1908, Chase walked off the team for the last month of the season. He came back the next year. Elberfeld did not. In 1910, Prince Hal smashed a teammate's bat to pieces, had a falling-out with another manager, George Stallings, jumped the team in the middle of a road trip, and returned to New York to appeal his case to Frank Farrell—who responded by firing *Stallings* and hiring Hal Chase to take his place. Stallings would lead the 1914 Boston "Miracle Braves" to a world championship. The Yankees plunged to sixth under Chase.

"God, what a way to run a ballclub!" moaned a teammate, Jimmy Austin.

Whatever his charms, there was, in the end, no denying Hal Chase's connection with professional gambling. This was not all that exceptional. Baseball was saturated with gambling. It was a time when, in nearly any billiards hall or smoke shop, a man could pick up a ten-cent "pool" ticket, betting on which team would win the most games or score the most runs in the coming week. By 1917, the Keystone pool alone was selling 165,000 such tickets every week, paying off the police to the tune of $17,000, and still netting $50,000. To this day, tabloids still carry "runs for the week" charts; in the 1910s, they were as important to many baseball bugs as the box score.

Gambling was everywhere. It was what men did for recreation, as ubiquitous as drinking. The ballpark was no exception. Fans wagered shamelessly in the stands, despite official prohibitions. During a game at Fenway in June 1917, dozens of gamblers grew so desperate to protect their bets against the home team that they stormed the field in the fifth inning, trying to force a forfeit. (Ironically, they were beaten back by some of the visiting White Sox, including Buck Weaver and Fred McMullin, soon to be banished for life in the greatest gambling scandal of them all.) Two years later, bookies in the third-base boxes at the Polo Grounds threw their straw boaters in the air with glee as the Cardinals staged a five-run rally. Suffice it to say, they did not have their money on the home team.

The players saw what was going on, and they wanted in on the action. The catcher Eddie Ainsmith later admitted that "everybody bet in those days because it was a way of making up for the little we were paid," but even the icons of the game were eager to get a bet down. Christy Mathewson, as noted, liked to wager serious cash with his teammates. John McGraw spent most of his waking moments away from the ballpark at the racetrack or the series of pool halls he owned. Following the 1904 season, Muggsy and an "associate" were arrested in the wide-open resort town of Hot Springs, Arkansas, after they spent several days hustling $2,300 from all comers. Their game? The manager of the New York Giants and his friend were pitching silver dollars at a bucket in a hotel lobby.

Gambling was nothing new in baseball, but it was an addiction that was beginning to eat away at its credibility. Some of the game's most prominent owners were sporting men themselves. Unable or unwilling to do anything about the plague of gambling, they resolved to ignore it. It helped that many of the fixed games seem to have been relatively meaningless, often played late in the season between teams that were going nowhere. If pressed, the self-appointed guardians of the sport palmed off the blame on familiar scapegoats. The fault was always that of "foreign elements," or a few bad apples, or others trying to make baseball look bad. A typically anti-Semitic *Sporting News* article characterized those giddy Polo Grounds bookies in 1919 as "Bolsheviki" and "the gents from the Ghetto."

What major-league owners refused to acknowledge was how its gambling problem was undermining the whole public perception of the game—much as baseball's owners many years hence would be glacial in acknowledging the damage caused by steroid use. Rumors flew about every important game or unexpected turn of events. Rube Waddell's injury in 1905, the Miracle Braves' 1914 World Series sweep of Connie Mack's Athletics, a win over the Giants that clinched the 1916 pennant for Brooklyn, a series of doubleheaders the White Sox won over Detroit to take the 1917 flag—all of these surprises and many more, it was whispered, were really payoffs. The fix was always in, the honest fan always being victimized by the inside game. This suspicion, as much as the real fixes, was ripping out the heart of baseball, the wonder and surprise that make all sport worth watching.

The team affected the worst was the Yankees, the most frankly corrupt club in the majors. For the public record, it was supposed to be a snake-bit or "cursed" franchise, much like the Red Sox of later years. Sportswriters wrote constantly about the Yankees' falling victim once again to "the Old Hoodoo," though like the Red Sox the Yankees' faults lay more in themselves than in their stars. By 1912, the team had slumped to last place at 50-102—to this day the worst record in the club's history—while attendance dropped to just a quarter million.

20

Ballyhoo

Franklin Pierce Adams was almost a caricature of a New York chauvinist. He dismissed anything and everything outside Manhattan as "Dullsboro" in his newspaper column, modestly titled "The Diary of Our Own Samuel Pepys." A relentless first-nighter, "F.P.A.," as his byline read, would prove sharp enough to trade quips around the Algonquin Round Table in the 1920s.

Yet before he began exchanging badinage with the likes of Dorothy Parker, Robert Benchley, and Alexander Woollcott, Adams was a sportswriter and, as a transplanted Chicagoan, a secret Cubs fan. When, on July 10, 1910, his New York *Evening Mail* editor informed him that his copy was eight lines short, FPA came up with the game's second most famous poem. "Baseball's Sad Lexicon" was a needling of Giants fans disguised as a commiseration:

These are the saddest of possible words,
Tinker-to-Evers-to-Chance
Trio of Bear Cubs fleeter than birds
Tinker-to-Evers-to-Chance
Ruthlessly pricking our gonfalon bubble
Making a Giant hit into a double

Words that are weighty with nothing but trouble
Tinker-to-Evers-to-Chance.

Adams was part and parcel of that other new force driving the popularity of baseball in the first decade of the twentieth century. That is to say, ballyhoo, as it was called at the time. In other words, hoopla, hype, publicity, *press.* New York was the world capital of it—so dominant that it could give the stars of *other* cities their lasting tributes. The country was moving into the golden age of newspapers, and nowhere was that culture more vibrant—nowhere was it more contentious, raucous, and just plain fun—than in New York. It was ballyhoo that got the masses to the ballpark in record numbers just as much as all those electrified trains and trolleys, those bridges and tunnels that whisked all the newly minted clerks and desk jockeys to their new pleasure centers.

With no broadcast media—no radio, no TV, and primitive newsreels just beginning to appear in the movie parlors—the papers were almost the sole source of news for a public with more time on its hands than ever before. There were eighteen newspapers in New York City, counting the Brooklyn dailies—and not counting most of the socialist press, the foreign-language press, the small papers serving the still scattered communities of Queens, the far Bronx, Staten Island.

They published in the morning and the afternoon, churned out endless extras hawked by legions of (often homeless) newsboys. They outdid themselves on Sundays when, for no more than a nickel, entire, separate staffs put out gorgeously colored, encyclopedia-thick editions replete with the funny pages and special supplements on sports, books, fashion, science, automobiles, gossip, and show business. Sections that, in writer Nicholson Baker's description, provided endless "cartoons, caricatures, 'gems of pictorial beauty'—layouts and hand-inked headlines that made your eyeballs bustle and bounce around the department-store display of every page."

This world had been roiled a few years before the turn of the century by the arrival in New York of William Randolph Hearst, a young man with an undertaker's eyes, a mountainous ambition, and a compulsion for collecting newspapers, mistresses, and objets d'art. The willful scion of a western mining magnate and senator, Hearst had come east armed with a big bankroll, stiletto instincts, and plans to turn a moribund rag known as the *Morning Journal* into a springboard to the presidency. Years later, Winston Churchill would size him up as "a grave simple child—with no doubt a nasty temper—playing with the most costly toys. A vast income always overspent: Ceaseless building and collecting."

He went right at the peripatetic genius of the New York print world, Joseph Pulitzer, who had himself reinvented newspapers on his arrival in the city from St. Louis, a generation before. Hearst quickly ripped away much of Pulitzer's matchless staff, right down to Richard Outcault, the brilliant cartoonist and inventor of *The Yellow Kid* comic strip (and thus, "yellow journalism"). The fight was personal, the *Journal*'s columns regularly sneering at Pulitzer's background, referring to him as "Jewseph" (at the same time that the *Journal* posed as an opponent of anti-Semitism and champion of the immigrant masses). All but blind, racked by neurasthenia, traveling constantly about the world in his specially soundproofed yacht, Pulitzer nonetheless rose to the challenge. The price of both dailies dropped down to a penny on weekdays, and the rest of Newspaper Row soon joined the battle royal.

It was a war fought out in inch-high headlines, in sensational deaths and overwrought patriotism, warmongering, political crusades, and gossip. Sports—and especially baseball—were a natural favorite, by their very nature exciting, frivolous, controversial, popular, and good for a new story every day. The press box at the Polo Grounds was soon filled with names that would become every bit as legendary as the players on the field: Damon Runyon for Hearst's new *American;* Grantland Rice and Adams of the *Mail;* Fred Lieb of *The Post* and *The Sun;* Bozeman Bulger and Irvin S. Cobb of *The Evening World;* Walter Trumbull of *The Sun;* Sid Mercer of *The Globe;* Heywood Broun of *The Morning Telegraph.* Even, occasionally, Bat Masterson, the fabled western marshal and former companion of Wyatt Earp who died not in a gunfight but over his typewriter at the *Telegraph,* where he presided as sports editor.

"There are those who argue that everything breaks evenly in this old dump of a world of ours," began Masterson's very last typed lines. "I suppose these ginks who argue that way hold because a rich man gets ice in the summer and a poor man gets it in the winter things are breaking even for both. Maybe so, but I'll swear I can't see it that way."

To look at any press-box photograph from this period is to see a group of men hell-bent on becoming characters. A brigade of cocked hats, jaunty suits, and ties, clenched cigars and toothpicks. They reveled in their ability to drink or—like Runyon—were conspicuous in avoiding liquor altogether, sipping endless cups of coffee. They traveled together, vacationed together, played elaborate practical jokes on each other, wrote stories for each other when they were too drunk or too hungover, stole scoops and ideas from one another. Like so many New Yorkers, almost all of them came from somewhere else, usually the South or the Midwest, and to look more closely at their cheeky, defiant faces is to see how young most of them really were.

Men of modest means, they had traveled to the big city intent on making their fortunes, and in the winnowing, Darwinian world of New York journalism they learned to be endlessly inventive. They filled their stories with slang, with jokes and anecdotes and nicknames; even, when the copy desk required it, some hastily scrawled lines of verse. Tom Clark, Damon Runyon's biographer, writes of how Runyon "never settled for the slightly adorned play-by-play accounts that filled most of his colleagues' daily pieces. He always distilled the event into a single conception, often outlandish but usually inventive and interesting. He sought continuously for fresh viewpoints, gimmicks, tricks—anything to avoid the tedium of the standard 'formula' baseball story of the day." Such gimmicks included reporting "an entire game from the viewpoint of a lady who had never seen baseball played, or that of a lizard or a group of yokels from Colorado."

"I always made covering a standard story like a big race or a ballgame more or less of a stunt," Runyon related. "When the great Pittsburgh slugger Honus Wagner came to town I covered the game, not from the press box, but from the bleachers and a rear view of Honus."

How good were they by current standards? It's hard to say. The sportswriters of the time weren't over-interested in the business of the game, in labor disputes and player salaries. Most strangely, by current lights, they didn't venture down into the locker room, and wouldn't for decades to come. They had little interest in the pedestrian quotations such trips usually produce, and there were pressing deadlines to make.

The clubhouses were, in any case, the players' preserve, and the writers were already friends with many players and managers—almost an inevitability considering all the time they spent together on trains. The day's sportswriters weren't about to dwell too much on their traveling companions' exploits in barrooms and cathouses. These wouldn't have been allowed in a family paper anyway, and for that matter the writers themselves tended to match their subjects drink for floozy. On the other hand, baseball writers of the early twentieth century did write about the game between the lines—much more than contemporary sports reporters do—and they could be piercing in their criticisms.

For all their affected cynicism, many of these knights of the press box quietly harbored greater literary ambitions. For decades to come, the sports pages would be the starting point for more "serious" writers, such as Runyon, John Kieran, Paul Gallico, Ring Lardner. They were writing not just to survive but to be noticed. Often, they succeeded. The results might seem comical to modern ears as, say, in some of Grantland Rice's more bombastic ledes or extended versifying—but a century later Rice is still remembered for labeling a Notre Dame backfield "the Four Horsemen of the Apocalypse." Just who the "Four Horsemen" were is largely forgotten.

Nor was all the ballyhoo confined to the pressroom. In the eventful summer of 1908, a twenty-nine-year-old vaudevillian named Jack Norworth watched the baseball bugs jam onto the Ninth Avenue el under a sign that read BASEBALL TODAY—POLO GROUNDS, and had an idea for a song. Norworth himself had never been to a baseball game, a singular omission for a red-blooded American male of the period. But he had already written the hit "Shine On, Harvest Moon," and now, hooking up with the thirty-year-old musician and arranger Albert Von Tilzer—also someone who had never seen a game in his life—he composed the epic of one "Katie Casey," a young lady who was "baseball mad."

Norworth added the song to his act, but its real success came thanks to a hybrid of the new, respectable entertainments: moving picture shows that used "song slides" to entertain their customers while the reels were being changed. Lyrics of popular songs were projected onto the screen, while hired crooners (including a young Jack Warner, and Sophie Tucker) led the crowd in singing along. Audiences ate up this turn-of-the-century karaoke. They made Norworth and Tilzer's "Take Me Out to the Ball Game" not only the sport's greatest hit but supposedly the third most played song in American history, after "Happy Birthday to You" and "The Star-Spangled Banner."

21

Bonehead

The whole country, it seemed—not just Katie Casey—was baseball mad. Total major-league attendance climbed to more than seven million in both 1908 and 1909, a peak that would not be scaled again in the dead-ball era. Measured as a percentage of the major-league cities' populations at the time, it would not be bested until baseball's attendance boom in the late 1980s. Up at the Polo Grounds, the Giants would draw a previously unheard-of 910,000 fans in 1908. Once again, the city's elite flocked to see and be seen: politicos and Wall Street bankers; businessmen and gangsters and police captains; and so many people from show business that McGraw himself was inducted into the Lambs Club.

They were drawn that year not just by the hype, or the scene, but also by one of the great pennant races in baseball history. Over the previous two years, FPA's Cubs had emerged as a powerhouse, shattering McGraw's record for wins in a season in 1906 and pummeling Ty Cobb's Tigers in the World Series the following year.

Chicago was built on much the same model as McGraw's championship teams, featuring a deep pitching staff led by Mordecai "Three-Finger" or "Miner" Brown, considered every bit as good as Matty in his prime, and the one man able to beat the Big Six as often as he lost to him. Brown's nicknames were bracingly literal. He was indeed a former miner, and as a child he had lost the index finger of his right hand to a corn separator. The middle finger of the same hand was left frozen in an S shape, and while still recovering from the accident, he had fallen and broken the remaining fingers, none of which healed right. The upshot was a misshapen paw perfect for throwing a deep-dipping breaking ball. (Asked if *he* thought his maimed hand made him a better pitcher, Brown replied with admirable frankness: "I don't know. I've never done it any other way.")

Yet the core of the team was indeed the trio of infielders—Frank Chance, Joe Tinker, and Johnny "Crab" Evers—that Adams's bit of doggerel would propel into the Hall of Fame. How good a double-play combination were they really? Nothing special. Nobody was. In the dead-ball era of continual running and slow grounders, double plays were little more than half as common as they are today. Even then, the Cubs never led the NL in twin killings in any year that Chance, Evers, and Tinker were with them. One could hardly expect them to, playing on a team that generally had some of the best pitching in the league. You can't double up a man who never made it to first base.

The statistics don't change the fact that the "trio of Bear cubs" were consummate players of their time: quick, versatile, and canny—the one constant on a Cubs team that still holds the record for most wins by a major-league club over any ten-year period. They were, as well, barely able to tolerate each other. Chance, the Cubs' manager as well as their first baseman and best hitter, ruled his team with an iron hand and was once acknowledged by no less than John L. Sullivan as "the greatest amateur brawler in the world." In a day when players did not wear so much as a batting helmet, he insisted on crowding the plate and was hit by pitches so constantly—137 times—that the beanings eventually shortened his career and cost him much of his hearing. (It also turned his voice into a grating whine that reportedly made whoever heard it grit their teeth.)

Joe Tinker was one of the best shortstops in the game, a superb fielder and base runner who would go on to a mercurial career as a Florida land tycoon. Early in his time with the Cubs, Tinker got into a fistfight on the field with Johnny Evers in a dispute over cab fare. The two men didn't speak again for thirty-three years, including the remaining seven seasons in which they played seamlessly beside each other. (The streak was broken when each man, unbeknownst to the other, was hired to help broadcast the Cubs' 1938 World Series against the Yankees. When they saw each other, both of the tough old ballplayers apparently broke down crying and hugged.)

Johnny Evers drove everyone crazy. Although he was five feet nine, when he came up to the majors, he tipped the scales at only 105 pounds, and he was never able to get his weight up past 125. Pictures show him looking like a refugee in the already baggy uniforms of the day, and Chicago sportswriter Hugh Fullerton wrote that "all there is to Evers is a bundle of nerves, a lot of woven wire muscles, and the quickest brain in baseball." His constant chatter was so annoying that even the nearly deaf Chance wished openly on several occasions that Evers would switch to the outfield. It was well known that the Crab could not wear a wristwatch. He had so much nervous energy that they just kept stopping.

Even at night, the little man would channel all that energy into the game. Staying up late in the team hotel, gobbling candy bars in more futile attempts to put on pounds, and poring over *The Sporting News* and the baseball rule book. Looking constantly for some kind of edge, somewhere, somehow, that no one else had ever spotted before.

It would be needed. Good as the Cubs were, dedicated as they were, by 1908 McGraw and his Giants had caught up. The season marked the apogee of the inside game, when runs were at a premium. As a *league* that season the NL had an ERA of 2.35, a batting average of .239, on-base percentage of .299, slugging percentage of .306—all record lows. This was McGraw's kind of ball, when the edge provided by a smart manager was likely to count for more than it ever had or ever would again, and as the season progressed, his Giants began to pull away from a season-long three-way race with Chicago and Pittsburgh. By September 18, Muggsy's boys were four and a half games up on Chicago with just sixteen left to play, and even so stalwart a player as Joe Tinker suggested to Chance that the race was over and that they might as well "break training and make a good night of it."

Chance thought it over, then declined the toot. "No," he told his shortstop. "We were good winners last year. Let's show them we are good losers and play the string out. We may win yet."

Even as he spoke, the Giants were beginning to stumble, slowed by their own injuries. McGraw was down to two reliable pitchers and resorted to pitching Matty to the limit, penciling the Big Six in to start every two or three days and often bringing him out of the bullpen on the days in between. Mathewson responded brilliantly. During one stretch in September, he started five times and relieved twice over the course of eighteen days, throwing almost 49 innings and allowing only three runs. Throughout the whole month he threw 110⅓ innings, remarkable even for the time. Before the season was over, he would rack up a career-high thirty-seven wins and five saves, with a league-leading 1.43 ERA. But not even Matty could keep up this pace indefinitely.

The Cubs began to catch up, and Johnny Evers found his edge. On September 4, the Pirates bested Three-Finger Brown and the Cubs in Pittsburgh, when Owen "Chief" Wilson singled in the only run with two out in the bottom of the ninth. A Pirate rookie, Warren Darst Gill, was on first when Wilson got his hit. Instead of running to second, once he saw the winning run score, Gill raced off the field—just as players had been doing for years in order to avoid the rush of fans the ushers let out on the field as soon as the game was over. Technically, Gill was supposed to touch second base, but no one ever did. It was one of those informal habits without any backing in the rule book, much like the catcher being allowed to block the plate.

Johnny Evers was having none of it. He scrambled to retrieve the ball Wilson hit, stepped on second base, then corralled umpire Hank O'Day and informed him that under Rule 59 of major-league baseball Gill was *out*—the third out of the inning. It didn't matter that the run had scored first: the play at second was a force play, negating the run. Gill had to touch the bag the same as he would in any other inning.

O'Day, a former major-league pitcher who had put in twenty years as an ump and was considered the best arbiter in the National League, thought it over for a moment, then ruled that the play would stand. He hadn't seen Gill *not* touch second base—a frequent occurrence in the one- or two-umpire system that prevailed at the time. The Cubs protested to no avail, as O'Day told the Crab, "Go home and take a bath, Johnny. The game is over." But that same night, O'Day sought Evers out and told him that in theory he was right. If he had seen the play, Gill would have been out, and the game would have continued.

Evers stowed that little vindication away for when he might need it next. Meanwhile, on September 22, Three-Finger Brown and Orval Overall pitched Chicago to a doubleheader sweep at the Polo Grounds. No finer combination of names has ever won a twin bill, and the Cubs were now tied with the Giants for first, with Pittsburgh just a game and a half back.

McGraw went back to his ace. Matty had just thrown a complete-game three-hitter against the Pirates on Monday—but lost, thanks to a call at first that the *New York American* insisted was "one of the worst ever seen on the [Polo] grounds." The umpire in question was O'Day, who was pilloried in verse on New York's sports pages:

When you made that rank decision,
When the thousands voiced derision,
Where in hades was your vision, Hank O'Day?

Now both O'Day and Mathewson were back out on the field, in what would be the most controversial baseball game ever played. The Big Six rose to his task, striking out nine, walking no one, and giving up only five hits. The Cubs scored a run when Turkey Mike Donlin tried and failed to make a shoestring catch on Joe Tinker and the ball got past him, the Cubbie shortstop circling the bases with an inside-the-park home run. Donlin got the run back with a single in the sixth, but otherwise the Cubs' side-winding lefty, Jack "the Giant Killer" Pfiester, matched Matty goose egg for goose egg.

With one out in the bottom of the ninth and the crowd of twenty thousand baying for a rally, Art Devlin singled for the Giants, but was forced at second by Moose McCormick. Two outs now, and up stepped Fred Merkle, the Giants' nineteen-year-old first baseman, playing because the veteran Fred Tenney had asked out of the lineup with a stiff back—the only game Tenney would miss all year. Merkle was one of a host of raw young players whom McGraw had insisted on taking north with him, an attempt to start rebuilding his team on the fly. Fred rode the bench for most of that 1908 season, appearing in only thirty-seven games, usually as a pinch hitter or late-inning substitute, but McGraw saw a kindred spirit in him. Chief Meyers would later aver that Merkle was "the smartest man on the club" in the years to come and that "McGraw never consulted anybody except Merkle on a question of strategy."

Now, under all the pressure of his last-minute substitution in a key game, Fred Merkle slammed a drive into right field. Running up the first base line, Merkle thought he had hit a double or a triple into the gap, maybe enough to score McCormick all the way from first. But Jack Hayden, a little-used Chicago sub, made an outstanding play to cut the ball off.

"At that, I could have gone to second easily, but with one run needed to win and a man on third, I played it safe," Merkle would remember.

It *was* the smart play, a mature decision for such a young ballplayer to make, and it would cost Fred Merkle for the rest of his life.

Al Bridwell, the tough Giants shortstop who had once knocked his manager down with a punch, stepped into the batter's box next and immediately noticed that the rookie who had run so cautiously was now taking too wide a lead at first. Bridwell, to his eternal regret, stepped out of the box and waved the busher back toward the bag. Then he lined a Pfiester fastball over second base, so hard that the other umpire on hand that day, Bob Emslie, threw himself to the ground to avoid being hit. McCormick scored easily from third, and the ushers opened the gates and let the big crowd race onto the field and into chaos.

There would be at least a dozen different accounts of what happened next. It played out like a scene in one of the new silent movies so popular in Manhattan, the jubilant crowd milling around obliviously while a few frenzied individuals fought their way back and forth through the mob. One can almost see the eyes of one player, then another, lighting up as they comprehended just what was going on and struggled to fight their way through the fans. All that was missing was the rolling baby carriage.

Merkle watched the winning run score, saw the crowd surging onto the field, and veered off toward the clubhouse in centerfield without bothering to touch second base, just as he had watched veteran players do many times before. Just as everyone had done for decades. It was the moment Johnny Evers had been waiting for. He called frantically for the ball, but the throw from Cub centerfielder Solly Hofman sailed over his head and landed near third base—where cagey old Iron Man McGinnity was standing in the third-base coach's box. McGinnity's famed arm had finally given out, but his mind was sharp enough to grasp at once what the Crab was trying to do.

According to most accounts, McGinnity grabbed up the ball and hurled it away, into the stands, anywhere beyond the grasp of Johnny Evers. Fred Snodgrass, another promising young Giant reserve with a tragic turn of his own yet to come, claimed that McGinnity threw the baseball clear over the Polo Grounds grandstand. The Cubs claimed that a little-used pitcher named Floyd Myron Kroh went into the stands and managed to retrieve the ball from a fan. Meanwhile, Christy Mathewson grabbed hold of Merkle in the vicinity of the distant clubhouse and rushed him back toward second. Everything seemed to move in slow motion, through the still milling crowd. But the Cubs had a new relay going, Floyd Myron Kroh to Joe Tinker, to Johnny Evers, who caught the ball—or at least *some* ball—and stepped triumphantly on second base in front of Bob Emslie—who refused to make the call.

Emslie pointed out that he had been flat on the ground during the play, avoiding Bridwell's line drive, and told Evers to appeal to his partner, Hank O'Day—the very same Hank O'Day to whom Evers had made the same appeal back in Pittsburgh. Chance now joined Tinker and Evers, the three Cubs beseeching the ump to not only call Merkle out but declare the game forfeit to Chicago since the mob on the field made it impossible to continue play. O'Day, all too conscious of the same mob, told Chance he would take it under advisement. Rather anticlimactically, everyone then hit the showers. But at ten o'clock that night, from the relative safety of his hotel room, Hank O'Day announced his decision. Merkle was out. The run didn't count, the game remained a 1–1 tie.

It was the most extraordinary decision by an official in the history of American sports. There really is no parallel to it: a critical game in a tight pennant race, decided hours after it was over by an umpire miles from the field of play.

It pleased no one. Charges and countercharges flew. Merkle claimed that he had indeed touched second base, and several of the Giants swore they never saw any ball get to Evers at second. The Cubs' president, Charles Murphy, maintained that the game should have been forfeited to Chicago. So did Chance, who also insisted that under league rules the tie game should be made up as soon as possible. Pushing this claim, he had his team show up at the Polo Grounds at 1:30 the following afternoon—two and a half hours before the scheduled game—and ordered the pitcher Andy Coakley to throw a few balls over the plate. He then declared, "Not only did the Giants forfeit this game, but they're subject to a $1,000 fine for refusing to play. Until that fine is paid, the Giants must forfeit every game."

McGraw countered that Floyd Myron Kroh's interference made the whole case moot. "Why was an unannounced Chicago player on the field? His mere touching of the ball rendered it dead." This conveniently ignored the fact that Joe McGinnity, a Giants coach, had hurled said ball into or over the grandstand. McGraw was on firmer ground in asking why, if the run did not count, O'Day had not announced his decision then, and called for the field to be cleared and the game resumed. Why the need for this call from the hotel room?

"I did not ask to have the field cleared, as it was too dark to complete play," O'Day wrote in his report to the league president, anticipating this very objection, but it was a dubious response. Night must have fallen awfully quickly that evening over the Polo Grounds.

In retrospect, it was O'Day's larger decision that was insupportable. Bill Klem, the gold standard among major-league umpires—and an old enemy of McGraw's—would nonetheless call the Merkle ruling "the rottenest decision in the history of baseball. . . . It was bad umpiring and gutless thinking at League headquarters." He was right. Hank O'Day, nicknamed "The Reverend," was a man of unquestioned integrity. As a pitcher, he was one of the very few white players to treat Fleet Walker as an equal. Though born in Chicago, O'Day had had his greatest playing days in New York, going 9-1 in the 1889 season for the Giants, then pitching two complete-game wins to nail down the first "Subway Series" against Brooklyn. As an umpire, he would make the Hall of Fame. But during the most important game of his life he had, without any prior warning, decided to erase the custom of decades in order to enforce an obscure rule, hours after play had ended. He had decided to do so, moreover, after discussing the idea with a player from only one of the teams involved.

"There is no set of fair-minded men in the country who would decide the game against us," McGraw, uncharacteristically sanguine, told the press when he appealed the call to the NL president, Harry

Pulliam, that same night. But Pulliam ruled in favor of O'Day, and so would the National League board of directors. Chance would not get his forfeit; the tie would be made up at the end of the season, if necessary.

Outrage ensued, at least at first. "If this game goes to Chicago, by any trick or argument, you can take it from me that if we lose the pennant thereby, I'll never play pro ball again!" threatened Mathewson. But a cooler Matty was soon acknowledging, "I don't believe Merkle touched second base. It could happen to anyone. There's no sense eating our hearts out. We'll just have to beat them again."

So they did. The very next day the Giants jumped out to a 5–0 lead and hung on for a 5–4 win before twenty-five thousand incensed fans who sat shouting, ringing cowbells, and tooting horns. Matty came on to save the game, and did so despite a Joba Chamberlain–like swarm of gnats that got into his eyes. By the ninth inning a fog had descended upon the Polo Grounds from the East River, one so thick that Mathewson had to walk in to see the signs from Roger Bresnahan, while in the stands the crowd made torches out of newspapers to drive the bugs away. There was no way Emslie, the umpire in charge, was going to call *this* game before the last out.

The Giants were back in first, but they wouldn't stay there alone. The Cubs went 8-2 in their remaining games, just enough to tie New York at the wire. The "Merkle game" would have to be replayed.

"I don't care whether you play this game or not. You can take a vote," Muggsy told his players. Several Giants actually voted no, but in the end they agreed to play, no doubt spurred on by a $10,000 bonus John T. Brush gave them to split among themselves, win or lose. The stage was set for a Götterdämmerung—at least in the eyes of New York's always excitable newspapers.

"Perhaps never in the history of a great city, since the days of Rome and its arena contests, has a people been pitched to such a key of excitement as was New York 'fandom,' " gushed *The New York Times.*

"Never before have two teams been tied at the end of a season. Never before has the race been so close. Never has it been necessary to play off the tie of six months' baseball in a single gigantic battle," intoned the *Herald.* "That the game will be a struggle to the death is certain."

The papers reported that as many as 350,000 fans went up to the

Polo Grounds that auspicious afternoon of October 8, 1908. They teetered along the cliffs on Coogan's Bluff, climbed up on the grandstand roof, perched upon the elevated train viaduct past left field. A fire company tried clearing the viaduct with hoses so that the trains could get through, but the soaked fans only fought their way back up to the tracks once the firemen left. One man fell to his death from the elevated; another fell from a telegraph pole out past centerfield and broke his neck. A mob of fans broke through a wooden fence into the outfield and had to be beaten back by mounted police. Later, they tried setting the fence on fire. The cops gave up and locked the stadium gates two hours before the first pitch, thereby keeping out many legitimate ticket holders.

The umpires, Bill Klem and Jimmy Johnstone, had an even more interesting time getting into the game. They had to literally push their way out to the field through the mob, and as they did, they were buttonholed by one Dr. Joseph M. Creamer, the Giants' team doctor and an intimate of McGraw's. Creamer showed them an envelope that he said contained $5,000 and told the two arbiters, "You know who is behind me and you needn't be afraid of anything." The stalwart Klem ordered Creamer out of his sight and reported the incident to the league office immediately after the game.

The Cubs took a fourteen-hour train ride to the old Grand Central Terminal on the 20th Century Limited, Mordecai Brown waving his famed pitching hand from the window to the crowds who gathered at every midwestern whistle-stop. On arrival, they got another type of reception. Thousands of New Yorkers jammed into the huge station just to jeer them. The Cubs were rushed up to the Polo Grounds with a police escort, forced to literally push their way through the crowds to get into the park. Once there, they were allotted no time for batting practice, and after only about fifteen minutes of warm-ups Iron Man McGinnity came on the field, ringing a bell and telling them that time was up. McGinnity continued on up to Chance at home plate, cursing the Cubs' leader, stepping on his toes with his spikes, even spitting on him—trying anything to get him to fight and get thrown out of the game before it started.

Chance cursed McGinnity back, but he wouldn't fall for it. The Cubbies and their manager had come to play. After Matty set Chicago down in order in the first, Jack Pfiester gave up a run and allowed runners to reach first and second with two out. Chance went to his bullpen at once, calling in his best pitcher from where he was warming up along the sidelines, surrounded by glowering Giants fans. Three-Finger Brown had pitched in eleven of the Cubs' last fourteen games, and he had received at least six death threats before this game, but when the call came, he calmly shouldered his way to the mound through the taunting outfield mobs.

"From the stands there was a steady roar of abuse," Brown said later. "I never heard anybody or any set of men called as many foul names as the Giant fans called us that day from the time we showed up till it was over."

Brown got the last out in the inning, but the Giants had a run and they had Matty, who had pitched twelve shutouts that season. The ecstatic fans kept screaming, "Fadeaway, Matty, fadeaway!" Little did they know, their hero already had. Before going off to pitch that morning, the Big Six confided in his wife, "I'm not fit to pitch today. I'm dog tired." That afternoon he made the usual, stately entrance from centerfield in his linen duster, working the crowd into a frenzy. But it took him an hour of warm-ups just to get his arm loose, and in the third inning all of McGraw's overwork caught up with his ace. The Cubs scored four times. Tinker tripled when the centerfielder Cy Seymour lost track of his drive thanks to the crowd on the roof behind home plate, Chance doubled, and Crab Evers drew a key walk.

"The Cubs beat me because I never had less on the ball in my life. What I can't understand to this day is why it took them so long to hit me," Matty admitted later.

Nonetheless, he kept the Cubs from scoring again, while the increasingly sullen fans brawled among themselves and tried to brain Chicago players with pop bottles. The New York *Journal* reported that the catcher Johnny Kling, chasing a foul ball, had to dodge "two beer bottles, a drinking glass and a derby hat." Supposedly, seven men were "carted away, raving mad."

There was almost one more opportunity to add to the legend that was already Mathewson. In the bottom of the seventh, the Giants loaded the bases against Brown with no one out. Matty, a good-hitting pitcher, begged to be allowed to bat with the game on the line against his greatest rival. McGraw demurred, sending up Larry Doyle, who had not played in a month, to pinch-hit. Doyle fouled out, and all the Giants could manage was a single run off Miner Brown. The Cub pitcher retired New York on four pitches in the bottom of the ninth, then ran for his life with the rest of his teammates.

They almost weren't fast enough. Pfiester was knifed in the shoulder, and Chance was punched so hard in the throat that he suffered broken cartilage, leaving him unable to talk and barely able to swallow for days. At least three other Cubbies were struck, and the NYPD had to hold the clubhouse doors against the mob with guns drawn. The cops advised the Cubs to dress and leave the Polo Grounds alone or in pairs, as inconspicuously as possible. Brown, afraid of being recognized, snapped at his would-be police escort, "You fellows get away from me!"

To say it was not the Giants' or the city's finest hour is an understatement. The *Chicago Tribune* huffed that the Cubs had "won not only decisively but cleanly and gamely, while their adversaries attempted to take cheap and tricky advantage of them in every way." Even Hearst's *Journal,* which claimed that the Cubs' "title is tainted," chided, "Is that baseball? Does that do New York any good? Gee whiz! If we can't lose a pennant without dirty work let's quit altogether."

The Cubs went on to pummel the Tigers again in the World Series. It was the last world championship they would win for 108 years. Their futility might have been called the curse of Fred Merkle—save that the curse was on Fred. *The New York Times,* under the headline BLUNDER COSTS GIANTS VICTORY, blamed Merkle's "censurable stupidity" for the lost game to the Cubs. Other New York papers were soon referring to Merkle as "the man who lost the pennant," and his failure to step on second became known as Merkle's boner, for a "boneheaded" play. For a time, making any sort of blunder was popularly called a Merkle. Fans hissed and booed him when he took the field, and he reportedly lost fifteen to twenty pounds just in the two weeks between his blunder and the end of the season. He told reporters, "I wished that a large, roomy and comfortable hole would open up and swallow me."

Instead, the abuse would go on and on, both the press and the fans refusing to let him forget the mistake that had not been a mistake at all before he made it. Merkle stuck it out through a long baseball career, but he would end up a recluse, living in the back of a fishing tackle shop in Daytona Beach, Florida, trying to dodge the reporters who just had to hear his story one more time. In one of the last interviews he did give, he concluded bitterly, "I suppose when I die they'll put on my tombstone, 'Here Lies Bonehead Merkle.'"

Fred Merkle was the victim of the irretrievable moment. The little, thoughtless mistake that lost everything and could never be retracted, the sort of thing that sends a thrill of dread through us all and that makes the games live in our memories—one more way in which baseball enables us to live (and die) vicariously. Small consolation to those involved. Al Bridwell, who had rapped the fateful hit that put everything in motion, later called it his only regret in baseball: "I wish I'd struck out instead. If I'd have done that, then it would have spared Fred a lot of unfair humiliation."

Yet Bridwell added, "Didn't get credit for that base hit. They decided it was a force out at second, instead of a single. Well, what can you do? Those things happen." An old shortstop, still thinking wistfully of a stolen hit, fifty years later.

John McGraw again took the loss with unaccustomed equanimity, at least in public. "My team merely lost something it had already won three weeks ago," he told the press. When Merkle sobbed to him, "Lose me, I'm the jinx," Muggsy gave him a $300 raise, praised his "gameness . . . through all this abuse" in the press, and told him, "I could use a carload like you. Forget this season and come around next spring." He made Merkle his chief lieutenant on the bench, and even a regular bridge partner with himself and Matty. Muggsy looked out for his ballplayers, but he was not one to give up a grudge. When Harry Pulliam, the forty-year-old NL president, suffered a nervous breakdown after the season and shot himself through the temple—blowing out both his eyes and leaving him to linger in terrible pain for hours before he could die—McGraw's only reaction was, "I didn't think a bullet to the head could hurt him."

Still, he had little to complain about. Nineteen-aught-eight was a very good year for the Giants, who now had the highest payroll in the game but earned a record $200,000 profit on the season. A theatrical benefit raised $3,700 for every player, and John T. Brush gave each one a gold medal reading "The Real Champions, 1908." McGraw got a $5,000 car from Brush, for which he hired a chauffeur, to get around town in style.

Muggsy also sold his share of his Herald Square pool hall and bought into another one nearby. This required the standard, $300-a-month payoff to the police, a fact that was neither hidden nor condemned. But the bribe presented no problem. If McGraw wasn't famous enough already, his new enterprise would get a huge shot of publicity from the man who would become his silent partner, a character as brilliant and as dazzling at his game as Muggsy was at baseball.

22

The Great Brain

At twenty-six, Arnold Rothstein was already one of the city's most notorious gamblers, and already a mystery—perhaps the biggest mystery in the whole byzantine history of the New York underworld.

He would be described, in countless cable TV documentaries, as a gang boss, or even the architect of the modern mob. It wasn't true. Arnold was never really a part of any organization, his own or somebody else's. Rothstein was sui generis—someone who funded the mob, just as he funded politicians, funded labor goons, funded rum-runners and dope runners, crooked cops and stone killers, Wall Street bucket shops and speakeasies, crooked card games and past-posting operations. Funded chaos and corruption in all its manifestations.

"A gray rat, standing in a doorway, waiting for his cheese," was how his own lawyer, Billy "the Great Mouthpiece" Fallon, famously described him.

Arnold hailed not from the Lower East Side or Brooklyn's Brownsville but from East Seventy-Ninth Street, where his pious, industrious, immigrant father was a successful cotton-goods wholesaler. Vexed by his parents' devotion to a precocious older brother, he rebelled against everything, dropped out of public school, dropped out of Hebrew school, and found his way back down to the seedy Bowery haunts his family had put behind them.

There he first came to the attention of Big Tim Sullivan, the Tammany chieftain, while running the table in a pool hall. Before long, Sullivan would count him as one of "my Jewboys," the bright young men he recruited from the demimonde to serve as his eyes and ears in the immigrant Jewish community, keeping it geared to the machine. It's easy to see why. Rothstein was a wizard not just with cards or a pool cue but with any kinds of numbers. He favored suits that were more appropriate for a banker or an aristocrat than for a pool hall sharpie. He never drank, his morning guzzling of milk of magnesia the only tell to the cost his profession exacted. And like most great gamblers, Rothstein never much cared for the vagaries of the game.

"He got no pleasure from watching horses run, or from Christy Mathewson striking out a batter at a critical moment. All he cared for, then and always, was the betting percentage," Carolyn Rothstein, a former showgirl and Arnold's oft-estranged wife, would write, or let someone write, after his death. "He got no thrill from close contests. Sport was merely a means of financial juggling to him."

By 1908, Rothstein was still working with Sullivan—*any*one who wanted to gamble in New York paid off to Sullivan—but he was also working on his own, a position he would always prefer. Save for a working vacation at the races in Saratoga every August, he could always be found at the glitzy new, electrified bars and restaurants around Times Square. At the Metropole and Jack's restaurant on Forty-Third Street, where the elite went to drink champagne and eat Irish bacon for breakfast after being out all night. Later Lindy's, immortalized by Runyon, who also immortalized Rothstein himself as Nathan Detroit in *Guys and Dolls* and as Armand Rosenthal, "the Brain." There he sat, deep into the fathomless Manhattan night, a slight, smooth-faced man with glittering brown eyes, taking phone calls, whispering into ears, eating sweet cakes, and drinking countless glasses of milk.

What was he doing? Making money, always making money. "He

lived only for money—he even liked the feel of it," one man who knew him well related. How did he do it? By listening, by watching. By butting in.

"Arnold Rothstein was chiefly a busybody, with a passion for dabbling in the affairs of others," according to Nat Ferber, reporter for Hearst's *New York American.* "He was also a fixer, a go-between, not merely between law-breakers and politicians, but between one type of racketeer and another."

He would become the master of the *other* Times Square, the world of backroom brothels and hidden depravities, of the illicit, floating crap games and card games that he practically invented. Everyone knew him, and usually by reverential, fearful names—"the Great Brain," "the Big Bankroll," "the Man Uptown." His feats became legendary, though they required little confabulation. He inveigled Broadway's leading ladies and used them to steer marks to his games. He once managed to make $850,000 manipulating a two-horse race out at Aqueduct. On another occasion he winged three police detectives who busted in on one of his floating dice games, mistaking them for robbers. In the end, he walked free. The detectives' captain was suspended and indicted.

Like all deities, he could make dreams come true, if solicited properly. The bankroll was indeed big; eventually, Rothstein carried at least $100,000 on him at all times, his lifelong ambition. Yet like many gods he was more dreaded than loved. According to his wife, he would trawl Broadway in the early morning hours, no matter what the weather, looking for men who owed him "amounts as low as fifty dollars."

"He wasn't right even with himself. For every friend he had a thousand enemies," one friend recorded.

Arnold Rothstein could always *buy* friends—buy chorines, buy pals, buy muscle. What he had to make for himself was a reputation. This was where McGraw's pool hall came in. In November 1909, a bunch of Rothstein's Times Square acquaintances decided to bring him down a peg by putting his much-vaunted ability with a stick to the test. They maneuvered Arnold into the classic sucker play, goading him into a match against a ringer from out of town, a wealthy Philadelphia stockbroker and pool shark named Jack Conaway.

The opening stake was $500, the place McGraw's new joint in the

Marbridge Building, next to the offices of the *Herald.* What more public a venue could there be in which to humiliate the cocky young gambler? The match started at eight o'clock on a Thursday night, and by closing time at 2:00 a.m. they were still at it. McGraw kept his doors open. The match went on, with the play close but Rothstein holding the lead. It continued, still, as the day resumed, and the bustle and flow of the city swelled up in Herald Square again. As word of the match spread, legions of sharpies and sporting men swarmed into McGraw's, laying down their bets. Still the game continued, on into Friday evening, the whole affair becoming a battle of endurance—one that might well have inspired the epic, fictional match between Paul Newman and Jackie Gleason, Fast Eddie Felson and Minnesota Fats, at the start of *The Hustler.*

It was the diminutive Rothstein, ironically, who played the Jackie Gleason role. Pacing himself, neither drinking nor smoking, eating little, he moved about the table with what a contemporary remembered as a "pantherish quickness . . . [a] catlike suavity of muscular coordination" that reminded the observer of Jack Dempsey, pocketing ball after ball with his "white, skilful hands." Closing time came and went again, with McGraw warning the participants, "I'll have you dead on my hands. And if you don't want to sleep, some of the rest of us do." They begged another two hours out of Muggsy, going on until 4:00 a.m. *Saturday*—thirty-two hours after their match had begun—when McGraw finally packed them both off to a Turkish bath. Rothstein was rumored to have won $4,000 on the contest. Far more important, he had become a somebody. His lesser reward was the chance to become partners with the impecunious McGraw, taking a stake in the pool hall where he had made his mark.

No one—including that part of the sporting press headquartered right next to McGraw's digs, at the *Herald*—saw any problem with the manager of the Giants being in business with one of the leading figures in the underworld. Nor had they associated any of this with the Giants' team physician trying to bribe an umpire before a critical game, the team's riotous makeup of the Merkle contest. An investigation was ordered into that particular incident, but nothing came of it, save for the Giants' quiet release of Dr. Creamer and an occasional item in the sports pages, asking, "Who were the men behind Doctor Creamer?"

It was a good question. Did McGraw try to fix a game that he felt he should have already won? Were the men behind the good doctor associates of McGraw's, from the gambling-soaked world he inhabited? No one knew, and no one cared to ask very hard. The sporting press soon dropped the subject altogether and looked forward to the next, incredible event in their city of unending entertainments.

23

Various Catastrophes

They would not be long disappointed. John McGraw's investment in his young rookies paid off sooner than expected. His Giants finally overturned the great Cubs dynasty and reeled off three straight pennants from 1911 to 1913. If this was not McGraw's most talented team, it was the one he would remember most fondly—"one which I selected and brought up myself," a typically steady, hustling outfit with few major stars. These Giants were adept at getting on base, and once they got there, they were off, stealing what is still a major-league record, 347 bases in 1911, followed by another 319 in 1912, and 296 in 1913—an average of more than two stolen bases a game for three years. They were a team that thrived on disruption, constantly bunting, hitting-and-running, stealing.

Once they got to the World Series, it was a different story. Not even Matty could stop one of Connie Mack's great Athletics teams in 1911 as he surrendered his first run in thirty-six innings of World Series ball. More heartbreak was in store the following year, in one of the wildest, closest, sloppiest, most enthralling World Series ever played. After seven games, three one-run decisions, and a combined twenty-three errors, the Giants and the Boston Red Sox were still tied, thanks to an extra-inning game called because of darkness.

The eighth and final contest took place at Boston's Fenway Park—

then completing its first season of use. Mathewson got the ball for the Giants, of course, and while Matty allowed an uncharacteristic five walks—a sure sign of fatigue for a control pitcher—he had enough to keep Boston off the board for the first six innings. His teammates, though, could manage only one run off the Red Sox starter Hugh Bedient, leaving eleven men on base.

With two outs in the bottom of the seventh, one Olaf Henriksen pinch-hit for Bedient. Henriksen, a native of Denmark, would have fewer than five hundred at bats in the major leagues, but now he took a tardy swing at a curveball and slashed a ball that hit third base and bounded off into foul territory, allowing a run to score (the New York *World* would call Henriksen "that confounded son of Thor" for this effort). The Big Six composed himself and got out of the inning. He got out of the eighth, and the ninth as well, while the Red Sox brought in Smoky Joe Wood, who had had a phenomenal year in the American League, running up a 34-5 record. The two great pitchers worked the game into extra innings, when none other than Fred Merkle ripped a single off Wood and scored the go-ahead run for New York. Finally, it looked as if Merkle might be redeemed. Nothing he could do would make the "bonehead" play go away, but now the story would serve instead as an inspirational sermon: the man who wouldn't give up, who came back and got the winning hit in the World Series.

Mathewson still had to get the last three outs in the bottom of the tenth. There is the feeling, as one traces Matty's career, that he was increasingly a great player asked to do too much to make up for the shortcomings of his teammates. This was a particular type of sports martyrdom, one that makes its victim more endearing than those heroes who are utterly unvanquished. In the latter years of his great career Matty always seemed to be on the mound in some key situation, overworked, toiling grimly to get McGraw one more world championship. In 1912, this made for a heartbreaking last inning that would be echoed by another great New York pitcher, nearly ninety years later.

Leading off the bottom of the tenth, Mathewson got Clyde Engle, pinch-hitting for Wood, to lift what Fred Snodgrass described as "a great, big, lazy, high fly ball halfway between Red Murray in left and me." He made no excuse for what happened next: "Well, I dropped the darn thing." The ball hit the center of Snodgrass's glove and popped out—another example of how the game of baseball can humiliate even its most skilled practitioners at the worst possible moment.

Engle wound up on second. On the mound, Mathewson swung his glove hand in frustration—as rare and telling a movement by the great man as DiMaggio kicking the dirt when Gionfriddo pulled in his long drive to center in the 1947 series. Snodgrass was mortified, but he was a McGraw-trained ballplayer, and he shook off his error and moved in to back up second, anticipating the expected, little-ball bunt that would surely come next. Instead, Boston's Harry Hooper hit away and lashed a line drive to left center, over Snodgrass's head. Digging up the first baseline, Hooper was certain he had hit a game-tying triple. Instead, to his dismay, Snodgrass just "*outran* the ball," making one of the finest catches many on hand said they had ever seen, pulling the ball in over his shoulder, then nearly doubling Engle off second.

Matty still had the lead, but he was obviously wearing thin. Facing Steve Yerkes, a .252-hitting middle infielder with no power, the Big Six somehow walked him on four pitches. Now he had to face Tris Speaker, one of the greatest centerfielders of all time, who had batted a gaudy .383 during the season. But Speaker showed himself a little too eager. He swung at the first pitch and lifted a weak pop-up into foul territory, between first and home.

Chief Meyers, the Giants' catcher, thought that Merkle at first or even Mathewson himself could have made the catch easily. But Merkle seemed to hesitate, confused perhaps by the bench jockeys in the Red Sox dugout yipping like hyenas for Mathewson, then for Meyers, to take it. Matty called for his catcher to get the ball, and the lugubrious Chief trundled down toward first, but the pop-up was just out of his grasp, falling to the grass between the three abashed Giants. Speaker, one of the most talented but also one of the most obnoxious players of his time, crowed at Mathewson, "Well, you just called for the wrong man. It's gonna cost you this ball game." He proceeded to rip a game-tying single on the next pitch, sending Yerkes to third and taking second on the throw. Mathewson walked Duffy Lewis intentionally, but Larry Gardner hit a fly ball to right that brought Yerkes home with the winning run.

Gardner's fly erased Fred Merkle's brief redemption, although the blame for this loss was not added to his shoulders. Instead, the headlines brayed about the ball Snodgrass dropped, "the $30,000 muff," as it was soon labeled, describing the difference in the total winners' and losers' shares for the series. As a twenty-year-old rookie, Snodgrass had sat on the Giants' bench and watched notoriety envelop Merkle, little suspecting that four years later the baseball furies would come for him. *The New York Times* advised its readers to "write in the pages of World Series baseball history the name of Snodgrass. Write it large and black. Not as a hero. Truly not."

McGraw typically gave him a $1,000 raise and defended his player, pointing out, "It could happen to anyone. If it hadn't been for a lot that Snodgrass did, we wouldn't have been playing in that game at all." Snodgrass stuck up for himself, too, insisting, "I never lost that World Series. I never took the blame for losing any World Series."

It made little difference. Fred Snodgrass had fallen victim to the irretrievable moment—even if he did follow it immediately by making one of the greatest catches anyone ever saw, in the tenth inning of a decisive World Series game. Much like Fred Merkle, much like Jack Chesbro, he would spend the next fifty years being introduced to men who asked, "Oh, yes, you're the guy that dropped that fly ball aren't you?" Guilty of the worst punishment that history can apply: a trivial villainy. Snodgrass was not about to become a recluse, making himself a wealthy banker and mayor of Oxnard, California, after retirement. But when he died, the headline on the *Times* obituary read, FRED SNODGRASS, 86, DEAD; BALL PLAYER MUFFED 1912 FLY.

Christy Matthewson, meanwhile, had stood on the mound for a moment, watching the winning run score, then walked slowly to the bench, tears streaming down his face. The spectacle was enough to make Sid Mercer of the New York *Globe,* one of those famously hardbitten sportswriters, bawl openly in the press box. Back in Manhattan, thirteen-year-old Specs Toporcer, who would be playing major-league ball himself within a few years, was standing on a platform, reading the ticker-tape accounts of the game aloud to a barroom on the Upper East Side. With each report from that mad tenth inning, the crowd grew more morose, until at the end young Specs "broke down and found it almost impossible to announce the tragic events. . . . After it was all over, I sat on the platform silently reading and re-reading the doleful news on the tape, as though repeated reading would erase the awful words."

It never would, as many another young baseball fan would discover. Christy Mathewson would never win another World Series. He had another great year, a typical Big Six year in 1913, and even pitched another ten-inning shutout against Connie Mack's Athletics. It was the only game New York would win, though, and in the final contest, trailing 3–1, Matty was removed for a pinch hitter to start the bottom of the ninth. Mathewson folded his small glove into a back pocket and started for the Giants' clubhouse, reversing the grand, theatrical entrance he had made across the Polo Grounds field so many times before. As Frank Deford describes it, a batboy ran out of the Giants' dugout and threw a mackinaw over Matty's big shoulders. But he never looked back, and "as the crowd watched, just before Big Six reached the clubhouse, the mackinaw fell loose from his shoulders and dropped to the ground, but he just kept walking, and then he disappeared from view."

24

The Flock Takes Flight

Three straight World Series losses were a little too much for John McGraw. He was still just forty years old, but he bore the physique, and the wear and tear, of a much older man. He seemed crankier than usual throughout the 1913 campaign, getting into yet another losing fistfight. Maybe it was all the intimations of mortality around him. In July 1912, on the tenth anniversary of his ascension to manager of the Giants, the owner, John T. Brush, had wired him, "My admiration for you has grown to love, because of your honor, loyalty, genius and indomitable determination to succeed." But Brush had already been reduced to watching games at the Polo Grounds from his automobile in the outfield, and that November his tortured body finally gave out.

"He was as tender as a dear girl, as resourceful as a man in the fullest of grand health. . . . What a wonderful—what a beautiful character—was John T. Brush," McGraw told his mourners.

Muggsy had lost the only real father figure he'd ever had, and that same fall Bugs Raymond, the hopeless drunk he had tried so hard to save, was beaten to death in a barroom fight near a Chicago ballpark.

McGraw himself had begun to turn to the bottle more often, and the night his team lost the 1913 World Series, he drank hard at a party he was hosting, a reunion for his old Orioles teammates. In the long history of New York baseball, alcohol and losing—or, for that matter, *winning*—have never gone well together. As the night wore on and he grew drunker, McGraw began to badger his old friend and business partner Wilbert Robinson. Uncle Robbie had been left holding the bag when McGraw abruptly departed from Baltimore with half his team back in 1902, and when Ban Johnson moved the Orioles to New York the next season, a bitter Robinson had to go back behind the butcher's block in the meat market he owned.

Six years later, Muggsy was looking for someone to tutor his youngsters in the sort of aggressive, hustling game their old Orioles used to play, and he hired on Robinson as what some consider the first true major-league "coach." Robbie helped raise McGraw's young players right, and McGraw even allowed him to buy into the pool parlor he owned with Arnold Rothstein. But now, in the wake of his third straight World Series loss, a drunk and belligerent McGraw began to openly berate his pal, blaming Robbie's coaching at third base for the failure of the Giants' running game. The amiable, roly-poly Robinson would have none of it, telling McGraw he had made more mistakes than the rest of the team put together.

"This is my party. Get the hell out of here!" ordered McGraw, firing Robinson on the spot. Robbie emptied his glass of beer over the manager's head and walked out. The two former friends would not talk again for another seventeen years. Betrayed once more, this time Robinson went looking for work in about the most inauspicious place imaginable.

—

On April 14, 1908, Henry Chadwick, the hectoring old prophet of the game, insisted on going to see the home opener of the Dodgers at Washington Park, despite suffering from a bad cold. Chadwick sat through the game in a "bitter east wind," then went home to record with typical propriety, "The bleacherites behaved abominably." Six days later, Father Baseball was dead of pneumonia, aged eighty-three.

It was just as well he was spared the rest of the season. Brooklyn went 53-101 and finished 46 games out of first place. "Hanlon's Superbas" were no more. New York sports pages now mocked the team as the "Suburbas," and Hanlon himself had been released as manager. By 1914, Brooklyn hadn't compiled a winning record for ten years, the monotony of its poor teams broken only by the occasional star such as the hard-luck southpaw Nap Rucker, who threw thirty-eight shutouts in ten seasons, had a lifetime ERA of 2.42, and ended up winning only as many games as he lost. Things were so bad that when the vaudevillian Jack Norworth introduced "Take Me Out to the Ball Game" at Brooklyn's Amphion Theatre, it was a flop. Who wanted to hear about baseball in Brooklyn?

Charles Hercules Ebbets, the former ticket taker, refused to give up. Ebbets had been with the team since its inception, and he had already saved the Dodgers for Brooklyn once. After John McGraw absconded from Baltimore, Hanlon had tried to buy out his ailing co-owner, Harry Von der Horst, and move the franchise to Maryland. Ebbets beat him to the punch, digging up a furniture dealer named Henry Medicus to buy Von der Horst out and make Ebbets himself the new, majority owner. Scraping for money, he refused offers from McGraw to take his best players off his hands for cash, insisting, "The Brooklyn fans deserve the best team I can give them."

Above all, Ebbets wanted a modern stadium to replace the sagging, wooden second incarnation of Washington Park. Nearby factories and the Gowanus Canal filled the park with an awful stench, and fans snuck up to the roofs of the new apartment buildings to see the games for free—when they bothered to look at all. Ebbets set out to find a better location. Like so many New York owners before him, what he discovered was garbage. In the heart of Flatbush, Ebbets ventured upon an ancient collection of shanties known as Pigtown, thanks to an enormous pit where local residents tossed their garbage and local farmers brought their pigs to graze on it. All in all, "the area smelled like sulfur and rotten fish."

Brooklyn in the twentieth century remained surprisingly rural in places, though the captive city continued to grow rapidly. It was home to more than a million residents and 100,000 factory workers, with its docks, its warehouses, its industrial plants all busier and bigger than ever. Within twenty years Brooklyn's population would more than double again, passing Manhattan's for the first time in their respective histories. Jews, Italians, Poles, Bohemians, Norwegians, African Americans, Russians, Germans, and all the other peoples who had jammed Manhattan's lower wards came across the river, changing the ethnic makeup of the borough—and its place in the American imagination—forever. It would complete its transformation from a high WASP redoubt to a place of urban characters, and caricatures—the Brooklyn represented in a thousand World War II movies as the melting pot personified, the new America.

Much of the country outside New York feared this new America, believing it to be a hotbed of crime and radicalism. In truth, the hyphenated Americans worked like horses and studied like monks. Most of them rushed to assimilate as quickly as they could. In the nickelodeon parlors, they stared spellbound at the "actualities," silent reels often made with no more than a camera set up in a truck bed, driving slowly through their teeming streets, showing *them.* Out at the great phantasmagoria that was Coney Island, they went to the "Fighting Flames" shows where an asbestos mock-up of a typical tenement was set aflame several times a day.

The other place where they came to America was the ballpark—at least on those few occasions when they could afford it. Why was this? Why did they not bring their own games, their own obsessions?

Mostly because they did not yet have them. English football—soccer—was spilling out from its home islands, but relatively few working-class immigrants played it yet. Sport was still largely out of reach, per the demands of work or religion. In the rush to assimilate, to Americanize, the children of the immigrants turned to baseball, playing it wherever they could, inventing whole new variations of the game in the streets.

The lords of baseball, in their usual wisdom, made absolutely no effort to accommodate them. They did not cut ticket prices, offer specials, let boys in for free, or schedule night games, even as their seats sat empty, and even though there were now more seats than ever. Between 1909 and 1915, nearly every major-league team replaced its old wooden field with a grander, more capacious, more permanent concrete-and-steel structure. The average cost of these new parks was more than $2 million apiece—at least $54.5 million in today's dollars—and they were built wholly with private money. They constituted a considerable commitment to the cities where they played—the very opposite of the grandiose stadiums extorted out of taxpayers today. They would also become the most beloved, beautiful, and eccentric parks the game would ever know, glossed with the lovely pretensions of Beaux Arts America, shaped by the random eccentricities of inner-city lots and sometimes shaping, in turn, the characters of their teams for decades to come. Sign a new pitcher or a slugger? Trade for a lefty or a righty cleanup hitter? Well, it all depended on which way your park skewed. Was there a peculiar little bend in centerfield where that last homeowner wouldn't sell? A small hill in left? A short porch in right? That was baseball, intimately tied to the cities where it was played.

In Manhattan, Polo Grounds III, the second park occupied by the Giants in Coogan's Hollow, had gone up in a ferocious blaze just three days into the 1911 season. The Giants accepted the Yankees' offer to play over at the Rockpile while Cleveland's Osborn Engineering Company built the team a new home on the old site. Within eleven weeks the Giants were back at the Polo Grounds, now another reinforced-concrete-and-steel grandstand capable of holding sixteen thousand fans. But the Osborn company did not really stop building it for years, adding another deck of grandstands that grew to be a hundred feet high and a thousand feet long, and a series of decorations that would loudly proclaim baseball's considerable ambitions. Along the façade of the new, new Polo Grounds' upper deck was a frieze of ballplayers in action. A repeating series of eight shields representing all the National League teams were hung from the roof. There were box seats modeled after the emperor's box in the Roman Colosseum, and iron scrollwork in the shape of the Giants' "NY" emblem on each aisle seat.

When building finally paused for World War I, the Polo Grounds was the imperial standard of baseball stadiums, with a capacity of thirty-six thousand. Yet it was also the most eccentric ballpark ever built, with a unique, horseshoe shape that would lead directly to two of the most dramatic moments in baseball history. The new Polo Grounds was only 257 feet down the right-field line, 279 to left field, before curving out a seemingly infinite 483 feet to where its multistoried clubhouse stood in dead center. The playing field was so enormous that both bullpens could be plopped out in the distant wastes of centerfield. It was a ballpark that would make stars out of hitters who could adjust to its bizarre dimensions and annihilate those who could not, enrage good pitchers and salvage poor ones. It was of such a size that it seemed to dwarf human capacity, but before it was through, it would be put in perspective by a lone figure, racing out across its endless field to give us one of the most scintillating moments in the sport's history.

Charles Ebbets lacked the resources to build a Polo Grounds even if he had wanted to. As it was, it took him three years to form a dummy corporation and quietly buy up the necessary lots for his new park. Ebbets was running out of money and in the midst of a permanent separation from his wife of more than thirty years, whom he had left for a woman he had been madly in love with for almost a decade. In the end, he was forced to hand over a half interest in the club, worth $100,000, to Steve and Ed McKeever, the local contractors who built the new park from plans by the architects Clarence Randall Van Buskirk and Alexander Leslie. It was a concession that would have dire consequences, but for now it brought Brooklyn a little gem of a ballpark, one that would be lovingly remembered even after the Polo Grounds was largely forgotten.

Ebbets Field rose on four and a half acres of real estate right in the heart of the borough, east of Prospect Park, and bordered by Bedford Avenue, Sullivan Place, Franklin Avenue, and Montgomery Street. Once the squatters were driven out, the garbage pit was filled in, and construction began on March 14, 1912. Charles Ebbets dressed up in his best overcoat and bowler hat for the groundbreaking ceremony.

"I've made more money than I ever expected to," he told reporters from Brooklyn's four dailies, "but I am putting all of it, and more, too, into the new plant for the Brooklyn fans. Of course it's one thing to have a fine ball club and win a pennant, but to my mind there is something more important than that about a ball club. I believe the fan should be taken care of. A club should provide a suitable home for its patrons. This home should be in a location that is healthy, it should be safe, and it should be convenient."

The writers suggested that Ebbets name the new field after himself. Supposedly thinking this idea over for the first time, he replied, "All right, that's what we'll call it. Ebbets Field."

He was entitled. No one had done more to keep baseball in Brooklyn, and this was his ultimate gift to the borough he loved.

Ebbets Field was cheaper than most ballparks of the era, but it would still cost what was then a whopping $750,000 just to build, never mind the price of ousting the porkers. It was not yet a neighborhood ballpark; the neighborhood would fill in around it in the years to come, which only confirmed its place in the hearts of Brooklyn fans. Initially, the double-decker grandstand extended all the way to the right-field corner, but only a little ways past third base, succeeded there by crude, concrete bleachers. In right-centerfield, the famous scoreboard, chain-link fence, and concave, concrete wall were not yet in place. There was only a high, plain wooden wall filled with the standard advertising of the day, for Fatima cigarettes and Bull Durham tobacco.

The park ran slightly uphill, from right field to center and parallel to Bedford Avenue, leading *Boys of Summer* author Roger Kahn to describe it as "a narrow cockpit of iron and concrete along a steep cobblestone slope." Its most gracious elements were its windowed façade and its fabled Italian marble rotunda, eighty feet in circumference, with twelve turnstiles and twelve gilded ticket cages, and tiled "stitches" in the floor to replicate a baseball. Above was a domed ceiling twenty-seven feet high and a chandelier with twelve arms in the shape of baseball bats, holding twelve globes shaped like baseballs.

The McKeevers had it ready in a year, despite a pig iron strike. In their rush, it was discovered too late that a press box had somehow been overlooked. The beat writers were forced to make do for the next sixteen years with a few rows of seats in the upper deck, behind home plate, where they were regularly bombarded with insults and worse by Brooklyn fans, including one "Apple Annie," a vociferous older woman who once bashed a sportswriter—Damon Runyon?—with her umbrella.

The park's very first game was an exhibition against the Yankees on April 5, 1913. Brooklyn won, 3–2, when a twenty-three-year-old former dental student from Kansas City hit an inside-the-park home run. Remarkably, Charles Dillon Stengel would perform the exact same feat in another New York ballpark, to win a much more important and memorable game against the Yankees, ten years later.

Stengel had come up to the Dodgers from Montgomery of the Southern League the September before, which meant that he would play or manage in *five* different New York ballparks, from Washington Park to Shea Stadium. The jug-eared, freckled, hot-tempered son of a Kansas City businessman and insurance agent, Casey—then nicknamed both Dutch and Irish—had dropped out of high school and later dental school for the chance to play professional baseball.

"I was a left-handed dentist who made people cry," he recalled. "I was not very good at pulling teeth, but my mother loved my work. Some of the people in the clinic didn't share her views."

Casey was homesick for Mom in the big city, but he never let it show. In his very first game—still back in Washington Park—he singled, doubled, singled, and then stole second. Up for the fourth time, he turned around and batted right-handed, just for the hell of it. He drew a walk and stole second again.

"The crowd was busy applauding the young man all afternoon," one account read, making him "the pet of the populace . . . the fair-haired youth."

This wouldn't last, only for another fifty-three years or so. Besides the showmanship, Casey was a good hitter, a swift outfielder with a fine arm who never backed away from a fight. He put a charge into the woebegone Dodgers, but not enough to get them out of the second division.

That began to change when Uncle Robbie came over from Manhattan. Ebbets seems to have felt he was getting another McGraw for his team, and back in his days as catcher for the old Orioles, Robbie had scrapped with the best of them. Soon after breaking in with the Athletics, he had been anointed the "official measurer of the bosoms" for the team's "Ladies Auxiliary"—an early group of baseball Annies. By the time he reached Brooklyn, though, Wilbert had four children and was devoted to "Ma Robinson," the unofficial team mother. Genial and lethargic, he was loved by all, if not necessarily respected. He formed a "Bonehead Club" to try to gently chide his players into paying more attention—one of its first members was Uncle Robbie, when he took the wrong lineup to home plate. He consented to take part in a spring training stunt by catching a baseball dropped from an airplane, only to have the pilot toss him a grapefruit instead. Robinson caught it in the flat of his catcher's mitt, where the fruit exploded, knocking him down and covering him in sticky liquid.

"Help, help," he called out to his watching players. "I'm bleeding to death. Help me!"

Unsurprisingly, Casey Stengel was widely believed to have been involved with this bit of hijinks.

Chief Meyers would describe Robinson as "just a good old soul," and as he aged, he would spend more and more of his time on the bench telling his players about the old days, or his exploits hunting and fishing down at Dover Hall, the winter camp he kept in Georgia. Yet his players also considered him "a sound baseball man and a good manager, especially when it came to handling pitchers."

Determined to show John McGraw what he could do, Robinson began to accumulate useful players, loading up the Dodgers with both young talent and still-serviceable, older players—some of them drawn from McGraw's own Giants. The team rose in the standings and was redubbed the Robins, after its big, cuddly skipper. It was a nickname that would live on for decades past Robinson's tenure, with headline writers referring to the Dodgers as the Flock right to the end of the team's stay in Brooklyn.

By 1916, attendance had reached nearly 450,000, a Brooklyn record, and Robinson had the team he wanted in place, the roster including the former Giants Merkle, Marquard, and Meyers. Its leading light was the left fielder Zack Wheat (brother of fellow major leaguer Mack Wheat), a superb curveball hitter who still holds the Dodgers' all-time records for games played, at bats, hits, doubles, triples, and total bases, and who was undoubtedly the most colorless

Hall of Famer ever to play ball in Brooklyn. But its spark plug was the irrepressible right fielder from Kansas City.

"It was Casey who kept us on our toes," claimed Chief Meyers. "He was the life of the party and kept us old-timers pepped up all season."

The Dodgers were embroiled for most of the season in a weird, four-team race with the Phillies, Boston, and, periodically, John McGraw's Giants. After finishing last in 1915, Muggsy made his team over with his usual speed and genius, but somehow he couldn't quite get it to click consistently. Baseball is a game of streaks, but the 1916 Giants were the streakiest in history. In an early road trip, they won seventeen in a row, and nineteen of twenty-one, then came back home and dropped ten of fifteen in New York. All but out of the race by September 8, lingering behind the Dodgers in a distant fourth place, they suddenly turned hot again, reeling off what is still a major-league record, twenty-six wins in a row—all at home in the Polo Grounds.

Incredibly, it wasn't enough. Despite winning twenty-six straight, the Giants not only didn't make it to first, they didn't make it out of fourth place. Robbie's Brooklyn veterans held steady, and despite their epic streak McGraw's Giants were already eliminated by the time they went to Brooklyn for a season-ending, three-game set at Ebbets Field. The Robins, meanwhile, stood to clinch the flag with a win in the first game of the series. With Brooklyn leading, 6–5, at the end of the fifth, McGraw couldn't stand it any longer. The Little Napoleon simply took off, leaving the dugout and not coming back for the rest of Brooklyn's pennant-clinching win.

"They missed my signs, displayed miserable judgment in every department of play, and almost turned the game into a farce," McGraw griped afterward. "I don't intend to take any of the blame. If the Giants are criticized, that is their lookout—not mine."

It was one more slap in the face of McGraw's old friend, who told the press for the record, "Manager McGraw's suspicions in this matter are ridiculous. His statement is very unsportsmanlike." Privately, Robinson snarled, "He pissed on my pennant."

In the World Series, the Flock fought fiercely, but was shown up by a younger, quicker Red Sox team with better pitching. In game two, they lost a fourteen-inning game, 2–1, to a tireless, big-boned twenty-one-year-old southpaw called Babe Ruth. Before long, Ruth would grow restless being able to pitch only every three or four days, and his demands to play every day would lead to seismic changes in the game. But in the meantime, baseball had to fight off new challenges, ones that threatened to throw it back into the scary old days of open competition.

25

The Other Game in Town

Two years before the Babe shut down Brooklyn, in 1914, the first challenge to the established major leagues materialized since Ban Johnson's creation of the American League in 1900. The Federal League, an amalgamation of two existing, midwestern circuits, signed a bevy of not-quite-first-rate American and National Leaguers, and set up shop in Baltimore, Buffalo, Pittsburgh, Indianapolis, Chicago, St. Louis, Kansas City, and Brooklyn. For the first time since the Players' League in 1890, the borough of homes and churches would have more than one major-league baseball team.

The Brooklyn Federal League team was owned by Robert Ward, a millionaire bread maker who took over the Dodgers' old Washington Park, added a big scoreboard in centerfield, and—for reasons that remain opaque—put American Indian symbols on the outside walls. Ward named his team the Tip-Tops, after his Tip-Top bakery, and vowed the Federal League would last forever. It lasted all of two seasons, and Ward's blatant commercialism in naming ball club after bakery so outraged sportswriters that they refused to accept it, insisting on calling the team the Brookfeds.

The Tip-Tops were nowhere near the tip of the top, finishing fifth, then seventh. Desperate to put a winning franchise in the New York market, the league allowed Indianapolis owner Harry Sinclair to move his Hoosiers, who had won the initial Federal League flag, to

Newark. This was the first and only time in major-league history that a team would move the season after winning a pennant—and the first and only season that a major-league club would play in New Jersey. The renamed Newark Peppers set up shop in hastily constructed Harrison Park, just across the Passaic River from where the New Jersey Performing Arts Center stands, and not far from where the Red Bulls' soccer stadium is today—a featureless facility that seated twenty-one thousand.

Sinclair, a gregarious oil tycoon, tried to fight or bribe his way into Manhattan. When the Giants and Highlanders colluded to block this, he offered John McGraw the stupendous sum of $100,000 to come over and manage the Peppers. McGraw turned him down, and Sinclair settled for trying to beef up attendance by staging bicycle races after home games. His Peppers contended for most of the season, but he transferred the Federal League's greatest star, a mouthy, flamboyant former Yankees outfielder named Benny Kauff, to Brooklyn, in payment of debts Sinclair had run up to the Tip-Tops.

"[Kauff] wore a loudly striped silk shirt, an expensive blue suit, patent leather shoes, a fur-collared overcoat and a derby hat," the sportswriter Frank Graham wrote in describing a typical outfit of Flashy Benny's. "He was adorned with a huge diamond stickpin, an equally huge diamond ring and a gold watch encrusted in diamonds, and he had roughly $7,500 in his pockets."

Thanks to his last name, Kauff was also thought to be the ne plus ultra for any New York team: Jewish. He was not, but if you think you've got the Jewish Joe Namath of baseball, why let him go?

Kauff led the Federal League in batting for the second straight year in Brooklyn, but it didn't do the Tip-Tops much good. The Team That Bread Made did manage to lure the old Players' League firebrand John Montgomery Ward away from his dogs and his guns out on Long Island, to serve as business manager. The resourceful Ward persuaded Federal League owners to open up a new front in their fight against the majors, challenging their cartel under the nation's newly revived antitrust laws. Victory in court would shatter the old National Agreement, and stood to make every player in the game a free agent.

The majors fought back as they always had, with money and guile. A severe national recession had left all sides hurting, and after the 1915 season many Federal League owners were just as glad to be bought out. Smiling Harry Sinclair, for one, reportedly collected $2 million to go away. (He would surface a few years later, as a major player in the Teapot Dome scandal.) The payoff seemed exorbitant, but the lords of baseball were in a hurry. The new league had managed to place its case in what looked like the perfect court, before a colorful federal justice in Chicago known for his outspoken opposition to the trusts.

Judge Kenesaw Mountain Landis had gained national headlines for imposing the largest antitrust fine ever on the Standard Oil Company. But like many of Landis's decisions, this one was largely voided on appeal. He might have been a mountain of integrity to the public and the press, with his shock of white hair and his glowering, Old Testament visage, but Landis was known as something of a loose cannon in legal circles. He was also an avid Cubs fan. When the case against baseball's monopoly came before him, he sat on it, quashing it until the rest of the Federal League went belly-up. It was a favor the owners would not forget.

No one was too much interested in the rights of another group left out of the national game—one whose talents might have helped the Federal League to survive. America as it entered the twentieth century was still moving backward from racial integration. In its infamous *Plessy v. Ferguson* (1896) decision, the Supreme Court had upheld Jim Crow in the South, allowing for the complete, legal separation of the races under the rubric of providing "separate but equal" facilities. Things were only a little better in the North, where de facto segregation mostly held sway.

Confronted with this impossible situation, Black leaders debated how African Americans might ever win a place for themselves in America. What most had trouble getting their minds around—a testament to their innate humanity—was that for most of America's whites the supremacy of their race was a closed issue. The white man had no intention of competing with Blacks, no matter how talented, honest, or industrious they proved to be.

African Americans were expressly excluded not only from "white" hotels, restaurants, trains, trolley cars, and almost any other social or public amenity but from almost all lines of work, blue collar and white collar. Any accomplishment despite this discrimination signaled white America only that still more segregation was necessary. When, in 1898, the all-Black Tenth Cavalry swept up San Juan Hill alongside Teddy Roosevelt's Rough Riders and received four Medals of Honor, the U.S. Army reacted by quietly moving Black troops out of combat units, relegating them almost entirely to supply and support battalions for the next half century.

"Let the Negro learn to clean stables, care for horses, feed and harness and drive them, run lawn mowers, make and keep gardens and also keep engagements," instructed *The New York Times* in a typical editorial in 1900, the same year that a brutal, police-led riot once again chased Manhattan Blacks from their own neighborhood.

The *Times*'s advice wasn't really meant to suggest a stepping-stone to anything. Black Americans were expected to stick to such lowly jobs, and to passively accept such insults, forever.

It was much the same in the new entertainments, so bent on assimilating all (other) comers to the melting pot. Ethnic acts abounded in the vaudeville halls, and their humor could be broad and crude. These could cut close to the bone, but everybody got in a dig, everybody got a turn on top—save for the Black man. African Americans were depicted on the turn-of-the-century stage as uniformly lazy, foolish, pretentious, dangerous, violent, rapacious, dishonest, childlike, fearful, and/or stupid—actually subhuman in most instances. They were the universal "other." As David Nasaw emphasizes in *Going Out,* the "negative qualities attributed to 'blackness' on stage served to unite the audience in a celebration of its own 'whiteness.'"

Baseball was no different. Blacks were still strictly forbidden to play anywhere in organized ball, majors or minors. Even in extremis, the insurgent Federal League never seriously considered integrating. When the aspiring United States League, a minor-league circuit with ideas, announced that *it* would not discriminate against Black players, the league's Baltimore franchise pulled out, and the whole endeavor collapsed.

The same strictures applied to players from the islands, from Puerto Rico and the Dominican Republic, and especially from Cuba, where a vibrant baseball culture had blossomed. When the foundering Cincinnati club was desperate enough to sign up a pair of leading

Cuban players, Armando Marsans and Rafael Almeida, New York's leading Black newspaper, *The New York Age,* dared to hope that "now that the first shock is over, it would not be surprising to see a Cuban a few shades darker . . . breaking into the professional ranks." Instead, the Reds assured their fans that their Cuban acquisitions were "Spanish," and "as pure white as Castille soap."

No one knew the level of Black talent down in Cuba better than John McGraw. He had followed up his very first year in professional ball with a stint on the island, where he quickly became a fan favorite, nicknamed *El mono amarillo*—"the yellow monkey." McGraw loved Cuba, and brought his white Giants back repeatedly for spring training games against the likes of José Méndez, "the Black Diamond," a small pitcher with incredibly long fingers, pinpoint control, a fastball hard enough to have killed one batter when it hit him in the chest, and a changeup that he threw from a variety of baffling, Tiantesque windups. Méndez regularly beat major-league teams in spring training, and Muggsy proclaimed him "sort of Walter Johnson and Grover Alexander rolled into one," speculating that he would pay $50,000 for him if the Black Diamond were a white man. But as a sportswriter of the time dryly noted, "Alas, that is a handicap he [Méndez] can't outgrow."

Muggsy had already learned his lesson, during his first spring training as manager of the American League's Baltimore franchise. Staying at the Eastman Hotel in Hot Springs, McGraw noticed the baseball skills of a young Black bellhop there. Charlie Grant was a slick-fielding, good-hitting second baseman for the Columbia Giants, one of Chicago's leading Black teams. Grant was also light-skinned enough, "with straight hair and sharp features," for McGraw to invent a whole new pedigree for him. Grant's name, he put out, was Chief Tokohoma, and he hailed from what was still the Indian Territory down in Oklahoma, with a living mother in Lawrence, Kansas. In fact, Grant was an African American from Cincinnati, and McGraw's scheme fell through when Chicago fans, familiar with his play around the Windy City, alerted the pinch-souled owner of the Chicago White Sox, Charles Comiskey.

"This Cherokee of McGraw's is really Grant, the crack Negro second-baseman, fixed up with war paint and a bunch of feathers," scoffed Comiskey, who threatened, "If he really keeps this Indian, I will get a Chinaman of my acquaintance and put him on third."

No doubt, it all drew a good laugh around the press box. McGraw left Charlie Grant in Hot Springs, telling him that he would soon find a way to call him up to Baltimore. He never did, and Grant returned to the peripatetic, ill-rewarded life of the Black ballplayer. Never again would McGraw attempt to sign a Black man. Nor would anyone else in charge of a New York club, until the return of a raggedy-armed former Yankees catcher named Branch Rickey.

By 1910, a vast multitude of African Americans, their hope and patience exhausted by the continuing white terrorism and American apartheid to be found in the South, had begun to make their way north, in what came to be known as the Great Migration. They would not stop until the end of the 1960s, by which time more than six million African Americans had left the South for the North and the West—what Nicholas Lemann would judge "one of the largest and most rapid mass internal movements in history—perhaps the greatest not caused by the immediate threat of execution or starvation. In sheer numbers, it outranks the migration of any other [single] ethnic group—Italian or Irish or Jews or Poles—to the United States."

Already by 1900, a majority of New York's Black population had been born outside the state for the first time in more than two hundred years. By 1910, the Black population of the city had increased tenfold, to more than ninety-one thousand, and within a few more years New York would pass Washington, D.C., as the leading Black city in the country.

The conditions these new arrivals found were horrendous. From 1895 to 1915, the Black death rate in New York exceeded the birthrate. The biggest killers were tuberculosis and pneumonia, diseases directly attributable to how they were forced to live. African Americans were charged the highest rents among the working poor in the city, an average of $2–$5 *more* a month than whites had to pay—and at a time when the typical Black worker made only $4–$6 a week; the average Black family, from all sources, brought in no more than $12–$15 a week.

To make the rent, African Americans often had to double and triple up. Most were not, in any case, allowed to live in "white" New

York neighborhoods, a rule enforced not by law but by custom. At the end of the Civil War, most of the city's Black population had been concentrated down in "Little Africa," along the narrow streets and back alleys abutting Minetta Lane in Greenwich Village. Over the next fifty years, African Americans would be pushed grudgingly up Manhattan by the new waves of white immigrants, settling first in what was known as the New Tenderloin and Columbus Hill. Running roughly from present-day Chelsea, through Hell's Kitchen to what is now Lincoln Center, these were wretched, poor, vice-filled blocks, reverberating with the rattle and roar of the West Side's new, elevated rail lines.

And yet, no matter how much they crowded in, no Black claim to property was considered really legitimate, no land occupied by Blacks went uncontested. Columbus Hill became known as San Juan Hill, thanks to the constant battles there between Blacks and the Irish toughs who would pelt them with rocks and bottles. Matters came to a head in August 1900, the hottest month yet recorded in New York City, when the NYPD led what was called a "n——r chase" through San Juan Hill and Hell's Kitchen, after a plainclothes cop was knifed in a brawl with a Black man. It turned into a twenty-four-hour rampage, in which the police encouraged a chanting, singing mob to smash windows in Black homes, dragged Black people off streetcars, and set upon any individual of color they happened to find on the street. At least eighty African Americans were badly beaten, many of them also arrested. Only a torrential rainstorm stopped the violence. Almost forty years after the lynchings of the Civil War draft riots, Blacks were considered as much a target of opportunity as ever.

Yet something was different this time. African Americans had sufficient numbers now to fight back, arm themselves, and protest from the pulpit and in the newspapers. The great exodus had brought dozens of ministers and sometimes their entire churches up together from the South, solidifying a sense of community. Intellectuals and successful entrepreneurs emerged, against all white opposition.

Most dramatic of all were the advances made by Blacks in show business. White New Yorkers had been mesmerized by Black culture—often despite themselves—for decades already. Now a whole new group of actors, dancers, songwriters, playwrights, and novelists stepped forward to wrestle for control over how they were depicted.

Often there was a terrible price to be paid for this, starting with the exaggerated minstrel makeup that Blacks, too, were perversely forced to wear when they finally began to appear onstage before white audiences.

Humiliations aside, the great song-and-dance team of Bert Williams and George Walker broke all the way through in 1903 with *In Dahomey,* the first Black-written and Black-performed musical ever produced on Broadway. *In Dahomey* would tour the country and go on to play the Palace—Buckingham Palace—before the royal family (though back in New York, Black audience members still had to enter the show through a separate entrance). Walker and Williams touted themselves under the brutally frank billing of "Two Real Coons." One can easily imagine the psychic toll this took, but it also made a statement: they were *real.* This was *their* music and *their* people, and in New York, at least, a public given a taste of real Black theater would begin to welcome more and more of it.

The artists and performers, the writers and thinkers, of New York's Black community would create a place, both physical and spiritual, for their people as the artists of no other ethnic group in New York—or anywhere else in America—ever really did. By the turn of the century a "Negro Bohemia" had taken shape on West Fifty-Third Street, the site of the Colored Men's YMCA and Marshall's Hotel, a popular watering hole. Here, Black artists, entertainers, and intellectuals of all stripes talked the night away in fervent discussions of race, art, and the role of the New Negro in the city around them.

"It was an alluring world, a tempting world," remembered the poet, intellectual, and activist James Weldon Johnson, but as the events of August 1900 showed, it was still not their own.

A new opportunity presented itself. Harlem had long been a sleepy, swampy community in the northern reaches of Manhattan, a semirural area with blocks of middle-class residents and patches of poor Irish, Italian, and Black residents living in areas with names such as Pig's Alley, and Goatville, and Canary Island. Beginning in the late 1880s, it experienced a building boom, in anticipation of the subway and the arrival of Manhattan's upper classes, making their own long march up Manhattan, ahead of the immigrant masses. Eager speculators snapped up land, evicted the pigs and goats, laid out broad, gracious avenues, and put up majestic elevator apartment buildings.

The developer David H. King Jr. went so far as to hire four of the top architects in New York, including Stanford White, to build two blocks full of elegant "King's Model Houses"—townhouses on West 138th and 139th Streets.

The speculators had gotten ahead of themselves. The rich were staying put in their Fifth Avenue châteaus, and the upper-middle classes already had plenty of fine apartments to choose from. Working-class Jews and Italians began to fill up blocks in lower and East Harlem, but there weren't enough of them to make back the developers' investment.

Whom to turn to—save the people who landlords could always charge more? In conjunction with a number of Black real estate agents—and over the vociferous objections of their white neighbors—African Americans were recruited to fill up central Harlem. By 1914, more than fifty thousand people of color were living there, and when the leading Black churches followed, buying up abandoned white places of worship, or building handsome new structures of their own—churches such as Black people had never owned before, anywhere in America—the foundation stone was laid.

Harlem would be *their own* place, a Black community, one as solidly grounded as the new stone churches. Before long it would be the capital of Black America, a neighborhood that white New York could no more take away than it could wrest Chinatown from the growing Asian population downtown. Black Harlem was, from the beginning, an overcrowded, underserved ghetto in which, like all ghettos, people of every profession and fortune were forced to live together. But it belonged unreservedly to African Americans, just as Black communities were being carved out in Chicago, Detroit, Cleveland, and other cities throughout the North. From these places would come ownership—ownership of the land, of the churches, eventually of institutions, including show business and baseball, which they would transform just as they did American music, theater, dance, and literature.

When it came to ball, though, there still was not enough capital in Black America to sustain a separate, professional league. Instead, Black players led a peripatetic existence, playing in Cuba or elsewhere in the Caribbean throughout the winter, taking on whatever teams they could find, Black or white, back in the United States.

"Where the money was, that's where I played," remembered John Henry "Pop" Lloyd, one of the greatest Black ballplayers to play regularly in the New York area before World War I.

On the road they bunched together in rattletrap automobiles, in Jim Crow railroad cars, in flatbed wagons. Traveling and even sleeping in their uniforms, finding food and accommodations wherever they could, bedding down in the ballparks where they played or in fields under the open sky. Often, they were forced to resort to promotions that bordered on minstrelsy; an outfit known as the All-American Black Tourists both paraded before the games and played in top hats and swallowtail coats.

Teams were temporary, fly-by-night operations, generally confined to the East Coast corridor between New York and Washington and to the Greater Chicago area. For backing, they were forced to rely on white sports promoters. The most prominent among them would spawn a promotional dynasty—one that culminated in Vince McMahon and World Wrestling Entertainment.

McMahon's grandfather and granduncle Roderick "Jess" McMahon and Ed McMahon were born to Irish immigrants and orphaned at an early age. While still in their early twenties, the McMahon brothers began to put together boxing and wrestling matches. It was they who would arrange the epic, interracial Jack Johnson–Jess Willard heavyweight bout in Havana in 1915. Described as "big, broad-shouldered . . . with curly iron-gray hair," Jess McMahon also grasped the opportunity to branch out into other areas in a rapidly changing Harlem. He and his brother moved into football and later basketball, sponsoring the fabled Commonwealth Big Five basketball squad, first of the great Black teams to play up in the Renaissance Casino.

The greatest team they ever assembled, though—one of the greatest New York teams ever assembled, in any sport—was a baseball team, the Lincoln Giants, later spun off as the aptly named Lincoln Stars. The club was a stunning amalgam of some of the biggest stars in the history of Black baseball. The shortstop and player-manager was Pop Lloyd, a devastating hitter and expert bunter and base stealer who started as a catcher and could play anywhere on the field. Nicknamed *El Cuchara*—"the Shovel"—in Cuba for his huge hands, he would fire volleys of pebbles across the infield along with the ground balls he scooped up. Connie Mack considered him the equal to Honus Wagner, one of the best players ever to take the field, while Babe Ruth called him "the greatest player anywhere."

Out in centerfield, for that matter, was "the black Babe Ruth," Oscar Charleston, a ferocious, fantastically talented, five-tool player who had enlisted in the army at fifteen and was known to brawl with everyone from Klan members to Cuban soldiers. Joining him in the outfield was "the black Ty Cobb," Spottswood Poles, a small but fleet fly chaser who was credited with a total average of over .400 during his fourteen-season, mostly year-round career and who would go on to receive five battle stars and a Purple Heart with the famous "Harlem Hellfighters" in France. On the mound were two of the greatest pitchers in the history of the Black game: Cyclone Joe Williams, a fireballer with great control whom some observers would consider better than Satchel Paige and who struck out twenty-seven Kansas City Monarchs in a twelve-inning, one-hit victory over the great Chet Brewer; and Cannonball Dick Redding, known as the Demon Pitcher, for a blazing fastball he would not hesitate to throw at anyone's head, and who once fanned twenty-five batters in a nine-inning game. The man catching them both was Louis Santop, a mountainous receiver who once accidentally broke three of Charleston's ribs with a friendly hug, could throw a ball over the centerfield fence from home plate, liked to call his home-run shots, Babe Ruth style, and batted .470, .422, .429, and .455 in his four seasons with the Giants/Stars.

Lloyd, Charleston, Williams, and Santop are in Cooperstown, while Redding and Poles should be. The rest of the Lincoln Stars were only great: the superb infielder and pitcher, Grant "Home Run" Johnson; the canny, power-hitting first baseman Bill Pettus; the speedy, deft-fielding outfielder Ashby Dunbar; the hard-hitting catcher–first baseman Pete Booker; the middle infielder George Wright; the tough, slick-fielding "Little Corporal" at third, Bill Francis; the lightning-quick, college-educated utility man Bill Kindle.

Few better teams, if any, have ever been assembled, on any diamond. And yet almost no one in the white public knew they existed. Their games generally went unreported in New York's many papers, and they played at Olympic Field, a small, crude, long-forgotten park up at 136th Street and Fifth Avenue, near the Harlem River. The

McMahons had them start each game with trick throws and "shadow ball" and mugging for the fans. When they got down to playing, they could beat anyone, dominating other Black teams in the East, playing Rube Foster's great Chicago American Giants to a standstill, frequently besting white teams from the semipros to the majors.

The respect all that earned was demonstrated in a contest where Louis Santop faced Jeff "the Bear" Tesreau, a big, hard-throwing spitballer for John McGraw's Giants. Santop and Tesreau hailed from the same hometown of Tyler, Texas, but when the Black catcher came up, Tesreau put the first pitch just under his chin. Jocularly, Santop called out to the pitcher, "Jeff, you wouldn't throw at a hometown boy, would you?" To which Tesreau replied, "All n——rs look alike to me!"

26

The End of the Inside Game

The spring of 1911 was the burning season in New York. Within weeks of each other, fires consumed two of the city's most beloved entertainment palaces. Just a month and a half after the Polo Grounds burned down, flames took the Dreamland amusement park out in Coney Island. The gleaming white park, owned by a conglomerate of Tammany businessmen and pols headed by the ubiquitous Big Tim Sullivan, went up in a spectacular, double-nine-alarm blaze. Within minutes, Dreamland's central tower was a pillar of flame visible all the way to Manhattan. Thirty-three separate fire companies rushed to the scene, including Dreamland's own Midget City company, a fire company composed entirely of little people, which acquitted itself admirably—but they were helpless against ocean winds that whipped the blaze into an inferno. Burning parrots dove through the air, shrieking in pain and terror, while a bleeding three-year-old lion called the Black Prince ran out into Surf Avenue and had to be shot dead by the police.

Grotesque a spectacle as it was, New Yorkers had already witnessed an infinitely worse tragedy in yet another fire that spring, at the Triangle Shirtwaist Factory in Greenwich Village. There, 146 garment workers died in the space of fifteen minutes. Many of the victims—almost all of them young women or teenage girls—ended up jumping from windows nine stories above the ground, dying out on the Greenwich Village sidewalk before their stunned friends, family, and neighbors. Much like the latter-day victims of the World Trade Center attack, they had no choice as the fire drew closer. The fire department, equipped with ladders that reached only to the sixth floor in a New York that already had at least eighty-eight skyscrapers, watched helplessly as they plummeted right through their nets.

This was too much, even in a city so inured to corruption. Over the previous two years, the young immigrant women who toiled so many hours at their sewing machines had organized the biggest strike in New York history, "the Uprising of the Twenty Thousand." Tammany had done its best to suppress the strike, having pimps and their prostitutes harass the women on the picket lines, then sending in New York's Finest to brutally beat and arrest the strikers for disturbing the peace. Now the men who ran the city stood exposed in their avarice, so bent on turning over their next dollar that they could not be bothered to even mandate proper fire ladders in a city full of loft factories.

Faced with losing the machine's voting base to the socialists, Tammany's more humane elements took charge. Big Tim Sullivan and his leading protégés, the state senate leader, Robert Wagner, and the head of the state assembly, a gregarious Lower East Side pol named Al Smith, pushed through critical reforms in working conditions and wages, at the behest of a remarkable social worker named Frances Perkins. Reform was firmly in the saddle everywhere—at least for a season. Liberal-left candidates of one stripe or another took a stunning 75 percent of the vote in the 1912 presidential election, and a national income tax soon followed. After it was passed, not a single new mansion was built along Fifth Avenue, and many that were there began their slow metamorphosis into museums, hotels, jewelry stores, and apartment buildings.

Tammany's reformers had saved the machine for the time being but doomed it in the long run. A city in which everyone, even the lowliest immigrant workers, had rights was not one that needed a machine. The Tiger was further wounded when, soon after his greatest triumph, Big Tim Sullivan's mind began to cloud, perhaps a victim of syphilis. With it went control over the seamier underworld elements that Tammany had long exploited.

When one Herman "Beansy" Rosenthal, a pudgy gambler who was one of Sullivan's "smart Jewboys," refused to make an expected payoff to the cops, it blossomed into a scandal that blew the top off all of New York's cozy little arrangements. Early in the morning of July 16, 1912, Rosenthal was enjoying a steak and ginger ale at the Hotel Metropole, on West Forty-Third Street and Broadway, when Beansy's fellow Sullivan protégé Arnold Rothstein persuaded him to step out to the curb. There, Beansy took four pistol slugs, three to the head and one to the neck, from men who then motored away, in what might have been history's very first drive-by shooting.

"I shall always remember the picture of that soft, fat body wilting on the sidewalk with a beer-stained tablecloth serving as its pall," Alexander Woollcott, who was in the Metropole that night, later wrote. "Just behind me an oldtimer whispered . . . 'From where I stand . . . I can see eight murderers.' "

This, like the Triangle Fire, was too much—too loud, too flagrant, the misfire of a machine that was breaking down. The reformers launched a crackdown on vice, and particularly Times Square. Yankees owner Frank Farrell's fabled House with the Bronze Door was forced underground. Arnold Rothstein rolled with the punches, as usual. Managing to evade any connection with Beansy's murder, good old reliable Arnold introduced the floating crap game and the floating card game, the high rollers reassembling every night at a different apartment or hotel room in Times Square. Besides providing Damon Runyon with the central plot point of *Guys and Dolls,* this had the advantage of greatly lessening the number of cops and politicians who had to be cut in for their piece of the action.

Yet the change also marked a dangerous independence for the criminals freed at last from Tammany's yoke—the beginning of a decades-long transfer of real political power in the city from the machine to the mobsters it once controlled. Mere anarchy was loosed upon the underworld. Even Rothstein's floating games, for all his gangster bodyguards, were stuck up repeatedly.

The Big Bankroll would never leave Times Square for very long, but he began to look into other diversions while he waited for the heat to die down. Rothstein started his own stable of racehorses, opened swank new gambling clubs out in Long Beach and up in Saratoga, even bought into a pair of joints in Harlem—one of them named the Cotton Club. He also began to spend time at Reuben's restaurant, located at West Seventy-Fourth Street and Broadway. Now instead of patronizing Lindy's, every night at seven he could be found in a back room there, eating his dinner.

Reuben's was a popular place with the show business crowd and would achieve immortality as the birthplace of the Reuben sandwich. But it was still far removed from the action down at the "Crossroads of the World." Its chief advantage was its location directly across Broadway from the Ansonia Hotel. No other residence in New York has so exotic a history as the Ansonia, an off-white Beaux Arts confection, seventeen stories high, that was and is the most beautiful and ornate of all the monumental apartment houses on the Upper West Side. It has housed a long and eclectic roster of celebrities in its time, from Babe Ruth to Enrico Caruso, Toscanini to Theodore Dreiser. Its fabled basement, complete with pool, harbored such unlikely establishments as Plato's Retreat, the heterosexual 1970s sex club of lore, and the gay Continental Baths, where Bette Midler got her start, accompanied on the piano by Barry Manilow, playing in nothing but a towel.

Rothstein wasn't interested in the Ansonia's architecture, though, or its potential as a venue for musical camp and anonymous sex. By the 1910s, baseball had become respectable enough for teams to stay in such an establishment when they were in New York. The Ansonia became a gathering place for ballplayers and their inevitable hangers-on, the bugs and the women, the gamblers and the suckers. Among the visiting teams that stayed there were the Chicago White Sox. Sometime in September 1919, eight of them gathered in their teammate Chick Gandil's room to discuss how they might fix the World Series.

They would get considerable guidance in this endeavor from the gray rat, eating his dinner just across Broadway.

27

"Gossip Is a Dangerous Thing"

Another Upper West Sider who could be found in the baseball crowd milling through the Ansonia's cavernous lobby and around its busy bar was John McGraw. Muggsy was still as active and inventive as ever, and after the humiliation of losing out to Wilbert Robinson's Dodgers, he managed to piece together another winner in 1917.

It was one of the Little Napoleon's more artful creations, a patchwork squad made up of both green, homegrown ballplayers and useful veterans, with a largely anonymous starting staff that somehow became the class of the National League and featured one of baseball's first real bullpens, full of effective pitchers instead of the old, the unready, and the weary. The lineup featured a recent McGraw addition, scooped up the year before when the Federal League folded.

"I'll make them all forget that a guy named Ty Cobb ever pulled on a baseball shoe," the splendidly attired Benny Kauff told reporters when he joined the Giants. "I'll hit so many balls into the grandstand that the management will have to put screens up in front to protect the fans and save the money that lost balls would cost."

Kauff, as usual, fell a little short of that boast, but in 1917 he did bat .308 and stole thirty bases. The Giants surprised everyone by coasting to the pennant before losing a hard-fought, six-game series to the heavily favored White Sox.

Yet something about the *way* his team had lost gnawed at McGraw. The usually reliable right fielder, Dave Robertson, had dropped an easy fly, and the star third baseman Heinie Zimmerman—another one of McGraw's famous reform cases, a highly talented player who had temporarily blinded a teammate with a bottle of ammonia back in Chicago—made a suspiciously bad throw and helped botch a rundown on a play that decided the series.

The rumors, ever louder at each Fall Classic, had it that these were more than mistakes. Nothing ever surfaced to confirm this, but they bothered McGraw, enough for him to lose at least one leading player who he was convinced had lain down during the series. At the same time, he retained his belief that he could solve anyone, get any player to perform up to his potential. In 1919, he indulged in what was surely his greatest act of hubris: he brought Hal Chase back to New York.

It was, perhaps, a favor to a friend. Christy Mathewson, McGraw's golden boy, had seen his destiny become entangled with that of his shadow opposite. In 1915, Matty's fabled right arm had at last begun to give out, and the following year McGraw engineered an opportunity for Mathewson to manage by trading him to the Cincinnati Reds, throwing in two valued players, Edd Roush and Bill McKechnie, to cinch the deal. On his final day in the Polo Grounds clubhouse, after sixteen seasons, Christy Mathewson bade goodbye to his manager, then silently sat down to a game of cards with his teammates. He played one hand, left his cards on the table, picked up his valise, and left without saying a word. The Big Six always did know how to make an exit.

Matty arrived in Cincinnati in the late summer of 1916—*too* late to keep the Reds from finishing seventh. One of the team's few bright spots was the thirty-three-year-old Hal Chase, who led the league in batting and still played a brilliant first base. What happened next between him and his new manager would have many ramifications, although some of the details are still immersed in the murk that followed Chase like his personal cloud. The two men seem to have maneuvered cautiously around each other at first, even striking up something of a friendship. Chase's game began to decline in 1917, but he was still a good player, and the Reds improved by eighteen games, moving up to the first division.

Yet there were also indications that Prince Hal was up to his old tricks, and things got much worse in 1918, a year when Chase seemed desperate for money, losing heavily in his extracurricular betting on the horses, dice, and cards. Rumors of fixed games and dirty dealings were rampant. The Reds' star third baseman, Heinie Groh, took to shouting across the diamond at Chase, "Who are you bettin' on today? I'd like to know how many errors I'm gonna have!" Chase seems to have recruited second baseman Lee Magee for his schemes, a conspiracy that led to a ludicrous game in Boston, where Cincinnati pitcher Hod Eller threw a two-hitter, but Magee kept making error after error to prolong the contest. The Reds finally won in the top of the thirteenth, when, with two outs, Magee reached base despite himself on a Braves error, then scored when Roush hit an inside-the-park home run, herding the dawdling second baseman ahead of him by screaming, "Run, you dirty son of a bitch!"

The Reds began to dissolve in acrimony. Matty apparently tried to take a page from McGraw's book on reforming ballplayers by inviting Prince Hal to join his running, four-man bridge game. Chase responded by persuading his partner, the pitcher Mike Regan, to help him cheat his manager and his teammates at the bridge table, then, having measured his man, offered Regan $200 to throw a ball game.

It all came apart back at the Polo Grounds. After a tough loss to the Giants on August 6, 1918, Mathewson snapped, confronted Chase in a "bitter quarrel," and suspended the first baseman for "indifferent playing and insubordination." The Reds owner, Garry Herrmann, backed up his manager, announcing that Chase would be banished for the rest of the season and that his remaining $1,600 in salary would be forfeited.

"The evidence we have gathered is appalling and will justify the decision to suspend him," Herrmann would tell the press, adding, "I rather think that his baseball career is completely ended."

But Matty had already had it. There was a war to be won over in France, and all through the 1918 season Christy Mathewson had been talking to his wife about how it was his duty to sign up and fight for his country. The idea probably seemed all the more enticing to him the more Hal Chase tore apart his team. Hours before he had it out with Chase, Mathewson had already started the enlistment process. By late September he was a commissioned officer, on his way to France.

His service was a nightmare from the beginning. Matty caught the influenza that was racking the world onboard ship and suffered terribly from seasickness. Once he reached France, he had to be hospitalized for ten days, but he pushed stubbornly on to Officers' Training School, as a captain in the "Gas and Flame" Division of the U.S.

Army Chemical Corps. It all seems horribly rushed in retrospect, but no doubt exceptions were made to get the great Matty on his way. His charge in the Chemical Corps was to drill enlisted men in preparing for attacks of deadly mustard gas, one more of the unspeakable innovations of World War I. The way the drill worked was that actual gas was released into a crowded room. The officers, being the last to put their masks on, were already at great risk of taking a hit of the stuff. One day, something went wrong and a signal was missed, the gas pouring in before anyone was ready.

"Men screamed to be let out when they got a sudden whiff of the sweet death in the air," Ty Cobb, who was a captain in the same unit, would remember. "They went crazy with fear, and in the fight to get out jammed up in a hopeless tangle."

Cobb felt the gas sear his throat and coughed up phlegm for weeks. For Matty, it was much worse.

"Ty, when we were in there, I got a good dose of the stuff. I feel terrible," he told the Tiger great.

The Big Six went back to the hospital, the war ending before he ever got to see action. His sacrifice had been useless. The influenza and the seasickness had weakened his immune system even before the gassing, but once he was out of the hospital, he was assigned to inspect shells in Flanders from which even more gas might have leaked. By the time he shipped home, he was wan and weak, a feverish shadow of himself. The doctors diagnosed chronic bronchitis, but Christy Mathewson, it would turn out, was suffering from the same ailment that had killed his younger brother two years before: tuberculosis.

Back in the United States, baseball was scrambling to keep the gates open, under the Wilson administration's "fight or work" edict. Baseball, ruled Provost Marshal Enoch Crowder in May 1918, was one of the country's nonessential "games, sports, and amusements."

The major-league owners responded by appealing Crowder's ruling while mustering every cheap display of patriotism they could manage. Ban Johnson hired drill sergeants to put his American Leaguers through their paces before each game, marching back and forth in their (baseball) uniforms and substituting bats for rifles. Both the Giants and the Dodgers seized the opportunity to start chipping away at New York's blue laws, scheduling Sunday games that were played after band concerts and marching exhibitions, with patrons paying only for the concerts and all proceeds going to war charities. To no avail: Secretary of War Newton Baker decreed that the game be shut down for the duration after September 12, 1918, with all players ordered to enlist, register for the draft, or find work that contributed in some way to the war effort.

As many as 38 percent of all major leaguers would put on a uniform, according to the historian Jim Leeke, including twenty-seven future Hall of Famers. (Some sources claim that professional Black players—including many of the best players on the Lincoln Stars—were more likely to sign up than major leaguers.) Few saw much action, mostly because the American stay in the war was so brief. The most prominent New York ballplayer to die in France was Captain Harvard Eddie Grant, thirty-five, a slick-fielding third baseman who had played for ten years with the Giants and three other teams, before leaving baseball for the law. Captain Grant was cut down by machine-gun fire in the Argonne Forest, leading troops behind enemy lines to relieve the "Lost Battalion"—a sacrifice that would earn him a plaque on a five-foot monument in deepest centerfield of the Polo Grounds.

With the end of the war, baseball went back to normal. Hal Chase had the chutzpah to sue the Reds for reinstatement, with back pay. Despite an affidavit from the hospitalized Christy Mathewson, detailing all of the subtle ways that Chase could and did manage to throw games, the Reds' owner, Garry Herrmann—also one of the three members of the National Commission that ran major-league baseball—was now worrying about the reasons for Chase's banishment going public. Ban Johnson agreed that "it would be a severe black eye for the game if the details became fully known."

John McGraw stepped in to offer a solution. His Giants had finished a distant second in 1918, and he was looking once again to retool his club. This was not unusual, but the method he chose was startling. It was almost as if Muggsy were bored and trying to set himself a challenge by fielding the shadiest possible outfit he could find—an all-star roster of game fixers, criminals, and chiselers. Pitcher Pol Perritt, who had been entangled in one of Chase's game-fixing schemes in Cincinnati, had shot and killed a hunting partner in the offseason, after supposedly mistaking him for a cougar. Pitchers Rube Benton and Jean Dubuc would later be banned from organized baseball for life, for threatening to fix a game and consorting with gamblers. The inimitable Benny Kauff would also be banned for life, accused of running a stolen-car ring out of his auto repair shop. Heinie Zimmerman would be blackballed from the game by McGraw himself for consorting with gamblers. Even McGraw's three young, supremely talented Hall of Famers to be, Ross Youngs, Frankie Frisch, and George "High Pockets" Kelly, would be accused of trying to fix a game in 1924. Pitcher Fred Toney, also brought over from the Reds, consorted with gamblers when he could, but his time with them was limited because he had spent much of the offseason in jail for draft evasion *and* violating the Mann Act.

With this crew of reprobates already on board, signing Hal Chase must have seemed like a final flourish—or perhaps it was just an attempt to get Chase out of Matty's hair. Whatever the case, the National Commission dutifully found Prince Hal "not guilty" and solemnly informed the public that "gossip is a dangerous thing, and sometimes must be recognized to clear up a situation." McGraw then acquired Chase from Cincinnati, gave the man his disputed $1,600 in back pay, and let loose his gang of thugs disguised as a baseball team.

The very strangest part of McGraw's 1919 Giants, though, had to be the man he now had sitting next to him on the bench: Christy Mathewson. Muggsy made his old friend a coach when he finally got back from France in March, and he began to make noises that he would retire before long and hand the reins over to Matty.

It was bizarre that Mathewson could be coaching on the same roster with Hal Chase. But Matty went along, now putting it out that it was Chase's teammates, not he, who had accused the Black Prince of throwing games. There were no incidents between the two men, although once when Matty was knocked down by a flung bat, Chase was conspicuous in being the only Giant not to rush to his side. Mathewson, for his part, just didn't seem to care anymore.

"In the summer of 1919 he developed a strange lassitude," his wife recalled.

For Hal Chase, the game was always afoot, especially as the aged

Giants began to drift out of contention. In mid-August, Fred Lieb of *The Sun* openly mocked Chase for playing "as though in a trance." Rumors swirled that he was fixing games yet again. They were stanched only by a series of injuries that forced Prince Hal out of the lineup for most of the last month of the season.

The Giants had dropped hopelessly behind Cincinnati, and McGraw left the team on September 16 on a scouting expedition—scouting oil wells in Texas, and a racetrack and casino in Havana that he wanted to buy. Mathewson was left to manage Hal Chase through the rest of the season, a downright weird turn of events, though it didn't seem to matter much. Chase's injuries left the former magician at first base limping pathetically about the field.

Yet Chase lingered in New York long enough for one last exercise in skulduggery. Like everything else to do with the man, the details of this venture are hard to discern, all the more so because it occurred in partnership with that other, professionally vague character, Arnold Rothstein.

28

The Big Fix

The fixing of the 1919 World Series was a tragedy that kept straying into farce. To this day, reconstructing any reasonably accurate chronology of the scandal can be maddening—probably because most of the major actors wanted it that way. We must rely on accounts that were related months, years, even decades after the events in question, many of which are completely contradictory. Even Eliot Asinof, whose *Eight Men Out* remains the seminal work on the scandal, got the sequence of events mixed up in places, putting players in the wrong city on the wrong day. Matters were further complicated by the fact that not one but likely *three* separate efforts were made to fix the series that year—yet another indictment of how deeply the gamblers had burrowed beneath the skin of major-league baseball.

What we do know is that sometime in July 1919, Chick Gandil, Chicago's roughneck first baseman, began putting out word that the White Sox were for sale. Irked by the stinginess of the owner, Charles Comiskey, Gandil and the clique of Sox players he headed let it be known that they would throw the World Series, if they made it. The White Sox were soon fielding offers from a veritable menagerie of gamblers, ex-ballplayers, ex-prizefighters, even a midwestern bookie and his blouse-making partner who went by the vaudeville-worthy monikers of Zelser and Zork.

Like one of the brand-new radio antennas starting to sprout from business buildings, Hal Chase picked up instantly on the rumors. One of them came from "the Little Champ," Abe Attell, once a great featherweight boxing champion and now a henchman of Arnold Rothstein's. Attell was also a friend of John McGraw's, in the all-too-cozy world of New York sporting life, and he liked to go up to the Polo Grounds and work out with the Giants. Chase told Attell that his plot was not the only one in the works, and the Little Champ passed the information on to Rothstein.

The Big Brain was spending his usual summer at the racetrack and the posh nightclub he owned in Saratoga Springs. He must have been nettled to hear the news from Attell. The more rumors got out about a fix, the less money Arnold was likely to make on one and the more likely he was to be the target of any investigation. As with any nasty virus, heat and light were anathema to Arnold Rothstein's work.

Late on September 15, the White Sox arrived in New York for a meaningless series with the Yankees and checked in at the Ansonia—again, just across Broadway from Arnold Rothstein's new favorite, Reuben's restaurant. Their game the next day was canceled on account of wet grounds, and looking to kill time, White Sox ace Eddie Cicotte, one of the leading conspirators along with Gandil, ambled into the Ansonia's bar. There he ran into one Sleepy Bill Burns, a former White Sox pitcher turned hustler who was known to have fixed an inconsequential set of games with a Philadelphia gambler named Billy Maharg in 1916. The player who helped them fix it? Reds first baseman Hal Chase, of course.

Now Burns and Maharg were after a much bigger score. They loitered around the Ansonia lobby for days, until Cicotte and Gandil told them they would throw the World Series for $100,000. That night, September 18, 1919, was likely when the eight ballplayers who would become known as the Black Sox met in a room in the Ansonia and decided to follow through with the fix. Burns rushed off to Montreal and Maharg went back to Philly, frantic to raise the money for the payoff.

They would have been better off just strolling across Broadway.

As Burns and Maharg discovered, the only man who had that sort of cash was Arnold Rothstein. And it was here that The Man Uptown drew all the strands of the World Series fix into his quick white hands.

Burns and Maharg—the Rosencrantz and Guildenstern of the piece—returned to New York on the night of Saturday, September 27, hoping for an interview with Rothstein concerning their little venture. Word arrived that he would not sponsor their fix. Crestfallen, the two men cooled their heels, back in the Ansonia bar. Lo and behold, who should stop by that Saturday night, no doubt accompanied by a ready smile and a whiff of sulfur? Why, none other than Hal Chase. Prince Hal urged the two gamblers not to take no for an answer, but to go talk to the great man in person. Chase just happened to know where Rothstein was dining that night: down in Times Square, in the Grill Room of the Hotel Astor.

This was a very strange place to fix a World Series, rather like meeting today at the Carlyle to fix the Super Bowl. The Hotel Astor was *the* posh establishment in Manhattan at the time, a five-hundred-room, gilded marble palace, complete with cavernous wine cellars, ballrooms, restaurants, private dining rooms fitted out to resemble yacht cabins—even an orangery. It was the gathering place for everyone who was anyone in New York: "Meet me at the Astor" was a password among the upper crust.

When Burns and Maharg barged in—as instructed—to make their pitch to Rothstein, they found themselves facing not only the Great Brain but three of his companions. One of these was later described as a prominent member of the bench. Another was Val O'Farrell, then a private detective, not long ago a policeman and the district attorney's chief investigator. This might seem a remarkable set of witnesses to a proposed felony, but Rothstein made no move to shoo his guests away while Burns and Maharg pleaded their case. Once the two men had outlined their plans to fix the premier event in American sports, Rothstein—according to the press reports widely planted by Val O'Farrell after the scandal had broken—indignantly ordered Burns and Maharg out of his sight, threatening them with violence if they ever so much as mentioned the idea to him again.

What Rothstein had done was to turn a headache into an alibi. The plot to fix the series was well known? Well, here was Arnold disavowing any role in it before witnesses, in the most prominent watering hole in New York, and adroitly passing the blame to a couple of other stiffs. The twist came the very next day. Abe Attell found Burns and Maharg at the Ansonia and told the two men that Rothstein had changed his mind and would back their play.

What had happened? According to the standard story of the fix, Abe Attell had decided to go it on his own, using Rothstein's name to raise cash. Rothstein got wise to this within a couple days, something that, according to Eliot Asinof, "could hardly have amused him, but there was nothing he chose to do about it at the moment." Arnold had already sent two other minions off to Chicago with $80,000 to put together his own fix. Faced with Attell's mutiny, he accepted it and sent more money on with the Little Champ, to finish paying off the ballplayers.

This account makes perfect sense—save for the fact that it jibes with absolutely nothing we know about Arnold Rothstein's personality or modus operandi. The Great Brain was hardly one to be buffaloed into the biggest venture of his life, with only hours to prepare, by a former pug he employed as his gofer and bodyguard. It was true that once the scandal did start to break, Rothstein put the finger on Attell. But at the same time, Arnold hired Billy Fallon—his very own, very expensive attorney—to defend the man. Had the Little Champ really double-crossed him, Arnold Rothstein would have sent other individuals he kept on retainer to deal with Attell, men with names like Legs Diamond and Lucky Luciano.

In the end, it's difficult to believe that Attell was doing anything else but Arnold Rothstein's bidding. Abe Attell and Dave Zelser met with Burns and Maharg in Burns's Ansonia room, probably on September 28, to settle the "details." There was no actual money forthcoming, which should have rung some alarm bells, but Burns and Maharg were so relieved to have Arnold backing them that they agreed to go to Cincinnati with Attell and Zelser and start lining up bets. Also at this meeting was Hal Chase, along with two more players from McGraw's rogues' gallery, the Giants pitchers Jean Dubuc and Fred Toney. Exactly what Chase's role was at this stage remains unknown, but it was more proof that he was working hand in hand with Rothstein and that his appearance in the Ansonia, just in time to meet Burns and Maharg the night before, was less than accidental.

Indeed, Chase's appearance at such key moments would later be taken as proof by some that it was *he,* not Rothstein or anyone else, who really instigated the World Series fix and that he came away with $40,000—maybe the equivalent of $720,000 today. These speculations don't hold water—Chase had little cash of his own to wager at the moment, thanks to a second, acrimonious divorce—but they do speak to just how suspiciously Hal Chase was regarded by his contemporaries.

More likely, Hal Chase was what he always was, a Johnny-on-the-spot when there was a fix to be made, this time for Arnold Rothstein, setting up the little farce played out at the Astor Grill. And Chase had other fish to fry during the World Series, accompanying his teammates on a postseason barnstorming tour of upstate New York, New England, and Quebec. There, during his very last days in a major-league uniform, Hal Chase once against distinguished himself by trying to throw an exhibition game in Vermont to a local, all-Black team.

Back in New York, Arnold Rothstein set about further covering his tracks and protecting his odds, in part by persuading his best friends and clients to make sucker bets on the White Sox. George M. Cohan supposedly lost $90,000. So did Harry Sinclair, the Teapot Dome oilman who had owned the Newark Peppers, though he would soon recoup with the U.S. government.

The afternoon the World Series began, on October 1, 1919, Rothstein walked out of the Ansonia lobby, took a taxi down to Times Square, and stood in the rain with the vast crowd watching the front of the Times Building. There, a giant, mechanical diamond was set up, across which spectators could watch outs recorded and runners advance as quickly as the wire service play-by-play was received. Rothstein stayed just long enough to see that the first batter for Cincinnati was hit by a pitch—the signal that the fix was in. The gray rat had his cheese. Rothstein walked over to his office and bet another $100,000 on the Reds to win the series.

Just how much money Arnold Rothstein made in all on the 1919 World Series will never be determined, although estimates start at $370,000 (or perhaps $6.5 million today), and the real sum might have been much, much higher. A *Chicago Tribune* reporter later remembered seeing Abe Attell standing on a chair in the lobby of a Cincinnati hotel before the first game of the series, his hands full of $1,000 bills, clamoring for any action on the White Sox. After the second game of the series, Burns and Maharg went to Attell and Zelser's hotel room, where Burns saw piles of cash "four to five inches thick" covering every surface.

"I never saw so much money in my life," remembered Maharg. "Stacks of bills were being counted on dressers and tables."

The week before, Attell had hocked his wife's wedding ring. Now he was swimming in greenbacks.

"Where did he get the money [to cover so many bets]?" wrote David Pietrusza. "To ask the question is to answer it."

Attell and Zelser had been sent out not to help Burns and Maharg, or to give them money to bribe players, *but to place more bets.* They commanded a platoon of at least twenty-five local bookies—yet another effort by Rothstein to at least partly hide his tracks.

Burns and Maharg, who made the mistake of betting everything on one of the three games the White Sox won in the series, lost their shirts. Maharg had to hock his diamond stickpin just to get back to Philadelphia. For their part, the Chicago ballplayers played their hand badly in the end and wound up with no more than $30,000 between them, of the $180,000 they had been promised at one time or another.

Arnold Rothstein, though, had done it. He had fixed the World Series, the apex of his gambling career. And his precautions were well advised. Almost as soon as it was done, the whole plot began to unravel.

Christy Mathewson did not have the pleasure of getting to watch

Hal Chase try to throw his last game with the Giants up in Vermont. Instead, Matty gave over his role as acting manager and went to cover the World Series as a special correspondent for *The New York Times.* Like everyone else, Mathewson had heard the rumors of a fix. Up in the press box, the columnist Hugh Fullerton of the *Chicago Herald and Examiner* asked the Big Six to circle in red ink on his scorecard all the plays that he found suspicious. Fullerton would do the same, and the two men would compare notes.

There Matty sat, coughing up his ruined lungs, circling each dubious play, watching grimly as inning by inning the White Sox set about destroying the game he loved. By the end of the contest, his scorecard was covered in red—the same red that flecked his spittle—but he could not quite acknowledge what lay before him. His final dispatches told *Times* readers in great detail that fixing a series was simply impossible: "The rumors and mutterings about the honesty of the Series are ridiculous to me."

Christy Mathewson was not alone. Despite qualms of their own, the White Sox owner, Charles Comiskey, and the American League president, Ban Johnson, also retreated into denial, and most of the press corps was willing to let the matter drop.

Only Hugh Fullerton, the Chicago columnist, refused to go along. When his own paper would not let him print his suspicions out of fear of a libel suit, Fullerton wrote a series of articles for the New York *World* in December 1919 beginning with the headline IS BIG LEAGUE BASEBALL BEING RUN FOR GAMBLERS, WITH BALLPLAYERS IN THE DEAL? Fullerton admitted he had no hard proof and did not even charge directly that the 1919 series had been fixed. But he did demand that baseball address the charges now engulfing it.

For his pains, Fullerton was shot at by a mysterious Chicago gunman and widely ridiculed by Comiskey and the baseball press. *The Sporting News,* of course, had its usual suspects—the Jews: "Because a lot of dirty, long-nosed, thick-lipped, and strong-smelling gamblers butted into the World Series—an American event, by the way—and some of said gentlemen got crossed, stories were peddled that there was something wrong with the way the games were played."

It was as if no one could quite believe what was right before their eyes. Nick Carraway, Fitzgerald's narrator in *The Great Gatsby,* reflected the prevailing credulity upon being told by Gatsby that the novel's Rothstein character, Meyer Wolfsheim, had put in the fix: "The idea staggered me. . . . It never occurred to me that one man could start to play with the faith of fifty million people—with the single-mindedness of a burglar blowing a safe."

Baseball's main response was to go about concealing its dirty laundry once again. This time, it was too much. The White Sox were back in the thick of the pennant race the following September, but now observers began to notice that Chicago lost every time the other contenders lost, won whenever they won. New rumors spread that the gamblers had so compromised the Chicago players in the World Series that they could make them do whatever they wanted.

Other long-drowned scandals began to bubble up, and an attempt to fix a routine game between the Phillies and the Cubs on August 31, 1920, went to a Chicago grand jury—the case pushed by Ban Johnson, now eager to demonstrate that corruption was not relegated to his American League. Giants pitcher Rube Benton was called to testify, and he told all about Hal Chase's attempts to fix games while he was on the Giants. Before long, the grand jury was looking into the World Series. One after another, the Black Sox were called upon to tell what they knew. Several of them began to confess. They were suspended before the end of the season, never to play in the major leagues again.

Hal Chase decided to stay in his native California and play with semipro outfits there in the hopes of being called up to the Pacific Coast League (PCL), the near-major league on the West Coast. He would never come east again, successfully fighting off an attempt to extradite him so he could appear before that Chicago grand jury. Prince Hal, it seemed, had beaten the system one more time. But the magician was missing his tricks now. Before the 1920 season was out, Chase managed to get himself banned from all PCL ballparks for orchestrating the worst gambling scandal in the league's history. Soon he was also banished from the Mission League, then even the San Joaquin Valley League.

So it would go for the last quarter century of his life, Chase sinking slowly through the lower fathoms of both baseball and general respectability, surfacing now and then for one more increasingly desperate hustle. In 1926, he tried to blackmail Aimee Semple McPherson, the radio evangelist—an epic battle of dueling frauds. But he was at a loss without any venue for his one legitimate talent. Chase talked periodically about trying to get back in the show, and he never was officially banned from the majors. But he never applied for reinstatement, and no one ever tried to sign him again.

By the time of his death in 1947, Prince Hal was a penniless alcoholic, estranged from his ex-wives and his only son, surviving on the kindness of strangers and his more distant relatives. His had become a life of spare bedrooms and drunk tanks, hospital beds and pool hall corners. Maybe he learned something. The interviews he gave to anyone who asked were peppered with words of remorse for his gambling, his womanizing, his game fixing. There was, in the end, at least some indication that he knew what he had lost—perhaps the worst punishment of all.

"When I die, movie magnates will make no picture like *Pride of the Yankees,* which honored that great player Lou Gehrig," he told *The Sporting News.* "I guess that's the answer, isn't it? Gehrig had a good name; one of the best a man could have. I am an outcast, and I haven't a good name. I'm the loser, just like all gamblers are."

Arnold Rothstein never figured himself a loser. The Brain had some tense moments as the secrets of the big fix unfolded, but Billy Fallon persuaded him to go to Chicago and face the grand jury head-on: "I want you to get on a train and walk right into the lion's den." Rothstein thought the Great Mouthpiece had gone bugsy, but listened to him in the end. He brazened it out before both the press and the grand jury, alternating between indignation and self-pity.

"I am in a position to prove conclusively that instead of profiting I lost heavily upon the outcomes of the games," Rothstein insisted. It was "Attell and some other cheap gamblers [who] decided to frame the Series and make a killing."

As soon as Attell and Burns told him of their scheme, Arnold claimed, he threw them out of his "office" and "told John J. McGraw . . . what had happened and asked him to notify 'Kid' Gleason, manager of the White Sox." The Brain was really the injured party here. "My friends know that I have never been connected with a crooked deal in my life," but he was so "heartily sick and tired of having my name dragged in" to any scandal that "I had made up my mind to retire from the gambling business." Rothstein insisted that he would now devote himself solely to his racing stable and his real estate interests. All the slanders had ruined his health and left him a "social outcast," but he was not so bereft that he couldn't issue an outright threat against the president of the American League: "Ban Johnson needs to watch his step: the most peaceful of men can be driven too far."

The grand jury failed to indict Rothstein, and somehow crucial evidence, including sworn player confessions, disappeared from the Illinois state attorney's office. For the crime of fixing the 1919 World Series, no one was convicted. Arnold Rothstein was free to turn his full attention to a lucrative rum-running operation made possible by the new Underworld Empowerment Act, otherwise known as Prohibition.

No doubt the saddest testimony before that Chicago grand jury came from John J. McGraw. It must have been a humiliation for Muggsy to have been called there, an indictment of how far his club had spun out of his control. Over the next four years, in the great shakeout that followed the Black Sox scandal, no fewer than six players and coaches from McGraw's 1919 roster were formally banned for life from organized baseball, and another three were unofficially blacklisted. If McGraw was shamed by this, though, he never gave any indication of it. He told the Chicago jurors that he had suspected Heinie Zimmerman and Hal Chase of throwing games, but he had no proof. He later claimed that he had chased both men out of baseball by offering them contracts so low that they disdained to return to the Giants, but this was a prevarication.

"In my opinion Chase deliberately threw us down," McGraw would admit sometime later. "I never was more deceived by a player than by Chase." And yet, even after the 1919 season, his contract offer to the first baseman was quite reasonable, considering his declining skills and playing time. Prince Hal had nailed his final pigeon.

"The Chase case gave many players the idea that they could play dishonestly and not be discovered, or if discovered or suspected, would be cleared," Hugh Fullerton would go on to write, blaming the Black Sox scandal on the absolution of Hal Chase before the season. "They believed the club owners feared publicity so much that they would be safe. The club owners have always adhered to the policy of secrecy and have whitewashed every scandal and charge of crooked work on the grounds that it was 'for the good of the game.' Their policy encouraged the crooked ball players and tempted the weak ones who until then had remained honest."

Christy Mathewson never did get to be manager of the New York Giants. By the winter of 1919–20 he was down to 150 pounds and was formally diagnosed with tuberculosis. This earned him $95 a month from the government's disability pension for disabled veterans and a spot in a sanatorium up at Saranac Lake. Treatment was a numbing regime in which the patient was largely forbidden to do anything that was deemed taxing, including reading, writing, walking, or talking.

"A fellow begins to feel that life is worth fighting for and to realize something of what it means to lose it," the Christian gentleman wrote. "Oddly, a fellow thinks less and less of himself and more and more of others. He has less dread of death. He sees that life is good and that death isn't bad at all."

Matty worked hard at recuperating and followed the doctors' orders. The would-be forester rekindled a keen interest in local botany and kept his chin firmly elevated for the sake of his wife and son. "It is a good old world," he wrote to Jane. He did a little hunting, worked on a "Big Six" board game, and made an occasional trip to the Polo Grounds, where he was mobbed. By the 1923 season, he had rallied enough for McGraw to use his Tammany connections and get him a job as president of the Boston Braves. On opening day, the two old friends embraced up at Braves Field.

Yet it was soon apparent that Matty wasn't even up to this titular position. He was forced back to Saranac Lake, getting away briefly to cover the 1924 World Series—the last World Series that McGraw would ever manage—and to visit the Giants' training camp the next spring in St. Petersburg. By the summer of 1925, though, he was obviously failing. For the press, he put out another jaunty release, keeping up his public image to the last: "Just say for me that I'll fan death again. He can't touch me, I'm sure of that."

To his wife he showed his real courage, telling her on his deathbed, "It's nearly over. I know it, and we must face it. Go out and have a good cry. Don't make it a long one. This is something we can't help."

He faded away for good at eleven o'clock on the night of October 7, 1925. The next day the news was announced at the second game of the World Series, in Pittsburgh.

"I do not expect to see the likes of Matty again," McGraw told reporters before leaving for his funeral. "Matty was my close friend. His passing is one of the great sorrows of my life. God rest his soul."

Muggsy was good at eulogies. The erudition the boy from Truxton had picked up in the big city shone through, but he had almost written one for the sport he loved. He had outlived his great friend and the best player he would ever manage. Now he would outlive as well the inside game that he loved—a game that he had, inadvertently, helped to kill.

Baseball was changing, would have to change in the wake of the Black Sox scandal, and Muggsy would have to change with it.

PART THREE

THE BABE IN NIGHTTOWN

1920–1929

From the first at-bat to the last old-cat
Was there ever a guy like Ruth?

—John Kieran

29

The City in the Air

In the portentous year of 1914, two teenage boys were released from juvenile institutions in two different southern cities. Louis Armstrong, just thirteen years old, had been sent to the Colored Waif's Home in New Orleans for firing a pistol into the air during a New Year's Eve celebration. George Herman Ruth, nineteen, had spent the better part of twelve years at the St. Mary's Industrial School for Orphans, Delinquent, Incorrigible, and Wayward Boys, for the crime of having parents unable to keep him away from the street life around the Baltimore docks.

Two young men, one Black, one white (perhaps), from the most humble backgrounds imaginable. Over the next few years, both of them would transform our popular culture. They would demonstrate in spectacular fashion the innate, creative power to be found in the American people. It was inevitable that before the 1920s were over, both young men would come to New York. Everybody else did.

Many fewer of them came from overseas. Antiradicalism and the fraudulent science of white supremacy, eugenics, had narrowed the torrent of immigrants through Ellis Island to a trickle by 1924. Congress slammed shut "the Golden Door" to almost all immigrants but those from "Nordic" European countries, who were deemed "scientifically" superior to all others. But no immigration law could stem the vast, *internal* migration to the city. More than two thousand men and women *a week* moved to New York in the 1920s, transforming the city's population once again and swelling it to more than seven million by the end of the decade. More than ever before—fleeing the Klan and Prohibition, Babbittry and Bryan—the best and the brightest, the wittiest and the most alienated, the most talented and the most ruthlessly ambitious, came to New York. With their help, the city would dominate the imagination of the whole world as it never had before, and never quite would again.

New York was now a city of not just one but many different whirlpools, many different, protean minglings of talent and energy. Choose your heaven. Up in Harlem, there was a renaissance. Down in the Village—also known as the Latin Quarter and Greenwich Thrillage—was a heady stew of radicals and bohemian artists: Max Eastman, Eugene O'Neill's Provincetown Players, Mabel Dodge's salon, Edna St. Vincent Millay and Katherine Porter, and Martha Graham proclaiming that "bodies never lie." Up on Broadway, there were no fewer than eighty-six live theaters between Twenty-Eighth and Fiftieth Streets by the end of the decade. They produced as many as 264 shows in a year, including works by O'Neill, Maxwell Anderson, George S. Kaufman, Robert Sherwood, Edna Ferber, Ben Hecht, and Charlie MacArthur. Just to the east, at the Algonquin Hotel, were the lunching wits of the Round Table, Dorothy Parker and Robert Benchley, Harold Ross and Alexander Woollcott, James Thurber and Will Rogers and Franklin Pierce Adams, escaped at last from the Polo Grounds press box.

The city was, as *The New Yorker* proclaimed in 1925, a "gymnasium of celebrities." It was the town of George Gershwin and Eubie Blake, Josephine Baker and Fanny Brice, Al Jolson and Fats Waller, Georgia O'Keeffe and Joseph Stella, A. Philip Randolph and Fiorello La Guardia, Jimmy Walker and Marcus Garvey, Ethel Waters and Ethel Merman. Even its gangsters lived by gaudy handles and crazy ambitions: Dutch Schultz and Lucky Luciano, Frankie Yale and Mad Dog Coll. At times the city seemed to run by hyperbole alone. New York was, in O'Neill's phrase, "a swirl of excited nothingness." To dean of commentators Walter Lippmann it was "a dissonance comprised of a thousand noises." To the city's new laureate, the young novelist F. Scott Fitzgerald, "the whole golden boom was in the air."

Sometimes this was literally so, as when the advertising guru Edward Bernays—a nephew of Freud, by now the reigning deity of the borough—put the first skywriting in the air above Manhattan in 1928 ("Smoke Lucky Strikes"). It was a city built for the sellers of smoke, revolving around the manipulation of money and ideas—a luftmensch metropolis, if you will. It was also remarkably modern. Manhattan, at least, had been deindustrializing since the end of the Civil War, when the great iron-mongering and shipbuilding concerns along the rivers were first squeezed out. It was a gradual process; by the 1920s the island still had 420,000 industrial workers, toiling in fifteen thousand factories and warehouses, but already *one-third* of the city's workforce could be defined as "white collar."

Instead of making physical products, as Ann Douglas points out in *Terrible Honesty: Mongrel Manhattan in the 1920s,* what the city specialized in was "packaging knowledge as information and dramatizing ideas as style." The city attracted "the country's best known musicians, composers, lyricists, and singers, its most important booking agencies, radio networks, recording studios and labels, and the theatrical enterprises in which songs, performers, and songwriters found their best showcase."

This synergy between performer and stage was vital. By the 1920s New York had begun to usurp the setters of fashion in Europe, its designers setting up shop cheek by jowl with the needle trades. It had lost most of the film industry to Hollywood, but by 1929 nearly a quarter of all American movies were still made in New York. They were shown in some eight hundred city movie theaters, many of them grand palaces that could each seat thousands of customers and that gave the magical new medium the setting it demanded, with full orchestras, cathedral-sized pipe organs, and fabulous interiors.

Soon a wholly new medium was emanating out of New York—appropriately, a medium of the air. In 1922, a local station broadcast the nation's first commercial radio ad (for real estate, of course). By 1926, David Sarnoff had lassoed some hundred stations into the National Broadcasting Company (NBC), the world's first radio network. Within three years it was reaching forty million listeners, pouring culture out into the nation. Now one could live almost anywhere, turn on a box, and hear the voices of the Metropolitan Opera, the strings of the New York Philharmonic, the big bands at the ballroom of the Waldorf Astoria (and even the World Series). The radio networks found a limitless source of content in the talent singing on New York's stages and in its clubs. They promoted in turn the more than $100 million worth of records the country was buying by 1921, the two billion copies of sheet music that sold every year in the city alone.

The boom was not confined to movies or radio. New York regularly invented and reinvented any number of entertainment industries in the years after World War I. Some six hundred magazines were published in the city, including *Time,* the first magazine to encapsulate the news of the week for those too busy to read a newspaper, and *Reader's Digest,* for those too busy or too distracted to read anything else. There were still *twenty* daily New York papers, where characters as diverse as Heywood Broun, Walter Lippmann, FPA, and a young Walter Winchell—writing "like a man honking in a traffic jam"—invented the modern editorial, society, and gossip columns. Winchell got his start at probably the most outrageous paper of all, the hilarious New York *Graphic,* which featured "cosmographs" of cut-and-paste, clearly fraudulent photomontages that might fairly be said to have invented camp. The slightly less sensationalist *Daily News,* billing itself as New York's "illustrated newspaper" and composed mostly of enormous headlines and photographs, instantly commanded a circulation of 1.5 million on weekdays and more than 3 million on Sundays—figures it would maintain for most of the next sixty years.

"Madison Avenue" was already a euphemism for the booming ad game, which was doing $3 billion worth of business by the end of the decade and battened on the city's inexhaustible supply of aspiring writers and artists. Parker, Edward Steichen, and Fitzgerald—eager to eat while pinning 122 rejection notices to the walls of his Claremont Avenue apartment—all worked apprenticeships in the selling biz.

"The whole world revolves around New York," pronounced another newcomer named Duke Ellington. "Very little happens anywhere unless someone in New York presses a button."

It was a life fueled by alcohol and speed, hard, exciting, and unrelentingly competitive. Despite—or rather, *because of*—Prohibition, there were at least 32,000 and perhaps as many as 100,000 speakeasies, blind tigers, blind pigs, "drugstores," or other illegal drinking establishments. By the late 1920s there were nearly 800,000 cars careening around the town—more than in the entire continent of Europe. Everyone in New York was in a hurry to get somewhere, probably to have a drink. The next sensation was always just around the corner, possibly waiting with a blackjack.

"There is nothing else in all the countries of the world like New York life. . . . It does more to people, it socks them harder than life in Paris, London or Rome possibly could," wrote James Thurber, who took New York as hard as anyone. The city's sensuality was visceral, something Fitzgerald captured in *The Great Gatsby:*

> I began to like New York, the racy, adventurous feel of it at night, and the satisfaction that the constant flicker of men and women and machines gives to the restless eye. I liked to walk up Fifth Avenue and pick out romantic women from the crowd and imagine that in a few minutes I was going to enter into their lives, and no one would ever know or disapprove. Sometimes, in my mind, I followed them to their apartments on the corners of hidden streets, and they turned and smiled back at me before they faded through a door into warm darkness.

"What the city could not supply, it could attract, seduce, and control," wrote Ann Douglas. "You 'made it' in New York, and everyone who was anyone knew it."

This was as true for sport as for any other entertainment, and the 1920s were the era in American life when any number of sports came into their own—when they, too, became a gymnasium of celebrities. The gods of the time are almost deadened by cliché: Jack Dempsey and Benny Leonard in boxing; Red Grange and Knute Rockne in college football; Bill Tilden and Helen Wills Moody in tennis; Bobby Jones in golf; the jockey Earl Sande, immortalized in Damon Runyon's verse as "a handy / Guy like Sande / Bootin' the babies in"; Gertrude Ederle swimming the English Channel; that greatest of nonhuman stars, the racehorse Man o' War. Even polo, for the first and only time in its history, produced a popular star in the war hero Tommy Hitchcock Jr.

Whole new professional sports, such as basketball and ice hockey, could be viewed uptown at Harlem's Renaissance Casino or down at the new Madison Square Garden. They had to be seen in the city to have any credibility. It was New York that provided the biggest newspapers, the most colorful sportswriters, the new radio broadcasters to bring it to the rest of the nation, enlarge it to a scale no one had ever seen before. It was here that the biggest college football games were usually played, in the vast reaches of the Polo Grounds or Yankee Stadium. It was here that the only American tennis tournament of significance was held late every summer, out in posh Forest Hills. Here where the biggest prizefights were arranged for the close, smoke-clogged atmosphere of the Garden, or out in the open at the ballparks, or in the enormous stadium thrown up overnight for Dempsey's record-setting gate against the French champion, Georges Carpentier, out in Jersey City.

That afternoon, July 2, 1921, might have been the apogee of the era, early as it was—at least when it came to sports. Dempsey thrashed Carpentier in four rounds at the center of the vast, jerry-built arena erected in Boyle's Thirty Acres—the pinewood planking so fresh that sap still oozed out of it in the broiling, summer heat—but missing from the unprecedented crowd of nearly ninety thousand was one of the champ's most ardent fans. Babe Ruth had to play baseball that afternoon before another huge mob up at the Polo Grounds. He went three for five in a doubleheader, with two home runs, three walks, and a stolen base, but hurried down to Manhattan afterward to celebrate with his pal Dempsey, two gods out on a spree.

"Beyond their accomplishments as performers, Dempsey and Ruth, c. 1920, were becoming commercial properties as no athletes had ever been," Roger Kahn wrote in his biography of the fighter, *A Flame of Pure Fire.* "It was not simply that they earned more money than their predecessors (or their contemporaries); the scale of their earning changed the dimensions of American sport."

Dempsey was a frightening puncher, another self-made man who captured the imagination of the public, and Kahn rated him "more prominent than any of his great sporting contemporaries," largely on the basis of the fabulous crowds and purses his fights would draw. But these were rare events, held sporadically throughout the decade, and boxing would never quite escape its association with the underworld or the queasy elements inherent in its nature, the spectacle of a proud man beaten bloody or unconscious before cheering throngs.

Baseball, by contrast, was still the national game, played every day by everybody, and it was Ruth who would drag it *out* of the mud. Countless more fans saw Babe Ruth play, either in a major-league game or in one of his endless barnstorming tours, than ever watched Jack Dempsey box, and in the end it's likely that the Babe outearned the Manassa Mauler, too. That's no rap on Jack. *None* of the new gods quite compared to Ruth. None of them so captured the public imagination. None of them—no other professional athlete, anywhere—transformed their sport the way that Ruth did his, merely by switching positions. Never had the man, the moment, and the city been so well met.

30

The Babe

It was always Babe Ruth's town, even before he got there. Its blatant exhibitionism, its rampant excesses, were ready-made for him. This was the New York of all-night bacchanals down in the Village's Webster Hall, "the Devil's Playhouse"; where twenty-four-hour Charleston "sprees" took place up at Roseland. It was the New York of Texas Guinan, the flamboyant speakeasy hostess who famously greeted her customers with "Hello, suckers!" and wore a necklace made out of miniature gold padlocks to symbolize all the times her clubs had been raided. It was the New York of the boulevardier and con man Wilson Mizner, who coined the phrase "Never give a sucker an even break"; the New York where Mae West starred in a Broadway hit with the bald-faced title of *Sex*.

It was the New York where—in between indulging her other addictions of reading compulsively and eating hot fudge sundaes—the teenage showgirl sensation Louise Brooks (nicknamed Louise Brooks No Restraint) could announce "I like to drink and fuck," and do both as blatantly as possible. One memorable weekend in 1925—when she was still just eighteen—Brooks, her much older lover, Charlie Chaplin, and their friends the showgirl Peggy Fears and the movie financier A. C. Blumenthal sequestered themselves in a hotel suite for an epic, three-day orgy.

The Babe liked to eat and drink and fuck, too, even if he wasn't so big on reading. (He claimed the only book he ever read through was the ghosted *Babe Ruth's Own Book of Baseball.* When a writer doubted him, he snapped, "Goddammit, I read it *twice*!") In fact, he liked to do almost everything, all the time, and on a scale that would have made Rabelais blush. He started his day with a bourbon and ginger ale, followed by a breakfast of a dozen eggs, a pound of bacon, and a loaf of bread. Lunch was six hot dogs eaten just before the game, although he might send the clubhouse boy out for more if he got hungry between innings. A large dinner followed, along with a supper of sandwiches prior to his 4:00 a.m. bedtime, and all of it washed down with countless gallons of beer, soda pop, bicarbonate of soda, and pitchers of iced tea drunk in one long gulp—tea, ice cubes, lemon slices, and all.

He carried thousands of dollars around on his person, just in case he saw something he wanted. He would change his silk shirts six or seven times a day, up in his eleven-room suite at the Ansonia—and maybe his custom-made silk underpants as well. He might also crash one of the monogrammed maroon 12-cylinder Packard touring cars he owned, or answer some of the two hundred letters a day he received—though he had people who did that for him, under instructions to put aside only checks and "letters from broads."

His sexual endurance would have made him a perfect playmate for Ms. Brooks. The Babe was said to have rented out entire whorehouses on the road for a night; the ladies revived him for another round by pouring champagne over his head. Not one but *two* teammates, eleven years apart, Ping Bodie and Jimmie Reese, said, "I don't room with Ruth, I room with his suitcase." His teammate Earle Combs remembered being ordered to stay in New York for a week after the end of the season by Ruth, and to buy up some freshly killed game at a specialty market. Ruth had told his wife that he was going hunting in North Carolina. Instead, he holed up in an apartment for three days with a pair of women, then brought in another pair for *another* three days. On finally emerging, he had Combs attach the dead animals to his touring car and was proudly photographed showing off the trophies of his "hunting trip."

"Can I go home now?" asked Combs.

Another teammate recalled playing cards with the Babe while they waited for their train to leave the station. A beautiful young woman with a baby on one arm kept walking up and down the platform, staring at Ruth through an open window.

"Better get away from here, lady," Ruth growled at her at last. "I'll put one in the other arm." It was a rare moment of Ruthian restraint. On a later trip, a woman chased a naked Ruth through the team train with a knife. It was the first time, his teammates joked, that Babe Ruth had ever run away from a girl.

These were only some of his appetites, in a life that seemed as if it were lived in frantic fast motion, like one of the silent movie comedies now filling the big screen. Ruth actually made several such comedies, including *Speedy,* the last feature to star the silent great Harold Lloyd. Why not? He did everything else. When he wasn't playing ball, he was touring the vaudeville circuit, hunting, golfing, chasing women, chasing booze. Fitzgerald's Gatsby stood on the dock and pined over Daisy Buchanan's green light at East Egg; the Babe would have dived right in and swum for it. A granddaughter later guessed that he had what would now be considered attention deficit hyperactivity disorder: "That's how he could eat so much, drink so much, and not be affected. He needed the energy. He would just burn it all off." No doubt she is right, but it seemed like the speed of normal life in 1920s New York.

Babe Ruth played more baseball games than anyone ever had before—at least any *white* major leaguer—and more than anyone probably has since, when you throw in all his barnstorming and exhibition tours. He made more money than any player ever had, endorsed more products, smashed up more cars, signed more autographs, shook more hands, romped with more kids, had more fun. He was the personification of the great American *more*—"our national exaggeration," as the sportswriter W. O. McGeehan labeled him. He was such a mythic figure that even the reactions to him sound apocryphal. When the venerable Yankees clubhouse man, Pete Sheehy, pointed out Ruth's locker to the rookie Don Mattingly in 1983, the Indiana-born Mattingly stared at him, incredulous.

"You mean Babe Ruth was real?" he asked Sheehy, a story that in itself sounds too good to be true, save for the many times that Mattingly has patiently affirmed it: "Honestly, at one time I thought Babe Ruth was a cartoon character. I really did."

How could one blame him? The Babe's longtime teammate Waite Hoyt put it best: "All the lies about Ruth are true."

He was, to begin with, the most important athlete in history. Others, notably Pelé, Muhammad Ali, Michael Jordan, have starred in more universally popular sports, become better known around the world. But it was Babe Ruth—even more than Dempsey—who first made professional sports big time, with all that would follow from that, everywhere. We still have trouble accepting this largely because the surviving Ruth—the Ruth we see on blurry, out-of-sync newsreels, usually near the end of his career—looks more like a Santa Claus figure than an athlete. Mincing around the bases with his peculiar, pigeon-toed stride, endlessly grinning and doffing his cap, his huge gut hanging over his belt. How could this man possibly have been an athlete, much less the greatest one there ever was?

The rare footage of the younger Ruth provides a different image: a sleek, muscular, six two and 185 pounds, tearing around the bases like a wild bull, a disturbing gleam in his eye. By the time he was twenty-one years old, he was the best left-handed pitcher in the major leagues, and he would win three-quarters of his decisions going head-to-head against the best right-hander, Walter Johnson. By the time he was twenty-three, he would hold a record for consecutive scoreless innings in the World Series by a pitcher—a record that would stand for forty-three years. When he turned his hand to playing every day in the outfield, he set records for home runs in a World Series, in a season, in a career; for on-base percentage, and slugging percentage, and walks, and extra-base hits, and runs batted in. In two separate seasons, he hit more home runs than any other single *team* in the American League. He was the first man ever to collect more than a hundred extra-base hits in a season, the first in the modern game to run up on-base percentages of over .500, or slugging averages of over .700—the only man ever to do it without the aid of all those performance-enhancing substances. (Beer does not count.)

How good was Ruth, truly?

"He was *better* than his legend suggests," insists Bill Jenkinson, a baseball historian who has meticulously tracked Ruth's career. "His real-life accomplishments transcend his myth."

The very gaudiness of the numbers suggests an era that was fundamentally different from ours, one in which conditions were so altered as to make all statistical comparisons meaningless. Baseball players today are undoubtedly bigger, faster, stronger than they were nearly a hundred years ago (if less polished or versatile, due in part to their shorter stays in the minor leagues). The Babe never had to deal with air travel, crossing multiple time zones, night baseball, specialty relief pitchers, or the constant probe of the internet. Almost no one threw as hard as they do today—but then, batters faced baseballs without body armor, or even helmets. And Ruth did play in an era of twenty-seven-hour Pullman car rides, of infinitely more primitive sports medicine and training, much more rudimentary facilities, and heavy, itchy, woolen uniforms. (The only sort of climate control the Babe knew was the wet cabbage leaf he put under his cap on extremely hot days, much to the amusement of fans and teammates.) He played at a time when teams scheduled exhibition games on "off days" *during* the season, before legions of newspaper reporters, who would and did write critically about every aspect of his life including, as Jenkinson notes, his "speeding tickets, traffic accidents, paternity suits, fishing and hunting without a license, violations of the child labor laws (he brought a child on stage during a vaudeville show)."

So how good was Babe Ruth?

Take home runs, his stock-in-trade. According to Jenkinson, Ruth hit at least 198 home runs of 450 feet or more. By way of comparison, Barry Bonds hit 36 shots of such length, and Mark McGwire, 74, even with their steroid-enabled bodies. Even more of the Babe's best shots died deep in the outfield; fences in Ruth's time averaged 28 feet *farther* from home plate than they are in major-league parks today. The Yankees tried to correct for this by building the Babe his own short porch next to the right-field foul pole in Yankee Stadium. But the Babe hit most of his balls into the power alleys, particularly *left* center, and he lost an estimated three home runs in the alleys for every one he dunked into the porch in The House That Ruth Built.

Beyond the disadvantage provided by the canyon-esque dimensions of the parks he played in, and a babble of idiosyncratic ground rules, *and* the fact that he spent the first five years of his career primarily as a pitcher, Ruth was uniquely victimized by a bizarre regulation. Under the rules of the time, umpires could decide that a ball hit out of the park entirely *would have* landed in foul territory, no matter where it actually left the field of play. Ruth was penalized again and again by this strange judgment call, hitting balls out of the park and out of sight, only to have an umpire give his considered opinion that they would have curved foul in, oh, the parking lot, or possibly Westchester.

So, given today's park dimensions and rules, how many home runs would Babe Ruth have hit? Jenkinson estimates 1,158, as opposed to the 714 he did hit in the regular season, and 23 in the World Series, as opposed to the 15 he swatted in the postseason. These totals would have included 86 home runs in 1920, 91 in 1927, and a ridiculous 104 in 1921; six seasons, altogether, in which he would have matched or exceeded Bonds's dubious record of 73 in a single campaign.

Babe Ruth was *that* good?

All speculation, of course. But how much more unbelievable is it than what we know Ruth *did* do, which was to alter the very nature of his game as no athlete has done before or since?

There are no comparable transformations. No all-star linebacker, say, who switched to quarterback and then began hurling so many ninety-yard touchdown passes that they changed the rules of football. No basketball guard who moved to center, then began to throw in so many half-court shots that they moved the hoop.

The Babe brought change overnight, and all by himself, just as his fellow New Yorkers were breezily altering architecture, music, theater, dance, radio, newspapers, and advertising. He did it in a fantastic manner, just like the other exhibitionists in his adopted city, hitting balls in gigantic, awesome parabolas, often out of sight. Baseball by

1920 had been critically wounded by how its proprietors had handled the war years, by the creeping corruption they had allowed to fester until the Black Sox scandal wrecked the 1919 World Series. By almost miraculous coincidence, Ruth was just then coming into his own, hitting the long ball that would sweep away the old, dead-ball game, the *inside game,* forever.

The key, as with all great performers, was timing. The Babe hit a record-breaking home run in his first *at bat* as a professional ballplayer. He hit .422 before the huge, baseball-starved crowds on opening day. He pitched and won the first major-league game he ever appeared in. He pitched and won the longest World Series game in history until 2018—all fourteen innings of it. He is one of only four men ever to hit three home runs in a single World Series game—and he did it twice. He hit the first home run in Yankee Stadium, The House That Ruth Built. He hit the first home run ever in the All-Star Game, hit a home run on his controversial "called shot." He hit a home run the day he married his second wife, with her in the stands cheering him on. He really did knock the cover off the ball, once opening up a two-inch gash in the horsehide. He really did promise to hit a home run for a critically ill boy in a hospital room. He hit the home run, and the boy really did get better.

He seemed to be at his best in the biggest games, on the biggest stages. After setting his scoreless-innings streak and going undefeated as a pitcher in two World Series, he hit under .300 in only one of the seven World Series he played in as a position player. In his last five World Series, a total of twenty-five games, he belted fourteen home runs.

Even his screwups tended to be colossal. He is the only man ever to be thrown out stealing to end a World Series. When he missed seven weeks with a mysterious ailment in 1925, it became "the bellyache heard round the world." Annoyed by an umpire's strike zone when he walked a batter to begin a game in 1915, he flattened the arbiter with a punch. He was tossed from the game, replaced on the mound by Ernie Shore. The man on first was thrown out stealing, and Shore went on to pitch the only perfect game of its kind in baseball history.

He brought to the game a charisma that no other athlete, then or now, could match, beginning with his classic pop face, "round and joyous, an invitation to the dance," as one writer would put it.

"Who has ever looked like him since Babe Ruth? Try to think of someone who looked like him," demanded Bill Gleason. "It's like he was created for this role that he was given, and he played it to the hilt."

It was a face that proved irresistible to photographers, and never—not even in the brazen New York of the 1920s—was a celebrity so willing to oblige them. As Ed Linn lists, there are pictures of him posing in cowboy gear and formal wear, boxing trunks and swimming trunks, golfing togs and football uniforms, derbies and Indian headdresses and endless crowns: "He posed with gorillas, with chimpanzees, and with lions. He posed riding horses and heifers. . . . He posed with leading musicians, blowing whatever musical instrument was shoved at him. He posed aiming a rifle, playing pool, drinking booze. He posed with everybody, and he endorsed almost everything."

Little boys found him even more irresistible than the women and the shutterbugs did. They mobbed him for autographs, sat with him in the stands, where he sometimes signed autographs between games of a doubleheader, romped with him in the outfield, clung to his arms and his bat even as he ran around the bases. He always indulged them. *The New York Times* described a spring training game in Waco, Texas, when, in the fifth inning, some three hundred children, "most of them barefooted and in overalls, charged out on rightfield and surrounded Ruth." For the rest of the game, "he gamboled on the grass, rolled on his back, and let the kids climb all over him."

When the Yankees played in Philadelphia, the team would leave the train at North Broad Street station and walk the five blocks to Shibe Park. When they did, a cry would go out: "Babe Ruth is coming! Babe Ruth is coming!" Adults would go to the windows to see, and the neighborhood children would surround him. He would arrive at the park laughing and waving, carrying a child or two in his arms or on his back.

Perhaps most remarkable of all, his fellow ballplayers felt much the same way about him. Somehow, Ruth seems to have played big-league ball for twenty-two seasons without making an enemy (with the possible exception of Leo Durocher, whom the Babe once accused, probably with cause, of stealing his watch from the Yankees' locker room). Even Ty Cobb, a rival who groused endlessly about how Ruth "took all the science out of the game," became a lifelong friend.

"Both teammates and opponents of Ruth vividly remember the times when they played with or against him. To be able to say that they played in a game with Babe Ruth gives them a special pride and satisfaction," found Lawrence S. Ritter and Mark Rucker. "In their old age it is apparent that they believe just having been on the same field with him validates their own careers, indeed to some extent their own lives."

"You know, I saw it all happen from beginning to end. But sometimes I still can't believe what I saw: this 19-year-old kid, crude, poorly educated, only lightly brushed by the social veneer we call civilization, gradually transformed into the idol of American youth and the symbol of baseball the world over—a man loved by more people and with an intensity of feeling that has perhaps never been equaled before or since," the superb Red Sox outfielder and Ruth teammate Harry Hooper told Ritter. "I saw a man transformed from a human being into something pretty close to a god."

Like all the best legends, especially baseball legends, he came out of nowhere. Ruth's origins were poor and working class, just like those other two Yankee outfield immortals, Joe DiMaggio, the son of an immigrant fisherman from California, and Mickey Mantle, the son of an Oklahoma lead miner. Between them, their careers in the city would span an amazing arc of forty-six seasons, during which time they would play on a total of twenty-nine pennant winners and twenty world champions. All three men were fragile in the field, prone to debilitating leg injuries. All had a flair for dramatic comebacks, for seizing the moment, and all three would come a long way to star in New York. But no one came quite so far as the Babe.

"He will be the patron saint of American possibility," wrote Leigh Montville, one of his later, and best, biographers. "His success will be a lottery ticket in every empty pocket. If he can do it, then why can't I? Or why can't my kids? He grew up worse than all of us . . . look at him now."

Unlike DiMaggio and Mantle, who at least hailed from intact families, the Babe had been all but abandoned to his fate. Until he was seven, Ruth lived in the rough Baltimore waterfront district known as Pigtown—at one point on what is now the field of Camden Yards.

His mother was dead of "exhaustion" by thirty-nine; his father, a lightning-rod salesman (!) and saloon keeper, would die in a brawl outside the bar the Babe had bought him, aged forty-five. Only one of his seven siblings lived very long, and for much of his life Ruth—just like Louis Armstrong—did not know his own birth day and year. As Montville writes, it's as if a fog settles in whenever one tries to delve too deeply into this past.

A few things can be deduced, even through the fog. The prodigious appetites came from a childhood of deprivation, both material and emotional. Ruth's parents seemed utterly unable to control him. He skipped school, shoplifted from local stores, threw rocks at deliverymen, and had his first shot of whiskey and chaw of tobacco by the time he was eight years old. His mother and father beat him brutally, then handed him over to St. Mary's and had little more to do with him. A fellow inmate would recall that no one ever visited the boy: "Babe would kid me and say 'Well I guess I am too big and ugly for anyone to come to see me. Maybe next time.' But next time never came." Ruth told another friend, "I think my mother hated me."

St. Mary's is usually depicted as the salvation of the lad. This is true. What's less understood is how Dickensian life at the institution actually was. The school was a complex of grim gray massive buildings, surrounded by a wall and iron gates, and in many ways it was run more like a prison than an orphanage. The eight hundred boys lived in barracks, two hundred to a floor, in beds placed end to end. They marched everywhere, were not allowed to talk during meals, were beaten with heavy leather straps for the smallest infractions, and were sometimes placed in solitary confinement. Breakfast was oatmeal or hominy grits, which is to say gruel. Lunch and dinner were soup and bread. The only exceptions were three small hot dogs and a pat of butter on Friday, and three slices of bologna on Sunday. There was little academic instruction; the main emphasis was on learning a vocational trade, and along with working real industrial hours, the boys themselves maintained the grounds and buildings, cooked the meals, and sewed their own clothing. To the end of his career, teammates would remember the adult Babe taking up a needle and thread to nimbly mend a shirt.

Many graduates, including Ruth's fellow future New York celebrity Al Jolson, hated the place. Fortunately for young George Ruth,

St. Mary's was practically a baseball factory. The school fielded no fewer than twenty-eight uniformed teams for all ages and abilities, and even produced its own baseballs in the machine shop. Boys—if they could—worked their way up the ladder to the top "Stars" team, which took on local high schools and colleges. As such, the system taught Ruth his vocation much as it taught other St. Mary's boys to be carpenters, shirtmakers, and steamfitters. He played every position, and often with a right-hander's glove, an experience that left the young southpaw almost ambidextrous. The Xaverian brothers who ran the school played alongside the boys. Their number included a massive, six-foot-six, three-hundred-pound native of Cape Breton, Brother Matthias Boutlier, whom all his charges looked up to and tried to emulate. It was from Brother Matthias that Ruth got his pigeon-toed stride, and perhaps as well the massive upswing that the brother used to hit countless fungoes.

This last is uncertain—at other times, Ruth said he modeled his swing after Shoeless Joe Jackson's, or that "I could always hit, but Brother Matthias taught me how to field"—but what was beyond dispute was that Ruth came out of St. Mary's a remarkably polished ballplayer. Signed to a $600 contract on Valentine's Day 1914 by Jack Dunn, the owner and manager of the International League Baltimore Orioles, he seemed so young and raw that his teammates dubbed him Babe the moment he set foot on a field.

Yet he was no novice. In his very first at bat with the Orioles, in an intra-squad game at Fayetteville, North Carolina, Ruth hit a 435-foot blast into a cornfield past the fence in right, breaking the record that another legend, the Olympian Jim Thorpe, had set for the longest home run at the field. Eleven days later, Ruth took the mound and pitched three shutout innings versus the Phillies. Eight days after that, he pitched a complete-game victory against Connie Mack's Philadelphia Athletics, the defending world champions, giving up just two runs. In an exhibition game against Casey Stengel's Brooklyn Dodgers, he so surprised Stengel with a long drive to center that Casey backed up considerably for his next at bat. Ruth still hit a triple over his head.

So it went. Pitching that first season in a top minor league and for the Boston Red Sox, Ruth won a combined total of twenty-four games. After he won the first game he pitched in the majors, it was put out that he was sent down to the International League for "more seasoning," but as his crusty manager, Bill Carrigan, later admitted, he was plenty seasoned: "He was already a finished pitcher, good enough for us or anybody else. But we were out of our pennant race and [the minor-league Providence Grays needed] to win theirs."

So they did, and soon Ruth was back in the show and running up ERAs that were at least half a run lower than the league's average, *and* batting and slugging averages that were seventy points higher. On a ball field, he could and would stand up to anyone, right from the start. Facing Walter Johnson in one of their epic duels, he went five for five at the plate, with three long doubles and a triple. When Ty Cobb came barreling in on Ruth when he was covering third, determined to spike him, the Babe nimbly dodged Cobb's cleats and tagged him so hard he knocked the Georgia Peach unconscious.

Off the ball field, he was considerably less mature. A teammate remembered that "when they let him out, it was like turning a wild animal out of a cage." He freely used roommates' toothbrushes, raced elevators up and down the floors of the team's hotels, spent his first paycheck to buy himself a bicycle, and married a sixteen-year-old coffee shop waitress he met the day he came to Boston. Soon he was buying motorcycles, then automobiles, and crashing them with frightening regularity. From time to time, his sense of fun interfered with his ability to give his very best effort at the park—not that it much mattered.

He could have had a second straight year with an ERA under 2.00 in 1917, but in the last inning of a game late in the year the Babe entertained a large crowd of soldiers he had met and brought to the park by deliberately surrendering three runs, before closing out the contest. His record World Series scoreless-innings streak might have been extended even further, but the day before his final start in the 1918 series the Babe decided to entertain himself by going through cars on the team train, smashing the crown of every straw hat he saw. The next day the knuckles of his pitching hand were bruised and swollen, and he gave up two runs, but won the game anyway.

Such incidents left the impression that he was a natural, or a freak of nature. Near the height of his career a couple of sportswriters prevailed on Ruth to undergo a thorough physical exam at Columbia

University, in order to see if he had any special physical advantage. All they found was that Ruth had above-average coordination, eyesight, and reaction times—to be expected in any major-league baseball player—and a six-to-seven-inch chest expansion, a figure that was more than three times the chest expansion of the average man but that counted to who-knows-what advantage on a baseball diamond.

Lost in all the lore of his "natural" ability is how much Babe Ruth *worked* at being a ballplayer—an ethic carried over from St. Mary's. At the peak of his career, he used a fifty-four-ounce bat, a hickory stick so enormous and top-heavy that contemporary ballplayers, used to the thirty-three-ounce, whip-handled, hollow-ended bats of the modern game, just shake their heads in disbelief when they pick it up at Cooperstown. Bats in Ruth's day were routinely forty-seven to forty-eight ounces. But even his contemporaries called the Babe's stick "the monstrous weapon." Where they were trying to use their bats just to make contact and nudge the ball through some pebbly infield, Ruth had figured out a way to swing for the fences.

"I copied my swing after Joe Jackson's. His is the perfect test," the Babe once told Grantland Rice. "Joe aims his right shoulder square at the pitcher, with his feet about twenty inches apart. But I close my stance to about eight-and-a-half inches or less. I find I pivot better with it closed. Once committed . . . once my swing starts, though, I can't change it or pull up. It's all or nothing at all."

There it is, the transition from the inside game to the power game of baseball, figured out to the half inch, in so thoughtful a soliloquy on hitting that it might have come from Ted Williams.

Ruth didn't think only about the game. He hired trainers during the offseason and ran, hiked, shadowboxed, and played golf—or at least he did until the Yankees, worried about his delicate legs, idiotically forbade him to engage in almost any form of exercise, thereby atrophying his body and probably shortening his career. As it was, he remained a dangerous hitter until he retired at forty. In his early years he was an excellent bunter and base stealer, and hit to all fields. He hit for the seventh-highest lifetime average of anyone who played their entire career after 1900 and came within four hits of batting .400 in 1923. He never struck out as many as a hundred times in a season. He stole home ten times in his career and hit ten inside-the-park home runs. He bunted for a hit at least forty-two times, including six bunt hits in a single monthlong stretch in 1921—the same year he broke his own home-run record again.

No less than Tris Speaker called Ruth "one of the half-dozen greatest outfielders I ever saw"—a sentiment echoed by many of those who played with and against him. Newspapers regularly held forth about his canny positioning, his rifle arm, and his "spectacular" catches in the outfield. He covered enough ground to finish as high as fourth in the American League in putouts in his halcyon season of 1921, surpassed by only three centerfielders. In 1923, he was third in putouts, along with throwing out twenty runners on the bases and swiping seventeen bags himself.

He was always honing his skills, even when he was showing off. Before games, Ruth and his equally strong-armed teammate Bullet Bob Meusel used to entertain fans by laying a towel over home plate and seeing how often they could hit it on the fly from deep in the outfield. Other times, Ruth and Meusel would play long catch across the outfield, with each of them using his non-throwing arm.

"When he was in a slump, he'd choke up a little on the bat, shorten his swing, and practice hitting to left," wrote Ed Linn. "He'd also pitch early batting practice and sometimes even put on the catching tools and go behind the plate to enable himself to get back the feel and rhythm of the thing."

For such a prodigious talent, for such a restless spirit, the role of being a starting pitcher, of appearing on the field only every three or four days, was soon inadequate. By 1918, while still winning thirteen games in the war-shortened season, Ruth was playing often enough in the field to tie for the league lead in home runs, with all of eleven—a standard mark at the time. The following season—1919, the plague year—he set the major-league record for home runs with twenty-nine, or two to three times the usual league-leading number. Ruth did this in another shortened season. Hitting the moldering, old "dead ball"—with so little spring in it, gray, and almost never replaced by the end of a game. Playing in a Fenway that then featured such distant outfield fences that he hit only nine of his round-trippers at home. The Babe was ready for something more.

—

By now, it was not just the pitching mound that made an inadequate stage. It was all of Boston. Most particularly his Red Sox team, which had won three of the previous four World Series but had fallen to sixth place. But it was Boston, too. The onetime intellectual hub of the nation had become a backwater, an often provincial, narrow-minded city, riven by the destructive conflict between its economically conservative Brahmins and its socially conservative Irish.

By 1919, Boston was a visibly tattered town, marred by both municipal corruption and parsimony, embarrassed by a tumultuous police strike and a catastrophic factory explosion that buried nearly forty people under a four-story-high landslide of molasses. Its gallery of municipal rogues, both Irish and Yankee, ranged from the Kennedy forefather John "Honey Fitz" Fitzgerald, to the immortal James Michael Curley, to Mayor Andrew Peters, who kept a prepubescent mistress—the tragic Starr Faithfull—on the side. Intellectually, the city on the hill's light was extinguished by a troglodyte Catholicism. The phrase "banned in Boston" had become a byword—and a selling point—for any controversial new book, play, or film.

None of this had a direct effect on Ruth. It wasn't that the Babe yearned for more intellectually stimulating theater or cleaner civic government. But all of these factors had combined to make Boston a place where the zeitgeist wasn't, to make it a small-time town, little different in outlook and excitement from his native Baltimore; a town where the Louise Brookses—and the Jack Dempseys, and the Duke Ellingtons, and the Satchmos of the world—never dreamed of settling. The Babe was never a small-time ballplayer. Of course he had to move on. All that was required was someone to set a better stage.

31

The Big Money

"Culture follows money," F. Scott Fitzgerald told Edmund Wilson at the start of the decade. Therefore, New York would presently replace London as the "capital of culture."

Fitzgerald was right. The nation's—and now the world's—money flowed to New York as never before. The war had been an incalculable boon to the city. Some 4.5 million tons of supplies had shipped out of its port to provision the American Expeditionary Force in Europe, and much of that had been manufactured right in town. Before World War I, the United States already produced over a third of the world's goods and services, or more than Germany, England, and France combined. *During* the war, corporate profits tripled, producing forty-two thousand new millionaires in America, most of them in the New York area.

But where "the Big Money," as John Dos Passos dubbed it, was really being made was down on Wall Street. Between just 1915 and 1918, America went from being the world's biggest debtor nation to the world's sole creditor. Following a severe postwar slump, the great bull market started gaining momentum in 1923 and stampeded on through the rest of the decade.

It was a period of easy and often funny money that overflowed the Street and floated any number of promoters, hustlers, and newly minted millionaires. Some were simply business sharps, like Joe Kennedy, prowling the Wall Street markets for killings. Others were outright con men, such as Wilson Mizner and Dickie Whitney, brother of a powerful Morgan partner, who would later be found to have used his post as president of the New York Stock Exchange to embezzle from everyone, including (literally) widows and orphans.

Most occupied a middle ground, like that other 1920s fixture, the Florida land salesman, teetering right on the edge of the law. They tended to be men of many parts, none of them too upstanding, and an inordinate number gravitated to the new growth industry that was sports. Men like C. C. "Cash and Carry" Pyle, the moustachioed manager of a Champaign, Illinois, movie house who noticed that a back at the local university named Red Grange ran like nobody anyone had ever seen before and was soon negotiating with a former Yankees outfielder, George Halas, for half of his football team. (When Pyle didn't get what he wanted from Halas, he started his own pro football team and his own league around the Galloping Ghost.) Men like Jack "Doc" Kearns, Jack Dempsey's manager, who bankrupted pretty much the entire state of Montana with a single fight, or Tex Rickard, Dempsey's promoter and a gambler, prospector, speculator, and sleaze who founded the New York Rangers hockey team and built the first Boston Garden.

Or like Harry H. Frazee, yet another hustler from the hinterlands who found his way to New York, in those days when it seemed as if they must have been running special grifter trains into Grand Central every hour on the hour. Frazee began *his* working life as a theater usher and bellhop from Peoria, Illinois (What *was* it about Illinois theaters that so tempted men to scheme?), and produced his first smash on the Great White Way in 1910, at the tender age of thirty. He followed that success with four more hits, all of them frothy musicals or comedies. Along the way he acquired the Cort Theater in Chicago, the Longacre Theatre on Broadway, stocks and real estate, and wrestlers and boxers, assorted. He kept a string of actress mistresses, hobnobbed with the glitterati, drank hard, dressed sharp, and talked fast.

Frazee also scooped up the world-champion Red Sox, in a heavily leveraged buyout just after the 1916 season. It was just a small part of his growing entertainment empire. It is instructive to understand exactly *how* small. As late as 1909, according to Henry D. Fetter, author of *Taking On the Yankees: Winning and Losing in the Business of Baseball,* the total receipts of all sixteen big-league teams was an estimated \$3–\$4 million, compared with a gross income of \$167 million *each* for the movies, live theater, and the sale of musical instruments.

Even after the sport's popularity exploded in the post–World War I years, the average major-league ball club had a profit margin of \$130,000 a year. A hit Broadway show, by comparison, could bring in \$10,000 *every week* for a year. Harry Frazee was willing to spend lavishly on the Red Sox for a couple of years and bought his team another World Series in 1918, picking up discarded members of Connie Mack's disbanded A's champions. But Frazee was disappointed to find that his leveraged buyout was not making the quick profits he expected—or required. For this he blamed the AL president, Ban Johnson, whom he accused of denying him access to all the star players he wanted to buy from other teams.

In this disappointment, Frazee would find common cause with an odd couple of colonels, neither of whom ever fought a battle. Colonel Tillinghast L'Hommedieu Huston and Colonel Jacob Ruppert were partners of convenience, joined by their common desire to own a ball team. The Colonels' names belied their origins. Despite his fabulous moniker, Huston was the self-made man, a civil engineer who acquired his first fortune by dredging Havana's harbor and building its sewer system after the Spanish-American War. A friend of John McGraw's, he was a corpulent man's man who liked to hunt and fish, wore suits until they stank, and kept his derby clapped so firmly on his head that sportswriters dubbed him "the Man in the Iron Hat."

Jake Ruppert was the silver-spoon dandy, dapper and compact, affecting a German accent even though he was born in Manhattan, in a lonely mansion amid what were then the wastes of Ninety-Third and Fifth. He was, to say the least, entitled, buying up a grand country estate across the Hudson from West Point, not to mention a series of yachts, thoroughbreds, purebred dogs, exotic animals, jade and porcelain, rare first editions, and very discreet mistresses. Yet the funny little Colonel with the old-world accent was also a first-class executive. His was the diamond-edged mind that—more than anyone else's—would build the greatest dynasty in American sports.

When he turned twenty-one, Ruppert made two brilliant business decisions. One was to join his father's brewing business, the other to join Tammany Hall. Before long, Ruppert Knickerbocker beer was featured in Tammany saloons all over New York. In return, young Jake served four terms in Congress from the East Side, the "Silk Stocking District," in order to secure the German vote for the machine. (The "Colonel" also came through politics, an honorific bestowed by a Tammany governor.)

Both Colonels had been looking to buy a major-league franchise for a while, and both hoped to grab up the glamour team of the time, the New York Giants. They were not available. There was some talk of Ruppert perhaps buying the Cubs, but he nixed the idea with typical hauteur. Chicago, Jake Ruppert let it be known, was "too far from Broadway." It was Ban Johnson who ultimately brought the Colonels together to take his perennial problem child, the Yankees, off his hands—the American League's most star-crossed team having fallen to new depths by the end of 1914.

New York's acting manager was its twenty-five-year-old shortstop, Roger Peckinpaugh. Its last permanent manager, Frank Chance, had quit after taking a swing at the co-owner, Big Bill Devery. The team had lost $30,000 on the season—in good part because it had no park of its own but rented space from the Giants in the Polo Grounds, for the considerable sum of $65,000 a year. Following the team's disastrous, last-place finish in 1912, the city had finally succeeded in driving a street through the middle of rocky Hilltop Park. Attendance had already fallen under 250,000, and Farrell and Devery had lost what little juice they had left down at Tammany.

Farrell had been making halfhearted plans to build a new park up in Marble Hill, at 225th Street and Broadway, a move that would have placed the Yankees in the Bronx ten years early. But he never put much effort into it, and instead of joining the many teams then investing in bold new parks, the Yankees became mere tenants of the Giants. Clearly, Farrell and Devery had lost any enthusiasm they might have had for the game, and they were delighted to palm the Yankees off on the Colonels for $460,000, or more than twenty-five times what the team had cost them just eleven years earlier. In a few more years both Farrell and Devery would be dead broke, and then just dead, their ill-gained fortunes returned from whence they sprang, to banquet halls and stuss tables, barrooms and bordellos.

Even taking that into consideration, many thought they had got the better of the deal. They might be dead, but the Colonels had to go on owning the Yankees. When Huston announced the sale at the Hotel Wolcott on New Year's Eve, a reporter told him, "Allow me to be the first one to offer you my heartfelt condolences."

(The new partners' first move was not propitious. Blue pinstripes having worked so well on the home uniforms, they added blue—and red and green—pinstripes to the gray road uniforms. This idea was discarded after the 1915 season, thankfully, and the leftover uniforms donated to the Sing Sing prison baseball teams.)

Yet no sympathy was required. It was Ruppert and Huston who had made the killing, mainly because they had the capital to turn their new team around. They exemplified the slow move of baseball from a sport controlled by men who had come up in it—men like Connie Mack and Charles Comiskey, who had started off as players and managers—to a business owned by those who had made their fortunes elsewhere. Both new Yankees owners had considerable resources independent of baseball, Ruppert in particular. Prohibition would put a dent in the brewing business, but the Colonel had already expanded into real estate; by 1929 his family fortune was estimated at $60 million. The ban on beer only increased the importance of his baseball franchise and concentrated his attentions.

It was under Ruppert that the Yankees became the first true corporation in American sports. It was Ruppert who would begin the long Yankees tradition of reinvesting his profits in the team, the key to sustaining it beyond the tenure of any individual star in management or on the field. It was Ruppert who would leverage his political connections and his place in the nation's biggest market to slip nearly all the restraints of baseball's cartel and remake the whole game in the best interests of his team.

He began by looking around until he found someone who knew the business. Ed Barrow, the moody, two-fisted manager of the Red Sox, had served in almost every possible baseball capacity during what was already a thirty-year career. Born in a covered wagon en route to Nebraska, Barrow started out writing for newspapers, selling soap, owning a movie theater, and clerking at a hotel desk—all perfect training, in their way, for being a baseball executive. After a brief partnership with the concessions magnate Harry Stevens, "Uncle Egbert" had gone on to posts as manager, business manager, club owner, and league president in the minors and majors. He knew the business side of baseball and he knew talent, having signed the great stars Honus Wagner and Pie Traynor to minor-league contracts.

Ruppert hired him as the Yankees' new business manager. He had already hired a new field manager, a scrappy ex-infielder named Miller Huggins, who also had a law degree—just the sort of hire a corporation would make, and one that went against the express wishes of Ruppert's partner, Colonel Huston. But The Man in the Iron Hat was away in France, making another fortune off World War I, and Ruppert turned the team over to Barrow. He had made the right call. Barrow installed a strict, vertical system of command on the Yankees. He barred the Colonels from the clubhouse after games and liked to say that he himself never set foot on the field during his first twenty years in New York. When Huston came home and tried his best to undermine Huggins, Ruppert bought him out for $1.2 million in 1922. It marked a profit of nearly $1 million in just over seven years for Cap, but Ruppert walked away with something much more valuable: complete control of the New York Yankees.

Ban Johnson was the next order of business. Ruppert, with what would become a perpetual Yankees sense of entitlement, believed Johnson had promised him the opportunity to acquire some of the biggest stars in the game when he bought the team. When this did not come about, Ruppert made common cause with the already disgruntled Harry Frazee and Johnson's old partner turned nemesis, Charlie Comiskey, accusing the American League president of funneling players he had promised them to the Cleveland club, in which Johnson now owned an interest.

The whole dispute became an extended, labyrinthine battle when Johnson tried to cancel Frazee's trade of a pitcher named Carl Mays to the Yankees on technical grounds. Johnson had the other five club owners on his side and was determined to use the dispute to drive both the Colonels and Frazee out of baseball. Instead, coolly wielding dollars and injunctions, Huston and Ruppert maneuvered the fight into the New York Supreme Court, where a Tammany judge—the future U.S. senator Robert Wagner—ruled the AL president guilty of a conflict of interest. Johnson's power was smashed for good.

"The time has come when the powers of Mr. Johnson should be curtailed," Ruppert remarked with icy indifference, referring to a man about to lose the work of a lifetime. "Ban Johnson will be put out of baseball."

Johnson and his erratic ruling commission were replaced by Judge Kenesaw Mountain Landis, the first commissioner of baseball. This was at heart another corporate move. For all of his dramatic mannerisms and his supposed omnipotence as the sport's new "czar," Landis knew better than to interfere in business between club owners, and Harry Frazee was looking to do business.

As corporate as Jake Ruppert was making baseball, it was still part of the show business. To get his franchise off the ground, to make it a real attraction as well as a contender, the Colonels needed a star, and Frazee had the biggest one there was. The Red Sox had slumped unexpectedly in 1919 and drawn badly at the box office, and the money Frazee owed the Sox's previous owner was past due. Meanwhile, Harry had his eye, as always, on the next production, the next theater.

"Someone asked me . . . if my club was for sale," Frazee told a reporter, displaying his own sangfroid. "What a ridiculous question. Of course, it is for sale. So is my hat and my overcoat, and my watch. Anyone who wants them can have them at a price. I will dispose of my holdings in the Red Sox at any time for my price."

At first, Harry Frazee seriously considered selling Fenway Park (of which he owned half, sort of) for its real estate value and moving the Red Sox into Braves Field. (Yes, Boston, it *could* have been worse.) Instead, he decided to sell the Red Sox off for parts, and almost exclusively to the Yankees, the one team that could afford to meet his price. What followed has been romanticized as "the Curse of the Bambino," but something much colder and much more typical of the time was taking place: the rationalization of yet another part of the entertainment industry, brought about by yet another collaboration of New York sharpies.

Frazee's biggest asset, of course, was Babe Ruth. Initiating what would become a long tradition in Boston, he set out to convince local sportswriters that he *had* to sell the Babe. Frazee put it about that his greatest star was undisciplined and unruly, breaking curfew and threatening to punch his manager. Ruth's public drunkenness and open cheating on his wife were embarrassments; he wanted to break his word and renegotiate his contract—almost the exact same sort of whispering campaign that would be used against one Red Sox "troublemaker" after another, into the twenty-first century. Most of the charges were true enough. They just ignored the fact that Frazee would have sold Ruth if he had been an ideal teammate or husband, much as he would have sold his own watch or coat if the price were right.

The price was right. On January 5, 1920, Frazee announced that Ruth would go to the Yankees for $100,000 in cash and notes. Frazee would also receive a loan of $300,000 to $350,000 from the Colonels, for which he put up Fenway Park as collateral. The amounts were staggering, well beyond what any ballplayer had fetched before. The $100,000 up-front price was the equivalent of $1.5 million today, and maybe much more, depending on how you figure it. Throwing in the loan, Ruth's true cost would have been at least $6.6 million in today's dollars.

Frazee accompanied the sale with a scorching, fifteen-hundred-word press release that called Ruth "without question . . . the greatest hitter that the game has seen" but went on to excoriate him as "one of the most inconsiderate men that ever wore a baseball uniform"; an "arrogant . . . bad influence" on the team who had "ruined" discipline and "hugs the limelight to himself." Not only was Ruth a one-man corrupter of youth and destroyer of virtue, but the Yankees had bought a pig in a poke, a player who was "taking on weight tremendously," who "doesn't care to keep himself in shape," and who "has a floating cartilage in his knee [which] may make him a cripple at any time." Frazee's grandson remembered similar diatribes, including Frazee's supposed rage that Ruth had dared to ask for a big raise.

"This just infuriated Big Harry," he recalled. "In the theater, he was used to people living up to their contracts."

In the theater, "Big Harry" had surely encountered a diva or two who wanted more money when they put fannies in the seats. And all his vituperation left unanswered the question of why he didn't get any players in return for "the greatest hitter that the game has seen." He would have "preferred" to trade for players, Frazee insisted, but "Huggins would have had to wreck his ball club." Indeed, "no club could give me his [Ruth's] equivalent in players without wrecking itself."

In other words, Frazee had just traded the Yankees a pig in a poke, an uncontrollable, dishonorable, prematurely broken-down wreck of a ballplayer—whose equivalent in players could not be found on any major-league club. Instead, he had to be sold for money. All of which went to Harry Frazee.

For the next three years, Frazee went on trading one Red Sox star after another to the Yankees: the pitchers Carl Mays, Waite Hoyt, Joe Bush, Sad Sam Jones, George Pipgras, and Herb Pennock; the catcher Wally Schang; the shortstop Everett Scott; the third baseman Joe Dugan—seventeen players in all. When the Yanks won their first World Series in 1923, half of the position players—Ruth, Schang, Scott, and Dugan—and six of the seven leading Yankees pitchers had come from the Red Sox.

Frazee tried to get respectable players in return for a while, but as the Sox continued to sink through the standings, the deals became more and more one-sided. Right from the beginning, there was almost always a telltale chunk of cash included—at least $155,000 altogether, on top of the supposed $400,000 to $450,000 in the Ruth trade—and the trades nearly always rid the Sox of established stars making big salaries in return for younger, cheaper players. When there was nothing left to be milked from the franchise, Harry Frazee sold it, too, for $1.15 million—nearly twice what he had paid for it, just seven years before. It was acquired by a syndicate with even less ready cash than Big Harry had, assuring that the Red Sox would spend most of the following decade in the cellar.

And in the end, it was even worse than it looked. For Boston. Harry Frazee was *supposed* to make 7 percent semiannual interest payments on that immense, $300,000 loan from Colonel Ruppert—the one secured by Fenway Park—for the next five years. By May of 1925, Frazee was then supposed to repay the entire loan. But he did not. Instead, Frazee had already sold the team. And before 1929 was out—with his usual, impeccable timing—Frazee had died, a victim of Bright's disease, at age forty-eight.

Technically, Jacob Ruppert could have assumed control of Fenway Park and done whatever he wanted with it. But the Colonel was much too shrewd to do any such thing. Instead, as Michael Haupert, a professor of economics and contributing writer to the Society of American Baseball Research (SABR) has detailed, Ruppert hung on to the property, benignly letting the Red Sox continue playing there—while collecting his high-interest loan payments. By the time someone with pockets deep enough to redeem Fenway Park finally owned the Red Sox—Tom Yawkey—total interest payments above the repayment of the loan had amounted to $276,920, by Haupert's estimates. Combined with another $10,000 the Red Sox had initially shelled out to help offset Ruth's salary, Boston had ended up paying *out* some $200,000 net, for the privilege of wrecking the franchise and getting rid of the game's greatest star.

The Hub had fallen prey to one more swift-talking, unscrupulous Broadway promoter. The Red Sox, to Harry Frazee, were simply another entertainment commodity, and a relatively minor asset at that, one to be manipulated for the maximum cash payoff, then discarded when there was nothing left to sell off. The money went not to the team but to buy that theater Frazee had his eye on and to back the comedy *My Lady Friends,* which he later made into the most popular musical of the decade, *No, No, Nanette,* featuring the hits "I Want to Be Happy" and "Tea for Two." When it came to baseball, Harry Frazee was one hell of a theatrical producer.

32

Death in the Afternoon

In his first spring as a New York Yankee, Babe Ruth quickly demonstrated that Frazee had been right all along. He was arrogant, self-centered, out of control, and a physical wreck. When fans in Jacksonville booed him for striking out twice in a spring training game, Ruth vaulted into the stands after a heckler more than a foot shorter than he was. The fan in question pulled a knife on him. Teammates saved the Babe from himself in that particular encounter. But soon after, he demanded and got a big pay raise and the right to play centerfield, where on opening day he let a fly ball sail over his head to cost his new team the game. In his second regular-season game, he struck out three times. He then went up to Boston as a Yankee for the first time and did almost nothing before sellout crowds as New

York was swept in a three-game series. Back in the Polo Grounds for his first home game, Ruth swung so hard in batting practice that he separated some ribs. He batted once, struck out on three pitches, and headed for the showers. It would be days before he returned. The club lost seven of its first eleven games.

"The Yankees' ancient hoodoo is still on the job," commiserated *The Sporting News.*

Ruth's slump lasted all the way until May 1, when he hit a colossal home run over the right-field roof of the Polo Grounds, off his once and future teammate Herb Pennock, the ball traveling more than five hundred feet. After that, he was back to form. More accurately, he was up to a new form that nobody had ever seen before in baseball, smashing home runs and reaching base with a previously unimaginable frequency. Before the year was over, Ruth would hit fifty-four homers, nearly doubling his record from the year before, and set modern records for runs scored, runs batted in, walks, on-base percentage, and slugging average.

The following year, 1921, he would go on to *exceed* many of those marks, driving his home-run record up to fifty-nine, scoring an impossible 177 runs, totaling 119 extra-base hits, and hitting .378. He also passed Roger Connor, a longtime Giants stalwart, who had retired with the most *lifetime* home runs—138—in 1897. The home run the Babe hit to break the mark is estimated to be the longest *ever* struck in a game, according to his chronicler Bill Jenkinson, who claims it traveled clear out of Navin Field (later Tiger Stadium). Ruth would hit another 575 home runs *after* breaking Connor's mark, a number that—in and of itself—only ten other major leaguers surpassed in their *entire* careers (and several of them enjoying dubious relationships with banned substances).

In the years to come, the Babe would go on setting records—many of which, more than a hundred seasons later, still have yet to be broken by anyone without the aid of an extended season or a body full of performance-enhancing drugs. The Yankees, bolstered by their new star and all of the other players Harry Frazee so obligingly sold them, became an immediate contender—their rise interrupted only by an odd, terrible incident that would also hasten change in the game.

—

On August 16, 1920, the Yanks were in the thick of a pennant race for the first time in a decade. New York was hosting one of the other two teams in the race, the Cleveland Indians, up at the Polo Grounds. On the mound was their ace, Carl Mays, late of the Red Sox, whose specialty was what had become known as a submarine pitch, a nearly underhanded pitch that he hurled by dropping down so close to the mound that he frequently scraped his knuckles on the dirt. The pitch worked almost as a knuckleball, as something completely unpredictable. Mays's own catcher, Muddy Ruel, remarked on how "some of the balls he throws take remarkable shoots, jumps, ducks and twists. . . . I have never known how I managed to catch some of them. I have never been able to understand how any batter ever gets a hit off him."

Among other things, they were too busy hitting the dirt. Mays led the American League in hit batters in 1917 and was known around the circuit as a headhunter. He denied the charge, claiming that it was just the "freak breaks" of his pitches that resulted in so many rung bells, and maintained with a typical dash of self-pity that "I merely wish to say that I am not a murderer, nor do I take unfair advantage of anyone."

Few believed him. In an era before batting helmets of any kind, a pitcher willing to throw hard inside had an enormous advantage, and it was one that Mays pushed to reckless extremes. He threw constantly at Ty Cobb, for instance, something that few men ever dared to do. Cobb raged at him, called him a "yellow dog," and charged the mound to wrestle with the pitcher. Mays kept hitting him. Cobb laid a bunt down the first base line and purposely spiked the back of Mays's leg, cutting it open and vowing, "The next time you cover the bag, I'll take the skin off the other leg." Mays kept hitting him. Completely mystified, Cobb went to talk to Mays about it, man-to-man, only to have the pitcher tell him, "No, I don't try to hit you, and I don't try to hit anybody, but if I do hit you, I don't care. I've had them try to hit me, and I've never squealed."

Carl Mays had evolved into a baseball version of Bartleby the Scrivener, perennially defiant for reasons that no one could quite comprehend. Mays had, ironically, arrived in the major leagues in the company of Babe Ruth, the two coming up together on the train from Providence to Boston. They were such polar opposites in outlook and disposition that Mays might have been considered the anti-Ruth. Where Ruth was expansive and amiable, Mays was diffident, pessimistic, combative. He had an unfortunate appearance: an enormous nose, beady eyes, and a perpetually down-turned mouth, as if he had just smelled something bad. His teammates disliked him right from the start, described him as "sulky," "not congenial," and uncommunicative. He got into locker-room fights, and on one occasion challenged Ruth to have a go at it—then failed to appear for their appointed rounds.

He showed his contempt for any teammates who drank or smoke, or chased after women, categories that often included everyone else in the clubhouse. He remembered every insult, every bad word from a sportswriter. In 1919, angry about lack of support, he jumped the Red Sox in mid-season, shouting at his teammates, "I'll never pitch for this ballclub again!" Earlier that year, when A's fans in Philadelphia kept banging on the visiting team's tin roof, Mays bolted off the bench and hurled a ball into the stands, hitting a man in the head and grazing a woman. He fled the city just ahead of an arrest warrant. And yet he remained baffled as to why he was not better loved.

"I always have wondered why I have encountered this antipathy from so many people wherever I have been," he told *The Baseball Magazine* in 1920. "And I have never been able to explain it, even to myself."

Mays's problems might have stemmed from his childhood. After his father, a jackleg preacher, died when he was twelve, Carl's mother raised him and his seven siblings on hardscrabble farms in Missouri and Oklahoma. The family was so destitute that he later claimed to have honed his pitching arm by killing squirrels and jackrabbits with rocks so they could have enough to eat. He was always tightly wound. He had wept in the Fenway locker room after stalking off the team, apparently distraught over domestic troubles and the fact that his new, uninsured house had just burned down. Mays was convinced that it was arson. Mays being Mays, he might have been right.

Now down in New York, all of his problems seemed to be behind him. He was the ace of a team in the thick of a pennant race. But in his start against the Indians on that humid, rainy August day, he fell behind, 3–0, going into the fifth inning. Carl could not have been happy. On the field, he was a ferocious competitor who often bawled out his fielders for making errors behind him. He might have decided to send a message.

Stepping up to the plate was Cleveland's quick, clever shortstop, Ray Chapman, in the midst of his best season yet. Chapman was the very antithesis of the pitcher he was facing, irrepressible and universally well liked, known for his beautiful tenor voice in an age when it was not unusual for men to break into song. He often led his Indian teammates in sing-alongs, had just had them belting out "Dear Old Pal o' Mine" on the elevated up to the Polo Grounds that afternoon. Ray was always merry these days. During the offseason, he had married a lovely young woman who was also heiress to an oil-and-gas fortune. His admiring father-in-law was urging him to quit baseball and join him in the business—the sort of postretirement sinecure that was available to precious few ballplayers of the time. His wife, Kathleen, was pregnant, and the future must have seemed unlimited.

One thing Chapman had never been able to do very well was to hit Carl Mays. Standing in against the Yankee pitcher on that overcast afternoon in 1920, he crouched down in the batter's box, trying to pick up Mays's submarine deliveries from a better angle. It was a mistake. He failed to see the first pitch from Mays at all. It hit his unprotected head with a crack so loud that when the ball rolled back out to the pitcher, Mays picked it up and threw over to first, convinced it had hit Chapman's bat. Shades of Roger Clemens and Mike Piazza, but this was tragedy, not farce. Ray Chapman stood where he was for a moment, then crumpled to his knees, grimacing in pain. The umpire Tommy Connolly, players from both teams, and a doctor from the crowd rushed over to him. They managed to get him up and walking toward the Polo Grounds' centerfield clubhouse, so far away, but after he passed second base, his legs gave out and his teammates had to haul him the rest of the distance, his arms around their shoulders. Once inside, he tried to write something on a pad of paper, but dropped the pencil. He did manage to call for his wedding ring and seemed relieved when it was placed on his finger.

Mays's pitch, it turned out, had cut a three-and-a-half-inch fissure along the base of Chapman's skull, driving a piece of bone down against his brain. Surgeons operated frantically to relieve the pressure, but found the brain already clotted with blood. Chapman slipped into unconsciousness, his last words to a teammate begging him not to tell his wife. He passed away early the next morning, just twenty-nine, but the tragedy continued for years. Kathleen Chapman remarried, but seems never to have recovered from her husband's death and died at the age of thirty-four—probably from poisoning herself. Her daughter, Rae Marie, born six months after Ray's death, died of measles at age eight, a year after her mother's passing.

Mays himself would be haunted by the death. At first he tried to pass the buck to almost everyone else: his manager and general manager, who should have known he was wild when he was "saved up for a special game"; the umpire Connolly, for not throwing out a ball that had "a roughened spot on it"; the weather, for making the ball wet, "which didn't make it any easier to control." He expressed his regrets, but did not attend Chapman's funeral, and insisted, "My conscience is absolutely clear." Unsurprisingly, he was booed on the road. At least five other American League teams threatened to boycott games with the Yankees if Mays were allowed to pitch. Before his start against Detroit a week after the beaning, his old friend Cobb sent him a note that read, "If it was in my power, I would have inscribed on Ray Chapman's tombstone these words: 'Here lies a victim of arrogance, viciousness, and greed.' "

Carl Mays went out that afternoon and beat Cobb's Tigers, 10–0. Save for a critical late-season series in Cleveland where the Yankees refused to let him appear, he pitched on in his dogged way, winning eight more games on the season, finishing with a record of 26-11 and a league-leading six shutouts. The next year he won twenty-seven games and helped pitch New York to its first pennant, but fate seemed to follow him like a malevolent dog. His manager, Miller Huggins, became convinced, with little reason, that Mays purposely threw games in the 1921 and 1922 World Series, and got rid of him as soon as he could. Mays's wife died at thirty-six, and he lost $175,000 in the stock market crash. In later life, he lobbied to make the Hall of Fame, a place he had a strong claim to, but the allegations of throwing World Series games—and Ray Chapman's death—undermined his efforts.

"Nobody ever remembers anything about me except one thing—that a pitch I threw caused a man to die," he complained bitterly near the end of his own life.

—

There have, by now, been some thirty-five to forty million pitches thrown in major-league baseball games, according to the calculations made by Mike Sowell in *The Pitch That Killed.* Only one has ever killed a man, although there were a few other fatalities in the minors. Ray Chapman's death was a brutal reminder of how primitive the sport could be, how dangerous. It also hastened the sea change in the game that Ruth had already begun, the start of another transformation that would bring it into the modern, corporate era.

Start with the ball. In spring training in 1920, players began to notice that it seemed livelier, bigger, easier to hit and to hit hard. A. J. Reach, the company that supplied all baseballs for American League teams, denied that any change had been made, but debate over the "juicing" of baseballs has gone on ever since. The real story seems to have been not so much the manufacture of the ball itself as a set of rule changes designed to make it easier to hit—the very rules Carl Mays complained the umpire wasn't enforcing.

When you hit a ball into the seats before World War I, you expected to get it back. As late as 1916, fans were being arrested at the Polo Grounds for concealing foul balls they had caught. After the war, in a rare burst of marketing savvy, the owners hit upon a new solution. They raised the price of tickets and let the fans keep the balls. Now umpires were commanded to replace a baseball whenever it got scuffed up. Even worse for the pitchers, they were no longer allowed to throw trick pitches. No more spitball, or emory ball, or licorice ball, or Vaseline ball. No more cutting the horsehide with rings, and belt buckles, or shaving it with concealed bits of sandpaper. The only exceptions were made for a single designated pitcher on each roster, who would be allowed to keep doing whatever he wanted to the ball for the rest of his career. No more would batters have to hack at—or dodge—a gray lopsided mess, one that blended in seamlessly with the twilight sky in the later innings.

The change was considered in part a matter of simple hygiene, in the post-influenza, germ-conscious 1920s. Who knew what you could catch? And what respectable person wanted to go to a game and see someone spitting on a baseball? Yet it also spoke to the game's great new innovation—one provided almost entirely by a single man. This was the home run. The owners had seen how Ruth had already transformed the game, how the fans had flocked back to the ballpark to see his mighty blasts, and they were eager to do anything that might improve the hitting—the *power game*—that the public seemed to prefer.

The purists—mostly sportswriters, in the mold of old Henry Chadwick—groused bitterly about the change, as they would about any and every offensive improvement, in every game ever played, for the next century: the home run, the forward pass, the slap shot, the dunk. Ring Lardner, already embittered by the Black Sox scandal and the general tilt of human existence, wrote satirically of "Baby Ruth" and of how the owners "fixed up a ball that if you don't miss it entirely it will clear the fence, and the result is that ball players which use to specialize in hump back liners to the pitcher is now amongst our leading sluggers when by rights they couldn't take a ball in their hands and knock it past the base umpire." *The Sporting News,* when it wasn't busy accusing Jews of ruining the national game, found all these home runs anti-American: "It seems to have reached the point where a ball is thrown out if it gets as much as a fly speck on it. This should not be. It's not patriotic, for true patriotism still demands economy and conservation."

The owners themselves soon began to worry about the cost of losing so many baseballs—worth \$2.50 at the time, or nearly \$40 apiece today. But the fans got to keep their souvenirs—a perk unique to baseball—and nobody was going to be making baseballs harder to see anytime in the near future. They might also have considered forcing batters to wear batting helmets—but that was still a couple decades ahead. Baseball could only move so fast.

33

The Franchise

Jacob Ruppert had taken a huge gamble, and now it would pay off. Going into the 1921 season—just six years after buying the New York Yankees—he possessed both the best-run team in the big leagues and the one commodity, the one star, that everyone wanted to see.

"It's almost as if when anybody hits a home run today they should pay Babe Ruth a royalty," wrote baseball historian Donald Honig. "It's like he invented it."

"His existence enlarges us just by looking at him, thinking about him, because you saw perfection," Heywood Hale Broun, author and son of the famous journalist, would marvel. "It was so glorious, it was almost painful. You were at the ballpark and Babe took that swing and the ball didn't fall down in the end, it whacked against a seat in the bleachers."

The fans flocked to the Yankees as they had never gone to see any baseball team before. In 1920, New York more than doubled its attendance from the year before and became the first major-league team to draw more than a million fans in a season. They would break the mark seven more times before the decade—and the big money—gave out, and they did nearly as well on the road. In September 1927, for instance, three meaningless Yankees games in Fenway drew fifty-eight thousand fans—nearly *20 percent* of the beleaguered Red Sox's *total* home attendance for the year. The fans came to see one thing, and they were not often disappointed. In the course of his career, counting regular-season, World Series, and exhibition games, Ruth hit the longest home runs ever recorded at the home fields of *every single major-league team, American League and National.* Often, he broke his own distance records, two or three or four times.

Nor did he stop there. He also hit the longest home runs anybody had ever seen in Baltimore and Providence and Fayetteville, North

Carolina, during his brief minor-league career. He hit the longest home runs ever seen throughout the South, in Memphis and Mobile, San Antonio and St. Pete, Charlotte and Waco, Savannah and Louisville, Richmond and New Orleans, as the Yankees wound their way slowly north each spring after breaking camp. He hit the longest home runs ever hit in Trenton, and Newark, and Paterson, New Jersey; in Johnstown and Haverhill; in South Bend and Sioux Falls; in Wheeling, West Virginia, and Wilkes-Barre, Pennsylvania; in Fort Wayne, Indiana, and Sleepy Eye, Minnesota; during the constant barnstorming tours and exhibition games he played in before, during, and after the Yankees' regular seasons. Like Jay Gatsby receiving his mysterious, bootlegger phone calls from points farther and farther west, Ruth went on breaking records in ever more distant places, the farther he and the Yankees traveled—in Denver and San Francisco and Anaheim, Vancouver and Honolulu and Manila, Tokyo, and Shanghai.

All told, Babe Ruth played some eight hundred exhibition games over the course of his career—what Bill Jenkinson would dub his "hidden career." He played games in six different nations, forty-two different states, and at least two hundred cities, towns, and villages. Some of these were on tours with friends and all-star collections, but most were with the Yankees, who scheduled an extraordinary number of exhibition contests *during* the season—as many as fifteen such contests one year. There was no site too distant, no venue too small, as long as it guaranteed a big gate. In July 1924, in the midst of a tight pennant race, the Yankees found themselves trailing Detroit by one run going into the ninth inning. The Yanks walked off the field and forfeited the contest to the Tigers. They had to catch a train for an exhibition scheduled the next day in Indianapolis. New York lost the flag that year to the Senators by all of two games.

The Yankees under Jacob Ruppert were, first and foremost, a business. Their primary goal was to make money, not to win pennants, and their players were worked almost as unrelievedly as those in any other American business of the time. In one not untypical stretch, during the greatest season they would compile, they had no days off at all between May 1 and June 6, 1927. Ruth—the supposed prima donna—was worked hardest, expected to play *every inning* in every exhibition. He was, as well, often expected to pitch the game, to sign hundreds of autographs, to perform any number of stunts and hijinks, and above all to hit a towering shot that everyone could go home and say was the greatest thing they had ever seen.

More often than not, the Babe obliged, homering more than three hundred times in these games that didn't count and hitting any number of other spectacular drives. In Fort Wayne, he called his game-ending shot, after walking to the plate in a crowd full of children. After a mammoth wallop in Albany, he led a Boy Scout troop off the field. He batted against a twelve-year-old girl and a seventeen-year-old girl, and played a game against the famous House of David touring team wearing a set of the same fake whiskers they played in. He signed the instrument of every member of the band in Chattanooga, broke fence planks with a clout in Memphis, turned a somersault at first base in Wheeling, West Virginia. In the Sing Sing prison yard, he hit three home runs, including a final, 520-foot drive that sailed over a forty-foot wall, past a machine-gun tower, and over the tracks of the New York Central, while a crowd of inmates wistfully watched it soar away.

Somehow the Yankees never seemed concerned that their big show might fold before they got it back to Broadway. Ruth was forbidden to work out during the offseason, but no one raised an eyebrow when he wrenched a knee pitching in an exhibition in Haverhill in 1923, or when he played with an injured ankle in a Baltimore exhibition the same year—*on the eve of the World Series.* He homered despite suffering from what turned out to be appendicitis in Binghamton, limped about with another bad knee in Bridgeport. Nothing, it seemed, could keep him down. Playing in Washington on July 5, 1924, he ran straight into a concrete wall in the fourth inning, chasing a foul fly ball in right field. Knocked unconscious for five minutes, visibly limping, he insisted on staying in the game, in which he had three hits, two of them doubles. Then he played all of the second game of the doubleheader as well.

"Whatever the owners paid him, it wasn't enough—it couldn't be enough," claimed his teammate Roger Peckinpaugh, but it's impossible to say he was really exploited.

Ruth signed the record contracts of his day—a pinnacle of $80,000 a year in 1930—and received half of all the exhibition receipts the Yankees got that year, money that must have exceeded most ballplayers' salaries by several times, *on top of that $80,000.* Not bad, in Depression-era dollars. He went on his own barnstorming tours after most seasons; a twenty-one-game, nineteen-city swing with Lou Gehrig in 1927 netted him another $70,000, or his salary all over again. He was shrewd enough to sign up Christy Walsh, an agent and promoter who proved adept at landing the Babe endorsements for just about everything, along with movie appearances and lucrative vaudeville tours.

Whole towns shut down when he came to play. Little Etowah, Tennessee, declared a holiday when his train made a whistle-stop. On the same trip, the state legislature adjourned to see him play in Nashville. More than a million people turned out for his welcoming parade through Tokyo's Ginza district on his 1934 trip to that new baseball convert, Japan. Newspapers ran regular columns headlined WHAT BABE RUTH DID TODAY, where they struggled for both new superlatives and nicknames. At least eighty of the latter appeared in print, many of them a real stretch. Ruth was not only the Bambino, and the Sultan of Swat, but also the Caliph of Clout, the Czar of Crash, the Maharajah of Maulers, the Prince of Punch, the Rajah of Rap, the Wali of Wallop, the Wazir of Wham, the Wizard of Whack, and the Infant Swatigy.

"Don't tell me about Ruth; I've seen what he did to people," remembered Waite Hoyt, describing the atmosphere of a religious revival that accompanied the man's junkets around the continent. "I've seen them—fans—driving miles in open wagons through the prairies of Oklahoma to see him in exhibition games as we headed north in the spring. I've seen them: kids, men, women, worshippers all, hoping to get his name on a torn, dirty piece of paper, or hoping for a grunt of recognition when they said, 'Hi ya, Babe.' He never let them down, not once. He was the greatest crowd pleaser of them all."

More than any ballplayer today, more than any of the great sporting stars of his era—more than Grange or Tilden or Bobby Jones, or even Dempsey—the poor kid from the streets of Baltimore seemed to understand this. Contrary to Harry Frazee's smears, the Babe was a trouper, a performer as well as a ballplayer.

And yet, even for Ruth, the demands of a life that was never offstage took their toll. He loved kids, but children swarmed him so avidly, at every opportunity, that he finally admitted, "They're hard on a fellow's health." His liked adults, but lived in a constant blur of new faces, all of whom wanted him to help them make money, touch him, shake his hand, get his autograph, get his story, go to bed with him. All men were "Keed" or "Joe," all women "mother" or "sister" (or something less respectful). By 1924 his first marriage was over, and he was keeping company with Claire Hodgson, charitably described as an "artist's model." She was remarkably able to keep him in line, but not always. There were flashes of temper and violence, usually directed at anybody who tried to rein him in. He feuded constantly with his manager, Miller Huggins; there was a rumor, unconfirmed, that he once dangled the diminutive skipper by his ankles off the caboose of a moving train.

During his frustrating 1922 season, when the Babe was suspended for thirty-nine games by Commissioner Landis for violating an arbitrary and temporary rule that had forbidden him to barnstorm the autumn before, Ruth scoffed, "Who does that big monkey think he is?" Finally reinstated, he promptly threw dirt in an umpire's eyes, chased a heckler into the stands, and stood atop the Polo Grounds dugout to yell at the crowd, "You're all yellow!" He was suspended twice more. In 1925, he was downed for seven weeks by his colossal, still mysterious stomachache, something that required abdominal surgery for what was described as an "intestinal abscess" and was rumored to be a venereal disease. More likely it was diverticulitis, or perhaps a hernia, or simple exhaustion and influenza.

Whatever his affliction, the Babe bounced back, as he always did. In 1929 there was a more serious breakdown. In January of that year, his long-estranged first wife died in a fire at a house in Massachusetts—a home where she was living with another man. This was considered a scandal at the time, and it left Ruth overwhelmed with feelings of grief and guilt. Then, on May 19, 1929, a violent thunderstorm set off a rush for shelter in the right-field bleachers at Yankee Stadium. The rush turned into a panic that killed one man immediately and injured another hundred fans, some of them very badly. The other players had already gone back to the clubhouse, but for some reason Ruth lingered in the dugout, and when he saw what was happening, he rushed toward the bleachers, calling for doctors. When he noticed a cop bringing out a fatally injured seventeen-year-old girl named Eleanor Price, he helped carry her into the Yankees' locker room, where he knelt beside her on the floor, stroking her head until she died.

The incident seemed to devastate Ruth, and it appeared as if the frantic pace he had led his entire adult life suddenly caught up to him. Still just thirty-four, he was reeling with exhaustion and missed the next three weeks of the season. Then he was back, just as suddenly as he had gone, blasting two home runs off the great Lefty Grove soon after returning to the lineup, batting .345, leading the league again in home runs and slugging.

The Yankees had found a seemingly inexhaustible treasure in Ruth, the player who would lead the team and the game into a shiny new era of entertainment. He helped them to switch the entire balance of power in the American League and to leave the once dominant Red Sox for dead. Now he would take on the Yankees' major rivals for New York.

34

A Giant Mistake

At a sportswriters' dinner following the 1922 season, a New York state senator named James J. Walker decided it was time to tell the Babe a few home truths. Ruth had just led the Yankees to their second consecutive pennant, hitting .315 with thirty-five homers and leading the AL in slugging. But he had misbehaved repeatedly, played a wretched World Series, and so undermined team discipline as to spark the immortal headline YANKEES TRAIN ON SCOTCH. Now, before the assembled banquet, Walker scolded him mercilessly, telling the Babe to his face that he had let down "the little, dirty-face kids." To the amazement of the attendant writers Ruth, sitting up on the dais, began to cry in shame.

"I'm going to work my head off," he swore, "and maybe part of my stomach, and then you watch me break that home run record."

The Babe would prove mostly true to his word, bouncing back to have one of his best seasons in 1923. Walker, for his part, had set the all-time record for chutzpah. Beau James was, if anything, even more of a perpetual boy than the Babe. A dapper little sprite of a man, Walker, his friend and biographer Gene Fowler would write, "played like a child, loved like a woman, hoped like a saint." His real dream was to make it on Tin Pan Alley, where he had penned the immortal tune "Will You Love Me in December as You Do in May?," but his Tammany father pushed him into the more secure—and lucrative—profession of politics. Elected mayor by mid-decade, he would come to personify 1920s New York, witty, insouciant, and brazen.

"Time," appraised Fowler, "has Jimmy on its hands."

Gentleman Jimmy, like the Babe, changed his vast wardrobe several times a day, spent his evenings gambling and going to shows, rarely made it to his city hall office before noon, and spent five of his first thirty months in office on vacation. When he gave himself a $15,000 raise, he quipped, "That's cheap. Think how much it would cost if I worked full-time." He was so unfailingly tardy for any appointment—he once kept Gandhi waiting forty-five minutes for a meeting in London—that reporters referred to him as "the late Mayor Walker."

It wasn't always so funny. Walker stuck around town long enough to scoop up at least $1 million in bribes and kickbacks over the course of his mayoralty. Another half a million in public funds went to convert an aged Central Park building into a fabulous Art Deco nightclub called the Casino, where Walker could hold court in a private upstairs room with his showgirl mistress. In the meantime, he allowed his subordinates to turn the city government into a circus of corruption—never mind the little kids with dirty faces.

Yet Jimmy Walker knew the people he represented. As a man who lived for little but pleasure, he understood their need for divertissement after all the sacrifice and economy of the war. By 1920, only one out of every six New Yorkers was still a native-born Protestant, and Tammany's predominantly Catholic constituency had never understood "Sabbatarian" measures against working people enjoying themselves on their one day off. Almost the moment the Armistice was signed, Walker, then still in the state senate, pushed through measures that legalized boxing and—more important—lifted the ban on Sunday baseball.

"Up to yesterday, baseball in greater New York was for the semi-idle, the floating population of New York City," the *New-York Tribune* rhapsodized after the first legal Sunday games, on May 4, 1919, drew thirty-seven thousand fans to see the Giants in the Polo Grounds, and twenty-five thousand to Ebbets Field—the largest regular-season crowds ever admitted to either park.

"Yesterday, those bleachers teemed with life. The men from the docks and the factories came, and they brought their wives and children. Those dark green benches held thousands of fans who never in their lives had seen a big league game."

Sunday baseball was a bonanza to the sport, in an era when most men still worked six days a week and all games were played in sunlight. The overflow crowds on what was once the Lord's Day (now Babe Ruth's) pushed major-league baseball's profit margins to more than 20 percent in the years just after World War I, figures never matched before or since, even after the advent of television. The Giants' thirteen Sunday dates in 1920 brought in 40 percent of the team's attendance that year—a gift from Tammany Hall to the machine's favorite team.

It must have seemed as if everything old were new again in those first fat years right after the war. The old synergy between the Giants and Tammany looked more powerful than ever. The push for Sunday baseball, realized by Jimmy Walker, had been started by a machine-appointed magistrate, Francis Xavier McQuade, who struck down the city's blue laws from the bench even as he was in the midst of becoming the Giants' minority owner and treasurer.

Conflict of interest? What conflict of interest? This was business!

McQuade's partner, and the Giants' new majority owner, was one Charles Stoneham, who had paid a record $1,030,000 for the privilege. Forty-two years old when he bought the team, Stoneham was already, in Charles Alexander's description, "grossly fat and somewhat bug-eyed," a man who "loved racehorses, gambling, and baseball, and [who] wasn't picky about his friends' reputation."

Charlie Stoneham ran a "bucket shop" down on Broad Street, a sort of imitation stock brokerage of the time, where "investors" gambled on whether certain stocks would go up or down, without any securities actually changing hands. Back in 1908, Stoneham had crossed even this tenuous line, getting himself hauled into court on charges of bilking the public with a dummy stock corporation. Other business activities included Havana's Oriental racetrack and casino, which he owned along with his manager, John McGraw, and occasional free-lance scams perpetrated with his old friend Arnold Rothstein, who was given a prominent seat in the new owner's box up at the Polo Grounds, the little matter of a fixed World Series notwithstanding.

Stoneham might have been something still worse—much worse. As Robert E. Murphy relates in *After Many a Summer,* not one but *two* wealthy widows of his close acquaintance killed themselves, apparently after he had led them on and/or bilked them of money. Charlie at first denied knowing either one. When, in one of these instances, he was quickly proven to be a liar, his friend McQuade stepped forward to tell the press that Charlie was distracted because his son, "little Horrie," had recently "drowned in the Morris Canal" (a fate countless Giants fans would come to wish upon Horace Stoneham).

Charlie Stoneham was also The Brain's type of gambler, which is to say, compulsive. Laid up with a bad leg one night in Saratoga, a bored Stoneham called Rothstein at his luxurious new casino, The Brook, and asked him, "What color came up last on the [roulette] wheel?" Rothstein informed him it was red, and Stoneham told him to put $1,000 on red again. He won his bet, then stayed on the phone with Rothstein for the next three hours, betting until he had lost $70,000 on the night.

Baseball, it seemed, had learned nothing. A known stock swindler and high-stakes gambler had been allowed to buy its flagship franchise and to seat the criminal who had initiated the sport's worst scandal in the front row. Judge Landis eventually forced Stoneham to chuck Rothstein out of the owner's box and to sell his gambling properties down in Cuba, but there was no further questioning of how Charlie Stoneham made his money, or of who his partners and intimates were. Stoneham at least had the good sense to retain the Giants' main asset. He made John McGraw a club vice president and even "lent" him $50,000 so Muggsy could buy seventy shares of the franchise himself.

It was the smart move—though it didn't necessarily look that way at the time. Maybe it was due to his humiliating blunder with Hal

Chase and how he was forced to confess it before a grand jury in the Black Sox case; maybe he was processing some vestiges of guilt and sorrow over what had happened to his great friend, Christy Mathewson, but McGraw's behavior had become increasingly erratic and alarming by the start of the new decade.

During the disappointing 1920 campaign—a race in which Wilbert Robinson's Dodgers again beat out the Giants for the pennant—Muggsy came almost all the way apart. One especially drunken night, he started a fistfight in the Lambs Club, then slugged a fellow member who was helping him home, knocking the man to the sidewalk and fracturing his skull. A police investigation followed, and McGraw narrowly escaped prosecution. His treasured ties to the show business were ruptured for good. He was kicked out of the Lambs and, McGraw being McGraw, retaliated by revoking all of the Lambs' Polo Grounds passes.

The incident was a harrowing one, for all his bravado, and it might have pulled Muggsy up short. Whether it was the challenge of the new game, or the wake-up call provided by nearly killing an innocent man in a moment of thoughtless, drunken anger, McGraw righted himself. He turned in the best managing job of his career in the early 1920s—the ultimate tribute to the man and the manager. From 1921 to 1924, the Giants would win an unprecedented—and still unmatched—four straight National League pennants. If no other figure so transformed his sport the way that Babe Ruth did in baseball, none adapted to the change as readily as McGraw.

Operating still as chief scout and chief operating officer of the Giants as well as their manager, McGraw pieced together a roster that retained capable veterans, such as shortstop Dave Bancroft and third baseman Heinie Groh, and added some of the best young players he had ever managed, including first baseman George "High Pockets" Kelly, outfielder Ross Youngs, and a fierce, savvy New York native who came directly to the Giants from college without playing a game in the minors, infielder Frankie Frisch, "the Fordham Flash." Batting cleanup was Emil "Irish" Meusel, a strong-armed outfielder who bore an almost uncanny resemblance to his brother, the Yankees star Long Bob Meusel, when it came to looks, statistics, and dour personality. (The two Meusels, who shared a house during the season, would become the only brothers to play against each other in three consecutive World Series.)

In many ways, it was a classic McGraw team, quick, opportunistic, slick fielding, and hard hitting. But in keeping with how baseball had changed, its competent but unspectacular pitching staff took a backseat. Now, instead of swiping more than two bases a game the way McGraw's old champions had a decade before, the Giants sprayed doubles and triples all over the Polo Grounds, and hit nearly as many home runs as the Yankees. Their manager acknowledged that "with the . . . ball being hit all about the lot the necessity of taking chances on the bases has decreased. . . . A manager would look foolish not to play the game as it is, meet the new situation with new tactics."

Beyond this concession to reality, Muggsy substituted and innovated brilliantly. If, in theory, the power game substantially diluted the importance of the manager, McGraw still found ways to count. He plastered over the few holes in his lineup, moving Frisch about as needed and working in another versatile infielder, Travis Jackson. Above all, he employed the strategy of platooning as it had never been used before. Blessed with two hard-nosed catchers in the right-handed Frank Snyder and the left-handed Oil Smith, he alternated them, to murderous effect. In the outfield, he did much the same with Billy Cunningham and a bowlegged, prematurely wizened fly catcher, that former toast of Brooklyn, Casey Stengel.

Casey had been banished from the Flock after Manager Robinson blamed him for the notorious grapefruit stunt, when Robbie thought he had been fatally injured by the falling citrus. In his first game back in the Ebbets Field outfield as a Giant, razzed and jeered by his old fans, he had doffed his cap—to let a pigeon escape, thereby inventing the most unique way yet devised to give the attendance the bird. Picked up by the Giants in exchange for an infielder named Goldie Rapp and a couple of other forgettables, he would become the next in a long line of unofficial McGraw player/coaches and surrogate sons. But none, save the departed Matty, were ever closer.

Stengel idolized McGraw and would go on to utilize much of what he learned from him in his own managerial career, particularly when it came to platooning. He would imitate every one of Muggsy's mannerisms, right down to the way he argued with umpires or bolted impatiently from the dugout to change pitchers. The two men, both champion spielers, could not seem to get enough of each other. The bachelor Stengel often went back with McGraw to his apartment after a game, where they swapped baseball tales long into the night.

"What on earth they gabbed about I never learned," Blanche McGraw remembered. "Of course, it was just an excuse to stay up all night. They spent most of the time in the kitchen, because it was nearer the food. Casey liked to cook bacon and scrambled eggs, which he did two or three times a night, and John liked to eat them."

In his time with the Giants, Stengel's lefty bat and his creaky navigation of the outfield limited him to only 552 plate appearances over three years, but as Steven Goldman points out, "they were the best 552 plate appearances of his career." Casey batted a cumulative .349, ran up a slugging percentage of .524, and reached base more than 40 percent of the time. He would also provide one of the greatest moments in New York's World Series history.

In 1921, the long-delayed showdown between the Yankees and the Giants, the match that had almost happened in the Yanks' second year of existence, finally came to pass. This was the first true "Subway Series"—but it was a monotonous trip. For the first time in World Series history, both teams played in the same stadium, the Polo Grounds.

It looked at first as if the new, corporate model for baseball would prevail. Carl Mays and Waite Hoyt, both acquired from Harry Frazee's Red Sox, opened the series by throwing back-to-back shutouts for the Yankees. The Giants dealt cautiously with Ruth, walking him four times in those first two games. In the fifth inning of game two, playing with his usual verve, the Babe tried to undermine this strategy by stealing second and third, but tore up his elbow avoiding Frankie Frisch's tag. Ruth attempted to hang in there, driving in two runs the next day, hitting a home run essentially one-handed in game four, and starting the game-clinching rally with a surprise bunt in game five. But he hurt the elbow again and it quickly became infected, blowing up, turning several dramatic colors (this was Babe Ruth's elbow, after all), and oozing pus that had to be drained with a tube. The Babe was able to make only a single pinch-hitting appearance in the last three games as McGraw's Giants coolly came back to win the best-of-nine series.

Many writers crowed that Ruth and the power game had been exposed. The Babe batted .313 on the series, played with an obviously disabled arm, and drove in four runs in sixteen at bats. Nonetheless, New York *Sun* writer Joe Vila mocked his "alleged injury." Others celebrated the debunking of the home run. *The Sporting News* informed its readers that "it wasn't real hitting and it wasn't the lively ball that enabled the Hugmen [Yankees] to break all home run records during the American League race. Punk pitching was the real reason." Once the Yanks and Ruth went up against the Giants, "the light was turned on and thousands of deluded fans suddenly realized how badly they'd been fooled by the so-called supermen wearing Yankee uniforms."

The writers were all the more gleeful the next fall, when the Giants won even more convincingly, sweeping the Yankees in four games, with a fifth called on account of darkness. The Babe was not injured this time but suffered the one truly bad World Series of the ten he would play in, hitting only .118. Vila called him "an exploded phenomenon," while Grantland Rice castigated "the once-mighty Bambino from Blooieland," who had "failed to hit the ball hard enough to dent the cuticle of a custard pie." W. O. McGeehan, the acerbic sports editor of the *Tribune,* wrote his professional obituary. The Babe, McGeehan concluded, was a "tragic figure" who had "flashed like a comet over all baseball fields. . . . [T]he most universal comment that he hears as his flaming star seems about to sink is, 'Ya big bum, ya.' "

This was the flip side of the big ballyhoo, the start of another venerable New York tradition: a sporting press that could flip like a short-order cook.

The Yankees, not for the last time, seemed to dissolve into a welter of recriminations after their 1922 series loss. Manager Huggins was convinced that Mays and Bullet Joe Bush had purposely thrown games to the Giants. Bush and Mays accused Huggins of calling the wrong pitches. Cap Huston, in his last days as co-owner, demanded once again that Huggins be fired. Ed Barrow threatened to quit as general manager if he was.

For McGraw, though, it was the pinnacle of his professional career. It was claimed that he had called every pitch his hurlers made to Ruth in the 1922 World Series, signaling them from the dugout—

vindication for Muggsy, whose previous failures in the postseason had been attributed to assertions that he was too controlling as a manager, turning his players into automatons. Now they had beaten the mighty Yankees in nine out of thirteen World Series games, and Mickey Face boasted that he had "the big monkey's number—just pitch him low curves and slow stuff and he falls all over himself."

"We yield to none in acknowledging the Napoleonic qualities of McGraw," wrote *The Sporting News*. "McGraw came as near to perfection in his strategy as man probably ever will come in baseball," confirmed another out-of-town scribe.

An ecstatic crowd waited for him outside the Giants' clubhouse after the last game of the series, eager just to touch him, patting his back and kissing his cheeks, stealing the hat from his head. McGraw thanked them, and then one elderly woman came forward to shake his hand and told the others, "I can go home now. I've seen the greatest manager in baseball."

Muggsy possessed enough humility to admit, some time after the fact, that "we caught Ruth in one of his slumps." But his success, and all the big, easy money, had begun to turn the heads of his employers. The Giants were making an average annual profit of $200,000—enough to declare a four-to-one stock split and finish enclosing at last the great, weird stadium that was the Polo Grounds with a double-decker grandstand, thereby sending gate receipts even higher. By 1923 the Giants had drawn the largest National League crowd ever, forty-one thousand, for a regular-season game. The 1921 World Series drew the very first million-dollar gate for the Fall Classic, adding still more bucks to the team coffers.

Just as it did on Wall Street, the big money only created a yen for more. The Giants might lead the National League in attendance every year, but thanks to Ruth their tenants were still outdrawing them. Thoughts of all the big Sunday crowds they *could* have if they didn't have to share the Polo Grounds with the Yankees became irrepressible. The Giants' owners noticed that over in Brooklyn the Dodgers got to play nineteen Sunday dates, while they got only thirteen, having to clear out so the Yankees could take on teams such as the Athletics and the Red Sox, in from cities where the blue laws were still in effect.

Soon, Stoneham and his co-owners had decided: the Yankees had to go. Before the first season of Sunday—and Babe Ruth—baseball in New York was even two months old, Judge McQuade announced that the Yankees' lease would be terminated at the end of the 1920 season. The Giants were now hoping to drive the American Leaguers out of town altogether, sure that it would be impossible for the Yanks to find a new site and build a new park before the next season started. It was an old-school Tammany move—a gangland move, narrowly focused on turf and territory. The Yankees were still paying $60,000 a year in rent—a considerable portion of the Giants' profit margin. Nor did the Giants' ruling triumvirate, still steeped in the world of the saloon and the pool hall, seem aware of the publicity that the teams' rivalry had created and what that meant at the box office. Their fellow owners understood it, even if they didn't. In an age of sudden colossal profits, baseball was hardly about to surrender the sport's greatest draw, in the nation's largest city.

The Giants were forced to back down and give the Yankees time to find a site and build a new stadium before kicking them out of the Polo Grounds. Tammany's team still didn't understand the new, corporate ways of the world, and it would cost the franchise dearly. But Jake Ruppert, once a Tammany congressman himself, saw it all with his usual, cold-blooded acuity.

"The Yankee Stadium is a mistake," he would say a few years later. "Not mine, but the Giants'."

35

Welcome to Goatville

The Yankees' search for a new home centered on Manhattan at first, particularly the site of the Hebrew Orphan Asylum, located between 136th and 138th Streets on Amsterdam Avenue. It's intriguing to guess what the team's nicknames might have become at a location with such a provenance, but the land was too expensive for the Colonels. Instead, they paid $600,000 for 11.6 desolate acres of an old lumberyard—appropriately enough—owned by the city's Ur-landlords, the Astors. The new site was not located in Manhattan at all, but at 161st Street and River Avenue in the Bronx.

"They are going to Goatville, and before long they will be lost sight of," gloated John McGraw, but he was wrong. The Yankees were going to the most dynamic borough in the city, and no one would ever lose sight of them again.

Muggsy was conjuring the bucolic Bronx of the nineteenth century, its population just fifty thousand by the 1880s. The highest structures in the whole borough were its grain elevators, the only industry a few factories, breweries, and coal- and lumberyards stuffed into its lower wards. Frequented mostly "by those who wish a rustic outing in the wild woods and pastures," according to *King's Handbook of New York City,* its northern reaches were so empty that the city—with a rare stroke of prescience—paid just $9 million to buy up four thousand acres of parkland, on which it would build such coming attractions as Van Cortlandt Park, the New York Botanical Garden, and the Bronx Zoo. Human habitation was limited to farms and sleepy villages, filled with German shopkeepers and Irish laborers—Melrose and Morrisania, Tremont and Wakefield, Highbridge and Kingsbridge and Williamsbridge. They hugged the routes of the New York and Harlem River Railroad and a trolley line so desultory it was dubbed the Huckleberry Horsecar, thanks to the ease with which its riders jumped off to pick berries along its way.

Everything changed with the subway. Within ten years of its arrival at 149th Street, the Bronx's population was 500,000, making it the size of the sixth-largest city in the United States, and its population would more than double again over the *next* fifteen years, to almost 1.3 million. The farmland buried under a vast grid of streets, highways, elevated rails, and (electrified) trolley, the sleepy villages transformed into complex urban universes, full of shops and synagogues, churches and cinemas. The former Goatville would soon be dubbed the wonder borough, while its daily newspaper, the *Bronx Home News,* urged its readers to "get a new resident for the Bronx" every day.

This was the "Little City" of New York, apart from the night world of Big City Manhattan. It was the city of neighborhoods, where most people worked long hours at industrial jobs. Yet it was also a city of strivers, and one of success. The people who filled it were immigrants who had made it—moving up from the squalid slums of the Lower East Side. Italians settling in Montrose and Belmont, and along Arthur Avenue; the Irish on Fordham Road, and so many Jews by the end of the 1920s—nearly 600,000—that Al Jolson kvelled about it to his mammy in *The Jazz Singer,* promising, "A whole lot of nice green grass up there. A whole lot of people you know. There's the Ginsbergs, the Guttenbergs and the Goldbergs. Oh, a lot of Bergs. I don't know them all."

Unlike Brooklyn, the Bronx had no history of itself as an independent, rival metropolis to brood over. It was a new place, its spine the Grand Concourse, a brand-new boulevard, its broad, tree-lined course inspired by Frederick Olmsted's grand parkways in Brooklyn and—as every new Bronx resident could tell you—the Champs-Élysées in Paris. The Concourse's southern terminus was an ornate white marble fountain, a tribute to Heinrich Heine's "Die Lorelei" poem, rejected by the anti-Semitic burghers of Düsseldorf but welcomed in the melting-pot Bronx. Here, people were transforming themselves as well as the borough, living in the fancy new apartments with central heating, electricity, gas stoves, refrigerators, and elevators. Living, more than ever before, with different peoples, eating different foods, practicing different religions.

"This is the newest New York," the best-selling English writer Arnold Bennett wrote on visiting one such Bronx apartment house. "And now I began to be struck by the splendour and the cleanliness of the marbled halls, tessellated landings and stairs . . . the whole producing a gorgeous effect. The people showed no trace of the influence of those older civilizations that seem to pervade the internationalism of the [Lower] East Side. The Bronx is different. The Bronx is beginning again, and beginning better."

This was, as Constance Rosenblum wrote in her perceptive history of the Grand Concourse, *Boulevard of Dreams,* the place "where janitors were called supers, where floors were covered not with linoleum worn thin from endless scrubbing but with glossy parquet—the 'true middle-class country,' as sociologist Samuel Lubell described that world." It was a place where wholly new dreams could take flight. The prestigious Lewis Morris Apartments, for instance, at 1749 on the Concourse, would soon come to be stuffed with offices of dentists and doctors—the educated children of all those uplifted garment workers, their families in apartments upstairs that ran to seven rooms or more.

(It was, too, a place to smash dreams, or at least gently euthanize them. Among the immigrant Russian Jews arriving every day was one Lev Davidovich Bronstein, a.k.a. Leon Trotsky, who moved his wife and two sons into a three-room apartment at 1522 Vyse Avenue during his wandering, prerevolution exile. The family lived there for a couple months in early 1917, while Trotsky churned out a propaganda sheet down on St. Mark's Place, only to have the Russian Revolution break out that spring and spoil everything. The Bronx must have presented disturbing insinuations of the possibilities of advancement within a capitalist society. A renegade fantasy has Trotsky choosing real estate over revolution. Staying in the apartment on Vyse Avenue or maybe moving up to a bigger one on the Concourse as the boys got older and a new child or two was added to the family. Arguing over socialism with his friends in the park like so many other graying, high-panted men. Taking his sons out to the big new ballyard on River Avenue, to sit in the sun in the bleachers and watch Babe Ruth play baseball, and shake his head over the silly American game but finding himself arching his neck, rising to his feet as the big man came to the plate.)

If the new apartment houses along the Concourse were not quite as expensive as the behemoths of Manhattan's Upper West Side, they were even more elaborate in their way, built by men even more desperate and dream-driven. No. 2665 on the Concourse, at Kingsbridge Road, was modeled after the Medici palace in Florence. No. 2700 was a medieval castle. The Theodore Roosevelt—which was really fourteen six-story buildings filling the entire block on the Concourse between 171st and 172nd Streets—was done up in a Spanish style complete with mansard roofs, marble floors, and little flags. Each building opened into an interior courtyard featuring a shady "Italian garden," complete with a fountain and a fifteen-foot statue of TR himself, "flanked by a sleeping lion and a sphinx." The developer of this particular fantasy was one Logan Billingsley, president of the Bronx Chamber of Commerce, older brother of Sherman Billingsley, the owner of Manhattan's Stork Club, "the New Yorkiest spot in New York." Logan was also, in another life, another state, a former bootlegger, former convict, former cop killer.

What drove him to develop middle-class housing on the Grand Concourse? "Maybe," his son would speculate many years later, "he just wanted to stay out of jail."

Billingsley's fellow developers, architects, and fantasists vied to outstrip him with each passing year of the golden decade. Andrew J. Thomas, an orphaned slum kid turned self-taught contractor and architect, wanted nothing more than to build for the working class.

"What better religion could there be than housing?" he liked to ask, announcing, "I'll abolish every slum in New York if I can gain the attention and help of charitable organizations, the state and society. . . . I'll raze nine or ten blocks at a time until the entire city is rebuilt."

He did not realize his goal, but by 1928 he had built Thomas Garden, another block full of five-story apartment houses on the Concourse, between 158th and 159th Streets. Intended originally as a middle-income cooperative, it included a communal playroom, dumbwaiters to take housewives' laundry to the rooftops, and, in *its* interior courtyard, a Japanese garden, complete with arched bridges over a goldfish pond and walkways lit with Japanese lanterns.

"It was tranquil. It was an oasis of beauty," remembered a young visitor, the longtime New York newsman Gabe Pressman, still filled with wonder more than half a century after the fact.

It was only appropriate to fit yet another palace into this fantasy city. If the Grand Concourse was the Bronx's Champs-Élysées, Yankee Stadium was its Arc de Triomphe. The last of the permanent, concrete-and-steel structures built by the original sixteen major-league teams, it was also something new, its design encompassing the revolution in the sport brought about by one man.

"Every other park in baseball had been built for the Dead Ball Era, with fences either so far away they were nearly impossible to reach or so close they provided little challenge to a slugger like Ruth," points out Glenn Stout. "Yankee Stadium was not built for the game that was, but for the game that baseball was becoming, the game of power and offense. It was the first modern ballpark."

The Colonels paid the Osborn Engineering Company—the same firm that had built Fenway Park and rebuilt the Polo Grounds—$2.5 million to construct their new park. Originally, Yankee Stadium was to consist of three fully enclosed decks, modeled after the Yale Bowl. But in a last grasp, Tammany dawdled with permissions to close city streets on the site until Osborn hired on White Construction, a New York contractor beloved by the machine. Building did not get under way for the 1923 season until May 1922—ironically forcing a more eccentric and elegant park upon the Yankees and sparing it something like Cleveland's Municipal Stadium, the oversized "mistake by the lake."

Yankee Stadium would still be immense, beyond the size of all but the biggest stadiums built to accommodate that other obsession of the 1920s, college football. In just 284 days, Osborn—and White—dug out 45,000 cubic yards of earth and replaced it with 13,000 yards of topsoil and 116,000 square feet of sod. Some 20,000 yards of concrete and 2,200 tons of steel went into the body of the stadium. The bleachers alone required 950,000 board feet of lumber and a million brass screws. It was a deep ballpark, with a left-centerfield far enough to stick a flagpole, and later actual stone monuments, right out on the playing field—but not so deep as to stunt the team's hitting. The right- *and* left-field lines offered short porches—but not easy enough to turn batters into pure pull hitters. The diversity of the field gave the team an edge by favoring neither pitchers nor hitters, nor any specialized game.

"The Yankees," as Stout notes, "never had to retool their game or style of play on the road"—something that would prove to be a distinct advantage over their rivals up in Boston.

Above all, the looming gray-white façade catered to a dream, the same way that all those battlements and flags and baronial lobby chairs did in the new apartment buildings along the Grand Concourse. It gave the stadium the aura of something grander and more important than a ballpark. Its most distinctive feature, the white filigree or frieze that hung from the upper deck, created an ambience of permanent celebration, like the icing on a wedding cake or bunting at a political rally. It also drew a veil across the upper deck, in a way that lent a sense of drama and grandeur to every big event. So much of the park looked shadowed and mysterious. Only the unenclosed outfield—the fortuitous result of one more Tammany extortion—let enough light in, the light of fifty Octobers, shifting about at deceptive, late-afternoon angles. And with it the real city just outside, the unmistakably urban landscape of apartment buildings and a courthouse on a hill and elevated trains rumbling by.

This was the new cathedral of baseball, in all its haughtiness.

On opening day, April 18, 1923, the announced attendance was seventy-four thousand. This was probably an exaggeration, but it might well have been sixty thousand, which still made it the largest crowd ever to see a baseball game up to that time. Most of the fans came by public transportation. Overlooking nothing, Colonel Ruppert had seen to it that three separate subway lines and the New York Central Railroad stopped at his new park, and to emphasize the point, he took the IRT to the game himself. (If any New York baseball owner has been on a subway since, it remains unrecorded.) Al Smith, now the governor of New York, was on hand to throw out the first ball, and John Philip Sousa led the Seventh Regiment marching band across the field during the pregame ceremonies. The opponent, appropriately enough, was the Boston Red Sox—with their owner, Harry Frazee, an honored guest, grinning from ear to ear beside the Colonels in their box throughout the festivities.

Babe Ruth claimed that he cried when the team left the Polo Grounds, he so loved to hit there. But now he walked out onto the field and looked around intently for a solid minute before muttering his verdict: "Some ballyard!"

The Ruth was pith. Privately, he told a friend that he would give a year off his life to hit the first home run in what Fred Lieb had already dubbed "The House That Ruth Built." The devil was never one to keep the Babe waiting. Batting in the fourth inning against the veteran Howard Ehmke, Ruth drove a pitch ten rows deep in the right-field bleachers for what proved to be a game-winning, three-run homer. The response was bedlam.

"The biggest crowd rose to its feet and let loose the biggest shout in baseball history," reported *The New York Times.* "Ruth, jogging over the home plate, grinned broadly, lifted his cap at arm's length and waved it to the multitude."

That autumn, the Yankees met the Giants for the third straight year. (Was *this* the first, true Subway Series, in that it was the first played by two New York teams, each in their own park, who "commuted" between them by subway? Well, you pays yer money and you takes yer choice.) It would also be the first World Series broadcast live, from start to finish, over a national network of radio stations. The earliest radio transmission of any ball game had been heard on KDKA in Pittsburgh in 1921. That same fall, the Yankees-Giants World Series had been on the air—but only by means of an observer relaying the action over the phone to KDKA, where an announcer engaged in what would become the venerable profession of "re-creating" a game over the radio.

Now, on October 10, 1923, the city in the air was on the air at last, all over the country, with Ruth facing his nemesis once again. McGraw expected the results to be the same, telling the press, "I believe that the same system which nullified his presence in the batting order in 1921 and 1922 will suffice."

It looked as if he might be right. Before a World Series–record crowd of over more than fifty-five thousand, in the opener at Yankee Stadium, a certain, well-known rascal stole the show. With the score tied, 4–4, and two outs in the top of the ninth, Casey Stengel whistled a long drive between Long Bob Meusel and Whitey Witt, into the wastes of deepest left center. As he churned around the bases, one of Casey's shoes started to come off, but he kept going, beating the throw home, in Damon Runyon's immortal description for the New York *Sun:*

> This is the way old Casey Stengel ran yesterday afternoon running his home run home. . . .
>
> This is the way—
>
> His mouth wide open.
>
> His warped old legs bending beneath him at every stride.
>
> His arms flying back and forth like those of a man swimming with a crawl stroke.
>
> His flanks heaving, his breath whistling, his head far back. Yankee infielders, passed by Old Casey Stengel as he was running his home run home, say Casey was muttering to himself, adjuring himself to greater speed as a jockey mutters to his horse in a race, saying, "Go on, Casey, go on."
>
> . . . The warped old legs, twisted and bent by many a year of baseball campaigning, just barely held out under Casey until he reached the plate, running his home run home.
>
> Then they collapsed.

Grantland Rice exclaimed, "Mudville is avenged at last!" while Heywood Broun mused that "it would have been a thrilling sight to see him meet an apple cart or a drugstore window."

Only Casey Stengel could manage to get himself described as an old horse, ready for the knackers, at the age of thirty-three. He had been married that summer, and later claimed his mother-in-law read such accounts with alarm.

"What kind of man did our Edna marry?" he imitated her. "Will he live long enough for us to find out?" He told the reporters, "I am really not old enough yet to go with crutches and I have done fairly good work this season, if I do say it myself."

When Stengel hit *another* game-winning home run in the same series—this one over the fence, before a *new* record crowd of more than sixty-two thousand at the stadium—he thumbed his nose at the

Yankees' bench after touching home plate, gloating later, "That's two for Stengel, one for the Yankees." Babe Ruth only laughed—"I don't mind. Casey's a lot of fun"—but Ruppert fumed and protested to Judge Landis. Even Landis refused to intervene: "Casey Stengel can't help being Casey Stengel."

Yet unbeknownst to anyone, it was the high-water mark for the New York Giants' franchise and for John McGraw. Over the next three games, McGraw's patchwork staff finally gave way as the Yanks battered their way to their very first world championship. Ruth hit three home runs, scored eight times, batted .368, and slugged 1.000 on the series. Many of the same scribes who had written his professional obituary the year before now praised him to the skies.

"Ruth is not only original, he is sometimes positively aboriginal," John Kieran chimed in, perpetuating the canard of Ruth as some kind of grand primitive. But Heywood Broun put it best: "The Ruth is mighty, and shall prevail."

For all of his insistence on running the Yankees like a modern corporation, Jacob Ruppert had nearly been undone by the tense final game of the series, going down to the Yankees' bullpen area and promising his amused pitchers that he would sign his businesses over to them if they would just beat the Giants. Afterward he wiped the tears away at the Yankees' victory party down at the Hotel Commodore, calling it "the happiest day of my life" and proclaiming, "Now I have the greatest ballpark and the greatest team!"

The Yankees bullpen was not added to the board of Knickerbocker beer. But the huge crowds at the new Yankee Stadium had brought in another record World Series gate. The Giants' owners happily raked in their share, without comprehending that they had created a monster.

Charlie Stoneham and friends had "forced" their bitter rival to move into the arms of a rapidly growing fan base, composed of many of the most prosperous, striving people in the city. Over the forty-five seasons from 1920 to 1964, the Yankees would not only enjoy unprecedented success on the field; they would also lead the American League in attendance thirty-six times. In twenty-six of those years, they accounted for more than one-fifth of the *total* league attendance, regularly drawing more fans than the bottom three teams combined. In 1932 and 1950, they outdrew the bottom *four* teams—or half the league. More important, for every season after 1919 save for three—1925, 1935, 1945—the Yankees would outdraw the Giants, usually by large margins.

The new stadium itself became a major tourist attraction; visitors to New York going out to see the park along with all the tall buildings and the museums and the jazz clubs. Its size and relative symmetry would make it a perfect venue for hosting any number of other events—college and professional football games, some thirty championship prizefights, papal visits, conventions of the Jehovah's Witnesses and the Knights of Columbus—thereby providing the team with still another steady stream of income for much of its stay. By evicting the Yankees, the Giants had not only forgone a sizable yearly rent but pushed their leading rivals into a commanding new position.

36

Dazzy and Daffy

The Bronx wasn't the only place where New Yorkers were going in the 1920s. Manhattan could at last begin to breathe again. After reaching an all-time high in population of more than 2.3 million people in 1910—more people than there were in thirty-three of the forty-six states in the Union at the time—the island would hold "only" 1.8 million souls by 1930. Robert Moses had already begun his dubious reinvention of New York as an automobile city, adding the Bronx River Parkway, the Hutchinson River Parkway, the Saw Mill River Parkway, the Cross County Parkway, the Holland Tunnel, and the George Washington Bridge to the city's infrastructure, between just 1923 and 1931.

In the age of the car, all of these new highways, bridges, and tunnels began for the first time to pull people *away* from the core of the city, as well as pulling them in. The new subways abetted the process; by the end of the 1920s, 91 percent of all New Yorkers lived within half a mile of a station. And while hundreds of thousands of them lived in the new, upscale buildings of the Bronx, more of them than ever went the other way—to Brooklyn.

The old city of homes and churches and ball clubs officially became the most populous borough for good in the 1930 census, with more than 2.5 million residents. Brooklyn's building boom would be a good deal more *haimishe* than either Manhattan's or the Bronx's, but just as sweeping. Between the end of the war and 1929, 117,000 new residential buildings rose in the borough. Some 13,000 of them were apartment houses; another 58,000 were Brooklyn's famous two-family houses, lining Ocean Parkway and filling in the central neighborhoods of Flatbush and Park Slope, Crown Heights and Brownsville, Brooklyn Heights and Clinton Hill and Williamsburg. Whole new developments went up throughout the southern tier of the borough to its coastal flats, in the old Dutch and English towns of Bensonhurst, New Utrecht, Gravesend, Canarsie, Fort Hamilton, New Lots.

If Brooklyn did not have Broadway, it still had its own movie company, the Vitaphone Studios, which churned out Warner Bros. shorts at East Fifteenth Street and Avenue M. If Brooklyn was not as upwardly mobile as the Bronx, it was still the working heart of the city. Its residents called their janitors janitors, made do with linoleum, and sought out their fantasy castles on Coney Island, where they now summered by the tens of thousands in a sprawling bungalow colony. It was in the 1920s that the cinematic stereotype of the Brooklynite—the good of heart, daft of head, whacky of diction, fiercely loyal, and charmingly ethnic—began to take shape. It would coalesce, in no small part, around the borough's abiding devotion to its ball team. The 1920s were the decade when the Brooklyn Dodgers first became a punch line.

At the start of the decade, they were still respectable—and still the Robins. The fans flocked to see the Flock in record numbers, while Uncle Robbie stitched together another winning combination of hobbled veterans and unknowns, led by a pitcher with the Dickensian moniker Burleigh Grimes.

(In 1934, wrapping up his career for the Yankees and the Pirates, Grimes would become the very last major-league hurler to throw a legally doctored baseball—in both leagues!—under the sport's grandfather clause allowing each team to name one designated spitballer until retirement. Grimes, also known as Ol' Stubblebeard, never shaved on days when he pitched. It seems the "slippery elm" juice that he spat on the ball would irritate his skin if it ran down his face—something that says all one needs to know about the aesthetic appeal of the spitball.)

The grizzled Grimes would make Cooperstown, largely on the strength of his slippery elm and a tendency—like that of Carl Mays—to throw at batters' heads. He won twenty-three games in 1920 and led the Robins into the World Series, where, as it happened, the team they faced was Ray Chapman's Cleveland Indians. Grimes's proclivities must have weighed on Cleveland minds. The Brooklyn pitcher didn't hit anybody in his first series start, but he did shut out the Tribe, 3–0, at Ebbets Field, despite surrendering seven hits and four walks. His luck would change back in Cleveland, when he started the pivotal game five, with the series tied at two games apiece. October 10, 1920—the auspiciously numbered 10/10/20—would be a day when all the baseball gods seemed to line up against the borough of Brooklyn for the first time and in the shape of a former seminary student. It would be a day of remarkable firsts—and every single one of them went against the Robins.

Before he could retire a single Indian, Grimes surrendered the first grand-slam home run in World Series history, failing to get his slippery elm ball past right fielder Elmer Smith. In the bottom of the fourth, Grimes then gave up the first World Series home run ever to a *pitcher,* a three-run blast by Jim Bagby.

Burleigh was mercifully yanked, but it didn't make much difference. The Robins managed to record thirteen hits and three walks against Bagby but scored only one run. They hit into three double plays but, in the top of the fifth, seemed finally poised to break through with two men on, nobody out, and a good-hitting relief pitcher, Clarence Mitchell, at the plate. Mitchell repaid Uncle Robbie's faith in him by lacing a ball toward centerfield, a line drive that had base hit written all over it. Both runners took off at once—but so did Ray Chapman's old double-play partner, a modest, light-hitting Cleveland native with the mysterious name Bill Wambsganss who had opted out of a life in the pulpit to play for his hometown team.

Wambsganss took three steps to his right and snagged Mitchell's liner. One out. His momentum carried him to second base, where he touched the bag, retiring Brooklyn's Pete Kilduff, who had taken off for third and never looked back. Two gone. Wambsganss then turned to see the runner from first, Otto Miller, "just standing there, with his mouth open, no more than a few feet away from me."

Wambsganss tapped him on the shoulder with the ball and ran into the dugout. The Dodgers' base runners and most of his own teammates stayed out on the field. In the stands, the Cleveland fans seemed equally dazed, sitting in silence even after Hank O'Day, the umpire from the notorious Merkle game, made the correct call this time. Then they erupted, the Indians racing into the dugout to mob Wambsganss. What they had just witnessed—too quick for most of them to comprehend—was an unassisted triple play, the rarest single play in baseball. To this day, it is the only one ever made in a World Series. Or as Ring Lardner quipped, "It was the first time in world serious history that a man named Wambsganss had ever made a triple play assisted by consonants only."

Brooklyn would score only one run in the rest of the series. The following day they were shut out by one of their own castoffs, a journeyman pitcher named Duster Mails—who liked to refer to himself as the Great Mails—and were blanked again in the seventh and last game of the best-of-nine series.

Once the Flock was eliminated, they would not be back in the Fall Classic for more than twenty years. After battling McGraw's Giants down to the last weekend in 1924, the team reverted to a numbing mediocrity, finishing sixth four times in a row to close out the decade, eleven times in all between 1922 and 1938.

This drop into perpetual drear was accelerated by the death in 1925 of Charles Hercules Ebbets, the savior of Brooklyn baseball. His death would prove a tragedy for his team and his borough, though one that would take a long time to work itself out. Ebbets had been grooming his son to replace him, according to Robert E. Murphy, but Charlie Jr. appears to have had a drinking problem and quarreled bitterly with his father—so much so that when Charlie Sr. died, he left his son an annual income of only $2,000, out of an estate valued at somewhere between $1.3 and $2 million. Junior died estranged from his wife as well, alone in an upper Manhattan apartment in 1944. The Ebbets half of the team went to some fifteen perpetually squabbling family heirs, scattered over three generations.

This left effective control of the team to the McKeever brothers, the contractors Ebbets had been forced to sign on with in order to get his park built, and who decided to make Wilbert Robinson club president as well as manager. A worse choice is hard to imagine. Uncle Robbie was old, obese, and moribund, his control over his ball team fading. The Dodgers, like the Giants, did not yet grasp that the game was now to be run like a big business, with a hierarchy of officers performing distinct tasks. At least life with Uncle Robbie provided some entertainment. This was when the team would first become known as the Daffiness Boys—although their reputation stemmed almost solely from a single incident involving the Flock's most talented players, Floyd Caves "Babe" Herman and Charles Arthur "Dazzy" Vance.

Babe Herman was a tousle-haired, bucktoothed outfielder with a perpetually furrowed brow and squinty gaze that made him look rather like a Neanderthal. This was unfair; Herman was in fact accepted at the University of California before signing with the Dodgers, but there is no denying he had occasional lapses in attention. Brooklyn's Babe was known to shove a lit cigar butt into his pocket and was once caught reading the newspaper on the bench. He adamantly denied ever having been hit on the head by a fly ball, but he was an awful fielder who led the National League in errors at first base and then in right field.

Herman was, by his own admission, "a pretty fair country hitter," a left-handed slugger who took advantage of Ebbets Field's short right-field fence to run up a lifetime average of .324. Yet it was his base-running that ultimately settled his reputation during his very first season with the Dodgers, in 1926. Playing at home against Boston, Herman hit a long smash with the bases loaded. One run scored, but the next runner held up at third. A second runner was soon on top of him and then Babe, seeing what he thought was a rundown, came plowing up, believing he had alertly grabbed an extra base. Before anyone could straighten it out, all three runners were on third base.

Herman, as it turned out, had plated the winning run on the play, but nobody remembered *that.* The pile-up on third base instantly became the stuff of legend, inspiring the story of a Brooklyn cabbie who supposedly shouted up to a fan, asking how the game was going when he passed Ebbets Field.

"The Dodgers have three men on base!" the fan yelled back.

"Which base?" the cabbie answered.

"Only time I can think of when a fellow drives in the winning run and the press makes him a goat instead of a hero," Babe harrumphed to Lawrence Ritter many years later. He also claimed that Brooklyn's third-base coach at the time, Joe Kelley, an old Orioles teammate of Uncle Robbie's, had confided to him, "Without my glasses, I can't even see who's pitching. But I won't wear glasses on a ball field."

"Why not?" asked Babe.

"Pride," explained Kelley.

For Herman the main culprit in the great third-base incident was Dazzy Vance, the runner who had stopped short for no particular reason after rounding third. Chick Fewster, the third runner on third, panicked and ran into the outfield, where he was eventually tagged. But Vance stayed where he was, flat on his back across the bag, addressing the crowd around him: "Mr. Umpire, fellow teammates, and members of the opposition, if you carefully peruse the rules of our national pastime you will find that there is one and only one protagonist in rightful occupancy of this hassock—namely yours truly, Arthur C. Vance."

Only Dazzy Vance could thwart a rally, immortalize a teammate, and reverse the order of his given names on a single play. Babe Herman never stood a chance against the pitcher, who quickly dubbed him "the headless horseman of Ebbets Field." Loquacious and genial, Vance had bounced around the minors for ten years, impressing scouts with his fastball, only to see his arm go dead by mid-season. After failed auditions with the Pirates and Yankees, he turned himself over to a surgeon, and a manager in New Orleans who hit upon the novel strategy of letting him rest for an extra day between starts.

This unprecedented coddling seemed to work, though no other manager would give in to such indulgence for another four decades or so, no matter how many great prospects ruined themselves. Breaking in with the Dodgers as a thirty-one-year-old rookie, Vance became the dominant pitcher in the National League in the 1920s, leading the circuit in wins twice, complete games twice, shutouts four times, ERA three times, and strikeouts a record seven times in a row, once by a ratio of nearly two to one over his next closest competitor. In 1924, his best season, he went 28-6, with thirty complete games and an ERA of 2.16—in a year when the league's earned-run average was 3.87.

During his sore-armed seasons in the minors, Vance had developed a big, snapping curveball, "like an apple rolling off a crooked table." He augmented it with an elaborate, high-kicking delivery and further distracted the hitters by wearing a red undershirt with the sleeves sliced to fluttering ribbons—except on Mondays. On Mondays, Dazzy Vance wore white.

"Then he'd pitch overhand, out of the apartment houses in the background at Ebbets Field," remembered Rube Bressler. "Between the bleached sleeve of his undershirt waving and the Monday wash hanging out to dry—the diapers and undies and sheets flapping on the clotheslines—you lost the ball entirely."

Such was baseball in the homey days of the Brooklyn Robins, with players piling up on third base and curveballs coming out of the washing at terrified batters. Meanwhile, the team continued to drift comfortably downward, its manager and president unperturbed.

"Uncle Robbie . . . was at least partially responsible for the image," Donald Honig would write. "He seemed to watch it all with a certain sense of detachment, as though he might have other, more serious business on his mind. He also seemed genuinely fond of his athletes, like a grandfather with too many rascally grandchildren bounding mischievously about, sighing at their boyish antics."

The team's perpetual money shorts didn't help. The Dodgers might play in the most populous borough of New York, but Ebbets Field was a bandbox, with less than half the capacity of Yankee Stadium or the Polo Grounds, and the team lacked any outside source of revenue. Instead, Steve McKeever took to squabbling over nickels and dimes with his players as the Depression came on. Dazzy Vance was shipped out and ended up on the "Gas House Gang" in St. Louis—providing the Cards at the same time with players called Dazzy, Dizzy, and Daffy. Babe Herman was traded for daring to protest when McKeever denied him a promised $800 raise after a season in which Herman batted .393. Returning to the Dodgers briefly at the very end of his career, the forty-two-year-old Babe hit a ball off the right-field screen to score two runs but slipped going around first base. The headline read SAME OLD HERMAN, TRIPS OVER FIRST BASE.

37

"Anything Can Happen Now"

On February 17, 1919, the Black soldiers of New York's 369th Infantry, the "Harlem Hellfighters," came marching home up Fifth Avenue. The Hellfighters had spent a longer time in combat—191 days—than any other unit of American fighting men in World War I, had suffered a fatality rate more than twice that of the white doughboys, and had emerged the most decorated single regiment in the American Expeditionary Force.

Now, as they crossed 110th Street into Harlem, James Reese Europe had the regiment's legendary band break into "Here Comes My Daddy Now." The crowds massed along the sidewalks "went wild with joy," reported *The New York Times.* "Each person in the throng seemed to be shouting to a particular soldier . . . until the unison of voices became a mighty roar such as Harlem had never heard."

It was a moment of unbounded hope in Harlem and Black America everywhere. Yet within three months of his return, Europe himself, the great bandleader and jazz composer, would be dead, knifed by a crazy drummer up in Boston. And the frenzied crowds along Lenox Avenue would find that as far as white America was concerned, the war had changed nothing at all.

The 369th included some of the best players on the New York Lincoln Stars, Harlem's own championship team. Having proven themselves over there, they must have considered it unimaginable that they would not at least be given a chance back here. Many Black leaders and intellectuals, including W. E. B. Du Bois, had supported the war effort at least in part in the belief that such support would make African American claims to equal citizenship undeniable. Instead, returning Black soldiers were greeted by an orgy of white-on-Black riots, beatings, lynchings, church burnings, and wholesale assaults on African American communities across the country. In what became known as the Red Summer of 1919, at least seventy-six African Americans were lynched. Even in the nation's capital, white soldiers and sailors roamed the streets, attacking Black citizens at random and killing five of them.

The violence was not limited to the southern states—one of the worst race riots of all that year was in Chicago—but it did accelerate "the Great Migration," the mass Black exodus, more than six million strong, continuing until the end of the 1960s, from the fields of the South to the cities of the North and the West. By the end of the 1920s, 40 percent of all African Americans lived in northern metropolises. Cleveland, Chicago's South Side, and Detroit's Paradise Valley, among others, all witnessed even greater percentage increases in their Black populations than did New York. But there was no place like Harlem.

"A blue haze descended at night and with it strings of fairy lights on the broad avenues," remembered the poet and novelist Arna Bontemps. "From the window of an apartment on Fifth Avenue and 129th Street I looked over the rooftops of Negrodome and tried to believe my eyes. What a city! What a world!"

By 1930, over 100,000 more whites had left upper Manhattan—replaced by over 200,000 people of color. Everywhere, it seemed, large signs reading JUST OPEN FOR COLORED were going up in storefronts. Neighborhoods remained largely Jewish or Italian in East Harlem and elsewhere on the periphery, but central Harlem, from Amsterdam Avenue to the Harlem River, 110th Street to 157th, was overwhelmingly Black. Where in 1890 only 1 in every 70 New Yorkers was of African descent, forty years later 1 in every 9 would be.

"It was New York that filled our imagination. We were awed by the never-ending roll of great talents there," wrote Duke Ellington, who arrived in 1923 for a twelve-year stint at the Cotton Club. "Harlem, in our mind, did indeed have the world's most glamorous atmosphere. We had to go there."

Go there they did. Of all the outstanding writers of the Harlem Renaissance, of all the leading sculptors and painters, and the great musicians and composers, only one major figure—the poet and writer Countee Cullen—was originally from the city. The rest might stay for only a few years, or months, or even weeks, before using Harlem as a jumping-off point to Paris, or points north, or even back south. But they had to come.

"I'd rather be a lamppost in Harlem," the new immigrants told one another, "than governor of Georgia."

The brave words belied just how hard life in the "Negro Capital of the World" really was. The NYPD might have hired its very first Black officers in the 1910s (something almost unimaginable in nearly all of America), but the city's most violent, venal, and uncontrollable cops were still reassigned to Harlem as a "punishment"—more for the people they were supposed to serve, it developed, than for themselves. Beyond the haze of the fairy lights, the crowding on many Harlem blocks approached that of the old Lower East Side as tenants doubled and tripled up to meet the extortionate rents white landlords charged.

They could get away with this because Blacks were allowed to live nowhere else in the city *but* Harlem, save for a few scattered enclaves in Brooklyn and Queens. It might be, as Bontemps claimed, that in Harlem it was "fun to be a Negro," but to take one step out of the neighborhood was to invite harassment and insult, in a New York where all of the best restaurants and hotels, the theaters and even the beaches generally turned away African Americans. Eugenics, the idea that the relative superiority of every race—or really, what we would now call every ethnic group—could be scientifically determined, had been reinforced for decades in universities, from the pulpit, even at county fairs that gave out prizes to the "ideal" white families. By the 1920s, it was being effectively used to keep Jews, Italians, and Slovaks out of the country, and it precluded any sort of contact with African Americans in what was considered polite white society.

The color line was drawn even within the community. Department stores along 125th Street, Harlem's Main Street, would not hire Black employees and would not allow Black shoppers to try on cloth-

The original New York Knickerbockers baseball club. The man with beard and stogie in the center of the first row is Doc Adams, the world's first shortstop, and the man who compiled the New York rules.

Esteban "Steve" Bellán, "the Cuban Sylph." The Fordham grad was the first Latin America–born player known to play professional baseball and would become "the father of Cuban baseball."

Thought to be taken at New York's Colored Orphan Asylum in 1863, this is perhaps the earliest photo of African Americans playing baseball. The asylum would be burned to the ground by a white mob that July, the children barely escaping with their lives.

Frank Grant, probably the greatest Black player of the 19th century, with the International League's Buffalo Bisons in 1887. None of his white teammates rest a companionable hand on Grant's shoulder. The following year, they would refuse to pose with him at all.

Smilin' Mickey Welch, star hurler for the 1883 New York Giants. Note the large team patch, with the city seal of New York on it.

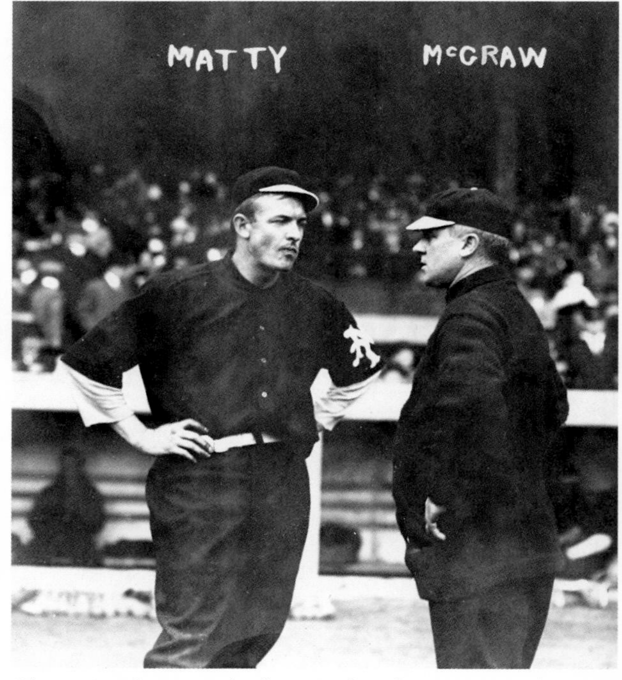

Christy Mathewson, the "Big Six," with manager and sometime roommate, John J. McGraw.

John Montgomery Ward, the man who started the Players' League, in a posed "action" shot.

Like all major leaguers who were deaf, Luther Taylor was called "Dummy." Taylor, who won 116 games in the majors, used to make his teammates sign him the jokes in vaudeville houses.

Orphaned at eight by a train wreck, "Turkey Mike" Donlin—named for his strut on a ballfield—was a dangerous hitter and a dangerous drunk, until he was tamed by actress Mabel Hite, for whom he left baseball for vaudeville.

John T. Brush, owner of the Giants from 1902 to 1912, in full Masonic regalia.

Outfielder Guy Zinn of New York slides back into first against Boston at Hilltop Park, 1912. The apartment buildings in the distance—still extant on W. 168th Street—were used by the Yankees to steal signs.

"Happy Jack" Chesbro, who won a record 41 games for the Yankees in 1904, but "lost" the pennant with a wild pitch.

Hal Chase, "the man with the corkscrew brain," playing for Buffalo in the Federal League, 1915, where he led the league in home runs.

Five American League club presidents, 1914, with league president Ban Johnson at center of front row. Yankees co-owner Frank Farrell, top right, seems to be looking for an exit.

The "dead-heads" on Coogan's Bluff watching the World Series at the Polo Grounds, October 10, 1905.

Angry Giants fans watch their team losing the makeup of the "Merkle game."

Hank O'Day, a World Series–winning pitcher, manager, scout, and Hall of Fame umpire, was one of the few white players to befriend the Black Walker brothers. But he would set off the Merkle controversy.

Cubs second baseman Johnny "Crab" Evers, the brain behind the Merkle call. He had so much nervous energy that it was claimed his watches stopped dead from the current emanating from his body.

Fred Merkle with, ironically, the Cubs. A savvy first baseman, he would play 16 years in the majors and for all three New York teams. But he would always be known as "Bonehead" for a single play.

Bat Masterson, the legendary western lawman turned New York sportswriter. "He died with his boots on"—at his typewriter.

A presidential golf outing. Left to right, President Warren G. Harding, Grantland Rice, Ring Lardner, and Undersecretary of State Henry P. Fletcher.

Opening day, April 10, 1915, for the Federal League at Washington Park. The Brooklyn Tip-Tops, in white, blew a 6–1 lead, then came back to win, 13–9, before 15,441 fans.

The great Louis Santop, Hall of Fame catcher for the New York Lincoln Giants, 1911 to 1916. A top hitter, he was known as "the human freight car," and once broke three of Oscar Charleston's ribs just hugging him hello.

Oscar Charleston, here with Cuba's Almendares club, played for 16 teams over 27 seasons, including the New York Lincoln Giants. Charleston neither drank nor smoked, but would fight anyone. Bill James named him the fourth greatest player of all time.

Wa-Tho-Tuk, better known as Jim Thorpe, a Sac and Fox Native American, was widely considered the greatest athlete of the 20th century. He played in 6 seasons and 152 games for the New York Giants, but hit only .252.

Carl Mays, inscrutable and unloved, the man who threw the pitch that killed Ray Chapman.

Opening day, 1923, at brand-new Yankee Stadium. Left to right are Yankees co-owner Jacob Ruppert, baseball commissioner Judge Kenesaw Mountain Landis, Ruppert's partner Tillinghast L'Hommedieu Huston, Red Sox owner Harry Frazee, and Ed Flynn, the future "boss of the Bronx."

The Babe in New York, game face on.

Jolly old Wilbert Robinson, the roly-poly, easygoing manager of the Dodgers for 18 years.

Martín Dihigo, perhaps the most multitalented individual ever to play the game. An outstanding hitter and pitcher, Dihigo played every position on the field, played year-round for 24 seasons, and played for Alex Pompez's Cubans in New York.

Alex Pompez, "El Cubano," being booked for running a numbers racket by Detective James Canavan after his extradition from Mexico. The owner of New York's Cuban Stars would bring many of the greatest Black and Hispanic players to the city.

The Dyckman Oval, in Inwood, seen from the intersection of Nagle Avenue and Academy Street. The refurbished home of Alex Pompez's New York Cubans, it was demolished for a parking lot for the Dyckman Houses.

The Newark Eagles' brain trust: Abe and Effa Manley. Abe Manley was a policy racket baron; Effa—the only woman in the Baseball Hall of Fame—an avid and sometimes severe student of the game.

The Giants' brain trust: Horace Stoneham, center, and Mel Ott, player-manager and later team executive.

The Yankees' brain trust. Left to right: farm system director and later general manager George Weiss, manager Joe McCarthy, and business manager and president Ed Barrow.

The Dodgers' brain trust. Left to right: Larry MacPhail, president and general manager; co-owner-to-be Branch Rickey; and manager Leo Durocher.

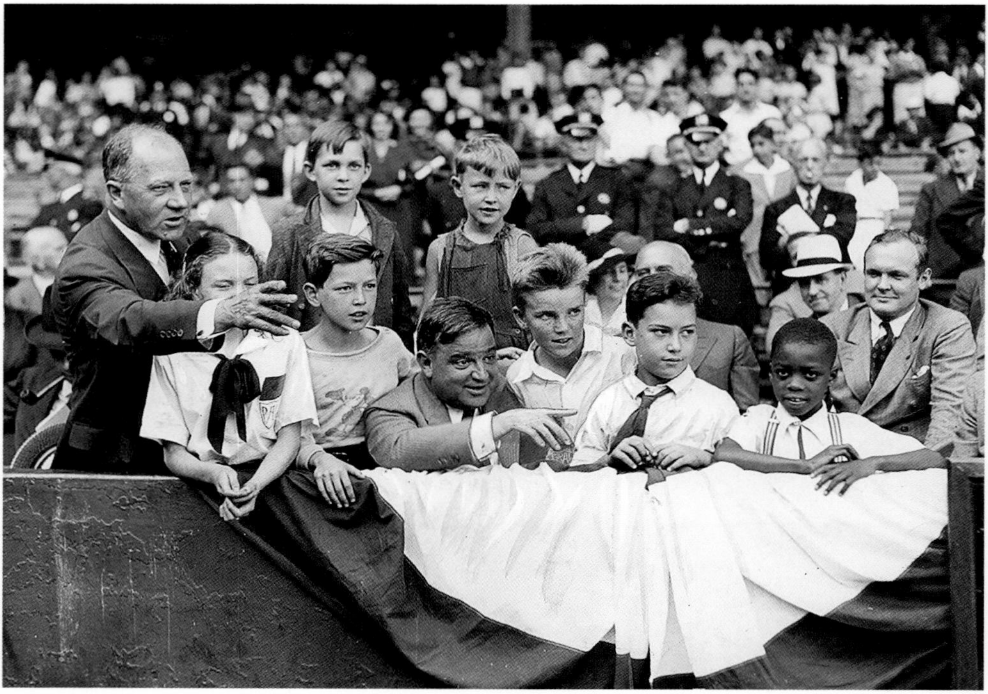

Mayor Fiorello La Guardia, "the Little Flower," center, and Police Commissioner Lewis Valentine, left, at the ballpark with children on a Police Athletic League outing.

The legendary Red Barber became the first to announce a professional baseball telecast anywhere.

Lou Gehrig, top, comforts his replacement, "Babe" Dahlgren, on the day Gehrig took himself out of the lineup, May 2, 1939. Ron Darling has called this the greatest baseball picture ever taken.

Joe DiMaggio kisses his elusive "ball bat" for *The Sporting News,* during his record, 56-game hitting streak in 1941.

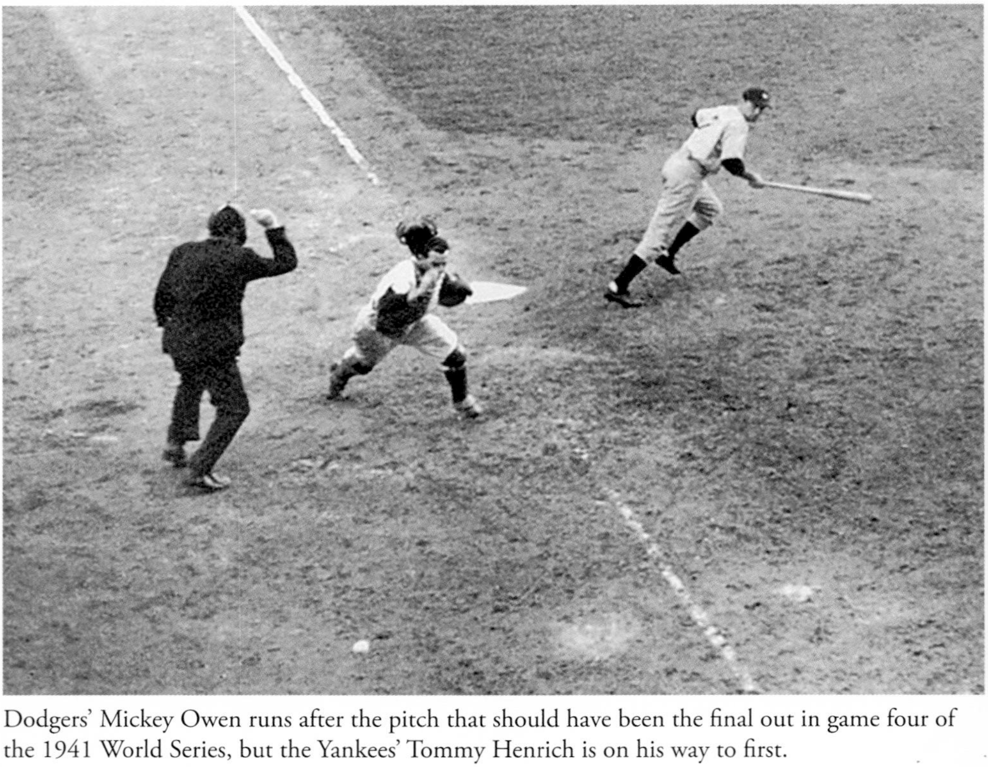

Dodgers' Mickey Owen runs after the pitch that should have been the final out in game four of the 1941 World Series, but the Yankees' Tommy Henrich is on his way to first.

ing. Nearly all Harlem movie theaters had special back stairways or fire escapes—some of which can still be seen today—where Blacks were forced to enter restricted seats in upper balconies, the sardonically labeled "n——r heaven." The street's leading theater, Hurtig & Seamon's Music Hall—later the Apollo—did not allow Black patrons at all. Nor did most of the fabled clubs, which might feature only Black performers but were usually owned by white gangsters. A visiting W. C. Handy was turned away from the door of the Cotton Club just as he heard one of his own songs being played. Inside, white "slummers" reveled amid a decor of "jungle trees," while limits on the skin tone of the performers were announced by the Cotton Club's signature song: "She's Tall, She's Tan, She's Terrific."

When African Americans were not turned away at the door, they were systematically dehumanized even by the keenest of observers.

"As we crossed Blackwell's Island a limousine passed us, driven by a white chauffeur, in which sat three modish negroes, two bucks and a girl," was how Fitzgerald described Gatsby and Nick Carraway passing into Manhattan. "I laughed aloud as the yolks of their eyeballs rolled toward us in haughty rivalry.

" 'Anything can happen now that we've slid over this bridge,' I thought; 'anything at all. . . .' "

Anything, apparently, save for an appreciation of Black Americans as something more than emblems of exotica and licentiousness. For all the slummers, it was true, there were more genuinely sympathetic white patrons than ever before, including the likes of Eugene O'Neill, Carl Van Vechten, and Nancy Cunard. Wealthy or well-connected men and women who opened the doors to major publishing houses, theaters, and music labels. Black singers and musicians, especially, experienced unprecedented crossover breakthroughs. In 1920–21, Mamie Smith's rendition of Perry Bradford's "Crazy Blues" sold more than one million records in the space of seven months, even at the then shocking price of $1 a record. It triggered a mania for the blues that saw 5,500 records cut by 1,200 African American artists over the next twenty years. No fewer than 211 Black women singers were signed up by white-owned record companies before the 1920s were over. In 1921, Ethel Waters sold 500,000 copies of the Fletcher Henderson arrangement of "Down Home Blues"; two years later, Bessie Smith's "Down Hearted Blues" sold 780,000 records.

It seemed that Du Bois's talented tenth might be able to wring recognition from the white establishment after all. But what success there was came more from Black push than white pull. Location was key; density was key.

Thanks to its antecedents as a planned suburb for well-off whites, Harlem, as James Weldon Johnson pointed out, was "not a fringe, nor a slum nor a quarter consisting of dilapidated tenements. It is a section of . . . handsome dwellings, with streets as well paved, as well lighted and as well kept as any other part of the city. It is a black city, located in the heart of white Manhattan, and containing more Negroes to the square mile than any other spot on earth. It strikes the uninformed observer as a phenomenon, a miracle straight out of the skies."

It was relatively easy for Harlem to become central. Central to the growing hordes of curious whites, looking for one thrill or another, cruising uptown in their limousines and touring cars, filling the clubs and the bars and the restaurants. Central to so much of white art and culture, above or below 110th Street.

"The nightclub capital of the world," Harlem had 125 legal clubs and cabarets and hundreds more illegal after-hours joints and blind tigers. They provided probably the most intense congregation of great music this country has ever seen, at Small's Paradise and the Savoy, the Cotton Club and Connie's Inn, the Clam House and Pod's and Jerry's Catagonia Club, and so many others. Black shows, in turn, spread down to Broadway, then leaped the Atlantic to Europe, where Le Corbusier compared their music to the fantastic skyscrapers of the New World: "Manhattan is hot jazz in stone and steel."

There were, as well, the ironic virtues of living in a ghetto. Not a slum, as interchangeably as the words are used today, but a real *ghetto,* much like the gated Jewish ghettos of Europe, a place where all members of a group were forced to live together, regardless of income, ability, or accomplishment.

Harlem was "the first concentration in history of so many diverse elements of Negro life," wrote Alain Locke, author of the Renaissance's seminal text, *The New Negro.* It had "attracted the African, the West Indian, the Negro American; has brought together the Negro of the North and the Negro of the South; the man from the city and the man from the town and the village; the peasant, the student, the businessman, the professional man, artist, poet, musician, adventurer and worker, preacher and criminal, exploiter and social outcast."

This Black diversity, this forcing together of so many elements, was one of the keys to its dazzling fermentation, just as it was in the white New York downtown. In Harlem it was more closely condensed, more fiercely lived, if only by necessity. Blacks in Harlem had no Bronx and no Brooklyn to aspire to, no more "away" they could aim for. Even in elite sections such as Strivers' Row and Sugar Hill, jazz musicians lived next to ministers, doctors with prizefighters, lawyers with writers and painters. Harlem's churches abutted its poolrooms, its nightclubs and dance halls.

Disgraceful as this form of northern segregation was, it forced a hugely creative cross-pollination and kept at least some money in the community. African Americans owned $60 million worth of real estate in Harlem by the end of the 1920s, a pittance compared with white wealth in the city, but a miracle for a people who had mostly arrived in New York less than a generation before and escaped slavery only the generation before that. The community had two profitable daily newspapers, its own array of fraternal organizations and lodges; its own YWCA and legendary YMCA on West 135th Street, domicile of so many great artists on their first night in New York. There were sixty Black churches in Harlem, many of them beautiful, capacious structures that had been built or bought for considerable sums. The Reverend Adam Clayton Powell Sr. induced his parishioners to erect and pay off the new Abyssinian Baptist Church on West 138th Street in record time; when it was done, he burned the mortgage in the pulpit. Before long, he would shepherd the largest Protestant congregation in the country.

The churches, and their many related social services and properties, were a stake in the ground, a freehold; the declaration by Black New York that it would not be moved again. Other movements, such as Walter White's NAACP, and A. Philip Randolph's socialist magazine, *The Messenger*—and later the Pullman porters' union he headed—started the next, long push for full civil rights and equality. Both were overshadowed for a time in the 1920s by Marcus Garvey's United Negro Improvement Association, which sought to weave an entire Black nationalist galaxy across the African diaspora, complete with its own king and court, government and creed.

Everywhere they could, Harlemites sought to carve out their own businesses, however painful the process. Two Black-owned record companies, Black Patti and Black Swan, wrested some of the booming record industry away from white control. W. C. Handy was the chairman of Black Swan's board and Du Bois was a member, Fletcher Henderson the recording director; the company made a healthy profit before selling to Paramount in 1924. There were also attempts to replace the ofay patrons from downtown. A'Lelia Walker, heir to Madam C. J. Walker's hair-straightening fortune, converted part of her mother's townhouse at West 136th Street and Lenox Avenue into the Dark Tower—Harlem's first true literary salon, decorated with murals by Renaissance artists and designed as a meeting place for the community's intellectual elite. The Dark Tower suffered from a multiplicity of purposes—it was supposed to be not only a salon but also a moneymaking nightclub—and its beneficiaries cruelly mocked both the pretensions of A'Lelia and what Zora Neale Hurston called "the n——rati." But the spirit of empowerment, of Black *ownership,* was ascendant.

It lagged, still, in baseball. Looking to fill their stadiums for those big Sunday doubleheaders that Jimmy Walker's legislation had made possible, New York's baseball teams were actively reaching out to non-Protestant white working-class fans. And all over town, different ethnic groups were battering down clubhouse doors.

McGraw signed up Jim Thorpe, hoping the Native American wonder could add baseball to the many sports he had conquered. It would prove to be a botched experiment, one of Muggsy's misfires. Thorpe—born Wa-tho-Huk, or "Path Lit by Lightning," into the Sac and Fox Nation of Oklahoma—had become the greatest college football player of his day, then amazed the world by winning both the decathlon and the pentathlon at the 1912 Olympics. With his (officially) amateur status exhausted, he turned to baseball, the highest-paying professional sport of the time, inking a sizable contract for $5,000. Yet something never quite clicked. McGraw kept him on the Giants for parts of seven seasons—trading him away or sending him down to the minors, only to acquire him again, as if he couldn't quite make up his mind.

Thorpe showed flashes of brilliance but—like so many before him, and Michael Jordan after him—struggled to hit a major-league curveball. McGraw kept him on the team but played him only sparingly, a strategy he used to bring along the likes of Fred Merkle and later Mel Ott. Thorpe's most recent biographer, David Maraniss, speculates that this was exactly the wrong approach for Jim, who thrived on work. Much like Ruth—much like so many great athletes—Thorpe figured out things about his sports as he played them, and in a stunning reversal of how things usually work, his baseball also seemed to improve as he aged. Remarkably, Thorpe batted .327 in his last major-league season (albeit in just sixty games), then went down to the International League and hit .360 and .358 over the next two seasons, with power and speed. But by then he was thirty-four and would play only one more season in organized ball.

The Yankees, meanwhile, got a leg up on the Italian community by signing Tony Lazzeri, and when told that the team had signed Lou Gehrig, manager Miller Huggins asked eagerly, "Is he Jewish?" The quest to sign a Jewish star had become something of a preoccupation with all three New York teams, leading McGraw to ink an enigmatic, intellectual backup catcher from Princeton named Moe Berg and to try an obscure slugger from the Southwestern League named Mose Hirsch Solomon, born on Hester Street, whom the press instantly—and predictably—dubbed the Rabbi of Swat. The Slugging Reb went three for eight in his brief major-league career, but apparently his fielding was less than echt. (Like everyone else in New York, he supposedly went on to make a killing in real estate.)

Yet for all this newfound tolerance, there was still not an inch of movement toward signing players of any darker color to play for the Dodgers, Giants, or Yankees. Black ballplayers in New York, unlike most other Black performers, were still shut off to the side—and under complete white authority. The McMahon brothers had moved on from the Lincoln Stars, but they had been replaced by Nat Strong, a crusty white booking agent, sporting goods salesman, and (inevitably) real estate dabbler.

It was the same old story: he who controlled the grounds, controlled the baseball. By hook or by crook, Strong had wrested control over almost every space where the game was played in New York, no matter how small or rudimentary: the Lincoln Stars' old stomping grounds at Olympic Field in Harlem; Sterling Oval and the Catholic Protectory Oval, in the Bronx; the Wallace Grounds, on the border of Bushwick and Ridgewood, where the Brooklyn Bridegrooms and Gladiators had once played. He was even in charge of scheduling games by Black teams at the big-league parks, when the Yankees, Giants, and Dodgers took to the road.

The pay to play was always the same: a stiff up-front fee, and 10 percent of the gate. When Nat Strong saw something he liked, he took it, shutting out white semipro teams entirely until they agreed to sell him partial or controlling interests in the clubs. He starved John W. Connors, a Black nightclub owner, out of his Brooklyn Royal Giants, installed them at Dexter Park in the Woodhaven section of Queens, and built a new Black major league around the team: the Eastern Colored League (ECL).

Dexter Park was a largely unadorned stadium that could seat up to eight thousand fans after Strong and Max Rosner, owner of the semi-pro Brooklyn Bushwicks, got through installing a steel-and-concrete grandstand. A wide, elongated park, it was distinguished mostly by the brilliant outfield billboard ad for an optician that read DON'T KILL THE UMPIRE—MAYBE IT'S YOUR EYES. Here merged all the different currents of baseball coursing through New York at the time: semiprofessional and industrial teams, high school and college nines, barnstorming major-league stars—and some of the greatest players in the Black game.

Homely and accessible as it was, some great feats of baseball took place at Dexter Park. Cyclone Joe Williams, one of the very best Negro League hurlers even at thirty-seven, once struck out twenty-five men in a twelve-inning game—and lost. Josh Gibson, the catching immortal, was said to have hammered a ball over the thirty-foot wall that stood 418 feet from home plate in left center.

Yet the ECL was a poor little brother to the Negro National League (NNL), the first Black major league started by a Black man, begun in 1920 by a big, wily Texas hurler named Andrew "Rube" Foster who scooped up most of the great Black stars for his Chicago American Giants team. What was left over was left to Strong, who ran his league as ruthlessly as he did everything else. Strong did employ his own Cadillac and seven-passenger Pierce-Arrow touring car to carry his

Brooklyn team on road trips, but he was too tightfisted to outbid Foster and company for the best players, and he would brook no dissent.

It took a young protégé of Strong's—and another overlooked minority—to save Black baseball in New York.

Alejandro "Alex" Pompez arrived in Harlem at the age of twenty, without money, friends, or prospects. Pompez had been born in Key West, Florida, the son of a lawyer, cigar manufacturer, and member of the Florida state assembly. When Alex was still just six, his father died suddenly, leaving his entire estate to the cause of Cuban independence—and his family destitute. Alex and his mother were forced to return to Cuba, but by 1910 he had made his way up to New York, where he found work rolling cigars for $20 a week.

Then the miracles began. Within a very short time Pompez owned a cigar shop on Seventh Avenue near West 126th Street, a store he would keep until his death in 1974. Soon, El Cubano, as he was called, had a closetful of stylish suits, a share in all sorts of local businesses, and an apartment up at 409 Edgecombe Avenue, the toniest building on Sugar Hill. The secret to his success was not cigars but Harlem's favorite new game, a private lottery known as policy, or the numbers. Anyone could play, and for as little as a penny. Bettors chose any three-digit number. If it matched some daily, predetermined number—usually the last three digits of the pari-mutuel payoff at a local racetrack; sometimes a stock market average—the policy bank paid off, at odds of six hundred to one.

It was a tempting enough jackpot, in those days before any official state lottery, and soon it had spawned an entire new industry. "Numbers runners" who fanned out around the city, taking bets. The writers of "dreambooks"—colorful volumes that converted every conceivable dream into the numbers you should bet the following day. Their prestidigitations were accompanied by all sorts of antique folk practices and sayings: how to make a dumb cake, and the secret of the Nine Keys, and the acorn charm, and how to divine the future through cards and dice and dominoes, and the lines in your palm, and the grounds in your coffee cup. (Their duller ancestors can still be found at some New York newsstands today, in the form of single, colored sheets—red or blue, yellow or pink—promising to pick you a winner in the lotto.)

Policy had an especially fervent following in Harlem, where hope was always a little desperate, and by the time he was twenty-six years old, Alex Pompez was grossing almost $3 million a year from behind the counter of his smoke shop. To this empire of pennies and nickels he added nightclubs and restaurants and then a ball team. He called it the Cuban Stars. There was already a well-known team by the same name, owned by Abel Linares in Chicago, but El Cubano didn't care. He accepted a challenge from Linares to play for the "right" to the name in a game in Puerto Rico. The New Yorkers won, 3–2, and refused Linares's demand for a rematch. Both clubs ended up keeping the name, but Pompez's would soon come to own it.

Nat Strong, a sort of mentor to Pompez, saw to it that his Cuban Stars became a charter member of the Eastern Colored League. But it was Pompez who knew his baseball, and he invested heavily in his team. After installing them in yet another bare-bones park, the Dyckman Oval, up at 204th Street near the Harlem River, Pompez expanded the Stars' new home to ten thousand seats. In 1935, he even installed lights—three years before any major-league team.

Above all, El Cubano insisted on fielding an all-Latin team and on maintaining his monopoly on Hispanic players. This drew howls of protest from the rest of the ECL. It also reflected the growing pains of the wider Harlem community. There were more than forty thousand immigrants of color from the West Indies and Latin America in New York by the 1920s—most of them concentrated between 112th and 118th Streets, where African Americans complained that Hispanic landlords would not rent to them.

The tensions between the different cultures would continue for decades. Many of the new immigrants considered themselves harder working and better educated than their neighbors and resented being grouped together with the sons and daughters of former slaves. In turn, African Americans mocked the Latins and islanders as "coconuts" and "monkey-chasers" and sneered at their pretensions.

Alex Pompez was already enough of a community leader that he chaired a neighborhood group "striving to bring about amity among all races and particularly the darker races with the native American Negro," as an editorial he signed in *The New York Age* read. The statement presaged his career in New York. Pompez strove always to bring great Cuban players to the city, but gradually expanded his alliances to recruit Dominicans, Puerto Ricans, and American-born Black players for his teams—as well as working more and more with a white-owned major-league club. Pompez didn't always win the greatest stars, Latin or otherwise, away from his rivals, but he got most of them to Harlem: the nifty little Puerto Rican infielder Emilio "Millito" Navarro; the legendary, all-Cuban outfield of "El Caballero," Alejandro Oms; Pablo "Champion" Mesa; and the volatile Bernardo Baró. Above all, he signed Martín Dihigo, the most versatile player baseball has ever seen.

There was nothing that "El Maestro" could not do on a ball field. A poll selected him as the second baseman on the all-time Black baseball team, but this was almost an arbitrary choice. Dihigo could and did play every other position on the field and was a dominating right-handed pitcher. A big man at six three and nearly two hundred pounds, he was extremely fast, hit for power and average, and had excellent range and an exceptional arm. Like so many of the great Negro League stars, Dihigo played wherever he could. In the summer, he signed on with one or another of the U.S. Negro Leagues, or down in the Mexican League, the *Liga Mexicana de Béisbol,* which debuted in 1925. In the winter, he was back in his native Cuba, or sometimes the Dominican Republic—a schedule at least as peripatetic as the Babe's, and one Dihigo kept up until 1945, when he turned forty, though he kept playing well into the 1950s in Cuba.

Sunny, genial, and gracious, El Maestro was well liked everywhere and a national hero back home, where Fidel Castro would make him minister of sport. Other stars of color were called the Black Babe Ruth, but only Dihigo matched—and even exceeded—Ruth's diversity on a ball field. He batted as high as .421 in the ECL, and *unlike* Ruth, Dihigo pitched more and more as his career progressed. He had a sizzling fastball, pitching no-hitters in Mexico, Venezuela, and Puerto Rico, and compiled a lifetime record of 261-138. Nor did he ever stop playing in between starts; like most Negro League ballplayers, he never had that option. In 1935, as player-manager of the New York Cubans, Dihigo took the team to the second-half title of the Negro National League, going 7-3 on the mound while hitting .372. In 1938, his top year in Mexico, he went 18-2 with an ERA of 0.90—

and batted .387. In 1937, playing in Santo Domingo, Dihigo was second only to Satchel Paige in wins and to Josh Gibson in batting average, hitting .351 while tying for the league lead in home runs. Johnny Mize, a future Hall of Famer who was playing with Dihigo that winter in the D.R., called him the greatest player he had ever seen, and remembered that teams would routinely walk El Maestro to pitch to Mize himself.

Dihigo's was a Persephonic existence, one in which for half the year he would be treated as the great star he was, while most of America had never heard of him. Just how good were the leagues he was playing in? And how good were the white major leagues without Dihigo and so many other outstanding players of color? What did all those gaudy statistics mean—on either side of the color line?

By the 1920s, it was possible to get some idea, because teams of Black and white all-stars played each other more frequently than ever before. The Black teams at least held their own, winning a little over half the contests by some accounts, as many as two-thirds, according to others. White major leaguers were frequently effusive in their praise, calling the top Black ballplayers some of the best they had ever played against.

(White fans all too often did not avail themselves of the opportunity to see Black talent, loath to venture to run-down ballparks in bad—or Black—neighborhoods. But again, twentieth-century racism was all about an *assumed* white superiority and *avoidance* of Black people. Any sign of Black superiority or even competence was generally met by removing Black people from the "competition." African Americans were more likely to go to see whites play ball—when they could afford it—and more and more, white teams began to rent out their ballparks to Negro League teams when they were out of town. Shamefully, white baseball would later cite those revenues as one more reason *not* to erase the color line.)

How good would even the very greatest white player, Babe Ruth (if he was "white"), have been with Black competition?

There's little evidence to suggest that the Babe's statistics would have been much diminished in an integrated major league. Facing local stars in Cuba after the 1920 season, for instance, the Babe went 11-32 at the plate, with an .839 slugging average—despite playing with a broken bone in his left wrist. In his recorded games against other

Black teams—games that were often played even more intensely than regular league games—Ruth was 25-55 at the plate, with twelve home runs, including a 4-4 performance against Bullet Joe Rogan, three homers in one game against Cannonball Dick Redding, and a towering home run in 1938, when he was forty-three years old and a coach with the Dodgers, off Satchel Paige . . . three of the greatest pitchers in the history of the game. Beyond the statistics, the Bambino drew raves from such great Black stars as Pop Lloyd, Judy Johnson, and Buck O'Neil.

Conversely, there is no reason to think that the great Black stars—who more than held their own against white major leaguers—would not have excelled in the white leagues.

A lingering question is whether the Babe himself was "the Black Babe Ruth." Speculation on the subject has abounded for years. Biographers have noted that Ruth laughed off the vilest abuse he was subjected to from fans and bench jockeys—save for the jibe "N——r lips," which had been his nickname at St. Mary's Industrial School. It incensed him to be called this, or any other variation on *that* word. What did this mean? Exploring it can rapidly become repugnant, dwelling as some have on Ruth's facial features, his skin tone, the texture of his hair, and worse.

And yet the notion is intriguing: the possibility that in America's national game—a game used in the 1920s to further the assimilation of all the *white* "races," a game where the color line was drawn with all the adamance of that eugenics-ridden, reactionary decade—its greatest star was "really" a Black man.

By the 1920s, New York's "mongrel culture," as Ann Douglas described it, had conquered the world but still could not be admitted at home. The exclusion of Martín Dihigo and Oscar Charleston and Josh Gibson and all the other great stars produced by the Negro Leagues did not diminish the greatness of Babe Ruth, or any other single team or player. It diminished baseball as a whole, diminished the nation that had invented the sport, diminished every official, every beat writer, every fan who watched it played without lifting a finger or a voice to include all who could play the game. It diminished every one of us, who never got to see just how great a Martín Dihigo, or so many others, could have been in the major leagues.

38

Out of the Shadows

The "great bellyache heard round the world" suffered by the greatest-white-player-who-might-have-been-Black in the 1925 season dropped the Yanks out of the first division of the American League, with a losing record. It would be forty years before they suffered either indignity again. General manager Ed Barrow reworked Ruth's supporting cast sufficiently to bring the Bombers home three games ahead of the Indians and into the 1926 World Series against Branch Rickey's St. Louis Cardinals, the great upstart team of the decade.

The series was another beaut, in a decade full of them, close and hard fought, with first one team gaining the upper hand and then the other. Ruth made up for all bellyaches, of whatever origin, with one of his greatest Octobers, playing brilliantly in the field and reaching base seventeen times in thirty-one times at bat as the Cards walked him again and again. He hit four home runs, including three monstrous blasts in one game at St. Louis's Sportsman's Park, two of them over the right-field roof and one to the bleachers in deepest centerfield, 430 feet away, leading the national radio broadcaster Graham McNamee to exclaim, "Babe's shoulders look as if there's murder in them."

Led by the closest thing to Ruth in the National League, the second baseman and player-manager Rogers Hornsby, the Cards kept battling back, tying the series at three games apiece in New York, then taking a 3–2 lead in the seventh and deciding game. But the Yanks loaded the bases with two outs in the bottom of the seventh inning, and Hornsby decided to pull the starter Pop Haines. He signaled for his best pitcher.

One of the most impressive qualities of Yankee Stadium was how venerable the ballpark appeared right from the beginning, particularly in the fall—some combination of the light and those deep gray shadows in the upper decks. By the afternoon of October 10, 1926, three years old and incomplete, the stadium still looked as if it had been there forever; as old as the Roman Colosseum, maybe, when Grover Cleveland Alexander walked in from the bullpen to face Tony Lazzeri.

"I can see him yet . . . walking in from the left-field bull pen through the grey mist," St. Louis's third baseman Les Bell would recall. "The Yankee fans recognized him right off, of course, but you didn't hear a sound from anywhere in that stadium. They just sat there and watched him walk in. And he took his time. He just came straggling along, a lean old Nebraskan, wearing a Cardinal sweater, his face wrinkled, that cap sitting on top of his head and tilted to one side—that's the way he liked to wear it."

What Bell saw was, like the home run, a relatively new phenomenon: the dramatic entrance of the relief pitcher with the game on the line. In the years to come, Yankee Stadium would provide the setting for more such entrances, by more great performers in more excruciating situations, than anywhere else—for Johnny Murphy and Joe Page, Sparky Lyle and Goose Gossage and Dave Righetti, and the great Rivera. For now, though, all eyes were on an opponent. They were about to witness the most unlikely confrontation ever to take place in a critical World Series moment, a duel between two future Hall of Famers—both of whom were epileptics.

Ol' Pete Alexander, it seemed, had been pitching in bad luck all his life. A head injury had delayed him from making the majors until he was twenty-four, though once there he was instantly the best pitcher in the National League, the start of a career that would see him tie Matty for the all-time NL record with 373 victories. While serving with an artillery unit in France, Alexander was traumatized by what he saw of battle, lost most of his hearing, and became afflicted with epilepsy. On his return he was still a remarkably effective pitcher, but he began to drink. He also took to carrying a bottle of ammonia everywhere he went so that when he had to leave the mound because of his fits, he could sniff it, revive himself, and try to return to the game.

"That takes a great deal of courage," his wife remembered, because the seizures "always left him so weak and, well, sort of hopeless."

His seizures were often (though not always) mistaken for

drunkenness—"Ol' Pete" was Prohibition slang for illegal booze—and his reputation suffered. He averaged almost eighteen wins a year for the Cubs in the 1920s, but manager Joe McCarthy cut him loose when he began to falter. According to his wife, "It was the lowest moment of Alexander's career. He thought he was through in baseball forever. Whenever he'd try to speak, tears would come to his eyes."

Branch Rickey, always on the lookout for a bargain, snapped him up for $4,000. Nearly forty years old, Alexander won nine games for the Cards down the stretch in 1926 and pitched superbly in the World Series, whipping the Yankees twice, including a 10–2 complete-game win just the day before, in game six. He told Hornsby that he could pitch in the final game if he needed him, but having celebrated his win in his customary fashion, he was sleeping it off in the pen when the call came.

"Yes, I am drunk. But I can get this guy out anyway," Ol' Pete supposedly told Hornsby when he met the manager on the mound. What they are known to have discussed was how to pitch to Lazzeri, with Alexander telling Hornsby that he intended to throw him fastballs inside—dangerously close to a hitter's wheelhouse.

"You can't do that," Hornsby protested, but Alexander insisted that his pitches would be too far inside for Lazzeri to do anything but foul them off. Once he had him set up, he would come back with his big curve on the outside. Hornsby worried over the idea for a moment, then decided to trust him: "Who am I to tell *you* how to pitch?"

Once on the mound, the weary, shambling Alexander turned into the picture of grace. He had a wonderfully fluid, minimal delivery, mixing speeds constantly and throwing both fastball and curve with pinpoint control. All it took was a couple throws to his catcher, Bob O'Farrell, and he was ready to proceed.

Tony Lazzeri had quietly put together an excellent rookie season for the Yankees. He had come to their attention in the course of hitting sixty home runs, driving in 222, and scoring 202 runs—all league records—at Salt Lake City, in the late, lamented Pacific Coast League. Lazzeri was not nearly that kind of power hitter in the majors, but he had whacked sixty extra-base hits, driven in 114 runs, and played a fine second base. One of the very few Italian American players in the game, he was quickly dubbed "Poosh 'Em Up Tony" and "the Mussolini of the diamond" by the press—both intended as compliments.

If he didn't like it, Lazzeri never complained, just as he never complained to anyone, or said very much at all in public. Back in the locker room, teammates found him "a very witty guy, full of fun. . . . A real nice guy."

Perhaps it was the epilepsy that kept him subdued in public. The disease would kill him at forty-two, when he fell down his cellar stairs during a fit, but throughout his entire fourteen-year career in the majors, he never had a seizure on the field. Now he stood in, facing a tight spot for any rookie, against the old master who shared his affliction. Alexander, apparently changing his strategy at the last moment, snapped a curve over at knee level for strike one. Ol' Pete missed outside with the same pitch, then came in with the fastball he had promised Hornsby.

Tony Lazzeri turned on the ball at once, driving it deep into the left-field stands—foul by a few feet. The crowd moaned in frustration. Later in the clubhouse, Alexander would tell reporters, "They're calling me a hero, eh. Well, do you know what? If that line drive . . . had been fair, Tony would be the hero and I'd just be an old bum."

While still out on the mound, though, Pete Alexander seemed unfazed by Lazzeri's smash, certain—as he had told Hornsby—that no one could hit that pitch fair. Now he had Lazzeri where he wanted him and the next pitch was perfect, another curve on the outside of the plate. Lazzeri swung and missed for strike three.

Alexander had worked out of the jam, but less remembered about the epic confrontation was that there were still two innings left to go in the game. Ol' Pete worked easily, retiring the Yankees in order in the eighth and getting the first two hitters in the ninth. That brought Babe Ruth to the plate. Refusing to give in, Alexander walked him on a 3-2 pitch, the Babe's eleventh pass of the series. Alexander was far from out of the woods. Bob Meusel, who had belted a double and a triple off him the day before, was up next, with Lou Gehrig after that. Then Ruth took off for second, only to be thrown out on a perfect strike from O'Farrell to Hornsby. It was probably the most unexpected and controversial play ever to end a World Series, one roundly condemned by some sportswriters at the time and most baseball historians ever after.

All the Babe would say, in his own defense, was that he had been "trying something." This was hardly sufficient for a few in the sporting press. The writer H. I. Phillips wrote that "it was the case of a behemoth thinking itself a gazelle," which was unfair but at least funny. Joe Vila, the Babe's old nemesis and a major-league hysteric, tried to drum up the annual rumors of a fix, claiming that Meusel and the pitcher Urban Shocker might have helped Ruth "throw" the series to the Cardinals.

There was not a shred of evidence for Vila's accusations, and most observers knew it at the time. Ruth was hardly a behemoth but in excellent shape. Most of the writers praised him to the sky for his play in the series, and for the bold chance he took. Meusel had had a bad series and had been in a slump for weeks, due to a nagging injury. Long Bob's double and triple off Alexander the day before had really consisted of a Texas Leaguer and a single that Cards' left fielder Chick Hafey let skip past him. The chances were in any circumstances that about the best the Yanks could hope for against Alexander, who was still pitching brilliantly, was a single. If Ruth were on second, such a hit might score him. If he waited on first—doing the safe thing, ready to lose by the book—it would have taken an extra-base hit or two singles to score him.

The Babe was simply trying to better the odds for his team. He was a fast if reckless runner, and he had easily stolen a base against Alexander and O'Farrell just the day before, on the same delayed steal he tried now. The field was a mire all day from overnight rains, and the ball O'Farrell threw was a soggy, heavy mess. It wasn't that Ruth blew it—or threw it. It was that O'Farrell made a terrific throw, just nipping the Babe when he put the ball in Hornsby's glove at his shoe tips.

Thomas S. Rice summed up the general feeling at the time, when he wrote in the *Brooklyn Daily Eagle,* "The play was close. Like Icarus, Ruth failed, but he failed in a great attempt"—which was putting it on a little strong. Suffice it to say that Ruth was playing without fear of failure—the quality that elevates the greatest performers over all others.

"He went on the ball field like he was playing in a cow pasture, with cows," remembered Rube Bressler. "He was playing in a cow pasture, with cows for an audience. He never knew what fear or nervousness was."

After the game, Alexander sat calmly amid the celebration in the visitors' locker room. The real excitement, he told the writers, "came when Judge Landis mailed out the winners' checks." Ol' Pete would pitch for several more years in the majors with distinction, but wound up having to tell the story of his greatest game over and over again for the tourists at the very heart of all the big-city ballyhoo, Hubert's Flea Circus in Times Square. He would die alone in a rented room, his shade receding into the shadows of the big park.

The Babe started at once on another barnstorming tour. When it reached Pennsylvania, he was told that a boy, Johnny Sylvester, was in a local hospital, and that he had been near death after a bad fall from a horse. Supposedly, little Johnny had been so energized by the three home runs Ruth had hit in a single game that he had made a miraculous recovery. Hearing this, the Babe had to go visit the kid where he was still in the hospital and swore that he would hit a home run for him the next day. True to his promise, Babe Ruth hit the longest home run anyone had ever seen in Wilkes-Barre. The kid recovered.

39

The Greatest Team, Part I

For Babe Ruth and the New York Yankees, there was always next year, and in the 1920s next year would always be better.

"The restlessness of New York in 1927 approached hysteria," Fitzgerald would remember in "My Lost City." "The parties were bigger . . . the pace was faster . . . the shows were broader, the buildings were higher, the morals were looser and the liquor was cheaper; but all these benefits did not really minister to much delight."

The city in the air seemed to soar ever higher. Before the decade was over, a hundred buildings of twenty stories or more would be added to the borough's already unique skyline. By 1929, fifteen Manhattan buildings rose at least five hundred feet above the ground, and there seemed to be no end, either to the number of new skyscrapers planned or to the heights they would reach. This was the era when Sunday supplements began to feature a fantastical *Metropolis* version of a New York built on many levels, threaded with sky bridges, and with airships zipping over and under them, and hangars and airfields on the roofs of buildings. Elsewhere in their pages, the papers played up one public spectacle after another: Lindbergh's flight across the Atlantic and the wild ticker-tape parade to welcome him home; a series of lurid domestic killings; the executions of Sacco and Vanzetti; the tell-all memoir by the late president Harding's mistress; the famous "long count" fight that confirmed the fall of that other icon, Jack Dempsey.

Not least among these sensations was the season put together by the New York Yankees. The team romped through the summer, compiling what was then an American League record, 110 wins—19 games ahead of an outstanding Philadelphia Athletics team—then swept the Pittsburgh Pirates in the World Series. They would make "the '27 Yankees" the catchphrase that, nearly a hundred years later, was still synonymous with something indomitable, the very best there ever was.

Were they the best?

Bill James tends to think so, citing the team as a major reason why he never wrote a book on the subject of what was the best team in baseball history: "At the end of the book the '27 Yankees win anyway, and everybody says, 'Well, what was that all about? Like we didn't *know* about the 1927 Yankees.' " (James does allow a possible exception for the 1998 Yankees, "since I do believe that the quality of play has generally improved over the years.") Rob Neyer and Eddie Epstein, making an in-depth study of teams that were great for more than a single year, in *Baseball Dynasties,* ranked the 1939 Yankees slightly ahead of the 1927 team. Over the years, others have also made cases for the 1961 Yankees, for Connie Mack's A's teams of 1929–31, for the 1942 St. Louis Cardinals, or the 1975–76 Cincinnati Reds.

But somehow, it always seems to come back to the 1927 Yankees.

Take the statistics first. At the plate, the Yankees in 1927 led the American League in runs, in hits, and in triples; in home runs, walks, batting average, on-base percentage, and slugging. Their combined on-base and slugging averages—the figure most analysts today consider *the* key hitting statistic—was a major-league record .872, one equaled only by the 1930 Yanks and easily surpassing anything put up by a team even in the steroid era.

On the mound, Yankees pitchers led the league in shutouts and ERA and surrendered the fewest hits, the fewest runs, the fewest walks, the lowest batting average, and the lowest on-base percentage of all American League teams. The team also was third in fielding percentage, committed the third-fewest errors, and stole ninety bases.

The 1927 Yankees outscored their opponents by 975–599, a margin of almost 2.5 runs *a game.* They outhit them .307 to .267, outhomered them 158–42. No other team in the entire American League hit more than 56 home runs; no other team in all of major-league baseball hit more than 100 home runs, save for John McGraw's Giants over in the Polo Grounds. The Yanks' team ERA of 3.20 beat out all other AL squads by at least .71, or nearly three-quarters of a run a game.

Individually, Yankee hitters led the league in on-base percentage, doubles, and triples. They finished 1-2 in slugging average, in combined slugging and on-base percentage, hits, and runs batted in; finished 1-2-3 in runs, in total bases, and in home runs, where Ruth led with his record sixty, Lou Gehrig followed with forty-seven, and no other American Leaguer hit more than the eighteen off the bat of Tony Lazzeri. Individual Yankees pitchers led the league in wins, saves, lowest batting average, and lowest on-base percentage, finished 1-2-3 in ERA and 1-2-3-4 in winning percentage.

Position by position, the team was strong almost everywhere, if not always spectacular. The catching duties were split between a couple of capable journeymen, Pat Collins and Johnny Grabowski. At third base, the veteran Jumpin' Joe Dugan was prized for his outstanding glove and his affable personality, but he was an old thirty, with a slowing bat. The shortstop Mark Koenig was a dependable player at the plate and in the field, with a fine arm and range. Lazzeri turned in a superb year at second and at bat, where he hit .309 with 102 RBI and twenty-two stolen bases. The outfield was one of the greatest in major-league history, with Ruth; Bob Meusel, who had a cannon for an arm and hit .337 with forty-seven doubles; and the centerfielder Earle Combs, "the Kentucky Colonel," who led the AL with 231 hits and twenty-three triples, hitting .356, scoring 137 runs, and running down almost everything hit into the stadium's cavernous outfield.

The pitching staff was excellent and deep, led by the veterans Waite "Schoolboy" Hoyt and Herb Pennock. Just behind them was a pitcher with perhaps the best name in all of baseball history, Urban Shocker. A control artist, who used a variety of wicked curves to complement his fastball, Shocker was also helped by a ring finger permanently bent during his early days as a catcher. He won eighteen games in 1927, even as his strength began to deteriorate from a heart condition that kept him out of the World Series and to which he would succumb a year later.

Behind Shocker were the old Dodger Dutch Ruether and George Pipgras, giving New York five reliable starters at a time when teams rarely had more than two or three. But the Yankees also had a new weapon. Wilcy "Cy" Moore was not the first hurler to be used primarily as a relief pitcher, but he quickly established himself as the best to date. Moore was a balding, thirty-year-old rookie by the time he made the Yanks' roster in 1927. He had wandered through the minors for years, until he hit upon the strategy of accidentally breaking his arm. This forced him to switch to a sidearm motion, his ball moving down and in to his fellow righties, down and away from left-handed batters. The scouts still ignored him because of his age, but when he went 30-4 at Greenville, South Carolina, Ed Barrow insisted on signing him anyway.

Once on the team, Moore seemed able to do whatever he was needed to do, to the point where he joked, "I ain't a pitcher. I'm a day laborer." Miller Huggins pitched him for 213 innings, including twelve starts on top of his regular, multi-inning relief stints. Moore's arm was aching by the end of the season, and he would never be the same pitcher again. But he won nineteen games—thirteen of them in relief—added thirteen saves, and compiled the best ERA in the league at 2.28.

The core of the 1927 Yankees, though, what put them so far above everyone else, was their number three and four hitters, Babe Ruth and Lou Gehrig. Ruth, now thirty-two, was back to his usual form, hitting baseballs for flabbergasting distances. And the Yankees had added someone who was almost his equal to hit behind him.

Lou Gehrig was a homegrown New Yorker, the son of German

immigrant parents, who had first come to national attention by hitting a ball out of Chicago's Wrigley Field, in a schoolboy all-star game between the two cities. The Yankees scout Paul Krichell spotted him at Columbia University, where Gehrig was working his way through the engineering school by serving the food his mother cooked in the fraternity kitchens. In those days, Columbia's diamond was still on its main campus, with home plate located in front of John Jay Hall, not far from 114th Street and Amsterdam. Gehrig hit a ball to the steps of Low Library across 116th Street—a blast of 450 feet—in a game against NYU. This was a distance record that Gehrig himself broke three weeks later, when he hit a 500-foot shot all the way to the steps of the Journalism School, not far from 116th and Broadway—*and to the opposite field.* Krichell, who had also signed Lazzeri and Koenig, and who would go on to ink Whitey Ford and Vic Raschi over the course of his fabled career, had already seen enough. Rushing to a telephone after the NYU game, the stout, bowlegged little scout told Barrow that he had found "another Babe Ruth."

Barrow was understandably skeptical, but his best scout was not far wrong. Like Ruth, Gehrig was one of those few athletes who seemed able to play at a major-league level from the beginning. Put on the roster for a few games in 1923 to see what he could do, Columbia Lou started crushing balls into the upper deck of Yankee Stadium in his very first batting practice. He hit .423 during his cup of coffee, whereupon the Yanks astutely farmed him out to the Hartford Senators of the Eastern League, in order to . . . what? Let him see if he'd prefer to work in the insurance business? Give the rest of the American League a respite?

When first baseman Wally Pipp hurt himself near the end of the 1923 season, the Yankees asked the Giants if they could bring Gehrig up for the World Series. John McGraw said no, and Gehrig stayed in Hartford, quite possibly costing the team the 1924 flag that they lost by three games to Washington. In 1925, though, Pipp was more seriously injured, hit in the head during batting practice by the former Princeton phenom Charles Caldwell. The story would be repeated for many years as an admonitory one, all about how Wally Pipp had sat out with a "headache" and how we must learn to play through the small hurts. Pipp had, in fact, been hit in the temple and was taken to the hospital in a semiconscious state. There he remained for two weeks and was still dizzy when he returned—a recurrence of the Ray Chapman tragedy narrowly averted. In the Darwinian competition of major-league baseball and 1920s New York, Gehrig took his place in the lineup and there he would remain for the next thirteen years, never taking a day off, while Pipp was shipped to Cincinnati.

Shy, studious, and unassuming, Gehrig was almost the diametrical opposite of the Babe in terms of personality, especially in his first years in the show. Columbia Lou had a sad, sweet smile and little to say. He still lived with his parents and rarely went out, preferring to invite teammates over for a home-cooked meal by his domineering mother.

At the plate, though, he combined with the Babe to form a one-two punch that no team was able to match—that no team would *ever* quite match. Gehrig was much more of a line-drive hitter than Ruth; he rarely hit the sorts of huge, soaring drives the Babe launched. But with his heavily muscled arms, low center of gravity, monstrously large, powerful thighs, and, well, *other parts*—his teammates called him Biscuit Pants, rather than the more romantic nickname the Iron Horse that the writers bestowed on him—Gehrig drove the ball with ferocious power, scalding doubles and triples as well as home runs about the spacious Yankee Stadium outfield.

The lineup these two left-handed monsters anchored was dubbed Murderers' Row, a nickname that had been attached to another, much less powerful Yankees team back in 1919. They were soon demolishing the rest of the American League at a pace that had the sportswriters gleefully scrambling for new adjectives. Ruth, James Harrison wrote in *The New York Times,* "went crazy and amuck" in a doubleheader pounding of Philadelphia on Memorial Day that left the Athletics "drawn, quartered, cooked in boiling oil and otherwise slaughtered."

"Folks, the existence of Santa Claus cannot be denied," wrote Paul Gallico, after Ruth and Gehrig hit back-to-back blasts to beat the White Sox in June.

The following day, trailing 11–5 going into the ninth, Tony Lazzeri hit a grand-slam home run, and the Yanks rallied to tie it, winning 12–11 in the eleventh. This was the start of what became known as the team's "five o'clock lightning," its seemingly uncanny way of coming on late in the game—though in truth it was little more than a talented lineup getting its third or fourth or fifth look at a tiring starter. But no matter.

Sportswriters and fans alike recognized at the time that they were witnessing something extraordinary.

Soon the pennant race had been supplanted altogether by another sort of race between Ruth and Gehrig. Someone was finally giving the home-run king a run for his money. Both men smashed their twenty-fifth of the season in a 13–6 rout of the Red Sox on June 23 that stretched the team's lead to ten games.

"There was a ball game at Yankee Stadium yesterday, but nobody paid the slightest attention to it," claimed Harrison. "Everybody knew that the Yankees would beat the Red Sox. It wasn't the ball game that drew the customers to the ball yard; they had come to see the great home run derby between G. Herman Ruth and H. Louis Gehrig."

On July 4, the contest between the two men drew 72,641 fans to the stadium, to watch the Yanks pummel the Senators, 12–1 and 21–1, running up thirty-seven hits. Two of these were home runs by Gehrig, who now pulled ahead of Ruth, 28–26. On July 26, they applied another merciless, twin-bill beating to the St. Louis Browns, 15–1 and 12–3, though this time the Babe hit two round-trippers to one for Gehrig and regained the lead. Gehrig hit two more against Cleveland, a couple days later, to take it right back.

Theirs was an easygoing rivalry, the two stars still friends at the time, Gehrig more than a little in awe of his gargantuan teammate. Lou determinedly dodged the spotlight, demurring when the front office suggested he showboat a little more: "I'm not a headline guy." But by September 6, he still had the home-run lead, 45–44.

Then Ruth took off, while Gehrig . . . did not exactly slump, finishing the season with a .379 average and 175 RBI. But Lou hit only two more home runs the rest of the way, while Ruth went on a new tear. By now the Babe had to carry his bat around the bases with him, to keep souvenir hunters from jumping down from the stands and stealing it. On September 22, when he hit his fifty-sixth home run as the Yankees edged Detroit, 8–7, Ruth had to haul the bat around the infield with a small boy clinging to it.

Five days later, Connie Mack brought the great Lefty Grove on in relief to try to preserve a meaningless win over the Yanks; Ruth hit a game-winning grand slam off him, for number fifty-seven. Two days after that, Ruth slammed the ball all about the stadium in a 15–4 rout of the Senators, hitting two more home runs and a triple. The next day, September 30, before an afternoon crowd of ten thousand, he picked out a slow screwball that Washington's Tom Zachary had aimed at his head, and drove it deep into the right-field bleachers, for the magic number sixty. Zachary protested vehemently that the hit was foul, but remained more frustrated that Ruth made contact at all.

"I don't see yet how he did it," Zachary recounted long after. "He never hit a worse ball in his life."

When he went back out to right field, the Babe was greeted with a sea of waving handkerchiefs in the bleachers, a tribute he returned with "a succession of snappy military salutes." Back in the clubhouse, he exulted: "Sixty, count 'em sixty! Let's see some other son of a bitch match that!"

They never would, at least not without eight extra games or who-knows-what aid to be found in a pill or a needle—not until 2022, and even then Aaron Judge would only match it. What other sports record remains essentially intact after nearly a century? Asked at the time if he could break his own mark again, the Babe shrugged and said, "I don't know and I don't care."

"Succumb to the power and romance of the man," wrote Paul Gallico. "Drop your cynicism and feel the athletic marvel that this big uncouth fellow has accomplished."

Ruth had, once again, outhomered every other team in the American League. Lou Gehrig, with a total of forty-seven, had outhomered four of them. Between them, they had dominated the league as no two players on the same team ever had, or ever quite would again.

"The performance of the Babe rather seems to dwarf the impending World Series," wrote William O. McGeehan, who had compared Ruth to a falling comet five years before.

Contrary to legend, the fine Pittsburgh Pirates team the Yankees played in the 1927 series did not give up after watching the mighty New Yorkers take batting practice. But the outcome was never in doubt. Ruth hit two home runs, drove in seven, and batted .400. Herb Pennock came within five outs of pitching a perfect game in the third contest, and Wilcy Moore finished the Yankees' four-game sweep with a complete-game victory, the winning run scoring rather unheroically on a wild pitch.

The next season the Yankees were back, and almost as good as ever. Gehrig and Combs again led the league in doubles and triples, respectively. Gehrig hit .374 and drove in 142 runs; Ruth tied him for the RBI title and hit fifty-four more home runs. Wilcy Moore was pitched out, but Waite Hoyt picked up the slack by adding eight saves to his twenty-three wins, Pipgras won twenty-four games, and Pennock led the league with five shutouts. The Yankees built up a big lead, held off a charge by an Athletics team that had seven future Hall of Famers on its roster, then got a measure of revenge by pounding Pete Alexander and his Cardinals in the series.

Despite being racked by injuries, the Yanks won in four games again. Gehrig hit four home runs and drove in nine, tying and setting, respectively, a pair of World Series records. He also batted .545, reached base twelve times in seventeen trips to the plate, and slugged a ridiculous 1.727. Ruth had a record nine runs scored and ten hits, reached base eleven times in seventeen trips, batted .625, and slugged 1.375.

The numbers were beyond gaudy. They were absurd, as ostentatious and astonishing a performance as anyone was putting on in the 1920s in New York, the city of perpetual astonishment. It was, and still is, the greatest two-man performance ever put together in the World Series, and there was little argument that—so far—their Yankees were the greatest team in major-league history.

40

The Brass Cuspidor and Paradise in the Bronx

If the Giants had failed to drive the Yankees from New York, at least they had Manhattan—and the Polo Grounds—to themselves again. On the field at least, John McGraw's team was second to none, taking an unmatched, fourth-straight National League pennant in 1924 and playing one of the weirdest and most exciting World Series ever, against the Washington Senators (of all teams).

The two teams traded wins back and forth with a succession of thrilling, late-inning rallies, through a riveting game seven in the nation's capital. The Giants were leading that final contest by 3–1, with two outs in the bottom of the eighth, but managed to lose in the twelfth inning after McGraw's veteran catcher, Hank Gowdy, got his feet tangled up in his mask and dropped an easy pop foul, and not one but two separate groundballs hit infield pebbles and bounced over the shoulder of eighteen-year-old Freddie Lindstrom, another McGraw wunderkind who had played an outstanding World Series.

The series was the only one that the Senators would ever win in Washington—and yet another excruciating defeat for John McGraw, who suffered more heartbreaking and downright bizarre losses in big games than any manager in the history of the sport. Muggsy was surprisingly sanguine in defeat, inviting the whole team and their wives to a gala party at the Biltmore Hotel after the long, quiet train ride back from Washington that night. There he led the singing himself, along with George M. Cohan and other Broadway stars who had managed to forgive him for his altercation at the Lambs Club.

In the years to come, though, McGraw's good humor would ebb away. The Giants remained contenders, and Muggsy continued to show a remarkable eye for young talent, starting four young players on Hall of Fame careers in the 1920s, including Lindstrom; the first baseman Bill Terry, who would be the last National Leaguer ever to hit over .400; a squat, hard-drinking outfielder with incredibly small feet named Hack Wilson; a stocky seventeen-year-old named Mel Ott, whom McGraw found playing for a lumberyard team in Gretna, Louisiana, as a left-handed catcher; and a laconic, Oklahoma southpaw named Carl Hubbell.

Yet physically and mentally, the burden of serving as the Giants' manager, de facto general manager, and head scout had begun to take its toll on John McGraw. Plagued by his chronic sinusitis, his obesity, and his usual physical mishaps, McGraw spent more and more time away from his team, skipping entire western swings. His patience with his ballplayers wore thin, and he hastily dealt away such old favorites as Stengel and Dave Bancroft. Frankie Frisch had always served as a whipping boy for the rest of the team, with McGraw calling him "cement head" and "dumb Dutchman." Now the criticism became more vituperative as McGraw fined him for the smallest mistakes and told reporters that the Fordham Flash "never satisfied me" as team captain.

The manager who had once stuck by Merkle and Snodgrass against the whole city was now hanging his best player out to dry. Frisch felt so maligned that he walked off the team, and before the 1927 season McGraw traded the man he had once regarded as a son to the Cardinals for Rogers Hornsby, a player he had coveted for years. "The Rajah" did not disappoint on the field, but his prickly personality spread discontent through the clubhouse. Adding to the darkening mood was the death of Matty from tuberculosis and of Ross Youngs, a wonderful little right fielder who contracted Bright's disease and died at just thirty years old, after a season of valiantly trying to play while attended by a trained nurse.

McGraw himself, it seemed, was beginning to give way at last. There was little to back him up. The Giants simply lacked the corporate structure and cold-eyed professionalism of the Yankees. The club secretary, James Tierney, enraged his manager by accidentally omitting Hack Wilson from the official roster one spring, allowing the Chicago Cubs to steal him. When Hornsby and Tierney feuded, Stoneham sided with his club secretary and dealt the Rajah, one of the greatest hitters in the history of the game, to the Boston Braves for five mediocrities—and a convenient $200,000 in cash. Hornsby ended up on the Cubs with Wilson, where the two men led Chicago to the 1929 pennant.

These careless and miserly moves were indicative of how the Giants were run under Charlie Stoneham. From 1920 to 1930, the Yankees made a combined profit of $3.5 million and paid out *no* dividends. In the town of the big money, Jake Ruppert kept reinvesting in his own franchise. The Giants, by contrast, made a profit of $2 million over the same years and paid back $1.5 million in dividends to their owners and Tammany stockholders. More and more, Stoneham used the team as his personal cash register, drawing a salary of $45,000 a year and taking $280,035 in unsecured loans from the franchise over the course of the decade.

"Stoneham made money from his team," judged Henry Fetter, "but Ruppert built a dynasty."

The Giants' front office would spend the better part of a decade immersed in a series of messy, costly lawsuits. McGraw got mixed up in the leading scam of the era, Florida land deals, when he tried to develop a "Pennant Park" community around the Giants' spring training facility in Sarasota. Stoneham tried to move out of the bucket-shop business and transferred many of his bigger accounts to another shady Wall Street brokerage, only to watch it collapse, $4 million in arrears. The Giants' owner was charged with conspiracy to defraud his investors. Then he was charged with perjury, when Billy Fallon, the now stuttering "Great Mouthpiece," inveigled him into a case involving yet another dubious financial firm.

It looked as if all his illicit connections might at last drag Stoneham off to jail. By 1925, Cap Huston and John Ringling of circus fame were preparing a bid to take over the Giants, so likely did it appear that Charlie would be forced to give up the franchise one way or another. Stoneham beat both raps in the end, only to plunge into a new legal battle for control of the team with Francis Xavier McQuade, when Judge McQuade objected to his partner making so many loans to himself. *Their* fight dragged on through the courts for nine years, through appeals and countersuits that grew uglier and uglier.

McGraw sided with Stoneham and testified that he had once seen McQuade punch his wife in the face, concluding, without a shred of irony, "I would say that when McQuade is in one of his rages, he is not in full possession of his faculties."

Lucille McQuade denied the incident ever happened, adding, "McGraw would not have known anyway, because he was so intoxicated that evening that he had to be carried to his room by players." Asked by counsel if the Giants' manager had been conscious or unconscious at the time, she gave one of the great one-word answers in the history of American jurisprudence: "Semi."

McQuade was ultimately ousted, at nearly the same time that he was thrown off the state bench for corruption. Charlie Stoneham and his descendants were in to stay—if not in New York.

"Baseball had come to be my pet hobby," Stoneham replied to rumors that he intended to sell the team, "and I have no intention of giving it up."

This was precisely the problem. Somehow, the Giants' principal owner seemed not to notice that baseball was now big business.

"The Giants represented the New York of the brass cuspidor," the writer and publisher Harry Golden would write years later. They were the team of "that old New York which was still a man's world before the advent of the League of Women Voters; the days of swinging doors, of sawdust on the barroom floor, and of rushing the growler."

Their owners were, in the description of one of their own lawyers, "all drinking men, all cursing men, all fighting men . . . management of the Giants was in the hands of a rough element."

The political ties that had sustained that element for a generation were finally beginning to snap. In 1926, Billy Fallon, all but penniless, befuddled with women and alcohol, was defending McGraw in a minor civil suit when he dropped to the floor of the New York Supreme Court, felled by a heart attack. The next day, feeling better, he tried to get up and make his way to the Polo Grounds to see his old friend's team play. Another heart attack killed him before he could finish shaving.

On the evening of November 4, 1928, Fallon's most notorious client, Arnold Rothstein, was found staggering down the stairs of the Park Central Hotel in midtown Manhattan, mortally wounded from a bullet to the gut. The Brain had been on a long losing streak, dropping a small fortune on yet another cheesy 1920s land deal, this one a development in Queens called Juniper Park. He had just lost almost

$10,000 an hour in an epic, three-day cards and craps marathon, then refused to pay up, claiming the game was rigged. One of the other players, a gambler and petty hood—a nothing, really—named George "Hump" McManus, was probably the sharpie who plugged him, though Rothstein refused to name anyone throughout his extended, agonizing death throes.

What the insiders grasped right away was that the investigation into the Brain's killing was liable to rip open the whole cozy inside world of New York politics. Informed of the gambler's death while attending yet another swank Jazz Age party, Gentleman Jimmy Walker left at once, hustling his mistress, Betty "Monk" Compton, out the door while musing, "Rothstein has just been shot. And that means trouble from here on in." He was more right than he knew.

By October 1929, though, the physical city was still rising. In the last, gorgeous penumbra from the boom years, the Bank of Manhattan Trust, Chanin, Daily News, and Chrysler Buildings were all soaring into the skyline. William Van Alen's seventy-seven-story Chrysler Building—the most beautiful of them all, and perhaps the most beautiful skyscraper ever erected—put a perfect cap on the era with its gorgeous Art Deco adornments, its stainless steel eagles and radiator cap decorations, its friezes of hubcaps, and its seven crowning spires of light. On October 16, 1929, even as the boom deflated almost hourly down on Wall Street, the final detail was bolted into place with a last insouciant Manhattan touch: a 185-foot, purely decorative steel spire that made the Chrysler Building the tallest building in the world (at least until the Empire State Building surpassed it a year and a half later). Already that July, work had begun on Rockefeller Center, the sleek Art Deco complex right in the heart of midtown.

So rich was the city that other fantastic buildings began to follow its people out of Manhattan. Not so much skyscrapers as the sumptuous movie palaces of the era, which would rival the nearly six-thousand-seat Roxy down in Times Square, "the cathedral of the motion picture." Theaters on this scale and with this level of adornment were soon dubbed atmospherics, for the way they strove to create an entire atmosphere for the moviegoer to escape into. There were soon hundreds of such theaters around the country, and five of Loew's remarkable "Wonder Theatres" in the New York area alone—with their Wonder Organs, seating for thousands, and hordes of immaculately uniformed ushers and usherettes—went up just in 1929–30.

The Wonder Theatre in the Bronx, the Paradise, opened its doors on the Grand Concourse, just below Fordham Road, on September 7, 1929. It took up an entire block, cost $4 million to build—$1.5 million *more* than it had cost to build Yankee Stadium—and like the stadium was divided into three decks, seating nearly four thousand patrons. The Paradise featured a mechanical Saint George slaying his dragon on the outside and lobbies stuffed to the rafters with Baroque effluvia. Those able to find their way through to the auditorium entered a Mediterranean palace courtyard with a deep blue Italian sky that gradually darkened into a starlit night before the movie came on.

For the new residents of the Bronx, it must have seemed that they had indeed arrived in paradise, that the dragons of worry and poverty and bone-wearying fatigue had been slain now and were terrors their children would never know. Surely, wonders would never cease, and even another implosion down on Wall Street, or the demise of a gangster, or the follies of another corrupt mayor, or even the mighty Yankees stumbling to second place was nothing to be truly concerned about, in a city that would continue to grow ever richer, bolder, higher, more fantastic every day.

It would take a little while, too, before the ball teams—at least the white major-league ball teams—felt the crash. Average per-game attendance for the majors reached its interwar peak in 1930, at 8,211. It was 13,573 in New York, where both the Yankees and the Dodgers (for the first time) drew more than a million fans on the year, and the Giants were fourth in the majors in attendance. This even though the Yankees had been left far behind in the standings by Connie Mack's Athletics teams—something that New York's fretful little lawyer-manager, Miller Huggins, had anticipated going into the 1929 season.

"It won't be necessary" to break up the Yankees, Huggins told the writers. "[The] law of averages will take care of us . . . the time will come when we will crash." He found another, more tangible culprit as well, in a story repeated so often it has gained the patina of truth. Too many of his ballplayers, Huggins insisted, were spending all their time following the stock market and no longer paying enough attention to the game.

In fact, it's doubtful that the Yankees were any more active as speculators on Wall Street than any other Americans. In the country at large, no more than a million people and "probably . . . much less"—out of a population of 120 million—actually played the market, according to the best estimates of John Kenneth Galbraith. Nor did most of the Yankees' sluggers play as if they were distracted. The Yanks in 1929 hit almost exactly as well as their Murderers' Row lineup had the year before and scored even more runs. Their fall to second place was due not so much to lack of desire or the distraction of the ticker as to that evil that is the usual source of misfortune in this world: no pitching.

Huggins consoled himself, at least, with the notion that he had found the solution to almost all of life's physical woes. During spring training in 1929, he posed for photographers in a new solarium on the roof of the Yankees' hotel and announced his intention to open one at the team's training camp. "He had become convinced that massive exposure to the direct rays of the sun was an ideal way to prepare for the season," explains Bill Jenkinson. Instead, by that September, Huggins was in the hospital with erysipelas, an infection of the skin tissue on his face described at the time as "blood poisoning." Within days, poor Hug was dead, just fifty-one years old. His passing stunned his team, and the wild decade would end in mourning at the big house in the Bronx.

PART FOUR

THE VIRTUOUS CITY

New York in the Great Depression

1929–1939

We were somewhere in North Africa when we heard a dull distant crash that echoed to the further-est wastes of the desert.

—F. Scott Fitzgerald, "My Lost City"

41

"Sluttish to the Last Degree"

It was appropriate that New York's decade in the air came to an end with a crash. The full significance of the Wall Street collapse was apparent only in retrospect. Despite all the fearful scenes from those fateful days in October 1929, despite the mobs of overcoated men jamming the street and the hillocks of ticker tape and the police on horseback holding back the crowds, the city wasn't quite lost yet, or even truly panicked. Only one person toppled off a building in the financial district, a clerk from Newark named Hulda Browaski who might have simply been dazed from all the hours registering "sell" orders and taken a break to clear her head. She left no note, and all of her money was safe. Contrary to popular lore, the suicide rate in the city actually *declined* that fall of 1929.

New York had witnessed such stock gyrations many times before. The sound and the fury signified nothing good; hard times always followed. But for every failure, a crash meant new beginnings, new opportunities for somebody.

This time would be different. This time, the bargain hunters, the bears who swooped in to pick cheap stocks from the carcasses of the bulls, fared just as poorly as their victims. The stock market's descent continued like an exercise in sadism, halting for just long enough to lure more investors in, then plummeting downward again. Meanwhile, the city's economy began to come apart. By the first winter after the crash, hunger was already a palpable presence in New York. When two bakery trucks made a delivery to a hotel near a Salvation Army breadline, they were mobbed by more than a thousand hungry people: "Bread and pastry were thrown into the street and the hungry men scrambled to get it." As many as thirty or forty men at a time took to entering large stores and demanding food. The store owners gave it to them, desperate not to let the incidents get into the papers.

By November 1930, the apple sellers, those iconic figures of the Great Depression, had begun to appear: six thousand of them on the streets of downtown Manhattan, selling their fruit at a nickel apiece. If they sold an entire crateful, they could net $1.85 on the day. Another seven thousand men and boys shined shoes for a nickel a pair. There was little alternative. Some ten thousand of the twenty-nine thousand factories in New York had closed by the end of 1930. Those lucky enough to still have a regular job saw their wages annihilated. In the sweatshops, a generation's worth of union gains were wiped out. Fifty thousand New York women crocheted hats for forty cents a dozen, or made aprons for two and a half cents apiece; sponged and threaded pants for half a penny a pair.

At such wages, family finances simply began to collapse. When they did, the victims were put out on the street. By 1933, seventeen thousand New Yorkers *a month* were being evicted. The meager furnishings of their apartments, their kitchen tables and beds and wooden chairs, usually bought on credit, were repossessed and piled up in warehouses. What happened to the people? Single men, if they still had ten cents to their name, "could sleep in a flophouse reeking of sweat and Lysol," in writer William Manchester's description. Others tried the sprawling new homeless encampment at the corner of West and Spring Streets, or the hobo jungle down by the rail tracks that ran through Riverside Park. In cold weather, the lucky ones slept amid the garbage on top of the municipal incinerator. During the day, Thomas Wolfe discovered homeless men fighting for space in the public latrine that used to exist in front of city hall. There, they gnawed at crusts of bread or "old bones with rancid shreds of meat still clinging to them."

"The sight was revolting, disgusting," wrote Wolfe, "enough to render a man forever speechless with very pity."

By the summer of 1931 people had begun to occupy the parks, settling into the ruins of the magnificent city that had existed just a moment before. In Central Park, where the Great Lawn is today, a little town sprang up. City workers had been demolishing the old receiving reservoir there, but the Parks Department ran out of money and the workers just walked away, leaving their work sheds, their tools, and their materials where they lay. Homeless New Yorkers converted these remnants into twenty-nine makeshift shelters, including a home twenty feet tall, built out of stones from the ruins of the reservoir. More men and women lived in the emptied water mains. Nearby, one man slept each night in a baby buggy, and a married couple camped for nearly a year in a cave.

Before long, hundreds of men and women were living in the Central Park Hooverville, and it had become a morbid tourist attraction, complete with regular performances by a tightrope walker. City authorities were worried enough to remove the sheep from the Sheep Meadow, afraid that the animals, grotesquely inbred though they were, would prove too tempting to the park's hungry squatters.

It was no joke. There were at least eighty-two separate breadlines in New York, with an estimated eighty-five thousand people lining up every day, desperate for anything to eat. Others could be seen scrambling over the mountains of garbage that lined the waterfront along the Lower East Side, battling the gulls and the rats for scraps of food. In 1931, New York hospitals reported at least 95 deaths from starvation-related illnesses, while the next year the city's Welfare Council reported that another 110 individuals—most of them children—had died of malnutrition. Some didn't make it to the hospital, such as an unemployed dishwasher who was found to have starved to death on a bench in Grand Central Terminal, amid the passing throngs, the hum and clatter of the Oyster Bar, the spectacle of the red carpet being rolled out to greet the arrival of the 20th Century Limited from Chicago every evening.

There had always been terrible poverty in the city. But now it had begun to afflict the sorts of individuals who had never been poor before—who had never feared being poor before. Andrew Freedman's home for the blue-blooded indigent up in the Bronx was at last filled with people who really had been rich. Amtorg, an arm of the Soviet government set up in Manhattan to recruit Americans for work in the U.S.S.R., put out ads for six thousand skilled workers. It was inundated with more than 100,000 applications from "plumbers, painters, mechanics, cooks, engineers, carpenters, electricians, salesmen, printers, chemists, shoemakers, librarians, teachers, dentist, a cleaner and dyer, an aviator, and an undertaker"—all willing to go live in Russia for the promise of a job.

Feelings of self-loathing and despair were pervasive. A man facing eviction told the *Daily News*, "Sometimes I feel like a murderer.

What's wrong with me, that I can't protect my children?" A federal relief worker in New York found that "almost every one of her clients . . . talked of suicide at one time or another." The Depression stunted ambitions—even the ambitions that people had for their children. Pete Hamill, growing up in what is now called the South Slope of Brooklyn, remembered that parents in his working-class neighborhood "didn't have their kids saying, 'Hey I wanna be an actor,' or 'I wanna be a writer.' They didn't want to hear that because they wanted them to get a civil service job, so if there was another Depression they'd be okay. They didn't want us to have our hearts broken."

It was the dream itself that was dying. New York would never really get over the Great Depression. The city would become rich again, grow again, come to dominate the nation's and even the world's culture again. But the easy confidence in its genius that had existed before the great slump was gone for good.

First, New York lost its economic hegemony. The Depression was when the ultimate financial power passed from Wall Street to Washington and the Federal Reserve. In its role as the New Deal's "model city," New York received a hefty helping of federal largesse—$1.1 billion from 1934 to 1939, or one-sixth of the entire federal budget for public works. But its relative importance still declined, along with its share of the national GDP, and New York's finances and its government would depend as it never had before on the federal government.

Even beyond the immediate economic devastation, the Great Depression tore up the social fabric of the city, exposing a deeper corruption. There was still no real social safety net in place. Governor Franklin Delano Roosevelt set up the first state emergency relief program in the country, but it was quickly overwhelmed. By April 1932, 1.25 million people—more than one in every ten New Yorkers—were dependent on public relief, with another 160,000 families awaiting their turn. Recipients got all of $8.20 a month—about one-fifth of the poverty level. People compensated however they could. In some neighborhoods, cops gave out food bought with their own money or donated by other municipal workers, both grateful and guilty to have a steady paycheck.

Wall Street and Tammany Hall, the traditional power centers of the city, were now ethically as well as literally bankrupt, their authority shattered. As the evictions kept multiplying, they were not infrequently "canceled" by the impromptu crowds that would gather, wait until all of a family's possessions were moved out on the sidewalk, then move them right back in. When the banks foreclosed on more than 60 percent of houses in Sunnyside, Queens, homeowners wrapped barbed wire and sandbags around their domiciles and bombarded the evicting sheriffs with pepper and flour. Even the father of Johnny Sylvester—the sick young boy Babe Ruth had "saved" by promising to hit a home run for him after the 1926 World Series—was hauled up before the congressional Pecora Commission and grilled on his unethical banking practices.

All of the glamour, all of the marvelous creativity and cleverness of Manhattan, could no longer conceal the fact that New York had become, in the phrase of La Guardia biographer Thomas Kessner, "a city without the soul of a commonwealth." Investigations uncovered a municipal government that had run completely amok. City employees routinely robbed the elderly and the infirm in public institutions and extorted massive bribes from businessmen. Park attendants ran dicing operations. City lifeguards spent most of their time cavorting with what we prefer to call "sex workers" today. It was probably just as well. Many of them were unable to swim. (The lifeguards, not the sex workers.)

The police were corrupted as they never had quite been before, even in New York, by both the politicians and the mob. Vice cops had taken to shaking down innocent young women by framing them for prostitution. The city's magistrates were shown to be the intimates of mob bosses or, like Judge Joseph Force Crater, simply disappeared with a cloud of undetermined scandal in their wake.

The Little City had been neglected to the point where it could no longer hold up the Big City. As more and more money disappeared into a few, select pockets, every civic accomplishment of the past fifty years looked about to be undone. Piers rotted. The city's waste and garbage washed back up on its shores; there wasn't enough money for a seaworthy scow. Parks decayed, forcing kids to play on the city's crowded, antiquated streets, with predictable results: 249 New York City children were killed by automobiles in 1933 alone. The Central

Park Zoo deteriorated to such a point that its attendants were given rifles and told to shoot escaping predators in case of fire.

The money had just run out, and in the East River stood the most poignant tribute to the city that was supposed to be, the unfinished bones of the great complex of bridges planned to connect Manhattan, the Bronx, and Queens by auto. There instead were only seventeen bare masonry piers, connected to nothing, like gigantic monoliths from some mysterious, vanished civilization.

"New York is colossal, astonishing, fascinating," journalist Alva Johnston would write about the fallen city. "But politically New York is a failure. As a municipality, it is corrupt, and sluttish to the last degree."

It was impossible for the city's game, so intimately tied to the political and economic culture of New York, to fare much better. These were the plague years for baseball. The Yankees, who had drawn more than 1 million fans for nine of the eleven seasons from 1920 to 1930, would not do so again until 1946. Attendance for the Giants and Dodgers sank to as low as 6,000 fans a game in the early 1930s. Nor were they even close to being the worst off in the majors. From 1932 to 1935, the average major-league crowd dropped below 5,000. In 1935, the St. Louis Browns drew a *total* of 80,922 spectators, or a little better than a thousand a game; they drew fewer than 1.2 million fans for the entire *decade.*

Throughout the Depression and the war years, major-league baseball would be in survival mode. Several teams veered close to bankruptcy, and for the first time there was talk of moving franchises, breaking up the old order of the same sixteen teams in the same eleven cities that had prevailed for thirty years. Club owners cut salaries by one-quarter, to an average of just under $5,700, and cut roster spots from twenty-five to twenty-three. The business structure of the game was fundamentally transformed, with major-league teams assuming full control over the minors and eradicating what little leverage the players had left. Sportswriters and fans alike suspended any concern over those at "work" on a ball field.

"A ball player in the majors these days—when men in other professions are laboring for a mere pittance—if they are working at all," wrote a Pittsburgh sportswriter, "is mighty well paid for what he does . . . and he should stretch a mite to give service for what he receives."

He was only echoing the general sentiment. If baseball salaries were cut by a quarter in the 1930s, the average national wage dropped by one-half. Even marginal players made \$3,000 to \$3,500 a year—not bad during the Great Depression for six months' work, with meal money and frequent hotel lodgings thrown in. Men were willing to do almost anything to keep such a job—and frequently did.

The Depression years were marked by constant beanings, spikings, collisions, and brawls on the diamond. Players spewed vicious epithets at each other from the dugouts to show they had "spirit" and suffered brutal, career-altering injuries. Earle Combs fractured his skull chasing a ball into a wall in 1935 and never played regularly again. Another great New York centerfielder, Pete Reiser, would inflict the same injury on himself a few years later. The Yankees' Hall of Fame catcher, Bill Dickey, fractured the jaw of Carl Reynolds after a particularly hard collision at home plate; Dickey's rival for the greatest catcher of the age, Mickey Cochrane, would have his career ended after he was hit in the head with a pitch. Nor were beanings limited to opponents. When the Athletics' rookie Doc Cramer belted an intrasquad home run off Lefty Grove one spring, the furious Grove hit Cramer in the head with a pitch his next time up and told his young teammate, "You didn't hit that one, did you, busher." The Tigers' shortstop Billy Rogell played the entire 1934 World Series with a broken ankle that he simply kept tightly wrapped, later remembering, "Hell, in those days you didn't want to get out of the lineup. Someone might take your job."

No matter how hard the ballplayers of the Depression went at it, the sporting press was always there to egg them on. *The Baseball Magazine* celebrated "an element of wholesome roughness about the national game which should not be suppressed," while *The Sporting News* lamented the "pink-tea brand of baseball" and claimed, "Restoration of the old game would help a lot." The very old idea that baseball was not what it used to be became pervasive, even embodied in an edict from Judge Landis by the end of the 1930s known as the Non-fraternization Rule, banning any friendly contact on the field.

The players needed no urging. They could see how things stood, if only through the windows of their Pullman coaches. Rud Rennie of the *Herald Tribune,* coming north with the Yankees in the spring of 1933, wrote of "Southern cities which looked as though they had been ravaged by an invisible enemy. People seemed to be hiding. They even would not come to see Babe Ruth and Lou Gehrig. They simply did not have the money to waste on baseball games or amusements."

And yet it was this haunted, fallen era that would become a focal point for nostalgia in the city, as it would throughout the country. Ballplayers of the time would become the template for how New Yorkers liked to think of themselves—tough, resilient, quietly determined. The old flash town had been submerged. It would surface again, but it could never compare in the memories of its people to the embattled, heroic city of the Great Depression.

42

The Virtuous City Is Born

Beginning in 1932, three years into the Depression, a series of morality plays would rewrite how New York City perceived itself and how it would be perceived. No longer would the city be seen as floating above the rest of the country, impossibly marvelous, arrogant, depraved, and more than a little alien. Unlikely as it sounded, New York would now become a light unto the nation, an example in reform.

At city hall, the old regime was finally ousted. Jimmy Walker was the first to go, the natty, elfin mayor trying to charm his way through one investigating committee too many.

"There are only three things in this world a man must do alone," he quipped to an adoring throng on the courthouse steps. "Be born, die—and testify."

The joke fell flat, as did Jimmy. He got the boot from no less than Governor Roosevelt, now trying to become President Roosevelt. On

September 1, 1932, Beau James buried his brother George out in Calvary Cemetery, then resigned his office. Nine days later, he sailed for Europe to meet up with his mistress—and to avoid any lingering possibility of indictment.

Tammany itself was the next to go. The machine had just opened a spiffy new Wigwam on Union Square in 1929. Before the next decade was over, it would be sold off to serve as a union headquarters and never replaced; no transition better symbolized the sea change in power that was taking place. Tammany would have another moment after the war as a twisted, mob-dominated shambles of its former self, but it would never fully recover, its main functions replaced by the powers and the prosperity the New Deal unleashed. In its place would stand a trinity of stern, efficient, progressive tribunes who would transform the city and epitomize the spirit of the new age: Robert Moses, Thomas Dewey, and Fiorello La Guardia.

Fourteen months after Walker's departure, La Guardia was elected mayor, using his own flying squads of *Ghibboni*—his "apes"—to slug it out with Tammany "poll watchers" at the ballot boxes. "The Little Flower" was a reformer, but unlike all the generations of effete, blue-blooded New York reformers in the past—and unlike the rather chilly figures of Moses and Dewey—he was a man of the people, a walking melting pot. The child of an Italian-Catholic father and a Jewish mother, he was brought up as an Episcopalian and gave campaign speeches in Italian, Spanish, Hungarian, Croatian, German, and Yiddish. Born on Varick Street, he had worked for years as a U.S. counsel in Trieste, processed new immigrants at Ellis Island, seen action as a fearless (if barely competent) pilot in World War I, and befriended Enrico Caruso, for whom he sometimes cooked spaghetti in his walk-up East Harlem apartment.

A boxy five two, La Guardia wore cheap suits and affected a wide, western hat from his days as the son of an army bandleader, when he grew up on posts in Arizona. He looked more like a burlesque-house comedian than a mayor, but he was smart, tireless, and incorruptible, unafraid of anyone or anything, including the sort of political gutter fighting that characterized New York City politics. "I invented the low blow," he liked to boast, and sometimes he meant literal blows.

On one occasion he attempted to throw a member of the city council out a window after the man called him a wop.

"I am inconsiderate, arbitrary, authoritative, difficult, complicated, intolerant—and somewhat theatrical," the unshrinking Little Flower said of himself, with considerable accuracy.

He was also possessed by a rage for social justice and an unyielding honesty. In the wide-open city of the 1920s, Fiorello had come across as a hysterical puritan, losing his first race for mayor to Walker by a record margin. Even in 1932, as an officially Republican congressman, he lost his seat to the Roosevelt deluge. Now, though, he seemed the perfect leader for the new, humbled city. La Guardia's New York was a hard place, an autumn place, where the light seemed perpetually dim—literally dim during the brownouts of the war. It was a time of deprivation and unspeakable fear. And yet it would burn brightly in the minds of New Yorkers for generations.

In part this was due to his good government instincts and scruples. "È finita la cuccagna!" he announced as he entered city hall on his first day as mayor, or, roughly: "The party's over!"—and he meant it. Tens of thousands of Tammany braves were immediately lopped from the municipal gravy train. In their place, La Guardia hired the best people he could find, including unprecedented numbers of Italians, Jews, and African Americans. He slashed his own salary almost in half, balanced municipal budgets, took New York out of receivership with the bankers, and built and built and built. He consolidated and expanded the subway system while maintaining the nickel fare. He gave the city its first two airports, its first public housing, and thousands of miles of roads and highways, along with new bridges, tunnels, schools, hospitals, parks, public swimming pools.

Unlike past reformers, he was not afraid to get his hands dirty cleaning up the town. "Drive out the racketeers or get out yourself," La Guardia ordered his new police commissioner, Lewis Valentine, an honest cop who had been banished to the wilds of Long Island City for his probity.

Officers were now encouraged to rough up known hoodlums on the street. La Guardia, along with Dewey's gangbusters, fought the mob to at least a draw, exiling Lucky Luciano to Italy, Owney Madden to Hot Springs, Dutch Schultz to the Newark chophouse where he met an inglorious end in the pissoir. He employed a similar ruthlessness with the force itself. One year he actually cut pay for the NYPD across the board, convinced the cops were making more than enough from the bribes paid out by bookies and madams (he was undoubtedly right). He canceled his bodyguard, sending the officer back to walk a beat. When a would-be assassin did approach him with a pistol, La Guardia leaped on the man, pulled the gun out of his hand, and pummeled him to the ground, where he sat on him until the police arrived.

New Yorkers loved the sheer, frenetic energy of the man, the way that he stamped his own pugnacious face on the vast, impenetrable workings of the city's government. He was ubiquitous, doing everything: breaking up illegal slot machines with a sledgehammer, dropping in unannounced on municipal offices to hector slothful city workers, helping firemen pull charred beams off trapped fire survivors; conducting the orchestras at the free classical music concerts the city sponsored at City College.

"It seemed as though the town had been invaded by an army of small, plump men in big hats," *The New Yorker* noted. "He was everywhere."

At city hall, Fiorello worked behind a thirty-two-foot-long table, swiveling about constantly in his chair, dictating to two or even three stenographers at the same time, jabbing at the six different buzzers before him. Even after he left the office for the day, his staff would stay behind, ready to take his further directives from the radiophone in his car. Constantly plying the federal government for money, he would routinely fly down to Washington in the morning and return by the afternoon. And yet there was more to him than energy alone. He was, at heart, a romantic, speaking of himself openly as "an artist or sculptor" in the mayor's office.

"Too often, life in New York is merely a squalid succession of days; whereas in fact it can be a great, living, thrilling adventure," he once wrote in a *Times* opinion piece, and he meant it.

Fiorello La Guardia, with considerable help from friends in Washington and Albany, created a New York where, for the first time, a collective democracy stood between individuals and the exigencies of life. He stopped most of the evictions and expanded the social welfare system. His public works programs employed hundreds of thousands of desperate men and women. By 1941, he had built the first sixteen thousand units of public housing in the country, most of it so good that New Yorkers still clamored to live in it eighty years later. But beyond all of that, he created a municipal government that was run for the Little City, the city of neighborhoods and working people.

In a time when there was no money, he brought into being an almost fantastic array of free possibilities for the people at their leisure. There was the sparkling new Jacob Riis Park in Queens and Orchard Beach in the Bronx, each one able to accommodate a quarter-million bathers on a hot summer afternoon. There were seventeen spectacular, "million-dollar," public swimming pools scattered around the city, each able to hold up to sixty-two hundred people at a time. There were the ten new municipal golf courses, the 240 new tennis courts, and, not insignificantly, fifty-one new baseball diamonds, including the first to ever breach Central Park.

There would be, now, the City Center of Music and Drama, and the City Opera, and the City Ballet, and special public high schools to promote learning in science, art, and music. There would even be a rebooted public radio station, WNYC, which would become La Guardia's most memorable bully pulpit. The site of those free concerts up in Harlem was the free City College of New York, "the Harvard of the working class," bastion of poor, ethnic New Yorkers largely excluded from the Ivy League. In its famous cafeteria alcoves they would "argue the world," in Irving Howe's phrase, and define the intellectual contours of America for a generation.

What stayed with New Yorkers above all was the impression that they were all in this together. There were significant exceptions to this feeling, of course. New York during the Depression and the war was marred by two riots in Harlem and by constant labor strife. It was a time when adherents of the fascist radio priest Father Coughlin attacked Jews on the streets of New York and even in their synagogues—often while police sympathetic to the attackers stood by and did nothing.

La Guardia could be slow to recognize outrages that did not jibe with his heroic view of his constituents. Yet if he could not solve all of the city's problems, he was at least capable of demonstrating what was possible. His style of rough, reformist justice would become the archetype for a thousand Hollywood melodramas of the time. His exuberance would enthrall the city at a time when everything that had been corny and naive suddenly seemed important again. He loved nothing better than cavorting with children, and a favorite activity was mounting an elevated platform at one of the innumerable park or playground openings that Robert Moses arranged for him and telling the assembled mob of youngsters, "Okay, kids, it's all yours!"

There was something earnestly childlike about La Guardia himself, as there was for so many of New York's heroes in this dark time, when comic-book superheroes first flourished. In an early, color home movie from the period, one that became part of the riveting *When It Was a Game* series of documentaries, the little mayor can be glimpsed between Joe DiMaggio and Lou Gehrig at Yankee Stadium before the opening of a World Series. All three men stand looking out over the field, smiling faintly, confidently, wearing Yankees caps—three rough but captivating faces that would come to personify class in the years ahead. The face of the common man, in all its beauty.

This was a key to the era, for both the city and the country. Together, these three men represented the transfer of the popular American ideal from the Anglo pioneer to the urban white ethnic. Fiorello H. La Guardia, Henry Louis (born Ludwig Heinrich) Gehrig, and Joseph Paul (born Giuseppe Paolo) DiMaggio were in the vanguard of a whole new breed, an opening of the country that had never quite been conceded before—certainly not on the fields of its favorite game.

43

"The Attendance Was Robbed"

Before that could happen—at least on the ball field—a troika of local heroes had to take their final bows.

The first to go was Wilbert Robinson. Lovable old Uncle Robbie's days in Brooklyn were numbered when Steve McKeever became the club's dominant owner, thanks to a typically weird Brooklyn chain of events. When they went to lay Charles Hercules Ebbets in the ground in 1925, it was discovered that, somehow, his casket was too large for its grave. Mourners had to wait for more than an hour in the rain while a bigger hole was dug, and in the delay one of Ebbets's main partners, Ed McKeever, caught pneumonia and died. (Only the Dodgers could lose two owners at one funeral.)

Uncle Robbie was elected team president as well as manager. But control of the team was now divided between fifteen Ebbets heirs and Ed McKeever's brother, "Judge" Steve McKeever, a hard-bitten former garbage collector and contractor who had been born in 1853 and literally helped to build the Brooklyn Bridge. Steve McKeever loathed Wilbert Robinson, who had been tickled to have a spacious office suite in his new capacity as club president—until he discovered that he had to pass through McKeever's office to get there. He rarely went upstairs after that, but McKeever fired him anyway, following the 1931 season.

It would not be the last time that a New York baseball owner fired a manager with no real plan in mind for improving the club. Robinson was banished just after Brooklyn had put together consecutive winning seasons for the first time in a decade, and only a year after the club had broken the one million mark in attendance for the first time.

No doubt, Uncle Robbie, who had begun his playing career in 1885, was an anachronism, but Steve McKeever replaced him with an even greater anachronism: Maximillian Carnarius, a.k.a. Max Carey, a onetime seminary student turned base-stealing whiz for the Pirates during the dead-ball era who insisted that his team play the brand of baseball that he had excelled at. Carey dealt away all of his club's top sluggers for a passel of high-average singles hitters, who could not run and could not hit the ball out of one of the coziest yards in baseball. Now Brooklyn was neither colorful *nor* good. Attendance plummeted.

"Brooklyn fans had shown they could forgive errors in the field and incompetence, but they wouldn't stand for dullness," wrote Harold Parrott in the *Brooklyn Eagle.*

—

This situation was partly rectified by replacing Carey with an old favorite from Washington Park days. Casey Stengel had completed his tutorial under John McGraw and spent the rest of the 1920s running minor-league clubs from Worcester to Toledo, where his Mud Hens won the American Association pennant but went bankrupt. When he caught on as a coach under Carey, the Dodgers' beat writers were ecstatic. Before he was even named manager, Ring Lardner had cemented the legend of Stengel as a spieler, spouting his wonderfully tangled patter of "Stengelese," in a serialized story for *The Saturday Evening Post.*

"Just keep talking, I'll get a story," Lardner liked to tell Casey, and the quips—or at least the turns of phrase—kept coming.

Tony Cuccinello, his aging second baseman, had "what you would call rather stagnant legs." "Mungo and I get along fine," Casey told the press about Van Lingle Mungo, his hard-drinking, histrionic pitching ace: "I just tell him I won't stand for no nonsense—and then I duck." When his infielders complained that their many errors were due to a hard infield, Stengel suggested, "Why don't you hit 'em on the ground to the other fellows and get on base that way?" He pointed out that his outfielders were just as unreliable: "They don't take bad hops in the air." He wasn't always devoid of sympathy. His players were "my little chitlins," "my bonny men," "my lambie-pies," and "my brave, young soldiers." When the Dean brothers held his squad to just three hits in a doubleheader, Casey looked at the bright side: "I didn't see a baserunner for eighteen innings, so I couldn't make any mistakes." After one bad loss, he claimed to have told his barber, "Don't cut my throat. I may want to do it myself later." After another, he conceded, "The attendance was robbed."

They rarely were, if Casey Stengel could help it. He would go into paroxysms arguing calls, sometimes clutching his heart, closing his eyes, and falling to the ground. Given a duck when the Dodgers played an exhibition game in Dayton, he named it "Goldberg," kept it with him in the third-base box all afternoon, then took it on the road when the team won. When he wanted the umps to call a game on account of rain, he brought out an umbrella. When he wanted them to call one on account of darkness, he actually brought out a railroad lantern—a shenanigan that became a *Saturday Evening Post* cover by Norman Rockwell. In Brooklyn, real life was once again running up the score on fiction.

"Casey was the best link or bridge between the team and the fans in the history of baseball," Branch Rickey would later write, although for the usual high church of baseball all of his jokes and shenanigans only confirmed him as a fool. *The Sporting News* referred to him even before his first game as a major-league manager as "a buffoon and a clown" and "the jester."

Nothing could have been further from the truth. Stengel was very serious about wanting to shake off what he called "Losing Dodger Complex." He did everything in his power to ensure his teams hustled, shifted his players around creatively, and platooned them at the plate—strategies he had learned in part from McGraw and that he would hone to a fine science in the years ahead. For all the quips, the desire to win was always there; Casey put his foot through a suitcase after a particularly aggravating loss in his first year. There was also a fierce desire to teach.

"He would have liked nothing better than to have ballplayers come home and stay with us so that he could work with them longer," Edna, his wife and invaluable helpmate, would recall.

The catcher Al López, one of the few serious ballplayers on Stengel's Dodgers, and later the only manager who would ever best him when he got his hands on a serious club, remembered that "on the ball field he had one great goal: to teach. . . . When he got . . . a kid with ability, he wanted to see him make it big. He'd stick with a young guy and nurse him along. Casey would sit and talk to them by the hour. He never had any children of his own, so he had a lot to give them."

They weren't always able to receive. By the mid-1930s, "The Dodgers were unique in the National League in not having a single marquee player, top-level pitcher, or run-producer who could not only win a few close games but also become a magnet for fan attention," according to Stengel biographer Steven Goldman. The team had mostly given up on acquiring good players, thanks to a standoff over money between the fifteen squabbling Ebbets heirs and the surviving McKeever.

"Every day the Dodgers are home," *Newsweek* wrote of Judge McKeever, "he clutches his silver-headed cane, walks a few blocks from his ten-room house to the park, and eases himself into a reserved seat directly behind home plate. There he puffs away on black cigars and reaches out his gnarled, jeweled hands for a glass of milk set in a ring on the arm of his chair. . . . Occasionally . . . [he] goes to his office and reads the tons of squawks and suggestions that fans send him. He answers most of them with a rubber stamp: 'Good Health and Luck—Steve.' "

"I'm in baseball because I love the game. I'm going to stay in it until I die," swore the judge, who had to rely on a colostomy bag as well as the cane. "And when I'm gone, my children and my grandchildren will carry on in my place."

He was as good as his word. McKeever heirs still owned part of the Dodgers even after they moved to Los Angeles. But the judge seemed to have little money or inclination to *do* anything with his team.

"What do you expect of a ball club with a board of directors like ours; a plumber, a hatter, a lawyer, and a butcher? We're lucky to keep out of an asylum," Uncle Robbie had complained before he was fired, but these were at least honest tradesmen.

Frank B. York, the team's lawyer, was another story. Replacing Uncle Robbie as club president, he went out to lunch one day in 1932 and never returned. It turned out that York had not only "borrowed" heavily from the club but busied himself in his spare time robbing a client's estate.

Judge McKeever's answer to all this was that Brooklyn should have a stadium "that would seat 100,000 spectators," announcing, "If I had my way I would spend a million dollars to give Brooklyn a winner again."

This was the most wishful of thinking and the start of a generation of Dodgers owners pining for a grand new stadium as the cure for all their troubles. But if McKeever could not swing his million-dollar dream house, the aging contractor did increase capacity at Ebbets Field to thirty-five thousand and turn the park into the one that Dodgers fans would always cherish—at least in memory. Gone was the old, open Ebbets, with its panorama of Brooklyn beyond the outfield fence; no more Dazzy Vance throwing his pitches out of the rooftop laundry. But those lost horizons were more than compensated for by this new, intimate space: the fans right on top of their heroes, the field now a neat little "cigar box," with a double-decker grandstand that ran from the left-field foul pole halfway into center. From center to the right-field line, there was now a high chain-link fence that topped a lower concave wall, and a forty-foot-high scoreboard.

This made for a veritable treasure trove of fun-house bounces, like something imported from Coney Island. Balls bounced crazily off the low concrete wall, got stuck in the chain-link fence, and at least once simply disappeared into the scoreboard, vanishing through a crack in the woodwork.

Yet the most famous addition to the ballpark was a sign for a local business. In the mid-1920s, Abe Stark, a clothier and borough politician, put up an ad for his shop at 1514 Pitkin Avenue, reading HIT SIGN, WIN SUIT. The sign cost Stark just $275 for an entire season and covered much of the right-field wall, but therein lay the problem.

"Many balls hit the original Stark sign," claimed Murray Rubin, whose father did alterations for Abe. "My father told me that some evenings, he altered more suits for players than for paying customers."

With the new fence in place, Abe Stark took the opportunity to stash his black-and-yellow sign *below* the scoreboard, where it was thirty feet long and just three feet off the ground. Stark claimed that it was *still* hit all too often, but most remembered just one man accomplishing the feat: the appropriately named Woody English, a slice-hitting shortstop for the Bums who hit the sign on June 6, 1937.

If the ballpark improved, the endless parade of ballplayers did not. Lonny Frey, later a solid infielder for a world-champion Cincinnati club, saw his career in Brooklyn founder when he committed sixty-two errors in a single season. ("There's an infielder with just one weakness. Batted balls," Casey Stengel commented.) Oscar "Ox" Eckhardt insisted on bringing a huge St. Bernard on the road with him. "If the dog goes, then I go with the dog," he insisted. Eckhardt hit .182 in his brief stint with the Dodgers. Both Ox and dog were gone. Freddie Lindstrom, after a Hall of Fame career with the Giants, came over the river and was so appalled at the ragged play that after one game as a Dodger he simply doffed his uniform and departed, leaving behind only a goodbye note.

The pitching was even worse. The Dodgers in the 1930s employed staffs full of hurlers with erratic abilities but consistently exotic names:

Van Lingle Mungo; Henry Clyde "Pea Ridge" Day; Cletus Elwood "Boots" Poffenberger, a.k.a. the Baron; Luke "Hot Potato" Hamlin; and the immortal Walter "Boom-Boom" Beck.

The last nickname stemmed from the sounds most commonly associated with Beck's pitching: the "boom" of bat hitting ball, then the "boom" of ball hitting wall. Boom-Boom compiled an ERA of 7.42 during his one, abbreviated season under Casey, but would not concede that his arm had unraveled. In his last start of the year, down in Philadelphia's cramped Baker Bowl, he allowed the first eight batters to reach base but refused to leave the game when Stengel came out to remove him. An extended argument on the mound ensued—so extended that out in right field, Hack Wilson, already exhausted from chasing several Beck offerings and his usual debauchery the night before, began to drift into a fugue state.

Wilson was a remarkable creation, five six and 190 pounds, with no neck to speak of and size 5½ shoes. Frank Graham claimed he "was a colossus from the knees up, but his knees seemed to start at the ground." His teammates called him Caliban. Hack had put in six seasons with the Cubs good enough to get him to Cooperstown, but like so many Dodgers he was at the end of his string—a string considerably shortened by his phenomenal capacity for alcohol. Now deep in his hangover nap down in Philly, he was oblivious when an enraged Beck turned and hurled the baseball high into right field. There it banged loudly off the high, tin-covered wall of the Baker Bowl—rousing Hack Wilson, who rushed over to field the ball and make a fine throw into second base.

Wilson and Beck were gone shortly thereafter, but it didn't much matter. The Dodgers' stalemated management kept sending in one new clown after another. Jersey Joe Stripp, who had the unfortunate tendency of sticking his gum on the end of his bat so he could reuse it afterward. Rosy Ryan, once a teammate of Stengel's on the Giants many years before ("McGraw is gone," Casey marveled, "but Ryan's curve ball lingers on"). The amazing Stanley George "Frenchy" Bordagaray, the first major-league ballplayer in a generation to sport facial hair, who once stopped to retrieve his cap while chasing a hit to the outfield.

"The cap wasn't going anywhere," Casey reminded him afterward, "but the ball was."

"I forgot," said Frenchy, who explained another botched fly thusly: "I lost it in the shade."

"George," Casey told pitcher George Earnshaw in response, "I'll hold him and you bite him."

Stengel finally put his foot down when the front office considered picking up the gargantuan catcher Shanty Hogan from the Braves. He could not play for the Dodgers, the manager decreed, because it was too late in the season "to get another tent made."

In Casey's second year, all the comedy blurred into freakish, inexplicable tragedy. Len Koenecke, playing in just his second big-league season in 1934 at the age of thirty, had a breakout year, hitting .320 and playing a terrific outfield. The next year he slumped and went down a bottle looking for his game. By August, Stengel had had enough, and when the club was in St. Louis, he demoted Koenecke to Jersey City, sending him back across the country with two other players on their way to the minors. They were supposed to look out for him, but they couldn't keep Koenecke from being put off their plane in Detroit for his drunken misbehavior. Koenecke chartered his own flight then, but en route reportedly began to make violent sexual passes at the pilots, who finally hit him over the head with a fire extinguisher—killing him instantly.

There would be a moment, at the end of Casey's first year in Brooklyn, when he got to show what he could do. Before the 1934 season, Giants' player-manager Bill Terry, still flush from his team's World Series victory the October before, assessed the rest of the league for the writers, but skipped the Dodgers entirely. Asked about Brooklyn, Terry snorted, "Brooklyn? Is Brooklyn still in the league?"

Casey and his Dodgers burned, but there seemed to be little they could do about it. While the Giants started right where they had left off, the Dodgers put on their new uniforms on opening day, only to discover that they were playing for "Brookyln." Things went downhill from there. In their first twenty games against the Giants, the Dodgers lost fourteen times.

With just two games left to play in the season, though, the Giants found themselves tied for first with St. Louis's irrepressible Gashouse Gang. Those two games were at the Polo Grounds—against the Dodgers. Casey pulled out every stop, giving his team inspirational pep talks, going over each opposing hitter and pitcher before the game, taunting the Giants from the dugout and the coaching box.

"Tough luck, Bill. . . . They're gonna say you kicked away the pennant!" he called out in the first game when Terry failed to handle a run-scoring grounder at first. Mungo shut down the Giants, 5–1, while the Cardinals won their game, and the Dodgers leaped around their locker room, yelling, "Brooklyn is still in the league!"

The next day, Dodger fans rode the subway en masse up from Brooklyn, to treat Casey to that venerable baseball tradition: an appreciation day. The "Section M Rooters Club" presented him with a suitcase, while the Section N Club gave him a pen-and-pencil set—poignant, Depression-era tokens of affection. When the game started, the Dodgers fell behind, 4–0, in the first, but battled back to tie it in the eighth and won it with three runs off Giants ace Carl Hubbell in the top of the tenth. The win set off another wild celebration in the visitors' clubhouse, while Casey told the press, "The Dodgers are still in the league, but not very still."

Even the tightfisted Brooklyn management rewarded Casey with a new two-year contract that included a $5,000 raise. Before dismissing his players for the season, Stengel sent them off with an effusive speech, ending in a tribute to their home borough: "There isn't a finer, sweeter, better gentleman or lady on God's green footstool than a Brooklyn fan. Three cheers for the Brooklyn fan, and the first mug that doesn't cheer gets a kick in the shins."

Yet the Dodgers made it only to fifth the next season, then slumped back down to seventh. The last straw came when the irascible, hard-drinking Van Lingle Mungo—"We can out-drink anyone in the league," Casey lamented—finally made good on his long-standing threat to jump the club. All the move did was kill an impending trade to the Cardinals for Mungo, who would later achieve immortality as the title for David Frishberg's wonderful novelty song, made up entirely of old ballplayer names. (Upon hearing it, the old pitcher asked Frishberg if there were any money in it for him. Frishberg replied that there might be, if Mungo wrote a song called "David Frishberg.")

It was also the end for Casey, who was released at the end of his third year on the excuse that he had let the team get out of control.

Instead, grizzled old Burleigh Grimes, the last spitballer, was hired to manage the club, and Brooklyn went back to losing drearily.

This was too much even for the fine, sweet fans of Brooklyn, who continued to stay away in droves. The team fell deeper and deeper into arrears—to the point where it eventually had to accept its main creditor, the Brooklyn Trust Company, as a partner.

It would prove to be the camel's nose under the tent. Everyone admired the Brooklyn Trust Company's president, George V. McLaughlin, a model of integrity and civic feeling. But George the Fifth, as he was called, had his smart young protégé—a recent law school graduate named Walter O'Malley—pore over the club's books. The young grad would soon provide an education for all concerned.

44

Last Call

The Babe would make a grander exit than Uncle Robbie, in several indelible acts. The most memorable was his "called shot." More than ninety years later, just what Ruth was doing on that October day in Chicago is still debated.

October 1932. The Yankees were back in the World Series and already half finished bludgeoning the Chicago Cubs into submission. There was bad blood between the two teams, created when his fellow Cubbies refused to vote a full share of their series earnings to the Yanks' former shortstop Mark Koenig, even though Koenig had hit .353 after coming over to Wrigleyville. Chicago fans then splattered the Babe and his wife with epithets and sputum when they arrived at their hotel before the third game of the series.

Of course it was the Babe who was their target. Of course it was the Babe who had been the loudest and bluntest in demanding justice for Koenig. It was the nadir of the Depression, but nearly fifty thousand fans turned out, the second-largest crowd ever to witness a game at Wrigley, more than ten thousand of them jammed into temporary bleachers built for the occasion. In the better seats a more subtle drama was playing out. Chicago's rough-hewn mayor, Pushcart Tony Cermak, was hosting his party's nominee for president, Franklin Delano Roosevelt, Pushcart Tony having backed Al Smith at the Democratic convention that summer.

When Ruth came to bat for the first time, the crowd was already so carried away they had begun to hurl big yellow lemons at the feet of the great man, an unimaginable extravagance at the time. The Cubs stood in their dugout, pouring on the abuse (much of it predictably racial). The Babe took it in stride. As the *Herald Tribune* related it, he "paused to jest with the raging Cubs, pointed to the right field bleachers, and grinned." Three pitches later, he hit a towering fly ball off the pitcher Charlie Root, right to the spot in the bleachers where he had pointed.

Somehow, no one has ever considered this blow to be a—or "the"—called shot. But on to the fifth inning, when it seemed that the Cubs and the crowd had begun to get to the Babe at last. Barking back at them now, Ruth was starting to lose his temper. The inning before, he had tried and failed to make a shoestring catch, a miscue that helped the Cubs tie up the game at 4–4. It was his second such flub of the series, and while neither cost the Yankees much, it must have seemed an intimation of mortality. For the first time that season, there were signs that the Babe, now thirty-seven, was beginning to slip. He'd had a fine year, to be sure: forty-one homers, 137 ribbies, a .341 average; 120 runs scored; leading the league in walks and on-base percentage. A fine year, a *terrific* year. But there were the little things. Only thirteen doubles—an indication that the legs were going. There were those flops in the field, and the fact that he was no longer the majors' home-run king, and in September he had been felled by yet another attack of "appendicitis" (the Babe, sui generis in all ways, seems to have had more appendixes than the *Encyclopaedia Britannica*). Adding insult to injury, Colonel Ruppert, with a cold-eyed look at the box receipts, had slashed his salary from $80,000 to $75,000 before the season began.

"Ruth hasn't a chance to get $80,000 in 1932, nor any other year in the future. Never again will any player get that much money for a year's pay," predicted Ruppert.

Now the Babe walked up to the plate again, his anger receding. A smile creased his face, and he waved his cap at the jeering, hooting fans as they worked themselves into a frenzy again. Just as he stepped into the batter's box, another big yellow lemon landed in the dirt before him, rolling to his feet. What happened next would forever be disputed, forever replayed.

We know that he gestured. That much is beyond doubt. It was captured on a grainy, black-and-white frame from a 16 mm home movie camera—from back when the movies first became something any American could do. We know that he gestured, it's there on the film: Babe Ruth, pointing his finger.

At what? At whom?

Well, certainly out before him. At Root, the pitcher, and maybe the bleachers again, and maybe the crowd.

"In no mistaken motion, the Babe notified the crowd that the nature of his retaliation would be a wallop right out of the confines of the park," *The New York Times* reported the next day.

Lou Gehrig, waiting on the on-deck circle, in the Babe's shadow as usual, later said that he was telling Root, "I'm going to knock the next pitch down your goddamned throat." Jolly Cholly Grimm, playing first base for the Cubbies, thought that Ruth was actually responding to Guy Bush, one of his chief tormentors on the Chicago bench and the next day's scheduled starter, telling him, "You'll be out there tomorrow."

This last scenario sounds a little elaborate. Why would Ruth point to the mound to tell off someone taunting him from the dugout? Over the years the stories have metastasized. Ruth himself, like any self-respecting immortal, left conflicting versions of the event, sometimes saying that he *had* "called his shot"—had declared he was going to homer off Root, at other times saying that he had only "waved to the fence" and "didn't point to any particular spot."

The pointing went on and on, to whomever and wherever, as Root worked the count to two balls and two strikes. The Babe making still more debatable gesticulations, seeming to indicate the count, seeming to point to Root, to the fence. Charlie Root claimed later that the Babe had *never* pointed to the fence, arguing, "I'd have put one in his ear and knocked him on his ass," and refusing to play himself in *The Babe Ruth Story* a few years later: "Not if you're going to show him pointing." But this doesn't pass muster. We can see him pointing on the home movie footage. What Root was clearly, clearly trying to do was something that would *really* deflate the big bum—to strike him out.

And Ruth, incredibly enough, Ruth was acting out the most renowned piece of fiction ever written about the game. He had become *Casey,* as in "Casey at the Bat." It was all there: the broad hand gestures, the awesome hubris, the mounting tension; everything direct from the iconic Ernest Thayer poem, the most famous text of the game. All made real, played right out on the field, *in the World Series.* It was a real player trying to alter a myth, a latter-day John Henry driving into the mountain, Casey Jones sticking to the throttle of his engine. It was the last stand of what the cultural historian Greil Marcus would call the weird, old-timey America, a place not quite real to us today.

And he did it. *He did it.* Where storybook characters tried and failed, Ruth succeeded, and what could be more American? Root tried to sneak a changeup past the fat old man, tried to make him twist his skinny, piano legs up in knots swinging at air. Instead, the huge bat—a little bit lighter now, another concession to the years—flicked out past the great gut and sent the longest fly ball ever seen at Wrigley sailing out over the flagpole to a small space between the right-field bleachers and dead center, almost 450 feet away.

At the moment, no one seemed to have any remaining doubts.

"The crowd, unmindful of anything except that it had just witnessed an epic feat, let loose with a great salvo of applause," reported the *Times.*

"What do you think of the nerve of that big monkey? Calling his shot and getting away with it!" Gehrig crowed later in the clubhouse. Lou followed with his own home run almost to the same place off Root, a laser shot that, typically, no one would remember. "It was like a flash of lightning and a clap of thunder," a reporter wrote, and for all intents and purposes the Cubs, and the series, were finished, the Yankees finishing the four-game sweep the next afternoon.

"You lucky bum. You lucky bum," Ruth later claimed he told himself as he scuttled around the bases, though it didn't keep him from taunting the Cubs as he ran along. In the locker room he was uncharacteristically restrained, almost coy, telling reporters, "Shucks, that big wind blowing toward the outfield helped me a lot." Later, after telling the story every which way, he would only say, "Why don't you read the papers? It's all right there in the papers."

In the papers, and in pretty much every contemporary account of the game, there was no doubt about it. Babe Ruth made an unmistakable gesture, pointing at least out at the pitcher and more likely toward the distant stands, indicating he was going to hit a home run. Even more incredibly, *he did it twice,* if the *Herald Tribune* account is to be believed.

If he did not, why did it become an immediate sensation? If he did not, why did tens of thousands of *Cubs* fans rise and roar their approval as one? As with so much else with Ruth, we have *diminished* his deeds with time, not expanded on them—diminished them because we cannot quite believe the reality.

Which included the fact that he had a legendary president-to-be in attendance as scenery. In the stands, FDR laughed and cheered. He would win election handily just over a month later, and some three months after that Pushcart Tony Cermak would be standing at the side of his car, still trying to make amends in Miami, Florida, when an assassin's bullet intended for Roosevelt went astray and hit him in the gut. Cermak was rushed to a hospital in the president-elect's car, with Roosevelt cradling him in his arms, telling him, "Tony, keep quiet—don't move. It won't hurt if you keep quiet." But it did hurt, and by March 6, Cermak was dead, just as a new age began.

The Babe's reward for his World Series heroics was a further $23,000 pay cut, down to $52,000. (Gehrig's salary was cut from $25,000 to $22,000, even though he drove in 151 runs and hit .349 in 1932.) Ruth's salary would be slashed yet again, in that hard age, to $35,000 (plus his usual slice of exhibition-game profits) the following season. By then the Babe was up over 230 pounds, the legs clearly going, substituted for constantly in the late innings.

"It's hell getting old," the Babe said with typical candor.

Still, he would not go quietly. In 1933 it was decreed there would be an "All-Star game," the first one in major-league history—or at least the first one since the Fashion Race Course in Flushing, in the summer of 1858. The 1933 game was organized by Arch Ward, sports editor of the *Chicago Tribune,* to help promote Chicago's Century of Progress Exposition and to benefit indigent retired players. It would be played at Comiskey Park, with the starting players selected by a vote of the fans and with Connie Mack and John McGraw, respectively, serving as managers of the American and National League teams. But everyone knew who the fans—hell, even the players—had come for.

"We wanted to see the Babe," remembered the National League starter Wild Bill Hallahan. "Sure, he was old and had a big waistline, but that didn't make any difference. We were on the same field as Babe Ruth."

When was the last time a major-league pitcher in an All-Star Game was there to see another contemporary player? Hallahan saw him, all right. The Babe hit the game's first home run, the very first home run in All-Star Game history, off the Cardinals southpaw. He also secured the victory for the American League, and his teammate Lefty Gomez, by making an outstanding running catch off Chick Hafey near the right-field wall in the eighth inning.

It was as if Ruth kept being dragged back for one more curtain call, like some beloved old vaudeville star. On the last day of the 1933 season he took the mound, as he sometimes liked to do, and pitched a complete-game victory over the hapless Red Sox—his final bit of payback. Ruth also hit his thirty-fourth home run in the game, which was his fifth Yankees outing as a pitcher. He won them all. Going along with the gag in the last game of the 1930 season, Gehrig had taken Ruth's spot in left field. They had five hits between them in that game, and made no errors, while Ruth pitched a complete game then, too, and even started two double plays, each time on "a smash hot off the bat." Gehrig finished that season at .379, Ruth at .359, and the Boston crowd was "visibly and audibly impressed," according to the *Times*'s account.

"It's incredible," Mets pitching coach Rick Peterson said when told of the feat nearly seventy-five years later, noting the time it generally takes to get a starting pitcher ready for his first start of the year: "That's why spring training is six weeks long."

Ruth showed what spring training was for in 1934, when he hit what some feel might be the longest home run ever, perhaps as much as six hundred feet in the air, off a Boston Braves pitcher named Huck

Betts and out of "the Other House That Ruth Built," the team's spring training park in St. Petersburg. After that season was over, there was a grand major-league tour of Japan, with 500,000 fans mobbing him in a parade down Tokyo's Ginza, held expressly to honor "Beibu Rusu." The Babe belted thirteen home runs in sixteen games, obligingly fanned against a local schoolboy sensation, and came home to discover that he was out of a job.

Ruth's only remaining ambition was to manage, but Colonel Ruppert famously told him, "How can you manage the team, when you can't even manage yourself?" He offered to let the Babe prove himself managing the Yankees' leading farm team, over in Newark. This was reasonable enough. What was not so forgivable, when he refused, was hoodwinking Ruth into accepting a job as player and "assistant manager" with Judge Emil Fuchs, an old Tammany hand now running the Boston Braves. Ruth agreed for $25,000 a year—and the clear understanding that he would soon realize his dream of managing with the Braves, a team so desperate that it had nearly stooped to installing an offseason dog track around the outfield.

It was all a shell game. Hugely overweight and out of shape, plagued by bad knees and bad colds, the Babe played sparingly and argued frequently with Fuchs. Still, when he was right, he could awe them at the plate. He won the Braves' home opener with a 430-foot shot off the great Carl Hubbell, then, on May 25, 1935, hit three massive home runs in one game in Pittsburgh, the last two off Guy Bush, who had put him on his ass in the first inning of the game after the Babe's "called shot." The final blow was the first ball ever hit out of Forbes Field, clearing the double-decked, right-field grandstand. As it left the yard, the Pirates players stood and watched, and the crowd let loose.

"It was the longest cockeyed ball I ever saw in my life. That poor fellow, he'd gotten to where he could hardly hobble along," Bush remembered. "When he rounded third base, I looked over there at him and he kind of looked at me. I tipped my cap, sort of to say, 'I've seen everything now, Babe.' He looked at me and kind of saluted and smiled. We got in that gesture of good friendship. And that's the last home run he ever hit."

A week later, Ruth got into yet another fight with Fuchs and retired. His wife later claimed, "From then on until the day he died, [he] sat by the telephone," waiting for an offer to manage a major-league team. It never came. Aside from a further snow job—a season coaching for the Dodgers—he never had another job in major-league baseball. Ruth was hardly a pathetic figure; thanks to the agent Christy Walsh, he even managed to beat the Crash, when it came to money. But it still seems incredible that nowhere, considering the desperate straits that all big-league teams were in during the Depression and the war—considering how many fetid editions of, say, the Braves, or the Browns, or the Phillies, or the Senators were trotted out, year after year, with no intention of even trying to contend—that *no place* in baseball could be found for its greatest, most transformative star to manage.

45

The Quiet Men

"It was a splendid game, wasn't it? Ruth? He was marvelous. That old boy certainly came through when they needed him."

Thus spake John McGraw after watching the man he used to call "the big ape" beat his National Leaguers in the first All-Star Game. Such a reaction could only mean that Muggsy was retired, which he was. McGraw had fielded contending teams right to the end, but by the early summer of 1932 he was finished—out of patience, out of ideas, out of health. More than ever, he yearned for the "tight pitching, sensational fielding, team play at the bat, base stealing and scientific methods" of his old, inside game—an impossible hope.

On June 2, Johnny Mac called into his office his star first baseman, Bill Terry—a player who had refused to speak to Muggsy for two years due to a salary dispute—and told him that he was turning the team over to him, if he wanted it. Terry did. The change was announced the next day. In his last official act as manager, McGraw filed a protest against his old nemesis, the umpire Bill Klem.

McGraw retired to his big, comfortable house in Pelham Manor, returning to the field only for that first All-Star Game. Before the start of the 1934 season, he would be dead of kidney and prostate cancer, weeks shy of his sixty-first birthday. There would be a funeral service at St. Patrick's, attended by some thirty-five hundred mourners, before his body was transported to its final resting place back in Baltimore—the city, ironically, that he had almost single-handedly bounced from the big leagues. There would be more tributes on opening day at the Polo Grounds and at the second All-Star Game there; at baseball's new Hall of Fame, where he was among the first class of inductees; and at Truxton, in August 1938, when his New York Giants took a train and then a school bus to John McGraw's old town, to play a semipro team, the Truxton Giants. Proceeds for the game paid for a monument to a "son of these hills" who had been "spawned for Destiny and Fame." This was a relief bust topped by a granite baseball, and it stood at the exact spot in the road where, so many years before, the teenage McGraw had fled from his father's rage to the inn of Mary Goddard, the kindly widow across the street.

When John McGraw died, it was as if he took all the color of the Giants with him. His most fabled contemporaries either had preceded him or would soon join him in the hereafter: Iron Man Joe McGinnity and his beloved Matty; Turkey Mike Donlin and poor Ross Youngs and Bugs Raymond; Rothstein and Fallon, the Brain and the Mouthpiece.

Charlie Stoneham, the porcine, bug-eyed, bucket-shop operator and literal lady killer who had fought so long and hard to keep control of his team, died in Hot Springs, Arkansas, McGraw's old roistering hole, in early 1936, aged fifty-nine. Miraculously, he had managed to hang on to the Giants through a decade of lawsuits, and now he passed it on to his son, Horace, a cherubic thirty-two-year-old who would become the youngest owner in modern major-league history. Young Horace "liked things soft and easy," in Charles Alexander's assessment. "His black-rimmed glasses and chubby pink cheeks," wrote author Michael D'Antonio, "gave him the look of a pampered prep-school boy"—which he mostly was.

After he put in a brief stint at Fordham, his father had sent young

Horrie out to California, to work for a while in a copper mine he owned. On his return, Charlie Stoneham had the boy sample every facet of the Giants organization: taking tickets, joining the grounds' crew in their eternal fight against the encroachments of the Harlem River. Despite these advantages, his life seemed to become more and more sad. There was the wife he was separated from for many years, unable to divorce her thanks to the strictures of his faith. A son who seemed to share his propensity for spirits. Inch by inch, like Charles Ebbets Jr. before him, Horace Stoneham began to sink into a whiskey bottle. Sitting up in the team's Polo Grounds offices out in centerfield with a highball, he would commandeer a drinking companion by crooking a finger at some subordinate and ordering, "Sitsee."

Young Horace's detachment meant, ironically, that the team was dominated more than ever by its manager. The Giants as an organization had learned nothing about division of management, or building a farm system, or the sorts of business models that would soon turn both of their city rivals, the Dodgers and the Yankees, into the most dominant organizations in baseball history. Instead, like some Tammany clubhouse, the franchise was simply turned over to the departing headman's designated choice, to do it all. Bill Terry was not only manager and first baseman but also the team's chief talent scout and its very first director of minor-league operations.

Terry was the polar opposite of McGraw in almost every respect: cold, blunt, and insular; a model of conscientiousness and self-discipline; a meticulous dresser and organizer who worked fourteen to sixteen hours a day and was prone to saying things after a big loss like "For the mistakes we made, I'll take the full responsibility." Reporters hated him because he would not give them his home phone number, but his players found him a welcome change after the constant carping of Muggsy's final years. The teams he shaped were steady, professional outfits, perpetual contenders and winners of three pennants and a World Series.

They were also the blandest, least remembered champions ever assembled in New York. If the Giants have receded in the city's collective memory, the 1930s Giants are a nullity. It's one thing to admit that most of their regulars would draw blank stares today: Jo-Jo Moore, the fleet, slap-hitting leadoff man and left fielder; Hank Leiber, a strapping outfielder with some pop who hit as high as .331; Gus Mancuso, an outstanding defensive catcher who handled the team's superb pitching staff; Rowdy Richard Bartell, the team's one touch of color, a fiery, 160-pound, journeyman shortstop with a quick bat and quicker fists who once got smacked flat in the chest with a tomato when he stepped in to bat at Ebbets Field. It's another to realize that even the team's stars and its three Hall of Famers—Mel Ott, Carl Hubbell, and Terry himself—have somehow slipped down the memory hole.

Terry had blossomed as a ballplayer only at the advanced age of twenty-nine, after McGraw finally moved him out from behind High Pockets Kelly at first. A superb fielder, "Smiling Bill" constantly led the league in chances, assists, double plays, and fielding percentage. He was a lifetime .341 hitter and the last National Leaguer to this day to bat over .400 in a season, a feat mitigated by the fact that in the year he accomplished it, 1930, the Giants as a team hit .309 and the entire *league* batted a record .303.

Ott had gone directly to the Giants from catching for a lumber mill team in the New Orleans suburb of Gretna, Louisiana. He was just sixteen years old when he arrived in New York, only five nine and 170 pounds, and the writers mocked him as "Master Melvin." But McGraw refused to send him to the minors, afraid of some lesser mind spoiling him, insisting, "Ott stays with me!" when Casey Stengel tried to snatch him for his Toledo Mud Hens. Master Melvin was Muggsy's last great project: McGraw breaking him in slowly, first as a pinch hitter, then moving him out from behind the plate to save his legs, teaching him to play right and center, third base and second.

The one thing he couldn't teach him was hitting. There was no need. The lefty-hitting Ott's stance made him look the perfect busher and drew open derision when he first came up. With each pitch he would lift his right leg—in a style later made famous by Sadaharu Oh—shifting his weight into the pitch. McGraw tried to change it, but he soon realized how it worked for Ott, bringing his bat forward in a quick, powerful swing.

"Just keep swinging that way, son," McGraw told him, and he did. By the time Ott was nineteen, he was a starter; by twenty he ran up forty-two home runs and 151 RBIs on the season. He would go on to bat .304 lifetime, lead the league in home runs six times, and become the first National Leaguer to hit more than five hundred homers. He played for twenty-two seasons and twenty-five years after he retired was still fifth on the all-time home-run list. His league career record for walks lasted forty years, until it was broken by Joe Morgan.

Bill James has pointed out that no other player's power numbers were so enhanced by the ballpark he played in, but this was at least partly by design. Ott deliberately practiced clearing the Polo Grounds' short porches of 257 feet to left field and 279 to right, hitting 323 of his 511 dingers at home. If he hit many fewer home runs on the road, his lifetime batting average in opposing parks was fourteen points *higher* as he drove doubles and triples into the gaps. He could hit it out on the road. In 1933, he won the Giants' only world championship of the era with a tenth-inning, two-out homer to centerfield in Washington's Griffith Stadium—no inconsiderable clout.

Off the field, Ott took a country boy's liking to Broadway, squiring Tallulah Bankhead to Toots Shor's famous watering hole. Perennially cheerful and accommodating to a fault, he liked to refer to the pitchers he mauled the most thoroughly as his "cousins," and he was always willing to do what the team needed, turning in one of his best seasons when he moved from the outfield to third base in 1938. The Giants rewarded his selflessness by cutting his already meager salary by $5,000, to just $19,500 and a few years later stuck him with the managing job when the team was in clear decline. Sportswriters passed him over for the two, or three, or maybe four MVP awards he deserved. It was Mel Ott whom Leo Durocher was talking about when he said, "Nice guys finish last."

He didn't finish last in the 1930s, thanks mainly to the Giants' strong pitching staff, led by the hard-nosed Fat Freddie Fitzsimmons (who at five eleven and 185 pounds could be "fat" only in the Depression), Prince Hal Schumacher, and the lefty ace King Carl Hubbell. Together, they led the Giants to a team ERA of 2.71 in that championship year of 1933—the lowest in major-league ball since the last dead-ball season of 1919. All three men were pugnacious competitors typical of their times, relying on guile and deception as much as velocity. Not-So-Fat Freddie throwing his knuckle-curve, constantly challenging hitters and umpires and even McGraw himself; Hubbell with his mysterious screwball. Prince Hal—the nickname a nice Shakespearean affectation, typical of baseball beat writers of the era—threw an overhand curve and a heavy fastball that made a gratifying pop in the catcher's mitt, at least before he blew out his shoulder and survived on a palmball for four more years. Pitching one terrible, hot day in St. Louis, Schumacher abruptly collapsed, and the trainer could not find a heartbeat. Only by hauling him off and packing him in ice did he manage to revive him and keep Schumacher from becoming the first major-league pitcher to literally die on the mound.

Palmballs, screwballs, knuckle-curves—these were the sorts of devices ballplayers of the era would come up with to keep from having to go back to the breadlines, or the unemployment lines, or the oil fields of Oklahoma, where Hubbell was originally spotted, hurling for a semipro industrial team. All three pitchers had workingmen's faces, weathered and narrow-eyed and faintly suspicious; perhaps also a little embarrassed at being photographed. Hubbell with his gaunt, Okie visage looked especially as if he could just as likely be found moving down Route 66 with the Joads as pitching in the Polo Grounds.

It was McGraw who let him throw his screwball at will, and he threw it with a big, slow delivery that helped him win more than twenty games every year from 1933 to 1937. Hubbell used it to lead the league in ERA three times and become the only pitcher outside World War II ever to win two MVP awards. The first came in 1933, when he won twenty-three games, pitched ten shutouts, and compiled an ERA of just 1.66—followed by a World Series when he nearly matched Matty's 1905 feat by allowing no earned runs in twenty innings of work. He was often at his best in big games, stopping the mighty Yankees in the first game of the 1936 World Series to break their series winning streak at twelve straight games and holding his own with the great Dizzy Dean in league games and Bob Feller in exhibitions. He was a workhorse and a model of consistency, his other nickname, The Meal Ticket, a consummate tribute in the Depression. Hubbell tied Rube Marquard's mark of twenty-four consecutive, regular-season wins in 1936–37 and threw forty-five straight innings of scoreless baseball down the stretch in 1933, including a critical eighteen-inning, 1–0 win over archrival St. Louis.

Unlike Dean's and Feller's, Hubbell's stock-in-trade was deception more than power, and he never had more than 159 strikeouts in a season. As Heywood Broun would write, he "moves through the world with . . . self-effacement" and "gains his effects with a minimum of effort and with precision rather than power." Yet Hubbell would always be remembered for a start that was the furthest thing from self-effacing, at the second All-Star Game, at the Polo Grounds, on July 10, 1934. The first two AL batters reached base against him. Hubbell then reared back and struck out Babe Ruth on five pitches, the last one a screwball for a called third strike. Next he fanned Lou Gehrig, having one of his greatest seasons, on four pitches. Then he struck out Jimmie Foxx with three screwballs. On to his second inning of work, King Carl struck out Al Simmons and then Joe Cronin, gave up a single to Bill Dickey, then struck out pitcher Lefty Gomez.

Two innings, six strikeouts, and five *consecutive* strikeouts of Ruth, Gehrig, Foxx, Simmons, and Cronin, five of the most feared hitters of his day. It was a feat that would not be matched until Pedro Martínez struck out Barry Larkin, Larry Walker, Sammy Sosa, Mark McGwire, and Jeff Bagwell in two innings of the 1999 All-Star Game, sixty-five years later.

Hubbell dutifully followed Terry and Ott into management once he retired, taking over as director of minor-league operations when Terry was kicked upstairs. He would hold development positions with the Giants in New York and then San Francisco for decades, including the years when the organization regularly churned out the best young players in the game. Even after he was felled by a stroke in 1977, he came back to scout and loved to watch the team in spring training—yet another perfect Giants hero, diligent, uncomplaining, in love with the game, and largely forgotten.

Terry and Ott and Hubbell all worked their way doggedly up the ladder, they paid their dues, they progressed from player to manager to front office much like Tammany braves climbing the ladder of the machine. But diligent though they might be, outstanding though they often were, there was no influx of fresh blood, no one recruited from outside the organization. Their roles as eternal Giants reflected a fatal dry rot within the team's management, as surely as Jimmy Walker and his cronies reflected the failure of the old clubhouse to deal with the exigencies of the Great Depression and the modern world in general.

The decline of the Giants was tied to that of Tammany in more than metaphor. As Tammany was eclipsed, the club lost its special relationship with city hall, its access to money and favors. And as the Irish assimilated into the melting pot of greater New York, ethnic rooting preferences changed, as they would throughout the city's history. Italians identified more with the Yankees, thanks to the presence on the Bombers now of the greatest Italian baseball star there ever was. Jews rooted for the Dodgers in Brooklyn, the Yanks in the Bronx.

The Giants, somehow, no longer seemed to be anybody's special team. There was no one especially Irish on the club after McGraw packed it in. As the 1930s progressed, the fans closest to the Polo Grounds became more and more those whom neither the Giants nor any other white team cared to appeal to. These were people of color, the rapidly growing population of Blacks and Hispanics in Central and East Harlem.

White fans became increasingly reluctant to venture uptown to the Polo Grounds, put off by the reports, mostly exaggerated, of crime in Harlem and the fact of the 1935 riot there. Already, the Giants had trouble providing sufficient parking for big crowds, and their patrons grew afraid to "risk" the subway. These problems festered and worsened for years, even decades, while the boys in the Giants' clubhouse—still playing "sitsee" through a whiskey-glazed afternoon, still blinking at the dust-speckled sunlight as it seeped through the drawn blinds—couldn't bring themselves to address any of it. The team's fortunes on the field slowly declined along with its attendance—although one potential answer to that, too, lay unheeded just outside the Polo Grounds' walls.

46

"The 'Coonsberry' Rules"

In 1938, an ugly incident indicated just how little progress had been made on race in major-league baseball. Jake Powell, a part-time outfielder for the Yankees, was asked by a White Sox radio announcer what he did in the offseason. Powell replied that he was a seasonal policeman in Dayton, Ohio, where he stayed in shape by "cracking n——rs over the head with my blackjack."

His remark at least sparked outrage among white as well as Black listeners, with a petition from African American leaders asking that Powell be banned from the game for life. Psychotic as the remark was, Powell wasn't even a policeman, in Dayton, Ohio, or anywhere else; it was his idea of a joke. There was something very wrong with Jake Powell. He ran up so many gambling debts that men with his markers once threatened to sue the Senators, his old team. While playing with the minor-league Dayton Ducks, he was caught trying to lift a circular fan, a bedspread, and even the drapes from his hotel room.

"He probably would have taken the mattress if he could have got it in his suitcase," his manager said.

Less amusingly, Powell was generally held to have deliberately run into Hank Greenberg at first base in 1936, breaking Greenberg's wrist and putting him out for the season. He was nonetheless valued for his relentless hustle and his aggressiveness, which usually would have been the end of it. But the African American community would not let Powell's "joke" go. After meeting with Black leaders, Commissioner Landis—hardly a paragon himself when it came to race—ordered Powell suspended for ten days. It was the first time any major-league player had ever been suspended for a racist remark, according to *The Sporting News,* which once would have ridiculed such a move. Black reporters urged a boycott of the Yankees, and when the team traveled to Washington, Black fans hurled pop bottles at Powell.

The Yanks, seeing their carefully cultivated corporate image threatened, issued their own apology and ordered Powell to visit bars and restaurants throughout Harlem, expressing contrition for what he had said. This was also previously unheard of, but it hardly indicated a great step forward in ending racism in baseball. Powell had been acquired from the Senators for Ben Chapman, who had worn out *his* welcome in the Bronx for his habit of turning to fans in right field in the stadium, making Nazi salutes, and calling them all a "bunch of sheenies." And after his punishment, Powell stayed on with the Yankees through the 1940 season. (Whatever demons were driving the man, they got the better of him in 1948, when he was arrested in Washington, D.C., for passing bad checks. In the station house, Powell drew a revolver from his pocket and blew his brains out.)

—

Things were changing, but not nearly fast enough. Blanche McGraw reported soon after the great man's death that she had found among his effects a list of all the outstanding Black players he would have liked to have signed for the New York Giants. When it came to race, even baseball's bravest hearts somehow failed in the clutch. But then, the same could be said for the city where McGraw's Giants played.

If the Great Depression hit New York hard, it all but crushed Harlem. Unemployment officially hit 50 percent among African Americans in the city, and in reality it might have reached 70 percent. Even if a person of color could find a job listed, it was most likely closed to him or her. Never mind positions that required a college degree or professional expertise; the most basic jobs were denied to people of color as a matter of course, in what remained a segregated town.

As late as 1935, no African Americans in New York were employed as milkmen, telephone operators, hospital or pharmaceutical workers. The charters of twenty-four different city trade unions specifically banned Blacks from joining. Even in Harlem, African Americans were routinely denied jobs. No Blacks drove the city buses that rolled through the neighborhood. None were employed at, say, the insurance giant Metropolitan Life, although it held more than 100,000 policies in Harlem. No Blacks were hired at the big department stores along 125th Street, not at Koch's or Blumstein's or S. H. Kress.

Instead, the many Black shoppers were still treated as potential criminals when they entered stores, usually refused permission to try on clothing, and followed closely by the house dicks. This turned to tragedy in 1935 when one Lino Rivera, a teenage boy of color, was caught trying to filch a penknife at Kress. He was carted off to the local precinct, but the rumor soon spread that he had been taken downstairs and beaten up by the store security (a not uncommon fate for Black shoplifters), or even killed. A crowd gathered and a riot ensued—the very first Black-on-white riot in the city's tumultuous history—and one that destroyed $2 million worth of property, left a hundred people jailed and thirty more hospitalized, and resulted in three fatalities (all of them Black people). A stunned mayor La Guardia rushed up to Harlem to try to personally restore order, and later he appointed a Committee on Conditions in Harlem, but its conclusions were deemed so incendiary that he suppressed the report.

La Guardia—after consulting with Alain Locke, the scholar and philosopher, publisher of the anthology *The New Negro,* and president of Howard University—did devote previously unknown resources to Harlem. These included one of the city's gigantic pools, parks, a new hospital, schools, and housing for African Americans. He desegregated much of the municipal workforce, fought discrimination in relief programs, and appointed the city's first Black magistrates and municipal employees, winning praise from both the NAACP and the *Amsterdam News,* the leading Black-owned paper in New York, for hiring "more Negroes to the big, responsible jobs in city government . . . than all other mayors of the city combined."

Yet it was far from enough. Living conditions in Harlem, always inadequate, deteriorated precipitously. Harlem Hospital provided only 273 beds and 50 bassinets for the community's 200,000 Black residents. Rooms there were so filthy, the death rates so high, that the hospital was popularly known as the Morgue, and rumors that its white staff was performing nefarious medical experiments abounded. (This did not happen in Harlem, though it proved to be all too true at this time in Alabama.) Harlem Hospital was eventually integrated and transformed, also on La Guardia's orders, but public health amongst African Americans continued to slide. Rates of pneumonia and typhus were twice as high as those for white New Yorkers, tuberculosis rates five times as bad.

Much of this reflected the fact that too many people were jammed into too little space, often without enough to eat. By the time of the 1935 riot, the community, with its broad avenues and spacious, modern apartment houses, had nonetheless passed the Lower East Side of Manhattan as the city's most crowded area.

"Harlem," wrote *Fortune* magazine, "is simply a vast rooming house." Its residents survived by doubling and tripling up, helping each other through with "rent parties," featuring down-home cooking and King Kong—home-brewed corn liquor. Anyone could gain admittance for twenty-five to seventy-five cents at the door, advertised through cards passed out on the street:

Many Folks Wonder Why My Baby Cries;
His Mama Eats Onions and Wipes Her Eyes.
Take This Card as a Gentle Hint,
I'm Giving a Party to Raise My Rent

Even the great jazzmen went, after their last set in the Latin Quarter, not about to leave their best stuff for the white folks downtown. Only here in someone's humble living room would they "cut" each other in earnest, some of the greatest musicians who ever existed, playing at their very best in a ghetto apartment. These were the sorts of terrible treasures that American apartheid would bring and that would never be seen again, that sort of talent so close to its seedbed, the music played strictly for and by those who loved it most.

Still, no matter who was playing, a rent party was not a substitute for a home, or a job. Banned, officially or unofficially, from most means of making a decent living, Black New Yorkers scrambled as best they could. African Americans were still largely prohibited from the Grand Concourse, save in the role of janitors, but not far from the great avenue—and often under the shadow of Yankee Stadium itself—sprang up "slave markets"—at Jerome and at Gerard Avenues and 167th Street, at Walton and 170th, at Simpson and Westchester—so named by the Black women who went there when they could find no other work. They showed up before dawn and could be found waiting in the early morning hours much like immigrant laborers today, sitting on old fruit crates or leaning against a building side. Dressed in the finest clothes they had—fake furs, stylish shoes, clever hats with a feather or two—trying to make a good impression.

It was a wasted effort. The white Bronx housewives who stopped by to hire them looked first for calloused knees, proof of a dedicated floor scrubber. In a buyer's market, they might offer all of seventy-five cents for a day's work, wages so low they sparked a running Harlem joke about the day maid who walks into her employer's apartment and immediately begins looking around.

"What are you looking for?" the white woman demands to know.

"I'm looking for something to steal," the maid tells her. "You paying me this little, you must be expecting me to steal something."

What they gave in return for these pittances was documented by Robert H. McNeill, one of the great photographers of Black life in America, and by Marvel Cooke, an investigative journalist for the *Amsterdam News* and W. E. B. Du Bois's *Crisis,* who went undercover to join these women at their work. In an article written with Ella Baker, later a leader of the civil rights movement in the South, Cooke told of a typical young woman at the "market" named Millie Jones who in the course of a day's work scrubbed and waxed an apartment's worth of floors on her hands and knees, using only a washcloth, beat the mattresses, washed fifteen windows inside and out, and laundered and ironed twenty-one men's shirts.

Alerted, belatedly, to the situation, La Guardia officially abolished the slave markets in 1941, in favor of the Simpson Street Day Work Office, where women like "Millie Jones" could go to be treated to the relative dignity of an employment bureau, with regulated hours and wages. It was a humane improvement, but the slave markets would return intermittently into the late 1950s.

Scattered protests took root, then grew. Adam Clayton Powell Sr., reigning power at his remarkable Abyssinian Baptist Church, described the 1935 riot as "an open, unorganized protest against empty stomachs, overcrowded tenements, filthy sanitation, rotten foodstuffs, chiseling landlords and merchants, discrimination in relief, disenfranchisements, and against a disinterested administration." His charismatic, roguish son and heir apparent, Adam Jr., led active street demonstrations as part of a "Don't Shop Where You Can't Work!" protest that made slow but real progress in at least integrating the drivers' seats of the buses and the sales staffs of the big department stores.

Nonetheless, the Depression had crushed Harlem's higher aspirations. Just as the city as a whole would never quite regain the confidence it had before 1929, Harlem's vision of becoming the world's Black capital would vanish in the hard struggle for survival. The 1930s and 1940s, like the 1920s, was a time of stunning accomplishment in Harlem. Jazz reached the zenith of its popularity in the big band era, and many of the great Harlem clubs and dance halls were at their peak, including Small's Paradise and the elegant, shimmering Savoy, where Chick Webb's house orchestra beat all comers—well, maybe not *quite* Duke Ellington's—in fabulous "battles of the bands." Harlem continued to produce first-rate literary talents, such as the fiction writers James Baldwin and Dorothy West or the likes of Cooke, Dan Burley, and many others at the *Amsterdam News*.

Yet the wider ambitions of Black artists and intellectuals were denied, turned back upon themselves. The stream of white patrons and editors from downtown dried up, along with the book contracts and the evanescent literary magazines they had sponsored. If anything, segregation stiffened, with whites more fearful than ever about holding on to jobs and homes. The 1930s marked the nadir as well as the zenith of a separate, Black America, one that lived more exclusively than ever within its own separate but unequal world with its own businesses, its own newspapers and movies, its own versions of Christianity, its own brilliance—and its own ball clubs.

As with everything else, Black teams, living so close to the edge, were hurt first and hurt worse than the white ones. Rube Foster's Negro National League went down after the 1931 season, while Nat Strong's Eastern Colored League collapsed even before the crash. Nevertheless, after a couple of false starts a new Negro National League arose in 1933, with a Negro American League following in 1937. The two circuits would resume the Negro World Series in 1942, but the annual highlight of Black ball was something else.

Beginning in September 1933, just two months after the first white All-Star Game—and in the same venue, Chicago's Comiskey Park—the first Black All-Star Game was played. It was and would remain an interregional contest, officially the "East-West All-Star Game," with participants chosen in voting sponsored by two of the leading Black newspapers of the time, the *Chicago Defender* and *The Pittsburgh Courier.* With a single exception, the game was played at Comiskey through 1950, and it would become, as one player put it, "the glory part of our baseball," both a showcase for the best Black ballplayers of the time and a major social occasion in its own right, drawing up to fifty thousand fans some years, including the leading Black performers and celebrities in the nation.

This was the heyday of the best and the most famous players in the Negro Leagues, of Satchel Paige, Josh Gibson, Buck Leonard, Cool Papa Bell, Martín Dihigo, Bullet Joe Rogan, Judy Johnson, Ray Dandridge, Chet Brewer, Jimmie Crutchfield, and many others. At the All-Star Game, they played before the likes of Joe Louis and Bill "Bojangles" Robinson, Cab Calloway and Billie Holliday. When teams came to New York, Buck O'Neil remembered, they stayed at the Woodside Hotel, where Count Basie's band played: "We would play ball in the afternoon and go down to Small's Paradise, go down to the Apollo that night."

Yet Black baseball was an even more desperate, even more Darwinian affair than white baseball in the 1930s. Black teams still traveled hundreds of miles between games, mostly in old cars over terrible back roads. They were still unable to stay in most decent hotels or eat in most restaurants; were still playing doubleheader after doubleheader on potholed, grassless fields with just fourteen to eighteen men to a side, for little money and less notice. Still, as O'Neil put it, "trying to prove to the world that we were as good [as] or better" than the best white players. The game they perfected, with vastly inferior equipment, under vastly inferior conditions, tended to be faster, headier, more opportunistic than the increasingly power-dependent game played in the white major leagues.

"We played by the 'Coonsberry' rules," recalled star infielder Newt Allen. "That's just . . . any kind of play you think you can get by with."

And yet, for all of their desire to prove they matched up, almost no one in the white world was paying attention. The door to the big leagues was closed tighter than ever, with no end to major-league Jim Crow in sight. Instead, sustenance for Black ball came from a dubious if inevitable source. In the 1930s, Negro League teams were often headed by attractive front men such as the wise old Homestead Grays' skipper, Cumberland Posey, or the dancer Bojangles Robinson, who founded the New York Black Yankees and would sometimes tap-dance on top of the team's dugout between innings.

Behind the scenes, though, almost every one of the Black baseball clubs was controlled by policy barons: James "Soldier Boy" Semler, owner of the Black Yankees; Rufus "Sonnyman" Jackson, owner of the Grays; Gus Greenlee of the Pittsburgh Crawfords; Tom Wilson with the Baltimore Elite Giants; Abe and Effa Manley of the Newark Eagles. To a man (and woman) they made their money in Black America's leading criminal enterprise, the numbers racket. It was not surprising that so much money should have ended up in the hands of such people, coming as it did from a ghettoized community barred from so many sources of legitimate income. They at least tended to be canny businessmen who put the Negro Leagues on a more solid footing than they had ever been before. In Richard Wright's appraisal, "They would have been steel tycoons, Wall Street brokers, auto moguls, had they been white."

No doubt—and no doubt their moral character was no lower than many of the individuals who have always run white baseball. Cum Posey would argue that Alex Pompez, for one, "had been a bigger benefactor in the life of Harlem than he has been a nuisance." But such absolutions are a little pat. The fact remains that El Cubano and the others drained their own communities of badly needed capital a few pennies at a time, eroding dreams, ensnaring youths—such as a young Malcolm X, then Malcolm Little, who worked as a Harlem numbers runner during the war—and bankrolling other criminal enterprises.

At least they provided their players with better wages and playing conditions than Negro League owners ever had before. The indomitable Effa Manley sponsored a winter team for her Newark Eagles in Puerto Rico and bought them an air-conditioned Flxible Clipper bus. The ambitious cutthroat Gus Greenlee had a soft spot for his Pittsburgh Crawfords, paying them to attend spring training and giving them $1.50 a day in meal money—previously unheard of in Black baseball. Greenlee, the main force behind the formation of the second Negro National League, spent $100,000 building Greenlee Field in Pittsburgh's Hill District, the first ballpark constructed primarily for a Negro League team. It was a crude amalgamation of tin and wood, brick and concrete, but nonetheless an impressive accomplishment in the teeth of the Depression.

In New York, however, no one outdid El Cubano. Alex Pompez had managed to keep his Cuban Stars afloat even after the demise of their Eastern Colored League. Renaming them the New York Cubans, Pompez had maneuvered his team into the Negro National League, where they remained the dominant team of color in the city. There was little competition. Robinson and Semler's New York Black Yankees had some initial success but soon plunged to the bottom of the NNL, where they remained for ten of their thirteen seasons, fielding aged sluggers such as Mule Suttles, Clint Thomas, and Fats Jenkins. The Black Yankees played occasional games at Yankee Stadium but spent most of their time at Hinchliffe Stadium, a football field in Paterson, New Jersey (save for one year at the equally unalluring

Triborough Stadium, tucked under Robert Moses's new bridge on Randall's Island). Abe and Effa Manley had more success, merging their Brooklyn Eagles team with the floundering Newark Dodgers and making it into a contender—but out in New Jersey.

Pompez was left alone to build his dream—for a while. He secured a lease from Jimmy Walker's Parks Department on the Dyckman Oval and would pour $60,000 into the cozy little Inwood park, built near the elevated line on a wedge of land bordered by Tenth Avenue and 204th Street, Nagle Avenue and Academy Street. Over the years, he expanded it from forty-five hundred to ten thousand seats, covered the grandstand, and installed lights in 1930, enabling the Cubans to become the first professional baseball team to play regular night games in New York City. He even added a beer garden once Prohibition ended, leaving *The New York Age* to proclaim, "There is no comfort that the fans can crave undone by Pompez Exhibition Co., Inc."

When the Cubans weren't at home, El Cubano staged prizefights, wrestling bouts, cricket matches, and motorcycle races. He started a Black professional football team, the Brown Bombers, named for the boxing great Joe Louis and coached by the former college star and first Black NFL coach, Fritz Pollard. Like the other, lower-level baseball venues around the city, such as Dexter Park, the Dyckman Oval was a place where all of the city came together for its entertainment. It hosted industrial teams as well, and semipro squads such as the "Treat 'Em Roughs," which had evolved out of a World War I military unit with the same moniker. It was at Dyckman and these other, smaller parks, too, where Blacks and whites played each other, white barnstorming teams that included Babe Ruth and other top stars from the majors taking on the leading Black teams of the day. This meeting ground, this shadowed place down by the Harlem River, where everyone could play together, so long as it wasn't too obvious.

Alex Pompez, too, continued to move between cultures, still bringing the top Latin players of color up to New York, remaining competitive with the powerhouse Crawfords. He even set up his own farm team, the Havana Cuban Stars, to keep feeding his New York franchise. Everything was running smoothly, until one night when Pompez suffered what might be called a business reversal.

Summoned to Harlem's Cayuga Democratic Club, Pompez was informed by a gunsel for Dutch Schultz that El Cubano and the

Dutchman were now partners in the numbers game. When this failed to impress Pompez, he received another visit late one Saturday night, this time in his Seventh Avenue cigar store, from a couple of truly frightening Schultz gunmen named Bo Weinberg and Lulu Rosenkrantz. They escorted Pompez to a West End Avenue apartment, where Schultz placed a gun on the table and proceeded to tear into Pompez:

"I hate a liar, and you are going to be the first n——r I make an example in Harlem, because I don't like nobody telling me lies. You promised to turn in your business and you has not done it, and we have been waiting for your business regardless. I don't care if you make a statement from here to the Bowery to the State Department. It ain't do you no good."

What Schultz was mad about was not simply Pompez's recalcitrance, but the fact that El Cubano had sounded out his fellow Black and Hispanic policy barons about forming a united front to resist Schultz's encroachments. The Dutchman's source was Henry Miro, a Puerto Rican numbers king he had already strong-armed. This gave the gangster an excuse to further terrorize everyone concerned, as the great crime reporter Paul Sann would write:

> El Cubano denied that he had ever said such a bad thing and a mobile unit was dispatched forthwith to bring in the Puerto Rican. Routed out of his sheets in the middle of the night and delivered to the scene with nothing under his Chesterfield but his rumpled silk pajamas, Miro had to stand for a dressing down in front of the whole company. The Dutchman, who didn't like him from an earlier script and often referred to him as 'nothing but a smart Spick,' called Miro some very bad names for reporting Mr. Pompez's position so carelessly.

Runyonesque patter aside, the encounter illustrates the plight of New York's Black and Hispanic communities. Now even the money from the numbers business would be siphoned out of the neighborhood by a white thug, operating with complete protection from the white politicians and police he had bribed. The wealthiest, most powerful men in the community could be snatched up with impunity from where they lived and worked, transported to a respectable white address, and threatened, mocked, and insulted. Pompez's fellow racketeers didn't dare resist Schultz, armed as he was with so much firepower and so many connections.

Of course, any partnership with Dutch Schultz was a limited one—extremely limited. Almost overnight, Pompez went from head of a policy bank that paid him at least $8,000 and sometimes as much as $34,000 *a day* in gross income, to a $250-a-month employee of the Dutchman's mob—allotted even that only to keep up a façade of color to draw business for the Harlem racket. Once he realized that no one was going to help him stand against Dutch Schultz, the loss of income spurred Pompez to concentrate more than ever on building his ball team. There was little else he could do, other than to wait out the fall of Jimmy Walker and Tammany, the election of La Guardia, and the appointment of Thomas Dewey as a special prosecutor to go after the mob.

Humorless, ruthless, buttoned-down Tom Dewey with his little pencil moustache and his towering ego was a man on the rise, about to go almost all the way to the White House and to become the archetype for a thousand cinematic urban crusaders. His first target was Schultz, who by now had consolidated his hold on all the policy rackets in upper Manhattan. This gave the Dutchman control of a staggering amount of cash, and he was trying to expand into still more neighborhoods, move in on still more rackets. Dewey pursued him with his usual zeal, forcing Schultz from the city and hitting him with one indictment after another. Schultz, never a subtle thinker, responded by informing Lucky Luciano, de facto chairman of organized crime in New York, that he was going to deal with Dewey as he dealt with all his problems, by making him disappear. Luciano, a more nuanced tactician, considered what murdering a nationally revered special prosecutor might mean for his own business operations and sent a couple members of Murder Inc. to gun down Schultz, Rosenkrantz, and friends in a spectacular hit at Newark's Palace Chop House in October 1935.

This turn of events liberated Alex Pompez and the other minority policy barons of Harlem. But Dewey was hardly about to stop, just because his chief quarry was gone. He was determined to unmask the whole corrupt alliance that had made Schultz's criminal empire possible, all the way up to Jimmy Hines, the local Tammany sachem and—not coincidentally—boss of the Cayuga Democratic Club, the place where Pompez had first been informed that his independent numbers career was at an end. To effect this, Dewey needed Pompez and his fellow racketeers to testify.

There was only one problem. El Cubano was nowhere to be found. Pompez had decided to go traveling for the sake of his health—viewing his potential testimony against some of the most desperate and violent men in New York as a grave threat to it. He went first to Canada, then to England, dropping from public view for more than a year. Finally, in January 1937, El Cubano was spotted again in his old Harlem haunts. Dewey secured an indictment and sent police to arrest him at his Lenox Avenue office. Pompez wasn't there, but the cops waited patiently for him to return, entertaining themselves by searching the place and turning up a large bundle of cash.

When Pompez finally did return to the building with Juanelo Mirabal, a former ace for the Cuban Stars now serving as the team's president and El Cubano's right-hand man, he immediately noticed something amiss. That was the elevator operator, who made a series of "facial gestures," variously described as "a strange twitch" and "a repeated raising of the eyebrows." Realizing that the man was not having a stroke or an epileptic fit, Pompez and Mirabal got off at a lower floor, where they hightailed it out a fire escape and off to freedom.

Or so the story goes. Whatever his means of egress, Pompez now took off for Mexico City, where he lived the high life for some months under the name "Antonio Moreno," before being arrested stepping into "a bulletproof car with Chicago tags"—one more El Cubano mystery. According to the *Amsterdam News,* Pompez's "fatal desire to communicate with Roy Sparrow secretary of the New York Cubans Baseball Club" inspired the feds to tap the phones at the park. El Cubano's strenuous efforts to fight extradition failed, and he was dragged back to New York in November 1937, just two days before Dewey won election to a full, four-year term as Manhattan district attorney.

Whether he was simply tired of fighting, or whether he could breathe a little easier in the new, virtuous, Dutch Schultz–free New York, Alex Pompez finally decided to give in and testify. James J.

Hines was convicted and sent off to serve five years in Sing Sing. Pompez was given police protection and a two-year suspended sentence from Dewey, who was, ultimately, a fair man. But it also meant that El Cubano, who had come to the city with nothing and created a multimillion-dollar business empire, now had nothing once more. His Cuban Stars had suspended play for two years. The city had refused to renew his lease on the Dyckman Oval and turned the site into a parking lot for public housing. Forty-nine years old, Alex Pompez would have to begin again from scratch.

47

The Powerhouse

As the 1930s progressed, the old Tammany face of the city was literally torn away, ripped down by La Guardia's demonic builder, Robert Moses, operating with $1.1 billion from the federal government and using plans he had kept in his head for twenty-five years, down to the smallest details.

Most of this was inarguably an improvement. It is difficult to adequately convey, despite all the tall new buildings, just how grimy, shabby, and even sordid New York City had become a few years into the Great Depression. Beyond the obvious excrescences, such as the open East River dumps, the shantytowns in Central Park and on the lower West Side of Manhattan, Moses also razed the likes of the monstrously oversized post office in City Hall Park. The cheesy, plaster replica of historic Federal Hall, festering in Bryant Park behind the public library, was replaced by a breathtaking, formal French garden. The dangerous, sooty, open railyards, hobo encampments, and oozing landfill along the Hudson were covered over by the original Olmsted-Vaux plans for Riverside Park but extended to three times their original size: a gorgeous, six-mile-long riverscape, complete with a parkway and a marina, tennis courts and ball fields, winding pathways and high, gracious trees.

It was "the finest single piece of large-scale planning," in the opinion of no less than Lewis Mumford, "since the original development of Central Park." For Moses, like La Guardia, was an artist of sorts, as his greatest critic, Robert Caro, would readily concede: "He saw New York and its suburbs—2,100 square miles, an area in which, when he was building, 12 million people lived—he saw it all as a canvas."

Over the years, he would paint in one element after another: bridges, tunnels, parkways, arterial highways, twenty thousand acres of new parkland. He even saw what wasn't there. Before he was finished, Robert Moses would add 25 miles of landfill to New York—25 miles, to a city of only 322 total square miles today. Thus "bringing it," in the words of Ric Burns and James Sanders, "fully into the twentieth century and making it the most efficient and best-run city in the country, if not the world."

"Robert Moses has made an urban desert bloom," cheered the *New York World-Telegram.*

There was collateral damage. The Moses of the 1930s remained largely a useful public servant, his imperial excesses and his runaway racism still checked by democratically elected officials such as President Roosevelt, who hated him and regularly tried to have him fired, and La Guardia, who needed him and cheerfully outmaneuvered him by ignoring Moses's many threats to resign.

"New York City is remarkably free of political control or influence," a federal report concluded in late 1934, the wonder almost palpable in the words. *Are we talking about the same New York?*

The question, unasked, was where all this building was leading to as Moses laid down a hundred miles of parkways within the city, the Henry Hudson and the Grand Central, the Belt and the Interborough. They were, at first, a welcome relief in a New York that had been choking to death on traffic, but before very long it was noticed that they only brought more cars. Like the sorcerer's apprentice, Moses went on building, linking them up to all the bridges and the tunnels and the suburban highways in Long Island and Westchester that Moses, with his many hats, was also building.

The ultimate realization of his vision—and the ultimate reassurance to New Yorkers of the 1930s—was his redemption of the Triborough Bridge, those forlorn totems of Tammany's failure, standing out in the East River. The completed Triborough (now the Robert F. Kennedy) was actually four bridges, and 13,500 feet of elevated viaduct, "a rendezvous of bridges," by the time Moses had it up and running in July 1936. The whole project was gargantuan. The bridges' anchorages were larger than the great pyramids, the concrete used sufficient to have paved a four-lane highway all the way to Philadelphia, the cost a then-staggering $50 million. Yet it was money that rippled on out through the Depression economy, employing five thousand men to build it, employing tens of thousands more in cement factories and steel mills, forests and lumberyards throughout twenty states and 134 cities.

It was also, as Robert Caro would note, "a traffic machine, the largest ever built." Not to mention a money machine. Under its great limbs, Moses set up his main headquarters, in an inconspicuous but luxuriously appointed office building on Randall's Island, a fiefdom from which poured forth still more plans, more money, more commands and directives—what came to be called, directly enough, the Powerhouse. Few people seemed to worry that, just over his head, all those new miles of bridge and highway were allowing drivers to go from upstate New York to Long Island, or from New Jersey to New England—without ever having to pass through the city.

This was the more problematic side of the virtuous city of the 1930s. It was—at least at times—a sort of imposed progressivism, made up mostly of hard white concrete, and impervious to the more organic growth of neighborhoods and communities. It excluded some people altogether. Even La Guardia, the heart in the new order and the polar opposite of Moses, coveted what was new and modern. He hated vehicles such as trolleys, which struck him as antiquated and European, banned organ grinders and their monkeys from the streets, forced most of the city's myriad pushcart vendors into covered brick markets. This was again mostly an improvement. The vendors would have bathrooms and shelter from the elements, and the covered markets would prove immensely popular and serviceable. Yet these were also more parts of the city's colorful street culture—some of them invaluable—that were removed to make way for the rampaging power of the car.

It all matched the spirit of the age. Jane Jacobs was still a girl, no one clamored to bid for "prewar" apartments, everything better had yet to be built—or so it was imagined. There was something indeed virtuous about it all and wonderfully optimistic as well. The reforms of the Depression would yield, in the end, a New York that was the greatest working-class *and* middle-class metropolis ever built, and it was an accomplishment that, against such great odds and with such a diverse population, has never been equaled before or since, in New York or anywhere else. It is the essence of democracy that no reform is forever, that freedom and opportunity have to be protected, reassessed, *adjusted* by each new generation.

Yet La Guardia had tied his vision irrevocably to the back fender of the automobile. What happened when the money for the perpetual building machine gave out—when Washington and Albany were no longer on the city's side? What did all those cars, those wonderful symbols of middle-class achievement, really portend?

Baseball, too, was entering its own corporatized era in the 1930s, one in which everything would be increasingly subjected to money and power. No team was better situated to take advantage of the fact than the team in the Bronx.

By the 1930s, the New York Yankees were the most successful, most profitable team in major-league baseball, and they would remain so throughout the Depression. But Jacob Ruppert, the team's shrewd, ruthless owner, was not satisfied. Over the course of the 1920s, the Yankees had netted more than $3.2 million in profits—over $1 million more than the next most profitable club in the majors. Nearly all of that money had been plowed back into the team, especially to acquire new talent. Ed Barrow, Ruppert's glowering general manager with the greasepaint eyebrows, had built up an impressive network of scouts for this purpose, led by the legendary Paul Krichell, the squat, bowlegged Bronx native who had previously served the St. Louis Browns as a catcher, coach, and minor-league manager.

Yet as good as Barrow and Krichell might be at finding talent, it remained too much of a hit-and-miss proposition. This was brought home in the first years of the Depression decade, when Ruppert signed a couple of surefire Pacific Coast League prospects in Jimmie Reese and Lyn "Broadway" Lary, the double-play combination of the champion Oakland Oaks. Between them, the two men cost $125,000 and proved to be one huge disappointment. Reese, born James Herman Solomon, was yet another failure as the great Jewish hope in New York baseball, never more than a capable backup and roommate for Babe Ruth's suitcase. Lary put in a respectable season as the Yanks' starting shortstop, driving in 107 runs in 1931, but went rapidly downhill from there, perhaps due to the temptations of the big town, as his nickname suggested.

It was not the first time, Yankee-haters would note, that the Bronx team had tried to "buy a pennant," nor would it be the last. But with the Depression settling in and beer still illegal, Ruppert felt the need to put his money to a more systematic advantage. Even in bad times, talent cost too much. Star inmates of Murderers' Row such as Earle Combs, Tony Lazzeri, and Mark Koenig had set the Yanks back some $50,000 apiece, buying their contracts from minor-league clubs. Lyn Lary's replacement, the weak-hitting shortstop Frankie "Cro" Crosetti, would cost $72,000.

A better corporate model was already in place halfway across the country, developed by a former Highlanders catcher now running the St. Louis Cardinals. What Branch Rickey had created was baseball's first real farm system, buying a controlling interest in minor-league teams all over the country and using them to develop and promote a steady flow of top young talent to his undercapitalized Cardinals.

There had been farm teams around since at least 1885, when John B. Day had used his New York Metropolitans as a feeder team for the Gothams. "Working agreements" between the big-league squads and maybe one or two minor-league franchises apiece had taken hold over the years, with the majors handing over surplus players to the minor-league franchises for seasoning while getting first crack at those ballplayers who were ready to serve.

It was only when Rickey went to a desperately poor Cardinals team in the 1920s, though, that teams embarked on building extensive minor-league *systems.* The whole idea was bitterly opposed by the minor-league owners, who feared losing much of their revenue and all their autonomy. Commissioner Landis, ever the romantic, accused Rickey and the Cards' owner, Sam Breadon, of "raping the minors" and destroying small-town baseball. At the same 1929 winter meetings, though, Ruppert declared that even the wealthy Yankees could no longer afford the prices the minors wanted for their talent. New York, he announced, was "going to be forced into owning minor league clubs, and so is every other major league owner in this room."

The Yanks started off by acquiring the Chambersburg (Pennsylvania) Maroons, in the Class D Blue Ridge League. Soon after, Ruppert purchased the International League's Newark Bears for $600,000. But more important, Ed Barrow had found just the man to run his system.

George Martin Weiss was the son of a German immigrant who owned a grocery store and meat market in New Haven, Connecticut. He briefly went to Yale but, like so many boys of his time, quit to support his family. When he was still twenty, Weiss organized a bunch of his former high school teammates into a professional team, the New Haven MaxFeds, that played in the independent Colonial League—a low-budget, outlaw "trolley league" that fed players to the equally renegade Federal League.

When the Federal League folded, George Weiss kept his franchise going, bringing in the game's top stars to play Sunday exhibitions and eventually scraping up the money to take over New Haven's Eastern League franchise and put them in a spiffy new park, named after himself, with a revolutionary electric scoreboard. The youngest owner in "organized" baseball at twenty-four, he turned the New Haven Profs into an instant hit on the field and at the box office, netted $200,000 by selling twenty-six of his players to the majors, and impressed Ed Barrow enough to eventually bring him to the Bronx.

George Weiss would always be one of the least-liked men in baseball. Authoritarian, unsociable, and "almost completely devoid of charm," he squeezed every nickel and every ballplayer who passed through the vast Yankee empire. More than any other individual, George Weiss would cement the Yankees' image as a cold, pitiless corporation.

"There is no second place," was a characteristic pronouncement. "Either you're first or you're nothing."

Yet Weiss was also the key figure in the Yankees' dynasty for almost thirty years, and as such would run up a record of success unmatched by any executive in *any* sport, save perhaps for Red Auerbach with the Boston Celtics. For most of his first decade with the club, Weiss spent much of his time on the road, looking over the Yankees' captive minor-league teams—a total of sixteen clubs by 1937, second only to the number controlled by Rickey's Cardinals. He would pore over every detail of each team's operations, until the stories of his inspection visits became legend.

"These kids were going to watch a Yankee farm team play in spring training for free!" Weiss raged at his underling Lee MacPhail, when he caught a couple of urchins scrambling over the right-field fence down in Florida. "Lee, this sort of thing must stop at once!"

Weiss would build on Barrow's network of the best scouts in the game, until he had a twenty-man staff headed by Krichell and including the likes of Bill Essick, Gene McCann, Tom Greenwade, and Johnny Nee. He was just as hard on them as he was with his junior executives, scrutinizing every line of their expense reports. When one scout drove him over the Golden Gate Bridge, Weiss noticed not the view but the twenty-five-cent toll.

"I just want you to know that you've been billing me 50 cents for each trip all these years," he told the man.

It was a mentality made for the Depression, and it paid off in both dollars and wins. The deals Weiss made could be dizzying, even byzantine. In one continuing set of transactions over the course of a year and a half, he turned a $500 expenditure into a $92,500 profit. Like many major-league executives of the era, Weiss got a cut of most transactions, and later a cut of everything he saved below the Yankees' projected budgets. It was a potentially corrupting arrangement. But with rare exceptions, Weiss saved the best of all for his own club, and it was through the players he *kept* that the team ultimately racked up its biggest profits. The great outfield that would roam the stadium by the end of the decade, Joe DiMaggio, Tommy Henrich, and Charlie "King Kong" Keller, was signed for just $25,000, $20,000, and $5,000, respectively. Much later, the versatile infielder and Rookie of the Year, Gil McDougald, would cost just $1,500. Mickey Mantle was signed for a $1,000 bonus, Yogi Berra for $500, Phil Rizzuto for a mere $75—or, according to some accounts, a twenty-cent lunch.

The acquisition of Rizzuto exemplified the Yankees' professionalism. Still just nineteen, only five six and maybe 140 pounds soaking wet, Rizzuto was the son of a streetcar worker, a native of Brooklyn who grew up in Glendale, Queens, and starred at shortstop at Richmond Hill High. When he showed up for a tryout at Ebbets Field, he was thrown all of five pitches from another nervous adolescent. The first one hit him in the back. When little Phil couldn't get the remaining pitches out of the infield, Brooklyn's manager, Casey Stengel, supposedly told him, "Look, kid, this game's not for you. You're too small. The only way you'll ever make a living is by getting a shoeshine box." It was a jibe Rizzuto never forgot or forgave. Next was a tryout at the Polo Grounds, where the Giants manager, Bill Terry, told him, "Don't even suit up, kid." Only the Yankees had the presence of mind to offer something relatively scientific: five straight days of games in which Rizzuto got to show off every part of his subtle, versatile game.

"My stats don't shout. They kind of whisper," the Scooter would say later.

The Yankees were able to hear that whisper, affording him the opportunity to show how he bunted and fielded his position, mastering all of the small, vital things in baseball that much more experienced players never did so well. At the end of the day, they had themselves a mainstay at shortstop for years to come—and one of their most beloved personalities.

This professionalism would show to even greater advantage in scoring the greatest prospect of the decade. Already a star in the top-flight Pacific Coast League at just eighteen, Joe DiMaggio tore up his knee in a cloudy off-field incident. Interest in him dived. It was 1934 and still a baseball culture where the top scouts—ivory hunters, as they were called—were men such as the Dodgers' Larry Sutton, who preferred light-haired players because he thought they remained stronger during the heat of summer, or Cleveland's Cy Slapnicka, who would never sign players he believed to be too well endowed.

The Yanks' Joe Devine and Bill Essick hired their own orthopedist to quietly examine Joe's injured knee. When he came back with a positive report, they let the Seals keep their top box-office attraction for another season, then acquired him for just $25,000.

Once the talent was rooted out, Weiss's extensive farm system polished it to a fine shine. At the top of the system was Newark, the gritty, golden-lit working-class city of Philip Roth's childhood. The Bears played in the humble, nineteen-thousand-seat Ruppert Stadium, located in the heart of the industrial, immigrant Ironbound district. There they reeled off seven International League pennants in eleven years. The talent level was simply ridiculous. Charlie Keller, for example, spent his first year out of the University of Maryland hitting .353 at Newark, with sixty-one extra-base hits. But there was no spot for him in the Yankees' outfield—so back he went, to hit .365, with sixty-four extra-base hits.

Newark's zenith came in 1937, when the Bears went 109-43, taking the league by 25½ games with a roster that boasted twenty-three players who would make the majors, including Keller, Tommy Henrich, the future Hall of Famer Joe Gordon, the future MVP Spurgeon "Spud" Chandler, Marius Russo, Atley Donald, and George McQuinn. In a preview of what was to come on the major-league level, they squared off in the "Little World Series" against the American Association champ, Columbus, the Cardinals' and Branch Rickey's top farm team, which featured Enos Slaughter, Mort Cooper, and Max Lanier. It was a battle between the best farm teams of the two most advanced franchises in baseball, and when the Bears stormed back to win four straight in Columbus after dropping the first three at home, many declared them the greatest minor-league squad in history.

It was the ultimate triumph for the Yankees' system. Until the following season, 1938, when Weiss added *another* top minor-league team—the equivalent of a team having *two* Triple-A franchises today—in the form of the Kansas City Blues. The Blues, who played in their own Ruppert Stadium, went on to take three pennants in four seasons and defeated the Bears in the Little World Series in 1938. Yankees versus Yankees, all playing for the title in their stadiums both named for the Yankees' owner! It was dominance of a sort to thrill the heart of any Yankees fan.

48

The Greatest Team. Again.

Once all those farmhands began filtering up to the big city, the Yankees would take off on a run that would never be matched by any other team, in any other sport. They simply won and won and won: a then-record four straight world championships from 1936 to 1939, followed by three more pennants and two World Series from 1941 to 1943. Then, after something so inconvenient as a world war got in their way, came the Yankees' ultimate run: fifteen pennants and ten world championships in eighteen years.

This was the age in which the Yankees turned the hullabaloo team of Ruth's 1920s champions into methodical dominance. In the American League, they were unrivaled. The National League usually fared little better. In a thirty-year run from 1923 to 1953, the Yankees met and defeated every NL team but the Braves, whom they did not get to play, winning sixteen of eighteen World Series and compiling a record of 68-26 in the Fall Classic, for a .723 winning percentage. The only World Series they lost at all in this period were to the Rickey-built Cardinals, in 1926 and 1942.

The corporate dynasty was set in stone. The uniforms settled, forever, as blue pinstripes on white at home, with the most elegant, stylized version yet of the old Tiffany interlocking "NY" on the left-hand side of the chest (over the heart!) and on the cap. A block-lettered "NEW YORK" that somehow looked even more formidable across the gray road kit. Numbers on the backs since 1929—the second such team to add them—but never anything so individualistic as a name. By the 1930s, too, they had added another flourish to the team logo: a red-white-and-blue "Uncle Sam" top hat they had borrowed from the most famous U.S. flying squadron in World War I, Eddie Rickenbacker's "Hat in the Ring" squadron. The Rickenbacker hat had been brim up, to keep in the good luck. Not so in the Bronx. When you were the New York Yankees, who needed luck?

The dynasty was never more dominant than at the end of the 1930s, when the Yankees reeled off consecutive seasons of 102, 102, 99, and 106 victories and lost a combined total of three games in four World Series triumphs. The streak culminated in a 1939 team that many would rank as the best major-league team of all time, ahead of even the 1927 Yankees.

There was never much question of how good it would be. The team took five of its first six games and didn't look back. By the end of May the Yanks were 29-7; by the end of June they were 50-14. Save for a brief pratfall before the All-Star Game, when the Yanks lost five in a row at home against Boston, they never stumbled. Much like the 1927 Yanks, they led the league in pretty much every major statistical category, including runs scored, on-base percentage, slugging average, home runs, complete games, shutouts, fewest hits and runs allowed, earned-run average, and fielding percentage. They hit over forty homers more than the next-closest American League team, committed over fifty fewer errors, and outscored all opponents by more than 400 runs (967–556)—the only time in the modern game that such a margin has ever been achieved.

At home, they were merely dominant. On the road, the 1939 Yankees ran up the third-best record, ever—*and batted .304.* The statistics wizard Nate Silver ranks them as the greatest professional sports team, anywhere, ever, by virtue of the margin by which they outplayed their opponents.

Time and again, this Yankees team simply clubbed its opposition into submission. In a June 28 doubleheader at Shibe Park, they battered the hapless Athletics by 23–2 in the opener, pounding a record eight home runs, then returned that same afternoon to hit five more homers, winning 10–0. Even the All-Star Game was pretty much an all-Yankees affair. It was played before nearly sixty-three thousand fans in Yankee Stadium and featured six Yankees starters—Red Rolfe, George Selkirk, Joe Gordon, DiMaggio, Keller, and Red Ruffing—who had half the American League's six hits in their 3–1 win, scored two of their three runs, and, thanks to DiMaggio, hit the game's only homer.

If anything, the club's talent was even better distributed than 1927's Murderers' Row. The infield was led by the gregarious Joe "Flash" Gordon, who slugged twenty-eight home runs, drove in 111 runs, and wielded what some consider the greatest glove ever seen down at second base. The Dartmouth grad Robert "Red" Rolfe had a career year at third, leading the league in runs, hits, and doubles and hitting .329. The outfield was among the very best ever assembled, a group of not three but *four* of the best fielders and most consistent hitters in the league. Tommy Henrich, "Old Reliable," a legendary clutch hitter and outstanding fielder, was reduced to being a role player behind a starting trio consisting of the great DiMaggio; King Kong Keller, who hit .334; and George "Twinkletoes" Selkirk, who belted twenty-one home runs, batted in 101 runs, and hit .306.

Behind the plate was the hard-bitten Bill Dickey, one of the greatest catchers of all time and an expert Yankee Stadium hitter, who added another twenty-four home runs and 105 ribbies along with a .302 average. Dickey handled what had already become a prototypical Yankees pitching staff, one that did not include the best starter in the league but that had far and away the most depth. (Only twice in the 1930s did the Yankees have the league leader in ERA—Lefty Gomez, on both occasions—but they led the league in *team* ERA six times, including every year from 1935 to 1939.) This was how it would go, year after year, with the Yankees machine pushed forward by generations of Marv Breuers and Johnny Broacas, Hank Borowys and Bill Bevenses and Tommy Byrnes, Johnny Kuckses and Tom Sturdivants and Art Ditmars.

The 1939 team was typical. The stars Ruffing (21-7, 2.93) and Gomez would make the Hall of Fame, but behind them were such consistent workhorses as Bump Hadley (12-6), Atley Donald (13-3, after starting the year 12-0), Monte Pearson (12-5, who would almost pitch a no-hitter in the World Series that fall), Oral Hildebrand (10-4), Steve Sundra (11-1)—seven pitchers in all who won ten or more games, plus Johnny "Grandma" Murphy, the outstanding reliever of the 1930s, who led the majors with nineteen saves in twenty-two opportunities. The team had so much pitching depth that its batting-practice pitcher, one Paul Schreiber, pitched and won a complete-game 4–1 exhibition victory over the International League's Toronto franchise.

Here was where the Yankees manager, Joe McCarthy, earned his salary. "Marse Joe" was hardly a quintessential corporate man. A mass of idiosyncrasies, he distrusted Poles, southerners, and anyone who smoked a pipe, which he considered a sign of complacency. He warned his players against drinking beer, which he felt left them weak in the legs, and urged them to stick to whiskey, which he did. Short, square-jawed, and stubborn, with penetrating eyes that could sometimes look haunted, he put in fifteen seasons as a minor-league infielder before giving up the dream of making the majors as a player. Taking over a floundering Cubs team, he drove it to a pennant in 1929, only to be fired a year later.

Both Barrow and the ubiquitous Paul Krichell took notice. They had had their eyes on McCarthy since his playing days and signed him on after getting the blessing of the Colonel, who invariably referred to him as "McCarddy." He shared their fierce desire to win, and McCarthy thrived in the Yankees' rigidly structured system.

A strict disciplinarian, he had the clubhouse manager break up the locker-room card table with an ax, convinced that poker losses caused bad feelings on a ball club. He refused to police curfews but substituted a mandatory 8:30 breakfast time on the road and insisted his ballplayers come to the park in jacket and tie, already shaved and showered and looking like professionals. He outfitted them in oversized caps, and uniforms cut half-a-size too large, hoping to make them look as big and formidable as possible. He was an expert on teaching the double play, had a prodigious memory for opposing players, rarely repeated mistakes, and refused to share his signs to his base coaches with his players, or his signs to his catcher with his pitchers.

Nearly all of his players respected him. Many adored him. "Never a day went by when you didn't learn something from McCarthy," judged no less than Joe DiMaggio.

His desire to win was such that it kept his team on its toes but threatened increasingly to derange him. An unimportant loss in Detroit one day in 1937 put him into a rage; when a reserve outfielder named Roy Johnson was heard to mutter, "What does that guy expect to do—win every game?" he was shipped out to the Siberia that was the Boston Bees. McCarthy *did* expect to win every game, internalizing Yankees perfectionism to a degree that had and would destabilize many another manager. But no other skipper won more than McCarthy's seven World Series titles or bettered his .614 lifetime winning percentage, which included not a single losing record or second-division finish over twenty-four seasons, with three different teams. Some, including Bill James, would call him the greatest manager in the history of the game. Others, such as the rival manager Jimmy Dykes, would sneer at such titles, pointing to the Yankees' abundance of riches: "What do you mean he's a great manager? All he's got to do is push a button and a better ballplayer comes off the bench. If I had a club like that, I wouldn't even go out to the ballpark. I'd just telephone in now and then."

The charge of being a "push-button manager" would plague McCarthy. It is hard to refute much of it. His four starting infielders in 1939, for instance, missed all of eight games between them. Year after year, when it came to the hitting part of the game, anyway, McCarthy's greatest chore was filling in a lineup from one of the best rosters in baseball. With the pitchers, though, he expertly exploited the Yankees' greatest strength. Like many managers of his time, McCarthy was suspicious of relief pitchers, even though he employed one of the finest. The Yankees led the AL in complete games year after year. But taking advantage of his team's immense depth, Marse Joe rarely employed a regular rotation, instead matching up starters to specific teams and situations and using as many of them as he could.

Very few teams, of course, ever had the pitching to utilize such a system. But it saved on wear and tear, leaving his best hurlers all the stronger for October. Red Ruffing led the 1939 team with only twenty-eight starts—a low total even today. When Ruffing—a hard-nosed, hard-drinking hurler who switched from the outfield to the mound after losing four toes in a mining accident—developed a sore arm down the stretch, McCarthy rested him for seventeen days, then started him in the first game of the World Series. He responded with a 2–1 win against an excellent Cincinnati Reds team. The frequently injured Pearson started the next day and did not allow a hit until the eighth inning. In the third game, Lefty Gomez strained a stomach muscle early and was replaced by Bump Hadley, who pitched the Yanks to an easy victory. For game four, Oral Hildebrand, Steve Sundra, and Johnny Murphy gave Ruffing the day off. The Yanks tied the score with two runs in the ninth, then won when DiMaggio singled in two runs in the top of the tenth. The second runner to cross the plate—burly King Kong Keller, who hated being called King Kong Keller—ran so hard into catcher Ernie Lombardi's shoulder (official version) or testicles (unofficial version) that Lombardi was left writhing in agony while DiMaggio swept all the way around the bases to score another, totally unnecessary insurance run, with a beautiful hook slide.

It was the perfectly arrogant, perfectly brutal, perfectly perfect ending to the Yankees' season, though incredibly the team could easily have been *more* dominant. DiMaggio missed six weeks after tripping and tearing a calf muscle. An eye infection and a knee injury later dropped his batting average from .412 to .381 over three weeks in September. Then there were the ones who got away. A decade earlier, Krichell had at last discovered the great Jewish box-office hope, right in the Bronx, at James Monroe High. The Yanks made Hank Greenberg a nice offer, but foolishly invited him to see a game at the stadium. Young Hank took one look at Lou Gehrig, decided it would be many years before he got to play first for the Yankees, and signed with Detroit. (Ironically, moved to left for the 1940 season, Greenberg found he preferred the freedom of playing the outfield.) The Yankees were even among the first to spot the great Ted Williams out in San Diego, but his Salvation Army mother reportedly refused to let him go play in Babylon.

An outfield of Greenberg-DiMaggio-Williams? The mind reels.

Certainly, Joe McCarthy thought that his team could have done better, even without any help. On the long trip back from Cincinnati after winning the 1939 World Series, some of his celebrating players paraded through the train, singing, dancing, and drinking. Marse Joe stuck his head out of his drawing room to chastise them: "Cut that out! What are you, a bunch of amateurs? I thought I was managing a professional club. Why, you're worse than college guys!"

Having squelched the celebration, McCarthy went back to what he had been doing: going over some of the forty-five games the team had lost during the regular season and explaining to some of his players how they might have been won.

What to do with such an organization? The other American League owners thought they had the answer. Desperate to stop the Yankees, they passed a rule at the end of the 1939 season that forbade the league champion to trade with any other AL team from the end of the World Series until it should next be eliminated from the pennant race.

Ed Barrow scoffed at the sanction, but secretly he must have been thrilled. Had the other owners even been paying attention? The Yankees had traded for all of nine ballplayers, of absolutely no consequence, during their entire four-year championship run. Almost the entire team had been brought up from the minors. (The no-trade rule ended once the Yankees missed the pennant by two games in 1940. They then won the next three pennants and two more World Series.)

Yet for New Yorkers, the more pressing question was, how to root for such a team? This bloodless, humorless corporate juggernaut. Here was the origin of the old saw: "Rooting for the Yankees is like rooting for U.S. Steel." If the Bronx Bombers were not a bunch of college guys, they also were not Ruth's merry band of marauders. In the fearsome uncertainty of the Depression, sheer domination and efficiency were not altogether unwelcome—hence the popularity of Robert Moses–style progressivism. But there needed to be more. There needed to be at least some evidence of a soul in the machine.

49

Biscuit Pants and the Dage

There was one great loss the Yankees suffered in 1939, one shocking enough to have flattened any lesser team. Lou Gehrig, still just thirty-five, was struck down by amyotrophic lateral sclerosis (ALS), known forever after as Lou Gehrig's disease.

It was Gehrig who, ultimately, made the Yankees human, along with the other player standing there with Fiorello La Guardia, in that snippet of old home movie. Reticent, wary, inscrutable to writers, teammates, and even loved ones, Lou Gehrig and Joe DiMaggio were very different individuals, but both were destined—often despite themselves—to break out beyond the game of baseball, to become legends that resonated in every corner of American culture.

They would be teammates for only a few productive years, but both their legends grew exponentially *after* their careers were over. Gehrig through his biopic, *The Pride of the Yankees,* for decades Hollywood's one successful attempt to depict the national game. DiMaggio in song and story that bordered on the mawkish—Paul Simon making him the embodiment of late-1960s angst and disillusionment: "Where have you gone, Joe DiMaggio? / A nation turns its lonely eyes to you." Or that went right over the line, with Ernest Hemingway's aged Cuban fisherman in *The Old Man and the Sea,* Santiago, urging the young Manolin to "have faith in the Yankees, my son. Think of the great DiMaggio."

Where Gehrig's heroic aura would only be confirmed in recent years by two outstanding biographers, Jonathan Eig and Ray Robinson, DiMaggio's would be annihilated by Richard Ben Cramer's *Joe DiMaggio: The Hero's Life,* which gave us Joe the relentless womanizer; Joe the grasping, mob-connected hustler; Joe the bad husband and the appalling father, abusing Marilyn Monroe. Joe, in his far-too-extended retirement, drunk out of his mind on the stairs of the Hotel George V in Paris with his dick out of his pants, still trying to talk a young beauty queen into sleeping with him. Joe living his life in ceaseless pursuit of his desires, and so rarely satisfied when he achieved them.

Both men were ready-made icons of their era. Where Babe Ruth was the avatar of the flash town from the 1920s, Gehrig and DiMaggio exemplified Depression-era New York. Both were publicly taciturn, stoic, uncomplaining. Both set records that were all about showing up every day and doing their jobs. Gehrig played in 2,130 consecutive games, a record that would stand until 1995. DiMaggio hit in his fifty-six consecutive games, a record that still stands today and is widely considered the hardest in the game to break.

Through Gehrig and DiMaggio, the ethnic became American, the American, ethnic. Casting Gary Cooper to play Gehrig in *The Pride of the Yankees* was an almost perfect fit; only Lou himself would have looked more the part of the frontier hero. Skin weathered and creased by twenty years of playing baseball in the afternoon, his face scrunched into a perpetual squint, and that sweet, sorrowful little smile, he looked like a man who had worked a lifetime on the prairie—instead of one who had grown up in the dense streets of Yorkville and Washington Heights.

DiMaggio had "eyelashes a yard long," the syndicated columnist Dorothy Kilgallen gushed, exclaiming, "Goodness, he's divine!" Yet he was more than that. With his wistful brown eyes, his thick mop of hair, his rugged features, even his slight buckteeth, he looked the part of a ladies' man, but also a man's man and a son—the triple crown necessary for full media acceptance. America was familiar with Latin lovers, another movie staple. Joe often looked like a small-town boy rather than a native of San Francisco's North Beach neighborhood, like every (Anglo-Saxon) mother's son. With his lanky, ballplayer's body, he was the "brown-eyed handsome man" John Fogerty would sing about. He was centerfield, and an act of transubstantiation to boot, the traditional American hero morphed into an immigrant's body.

For both men, their official nicknames would be suitably mythic, drawn from the nation's past and its literal mobility, the Iron Horse and the Yankee Clipper—though in the leveling earthiness of the clubhouse they were simply Biscuit Pants and the Dago. Biscuit Pants was Gehrig, of course, so named for the almost freakishly thick thighs, hips, and buttocks from which he generated so much of his tremendous power. Fourteen pounds at birth, his physique was doughy and unresponsive. A grammar school friend remembered how "his body behaved as if it were drunk," while a high school typing teacher recalled that "his thick fingers just couldn't seem to find the right keys."

Young Lou took charge of his life and his sluggish body, training relentlessly at his father's turnverein, a sort of German gymnastics club. By the age of eleven, he was strong enough to swim the deceptive currents of the Hudson, from Washington Heights to the Palisades *and back.* By the time he enrolled in the High School of Commerce on Manhattan's Upper West Side, he was coordinated enough to have mastered football, basketball, soccer, billiards, and his favorite sport, baseball.

Simply finding the time to play all these games was no mean feat for an immigrant's son. He owed it mostly to his mother, a debt he never forgot. Pop Gehrig was a metalworker with a greater propensity for the gold rail or the sickbed than the mill. Ma Gehrig, often dismissed as a large, smothering ethno-mother, was also one of the heroic immigrant women to be found all over New York at the turn of the century, keeping her family together through incessant toil. She took on all the work she could find, cooking, cleaning house, washing other people's laundry. Having lost three of her four children in infancy, she concentrated all her worry, love, and ambitions on her one surviving son.

"He's the only big egg I have in my basket," she liked to say. "He's the only one of four who lived, so I want him to have the best."

Lou dutifully labored alongside her, delivering and picking up the laundry, working at a local grocery store and butcher shops, filling in for his father in a janitorial job—later picking up as much as $10 a game playing for the Minqua, the local Tammany ball club. By the time he was twelve, he was, in Paul Gallico's description, a "shy, harassed, worried youngster, in castoff clothes." If he always had enough to eat in Ma Gehrig's kitchen, young Lou was never seen to wear an overcoat or a hat, even on the coldest winter days, probably because he did not own one.

No one would have described Joe DiMaggio as "shy, harassed, worried," at any time, ever. According to his childhood pals, he had an almost preternatural ability, right from the start, to accumulate friends, favors, money, smokes, girls, just by feigning indifference. Cramer makes the case that this was largely a cover, a defense mechanism cultivated out of fear of ever being "exposed" as ignorant, awkward, or helpless. Joe D. discovered early just how little leverage he had as an immigrant fisherman's son who was neither studious nor particularly industrious.

Socially promoted through the eighth grade, Joe dropped out almost immediately upon reaching Galileo High School. The rumor was that he never set foot in its classrooms. He hated the motion of the sea and the smell of the fish on his father's boat. (The hardness of a fisherman's life has played an outsized role in the success of the

Yankees over the years. Mariano Rivera recalled setting his sights on baseball when he first went out on *his* father's boat and could not believe how hard the work was. Maybe Hemingway was onto something after all.) It didn't matter. Pappa Giuseppe's boat was confined to the San Francisco Bay, too small to go out through the Golden Gate and fish for crab and salmon, the big catches that might bring some chance for a better life. Besides, there were two older brothers already at work on board.

The closest that Joe, the fourth of five sons, came to regular work was selling newspapers at trolley car stops. This was a serious problem. Italians—especially *southern* Italians—were barely considered "white" when the DiMaggios arrived, with all the added discrimination that implied.

"There has never been since New-York was founded so low and ignorant a class among the immigrants who poured in here as the Southern Italians who have been crowding our docks during the past year," *The New York Times* had editorialized not long before Giuseppe DiMaggio arrived in California from Sicily. In 1911, three years before Joe was born, the Dillingham Commission, an official committee investigating immigration, pointed to the Italian sociologist Alfredo Niceforo's description of "the South Italian as excitable, impulsive, highly imaginative, impracticable; as an individualist having little adaptability to highly organized society."

The idea of Joe as still the "other," still not a real American, can be seen in how long the press struggled simply to get his name right (Di Maggio, De Maggio, Demaggio, D' Maggio . . .). In their seeming obsession with having him pose making or eating or draining spaghetti.

"Italians, bad at war, are well-suited for milder competition," *Life* would write of DiMaggio himself, in what was intended as a laudatory 1939 profile. "Although he learned Italian first, Joe, now 24, speaks English without an accent, and is otherwise well adapted to most U.S. mores. Instead of olive oil or smelly bear grease he keeps his hair slick with water. He never reeks of garlic and prefers chicken chow mein to spaghetti."

As American as chicken chow mein!

How was a quiet, virtually unlettered boy with a bad sea stomach to make his way against such hurdles? *Supposedly,* he wasn't even the best ballplayer in the family; that honor lay with Tom or Mike, out working the boat (though you hear such stories a lot in tales of the great). Tennis was Joe's game, but who could make a living out of tennis in the 1930s?

Like many of his friends, Joe was slowly drawn into a life of small hustles, stripping copper from abandoned buildings to sell to the junkman, filching fruits and pies from the local vendors, rushing the doors at the Acme or the Peni-a-cade, the local bijous. Salvation came from the network of neighborhood and semipro industrial baseball leagues that crisscrossed all big cities in the 1930s. It came with astonishing ease and speed, just as everything would seem to come to DiMaggio so naturally when he turned his hand to baseball. He was still just sixteen when a bunch of schoolyard pals persuaded him to join their new neighborhood team, the Jolly Knights. From the Jolly Knights, it was on to Rossi Olive Oil, from Rossi Olive Oil to Sunset Produce, and from there to the San Francisco Seals of the Pacific Coast League at just seventeen, back in the day when many of the best western ballplayers never bothered going east and the PCL was nearly another major league.

Lefty O'Doul, an early coach and mentor of Joe's—and nearly a .400 hitter in the majors himself—claimed that his only contribution to Joe as a hitter was to "change nothing." Throughout his career, DiMaggio seemed genuinely perplexed that there was such a thing as learning to hit, once impatiently telling his favorite whipping boy, Yogi Berra, "Just walk up to the plate and *hit* the ball. There's no talent involved."

At eighteen, he switched from shortstop to playing the best centerfield anyone had ever seen, and ran up his first record batting streak in the PCL, some sixty-one consecutive games. "Give him a couple of years . . . and Di Maggio is going to be one of the greatest ball players in the country," the Seals owner, Charlie Graham, proclaimed.

A mysterious knee injury, in which he tore cartilage in four places, perhaps getting in or out of a cab, delayed his arrival on the Yankees by what could have been a critical two years. As it was, he came to town as the most hyped athlete in the city's history. No other New York athlete has ever raised such expectations before his debut, for so extended a time—not Joe Willie Namath or Patrick Ewing or Bill Bradley, not Mickey Mantle or even Babe Ruth.

DiMaggio, according to the New York press corps, was "brilliant," a "sensational outfielder," "the greatest ballplayer [ever to] graduate from [the] Pacific Coast League," "the replacement for Babe Ruth," even certain "to be Cobb, Ruth, Jackson in one," before he ever stepped on a ball field for the Yankees. The hoopla grew so loud that the press began to worry itself. DI MAGGIO COMES UP WITH TWO STRIKES ON HIM AS INNOCENT VICTIM OF LAVISH NEWSPAPER BALLYHOO, read one *Sporting News* headline.

When, after a solid year of this, the anointed one finally appeared in camp in the spring of 1936, Ed Barrow cautioned him not to get too excited. "Don't worry, Mr. Barrow," Joe, still just twenty-one, reassured him. "I never get excited."

It was more of the phlegmatic cover that would serve him well, avoiding the embarrassments he so hated. Asked for a quote by the first writer he saw in spring training, he muttered, "Don't have any." (He thought "quote" meant a soft drink.) The story of his long cross-country drive with his equally closemouthed Italian American teammates from the Bay Area, Tony Lazzeri and Frankie Crosetti, soon became just as legendary. The three ballplayers were reputed to have said nothing the entire way, save for one evening sitting around a hotel lobby, when DiMaggio cleared his throat. "Whadidya say?" asked Lazzeri. "He didn't say nothin'," replied Crosetti. "Shut up."

His debut was delayed again, for more than a month of the 1936 season, by another freak injury in spring training. But in his very first contest, a 14–5 win over the St. Louis Browns, Joe lashed two singles and a triple. The Yanks drew twenty-five thousand fans, their biggest crowd since opening day. In his fourth game, he caught a fly at the warning track in Yankee Stadium's left field and cut down what would have been the tying run for Detroit, on a throw Ed Barrow said was the best he had ever seen. His first home run, against Philadelphia, helped move the Yanks into first place. Two days later, his rolling block took out a Cleveland infielder to break up a double play—and set off a brawl. On the final day of May, he was hitting .411 and clinched the Yanks' fifth straight win by singling in the tying run against Boston in the seventh and tripling in the winner in the twelfth. Some forty-two thousand fans showed up, including Mayor La Guardia.

June brought an eighteen-game hitting streak. By July, he had finished ahead of all other American League outfielders in the All-Star balloting: HERO NO. 1, proclaimed the tabloid headline. The comparisons to Ruth proliferated. By the end of the year, he had batted .323, with twenty-nine home runs and 125 RBIs, and the Yanks were back in the World Series for the first time in four seasons. He hit .346 for the series and scored the clinching run in the final game with an almost miraculous leap *over* the catcher Harry Danning, as the Yankees steamrolled the Giants.

The truly indelible image came at the end of the second game, an 18–4 romp over the Giants, in which the Yanks set a record for runs in a single World Series game that has yet to be broken. DiMaggio got a terrific jump on a rocket hit by the Giants catcher Hank Leiber, running it down nearly at the end of the Polo Grounds' limitless centerfield before making an incredible, over-the-shoulder catch that carried him to the steps of the clubhouse there. Because it was the final out of the game, he kept on going, up the stairs, toward the locker rooms—until he remembered that President Franklin Roosevelt, on hand for all nine innings, was supposed to be making his departure by car through the centerfield fence. DiMaggio turned and stood on the little porch, the balcony at the top of the stairs that made such a natural stage. He stood at attention, ball in his glove, as the president drove past. FDR, then at the very peak of his popularity, just a month away from the most overwhelming triumph in presidential history—and somehow, once again serving as a supporting player for a Yankees great—saw Joe there in turn, and laughed and touched his hat, and gave him a big wave as he passed out of the park.

"And from the crowd there was a final, rippling cheer, as the Dago boy from Fisherman's Wharf was saluted by the President of the United States," Richard Ben Cramer would write. Joe DiMaggio—and the Italians—had arrived.

The idea of Lou Gehrig's debut, or anything else in his life, attracting such attention would have been mystifying—and no more so to anyone than to Gehrig himself. Throughout his life, Lou would demonstrate an uncanny ability to linger in the background, beginning with the fact that he played almost his entire career in the shadow of two of the most charismatic players ever, Ruth and DiMaggio.

It became almost comical. When Gehrig hit .545 in the 1928 World Series, Ruth hit .625. When Gehrig hit .529 in the 1932 Series, Ruth hit his famous "called shot" home run. Lou belted two home runs that same afternoon, both of which were largely ignored. Even when he became the first man in the modern game to hit four home runs in a single game, also in 1932, and was robbed of number five—*five!*—only by a circus catch by Al Simmons, it happened to be the same day John McGraw announced his retirement.

Back at Commerce High, Lou had starred on the baseball team, which was the best in New York, and was selected by that brand-new "photo newspaper," the *Daily News,* to defend the city's honor against Lane Tech, the best of Chicago. It was a dream trip aboard the celebrity-filled 20th Century Limited to Chicago, one that included a pep talk from former president Taft, followed by a parade through the Second City in the backs of open convertibles. Commerce won the big game, with the crowning blow a grand-slam home run that Gehrig, still just seventeen, hit in the top of the ninth, knocking the ball all the way out of Wrigley and onto the porch of a house across Sheffield Avenue. A cheering crowd of five thousand people, complete with brass band, greeted the team when they returned to Grand Central the following day, and Lou's deed was celebrated in both New York and Chicago, *The New York Times* exulting that "the real Babe Ruth never poled one more thrilling."

One might have assumed the scouts would be breaking down the Gehrig tenement door. None showed up. Perhaps it was because the *Times* couldn't even get his name right, spelling it "Gherrig." So did his own high school yearbook.

Once again, Ma Gehrig came to the rescue. She saw to it that Lou finished high school in an age when only about 5 percent of the city's children did so, then got herself a job cooking and cleaning at a Columbia University fraternity. There, amazingly, this large, stout German immigrant woman with a thick accent was able to "network" her way into befriending the graduate manager of the school's sports teams, who agreed to go watch her Lou play ball.

Gherrig got a football scholarship to Columbia, albeit one that still meant he had to work full time in the summer and part time during the school year. He pledged a fraternity, but every night Mrs. Gehrig's one egg went over to wait and clear tables and wash dishes at the rival frat where his mother hen cooked—an almost gratuitous act of self-abasement. On the gridiron, he was a tackle, an excellent punter, and a bruising halfback with surprising speed, but no one compared him to Christy Mathewson. Playing baseball in the spring, he proved to be not only an able first baseman but also a surprisingly good outfielder and an excellent college pitcher, striking out ten or more batters in five of his eleven starts and whiffing seventeen Williams hitters to set a Columbia record that still stands. But no one talked of him becoming a major-league pitcher like Babe Ruth.

Where his talent could not be ignored was at the plate. Gehrig hit with tremendous, frightening power, not only batting .444 in his one Columbia season, but also slugging a silly .937, with fifteen extra-base hits in just sixty-three at bats.

(Undoubtedly, too, Lou could have been a major leaguer as a teenager—much like the Babe, Mantle, Mel Ott, and so on. Such prodigy breeds suspicion, casting doubt on the game's overall talent level in the past. What all these "naturals" had in common, though, was that they played all the time, back in the day when baseball was still the national passion. Gehrig always played sandlot ball with local boys, even when he was with the Yankees, while DiMaggio rented himself out to other industrial league teams when Rossi Olive Oil or Sunset Produce had the afternoon off.)

The stinging, rising line drives that first caught Paul Krichell's attention would soon be replicated endlessly on major-league diamonds. Over the course of his career, Gehrig would nearly match the Babe with a .340 lifetime batting average and might well have broken Ruth's home-run record if not for his rare illness.

As it was, he spent an entire career hitting frozen ropes. For thirteen years in a row, he scored at least 115 runs and drove in at least 107. For twelve years in a row, he hit .300 or better, had at least twenty-seven home runs and sixty-six extra-base hits, and compiled an on-base-plus-slugging (OPS) total of over 1.000. He racked up more than two hundred hits in a year eight times, hit at least thirty doubles twelve times, hit at least ten triples nine times, drove in more than 150 runs seven times (including an AL-record 184 in 1931), set a mark for grand-slam home runs at twenty-three that has only been broken by juicers—all while never striking out as many as a hundred times in a season. In the World Series, Gehrig picked *up* his game, hitting .361

in seven series, with ten home runs and thirty-five RBIs, and an OPS of 1.208, driving in the winning run eight times in thirty-four games.

It didn't hurt, of course, that Gehrig spent so much of his career getting to drive in a couple of the greatest hitters in existence, the Babe and Joe D. But this worked both ways. Both of those men drew many fewer walks than they would have otherwise, saw many more fat pitches to hit with Lou Gehrig batting behind them.

The key to Lou's consistency was, as always, hard work: keeping up the rigorous physical regimen he had practiced since he was a boy. Almost to the end of his career, he boasted rock-hard abs and upper arms that looked as though they could only have come from the steroid era. Most impressive of all was his "lower body [which] appeared to belong to another species, neither man nor ape," in Eig's awed description. "Each thigh was bigger than many a man's waist, each calf the size of a Christmas ham." In a filmed workout session with the former heavyweight champ Jack Dempsey, Gehrig can be seen easily outpacing the boxer, moving effortlessly through endless sit-ups and push-ups.

He was about as tough, too, playing through painful bouts of what was diagnosed as lumbago in his lower back. Before he retired, it was determined that every one of his fingers had been broken, many of them hurting so routinely that he didn't realize they'd been fractured until X-rays were taken years later. At the end of the 1930 season—a campaign in which he hit .379, with forty-one home runs and 174 RBI—he had to be hospitalized for a week with a broken finger and bone chips in his elbow, another recurring injury. In 1934, during one of the greedy Yankees' exhibition games with their own farm team in Norfolk, he was beaned so terribly by a mouthy busher named Ray White that he had to be rushed to the hospital. White, who had also attended Columbia (and Phil Rizzuto's Richmond Hill High), had been offended by Lou's limited social skills and the fact that Gehrig had homered off him.

"I guess the streak's over now," he bragged to his teammates after the game. "I didn't throw at him, but somebody had to end that streak."

The next day, the Yanks traveled to Washington, where they had to find Lou a new cap to let him play because his head was still so swollen. They settled on one of Babe Ruth's—with the seams split in the back. That afternoon, Lou hit three triples in his first three at bats. That year he won the triple crown.

He played every day. He not only played but hustled doggedly, diving into the stands after balls, stopping throws with his bare hands, conscientiously backing up everywhere. As would be the case with Cal Ripken Jr., the man who would break his record, some of the bright boys in the press box would periodically suggest that he was hurting himself and the team by never resting.

"This Iron Man stuff is just baloney," pooh-poohed the Babe himself. "I think he's making one of the worst mistakes a ball player can make. The guy ought to learn to sit on the bench and rest. They're not going to pay off on how many games he's played in a row. When his legs go, they'll go in a hurry."

The knock drew a rare burst of anger from Gehrig: "I don't see why anyone should belittle my record or attack it. I never belittled anyone else's. I'm not stupid enough to play if my value to the club is endangered. I honestly have to say that I've never been tired on the field."

By then the two superstars had reached an impasse in their relationship that would make Derek Jeter and Alex Rodriguez look like bosom buddies. They had been close at first, as close as Gehrig ever let anyone get, with the Babe spending evenings over at the Gehrig household, charming Ma Gehrig and downing huge portions of her dense German cooking. The falling-out remains slightly mysterious, something that came about perhaps over a careless remark about Lou's mother, perhaps over a comment Ma made to the second Mrs. Babe Ruth; most likely, over a shipboard incident during the 1934 barnstorming trip to Japan when Lou's new wife, Eleanor, fell in with Claire Ruth and accompanied her back to her cabin. There, it seems, the Babe was enjoying a vast feast of champagne and caviar and, as Eleanor would explain, "I'd never been able to get my fill of caviar." Two hours later, after Gehrig had led a frantic, ship-wide search, fearing that his bride had gone overboard, she was discovered drunk (and perhaps worse) in the Babe's stateroom.

Whether there was worse remains unknown, but Lou would never forgive his old friend. There might *not* have been worse, because Gehrig, thirty-one by this time, remained oddly childlike in many ways, in almost a state of arrested development. Unlike DiMaggio, who was familiar with the inside of whorehouses from a tender age and whose standard clubhouse report on later dalliances was a nonchalant "I gave her a good pump," Lou might have been a virgin when he married. He was good-looking enough to attract women, but once they tried to talk to him, "they saw the fear in his eyes, the look of a little boy lost in a big man's frame," as Eig put it.

This was apparent in his choice of Eleanor, a fading Chicago flapper and one of the Yankees' "circuit girls." Gehrig would marry a "baseball Annie." He watched her from the edge of a party for most of a night—a party on the eve of the "called shot" game at Wrigley, the park around which so many of the significant moments in his life would revolve, then walked her home without offering so much as a handshake at the door. A week later, he sent her a wildly expensive diamond necklace. Several months of wary correspondence followed, then a dinner with a big group when the Yanks swung through Chicago the following May, and the next morning—out of the blue—a marriage proposal. He had not yet kissed his bride-to-be.

Eig attributes this sort of aching boyishness to his mother's domination, but it might have run even deeper. Guilt, perhaps, at being the only child in his family to have survived, or the financial burden he was to his parents. Childhood friends remembered that "he seemed from an early age to be carrying with him a sense of his own worthlessness," and even when he was making his sizable top salary of $39,000 a year, Lou remained parsimonious and nervous, smoking and chewing gum constantly. Sensitive and unfailingly considerate, he was one of the very few white ballplayers of the time to speak openly against the sport's color line ("There is no room in baseball for discrimination. It is our national pastime and a game for all."), but teammates and opponents alike found him aloof and distracted until they got to know him better.

Others wondered if he was simply dumb. *Life* magazine called him "one of the slowest-witted athletes in history." He often seemed strangely befuddled, as when he blew a lucrative radio commercial for a cereal named Huskies by calling it Wheaties on the air. He possessed a mind agile enough to excel at philosophy and history at Columbia's engineering school, and enough sensitivity to weep at Wagner's *Tristan und Isolde*. Yet he often seemed to be killing time away from a ball field, riding the roller coaster at Rye Playland for hours by himself on rare off days. Returning from the stadium to his parents' home, he sometimes rounded up the neighborhood boys and played ball in the street with them until it was too dark to continue.

He appeared to open up and mature after his marriage, and once the Babe retired, his amazing playing streak began to gain recognition. Eleanor was an able manager and promoter (and the one woman he had met with the brass to stand up to his mother). He was named captain of the Yankees, feted at banquets, signed to endorsement deals. He even went out to Hollywood to take a screen test and play a small role in a Western one offseason, which delighted him. His popularity should not have been a surprise. Lou Gehrig was the model ballplayer for the Depression, the shy, modest man who did his job and soldiered on, through any and all adversity. He had moved at least a little into the limelight, and he seemed to like it. Going into the 1938 season, captain of a seemingly indomitable team, beloved around America, he had everything going for him.

So, it seemed, did Joe DiMaggio. His second year with the Yankees was even better than his first. He batted .346 in 1937, led the AL in runs and total bases, finished second in hits and RBIs, continued to play the best centerfield anyone would witness before the coming of Willie Mays, and deserved the MVP reward he finished four votes short of winning. He even challenged Ruth's home-run record for much of the season before the old Yankee Stadium's daunting distances to left center forced him to "settle" for forty-six, making him the only righty ever to win a home-run title in the park, a feat he would repeat.

The Yankees cruised to another pennant and World Series triumph. Their centerfielder had made a start to his career the way no one ever had in baseball, and the next contract from Ruppert and Barrow offered to raise his salary from $17,000 all the way to $25,000. Joe had just bought a restaurant with his brothers, a house for his parents. He held out for $40,000. For once his timing was off. Nineteen thirty-seven marked the beginning of "the Roosevelt Recession," the double-dip slump in the Depression occasioned by FDR's attempt to rebalance the federal budget prematurely. Unemployment shot up again. Salaries plunged. At a time when the average wage was $1,138 and the government's Works Progress Administration paid all of $33 a month, such a demand by a ballplayer not named Babe Ruth seemed astronomical, even preposterous.

Barrow and Ruppert refused to budge and deliberately humiliated their young star in the press. After two years of superb play, after battling through serious injuries (one of them caused by the team itself), after two years of the only championships and the biggest crowds the Yankees had managed since Ruth had departed, all Joe was asking for was *half* of the Bambino's peak salary. But between the reserve clause and the Yankees' deep roster he had no leverage, and Ruppert, the cold heart of the sport's cold, corporate giant, exploited that advantage to the hilt.

"DiMaggio is an ungrateful young man, and is very unfair to his teammates, to say the least," he told the press. "I've offered him $25,000, and he won't get a button over that amount. Why, how many men his age earn that much? As far as I'm concerned that's all he's worth to the ballclub and if he doesn't sign, we'll win the pennant without him."

Joe might have pointed out that even fewer young men get to inherit their father's mansion and brewery. But the same columnists and reporters who had written so worshipfully of him now told readers of his "greed." Even when Joe finally cried uncle, the Colonel was far from magnanimous, making sure the press knew he had not handed over that extra "button," docking DiMaggio his $150 a day in salary until he "got into shape," and charging him train and hotel fare and meal money until he was restored to the lineup.

"I hope the young man has learned his lesson," he told the papers. But just to make sure, the lesson went on and on. The fans, whipped up by the Yankees' management and the papers, jeered their idol mercilessly when he made it back to the field.

"I hear the boos," a resentful DiMaggio admitted. "I read in the papers that the cheers offset them, but you can't prove that by me. All I hear is boos. . . . And the mail! You would have thought I kidnapped the Lindbergh baby, the way some of those letters read."

Booed when he dared to ask for more money after one of his greatest seasons, he would be booed again the year *after* his record hitting streak, when he briefly slumped while in the middle of a divorce—booed yet *again* when he seemed to lose a step after returning from the army ulcerous and underweight, the pain from a bone spur knifing through his heel. The moment it looked as if he might be through, the team he had been with for his whole career would try to trade him—to Washington, for Mickey Vernon (*Mickey Vernon!*); to the Red Sox (*the Red Sox!*) for his archrival, Ted Williams.

He would never complain again, at least not in public. There would be no raise again in 1939, another great season, a fourth straight world championship notwithstanding. The Colonel had died of phlebitis, aged seventy-one, calling on his deathbed for his old bad boy, Babe Ruth—much as another imperious Yankees owner, George Steinbrenner, would be assuaged near the end only by the presence of *his* brilliant, controversial acquisition Reggie Jackson. (The Bambino reported that it was the only time Ruppert ever called him "Babe," instead of his usual, peremptory "Ruth.") Paying *anyone* more money under the circumstances would have been unseemly, explained Ed Barrow, who had just inherited three hundred shares and effective control of the team with Ruppert's death.

DiMaggio didn't squawk. That September 1939, Joe McCarthy, insisted on keeping him in the lineup—and costing him his best chance to reach the magic .400 mark—even though he could barely see the ball due to an eye infection.

"People might've said you were a cheese champion," Marse Joe explained.

Joe said nothing, even though it was neither the first nor the last time the Yankees played fast and loose with his health. His rookie debut had been delayed still further because he'd bruised a foot, and the reigning quack in the Yankees' clubhouse inflicted first-degree burns on it with a diathermy machine. (The team blamed DiMaggio, for having an excess of blood sugar in his foot.) There was the bizarre case of tonsillitis (or so it was diagnosed) that inflamed his nerves all the way down to his throwing arm and cost him the first month of the 1937 season; the torn calf muscles that cost him the first month of the 1939 season. There would be more torn cartilage that made his 1946 season so miserable, the bone spurs in his ankle that would cost him almost half of 1949 and plague him through the last three years of his career. The team's traveling secretary remembered how "grotesque" Joe's injured heel was after visiting the doctor the club had recommended: "It was stitched up like a bad shoemaker had fixed it." Later, live maggots were sewn up in the same heel to eat away the dead flesh, as if he were living in the Middle Ages, instead of the city with the most advanced medical care in the world.

More than once, and from an early age, Joe was laid up with sudden, devastating injuries that threatened his entire livelihood as a ballplayer—was forced to lie about for days and weeks and months, wondering if it were all over and what that might mean. He knew how quickly it could all go away, how quickly everyone could turn on him. One could divine that by his stomach, no matter how private he tried to be. By the ulcers, and the steady stream of cigarettes, and the "half-a-cuppa-coffee" he kept demanding from Pete Sheehy, the Yanks' ageless clubhouse guy, for hours before each game.

The existence that Joe DiMaggio—and Lou Gehrig—often *seemed* to be living in the 1930s was that of a boys' adventure story, with Fiorello La Guardia and Franklin Roosevelt and an endless host of other celebrity admirers constantly popping up in the background. Yet the reality was that both ballplayers, no matter how great their talent, were engaged in their own Darwinian struggle just like everyone else in Depression New York.

Joe DiMaggio had come to understand, very quickly, how much other men were making off his talents. If he, too, could seem cold and grasping, if he was perhaps too afraid that some part of him might be given up for nothing, if the great DiMaggio could be all too human after all, well, he had been taught by both the Yankees' owners and their fickle fans. To be caught up too much by his personal failings is to join the ranks of the permanently aggrieved, always disappointed that an artist's grace does not match his talent. What Joe DiMaggio wanted was things on his terms, whenever he could get them. This was not so unreasonable a demand from so great an artist.

"He is the greatest player in baseball. Not alone as a hitter. His fielding has been marvelous, his throwing grand," wrote the men who watched him play every day and inevitably fell in love. "Every time you see Joe DiMaggio take that effortless swing of his or race back against the boards to rob some luckless batter of a triple, you can't help getting a sneaking feeling that here, perhaps, is the greatest all-around ballplayer there has ever been."

Was he *that* good?

Stronger statistical arguments, over the course of a whole career, at least, would be made for Mantle, Mays, Junior Griffey, Barry Bonds.

In his own time, Ted Williams was a better hitter, Musial lasted longer, and then there were all those barred greats from the Negro Leagues—Martín Dihigo and Oscar Charleston, for starters. And there was the incontrovertible fact of Babe Ruth. Joe DiMaggio never pitched a game, in any pro league.

Yet he played ball for thirteen major-league seasons, and in that time his teams took ten pennants, came within a combined five games of taking two more, won nine World Series, and ran up a postseason record of 37-13. He retired as the leading active player in home runs and with a lifetime OPS of .977—although undoubtedly his most remarkable record was the fact that his ratio of home runs to strikeouts was nearly one to one (361-367). In other words, a fan was just as likely to see him hit a home run as to whiff, and two and a half times more likely to see him hammer an extra-base hit than strike out.

Power hitters simply don't hit with that sort of bat control. Not Ruth, who fanned nearly twice as often as he homered. Not even Williams, who hit 521 homers and struck out 709 times. Who knows what stats DiMaggio might have run up with a more conducive ballpark, or if he had gone up to the majors when he was first ready. Or without all the time lost to injuries, or the three years sacrificed to the army during World War II.

Beyond his hitting, his contemporaries would claim that Joe could have stolen bases by the bushel, had he not played in the era when that skill was least valued, and the writers would claim, "DiMaggio never makes a mistake on the bases." Out in centerfield, the ground he could cover was amazing, at least before the Yankees and the army finished butchering his legs. In 1938, fresh off the boos from all the Yankee Stadium faithful, he outran a Hank Greenberg fly ball all the way to the edge of the endless stadium, out to the 461-foot mark in deepest center—out past the monuments there, to make an over-the-shoulder catch. It was a play that astonished even Joe so much that he ran in with the ball instead of throwing it back to the infield, forgetting in his glory how many outs there were.

"He did everything so easily," marveled Joe McCarthy. "You never saw him make a great catch. You never saw him fall down or go diving for a ball. He didn't have to. . . . The idea is to catch the ball. The idea isn't to make exciting catches."

People found a lot of DiMaggio's catches exciting, but the point is well taken. It was not just his statistics or his raw ability that made even cynical sportswriters swoon over Joe DiMaggio. It was always his ineffable style, what Richard Ben Cramer aptly called his "beauty." Joe DiMaggio "looked like a ballplayer," in the common parlance, which is to say that he looked like what we felt a ballplayer *should* look like: tall and loose framed, angular and wiry and sharp-featured. A look, it should be noted again, that like Lou Gehrig's face coincided very much with the ideal of the American frontiersman, the cowboy and the rancher, the yeoman farmer and the long rider.

It was this grace that always won them over, the fans and the writers (at least until he next faltered for a moment or two). They dubbed him Joltin' Joe, a nickname that perfectly embodied his physical style. By 1939, the writer Arch McDonald was calling him "the Yankee Clipper" after Pan American's transatlantic airliner, already a wistful tribute to world togetherness, introduced on the brink of the war. To Americans of the time, it symbolized power, class, *style,* much as the old "Big Six" fire engine meant indomitable power to the fans of Christy Mathewson's day. Yet there was as well grace, desire.

"I always think, there might be someone out there in the stands who's never seen me play," Joe would tell the sportswriter and confidant Jimmy Cannon about why he played hard every day—finally producing that quote the writers wanted, one that would define his legacy.

"DiMaggio plays ball with a grim intensity," a West Coast reporter had noted even at the beginning, seeing through the pretense of nonchalance. It was an intensity he brought back to the clubhouse, something that grew harder and sharper the older he got.

Throughout his tenure, DiMaggio's Yankees were a club full of tough, veteran players, quick to jump on any young player they believed wasn't putting out. But it was DiMaggio they feared and respected most of all, DiMaggio who could shred them with a look or a word. After the war, he would famously whip a young Berra into physical and mental shape, giving him a tongue-lashing when his failure to run out a pop-up cost the team a game; cursing him to his face when Yogi—but not Joe—sat out the nightcap of a grueling, midsummer doubleheader in the Washington heat: "What's a matter, you *tired*? What kinda fuckin' bullshit is this—*you can't play two games?*"

Berra would become the most durable catcher in major-league history, averaging 140 games behind the plate for the next eight years. DiMaggio would keep playing as hard as his own body would let him, covering his legs with more and more tape before each game as the years went by, insisting he felt fine. But whether on the field or just sitting in the dugout, he would earn the ultimate encomium from his teammates, the old ethnic insult turned tribute. Their undisputed leader, their king, the man they looked to always when things got tough was the big guy, the best player they'd ever seen. Or simply "the Dago."

50

"And Always We Played the Game"

The spring of 1938 started off badly for Lou Gehrig, too—though not, of course, because of anything so outlandish as a holdout for more money. Instead, he felt unaccountably sluggish and awkward, with constant pains in his hands, arms, and shoulders. He looked strangely uncoordinated, both in the field and at the plate, as if his body were devolving back to that of the ungainly boy he had been, before he had whipped himself into shape with so many years of hard work. It was a tribute to that work, and to his smarts as a ballplayer, that he was able to keep playing at all, compiling what would have been a very good season for almost anyone but himself.

Gehrig was thirty-five by now, and most observers assumed he was simply another ballplayer who had grown old all at once. But it was more than that. Suddenly his uniform seemed to sag on him, with his weight dropping and his muscle mass falling away, his legs slowing badly. In the World Series that year, another sweep of the Cubs, he managed only four weak singles and after it was all over sat in the back of the locker room, quietly smoking a cigarette and watching his teammates sing their traditional victory songs of "Roll Out the

Barrel" and "The Sidewalks of New York." Prying writers were told he would be fine again next year.

Instead, that offseason Lou tripped so often, dropped so many routine objects, that Eleanor feared he had a brain tumor. A visit to the doctor produced only a diagnosis of "gall bladder trouble" and a prescription for more roughage in his diet. By spring training in 1939, he was in agony, his coordination visibly deteriorating. There were brief flashes of the old Gehrig—an exhibition against minor leaguers where he drove in six runs, another when he made a great grab of a line drive, a contest against the Dodgers when he hit two home runs off Fat Freddie Fitzsimmons. But when one of his teammates asked how he felt, he muttered, "Like hell," and others could see that something was wrong.

"He was tired," remembered one of his replacements-to-be at first base, Johnny Sturm. "It was like a match burning out."

Once the season started, the writers cheerfully anticipated his demise. "Gehrig's ambition to play in 2,500 consecutive games," jeered Jack Miley of the *Post,* "is slimmer than a bathing beauty's ankles." Jimmy Powers of the *Daily News* joked that Lou seemed "pretty cheerful for a corpse."

What everybody else saw was the dying animal, and it shook them. The fans booed, then went silent with foreboding. Now, when Lou made contact, the ball barely rolled to an infielder. He kept falling down at first, and he barely seemed able to run at all.

The worst came in a game against the Athletics at the stadium on April 25. Leading off the bottom of the eighth, he lofted a fly into left that had all the makings of a double. Instead, the throw to second beat him by ten yards. When it did, Gehrig neither tried to scramble back to first nor charged ahead into second. Instead, he simply dropped his head and trotted back into the Yankees' dugout. The crowd went silent, while A's second baseman Dario Lodigiani was too stunned to follow him and put the tag on. Back in his own dugout, Lodigiani asked his manager, Connie Mack, who had been in the majors as a player or manager for nearly half a century, if he should have tagged him. A shaken Mack said he didn't know, that he had never seen anything like it.

Five days later, Lou made a routine flip to Fireman Johnny Murphy to retire the side in the ninth, on a play where he could not run two feet to record the out. His teammates congratulated him as if he had personally won the World Series.

"Heavens, has it reached that stage?" he asked himself.

It was time to go. On May 2, in Detroit, he asked Joe McCarthy to take him out of the lineup. Ironically, the retired Wally Pipp was on hand that day and told the press, "Lou looks ill to me." A choked-up McCarthy called it "a black day for me, and the Yankees." He sent Gehrig up to the plate with the lineup card, where he received a huge ovation from the Detroit crowd. He tipped his cap, went back into the dugout, and tried to hide how hard he was crying by taking a long, long drink at the water fountain. Typically, though, a photograph caught him giving his replacement, Ellsworth Tenney "Babe" Dahlgren, a consoling hug in the dugout.

He would never play in a major-league game again, although he did start one more exhibition contest, on June 12, against the Yanks' Kansas City Blues farm team. He grounded out softly to second, missed two balls at first, then caught a line drive that knocked him over. That was it. He pulled himself from the game after three innings and made his way to the Mayo Clinic in Rochester, Minnesota, where he would at last find out what was wrong with him. What he had, of course, was ALS, a degenerative brain disorder.

Or did he?

More recent research posits that Gehrig might actually have been suffering from chronic traumatic encephalopathy (CTE), a very similar, degenerative condition caused by repeated concussions and other head injuries, which might account for the seemingly disproportionate occurrence of "ALS" among athletes. If so, this would have been particularly cruel. It would have meant that Lou's very persistence, his relentless will to play and play through anything and everything, might have hastened his demise, his disease a consequence of all the head-on collisions he had as a college football player and the beanings he had taken from the likes of Ray White in a sport that—twenty years after Ray Chapman's death—*still* had not seen fit to adopt batting helmets.

It is impossible to ever truly know just what set of deadly initials Gehrig had—ALS? CTE?—because his body was cremated. On at least four documented occasions he was knocked cold on a baseball field, but then his chronic "lumbago," according to other neurologists, might have indicated the first symptoms of ALS after all. There was confusion enough about what Gehrig had at the time, thanks to a poorly worded press release from the Mayo Clinic that described ALS as "a form of chronic poliomyelitis (infantile paralysis)." Few fans or sportswriters had ever heard of ALS, and few bothered to inform themselves about it. Everyone knew what polio was, though: a fearsome, highly contagious disease that terrorized parents each summer in those pre-vaccine days. Proceeding on this notion, Jimmy Powers—the same press-box wit who had called Gehrig a corpse—blamed the Yankees' fall from first in 1940 on a massive polio epidemic caused by the Iron Horse.

The charge so outraged Gehrig that he sued, forcing a settlement and an apology out of Powers and the *Daily News.* But the confusion did not end with the scribes. ALS (or CTE) is *not* polio and *not* communicable. What it *does* do is kill the motor neurons of the body, destroy coordination, cause muscles to atrophy and decay. Victims lose control of their hands and their legs, become unable to speak, eat, swallow, or breathe. For some reason, though, Lou *himself* did not seem to understand this. The doctors at the Mayo might have been less than forthright with him, which was often the case at the time; patients with fatal diagnoses were often not told just what they had. They might have wanted to keep his spirits up, or been genuinely unsure about how long the disease would take to work its course. Or perhaps Gehrig himself was stunned into denial—or was trying to soft-soap things for his wife and mother. He accepted the news that his playing career was over, but told Eleanor, "There is a 50-50 chance of keeping me as I am. I may need a cane in 10 or 15 years."

It was a notion that he stuck to—or at least seemed to stick to—almost until the end, even as his body fell apart. Relieved to at least know what was ailing him, Lou returned to the Yankees, determined to do something to justify his salary, even if it was only rooting from the bench. Cheered madly by fans whenever he ventured onto the field or even when he so much as passed through a train station, he insisted, "I'm not going to make that play for sympathy," and literally retreated to the shadows again, hanging back in the dugout.

It was too late for that. Death, in its approach, had made him luminous. The Yankees decided to throw him the biggest display of sympathy in the history of baseball, a well-intentioned public celebration that was by turns poignant and painfully thoughtless. Scheduled for a July 4 doubleheader against the Senators, it was designated Lou Gehrig Appreciation Day, but was also the first Old-Timers' Day in major-league baseball. Ed Barrow had Yankee Stadium decked out in red-white-and-blue World Series bunting and brought in every member he could find of the great 1927 team, plus Mayor La Guardia, Postmaster General James Farley, and—rather oddly—Wally Pipp.

The choice of teams was a good one at least, underscoring as it did the greatness of Gehrig, the only ballplayer to link two of the very greatest teams in baseball history. Lou wanted desperately to get out of it, unsure if he could bring himself to say anything without tearing up. Others wondered if he could stand up. He seemed so frail and awkward now that Barrow, making a rare venture onto the field, stood with an arm around Gehrig's shoulder—to make sure that he would stay up throughout the long ceremony.

Most of it was the standard ritual for a ballplayer's "day." Lou received a small mountain of useful, homey presents from fans, teammates, writers, and other teams—silver candlesticks and a fruit bowl, a rod and reel, a serving set, a plaque. La Guardia called him "the best to be found in sportsmanship and citizenship," Farley rather awfully claimed he would "live long in baseball," and Babe Ruth chattered away happily about his old friend for a few minutes, as if the years-long feud between them had never happened.

Yet this was not any day, and it would not proceed normally. A heavy, engraved trophy topped by a silver eagle was presented to Gehrig by McCarthy on behalf of his teammates—the trophy so heavy that Lou had to put it down on the stadium grass almost immediately. Inscribed on its side was a John Kieran poem that began,

We've been to the wars together;
And we took our foes as they came,
And always you were the leader,
And always you played the game.

It ended, "Your pals of the Yankee team." McCarthy broke down in sobs, before relating a conversation in which Lou had told him he was "quitting as a ballplayer because you felt yourself a hindrance to the team. My God, man, you were never that."

Through most of the ceremony, Gehrig himself stood twisting his cap in his hands, head down, feet pawing at the turf, periodically wiping at his face with a handkerchief. When the other speakers were finished and the sixty-two thousand fans in the big house started to chant, "We want Lou! We want Lou!" he turned away, and the master of ceremonies, Sid Mercer, announced that Gehrig was too moved to speak. The crowd went on chanting. Lou's parents were openly sobbing as well now in the stands, and Eleanor was trembling. McCarthy whispered something in his ear, and Gehrig moved obediently to the microphone, where he delivered the short speech that became the most famous piece of oration in baseball history.

"For the past two weeks, you've been reading about a bad break," he began. "Today I consider myself the luckiest man on the face of the earth."

Gehrig's head was still down, his voice breaking, the words rolling about the still ballpark and echoing off the fences. He paid tribute to everyone around him, to his manager and his teammates, and his old manager and his old teammates, to the fans, and the writers, and the groundskeepers, and Ruppert and Barrow, and the vendors and even the New York Giants, who had sent a gift. He worked a laugh line into a tribute to his wife and his parents and to his mother-in-law. (He had even planned a line making fun of his infamous Huskies/Wheaties flub, but forgot it—or thought better of it—in the rush of emotions.)

He closed with the perfect statement for the Depression, at the end of the hard decade: "I might have had a bad break, but I have an awful lot to live for." A band started to play. The fans went wild and the Babe pumped his hand, then wrapped him up in a bear hug, his big moon face melting while Gehrig's small smile never wavered. (Only Bill Dickey, Gehrig's roomie and best friend on the team, noticed that Gehrig did not put his arm around the Babe: "Lou just never forgave him.")

Then it was over, Gehrig stepping down into the Yankees' dugout again. It was a moment perfectly captured by Sam Wood, director of *The Pride of the Yankees,* who put a stunning coda on what was otherwise a standard, overlong Hollywood weeper. Gehrig/Cooper makes his final speech, then steps down through the dugout and disappears. He is gone, the camera lingering silently on the empty dugout for a long, awful beat, bringing home the finality of that absence. Released in 1942, the movie seemed to speak to what all of America was going through, a war right on the heels of the Depression, one that would bring so many of its own lingering absences.

Real life rarely offers such perfect conclusions. Gehrig, ever dutiful, stuck around like a good team player to watch the Yanks beat the Senators in the second game. He kept traveling with the club for the rest of the season, going to every game save for further visits to the Mayo Clinic. Much as he was determined to support his teammates, his presence must have weighed on them. (Not so coincidentally, the Yankees' one real slip that year—the five-game series loss at home to the Red Sox—followed immediately on the "luckiest man" game.)

Bob Feller, coming upon a half-naked Gehrig in the locker room, found him "shockingly thin." Joe DiMaggio remembered that his deterioration advanced so quickly that "at the beginning of [a long road] trip, Gehrig shuffled the cards with difficulty, but before the trip was over someone had to take over his deal for him." Members of the Cincinnati Reds remembered him driving up to the stadium for the World Series, getting out of his car, and immediately falling down.

More accolades followed. He was named captain of the AL all-star team and became the only player who would ever be voted into the Hall of Fame the same year he retired, in a special election. He was voted a full share of the team's winning World Series money, and joined his teammates in a final rendition of "The Sidewalks of New York," but it was clear that he needed to do something else now. La Guardia came through with a job as parole board commissioner—one that Lou seemed excited to accept and worked at diligently.

To the end, as his muscles slowly rotted away and he lost the abilities to drive, then to walk, then to write, Lou hung on to his original idea that he had a "fifty-fifty" chance of beating the disease. He tried injections and massive doses of vitamins, and any other experimental cure he heard of, and talked to other ALS victims who seemed to be doing better. His letters to his doctors are almost heartbreaking.

"PLEASE reveal to me the honest opinions. . . . What is your conclusion? And honestly, please . . . an honest opinion coming from you people is of vital importance to me," he begged them, as one hope after another fell away. Above all, he wanted them to understand that he was not giving up: "Please don't judge me a cry baby, or believe me to be losing my guts . . . as you know, I am not a cry baby. . . . I am not dumb, or unreasonable enough to ask the impossible. . . . Please don't think that I am overly depressed, crying, or quitting, for I am not."

Always he played the game. His teammates were convinced he knew the truth, visiting him in the small, first-floor bedroom of the Riverdale house where he was confined by the end. He could no longer get out of bed, and his weight had dropped to 125 pounds, but his mind remained sharp. Maintaining "confidence" and morale was a staple of 1930s medicine, and Gehrig could not let himself be seen as giving up. Or perhaps the brave front was for his wife. Movies of the time were full of noble sacrifices, dying spouses valiantly hiding the truth from their loved ones; Jimmy Cagney dying yellow at end, feigning a fear he does not feel so the Dead End Kids won't follow his path to a life of crime. Lou Gehrig went down, on June 2, 1941, still mouthing the words "fifty-fifty" to his wife when he could no longer speak. Was it irony or a grand gesture? The movies, to which he now belonged, would have let it be both.

PART FIVE

SINGING IN THE DARK

The City in Time of War

1939–1945

And these few precious days I'd spend with you.
These precious days I'd spend with you.

—"September Song" from *Knickerbocker Holiday,*
Kurt Weill and Maxwell Anderson

51

The Waiting Game

When *The Pride of the Yankees,* starring Gary Cooper and Teresa Wright, was released in the summer of 1942, the gigantic poster for it in Times Square did not go up in lights. Instead, it lit itself, composed as it was of thousands of one-inch-square glass tiles, designed to catch and reflect what ambient light remained in what had once been the Great White Way.

There was little enough, in this place where electric light had first been displayed to such dazzling effect not forty years before. The Wrigley's gum sign with its famous aquarium of wriggling angelfish was gone now, sold for scrap metal. So were the Planter's peanuts, pouring perpetually out of their electric bag; the red roses blossoming under Four Roses whiskey; the effervescent bubbles of the Bromo-Seltzer sign in their nine-foot glass. The marquees of all the theaters and the movie palaces along the Great White Way were dark, as were the clocks on the Paramount and Metropolitan Life buildings, the red neon signs that had just started to decorate countless bars, restaurants, and stores.

Even the lit ball that dropped every New Year's Eve from the old Times building was stored away, replaced by a set of chimes. At the stroke of midnight on Sunday, May 17, 1942, the famous news zipper around the Times Tower ran a polite adieu: THE NEW YORK TIMES BIDS YOU GOODNIGHT. Then its 14,800 bulbs went dark for the first time since their installation in 1928.

The lights were going out all over New York. Dark now were the Chrysler Building, and the Empire State, and all the other skyscrapers. The cleaning staffs had to work by reduced light inside, with blackout shades drawn. Trains entering New York had to pull their shades, too, and once they reached Penn Station, the skylight of its great Concourse had been painted over in black, along with the globes of light that had illuminated its roof. Riders had to inch their way down the darkened subway entrances now; on the cars themselves—and on the city's remaining trolleys—the lightbulbs had been dipped in more black paint, save for a narrow ring around their necks. Out at sea, the Fire Island Lightship was turned off, as was the Scotland Lightship by the Verrazzano Narrows and the entrance to New York Harbor. All the bright lights of Coney Island's remaining playgrounds were shut down, and the torch of the Statue of Liberty—liberty's very beacon—was covered.

Unlike many wartime measures, such as the largely symbolic metal and rubber drives, there was good reason for the blackout. Since the U.S. entry into World War II, the bright lights of towns and cities up and down the Eastern Seaboard and the Gulf Coast had helped turn coastal waters into a shooting range. By March 1942, fifty-four Allied freighters and oil tankers had been sunk between Maine and Florida by the German U-boats lurking offshore. Much of this slaughter took place within sight of land, with debris and bodies washing up on the beaches; one such encounter occurred so close to a stretch of the Jersey shore that a torpedo even careened up onto the sand and exploded—the only Axis assault known to have hit American soil along the Atlantic.

New York made the best backdrop of all, the city's glow visible thirty miles out to sea and two hundred miles away at bomber height. Since Pearl Harbor, its residents, like most Americans, had largely ignored the blackout regulations, even though their mayor was also codirector of civil defense for the entire country. By April 1942, La Guardia had had enough, and he brought in the army to help enforce a twenty-minute, citywide blackout.

On April 30, thousands of New Yorkers poured into Times Square to witness a truly modern anomaly: darkness at night. The results were not encouraging. With a full moon out, a persistent "sky glow" still left much of the city highly visible. A furious La Guardia led a further crusade to cover every inch of the town with still more blackout paint, "blackKraft" blackout shades, and other camouflage. But even at the city's most diligent, it made little difference. Night photographs of Manhattan with just the minimal amount of illumination necessary to allow people and vehicles to move safely through the streets still captured golden rivers of light, up and down the island.

New York in the modern world was just too big to hide under a bushel.

It wasn't that there was no threat.

"Hitler . . . imagined New York 'going down in a sea of flames,'" Manfred Griehl would claim in *Luftwaffe over America.* "He visualized the skyscrapers as gigantic 'towers of flame' and as 'blazing bundles of firewood' . . . [that would leave] Manhattan a 'bursting city.'"

This was to be effected by a long-range, four-engine transport flying a light bomber across the Atlantic under its fuselage. As they approached New York, the bomber would drop off and deliver its bombs, then ditch at sea, where the pilot would be picked up by a Nazi sub. It was a plan fantastic in every respect. But German schemes developed near the end of the war envisioned much more viable implements of mass destruction, such as a submarine that could surface and fire off rockets. A little more work on this idea than, say, the "buzz bombs" that devastated London and thousands might have died in New York, instead.

As it happened, a U-boat raiding the East Coast in January 1942 was able—much to its commander's surprise—to navigate its way right past Coney Island and to the brink of Lower New York Bay, close enough to see Manhattan laid out before him.

"I cannot describe the feeling with words, but it was unbelievably beautiful and great," the twenty-eight-year-old commander, Reinhard Hardegen, recalled. "I would have given away a kingdom for this moment if I had one." Hardegen had visited New York once as a child, and now, at his periscope, he fantasized about landing and walking about Times Square: "[I] wondered what form the life of the city was taking at that hour. . . . Were the Broadway shows just letting out? Were the jazz clubs just getting started? Were the newsboys hawking the last editions—or the first?"

New York was fated not to be one of the war's heroic citadels, a London or a Leningrad, but to remain the epitome of a culture that still tempted the whole weary world. In one of the more slapstick incidents of the war, another German U-boat landed four saboteurs, complete with explosives and $90,000 each in cash, on the sands near Montauk. They managed to dodge past the beach defenses and make their way into the city, where they behaved pretty much like any other rubes out on the town. The Nazi saboteurs occupied themselves visiting Rockefeller Center and Times Square, ate at an Automat and a deli, bought spiffy new duds at Macy's and elsewhere—one of them picked up a sharkskin suit!—spent an afternoon at the newsreel theater in Grand Central, engaged in an all-night pinochle game, made plans to go out to Coney Island or Palisades Park, and even visited Grant's Tomb.

Two of the saboteurs, who had spent years living in the United States before the war, confessed to each other that they had planned to betray their mission all along, overwhelmed as they were with nostalgia for their time in America. They turned the rest in, along with four saboteurs who had landed in Florida—two of them arrested in a bar outside Grand Central.

The New Germany, it seemed, was no match for Old Manhattan. As the saboteurs' experience implies, the war was—at least on the surface—a helluva good time for many New Yorkers, just as it was for so many other Americans on the home front. Of course, there was more to it than that. By 1944, nearly one million New Yorkers were serving in their country's armed forces; sixteen thousand of them would die. More than most other Americans, they were forced to worry about relatives and loved ones trapped over in Europe, especially Jews caught up in Hitler's programs of extermination. Like all other Americans, New Yorkers in the war years worked harder and longer than ever, tested the limits of their courage and skill and endurance.

New York's contributions to the war effort were material enough. Factories throughout the region poured out guns, ammunition, airplane parts, tanks, ships, uniforms, medical supplies. Before the conflict was over, three million servicemen and -women had been transported through the Port of New York, along with sixty-three million tons of war supplies. That is, *one-half the personnel and one-third of the matériel that the United States shipped overseas during the war went through New York Harbor,* making it "the greatest war port in history," in James Sanders's estimation.

It was the very pinnacle of New York as a seafaring city, the great convoys for Europe forming daily, far up the Hudson, and swinging slowly around before they headed out to sea. Workers swarmed over the city's eighteen hundred piers, forty shipyards, and thirty-six dry docks. (Crime plunged as the young men went off to war. By 1943, there were only 201 homicides all year, in a city of more than 7.5 million people.)

Immigrants were back, and in sizable numbers for the first time since Congress slammed shut the Golden Door in 1924. All through the later years of the 1930s, their numbers increased—Jews and gentiles alike from Europe, desperate and grateful to make it out alive. In a strange reversal, "enemy aliens"—241 Japanese, 165 German, and 65 Italian nationals—were rounded up by the FBI within four days of Pearl Harbor and shipped off to Ellis Island, where many of them would sit out the war. These were mostly stranded businessmen and sailors and random unfortunates such as the opera singer Ezio Pinza. Unlike "the wretched refuse" of the past, the new immigrants from Europe were disproportionately successful, cultured, urbane, and well educated—doctors and lawyers, professors and scientists, writers and artists. Many of these individuals were eagerly absorbed by New York's now world-class cultural institutions.

Kurt Weill, to name just one extraordinary case, worked with Ira Gershwin, Moss Hart, and Maxwell Anderson. Between them, they turned out Broadway hits such as *Lady in the Dark* and *Knickerbocker Holiday,* with its melancholic hit "September Song"—sung by no less than Peter Stuyvesant! Becoming a naturalized citizen during the war, Weill wrote and performed his "Buddy on the Nightshift" for munitions factory workers on the touring *Lunch-Hour Follies.* Lotte Lenya, his longtime muse and wife, starred in the theater and at such sophisticated clubs as Le Ruban Bleu and the Village Vanguard.

Up on West Fifty-Seventh Street, the Art Students League, already at the cutting edge of the art world, would absorb a dazzling array of European painters and sculptors for its faculty, preparing the seedbed for the rise of Abstract Expressionism and Pop Art after the war. The New School's "University in Exile" took in many of the leading European minds in the social sciences, while Columbia's Institute of Social Research housed the transplanted Frankfurt School from Germany. Just across campus—and five stories beneath Pupin Hall—Enrico Fermi, refugee from Mussolini's Italy, led an international team of physicists in conducting America's first successful experiment in nuclear fission, splitting a uranium atom.

Developing that breakthrough into the world's first atomic bombs would be the object of the Manhattan Project, so named for its original headquarters on the eighteenth floor of 270 Broadway, an innocuous building across the street from city hall. Material for the bombs, some 1,250 tons of uranium, had already been safely spirited away from the Congo by still another refugee, the Belgian engineer Edgar Sengier, and stored at warehouses in Port Richmond, Staten Island, and at West Twentieth Street in Chelsea—where it would lie forgotten for the next forty years.

Other refugees, less brilliant or well connected, had to scramble to get by however they could. As Lorraine Diehl relates in *Over Here! New York City During World War II,* middle-aged professionals and academics worked as janitors, waiters, busboys, fur packers, messengers, hospital orderlies, errand boys, secretaries, maids, and butlers—even dishwashers, in a New York version of *Casablanca*'s Café Américain.

"They cleaned offices, they worked, as I did, in a factory," a fictional "emigrant wife" recounts in the novel *Die Engel weinen* by Bella Fromm, a leading Jewish German journalist who arrived in New York in 1938. "They became housekeepers or cooks, and if luck was with them, they got a housekeeper's position with room and bath where their husbands could live with them. If he was capable of being a butler, all the better."

Finding a place to live was a growing problem, even as the war neared. Some refugees smashed through the anti-Jewish restrictions of Queens garden-apartment communities in Forest Hills and Jackson Heights. Others, such as the Kissinger family, moved into Lou Gehrig's old Washington Heights neighborhood, now so heavily German it was called Frankfurt on the Hudson and the Fourth Reich. Many, such as Isaac Bashevis Singer, wound up in the great apartment houses such as the Belnord, or cheaper rooming houses and hotels like the Milburn and the Marseilles, on the Upper West Side of Manhattan. There, in what became known as "the gilded ghetto," they formed an intellectual's café society along West Seventy-Second Street, dining and arguing daily at the local Automat, the Famous Dairy Restaurant, or Viennese bakeries such as the Café Éclair.

Once the war began, still more refugees made their way to New York. The great transatlantic liners, the *Queen Mary* and the *Queen Elizabeth,* the *Mauretania* and the *Antonia* and the *Normandie,* sped past the U-boat wolf packs one last time, to be converted into troopships. Thousands of evacuated British children were brought over.

A Canadian millionaire, William Stephenson, code-named Intrepid, arrived at the instruction of Winston Churchill to set up a highly effective spy ring and propaganda service for the British Empire, from his headquarters at Rockefeller Center. A young Ian Fleming, working with British Naval Intelligence, accompanied Stephenson's men as they broke into the Japanese consul general's office, two floors down, and microfilmed the codebooks for its radio transmissions to Tokyo.

All of them, immigrants and spies, Jews and fascists, brilliant scientists and newly minted housemaids, schemed and worried and waited and hoped, along with the millions of others who were their hosts. New York, in the strange interregnum between September 1, 1939, and December 7, 1941, would come to understand what so many cities around the world also came to know, the tense, almost giddy sensation of waiting for war. New York would experience that anticipation for longer than any of the others, and in this stolen time the city would revive, set about recharging its creative energies, set about *playing* again with an almost ferocious vigor. In baseball, this meant one last, particularly sweet season before the United States was drawn into the war. But first the city's attention would be drawn to another spectacle, a distraction in which it would defiantly reassert its own vision of the future—and leave unwitting clues as to what that future would actually be.

52

The World of Tomorrow

"Sometimes at night I lie awake in the dark and try to recapture the vision and the sound of the World of Tomorrow," the great reporter and chronicler of New York, Meyer Berger, would write. "I try to remember how the pastel lighting glowed on Mad Meadow in Flushing: soft green, orange, yellow, and red; blue moonglow on the great Perisphere and on the ghostly soaring Trylon."

Nothing else, from a time that became the object of almost unbroken nostalgia, would shine brighter or longer in the memories of New Yorkers than the 1939–40 World's Fair. "The World of Tomorrow," with its charming orange-and-blue buses, its tea-shaped cars that might have been designed by Buckminster Fuller, the ubiquitous monolith and orb that served as its trademark, would create a uniquely twentieth-century phenomenon: a love of the future as it was conceived in the past. The bittersweet remembrance of a worse, happier time; the sentimental longing that would come to dominate the New York psyche—not to mention the psyche of baseball—in the decades after the war.

The fair promised harmony, peace, rationality—and urban planning, with more than two hundred buildings situated on the equivalent of 370 city blocks. Its broad, bombastically named streets radiating away from a central hub: the Avenue of Pioneers and the Avenue of Patriots; the Avenue of Labor and Rainbow Avenue; the Court of Power and the Plaza of Light, Constitution Mall, and the Court of Peace, and the Lagoon of Nations. Pavilions were divvied up into "seven thematic zones featuring the aspects of modern life that wed man and machine."

Critics might point out that the fair's more memorable architecture was favored by radical, foreign ideologies, Trylon and Perisphere lifted directly from the notebooks of Russian Constructivists and

Gropius at the Bauhaus. They might scoff at the many commercial pavilions advertising the brave new world of Coca-Cola and Sealtest, Heinz pickles and Planter's peanuts, or note that the fair's most popular attractions were nothing so high-minded at all but the sleazy collection of freak shows and girlie peeps along a nearby midway.

"The road to Tomorrow leads through the chimney pots of Queens," scoffed E. B. White. "It's a long, familiar journey, through Mulsified Shampoo and Mobilgas, through Bliss Street, Kix, Astring-O-Sol, and the Majestic Auto Seat Covers."

New Yorkers—and out-of-towners—were enthralled nevertheless, and always would be. If the fair was grandiose, it was also dazzling, its colors and forms changing with the passing of the hour. Nor did visitors mind that the utopia it touted was linked inextricably to the automobile. Far and away the fair's most popular exhibit, still regarded with awe by visitors decades after they had seen it, was General Motors' Futurama, a thirty-six-thousand-square-foot model designed by Norman Bel Geddes (who would presently resurface in the service of a certain Brooklyn baseball team). It was supposed to depict a typical chunk of the United States in 1960—one that was, unsurprisingly, all about *cars:* cars moving at a hundred miles an hour, on fourteen-lane highways. Cars zipping around towering skyscrapers; cars racing out to well-spaced, single-family homes in the suburbs. Everything was in motion, even the visitors circling the display in moving chairs, all without one bus, subway, or other public conveyance in sight.

Visitors leaving Futurama were presented with a pin reading, "I Have Seen the Future." If they still didn't get the point, they might visit the Perisphere and an auditorium twice the size of Radio City Music Hall's. There they were treated to six minutes of "Democracity," the planned utopia expected to exist by 2039. The man of a hundred years hence would live in high-rise garden developments called Pleasantvilles, work and play and educate himself in Centerton hubs, with all factories banished to Millvilles, separated from residential areas by greenbelts and farming areas.

It was, in short, just about every notion of city and suburban development that would repel actual people in the decades ahead. None of which did anything to dim its appeal—or its memory in the public imagination.

"General Motors has spent a small fortune to convince the American public that if it wishes to enjoy the full benefit of private enterprise in motor manufacturing," Walter Lippmann noted caustically, "it will have to rebuild its cities and its highways by public enterprise."

Well, exactly. This was, not so coincidentally, Robert Moses's vision of the future, and the World of Tomorrow was designed in good part to serve Bob the Builder's master plan. The fair itself was bisected by Moses's brand-new Grand Central Parkway, its immediate purpose to eliminate an eyesore, the Corona Dump. This was a fantastic mountain range of ashes from Brooklyn incinerators that Fitzgerald had immortalized in *The Great Gatsby.* It was the domain of John "Fishhooks" McCarthy, an old Tammany holdout who famously went every morning to St. James Church on the Lower East Side to pray: "O Lord, give me health and strength. We'll steal the rest."

Moses finally ended Fishhooks's ash heap contracts and hoped to make the fair a permanent exhibition of wonders, an anchor for his further development of Corona and Flushing. It was not to be—at least not yet.

The World of Tomorrow drew an estimated fifty-five million visitors in its two summers of existence, but this was well below what its planners had counted on. Before the fair even opened, its unflagging optimism had begun to give way before the realities of a world plunging into war. By the time it closed, the pavilions of Czechoslovakia, Poland, Norway, Belgium, the Netherlands, and France had lost their funding as those countries were gobbled up by the Nazis. Moses would have to find something else for his 1,216 acres of spanking-new parkland.

There was another intimation of the postponed future at the World of Tomorrow. The fair was opened by President Roosevelt, broadcast to a—somewhat—wider audience, thanks to a new technology that had been developed in the United States even before the Great Depression, but had lingered in the shadows ever since. This was the new "picture radio" in the RCA pavilion.

Television had become a reality in the 1920s, with experimental stations running regularly scheduled programming in New York by 1928, but by 1939 there were still only an estimated two thousand sets in the New York area. That year, W2XBS—later WNBC-TV—began broadcasting as many as fifty-eight hours of programming a month. Outdoor events still could only be covered within ten miles of the station's transmitter (they had finally found something to do with the Empire State Building's planned blimp mooring) and could only be viewed within a radius of forty to fifty miles.

This covered a population of some ten million people, to be sure, but reception was only a crude gray 441-line affair. Television remained mostly the preoccupation of cranks and amateur enthusiasts, much like ham radio—none of which was enough to stop W2XBS from taking a crew up to the northern tip of Manhattan Island on May 17, 1939. There at Baker Field, where Columbia's baseball diamond had been moved in the years since Gehrig had bounced drives off the library steps, the fledgling station made the very first television broadcast of a baseball game.

The telecast emanated from a single camera, mounted on a twelve-foot-high wooden platform behind a fence and just to the third-base side of home plate. The announcer was a local radio personality, the mawkish, pill-popping, one-legged Long Bill Stern; the audience, whoever happened to be clustered around the four hundred primitive sets that carried the game. They saw Princeton defeat a Columbia squad with the NFL star-to-be Sid Luckman at shortstop, by 2–1, in ten innings—that is, when they could see anything at all. The baseball was all but invisible, the players a blur. It rated one line in the next day's *New York Times,* which was soon reporting that retailers had given up on moving their boxy TV sets for the year, in favor of more elaborate home radios.

53

The Redheaded League

There remained those who saw a future for television. One was David Sarnoff, the brilliant, ruthless, self-aggrandizing Russian immigrant who had worked his way up from office boy to found NBC Radio and become head of RCA. Sarnoff understood that television's time would come after the war, and he saw that one of its biggest attractions would be professional sports, which at the time meant baseball.

To that end, a more important broadcast was made that same, fateful summer. On August 26, 1939—just three days after the signing of the Hitler-Stalin pact made World War II inevitable—W2XBS televised a doubleheader from Ebbets Field, the Cincinnati Reds against the Brooklyn Dodgers. It was an appropriate match, harking back to the day in 1870 when the original Red Stockings saw their eighty-one-game undefeated streak snapped at the Capitoline Grounds. This time, the Reds won the opener, 5–2, while Brooklyn took the nightcap, 6–1.

Two cameras were used (as opposed to fifteen for a game today); one of them behind home plate to give a better view of the whole playing field. The audience was now estimated (somehow) at five to eight thousand, including a filled theater at the World's Fair. And this time the broadcaster was a considerably smoother presence, a thirty-one-year-old southerner who introduced himself with the first words ever spoken on a television broadcast of a professional baseball game: "This is Red Barber speaking. Let me say hello to you all."

Barber worked that first game without the help of a monitor, broadcasting from the second deck, right among the fans. He had to ad-lib the spots for the game's sponsors, Mobil motor oil, Ivory soap, and Wheaties. Harold Parrott would complain in *The Sporting News,* "The players were clearly distinguishable, but it was not possible to pick out the ball." A million televisions sets would be sold in the United States in 1941 as commercial broadcasting at last began to take off, but any further development would have to wait for the end of hostilities.

"Everybody knew it was the beginning of something big," Barber would remember. "We just didn't really know what."

Wanting some memento of his historic broadcast, he asked NBC for a souvenir, and the network promptly responded with an engraved silver cigarette case, reading "In Grateful Appreciation." Inside it, instead of cigarettes, was a bill for $35, or about $500 in today's money.

It would be hard for two men to be any less alike than Walter Lanier Barber and Larry MacPhail, the new president of the Dodgers who had made all this possible, save for the color of their hair. But between them they were about to usher in the heroic era of Brooklyn baseball.

For all of the Yankees' ruthless professionalism, for all of the team's efficiency at identifying, signing, and developing young talent, the Bronx team was a laggard when it came to promoting itself and maximizing attendance. So were most major-league teams, which seemed determined to make fans prove themselves worthy by fighting their way past every conceivable obstacle to see a game. Well into the Depression, the Yankees held precious few promotions, and they certainly weren't interested in giving away anything. Decades later, George Weiss would still be lamenting the idea of Cap Day, feeling it diminished the brand of the Yankees to have poor urchins running around the street in their own "NY" caps.

Most clubs in the 1930s did not want to so much as entertain the idea of night baseball. Black baseball teams had been playing night games since the 1920s, and in 1930 the increasingly desperate minor leagues followed suit. It was a tremendous success; attendance for the Pacific Coast League tripled for night games. But the majors scoffed at the idea, offering rationales that became downright bizarre. Playing night ball, feared the National League president, John Heydler, would mean getting baseball "into the show business, which, after all is said and done, is all that night baseball can ever be."

"The man who goes to night baseball after he has eaten a hearty meal is apt to have indigestion if he is nervous or excited; the disturbed and misanthropic fan will not sleep well after a night game," worried J. G. Taylor Spink in *The Sporting News.*

In New York, there was even a living, breathing example of what a difference night baseball could make. Max Rosner's semipro Bushwicks, playing Wednesday and Friday night games at little Dexter Park in Queens, reportedly drew a total of 350,000 fans there in 1931—more than the home attendance of four major-league teams. But midway through the decade, there were still no lights in any major-league park.

"Night baseball is a passing attraction which will not live long enough to make it wise for the New York Club to spend $250,000 on a lighting system for the stadium," insisted the Yankees' Ed Barrow.

If night baseball was out, radio was an abomination. If people could listen to the games on the radio, why would they ever come to the park? The baseball owners' fear was understandable. Everybody knew that once radio had started broadcasting music, nightclubs, concert halls, and juke joints had all closed up, and everyone had stopped buying records. Broadcasting the World Series over the radio had originated with another "nickel series" in New York in 1922, and Hal Totten had been announcing regular-season Chicago Cubs games over the radio since 1924. Since that time the club's gate receipts had soared, with the Cubs leading the NL in attendance every year from 1926 to 1932. But why let facts get in the way? Baseball's owners nearly voted to ban the broadcast of games entirely after the 1933 season, stayed only by the Cubs owner William Wrigley Jr.'s insistence on keeping it. As it was, each team was given the choice of whether to broadcast its games or not, and the decision by all three New York teams was an emphatic *No!* It was agreed between them that not a word of precious baseball would leak out over the airwaves for the next five years.

The sport's newest owner had some very different ideas. It might be said of Leland Stanford "Larry" MacPhail, as of Byron, that he was "mad, bad and dangerous to know." But he sure was good for Brooklyn.

"MacPhail was a genius," acknowledged Leo Durocher, whose battles with the man were epic. "But there is a thin line between genius and insanity and in Larry's case it was so thin you could sometimes see him drifting back and forth."

James Reston remembered MacPhail as the only man he was ever physically afraid of when he went into a rage, and his rages could be triggered by nothing at all. He got into regular fistfights, including one with beat writer Red Patterson from the *Herald Tribune.* The mild-mannered Red Barber remembered him cursing and "roaring" with anger after he asked the radio announcer about the abilities of a ballplayer and didn't get the answer he wanted. Like many such "mysterious" mood swings, MacPhail's rages had a simple enough source.

"Never again did I stay around him one minute after I saw him take the first drink—from then on I was already late for an appointment. Very late," recalled Barber.

When sober, MacPhail was considered an exhilarating, even charming presence, something that is hard to understand from our perspective today. In pictures from his New York days, he always looks very much the epitome of the mean drunk: rubber-faced and hard-eyed, his hair mussed and his suits rumpled. Writers of the time were mesmerized by him—at least at first—due perhaps to his ability to spin legend from his colorful past.

MacPhail was the son of a onetime grocer and loan shark who had somehow managed to parlay those enterprises into a chain of twenty-one Michigan banks. Larry himself had been talked out of attending the U.S. Naval Academy by his parents, going instead to law school, then turning around a failing Nashville department store. Enlisting in World War I as a private, he rose to the rank of colonel of artillery and was gassed and wounded in France. After the Armistice, he joined his commanding officer in a harebrained scheme to kidnap the kaiser from his Holland exile and put him on trial for war crimes—a caper that nearly got him court-martialed but supposedly allowed him to purloin a Hohenzollern family ashtray from the kaiser's desk. (The imperial ashtray would put in a long career in his office, a consummate conversation piece.)

After the war, MacPhail dabbled in the law again and skipped from business to business. A college baseball player, he was always obsessed with sports, and he worked Saturdays as a Big Ten football ref, where some credit him with having invented the use of hand signals to let the crowd know what the call was. In 1931, aged forty-one, he decided at last to devote himself to what he loved most, borrowed $100,000 from his father to buy the Columbus Red Birds minor-league franchise, then flew to St. Louis, to offer the club to Branch Rickey and the Cardinals. Rickey, impressed by MacPhail's energy and ambition, agreed to buy the Red Birds and hired him to run the team. He would not be disappointed—right away. MacPhail built Columbus a new park and put the Red Birds both literally and figuratively on the air, broadcasting their games and flying them to road games (never mind the number of players left too airsick to play). He also introduced night baseball to the Ohio capital. It was a winning formula he would employ repeatedly throughout the decade. Attendance increased more than 50 percent in one year, and by 1933 Columbus had won its first pennant in twenty-six years.

MacPhail was not around to see it. There were always problems with Larry working for somebody else, which were that he tended to spend their money freely, ignore their rules, and refuse any direction. Then there was the drinking—something that appalled the abstemious Rickey.

"With no drinks, he was brilliant, with one he was a genius. With two, he was insane," one writer remembered. "And rarely did he stop at one."

Both sides of MacPhail would soon be on display. After swearing off alcohol for a year, he got Rickey—always a soft touch for a repentant sinner—to recommend that he take over the day-to-day operations of the Cincinnati Reds from their bankrupt owner. MacPhail then prevailed on inventor and industrialist Powel Crosley Jr. to buy a majority stake in the team. Crosley owned a company that manufactured refrigerators and radio sets. In a 1930s example of synergy, he also owned two radio stations—including what was then the most powerful station in the world. MacPhail convinced Crosley that he could use his station to sell his refrigerators and his baseball—and up the sales of his radio sets in the bargain.

The man chosen to put the Reds on the air was a soft-spoken Mississippi native who had spent the last five years broadcasting University of Florida football games. Red Barber took a pay cut to $25 a week in his new job, but it was the best sacrifice he ever executed. "The Old Redhead" was an immediate hit in Cincinnati, with his warm, relaxed southern voice and seamless delivery. MacPhail repeated his winning formula, sprucing up what was now Crosley Field, building a farm system for the Reds, and spending money to acquire proven players. In June 1934, he chartered a plane to fly a major-league team to a game for the first time, bringing the Reds home from Chicago. And on May 24, 1935, President Roosevelt tapped a golden key at the White House, activating a signal that lit up a major-league ballpark for the first time.

"No pun intended, but there was electricity in the air—in the air, on the field, in the stands, and in the dugout," remembered the Reds' Billy Sullivan. "Ballplayers did not get blasé. They got fired up."

Players and fans alike had discovered the strange exhilaration, the sense of wonder and intensity that night baseball conveys. The Reds' crowd that evening was more than six times the average for an afternoon weekday game, even though it had been delayed until 9:00 p.m. to make the effect of the lights all the more dramatic. Attendance more than doubled from the year before, the team began to rise steadily through the standings—and Larry MacPhail got himself beaten black and blue, brawling in a hotel elevator with a pair of police detectives. Another yearlong sabbatical from baseball and alcohol followed, succeeded by Branch Rickey telling yet another floundering team that he knew just the man who could save them.

In Brooklyn, Judge McKeever had finally passed away at age eighty-four, breaking the long stalemate in the Dodgers' front office. The ownership was still divided between the heirs of Charlie Ebbets, the heirs of the McKeevers, and the Brooklyn Trust Company, but all were now desperate to make back some money from this white elephant of a ball club. Steve McKeever's daughter, Dearie Mulvey, and her husband, Jim Mulvey, wanted to hire Rickey himself, but Rickey, still comfortable in St. Louis, suggested his redheaded stepson.

If the Dodgers' owners thought Larry MacPhail was going to act like an abashed reprobate who had managed to drink away his last two jobs, they were very much mistaken. All MacPhail demanded was total control of the club, and enough of other people's money to turn it around. *Spend money on the Dodgers?* Such an outrageous thing had never been attempted before! When the assembled Brooklyn owners balked, MacPhail looked at his watch, slammed a hand on a desk, and announced, "If I can't do business here, I know where I can. Well, what about it?" The owners caved, and MacPhail told an associate, "I'm going to turn Brooklyn inside out, upside down, and win pennants every year."

He started, as usual, with the ballpark itself, spending a reported $200,000 to refurbish what had become a shabby, neglected Ebbets Field, beginning with a spacious office for himself. A corps of ushers and vendors was decked out in bright uniforms, an army of contractors hired to make everything shiny and new.

"The first thing he did was to paint the park over and made it clean and give you a toilet that you could visit without your feeling like a horse going to a horse trough," remembered the Brooklyn fan Bill Reddy, in an interview for Peter Golenbock's *Bums.* "You could go to the bathroom and take a leak and not have to worry about worms crawling up the walls and biting you. And you could buy a program or a beer from a guy who didn't look like a fugitive from a chain gang."

Next came the lights. Here he got lucky. The very first major-league night game played in Brooklyn—the first played in any major-league park in New York City—took place on June 15, 1938. It was—once again—Brooklyn against the Cincinnati Reds. This time, the pitcher for Cincinnati was not Asahel Brainard with his "scientific pitching" but a wild, hard-throwing young southpaw named Johnny Vander Meer, just four days removed from a no-hitter at Crosley Field against the Boston Bees. Vander Meer, "the Dutch Master," was a native of little Midland Park, New Jersey, where he had grown up worshipping King Carl Hubbell, and signed his first pro contract with the Dodgers. Several hundred of his former neighbors chartered buses into Brooklyn to honor their hometown hero, but they would have to wait awhile.

"MacPhail kept selling tickets," Vander Meer remembered. "The ballpark was overcrowded. They were sitting in the aisles and everywhere. The fire marshal wouldn't let the game start because of the crowded conditions."

The starting time was pushed back to 9:45 as MacPhail packed 38,748 ticket buyers into Ebbets, the most it would ever hold. While they waited, they listened to speeches and marching bands and watched races between the Olympic champion Jesse Owens and various Dodgers. Then a thoroughly forgettable Dodgers hurler named Max Butcher threw the first pitch of the first night game in New York's major-league history.

"I don't know how many pitches I threw by the time the game started, but when I got up to get ready for the first inning, it was the fourth time that I was up and throwing," complained Vander Meer.

He found early on that he was hanging his curve a little, "so I threw about ninety percent fast balls" for most of the game, and as such quickly turned the contest into a catch with receiver Ernie "Schnozz" Lombardi, the erstwhile Dodger. Some hitters preferred night games right from the start, because they eliminated outfield shadows and the glare off white shirts that used to be common, in the days before teams routinely provided a centerfield backdrop devoid of fans. But the first lights provided only a fraction of the illumination that modern stadium lights do. The Dodgers had trouble seeing Vander Meer's fastball, but then he seemed to have equal trouble seeing the plate, walking eight while striking out seven but not surrendering a single hit. Meanwhile, the Reds chased Butcher to give him a comfortable 6–0 lead. The fans tried to jinx Vander Meer by letting him know that he had another no-hitter going: "In Brooklyn, they let you know in the first inning."

By the bottom of the ninth, Vander Meer "figured I had twenty-one good pumps left," and decided to let fly with his best fastball. It almost ruined him. After a groundout to start the inning, he walked three men in a row, the tension in the packed park rising giddily.

If only anyone outside the park could have heard it. Thanks to the New York–wide ban on broadcasting, the dean of all broadcasters, Red Barber, was back home in Cincinnati, where excited fans kept calling him to tell him how the game was going. In 1979, Red would repay the Florida Association of Broadcasters for the Gold Medal award they gave him, by making up a tape with his "vivid recap" of those first eight innings. Then he added three minutes' worth of excitement, broadcasting the end of the ninth inning as if he were actually there:

> There's no one warming up in the bullpen. It's going to be Vander Meer going all the way. It has to be. He pitched a no-hitter four days ago at Cincinnati against Boston, and tonight is

> his night. His father and mother are here. The girl he's going to marry. They're all here. And this crowd is now for him. They've turned their backs on their ball club, the Dodgers. They want him to do it.

Vander Meer got Ernie Koy, a swift rookie centerfielder, to ground into a force at home. That brought up Leo Durocher, who would hit only .219 in 1938 but was just annoying enough to break up a no-hitter. On Vander Meer's first pitch, he shanked a sinking drive into right field.

"Durocher swings, and it's a hard line-drive going down the right field and it's foul just by a couple of feet in the right-field corner," Red Barber re-created.

Three pitches later—just after the hour of midnight had passed, unheard of for a baseball game then—Durocher flied out softly to Harry Craft in center. In New York City's very first major-league night game, Johnny Vander Meer had pitched his second consecutive no-hitter, a feat unmatched before or since.

Somehow, there were no reports of any hearty eaters or misanthropic fans being disturbed. Baseball was now all in with the show business, and MacPhail decided to make the most of it. At the end of the year, he informed the Giants and Yankees that he would not be renewing the citywide, five-year pact banning any baseball broadcasts. He had already lined up a sponsor, General Mills, the maker of Wheaties, which agreed to pay $70,000 for the right to broadcast Dodgers games over WOR. Brought in from Cincinnati at a salary of $8,000 to become the voice of the Dodgers—at MacPhail's insistence—was Red Barber. It was the start of a career in New York that would last for twenty-seven years and would end in what was both the most shameful and the most honorable moment in the history of New York sports broadcasting.

54

Brooklyn Becomes the World

All that was far in the future. For now, the world was still young, and Brooklyn fell in love with the Old Redhead right away. What was not to love? Barber was, above all, a consummate professional, erudite and precise, careful to watch the outfielders on fly balls. He came to the park three hours before the first pitch and spent that time down on the field viewing batting and fielding practice, picking up everything he could use on the air. Once in the broadcast booth, he sprinkled his patter with catchphrases from his Deep South background that became immortalized around baseball and beyond.

A "rhubarb" was a fight or dispute. Teams in the middle of a big rally were "tearin' up the pea patch." A high but easy fly ball was a "can o' corn." Winning teams were "walkin' in the high cotton" and had easy wins "tied up in a croker sack." A close game was "tighter than a new pair of shoes on a rainy day," while graceful players moved "easier than a bank of fog" but sometimes bobbled balls that were "slicker than boiled okra." The bases were "COD"—"Chock-Full O'Dodgers"—or "FOB," "Full of Bums." Players were "Big fella" and "Mister," "Colonel" and "Old ——," and an exciting play was punctuated with a cry of "Oh, doctor!"

"He was a showman," remembered Bob Edwards, a newsman who almost half a century later hosted a weekly segment with Barber on National Public Radio. "When he was a kid, he wanted to be in vaudeville."

Far from declining, the Dodgers' attendance shot up almost 50 percent the first year Barber was on the air. The Giants and Yankees, scrambling to catch up, reached an agreement whereby whichever of the two teams was at home would also be on the air. As a result, neither team could build a consistent radio fan base for years—at least none that compared with the Dodgers'.

"They did not realize at the time the beneficial effect of radio, that it would be making families of fans," wrote Barber himself.

He understood that what he had created was the new radio world of baseball—a world beautifully realized in a borough full of two-family homes, porches, and brownstone stoops, where boys and girls would remember walking home and catching every pitch from the radios playing in the summer twilight; a whole city bound together by the soft, southern voice of the Dodgers.

"And the men would spend their evenings sitting on their stoops in their strapped undershirts, and women would be together on a different stoop, gabbing, and the radio would be blaring Red Barber and the Dodger game, and when it got dark, the kids began playing ring-a-levio or Kick the Can, or Three Feet to Germany, all the exotic games which disappeared with the emergence of the automobile," remembered the Brooklyn fan Joe Flaherty, in a stream of consciousness for *Bums.*

Within three years of Red Barber's arrival in Brooklyn, his patter would inspire one of James Thurber's wickedest short stories, "The Catbird Seat," named for the Barberism "sittin' in the catbird seat" (that is, "sittin' pretty"). Or did he? Barber's daughter would claim that her father picked up the expression *from* Thurber's story, which would have been an intriguing example of intellectual cross-pollination, though Barber himself said he learned it in a Memphis card game. The larger point was that it was *Thurber.* Here was Brooklyn, grim and gray—Brooklyn, the fallen city, coldcocked by the Depression—drawing the highbrow attention of the *New Yorker* set.

(Technically, it was *not* the first penetration of the publication by the Dodgers. That honor belonged to George C. Price's wonderful cartoon take on Abe Stark's HIT SIGN, WIN SUIT sign. In the cartoon, an outfielder leaps to catch a fly ball near the wall, in front of the famous sign. Just behind the outfielder is a middle-aged man in a suit, with a baseball glove on both hands, desperate to keep ball from hitting sign.)

It was another triumph that reflected the Americanization of Brooklyn—or more accurately, the acknowledgment that the *haimishe,* polyglot borough of Brooklyn might be the real heart of the nation. Brooklyn, drawn from all over the world. With the onset of the war—a war against the forces of racial purity and absolutism—

the borough's ethnic composition became an active virtue. Became, even, a cliché of the B war movie, where in a platoon made up of men from any number of (white) ethnic backgrounds, one of the grunts was always from Brooklyn—and always a Dodgers fan.

It was not that far from the truth. Brooklyn led the war effort in New York, sending 327,000 men and women to fight, of whom 7,000 would die. Brooklyn contained seventy-two defense plants, with almost fourteen thousand workers. Brooklyn even outproduced Japan—*all* of Japan—by itself at the Brooklyn Navy Yard, where seventy-five thousand workers, including women riveters, women welders, and women shipfitters, toiled around the clock, three shifts a day, seven days a week, building and refitting more ships of war than America's Axis enemy would make throughout the conflict.

And yes, their team was the Dodgers. The triumphs of Gehrig and particularly DiMaggio might have helped legitimize the American immigrant. But the Dodgers under Larry MacPhail had set about building a whole *team* of outlanders, a club that—with a couple of huge exceptions—reflected the mixed ethnicity of the borough they played in.

Not least, MacPhail had put together a modern farm system and hired the son of the master himself, Branch Rickey Jr., to run it. By 1940, the Dodgers controlled eighteen farm teams—more than even the Yankees, more than any club but St. Louis—and the system would eventually produce its own dynasty. Neither MacPhail nor Brooklyn had the capacity to wait. Instead, the borough's new enfant terrible estimated that he spent $1 million to bring in an entire odd lot of ballplayers—castoffs, stars, promising rookies bottled up behind veterans. All of them got a second chance in Brooklyn.

"Our ball club was a very unusual one," remembered Pee Wee Reese, "everybody came from some other team. I don't think anybody at all came up through our farm system."

There were more ethnics, men with the sorts of names still rarely heard before in major-league baseball. Dolph Camilli was a graceful, thirty-one-year-old first baseman and power hitter whom MacPhail brought over from the Phillies for $50,000. The Dodgers' managing board swallowed hard but signed the check. Camilli, a former boxer whose brother was killed in the ring by the heavyweight champ Max Baer, was a quiet, solid presence on the field who became the team's leader and captain. Away from the park he seethed, walking the streets for hours after making a poor play or going hitless at the plate, trying in vain to calm his stomach and leave the game behind.

From the Cubs, for $65,000 and a couple of throw-ins, came the best National League second baseman of the era, William Jennings Bryan Herman, a lifetime .304 hitter—considered maybe the best hit-and-run man ever to play the game. Harry Arthur "Cookie" Lavagetto had already been acquired in a straight trade from Pittsburgh to play third, while filling out the infield was a man whose name would be revered in Brooklyn.

Harold Henry Reese, the "Little Colonel," actually stood five ten and weighed 160 pounds, a perfectly average big leaguer for the time. His nickname came from his boyhood triumphs as a champion marble shooter. The Red Sox owner, Tom Yawkey, had bought the entire Louisville Colonels team in order to acquire him. But Pee Wee posed a threat to Boston's reigning shortstop, the player-manager Joe Cronin, and was soon dealt to Brooklyn for the pitcher Red Evans and $75,000. Reese would anchor the Dodgers' infield for most of the next seventeen years, was an outstanding leadoff hitter, one of the best fielding shortstops in the National League, and a natural leader who would succeed Camilli as the team's captain.

He led a large southern contingent on the Dodgers that included Fred "Dixie" Walker, a right fielder from the Yankees' system who was soon redubbed "the Peeple's Cherce," for his prodigious hitting against the hated Giants. On the mound was the gregarious Kirby Higbe from South Carolina, whom MacPhail ponied up $100,000 and three players for. Whitlow Wyatt, a literal rambling wreck from Georgia Tech, much injured, much traded, and enamored of the beanball, came from the Indians' system. Hugh Casey, the relief ace, was a quiet, hard-drinking spitballer who would become renowned for pummeling Ernest Hemingway during a boozy, late-night boxing match one spring when the Dodgers were training in Cuba.

"Ernest would belt Case one, and down he would go," recalled Higbe, a witness. "Case would belt old Ernest, and down he would go. . . . The furniture [really took] a beating."

(A few years after the war, Casey would precede Hemingway in his way out of this world. Despondent over his failing marriage and a paternity suit, Hugh put a shotgun in his mouth while on the phone with his wife and blew his brains out, aged just thirty-seven. His wife, who was pleading with him not to do it, told police, "He was just as calm about it as if he was about to walk out on the ball field and pitch a game.")

Finally, MacPhail grabbed as many players as he could from the master himself. He scooped up the great Pete Reiser for centerfield, handed Rickey and the Cards $65,000 and two players for a good-fielding catcher named Mickey Owen, and sent over four more players and $125,000 for Curt "Coonskin" Davis, a capable veteran starter, and left fielder Joe "Ducky-Wucky" Medwick. A Jersey boy, Medwick hated his avian nickname, which was courtesy of a female fan. In fact, he hated most things and most people and was widely hated in return as a selfish, irritable ballplayer known for getting into fights with opponents and teammates alike.

"The trouble with that Medwick is, he don't talk none, he just hits you," Dizzy Dean said of Ducky, who once chased both Dizzy and his brother Daffy with a bat, in what sounds like nothing so much as the plot of a Warner Bros. cartoon.

A classic bad-ball hitter who supposedly inspired Yogi Berra's style at the plate, Medwick was also known as Muscles for his formidable guns, and he had spent years whacking extra-base hits around St. Louis's Sportsman's Park. The last National Leaguer to this day to win the Triple Crown, he was still just twenty-eight years old when MacPhail finally acquired him in 1940. But six days after arriving in Brooklyn, Medwick got into another spat with an old teammate and was beaned so badly by Cardinals pitcher Bob Bowman that afternoon at Ebbets Field that it was briefly thought he might die. The beaning was horrific enough that baseball—a mere twenty years after Ray Chapman's fatal head injury—decided to seriously think about requiring batting helmets. In the spring of 1941, the Brooklyn Dodgers became the first club to have all of their players wear some kind of protective headgear.

It was not just Medwick, though, loathed as he was. Dodgers were constantly getting hit by pitches. Between 1940 and 1942 alone,

Medwick, Reese, Reiser, and Owen suffered potentially career-ending beanings. The reason for this was yet another MacPhail pickup from St. Louis.

Hitting batters was just the way Leo Durocher believed in playing ball. Dodgers pitchers plunked so many opposing hitters once he took over that six of the other seven National League teams filed official complaints with the league office. When constant warnings failed to accomplish anything, they started throwing back. Leo the Lip didn't care. It wasn't *him* being thrown at.

"You're on a raft with Leo in the middle of the ocean. Leo falls overboard. You leap in and save him, but a shark comes along and takes your leg. The next day, you and Leo start out even," was how sportswriter Dick Young would describe life with Durocher.

The Lip had come over to Brooklyn as a slick-fielding shortstop, then bullied his way into the manager's job. Babe Ruth, whom MacPhail had hired as a first-base coach and sideshow attraction, had thought he would be the next skipper, but Durocher made a big play of backing the incumbent manager, Burleigh Grimes, even picking a fight with the Babe in which he knocked the big guy's clubhouse stool out from under him, then leaped on him and started slapping his face. If this was a cruel way to treat the game's greatest star, it was Leo all over: fearless, underhanded, and stunningly aggressive. Early in his career he had even challenged Ty Cobb, hip checking him when Cobb went around second base, then taunting, "You're an old man. The game has passed you by. You ought to get out."

Leo had never known any other way to behave, even if he had been an altar boy. Emerging from a Springfield, Massachusetts, slum, he had hustled pool at a "billiards academy" and run with the local sharpies. Bounced from his very first minor-league team for stealing money from his teammates' clothes, he would do the same to Ruth as a rookie with the Yankees in 1928, filching the Babe's watch from the clubhouse. Like his fight with Ruth in Brooklyn, this might have been a calculated ploy, designed to impress his manager—on this occasion, Miller Huggins, another scrappy infielder who harbored no love for the Babe. Huggins took Durocher under his wing and helped turn him into one of the best gloves in the majors, while Leo reveled in the bright lights of Manhattan, haunting Times Square and Larry Fay's El Fey nightclub; spending every night at expensive restaurants and Broadway shows, making such dubious friends as George Raft and Billy Rose; earning the nickname Fifth Avenue for the garish suits he delighted in.

Unlike Ruth, though, Durocher was never more than a Punch-and-Judy hitter, and after Huggins died, he made so bold as to tell Ed Barrow to "go and fuck yourself" during contract negotiations. Shipped out to Cincinnati, he fell deeper in debt, kited checks everywhere, and found himself forced into a brief marriage that probably owed much to his characteristic dating style. The secret to success with women, Durocher once advised a young sportswriter, was "make sure you put your hand on their snatch" within five minutes of commencing a date: "No go? Tough, but it's still early yet. Plenty of time to call another broad. But suppose she don't knock your hand off. Well, then hello dear. You know you're in, an' you ain't gonna waste the evening."

By the time he washed up in St. Louis in 1933, the old Durocher charm had somehow failed to deter thirty-two separate creditors, all of whom were threatening to sue. Leo—not for the last time—was in imminent danger of being tossed out of baseball for his moral failings. Branch Rickey took him in hand, set up payment plans with all his dunners, and kept him on a strict budget. Always quick to give a backslider a second chance, Rickey even arranged an offseason coaching job for his young reprobate and encouraged him to marry a responsible career woman the Lip had fallen in love with in St. Louis. Durocher became another spark plug on his 1934 championship team, supposedly giving the squad its famous nickname when the writer Frank Graham overheard him telling Dizzy Dean, "They wouldn't let us in the other league. They would say that we are a lot of gas house ballplayers."

The Gashouse Gang nickname stuck, thanks to the penuriousness of the Cardinals' management, which was loath to provide the players even with clean uniforms. But it spoke as well to a growing divide between the two major leagues, one that would become more and more evident as the years proceeded and has still not quite faded away.

The American League had accumulated the most talent by the 1930s, thanks in large part to a few deep-pocketed owners, such as the Yankees' Ruppert and Thomas Yawkey up in Boston. But it was an advantage that would express itself in a muscle-bound, bludgeoning style. The AL was a league full of power hitters and power pitchers, beating down all opposition. From 1927 to 1942, there were only three true pennant races in the junior circuit. The winning club—usually the Yankees—tended to sweep all before it, and they usually beat the National League's best, with the AL taking eleven World Series and seven of the first ten All-Star Games in that period.

Yet because they had to scramble, the National League teams began to develop a more varied, imaginative style of ball, one that had not yet abandoned the hit-and-run or the bunt—a style that pleased the fans, was eminently suited to the scraping-by 1930s, and always seemed to produce a thrilling pennant race. NL teams brawled more, threw at each other more, got their uniforms dirtier. They developed an opportunistic, underfunded style of ball that fit in more and more closely with the kind of baseball that Negro League teams were playing—a style of play already pointing in the direction of where the color line would first be broken.

Durocher brought this hyperactive, scrappy style of play to Brooklyn. The team reflected the man, though they didn't necessarily like him. Leo played favorites among his players and otherwise manipulated them; on at least one occasion he brought them to the verge of mutiny for slamming them in the press and then lying about it. Billy Herman claimed that he once deliberately bounced a throw into the dugout that hit Durocher square between the eyes and knocked him out.

Leo's fights with the volatile MacPhail, Branch's other bad boy, were Homeric, part of a relationship that often made the George Steinbrenner–Billy Martin folie à deux seem like a badminton match. Durocher later estimated that MacPhail fired him sixty times in their four years together. He fired him for insubordination, for playing bingo, for standing up for his coaches, on one memorable occasion for not ordering a train to stop. He fired him when Leo punched out a golf caddy who dared to talk back to him. Incredibly, he did *not* fire him when Durocher punched *him* out, after MacPhail refused to stop calling him names. Instead, the owner picked himself up, hugged Leo, burst into tears, then went to the ballpark with his manager.

"I'm glad we had our little talk yesterday," he told Durocher the next afternoon. "I really feel we understand each other better now."

55
The Stolen Season

No one ever really understood MacPhail, or much liked Durocher, but between them they made Brooklyn a contender. The team climbed to third in 1939, then second in 1940, and in 1941 found themselves in a pennant race with no less than Mr. Rickey's Cardinals. Brooklyn was truly back in the big leagues at last, but Rickey had rebuilt the Cards into yet another dynamo, stacked with both veteran stars and a host of terrific young players from that Columbus farm club MacPhail had refurbished. They looked unbeatable.

Yet the Dodgers broke out on top, winning twenty of their first twenty-six games, while Cardinal after Cardinal went down in a welter of injuries. Wyatt, Higbe, Davis, Luke Hamlin, and Hugh Casey, in a rare start, all pitched shutouts in those first twenty wins. The Bums had the best infield *and* outfield in the league. Dodgers fans were ecstatic. No one had ever seen a Brooklyn team this talented, or this spirited. Their enjoyment was shadowed only by the intimation that this was likely to be the last normal season for some time to come. The waiting game was almost over.

"The war threat concerned us deeply," remembered Red Sox pitcher Broadway Charlie Wagner. "It was always on your mind. You talked about it all the time. On the train or in the hotel lobby we'd ask each other, 'What are they doing overseas now?' You knew it was coming."

"Most of us were making our minds up during the season what we wanted to do," recalled Bob Feller. "If you weren't, you had to be living in a cave somewhere."

Already, ballplayers such as Hank Greenberg were being called up in the nation's first peacetime draft. Major-league clubs began the tradition of playing "The Star-Spangled Banner" before each game. Lucy Moore sang it at Yankee Stadium on May 18 to celebrate "I Am an American Day," while that same afternoon down in Central Park,

Mayor La Guardia led a rally of 700,000 New Yorkers. On the night of May 27, play was halted for forty-five minutes at the Polo Grounds while fans and ballplayers alike stood and listened to President Roosevelt declare "an unlimited national emergency," openly siding with Great Britain and claiming a new Atlantic sphere of influence from Greenland down to the Cape Verde Islands and the Caribbean.

For all the anxiety, on the field an extraordinary season was unfolding. This would be the summer of the great DiMaggio's great streak; the year that Ted Williams, just twenty-three, would become the last man to hit over .400, and Feller, still just twenty-two, would win twenty-five games and lead the AL in strikeouts and shutouts. This was a year that, like the World's Fair, would become instant nostalgia.

Maybe it was a function of all the European refugees living among them, or seeing the tools of war pouring out of New York's factories and passing through their docks. Maybe it was living in the media capital of the country, with the city's eight dailies conveying one fresh horror after another from Europe or Africa or Asia. But for whatever reason, New Yorkers seemed to grasp more than other Americans what a rare, fleeting time this was, and tried to hold on to any remnant of normal life for as long as they could. The city's three ball teams would finish 1-2-3 in major-league attendance in 1941, as if their fans were savoring them all, even the stumbling, fifth-place Giants up in the Polo Grounds.

Yet no one seized this last, haunted summer with both hands the way that the fans of the Brooklyn Dodgers did. A club-record 1.2 million came out to Ebbets Field, over a quarter million more than the second-highest draw, at Yankee Stadium, and the most fans *any* New York team had drawn since the Yanks in 1920–21, Babe Ruth's first two years in New York. But they did more than just show up. They made baseball in Brooklyn a spontaneous communal enterprise, such as it had never been before around any New York sports team and would not be again until the rise of the Mets.

None of it was staged; none of it was orchestrated. None of it had to be. The Dodgers in those days lived among the fans, in the shady streets of Brooklyn, to an extent unheard of today. The fans in turn treated them as their friends and neighbors—particularly when they began to win. They would throw days for them, feed them at local restaurants, bring birthday cakes to their clubhouse, and toss little vials of holy water and religious medals down to them from the stands. The players in turn would freely sign autographs, wave to and chat with their admirers before games, and discuss strategy afterward, even thrill their kids by taking them along to dinner sometimes.

"And in the evenings, thousands of fans, literally, would walk across Prospect Park to the night games, past the Swan Lake and the Zoo and out onto Flatbush Avenue, joined together by this odd faith," Pete Hamill would write of this time. "They were *part* of an experience larger than themselves." Ebbets Field had become, wrote Dave Anderson of the *Times,* "a palace forever."

The Dodgers were of their fans, and with them, not superstars making incalculable amounts of money. They were "Dem Bums," a loving caricature created by the newspaper cartoonist Willard Mullin at the *New York World-Telegram* (or was it first Leo O'Mealia, competing cartoonist at the *Daily News*?), who heard the cabbies and the bookies and the vendors around Ebbets Field asking how "dem bums were doin' " and drew up a full-blown, happy-go-lucky hobo with unshaven face, cigar stub, the ragged remnants of a suit, and maybe three teeth below his bulbous nose.

It was the face of a ragged time, and it stuck, picked up by a quintet of fans who dressed as hoboes themselves and lugged instruments into Ebbets Field. There they played "Three Blind Mice" when the umps missed a call, played "The Worms Crawl In, the Worms Crawl Out," when the visiting team changed pitchers; danced and played ragtime throughout the stands and on the roof of the dugout as "The Dodgers Sym-Phony."

There were so many characters. Dodgers home games became three-ring circuses, with the fans at least two rings of the entertainment. They seem to have started some of the game's most enduring traditions. It was a member of the Sym-Phony who is supposed to have first played a cavalry charge on his trumpet, evoking a roar of "Charge!" from the fans. After each home run, the sponsor Old Gold would slide a pack of cigarettes down the screen over the stands behind home plate. As it came down, the Dodgers' fans made a collective "Woooo!" sound—one that all fans would eventually make about all foul balls rolling down the backstop screen.

They snorted at the malapropisms of the public-address announcer Tex Rickards, who used to advise them, "A little boy has been found lost," and ask, "Will the fans along the outfield railing please remove their clothes." They tapped their feet—beginning in 1942—to the organ music of Gladys Gooding, discovered by MacPhail at Madison Square Garden, and later the answer to that New York trivia staple, "Who was the one person to play for the Dodgers, the Rangers, and the Knicks?"

The most devoted fans were almost as memorable as the players—often more so. Jack Pierce, a restaurateur by the St. George Hotel, who would always buy three seats: one for himself, one for a pile of balloons, and one for the bartender from his restaurant, whose job was to spend all game blowing up the balloons—at least until Pierce switched to a helium canister, which took over the third seat. The balloons all had a message, as did the cards Pierce would pass out to anyone who took them. It was "Cookie for President. Always good in the clutch." Pierce's extended, neurotic cry of "Loooookie, loooookie, loooookie! Here comes Cooookie!" resounded throughout the small park.

Out in the centerfield bleachers was the immortal Hilda Chester. The stereotype of a working-class Brooklyn housewife, Hilda was a large, cheerful woman with a shapeless, flower-print dress, a perpetually red face, and a mane of limp gray hair. She claimed to have been a softball star as a girl who dreamed of making the big leagues. The closest she came was working as a peanut sacker at Ebbets Field, shoveling the peanuts out of their fifty-pound sacks and into individual bags for the vendors. Afterward, she would sit in the stands and yell for the Dodgers, and if the Dodgers weren't at home, she would go to the track.

In the late 1930s, Hilda suffered a heart attack, and when her doctors advised her not to yell, she took to banging on a frying pan with a ladle and occasionally leading conga lines through the stands. Dodgers players, apparently driven to distraction, presented her with what would become her trademark cowbell instead, and after she suffered another heart attack in 1941, they visited her in the hospital, led by Durocher. Hilda, who would live for only another forty years, became a staunch fan of the manager, even trying to perjure herself on his behalf, after Leo hit another fan with a set of brass knuckles.

"This man called me a cocksucker, and Leo came to my defense," Hilda told the court. At the ballpark, she was slightly more demure.

"Ain't it t'rillin'?" she liked to say. "Home was never like dis, mac."

It sure wasn't. But the Dodgers still could not shake the Cardinals, who took over first place by two percentage points at the end of August. St. Louis seemed indomitable. When the hustling right fielder Enos "Country" Slaughter broke a collarbone chasing down a fly, the Cardinals simply reached down into their seemingly limitless collection of talent on the farm and pulled up an amiable twenty-year-old whippet of a hitter from Pennsylvania named Stan Musial. Stan the Man, as his reluctant admirers in Brooklyn would dub him, went two for four in his very first game and hit .426 down the stretch.

56

The Streak

How could the Dodgers prevail against such an organization? And even if they did manage to beat out the Cardinals, they would still have to face the Yankees, back at the top of their game after faltering in 1940 when seventy-two-year-old Ed Barrow, in a rare error of judgment, failed to bring up his twenty-cent beauty, Phil Rizzuto, to replace a declining Frankie Crosetti. Little Phil made the team in 1941, hitting .307 and forming one of the greatest double-play combinations ever seen with the acrobatic Flash Gordon at second. DiMaggio, Charlie Keller, and Tommy Henrich became the first outfield ever in which every man hit thirty or more home runs, and the typically deep if unspectacular pitching staff dominated the American League.

The Yankees' season, though, was defined by DiMaggio's hitting streak, the crowning glory of "the Dage's" career. In an almost supernatural passing of the guard, the streak coincided with Lou Gehrig's death, but Joe's record would outlast and outstrip even Gehrig's. It meant not just appearing but delivering in every single game, without fail.

The day that Gehrig died, DiMaggio hit a single and a double off Bob Feller as the Yanks broke up Feller's streak of thirty-one consecutive scoreless innings (DiMaggio was, by Feller's own admission, "the only righthanded batter who could hit me with any consistency." He batted .344 lifetime against Rapid Robert; the left-handed Ted Williams hit only .270 against him). DiMaggio's own streak of getting at least one hit in every game had reached nineteen games in a row by this time. New York sportswriters began to take notice as he approached, then broke, Roger Peckinpaugh's club record of hitting in twenty-nine straight games. This he did as well against Feller, with a double that ruined Robert's eight-game winning streak before forty-four thousand fans at the stadium. (Joe was the only batter who wouldn't give in to him, wouldn't back away from Feller's hundred-mile-per-hour fastball or terrifying curve.)

As DiMaggio moved past thirty games, the whole country began to indulge itself with this foolish thing, the streak moving from the sports page to the front page even as the war news turned from bad to awful. Before June 1941 was out, Hitler had flung 4.5 million Axis troops against 3.2 million Soviet soldiers along a nineteen-hundred-mile front, making war on a scale never seen before in human existence. The sheer numbers were incomprehensible; what it meant for the world of tomorrow all but overwhelming.

For many Americans, helpless before the sight of such colossal slaughter, baseball—and the streak—were what they preferred to talk about when the day was over. A debate was even stirred—a wonderfully frivolous, inconsequential debate—when DiMaggio's skein had to pause for the All-Star Game on July 8, at Detroit's Briggs Stadium: Should it count, too? Not quite an argument over whether the United States should intervene in a conflict between the world's leading totalitarian powers. In any case, Joe hit a double, putting the whole question to rest. In the ninth inning, he used his considerable speed to just beat out a relay throw to first on what seemed to be a sure double play, keeping the game alive. Ted Williams then stepped up, hit a three-run homer to win the contest, and loped gleefully around the bases.

What a world. What a world away from the "bloodlands" of eastern Europe.

In Brooklyn, some people wanted to have another debate, to invite Charles Lindbergh and his troupe of traveling isolationists, "America First," to rally at Ebbets Field, just as they were doing all over the country. They hadn't counted on Larry MacPhail, the man who stole the kaiser's ashtray. William T. Leonard, head of the Brooklyn America First Committee, complained publicly that MacPhail had "applied unseemly terms to such outstanding Americans as Colonel Lindbergh, Senator Wheeler, Senator Nye, and to the entire membership of the America First Committee."

MacPhail promised to apologize at a future date: "Yes, indeed. Right on the steps of Borough Hall in the year 1999, if the America First Committee is still in the National League."

Ebbets Field remained unsullied by appeasement. Meanwhile, DiMaggio suffered in silence, his stomach churning even as his roommate, Lefty Gomez, cracked to the writers, "You could hang him on a coat hanger in the closet and he'd fall asleep." Joe holed up in his hotel rooms, trying to get lost in the *Superman* comics that constituted much of his reading matter. He was Superman himself now, the writers taking "El Goofo" at his word and describing Joe as "probably the least excited guy in America" and "cool as a Good Humor man in Alaska."

The inevitable disparagers were already out and about. They would never really stop. Ty Cobb, while describing DiMaggio as "wonderful," sniffed that *he* had hit in forty straight games back in the old dead-ball era, and added, "When a team's leading hitter is after a batting streak record, I don't care how good a competitor he is, he's thinking about himself more than usual." Whitlow Wyatt, over in Brooklyn, apparently laboring under the impression that the likes of Lefty Grove and Bob Feller were cream puffs, scoffed, "In our league he would have to do most of his hitting from a sitting position." On and on it would go, for years to come, with various objections popping up on one sports page or blog after another, even down to *The Nation* magazine—*The Nation*!—on the fiftieth anniversary of the streak. "Debunkings" made by individuals complaining about this scorer's call, or what that pitcher had thrown, and always about games that the writers themselves had never seen and that were never recorded on film.

DiMaggio managed to face down the player-haters and keep hitting. One Johnny Babich, an old rival from the PCL, boasted that if he got the Dago out once, he would walk him every other time up, public uproar be damned. He tried—and Joe leaned across the plate, flicked his bat out at a ball far off the plate, and lined it back between Babich's legs, nearly gelding the pitcher.

"Babich was white as a sheet," DiMaggio noted with satisfaction as he pulled in to second standing up.

Many more rooted for him to go on, coming out to see the Yankees in Washington, in Cleveland, in St. Louis in numbers greater than had shown up all summer. Before the year was over, Les Brown and His Band of Renown—no minor novelty act, but a big band headliner—had recorded the carefree, swinging "Joltin' Joe DiMaggio." Lou Gehrig, the hero dying young, might have his movie (already under the cameras), but Joe had his song, capturing perfectly the defiant insouciance of a country staring down the gun: "He started baseball's famous streak / That kept us all aglow . . ."

The streak went on, but to what end? What *was* the longest hitting streak ever?

First the scribes dug out George Sisler's mark of forty-one consecutive games, set almost twenty years earlier and the most by any player since 1900. Joe tied it with a single in the first game of a doubleheader, played down in Washington's Griffith Stadium in hundred-degree heat. Then, calamity: when he came back out for the second game, he discovered that his dark "ball bat"—the bat he had been using throughout the streak, as opposed to batting practice—was gone, stolen right from the Yankees' bat rack, in the sort of theft that wasn't supposed to happen in America in 1941. After hitting the ball hard but making out in his first at bat, he was heard to mutter, "If that'd been my ball bat, it would have been in there."

Finally utilizing a similar bat reclaimed from Tommy Henrich, he singled to break the record. The ball bat would eventually be returned by the thief, who supposedly hailed from somewhere in New Jersey. Rumors flew about how that happened. Richard Ben Cramer hints darkly that the recovery was brought about by "a gofer for Newark's First Ward rackets boss." Whatever. DiMaggio took it back and gave up the bat he had borrowed from Henrich to be raffled off for $1,678 to the USO, which was already caring for America's rapidly growing peacetime army.

Meanwhile, the writers had dug up a new record: Wee Willie Keeler's forty-four-game mark, achieved in 1897.

"Hell, I thought they made it up," Joe's younger brother, Dom, already starring in the majors with the Red Sox, remembered. "Well, maybe Joe would break that one, too."

He did—and then someone discovered that Keeler had hit in the last game of *1896,* for *forty-five* straight games. A consecutive hitting streak with a whole offseason in between? Really? No matter. Joe swung right through, to forty-six, forty-seven, forty-eight, all the way up to the night of July 17 in Cleveland. That same day, a new offensive saw nine million men fighting on the Russian front. In Cleveland, a mere 67,468 came out to watch the great DiMaggio stopped at fifty-six consecutive games by a pair of capable but unremarkable pitchers, Al Smith and Jim Bagby, and a superb third baseman, Ken Keltner, who played deep behind the bag and made a couple of fine stops on tough ground balls.

The streak was over at last, and Joe promptly started another one the next night, banging a single and a double against Feller, his whipping boy, going on to hit in 16 more consecutive games, for seventy-two out of seventy-three. Before the season was out, he would have hits in 114 of the 139 games he played, but it was the streak that put him over the top as an American icon, and the Yankees over the top in the AL pennant race.

Joe hit .408 during those fifty-six games, his average no lower than .300 against every American League team (and as high as .524 against the Athletics). Again, his bat control was otherworldly for a power hitter. He belted fifteen home runs, totaled thirty-four extra-base hits, and drew twenty-one walks, for the duration of the streak, while striking out only five times. The Yankees compiled a record of 41-13 (with two suspended games), and a crescendo of 20-2 that put the pennant race out of doubt. The team would go on to clinch the American League flag on September 4, just three days after Labor Day—the earliest any pennant or division title had ever been decided, the earliest it ever *has* been decided to this day.

57

Brooklyn's Own DiMaggio

As Hilda Chester would say, "Eacha heart out, ya bum." Joltin' Joe DiMaggio wasn't keeping *Brooklyn* all aglow. Brooklyn, in 1941, had its own DiMaggio.

His name was Pete Reiser, and he would come to embody all of the wistfulness, all of the lost promise of that time just before the war, the world of tomorrow that never came. Never before had two such young, exhilarating talents, both at the top of their game, played at the same time and the same position in New York. Never would they again—save for when those *three* legends, Mantle and Mays and Snider, took the field together ten years later.

Reiser, like DiMaggio, *looked* like the ideal of a ballplayer. He had Joe's basic body type if a little smaller: a loose, lanky five eleven and 185 pounds. Branch Rickey had spotted him first, of course. No ballplayer from the St. Louis area who looked that good was going to be signed by anyone else. Then, in 1938, Judge Landis made another of his random assaults on Mr. Rickey's farm system, declaring that some hundred Cardinals farmhands were free agents, eligible to be signed by any club. Reiser was the only one Rickey cared about. He called in a favor from MacPhail to try to hide him, getting the Dodgers to sign the kid for just $100 until the day he might be quietly shuffled back to the Cards in another deal. But it would never be possible to hide Pistol Pete Reiser under a bushel.

He was, thought Leo Durocher, "another Ty Cobb." Others would compare his natural ability only to that of Mantle and rank him even above DiMaggio. Like Joe, he was a five-tool player, able to catch, throw, hit for power, hit for average, and run fast enough to steal home a record seven times in one season. Like DiMaggio, he had an unaffected charisma, in this case a handsome midwestern look, with his big ears and infectious grin, and a rare dash and verve on the playing field. Unlike the more fluid, contained DiMaggio, he seemed to do everything with a raw, manic energy.

"He smoked a lot of cigarettes—he was a chain smoker—and he drank a lot of Cokes," recalled his roommate, Pee Wee Reese. "He played hard—*damn,* he played hard. If he hit the ball back to the pitcher, he'd run down the first base line just as hard as he did when he got a base hit. He ran out to centerfield like that, and he ran in the same way. No one hustled any more than Pete Reiser did."

The abandon with which he played would lead to tragedy, but in the spring of 1940, Reiser was still a twenty-one-year-old wunderkind out of nowhere—reminiscent of the protagonist in *The Kid from Tomkinsville,* the famous John R. Tunis boys' story published the same year, when art still imitated baseball. MacPhail—still hoping to hide him—ordered Durocher not to play young Pete, but this only led to Leo's aforementioned slugging of his boss. In the end, Rickey was forced to accept defeat and a settlement from the Dodgers, rumored to be as high as $250,000. Reiser was called up later that same season, to play sensationally at short, third, and the outfield—any position he put his hand to.

By the 1941 season, he had settled into centerfield, where he simply dazzled, smashing hits all over the oversized pinball machine that was the Ebbets Field outfield. Before the year was over, he had accumulated seventy extra-base hits, leading the league in runs scored, doubles, triples, and total bases, and slugging and batting average—the first rookie ever to lead the NL in batting. He might not have possessed quite the power or the plate discipline that DiMaggio had, nor quite the same skill in centerfield, but then he was younger, just twenty-two years old in 1941.

"He was a heck of an athlete," Reese remembered. "He wasn't the most graceful player you ever saw. All he could do was catch the ball—and hit and run. I always had a great deal of admiration for Musial, who I thought was one of the top players of my time or any time, but I think Pete would have been right there."

He was slowed only when the Phillies' Ike Pearson nailed him in the back of the head in the season opener, a beaning that sent him to the hospital. It was a foreshadowing, but for the time being Pete was saved from worse damage by the stiff plastic cap inserts that MacPhail, unable to halt Leo's beanball wars, had forced every Dodger to wear.

Reiser was back within the week, delighting fans again with his all-out play. He would lead the league in being hit by pitches that first year. More perilously still, he would run into walls with abandon, crash into concrete and wire fences as if he weren't even aware they were there. Somehow, he always seemed to bounce back—invincible, a Superman like DiMaggio. He would be the emblem of this stolen season, as much as the Dage or Williams, or Bob Feller, this young man of limitless talent, streaking heedlessly across a darkened field, toward a looming, faceless danger.

58

The Wait for Next Year Begins

Hard as the Cards charged, Dem Bums would not fold. Setting out for a long western swing in a sparkling-new chrome-and-aluminum train on the Pennsylvania Railroad—another MacPhail feature, complete with individual compartments for each player, how the managing board must have raged!—they played like champions. Volatile, heavy-drinking Johnny Allen, the former Yankees' phenom, threw fifteen shutout innings at Cincinnati, and the Dodgers finally broke through in the top of the seventeenth with five runs—led by a Reiser home run. In St. Louis, they took two of three, with Whitlow Wyatt beating the Cards' ace Mort Cooper, 1–0—thanks to a little help from Leo and his bench jockeys.

"We won that series because we rode the younger St. Louis players into the jitters," crowed Dixie Walker.

Back in Philadelphia, with a chance to clinch a tie for the pennant, the Dodgers lured five thousand fans down from Brooklyn, including Leo's show business friends George Raft and Betty Grable, for a doubleheader in Shibe Park. The Brooklyn fans even sat on the Dodgers' bench, where they talked with Durocher before the game.

Brooklyn only split a doubleheader in Philly, but hundreds of the faithful followed them in nine chartered airplanes up to Boston. There, they watched the Bums win their first pennant in twenty-one years. Wyatt pitched his seventh shutout of the season. Pete Reiser hit a home run—again. Billy Herman made a great catch. On the train home, they staged the most raucous team celebration in New York baseball history until the Mets nearly tore their plane apart, coming back from Houston after winning the National League pennant in 1986.

"Tony Martin, the movie guy, got up to make a speech, and somebody hit him smack in the face with a hot steak," Durocher recalled. "The gang yelled, 'Sit down, ya bum, this isn't your party,' and from then on it was a riot."

The Dodgers downed $1,400 worth of booze, cut off each other's ties, and literally tore the shirts off each other's backs as their fancy new train sped toward New York. Their fans were racing up by subway to greet them, a veritable invasion of Manhattan by Brooklyn, thousands pouring into Grand Central to hail their conquering heroes. MacPhail, accompanied by Rickey, who happened to be in town, wanted to join the grand entrance. He planned to board the train at its 125th Street stop in Harlem, but Leo Durocher claimed never to have got his wire. Instead, saying he wanted to keep all his players on board to greet their fans, Durocher ordered their special train to skip the 125th Street station. It zipped past an astonished MacPhail on the platform, humiliating him in front of Rickey, and went directly to the tumultuous reception waiting at Forty-Second Street.

The foul-up enraged MacPhail and cost Durocher his job again—for a night. But three days later the Dodgers won their hundredth game of the season at Ebbets Field, then celebrated their whole miraculous season with a giddy parade from Grand Army Plaza to Brooklyn's Borough Hall. The fans dodged around the mounted police and threw themselves into the convertibles carrying their heroes.

"It was parade, carnival and mardi gras rolled up in one," wrote *The New York Times,* "unmatched in Brooklyn's history for sheer spontaneous madness."

Not a one of those fans could have imagined Brooklyn losing the World Series against the *Yankees,* in what would now—coming on top of the first Carriage Series, the Streetcar Series, the One-Park Series, and the Subway Series—be the very first *All Outer-Borough* Subway Series.

The Yanks, it was true, had gone an incredible 28-3 in World Series games dating back to 1927, winning their last seven straight series. But the Dodgers and Durocher didn't look in the least intimidated. In fact, they seem to have gotten inside Yankee heads.

"We just didn't want to lose to Durocher," remembered Tommy Henrich. "He was the kind of guy who would run over you to win."

The Dodgers lost a close series opener, 3–2, in Yankee Stadium, but came back to take the second game by the same score, breaking the Yankees' ten-game winning streak in the World Series. The catcher Mickey Owen made sure to plow into Phil Rizzuto while trying to break up a double play, outraging the lordly Yankees.

"He must have gone ten feet out of his way to smack Phil down," seethed DiMaggio. "He tried to cut Phil down. He played dirty ball," protested the pitcher Atley "Swampy" Donald.

Eacha heart out. Now the series moved down the East River to Brooklyn, where anything might happen—and it did.

Before the borough's first World Series game in more than two decades even began, Billy Herman took a vicious cut at a batting practice pitch and all but disabled himself, tearing a rib-cage muscle. Once play did get under way, Fat Freddie Fitzsimmons, the old Giant who had won six games for Brooklyn down the stretch, matched the Yanks' Marius Russo zero for zero, for seven innings. Then the Brooklyn-born Russo—who had played ball at Brooklyn College and LIU, for crying out loud!—Russo the Brooklynite, Russo the pitcher who compiled a lifetime average of .213 as a hitter, whacked a drive off Fat Freddie, an outstanding fielder, that broke his kneecap. Fitzsimmons was done for the series, and the Yanks managed to eke out two runs off Hugh Casey in the eighth and hold on for a 2–1 win—as Russo pitched a complete game.

If this seemed like cosmic bad luck, the following day, October 5, 1941, would live in infamy for Brooklyn fans. The Brooks came back from a 3–0 deficit and held a 4–3 lead going into the ninth, thanks to a two-run homer Pete Reiser belted over the right-field scoreboard. Hugh Casey, pitching heroically, was throwing his fifth inning of shutout relief and "making a hollow mockery of the vaunted Yankee power," as a young columnist for the *Philadelphia Record* named Red Smith wrote. (Just how many talented redheads *were* there operating in Brooklyn at this moment?)

After retiring the first two hitters in the inning, Casey might have decided he needed a little something extra. He worked the count to 3-2 on the Yankees' Old Reliable, Tommy Henrich, then threw a pay-off pitch that will forever be a matter of contention.

"It was a little wet slider," thought Pee Wee Reese out at short-stop that day. The catcher Mickey Owen disagreed, maintaining later, "Hugh never threw a spitball in his life because he didn't have to," claiming the pitch was his patented "big overhand jug handle" of a curve.

Henrich called it simply "a very good high curve. . . . It was a beauty, one of the best and craziest curveballs I've ever seen. It was definitely not a spitter, as some people have claimed. I thought it was going to be a strike, so I started my swing. And then that pitch broke sharply down. I tried to hold up, but it was too late. I'd committed myself. The funny thing is even in that instant, while I was swinging, I thought to myself that if I'm having this much trouble with the pitch, maybe Mickey Owen is, too. So I looked around behind me after I missed the ball"—a memory confirmed by an AP photo of the play, Henrich glancing over his shoulder even as he is already sprinting to first, the bat still in his hand. Owen is throwing back his mask, running for the ball, all the split-second magic of baseball captured in that one picture.

Owen didn't struggle with many pitches. That season he had set a National League record for catchers by handling 476 consecutive chances without committing an error. But now Casey's curve, wet or dry, broke sharply down to the right, ticking off his glove as it rolled toward the backstop. Mickey Owen, as the *Herald Tribune* would recount, did "a vivid imitation of a man changing a tire . . . grabbing for monkey wrenches, screwdrivers, inner tubes and a jack and he couldn't find any of them."

"I saw that little white jackrabbit bouncing and I said, 'Let's go,'" Henrich would remember. "It rolled all the way to the fence. I could have walked down to first."

As it was, he reached the bag as the cops and some delirious Brooklyn fans started to rush the field around him. Once again, just as when the Atlantics ended the Red Stockings' famous winning streak, just as happened in the infamous Merkle debacle of 1908, a critical New York game would not be over even when it was over, the action dissolving into chaos, with everyone coming out of the stands to take part. It was an instant legend. Mighty Casey had thrown wild, and Old Reliable was a-huggin' first.

"Give those Yankees a reprieve and they climb right out of the electric chair and execute the warden," wrote New York's lefty, advertising-free daily, *PM.*

"The minute that happened, as soon as Owen dropped the ball, you knew somehow the Yankees were going to win the game," remembered Roger Angell, then a young Harvard student down from Cambridge for the game. Pee Wee Reese felt much the same way out at shortstop: "We had it in our pocket, and I'm saying, 'It sure looks as if we're going to get our ass beat.' And we sure did."

The end wasn't inevitable. Casey still only needed one more out, and the Dodgers were playing at home. But the Flock seemed flummoxed, and no one more than Durocher, who failed to go out to the mound and give both his pitcher and his catcher a few minutes to recover themselves: "I sat on my ass and didn't do anything."

Left to his own devices, Casey gave up a single to DiMaggio, then fooled King Kong Keller with two more pitches, making him swing awkwardly. Keller had sprained an ankle so badly before the series that he had to wear a cast up over his ankle, but he later explained how he had managed to round into playing shape: "I ripped the cast off."

Now he pulled the next pitch from Casey off the chain-link fence in right, the ball hanging up there for an agonizing extra few seconds, dropping at last to the concave concrete wall beneath it and rolling down so slowly that not only Henrich but DiMaggio had time to steam around the bases, the Dage crossing home with a slide so fierce Henrich claimed it carried him six feet past the plate. A walk and another double by Joe Gordon scored two insurance runs, and Johnny Murphy put the Dodgers down in order in the bottom of the ninth, to secure a stunning, 7–4 victory.

"I thought, 'Why, God, why?' Why had God done it to us and given it to them? Why?" wailed the eleven-year-old Brooklyn fan Joel Oppenheimer, walking through Yonkers that afternoon while he listened to Red Barber describe the game. (Eleven-year-old Joel was a model of stoicism compared with the Dodgers' owner, Larry MacPhail, who wept openly at the press room bar.)

The next day Ernie "Tiny" Bonham shut down the Dodgers on four hits, to complete a sweep of all three games in Brooklyn and clinch the series. Afterward the Yankees, having regained their swagger, evinced a spectacular lack of charity toward the beleaguered Owen.

"As long as there had to be a goat, I'm glad it was him," insisted an unforgiving DiMaggio. "We are not a bit sorry for him."

"Sure it was my fault. The ball was a low curve that broke down. It hit the edge of my glove and glanced off, but I should have had him out anyway," Owen acknowledged freely, before trying to get in one last dig at the boys from the Bronx: "But who ever said those Yanks were such great sluggers? They're the real bums in this Series, with that great reputation of theirs."

Unfortunately for Owen, history would decide otherwise. But when all of Brooklyn had finished crying, the fans saw no reason not to keep their heads up. After all, they still had a terrific team, the headiest manager in the game, and a genius running the club. For the first time, a headline in the *Brooklyn Eagle* summed up their attitude: WAIT 'TIL NEXT YEAR!

59

Hail and Farewell

Larry MacPhail managed to pull himself together after his initial crying jag over Owen's flub, and once the game was over, he went down to the locker room to console his catcher. Soon after the series ended, though, it was rumored that he was still so mad at his club that he had offered to swap rosters with the perennially cellar-dwelling

St. Louis Browns, if the Browns' owner, Don Barnes, would throw in $3–$4 million.

The story was probably apocryphal, though another "exchange" between the Dodgers and the Browns almost *did* take place after the 1941 season.

Barnes had persuaded Phil Wrigley to sell the Cubs' minor-league Los Angeles Angels franchise to him for $1 million. It wasn't so much the team Barnes was interested in as the territory. That winter he went to baseball's annual meetings with a plan to move his woebegone Browns to Southern California. This, too, might have seemed implausible in the days before jet planes, but Barnes claimed that existing airline schedules would make it possible.

The Los Angeles *Browns*? Could it have happened? Barnes claimed to have L.A. backers lined up who would guarantee to make good any losses if attendance didn't reach 500,000. The possibilities are intriguing. Such a move might well have kept Dem Bums from leaving Brooklyn sixteen years later. But alas for Barnes, alas for Brooklyn, the winter meeting where he broached the plan took place on December 8. With all the confusion and uncertainty after the attack on Pearl Harbor, the big move would be tabled.

MacPhail, meanwhile, went on fretting and fuming throughout the 1942 season, although it was hard to understand what was bothering him. The war had arrived, but by the spring, even with the draft, just forty-one American League players and twenty National Leaguers had entered military service. (Hank Greenberg, having just completed his year's commitment to the draft, went back and enlisted the day after Pearl Harbor.)

Save for Cookie Lavagetto at third, replaced capably by the veteran Arky Vaughan, the Dodgers were able to field the same lineup as they had in 1941, and they got off to an even better start. Pete Reiser took up where he had left off, hitting .364 by mid-July, running as wild as ever on the bases and in centerfield. The team built up a hefty lead on the Cardinals, but MacPhail remained unsatisfied, harassing Durocher more harshly than ever about his players' drinking and gambling, leading to new fights and firings and tearful outbursts. After yet another win, MacPhail called a team meeting and warned his players,

"I'm telling you boys, the Cardinals are going to beat you out if you're not careful. You guys are getting lackadaisical, you think you have it clinched, and before you know it, they are going to beat you out."

Afterward, this prediction would be regarded as the vision of a prophet, though more likely it was the paranoia of a drunk. For all their carousing, there is no evidence that the Dodgers got lackadaisical at all, nor did they stop winning. But then, on July 19, in a game in St. Louis's Sportsman's Park, what everyone had been dreading occurred. It was the second game of a doubleheader in which the Cards had taken the opener, a back-and-forth contest in which Brooklyn led early, fell behind by 6–2, then tied the game in the fifth. It was still 6–6 into the bottom of the eleventh inning, when Country Slaughter hit a tremendous drive into deep centerfield off Johnny Allen. Pistol Pete Reiser took off after it like a greyhound, even grazing the flagpole in center as he ran. He went on undeterred, actually sticking out his glove and making what would have been a fantastic, over-the-shoulder catch. Then he hit the concrete wall.

"It felt like a hand grenade went off inside my head," he would say.

The play was so traumatic, lingered so heavily in the minds of many Dodgers fans that years later they remembered "seeing it" in Brooklyn, at night—even though there was no flagpole on the field in Ebbets. While the ball fell out of Reiser's glove and Slaughter raced around the bases for a game-ending, inside-the-park home run, Pete lay unconscious on the field. He was able to eventually walk back to the clubhouse, but collapsed again and was rushed to the hospital. There he was told that he had a fractured skull and concussion and that his season was over.

It should have been. Instead, Pete Reiser was betrayed by two older men of authority, who knew better but whose only thought was to win more ball games. Larry MacPhail concluded that Reiser's injury was somehow another plot by Branch Rickey and that he was all right to play. Three days after hitting the wall, Pistol Pete was back in uniform, even though he was suffering from double vision and horrible head pains. Leo Durocher assured his doctor that Reiser would be in the dugout only to lend moral support and to serve as a decoy. But six days after fracturing his skull—*less than a week*—Reiser was back in the starting lineup. Incredibly, he even continued to excel at the plate, banging out ten hits in his first seven games back, playing entire doubleheaders, and stealing bases. The Dodgers upped their lead to ten games.

Even in the rough-edged game of the time, this was madness.

Reiser, feeling dizzy again, had to miss eight days in early August, then another week near the end of the month. The Dodgers' doctors told Durocher and MacPhail once more that Reiser should not play again that season. It didn't matter. The Cardinals were making another late-season push, and the Bums had to have their best player out there—even if he was no longer their best player. Reiser hit only .221 for the rest of the year. His double vision continued, and he looked wobbly in the field, making five errors, but it didn't matter. A pennant race was on.

"I have never, ever blamed Leo for keeping me in there," Reiser would later tell Peter Golenbock. "I blame myself. He wanted to win so badly it hurt, and I wanted to win so bad it hurt."

As usual, it hurt someone else much worse than Leo. Reiser would finish sixth in the MVP voting in 1942, another indication of how good he was—and would never be again. He would play for another seven seasons and show flashes of his old brilliance, leading the league in stolen bases again in 1946. Yet his recklessness more and more looked like an effort to compensate for his lost talent. On nine different occasions Pistol Pete would be carried from the field on a stretcher, until even he began to joke about it. Asked by a radio reporter one spring, "Where do you think you'll finish the season?" Reiser replied, "In Peck Memorial Hospital."

It was no joke. Neither Durocher nor MacPhail took the care they should have to protect their charge. Nor did the Dodgers' doctors, nor did the beat writers bother to look closely into Reiser's desperate condition. Only Branch Rickey, watching from afar, found the appropriate outrage for what he felt Larry MacPhail, above all, had let happen to his greatest find: "That character should never have been entrusted with something that fine."

This time, without Pistol Pete, when the Dodgers' streamlined "Victory Special" took its last western swing, the team lost three of four to the Cards, including a 2–1 loss in fourteen innings and a 1–0 loss in ten. The Dodgers still didn't fold, going 20-5 in September 1942 and setting a record for wins by a second-place team with 104. But the Cardinals, who would prove to be one of the greatest teams ever assembled, took the pennant by two games.

The Yankees had suffered a few puzzling bumps along the road themselves in 1942, mostly when Joe DiMaggio experienced the most extended slump of his career, laboring along at .255 well into the season. His marriage was dissolving, and he was anxious and distracted about whether he would have to go into the military for the duration. But Yankees fans helped by booing him lustily at every turn, and by year's end he was back among the league leaders in almost every hitting category. Joe Gordon played brilliantly at second and won the MVP award, Charlie Keller continued to star, and the Yanks' deep pitching dominated the AL once more. The team won 103 games and coasted to its sixth pennant in seven years.

Taking on the Cards in the World Series, it looked as if they would romp to another world championship. In game one, they jumped off to a 7–0 lead, and thirty-seven-year-old Red Ruffing came within four outs of a no-hitter. Then he faltered, giving up four runs in the ninth, leaving Spud Chandler to retire Musial with the bases loaded for the final out. De-jittered, the Cards proceeded to outhustle, outpitch, and outhit the Yankees for four close wins in a row. There would be no more choruses of "Roll Out the Barrel" this year; in the stunned and silent Yankees' dressing room afterward, Joe McCarthy snarled at the writers, "What's the matter? . . . What do we have to do, win all the time?"

It was not so much that the Yankees had lost as that the Cardinals had beaten them. The 1942 Cards were the culmination of more than twenty years of work by Branch Rickey in St. Louis, combining another powerhouse lineup with a dominant pitching staff. The small-market, undercapitalized Cardinals had been built on a fraction of what it had cost the Yankees and, especially, the freewheeling MacPhail to build *their* contenders.

The lesson was not lost on the stockholders of the Brooklyn Dodgers, especially the board of the Brooklyn Trust Company. They were especially upset when MacPhail disobeyed their direct orders and paid $25,000 to acquire the journeyman pitcher Bobo Newsom as "pennant insurance" down the stretch. On September 24, 1942, the Dodgers' problem child suddenly announced that he was entering the

U.S. Army as a colonel. In his farewell press conference, MacPhail admitted his spendthrift ways, but took credit for the team's turnaround, claiming that he had managed to pay off most of the Dodgers' debts, put $300,000 in the bank, and sign a new radio contract for $150,000 a year. He concluded, "The future of the club is bright, even under wartime conditions." MacPhail was not wrong, even if he said so himself, but it must have galled him to learn a few weeks later that his replacement would be Branch Rickey.

60

The Cave of the Winds

"Luck is the residue of design."

It was one of his favorite aphorisms, and aphorisms seemed to flow as freely from Branch Rickey's mouth as cigar smoke. Surely, it was the strangest chance that brought Rickey back to New York in 1943, but then the city always did seem to draw the best, however unwillingly, to test themselves against it.

There was no more unlikely Brooklynite than Branch. The quintessential midwesterner, he had spent more than thirty years in St. Louis, trying to save first the poor Brownies, whom neither luck nor design could help, and then the Cardinals, with whom he had made a small fortune. But here he was, back in the big city he had left after 1907 as a sore-armed, washed-up catcher for the Highlanders, lecturing the local Rotary Club about Brooklyn pride.

"The Brooklynites resent Manhattan getting all the credit. They have a real pride in their own and refuse to become parasitical," he explained soon after his arrival. "When anything comes along distinctly Brooklyn, they rally behind it because it is an expression of themselves, even an entity as lowly as a baseball club. 'Poo on the

Giants they say,' and they are right. It is the pooling of support behind the team, by George, which makes it successful."

Poo on the Giants? An entity as lowly as a baseball club? And what did *Branch Rickey* know about "Brooklynites"?

Rickey was probably born delivering an after-dinner speech. This was a typical performance, full of bluster and piety, sly condescension and self-disparagement at the same time. The New York press was bemused, as it always would be by Rickey. His huge head, big, gnarled ex-catcher's hands, and potbelly—not to mention his pomposity—made him inherently amusing and not a little endearing, at least if you did not have to depend upon his largesse to put food on your table. He wore colorful, extra-wide bow ties custom-made for him at Brooks Brothers and Lord & Taylor, but that was his one concession to (a sort of) fashion. "Even his shoes looked rumpled," as Jonathan Eig would write, and he consumed his meals with so little care that his assistants joked, "Everything the boss eats looks good on him."

Where he had been called The Brain in St. Louis, in New York he would be dubbed the Mahatma, after Gandhi. Also, less flatteringly, the Great White Father, the Cave of the Winds (after a Coney Island ride), and "El Cheapo," by Jimmy Powers. There was truth in all of it. Rickey, as sportswriter Tom Meany put it, was "an incredible combination of Jesus Christ, Tammany Hall, and your father." Others joked that he was "a man of many facets—all turned on."

Rickey came from a poor but deeply religious Ohio country family, the son of a devout Methodist mother and the grandson of a one-eyed Civil War horse trader. Both personalities would reside quite happily together within Branch for his entire life. He would keep his promise to his mother never to go to the ballpark on Sunday. The remaining six days of the week he spent skinning the other general managers around the National League.

The first member of his family to go to college, Branch worked his way through school, and later law school, usually by coaching and teaching. In college, he excelled at football as well as baseball, loving the camaraderie and the collective effort of the sport. He could come off as little more than a collection of pieties and homilies, never swearing or drinking even if he was rarely seen outside a whirl of cigar smoke. This was certainly a part of him, but never *all* of him. Branch

Rickey was, more accurately, a George Babbitt with the mind of a Napoleon.

There was a drive in the man, a desire for recognition that once led him to write to his parents, "My greatest joy is not the paltry job . . . but the fact of being known by men of such standing and character that their commendation places me above the pull and push of the other fellow."

Throughout his adult life he would dabble in politics, in public causes from temperance to raising war bonds. He never seemed to sleep and read incessantly, keeping copies of Shakespeare, Plutarch, Boswell's biography of Johnson, and the Bible on prominent display in his office. He claimed to own every book on Lincoln ever written. He never could seem to shake the idea that baseball was below him, calling it "a sort of disgraceful profession," even after he had made the major leagues.

Once there, he lasted only two full seasons as a catcher—one of them a year with the Yankees né Highlanders, where a sore throwing arm led to his surrendering thirteen stolen bases in one game—briefly a major-league record—and forced his retirement as a player. A harrowing bout of tuberculosis that laid him up at Saranac Lake for a year only fed the flame of ambition within. Years later, during World War I, though already an established baseball executive and a father, he volunteered for the artillery in France—in good part to prove to himself that he had conquered the TB.

"I want to get out and do something—some one thing and bend every effort," he wrote soon after leaving the sanatorium. "I may fizzle about for a while, but if I get a good grip on some *one* thing—and have a purpose . . . I guess I'll do my best not to make God as ashamed of me as he has been these last few years."

To that end he put himself through Michigan's law school, and briefly tried to set up a practice out in Boise, Idaho, where he thought the mountain air would be good for his lungs. There, as he told it, his one and only client was an odious criminal who hadn't even asked for a lawyer: "I never knew a man could be so guilty of so many crimes." He gave in to his natural calling and after World War I became, successively, the manager, business manager, and general manager of a threadbare Cardinals team that had never won a pennant. Rickey put together a club that took six flags and four World Series in seventeen years, the only team in the majors that could regularly stand up to the Yankees. He did just about everything to reinvent the team, right down to personally designing its classic logo of two cardinals perched on a baseball bat. As a judge of talent, Branch Rickey was unequaled, always able to see what he couldn't do. As one St. Louis sportswriter conceded, no one was "as quick to see fine knee action in a runner, rhythm in a throwing arm, and timing at bat."

Rickey would find, develop, or trade for legions of outstanding ballplayers during his time in St. Louis: George Sisler, Urban Shocker, Rogers Hornsby, Frankie Frisch, Chick Hafey, Pepper Martin, Dizzy Dean, Jim Bottomley, Johnny Mize, and the whole, remarkable squad that had just bested Brooklyn *and* the Yankees. It wasn't luck. No one in the game labored as long as Branch Rickey. Working out of a small office decorated mostly with a rug he had brought from home, he crisscrossed the country incessantly by car and train, discovering player after player, often wiring ahead to have the hotel buy a shirt for him rather than stop and get one cleaned. He once took in eleven games over the course of two days and nights. After conceiving the idea of the farm system, he warred constantly with Judge Landis to keep the Cardinals' minor-league pyramid intact, building it up to an unequaled thirty-three teams by 1937. And he worked smart. As manager, Rickey devised any number of innovations for teaching players, from sliding pits to tethers that would keep them from overstriding. It was Rickey who came up with the system of scoring prospects on a numerical scale of 20 to 80 for pitching, fielding, running, hitting, and hitting for power—a system still used by major-league scouts to this day.

The triumph of Branch's brilliant young 1942 team marked the pinnacle of his success in St. Louis, but it was not enough. It's difficult to believe today that a Branch Rickey would not be considered an immovable icon, but in the 1940s all that mattered was his relationship with Singin' Sam Breadon, the Cardinals' prickly owner. Breadon, the son of an Irish immigrant, had left school in the fourth grade and worked his way up from the waterfront districts of Greenwich Village to a successful car dealership in St. Louis, where he liked to sing in barbershop quartets. Branch Rickey had made his franchise for him, but all the credit The Brain got rankled Breadon, and the deal Rickey had cut for himself rankled even more. Rickey was probably the highest-paid executive in the sport at $50,000 a year, but he also got 10 percent of all player transactions—much as George Weiss did with the Yankees.

In a lesser individual, this might have proved a fatal conflict of interest. With a baseball man of Rickey's integrity and acumen, it was a useful incentive. No other general manager has compiled such a long record of successful deals.

"There's only one way to get the best of that Rickey," Casey Stengel advised. "You let him talk for three hours on the strong and weak points of the players he wants to scoop. Then when Branch says, 'Is it a deal?' you snap 'No!' and walk out on him."

Yet when Rickey's contract came up for renewal after the 1942 season, Breadon told his general manager that the war made it impossible to justify his salary. He calculated that he had enough Rickey talent accumulated to last him for years to come, and that The Brain's ability would be wasted while most of the players were away at war. This was accurate enough for the short run. St. Louis would win three more pennants and two more World Series over the next four seasons—then endure an eighteen-year pennant drought.

Brooklyn, meanwhile, represented an opportunity for Rickey to work with his son, Branch Jr., who was already running the Dodgers' minor-league system. The club was reorganized again, with Branch Sr. putting down $82,000 to buy one-quarter of its stock. Another quarter remained in the hands of Jim Mulvey and Dearie Mulvey, the McKeever heirs. A third quarter was bought by John L. Smith, head of the Pfizer chemical company, flush with money from its production of the new wonder drug, penicillin. Smith was also a devout Christian who got along well with the pious Rickey.

The fourth quarter went to an unknown, a representative of the Brooklyn Trust Company who had been on the team's management board since 1933. Walter O'Malley was a rich man's son who had been educated as an engineer before getting his law degree at Fordham. A shrewd investor, he had made himself useful as the right-hand man to the president of the trust company, George V. McLaughlin. His ownership in the Dodgers was a reward for all his faithful service—a veritable gift, to be repaid out of future earnings. O'Malley said nothing at the press conference announcing the new arrangement and was widely thought by the writers to be no more than McLaughlin's eyes and ears.

For the time being at least, Rickey got to run the baseball end of the business without interference, and he went about it much as he always had—with one key twist. Where other teams were cutting way back on scouting and development, he *expanded* the Dodgers' recruiting budget, setting up tryout camps around the country, telling his most trusted scout, Clyde Sukeforth, "If we win the war, it will be worth it. If we lose the war, what difference does it make?"

"The other clubs dropped all but about five of their scouts," the Dodgers' front-office man Fresco Thompson claimed. "They figured there wasn't any sense in signing young players who would soon be drafted. Mr. Rickey said, 'We'll gamble. We'll sign every good young player we can get our hands on.' "

Rickey and the Dodgers got their hands on a sixteen-year-old outfielder from Compton, California, named Duke Snider, who the Dodgers' traveling secretary, Harold Parrott, claimed "was the first player who ever asked me for candy money." They picked up a hard-throwing pitcher off the NYU campus named Ralph Branca. They inked Carl Erskine, George Shuba, Gil Hodges, Clem Labine, and Rex Barney—a dynasty in the making. If most of these players were years away from playing in the majors or about to enter the armed forces, so much the better. Let Uncle Sam foot the bill for their upkeep until they were ready.

To make room for the kids—and save still more money—Rickey cleared the team's expensive, aging veterans from the roster. Dodgers fans watched their feisty, lovable team dissolve and were restive, especially when Jimmy Powers pressed the idea that "El Cheapo" was just doing it for the money. When Dolph Camilli was traded, Rickey needed a police escort home, and fans picketed Ebbets Field with signs reading, RICKEY THE WRECKER, GO BACK TO ST. LOUIS, YOU BUM, and—from the more literate side of Flatbush—LEAVE US HAVE MACPHAIL.

"In less than a year the new leadership has dismembered a magnificent baseball team and smothered its vitality," a fan wrote to *The*

New York Times. "With Branch Rickey still in power we may look for further mutilations."

"I could be tempted to join the howling fans, but the fact remains that whatever changes were made were calculated to help the club," Rickey replied with unwavering self-confidence. "I do not propose to deviate from such calculations."

The next generation was on the way. The trick was finding enough bodies to bridge the gap. The Mahatma's solution was a combination of veteran castoffs who could be had cheap, such as Augie Galan, Paul Waner, and Arky Vaughan, and those new kids who had not been drafted yet, including Branca, Clyde King, Vic Lombardi, Luis Olmo, Eddie Miksis, Bobby Bragan, Gene Mauch, and a heady, foul-mouthed middle infielder from Philadelphia who was nearly as brash as Durocher himself, Eddie "the Brat" Stanky.

"Tell Rickey to back up the truck and unload another batch of kids," Durocher would periodically exclaim in frustration.

Things grew so desperate that Durocher himself laced up his spikes for a few games. Even Frenchy Bordagaray came back, sans goatee. For a good part of 1945, the Dodgers' shortstop was Eddie "Bazooka" Basinski, a symphony violinist before and after his stint with the Bums. Durocher for some reason refused to believe this, even though Basinski—no doubt the one and only virtuoso ever nicknamed Bazooka—would bring his violin on the road in order to practice. Leo once challenged him to play before the team, promising him a suit if he did. Basinski played, Durocher had to cough up a suit, and Bazooka's nickname changed to Fiddler. (There is no indication that he ever played with the Ebbets Field Sym-Phony.)

Despite the improvement in background music, the Dodgers did not contend for the duration. They were a catch-as-catch-can aggregation, often with no catching at all. Spelling Basinski at shortstop was one Tommy "Buckshot" Brown, a Brooklyn boy who'd had to quit school and go to work on the docks with his uncle at the age of twelve. At fifteen, he went to a Dodgers' tryout and made his major-league debut in 1944 at just sixteen years and eight months of age—the youngest man ever to play for a major-league team in New York. Brown would also become the youngest player ever to homer in the majors, but because he was still just seventeen, Old Gold refused to give him the carton of cigarettes that every Dodger got for hitting a home run.

Buckshot Brown would last as a utility man in the majors for nine seasons, although, as his nickname implies, his fielding could be erratic; he once hurled a throw to first all the way into the upper deck. Washed up at twenty-six, he put in thirty-five years in a Ford plant in Nashville, but had few complaints: "Being 12 years old, working on the docks and playing street ball, I didn't have much time. That's the only thing I missed, was being a kid."

61

Life During Wartime

This was baseball during the war—comic, ragged, more than a little poignant. The St. Louis Browns actually brought up a one-armed outfielder named Pete Gray for seventy-seven games in 1945 (Gray was good enough to hit .218, but spent a lot of time getting beaten up by his teammates, apparently defending the honor of the fully armed community). Some entrepreneurs even resorted to letting *girls* play, forming the now storied All-American Girls Professional Baseball League. But this would be confined entirely to the Midwest.

Some owners considered shutting down the game altogether for the duration, but President Roosevelt insisted that baseball continue: "I honestly feel that it would be best for the country to keep baseball going. There will be fewer people unemployed and everybody will work longer hours and harder than ever before. And that means that they ought to have a chance for recreation and for taking their minds off their work even more than before."

There were travel restrictions, just as there were for all Americans. The All-Star Game was canceled in 1945. Judge Landis ruled before the 1943 season that all spring training camps would have to be held north of the Potomac and Ohio Rivers and east of the Mississippi—a decision that one writer would joke "sounds like a treaty with the French and Indians."

For the Dodgers, this meant spring training at the Bear Mountain Inn, near the Catskills, fifty miles north of New York. There the team could use the indoor field house at West Point when it was too cold or snowy to go outside. Their lodgings became known as the day nursery, and for entertainment the fuzzy-cheeked, apprentice Bums were bused off to the movies or spent evenings listening to cheery, bighearted Dearie Mulvey, a co-owner, play the inn's piano. The Giants had similarly homey accommodations at Lakewood, New Jersey; the Yankees, first in Asbury Park and then in Atlantic City. Neither of these summer resorts was really adequate. The proud Bombers were forced to train on high school fields and basketball courts, in empty armories and abandoned air hangars. They shivered at night in underheated hotels or paced along blacked-out boardwalks.

Nonetheless, the team's tremendous depth would help it to one more championship under "Uncle Egbert" Barrow. Baseball in 1943 was baffling to many players, especially hitters, because wartime shortages extended even to baseballs, which became suddenly spongy and difficult to hit for long distances, almost as if the dead-ball era had returned overnight. The change could be seen in the sudden drop-off in production by players such as Flash Gordon, who went from hitting .322 as the AL MVP in 1942 to just .249 a year later. But the Yankees were able to romp to another American League pennant by calling up rookies such as the free-spirited outfielder Johnny Lindell, the speedy infielder George "Snuffy" Stirnweiss, and a sterling third baseman named Billy Johnson to complement the veterans Charlie Keller and Bill Dickey. Canny Barrow acquisitions such as first baseman Nick Etten, acquired from the Phillies for $10,000, and various nonentities filled in the rest of the roster.

The Cardinals brought back most of their stellar 1942 team, en route to winning another 105 games, but this time they were overwhelmed by the Yankees' starting staff of Spud Chandler, Marius Russo, Hank Borowy, and 215-pound "Tiny" Bonham in the World Series. Brooklyn's Russo pitched another masterful complete-game victory in the series, just before leaving to join the army, while Chandler, who had taken the AL MVP award with a 20-4 record and a 1.64 ERA—the lowest in Yankees history for a starter—won two games, the last of which was a complete-game shutout in which he allowed ten singles and two walks. Spud spun his way through, thanks to a two-run homer by Dickey, the Yanks' great receiver for so many years, who had figured out a way to hit .351 in a circumscribed season and was now playing in his very last World Series game.

They sang the old songs again in the Yankees' locker room, champions for the tenth time in the last twenty-one seasons, but they must have hit some somber notes. Dickey would lay down his mitt to become a coach for the next two years, while Gordon and Keller got their draft notices. Chandler went to work in a munitions plant. The teams Barrow would patch together in their stead would contend in 1944 and 1945, only to stumble in September, in a most un-Yankee way. This was the baseball world the war had turned upside down, with teams such as the Browns and the Senators breezing by the mighty Bombers now.

Back in New York, the war continued to make time go backward. Manhattan's broad avenues—all of them still two-way then—emptied out, due to the lack of new cars for the duration. Some merchants even tried replacing their delivery vehicles with horses, which didn't work out so well, the art of the teamster having been lost in less than a generation.

The city got greener, with victory gardens to augment wartime rations springing up in backyards and schoolyards, on rooftops and terraces, in parks and vacant lots. In Jackson Heights and other, more open parts of Queens and Brooklyn, these enterprises were nearly the size of real truck farms. But there were also peas growing on the lawn of the Charles Schwab House along Riverside Drive, one of the last mansions in Manhattan, and tomato plants rising above the skating rink in Rockefeller Center.

There were constant parades, rallies, speeches, special broadcasts, exhibitions, displays of captured enemy tanks and planes. All designed to see the troops off, or to sell war bonds, or to salvage or save rubber, metal, fat, gasoline. A rather lurid *Nature of the Enemy* exhibition in Rockefeller Center "featured huge installations depicting a shuttered church, a group of gun-toting children in gas masks, and a vivid image of a concentration camp." Many of the salvage drives proved less than useful, particularly when it came to recycling old tires and kitchen pots and pans, but they achieved their primary goal of keeping everyone involved in the war effort. More practically, women were now to be seen working in almost every job there was outside the home. They drove buses, trolleys, streetcars, trucks, and taxis; tended bar and waited tables; ran errands and elevators; delivered the milk and the mail. Tens of thousands of them in the New York area alone worked making explosives and ammunition, riveting and drilling together planes and ships and tanks. Still others in the Waves and the Wacs, the SPARs and the Civil Air Patrol flew scout planes and patrolled in ships, keeping the watch along the coast.

Baseball tried to do its part. More than 350 major leaguers were officially in military service, but by early 1944 it was discovered that more than 300 of them were still stateside. Only two were killed, Elmer Gedeon and Harry O'Neill, who had played a grand total of six big-league games between them, though stars such as Hank Greenberg, Bob Feller, and Harry "the Hat" Walker did see considerable action. But the vast majority spent the war playing ball for their delighted commanders, going on "morale" tours or war bond drives. Base teams such as the Norfolk Naval Training Station, DiMaggio's Santa Ana Army Air Base, the Army Seventh Air Force in Hawaii, and the Great Lakes Naval Station were where the best baseball in the world was being played now. Players were even traded between them; when Phil Rizzuto beat out Pee Wee Reese for the shortstop spot at Norfolk, Reese was "transferred" to another base.

This was not, to be sure, the players' fault, and it might have been just as well. Who, after all, wanted to read a steady litany of death notices for America's most beloved athletes—or movie stars, or singers and musicians, for that matter? There were complaints, but the players—in war as in peace—had little control over where they went.

Meanwhile, all players, coaches, managers, and baseball officials took 10 percent of their salaries in war bonds. Servicemen were generally allowed into ballparks for free. Fans, too, if they brought scrap metal to the Polo Grounds, or cigarettes—"Smokes for Servicemen"—to Crosley Field in Cincinnati. The three New York teams played a six-inning round-robin at the Polo Grounds to raise money for war relief in 1944. It drew more than fifty thousand fans, featuring as it did fungo-hitting, throwing, and running competitions between players from the Yankees, Giants, and Dodgers. Milton Berle did a routine, and so did Al Schacht, "the Clown Prince of Baseball," and there were some tunes from a Coast Guard band, and when five hundred wounded servicemen were brought in, they drew a huge hand. The event raised $4.5 million in admissions and another $56.5 million in war bond pledges, including $50 million by La Guardia from the City of New York, or the equivalent of more than $750 million in today's dollars. Babe Ruth, who had angrily thrown all the Japanese memorabilia from his 1934 trip away when he heard the news of Pearl Harbor, came back to Yankee Stadium for another fundraiser in a game between retired greats, belting a ball into the lower right-field stands off Walter Johnson.

"The fans didn't come to see me strike anybody out," Johnson later explained as to why he had not thrown harder. "They came to see Babe hit a home run."

In an early version of Rotisserie baseball, the three New York teams encouraged groups to "obtain" a favorite player in an auction, by pledging to buy a certain amount of war bonds. They then bought even more bonds depending on his performance: $2,500 for each single, $5,000 for a double, $7,500 for a triple, $10,000 for a home run, $25,000 for a pitching win, and $50,000 for a shutout. Before it was all over, this promotion had raised a startling $123,850,000 in war bonds in New York alone. The individual player who brought in the highest amount proved to be—logically enough—"the Peeple's Cherce," Dixie Walker, who drew $11,250,000.

Much of the new discretionary income being earned by war workers did go to baseball tickets now. But the day shift was out of luck, once La Guardia ordered the "dim out" early in the 1942 season. No more night games. It was yet another setback for Horace Stoneham, who had finally installed eight enormous steel towers at the Polo Grounds in 1940, making it the best-lit park in the majors. The Giants resorted instead for a time to that romantic invention, the "twi-night" doubleheader, beginning in the late afternoon and ending in the long summer dusk. But Stoneham angrily ended these, too, when the Dodgers escaped late Giants rallies with a win and a tie on consecutive evenings, thanks to the city's dimout rules.

The Giants needed all the help they could get. In August 1943, King Carl Hubbell won his last game, then took over the team's farm system. The Giants won only fifty-five games and finished last for just the second time since John McGraw had come to town in 1902. Bill Terry had already stepped up to the front office, as general manager, to be replaced by Mel Ott in the dugout. Master Melvin—still just thirty-six in 1945, still one of the best hitters in the National League—soldiered on, playing right field and managing a mostly faceless, listless team, though there were exceptions. Eccentric Danny Gardella, a native of Fordham Road—described by Jimmy Powers as "not much taller than a fire hydrant" but one of the first players ever to pump weights—was brought over to entertain the fans with some occasional power hitting and stunts such as walking on his hands before games.

Gardella had labored as a boxer, longshoreman, elevator operator, trainer, and masseur before making it to the majors, where he seemed to work overtime to attract attention. The outfielder did splits in the shower, quoted Plato to the writers and hauled poetry anthologies along on the road, strapped himself into train luggage racks to sleep on occasion, and liked to walk the streets of Lakewood during spring training, singing arias in his "rich baritone." His hitting was a sensation when he first came up—inciting the *Daily Mirror* headline GARDELLA, YOUNG FELLA, LIFTS GIANTS OUT OF CELLA—but his fielding left much to be desired, due mainly to his wandering attention. On one memorable occasion, Gardella managed to flip his cap down over his eyes instead of flipping his shades up; on another, a fly ball caught him in the midst of adjusting his belt, and he went running after the ball with one hand holding up his pants. He did not make the catch.

Bolstered by such entertainment, the Giants in 1945 drew more than a million fans for the first time. The Polo Grounds had already hosted the All-Star Game in 1942, with all proceeds going to war charities. The scheduled 6:30 start was delayed by rain for nearly an hour, though, and while lights were allowed, La Guardia had scheduled a citywide blackout drill for that same evening, All-Star Game be damned, and the last out was not recorded until just before the drill's 9:30 start.

"As the contest ended, everything went dark—streets, stands, elevated stations, locker rooms, everything," David Pietrusza would write. "Both teams lingered in darkened clubhouses for 20 minutes before lights returned. Thirty-five thousand fans tarried in their seats, amusing themselves with a community-sing while they waited to leave the park."

It was a heartwarming moment and how we wanted—how we *still* want—to think of ourselves in America, in New York, during the war.

"All Americans felt they had to do their share, thereby enhancing each American's sense that her commitment and contributions mattered," the political scientist Robert Putnam would write. "As one said later in an oral history of the home front: 'You just felt that the stranger sitting next to you in a restaurant, or someplace, felt the same way you did about the basic issues.' "

It wasn't always so. The war also brought conflict and social turmoil. For all the scrap-collecting kids, the cops had to shoo away bevies of underage "victory girls" patrolling Times Square. With Pop at war and Mom at work, more and more children returned from school to empty homes. This was the moment when the term "juvenile delinquent" first came into common parlance. La Guardia had the city provide as much day care as it could, but the whole idea was opposed by the Catholic Church, suspicious that it was all a plot by the state to take over child rearing.

Out on the West Coast, Hollywood had been planning another baseball biopic, *The Great DiMaggio,* the story of a humble, immigrant fisherman from San Francisco whose three boys grew up to be major-league baseball players. But Giuseppe DiMaggio had never become an American citizen, and so he was officially a "suspect alien" like other unnaturalized Italian Americans—forbidden to go within half a mile of the shore, where his boat and the family restaurant at Fisherman's Wharf were; forbidden to travel more than five miles from home, or go out at night or even own the radio with which he had always followed his sons' exploits. He was at least better off than the seventy thousand Issei and Nisei, the DiMaggios' Japanese American neighbors on the West Coast who were so infamously carted off to detainment camps in the interior.

Yet as painful a chapter as the detention of the Nisei would become, the worst fissures of the war would open along older racial lines.

62

The Fire This Time

New York was never more truly the crossroads of America than during World War II. In 1945 alone, 109 million people passed through "the building vast enough to hold the sound of time," Penn Station—many of them in uniform. Servicemen were everywhere, not only shipping out to Europe, but on their way to different training camps or pouring in from Jersey bases for a few hours' leave. They could be found dozing on the stairs and escalators of the great station, or saying their heartbreaking goodbyes, or scrambling through the soaring marble hallways to the lilting Irish tones of the train announcer Ann Gavin—another wartime fill-in who would become an institution—as she read off their connections.

"The atmosphere in the station was sad and exciting, and many people were crying," Alfred Eisenstaedt remembered from snapping pictures there for *Life* magazine. "The men were very shy—it was difficult for some of them to embrace in public. Their mothers couldn't go beyond the train gates, and they stood there, looking down at the tracks, crying."

The city went all out to accommodate the servicemen, providing USO and Red Cross hospitality services, the famous Stage Door Canteen, where Broadway stars served and entertained and danced with the troops; another, the Steno Canteen, was run by the women office workers of the city. The troops could get free or discount tickets to see shows all up and down the Great Dim Way—maybe even get in to see that young crooner, Frank Sinatra, who was delighting all the bobby-soxers. New Yorkers took the fighting men into their homes for Thanksgiving or Christmas dinner, and in the summer, of course, they could have their pick of ball games.

The place they really wanted to go, though—more than anywhere else—was Harlem.

This was the last moment that it would still be a destination, a place for tourists to come. In purely material terms, the coming of the war was a godsend for Harlem, which had suffered more than any other part of New York through the Great Depression. Soon the broad uptown avenues were mobbed with men in uniform, where they could see the final, glorious bloom of a culture that would never be quite so exquisite—or quite so separate—again. It was a cornucopia for the senses, for young men, Black or white, who had never been more than a few miles from home or the family farm. Listening to the swift, clever patter of the new jive. Gawking at the "Thursday girls," the "kitchen mechanics" and "domestic engineers"—cooks and maids—dressed up to the nines on their one free night a week, smoke billowing from the beauty salons where their hair was literally ironed. The street vendors peddling hot yams with melted butter and brown sugar in the winter, ice cream and charlotte russe in the summer; fruits and vegetables. The fish and clam men shouting "Wahoo! Wahoo! Wahoo!" at the top of their lungs, or singing their own adaptations of one popular song or another to sell their wares.

The soldiers and sailors lined up to get into the fabled bars and restaurants and dance clubs: the Kozy Korner and the New Thrill, Bowman's and the High Hat, Henry's Sugar Bowl and Jimmy's Chicken Shack, the Apollo, and the Renaissance Casino, and Small's Paradise with its renowned oval bar and fabulous Clover Leaf Bar. Best of all, if they could get in, was to go stompin' at the Savoy, the block-long club at Lenox between 140th and 141st Streets with its *two* house bands, one on either end of a 250-foot-long, polished maple-wood dance floor. With its cut-glass chandeliers and its marble staircase and orange-and-blue walls; its haughty, beautiful hostesses; and the amazing jitterbugs; it was where everyone, Black and white, wanted to go even if they could not dance a step.

This was what disturbed the authorities, especially in the military. Jitterbugging was wild, "jungle" dancing that led inexorably to "race mixing." In response, the military declared more and more of Harlem "off limits" to white servicemen, sending legions of military police to contain the throngs of soldiers and sailors who still insisted on coming uptown. The excuse was usually "vice"—though the Savoy, at least, went to great lengths to preserve their virtue, refusing to serve alcohol for the duration, and Harlem during the war could not lay a finger on the "vice" to be found in wide-open, all-white towns outside military bases around the country.

Nevertheless, the idea of Harlem as the font of all depravities—especially in darkened, dimmed-out New York—could not be surmounted. Macy's sold silk-tasseled "mugging sticks," ten to nineteen inches long, with a flashlight on one end, designed to ward off or prevent the assault one was bound to be subjected to uptown. Finally, on April 21, 1943, the military not only declared the Savoy off limits but ordered it closed, costing ninety local residents their jobs. Harlem was stunned. "The Track," "The Place of Happy Feet," had been shut down by military fiat, because the brass did not want white American servicemen fraternizing with African Americans. Nothing could have made a clearer statement about how people of color were regarded in an America fighting a life-and-death struggle against the forces of racial supremacy.

There was some progress being made—forced, really—by African Americans themselves. The Reverend Adam Clayton Powell Jr.—elected New York's first Black congressman in 1944, and now ensconced in his father's old positions in both the pulpit of the Abyssinian Baptist Church and at the head of Harlem's "Don't Buy Where You Can't Work" campaign, wrung jobs for Black people on neighborhood bus lines, with public utilities, and, finally, even from the notoriously racist department stores along 125th Street.

Nationally, the tenacious socialist agitator A. Philip Randolph, leading the all-Black Brotherhood of Sleeping Car Porters from a small apartment on 140th Street, had struck a stunning blow for civil rights when he threatened President Roosevelt with a massive protest—a "March on Washington," twenty-two years ahead of the one that Dr. Martin Luther King Jr. would lead—if Black workers were not given equal opportunities to work in the war industries. In response, Roosevelt issued Executive Order 8802, the Fair Employment Act, leading to an unprecedented desegregation of the workplace during the war.

This was no small victory, with more than one million Black men and women winning defense industry jobs within two years of Pearl

Harbor, significantly boosting Black employment, wages, and earning power. But like all other gains for African Americans, it would have to be affirmed in the street. Before World War II was over, there were forty-seven race riots in the United States, nearly all of them attacks by whites on Blacks and, occasionally, Hispanics, for daring to accept the jobs they had earned in defense industries.

The government tried to cool things off by banning the use of the n-word on military bases and showing films highlighting the proud history of Black U.S. soldiers. Nonetheless, the conflicts in defense plants cost an estimated one million production hours and served as excellent Axis propaganda. *Signal* magazine, the Nazis' version of *Life*, published in many languages throughout occupied Europe, featured pictures of rampaging white workers and mocked "the fight between whites and Negroes in the country of equality."

Things came to a head on June 20, 1943, in Detroit, when mobs of whites, enraged that Black defense workers and their families had been allotted *any* of the jobs and the new housing units flung up for the war effort, attacked African Americans throughout the city—usually with the passive or even active support of the police. Federal troops had to be rushed in to impose order, but not before thirty-four people were killed (twenty-five of them African Americans) and hundreds more were injured and arrested.

Looking on uneasily, Mayor La Guardia warned on the city-owned radio station he had created, WNYC, against "snake agitators" and appealed "to all to be calm." But that very summer, the Metropolitan Life insurance company announced its plans to build what would become Stuyvesant Town and Peter Cooper Village, block after block of model, affordable, downtown housing for returning veterans—all to be reserved exclusively for white people. La Guardia would dragoon Met Life into eventually building the Riverton Houses, an all-Black housing development in Harlem, but tensions in the city only ratcheted upward. The Little Flower urged Harlem to "keep cool" and inveighed against "those who try to use this issue to manufacture a problem." But Black New Yorkers didn't need to have anything "manufactured." They could see the vast injustices that were all around them, could taste the insults and the degradations they were subjected to on a daily basis. Then there were the eyewitness accounts from their own sons and husbands and brothers in uniform, many of whom, used to discrimination though they were, had never been subjected to anything like the indignities of the Jim Crow South before.

Black troops were so terribly treated, not only by southern cops and sheriffs, but also by white officers and enlisted men, that bases frequently became armed camps—armed against each other. The constant arrests, clubbings, and shootings of Black soldiers by white MPs and local police became so egregious that Reverend Powell Jr. wrote an editorial for the Harlem *People's Voice* headlined MR. PRESIDENT, JUST WHAT IS IT WE ARE FIGHTING FOR? Black soldiers at Camp McCain in Mississippi were so fed up with their treatment in nearby Duck Hill—scene of a barbaric double lynching just a few years before the war—that on the Fourth of July 1943 they marched into the tiny delta town and unleashed a twelve-minute fusillade, while the locals cowered behind doors. Somehow, no one was injured, and the army was so flummoxed, it simply refused to discuss the incident.

That sort of desperate defiance was becoming more widespread. World War II also saw the creation, for the first time in U.S. Army history, of large numbers of Black commissioned officers, although these men were often treated just as shabbily as Black noncoms. One of them was a young, college-educated lieutenant at Fort Hood, Texas, ordered to sit in the back of a bus by the driver, even though it was a special army bus, run for the express purpose of evading the South's Jim Crow laws. Lieutenant Jack Roosevelt Robinson was the son of sharecroppers and the grandson of slaves, but he had been raised in relatively integrated Southern California, and he knew his rights.

"I walked up and put my finger right in his face. I figured the best thing to do was not to shrink in a case like this," Robinson would write. "I put my finger right in his face and told him to leave me alone."

Robinson was arrested and court-martialed on multiple offenses, including drunkenness, though he was a lifelong teetotaler. An all-white court of nine officers found him not guilty on each charge, but his unit, the 761st "Black Panthers" Tank Battalion, had proceeded overseas without him, where it became the first Black tank unit to see action in World War II.

Honorably discharged in November 1944, Robinson found himself at loose ends. He had been a star athlete at UCLA, the first man there ever to letter in four sports, and had won the NCAA national long jump championship. But afterward the only work he had been able to find in professional sports was with the Honolulu Bears and the Los Angeles Bulldogs, a pair of semiprofessional football teams. Out of the army, he played a little with the Bulldogs again and coached basketball before a friend suggested he try Negro League baseball.

Baseball had been Jackie's worst sport at UCLA, but he decided to give it a try anyway—it was still the only American sport that might really pay off—and was appalled by what he found. He had had no experience akin to what he encountered barnstorming with the Kansas City Monarchs through the South, where the team was lucky to find private homes to stay in and a restaurant to serve them out the back door. Gas stations refused to let the players use their bathrooms even while they were filling up the team bus.

"We . . . pulled up in service stations in Mississippi where drinking fountains said black and white, and a couple of times we had to leave without our change, he'd get so mad," recalled Robinson's teammate Othello Renfroe.

Robinson hated as well the extreme informality of Negro League baseball: the games left half-finished because of scheduling demands, what he judged to be the lackadaisical attitude in unimportant contests. Such laxity was unbearable for Jackie, who burned always.

"Robinson fit in like a schoolmarm in a brothel," biographer Jonathan Eig would write.

Nonetheless, he hit five home runs and stole thirteen bases in forty-seven games at shortstop for the Monarchs, hitting .387—and .434 in official Negro American League games. It was good enough to get him into the prestigious East-West All-Star Game at Comiskey Park. He reportedly had a little difficulty making plays in the hole, but otherwise showed an amazing improvement over his college play—a testament, perhaps, to the amateur baseball he had kept playing over the years.

Financially, the war helped Black baseball rebound just as it had with the majors, but conditions were little better than they had been twenty years before. The teams played erratic schedules of anywhere from thirty to seventy "official" league games, plus the usual, endless barnstorming excursions.

Around New York, the Black Yankees continued to putrefy out in Paterson. But Alex Pompez had found yet another new life for his New York Cubans, signing a deal in 1943 with Horace Stoneham to have them play in the Polo Grounds, where they remained a winning team. The rising force in the area, though, was the Newark Eagles, playing out in Ruppert Stadium under the guidance of the most unusual owner in baseball history.

Effa Manley was a woman who would perpetuate an aura of mystery through much of her life, right down to the year of her birth and the nature of her race. She was born in Philadelphia to a seamstress mother who was of both white German and (Asian) Indian descent and to the white man who was her mother's employer. Raised in a household with a Black stepfather and stepsiblings, Effa would live as "Black," although she described herself in old age as "white."

No life could better underscore the essential absurdity of all racial constructs. Whatever color she was, Manley was undeniably glamorous, alluring, bold, and competent. Moving to New York to work in the millinery business, she soon married Abe Manley, a Black policy baron and real estate investor who bought the Eagles' franchise with her.

"Babe Ruth made a baseball fan of me," she liked to say. "I used to go to Yankee Stadium just to see him come to bat."

A keen businesswoman, Effa ran the Eagles while her husband put up the capital. Monte Irvin, one of her top players, described her as "unique and knowledgeable and effervescent. She ran the whole business end of the team." The male owners, generally men from the numbers racket, were less than enthralled to have a confident, strong-willed woman in their ranks. The usual stereotypes would be affixed. Mrs. Manley was either harridan or whore, and often both. She was "aggressive" and full of unwanted advice. Stories abounded about how she henpecked her husband and controlled their team, even flashing bunt signals from her box by "crossing and uncrossing her legs." Her real objective in owning the Eagles was said to be her dalliances with younger players, including a fiery affair with one of the leading Black pitchers of the day, flashy Terris "Speed" McDuffie, a.k.a. Terris the Terrible. She was rumored to have ordered her managers to pitch McDuffie on days she brought her women's club to the park, just to show him off. After one lovers' quarrel, Terris the Terrible is supposed to have knocked Manley to the floor of a Penn Station platform and kicked her as she lay there—after which he was exiled to the New York Black Yankees "for two old bats and a pair of used sliding pads."

Her personal life aside, Manley seemed to contain many of the traits of male baseball owners, particularly in New York. Imperious, benevolent, and temperamental, all at the same time, she could be generous to her players and solicitous about their welfare, even setting them up in business, but would also "call you in and tell you how to dress, what to do, who to associate with," according to Eagles first baseman George Giles.

"When she was displeased, the world came to an end. She'd stop traffic," claimed Giles. "Mrs. Manley loved baseball, but she couldn't stand to lose. I was a pretty hard loser myself, but I think she'd take it harder than anybody."

Owners such as Manley had built the Negro Leagues into a $2 million enterprise by the end of the war, making baseball into one of the biggest Black-owned businesses in the country. Effa also campaigned for civil rights, joining Powell's "Don't Shop Where You Can't Work" campaign, holding an "Anti-Lynching Day" at Ruppert Stadium in 1939, and serving as the local treasurer of the NAACP.

Yet all the crusading in the world still could not get the major leagues to seriously consider integration during this time of national emergency—even as they sponsored (white) women's teams and called up a one-armed white man ("The only thing a one-armed white ballplayer can do as well as a black player," went the bitter joke in Negro League circles, "is scratch the side that itches"). Branch Rickey, it was murmured, had told the Brooklyn Dodgers' board that he was looking to develop a Black ballplayer. But many writers dismissed this out of hand as another piece of legerdemain from the Cave of the Winds, designed to slip the increasing political pressure to integrate.

Such hopes and rumors could no longer appease a people still being treated as second-class citizens, even as their country recruited them to fight a global war for freedom. Once Detroit exploded, everybody could see another conflagration in the offing in Harlem. James Baldwin would write in "Notes of a Native Son" that he remembered "the strangest combinations" of people gathering on the stoops and the street corners, both devout churchgoers and "the most flagrant disbelievers; something heavy in their stance seemed to indicate that they had all, incredibly, seen a common vision, and on each face there seemed to be the same strange, bitter shadow."

Mayor La Guardia could see it, too, lamenting on the radio at the end of June, "How many times have I said in the last two years that I fear panic more than enemy bombs? . . . How many times have I stated that a rumor, skillfully spread, might cause great consternation among groups of our people?"

He conferred with civil rights leaders, urged clergy to speak out against racism, announced plans for two new Harlem housing projects, and pushed for immediate rent controls. After speaking with the commissioner of police, he sent extra squadrons of motorcycle police to roar ostentatiously through the uptown streets. But this noisy show of force only further increased tensions.

Then the match was lit, an altercation at the seedy Braddock Hotel, once a favorite destination for Harlem headliners, situated just behind the Apollo Theater. A white cop shot a Black soldier in the arm, when the soldier tried to help a Black woman arrested on charges of being drunk and disorderly in the hotel lobby. The serviceman was not badly wounded, but once again rumor raced past reality. Soon people were running up and down the streets, breaking bottles, smashing windows, setting fires, looting stores, and shouting, "White man kill Black soldier! Get the white man! Get the white man! He's to blame!"

Instead, the riot devastated Harlem itself, resulting in nearly six hundred arrests and damaging fifteen hundred stores. Five people were shot dead—all of them Black men.

La Guardia worked feverishly throughout the night to extinguish the riot, rushing up to Harlem to join Black leaders. Together they roamed the streets in a WNYC sound truck, trying to dispel the rumors, urging everyone to go home. Spotting people looting a shop, La Guardia ordered, "Put that stuff back!" He was nearly struck by a "missile," and bricks and bottles crashed against the sound truck for hours. But in the end, the riot was contained at much less human and material cost than what had happened in Detroit.

Many Black leaders blamed "hoodlums," and the *Amsterdam News* called the rioters "a disgrace to their race, a disgrace to the city and a disgrace and a shame to the nation of which they are citizens." Others noticed how many of the looters took simple foodstuffs.

A new peace was patched together by La Guardia, new attention was paid, new investigative committees hired. In October, the Savoy was even permitted to reopen. And when the war ended, Harlem joined in the wildest, most raucous celebrations New York had ever seen, the almost frightening victory bacchanals that broke out as the Nazis, then Japan surrendered. The lights came back on, sailors kissed nurses in Times Square, they hanged Hitler in effigy in Brooklyn, and a group of foreign servicemen formed a line in front of the Hotel Astor and belted out a chorus of "God Bless America."

Yet there were a few who recognized a hollow spot in the victory, a lingering wound that had to be dressed, both in New York and in the country as a whole. No longer would commission reports and railing against rumors and snake agitators serve. In the new postwar world, something would have to be done to make all of New York's people true citizens if the city was to survive. That change was coming, and baseball would play a small but vital role in making it happen.

Acknowledgments

There are so many people I have to thank for their help in bringing *The New York Game* (finally!) into print.

They start with my agent, Henry Dunow, and my editor, Andrew Miller, whose patience and encouragement were extraordinary. This was a book that we first dreamed up so long ago that I remember the three of us going to a Yankees game and watching Orlando Hernández literally get stopped and frisked afterward, in the crazy, fraught weeks after the 9/11 attacks. It ended up being written over so many years due to other professional commitments and extended family obligations. But they stood by it through everything, for which I am grateful.

My wife, Ellen Abrams, was also persistent in seeing me finish this book, even to the point of being adamant. She was of invaluable service as a reader, consultant, and pictures editor, and remains, as ever, my trusted friend, love, and helpmate.

John Freeman provided me with an outstanding, final edit of the manuscript and constant encouragement. Sarah Perrin and Isabel Ribeiro were patient, helpful, capable, and amiable in coordinating the photo spreads, index, and back and front matter. I have John Gall to thank for the outstanding jacket design. Nicole Pedersen, the production editor on the book, and the production team—copyeditor Ingrid Sterner, text designer Michael Collica, and production manager Lisa Montebello—did an amazing job of copyediting, fact-checking, and producing what must have been a challenging manuscript.

John Thorn, the dean of baseball historians, my longtime friend and colleague Gail Buckland, and our dear family friend, Lili Schwartz, were incredibly generous and forthcoming with their time and advice, in helping me secure pictures and permissions. While Allen Barra's wonderful books on baseball were largely set outside the time that this volume encompasses, I learned something from every single thing he wrote about baseball—and history. And a great big shout-out to Jonelle and Maggie, too.

I have been blessed, all my life, with wonderful friends and family, many of whom have whiled away pleasant hours with me at the ballpark. In the first week of August 1967, and shortly before we moved away to Red Sox territory, my father, Kenneth Baker, took me to see the Yankees at the original stadium so I could see Mickey Mantle play there, and my beloved uncle Bruce Baker took me to Shea Stadium, to see Tom Seaver pitch against Willie Mays and Willie McCovey. They are indelible memories, as were the games my father later took me to at gorgeous, thankfully preserved Fenway Park. My mother, Claire Baker, was also good enough to sit through a game at Fenway, even if she never did approve of the base coaches, whom she insisted on calling "cheater men."

Rockport, Massachusetts, the beautiful town where I was lucky enough to grow up, was also where I learned to write professionally. I am very grateful to the coaches of the high school teams I wrote about there: Dick Baker, the late Jade Donaldson, and George Ramsden and Steve O'Connor, the very patient coaches of our overmatched baseball teams. Also to Rick Cabral, who went with me to see Henry Aaron play at Fenway, and Tom and Todd Balf, Christmas tree entrepreneurs.

In New York, there has been my favorite family of fans, Chris Spelman and Ann LaForge, and their wonderful sons, Gus, who had hope when others did not, and my godson, Teddy, who once wreaked havoc with a bat on the playing fields of Central Park and who will be a superb writer. My whole, terrific Horace Clarke crew of friends, Yankees and Mets fans both: James Gray, with whom I have spent so many moments of triumph and despair on the phone. Dan Conaway, who once tried to root the Mets home with his imitation of Howard Beale. Jack Hitt, who always knew when to cheer. Darin Strauss, still angry about 2004. Rick Feeley, with whom I saw probably the worst Mets doubleheader ever. Andy Staub, who christened the Piazza Metropolitana. Marc Aronson and Steve Hubbell, distant relation to Carl, who is a friend indeed.

And so many more: the magnificent Condons, Tom and Anne and Clare and Jack, the "headhunter." Kevin Hench, Nathan Ward, and

Gillian MacKenzie, all good friends even if they, too, come from Red Sox territory. Nicky Dawidoff, to whom I apologize both for scribbling on his Sox shirt and for what I said in 2001. Johnny Abady, rallying the faithful on the subway. Dan Larkins and Frank Citera, who overcame the fear of loge with me.

Thanks, too, to so many family and friends, fans or not, who have made my life such a pleasure: my sister, Pam Baker, and her (long-suffering) husband, Mark Kapsch. My treasured Brooklyn in-laws, Matthew Brinckerhoff and Sharon Abrams, Anik, who loves cats (and wore the World Series–winning onesie), and Jackson, who loves chess. The great West Coast crew: Ari and Larry, who took me to the Oakland–Alameda County Coliseum, and the incredible Susan and Esther and 10Ben. The Whitney-Wallaces, with whom I could conquer the world, Cathy and Cindy and John and Dan and Tricia, and all of their amazing, constantly expanding clans. The old Maine contingent, Missy and Scott, and Zoë and Julian and Griffin, and Oliver.

To Amanda Robb and Andrew Chesler, dearest of dear hearts. To Steve Sherrill, who prefers basketball, and to all the fantastic Hitt-Sanderses, Dr. Lisa, and Yonce, and my goddaughter, Tarpley. To the Out with the Trash Club, Kay and Ben, Fred and Erica, Ed and Ed, Nancy, Warren, Gina, Martin, Pamela, Lauren, and Michael, and so many others at the Century. To all of the great friends I have made at the Remember the Triangle Fire Coalition and the Living New Deal, too numerous to list here but whose fellowship I have so enjoyed.

And to the Old One, Ann Baker, soon to be at the heart of the Tenafly Historic District, all my love.

Bibliographical Essay

It seemed faintly ridiculous to insert footnotes into this highly subjective fan's take on both New York City and the game it invented, baseball. Yet no sport, anywhere, has attracted more outstanding writers, and I have gained immeasurably from their words, as well as from listening to the games, watching the games, going to the games. When it comes to the city, well, the words that New Yorkers alone have expended on it form an archive that will never be plumbed. What most of them have written is impassioned, sincere, inspired, funny, angry, and hopeful—as I hope my own words are.

Much of what I have depended on in the first volume of *The New York Game* has been the city's own vast, varied, and fabled newspaper culture—most of it now, sadly, defunct. This has included the four daily papers still standing—*The New York Times,* the New York *Daily News, The Wall Street Journal,* and the *New York Post*—and so many of those legendary, departed publications: the *Herald Tribune, The World, The Sun,* the *Mirror,* the *Telegram,* the *Journal,* and the *American,* and all permutations and hyphenations thereof. But also the great Black newspaper, the *Amsterdam News;* its less heralded predecessor, the weekly *New York Age;* the greatest newspaper ever published in the Yiddish language, *The Jewish Daily Forward* (*Forverts*); outer-borough stalwarts such as the original *Brooklyn Eagle* and *Newsday;* and upstarts like the defiant *PM* and even the communist *Daily Worker.*

New York–based magazines, in particular *The New Yorker* and *Harper's,* were also splendid sources, as was the national sporting press, led by *The Sporting News* (odious though "The Bible of Baseball" often was back in its bigoted youth).

The internet was of course a very useful tool to quickly ascertain facts and figures—with reasonable caution and judgment. (Looking at you, whoever you wags were, who tried to fool Wikipedia into believing that Wally Pipp was a young Jewish immigrant named "Pipik.") And I learned something, always, every day, from the very best baseball blog on the web, *It Is High! It Is Far! It Is . . . Caught.*

Far and away the most irreplaceable site of all online, though, was baseball-reference.com—especially if we must now live in a world without *The Baseball Encyclopedia.* Baseball Reference is a wonder in and of itself, a joy and a blessing to all of us who follow the game.

The following, selective bibliography, though, is one solely of books. References books or volumes that, as well as giving me enormous pleasure to read, helped me throughout this first volume of *The New York Game*—and its successor. Books that pertained only to a single player or team or season, to a single episode or a span of years or an era. Books, books, books—about the city and the game.

I hope there is room for one more.

General Reference, Anthologies, and Works Spanning the Course of This Book, Pertaining to New York City

New York: An Illustrated History (New York: Alfred A. Knopf, 1999), by Ric Burns and James Sanders with Lisa Ades, is a superb companion volume to Burns's equally superb documentary about the history of the city. I used Kenneth T. Jackson's *Encyclopedia of New York City* (New Haven, Conn.: Yale University Press, 1995) so often even before I embarked on my book that I had to get the 2010 edition. Eric Homberger's *Historical Atlas of New York City* (New York: Henry Holt, 1994) is another indispensable reference book, mapping hundreds of years of change in the city. The collections *Writing New York: A Literary Anthology,* ed. Phillip Lopate (New York: Library of America, 1998), and *Empire City: New York Through the Centuries,* ed. Kenneth T. Jackson and David S. Dunbar (New York: Columbia University Press, 2002), are a delight to have at one's fingertips.

Also quite enjoyable and of use was *The Encyclopedia of New York State,* ed. Peter Eisenstadt, Laura-Eve Moss, and Carole F. Huxley (Syracuse, N.Y.: Syracuse University Press, 2005).

When it comes to Black uptown New York over the first half of the twentieth century, I am indebted to Jervis Anderson's *This Was Harlem: A Cultural Portrait, 1900–1950* (New York: Farrar Straus Giroux, 1981). Concerning the old political establishment that baseball in New York was so closely linked to, I not only relied on but also greatly enjoyed Oliver Allen's *Tiger: The Rise and Fall of Tammany Hall* (Boston: Da Capo Press, 1993); Alfred Conable and Edward Silberfarb's *Tigers of Tammany Hall: Nine Men Who Ran New York* (New York: Holt, Rinehart and Winston, 1967); and more recently, Terry Golway's *Machine Made: Tammany Hall and the Creation of Modern American Politics* (New York: Liveright, 2014).

On the theme of general entertainment—high and low—there were David Nasaw's *Going Out: The Rise and Fall of Public Amusements* (New York: Basic Books, 1993); James Traub's *Devil's Playground: A Century of Pleasure and Profit in Times Square* (New York: Random House, 2004); and Alice Sparberg Alexiou's *Devil's Mile: The Rich, Gritty History of the Bowery* (New York: St. Martin's Press, 2018).

To understand, as much as possible, the zeitgeist of a past era through *its* idea of history, I leafed through *"Manna-Hatin": The Story of New York* (New York: Manhattan, 1929), an anonymous, promotional account of New York history by the Bank of Manhattan Trust Company—complete with foreword by Mayor James J. Walker, shortly before the company and the rest of Wall Street plunged into the abyss.

Works on Baseball

My battered, dog-eared copy of *The New Bill James Historical Baseball Abstract* (New York: Free Press, 2001) proved invaluable—if constantly distracting. Nearly as valued was *The Bill James Guide to Baseball Managers from 1870 to Today* (New York: Scribner's, 1997). Mr. James has truly transformed how we see the game—for the better—and even on those rare occasions when I disagreed with his conclusions, I always respected his reasoning.

Just as insightful and distracting was *Baseball: An Illustrated History* (New York: Alfred A. Knopf, 1994), Geoffrey C. Ward's companion volume to Ken Burns's seminal documentary, and its 2010 updating including *The Tenth Inning,* which I had the privilege to contribute to.

My parents bought me my first *Baseball Encyclopedia* when I was ten. I still have it. I still have all of them: a beautifully bound 1969 Macmillan first edition with its own box (David S. Neft, Lee Allen, and Robert Markel, eds.) that must have cost my folks more than they could easily have afforded; the 1979 fourth edition (Macmillan, Joseph L. Reichler, ed.); the 1997 fifth edition, now Viking's *Total Baseball: The Official Encyclopedia of Major League Baseball,* ed. John Thorn, Pete Palmer, Michael Gershman, and David Pietrusza; and the seventh edition, also *Total Baseball,* ed. Thorn, Palmer, and Gershman with Matthew Silverman, Sean Lahman, and Greg Spira (Kingston, N.Y.: Total Sports, 2001)—once again, elegantly designed and loaded not just with statistics but excellent historical articles.

Favoring words over statistics for individual major-league players—all of them, at least up to thirty-five years ago, along with many Negro League players—*The Ballplayers: Baseball's Ultimate Biographical Reference,* ed. Mike Shatzkin (New York: Arbor House, 1990), lives up to its name, with fine capsule bios of some six thousand players, the great and the good and the completely obscure.

Another terrific reference book was Joseph L. Reichler's *Baseball Trade Register* (New York: Macmillan, 1984), which, incredibly, contains exactly what it advertises: "Every Trade, Sale, and Free Agent Signing from 1900 On." Like many of my best book acquisitions, I was lucky enough to see it being sold on a New York sidewalk for a dollar. Other useful works I relied on included Dennis Purdy's *Team by Team Encyclopedia of Major League Baseball* (New York: Workman Publishing, 2006).

Jonathan Schwartz's *Day of Light and Shadows* (Pleasantville, N.Y.: Akadine Press, 2000) focuses on one game and one season—1978—that is outside the purview of this book. But it remains to this day, by my lights, the best book ever written about what it means to be a fan. *Baseball: A Literary Anthology* (New York: Library of America, 2002), ed. Nicholas Dawidoff, is a tremendous asset to any fan of baseball—or literature. And Jules Tygiel's *Past Time: Baseball as History* (New York: Oxford University Press, 2000) puts the game under a sociological lens.

Douglass Wallop's *Baseball: An Informal History* (New York: W. W. Norton, 1969) was published in time for one of baseball's many commemorative years—this one the hundredth anniversary of (openly acknowledged) professional ball. The ninety-five-cent Bantam paperback of this book was one of my prized possessions as a boy.

In tracing those excluded from the national pastime for so long,

Robert Peterson's *Only the Ball Was White: A History of Legendary Black Players and All-Black Professional Teams* (New York: Oxford University Press, 1992) is an irreplaceable survey of Black (and Black-Hispanic) baseball—starting from well before the Negro Leagues. James A. Riley's *Biographical Encyclopedia of the Negro Baseball Leagues* (New York: Carroll & Graf, 1994) is another matchless resource on the same subject.

Adrian Burgos Jr.'s *Cuban Star: How One Negro League Owner Changed the Face of Baseball* (New York: Hill and Wang, 2011) was a happy find, with its all-but-incredible story of Alex Pompez, whose career as the owner of America's greatest Hispanic team and a Harlem policy baron runs like a bright thread through so much of New York baseball history. Peter Levine's *Ellis Island to Ebbets Field: Sport and the American Jewish Experience* (New York: Oxford University Press, 1992) was also highly enjoyable.

When it comes to where the game was played, *Take Me Out to the Ball Park* (St. Louis: Sporting News Publishing, 1983) is the greatest of tributes to old ballparks, with a lively text by Lowell Reidenbaugh and fine photos—but above all the artist Amadee's (Amadee Wohlschlaeger's) illustrations of the parks over the course of his long career as a sports cartoonist. This sort of book simply doesn't exist anymore. It should.

Other works on ballparks I would recommend—New York and otherwise—are Paul Goldberger's architecture critic's take, *Ballpark: Baseball in the American City* (New York: Alfred A. Knopf, 2019); Stew Thornley's *Land of the Giants: New York's Polo Grounds* (Philadelphia: Temple University Press, 2000); Lawrence S. Ritter's *Lost Ballparks: A Celebration of Baseball's Legendary Fields* (New York: Penguin Books, 1992); Neil J. Sullivan's *Diamond in the Bronx: Yankee Stadium and the Politics of New York* (New York: Oxford University Press, 2008); Joseph Durso's *Yankee Stadium: Fifty Years of Drama* (Boston: Houghton Mifflin, 1972); and Ray Robinson and Christopher Jennison's *Yankee Stadium: 75 Years of Drama, Glamor, and Glory* (New York: Penguin Studio, 1998) (even more drama!).

When it comes to the history of teams, works on the Yankees, unsurprisingly, proliferate. Mark Gallagher and Walter LeConte's *Yankee Encyclopedia,* 5th ed. (Champaign, Ill.: Sports Publishing, 2001), was only one edition of a very useful resource that kept getting bigger and better. I was also aided greatly by Marty Appel's comprehensive *Pinstripe Empire: The New York Yankees from Before the Babe to After the Boss* (New York: Bloomsbury, 2012); Ray Robinson and Jennison's *Pennants & Pinstripes: The New York Yankees, 1903–2002* (New York: Viking Studio, 2002); and Donald Honig's *New York Yankees: An Illustrated History* (New York: Crown, 1987).

Glenn Stout and Richard A. Johnson's *Yankees Century: 100 Years of New York Yankees Baseball* (Boston: Houghton Mifflin, 2002) is an outstanding illustrated history of the Yankees. Stout's *Red Sox Century: The Definitive History of Baseball's Most Storied Franchise* (Boston: Houghton Mifflin Harcourt, 2004) is equally helpful here, and nearly as good. I differ sharply with the author's argument for why Babe Ruth "had" to be traded, but I respect his opinion and enjoy his work immensely. Speaking of the Yankees and their leading rivals, Ed Linn's *Great Rivalry: The Yankees and the Red Sox, 1901–1990* (Boston: Houghton Mifflin, 1991) is worthwhile for the outstanding writing alone. Peter Golenbock's *Fenway: An Unexpurgated History of the Boston Red Sox* (New York: G. P. Putnam's Sons, 1992) goes back even beyond the eponymous ballpark, to the very start of the American League (and the rivalry).

In ranking teams great and otherwise, Rob Neyer and Eddie Epstein's *Baseball Dynasties: The Greatest Teams of All Time* (New York: W. W. Norton, 2000) is a relentlessly intelligent ranking of the best teams what ever was. Also helpful was Howard Siner's *Sweet Seasons: Baseball's Top Teams Since 1920* (New York: Pharos Books, 1988); while George Robinson and Charles Salzberg's often hilarious *On a Clear Day They Could See Seventh Place: Baseball's Worst Teams* (Lincoln: University of Nebraska Press, 1991) took the opposite perspective. Dave Anderson's *Pennant Races: Baseball at Its Best* (New York: Doubleday, 1994) is a handy guide, written as it was to commemorate that now abandoned and deeply missed phenomenon, the winner-take-all pennant race.

When it comes to a pair of titans who kept appearing or reappearing in one role after another in New York City for the better part of a century, I was pleased to turn to Lee Lowenfish's comprehensive, standard-setting work, *Branch Rickey: Baseball's Ferocious Gentleman* (Lincoln: University of Nebraska Press, 2007) and Jimmy Breslin's deft *Branch Rickey* (New York: Viking, 2011). Steven Goldman's smart, insightful, and typically well-written *Forging Genius: The Making of Casey Stengel* (Sterling, Va.: Potomac Books, 2005) was my favorite Casey bio, though Marty Appel's *Casey Stengel: Baseball's Greatest Character* (New York: Doubleday, 2017) was also well worthwhile, as was Harvey Frommer's *Baseball's Greatest Managers* (New York: Franklin Watts, 1985).

Turning to the ledger, Henry D. Fetter's *Taking On the Yankees: Winning and Losing in the Business of Baseball, 1903–2003* (New York: W. W. Norton, 2003) is the best single book I have ever read on the business of baseball. Other baseball business books I was grateful for were John Helyar's *Lords of the Realm: The* Real *History of Baseball* (New York: Villard Books, 1994); Andrew Zimbalist's *Baseball and Billions* (New York: BasicBooks, 1992); and Mark L. Armour and Daniel R. Levitt's *In Pursuit of Pennants: Baseball Operations from Deadball to Moneyball* (Lincoln: University of Nebraska Press, 2015).

Era by era, section by section, the books that I found most helpful included the following:

Up to the Twentieth Century—New York

Edwin G. Burrows and Mike Wallace's *Gotham: A History of New York City to 1898* (New York: Oxford University Press, 2000) is, of course, the nonpareil here.

Jacob A. Riis's *How the Other Half Lives* (New York: Dover, 1971) is the classic look into slum life in the nineteenth century, while Barnet Schecter has written the preeminent work on the 1863 draft riots, *The Devil's Own Work: The Civil War Draft Riots and the Fight to Reconstruct America* (New York: Walker, 2005).

Luc Sante's tour of the demimonde and the underworld, *Low Life* (New York: Vintage, 1991), is a delight to read—something I often do, still, just for the enjoyment of it. Herbert Asbury's *Gangs of New York: An Informal History of the Underworld* (Garden City, N.Y.: Garden City Publishing Company, 1927) is, of course, a legend. A copy of the original was handed down to me by my father, after it was handed down to him by his father. Also of great help was Asbury's *Ye Olde Fire Laddies* (New York: Alfred A. Knopf, 1930).

Focusing a little more closely on nineteenth-century machine politics, readers won't be disappointed by digging further into Kenneth D. Ackerman's *Boss Tweed: The Rise and Fall of the Corrupt Pol Who Conceived the Soul of Modern New York* (New York: Da Capo Press, 2005); Alexander B. Callow Jr.'s *Tweed Ring* (New York: Oxford University Press, 1965); or Dennis Tilden Lynch's *"Boss" Tweed: The Story of a Grim Generation* (New York: Boni and Liveright, 1927).

Climbing up into high society, I enjoyed Eric Homberger's *Mrs. Astor's New York: Money and Social Power in a Gilded Age* (New Haven, Conn.: Yale University Press, 2002) and Justin Kaplan's *When the Astors Owned New York* (New York: Viking, 2006).

Nineteenth-Century Baseball

The incomparable John Thorn's *Baseball in the Garden of Eden: The Secret History of the Early Game* (New York: Simon & Schuster, 2011) is a wonderful read (and Thorn is not only a terrific writer but also a mensch). Of great help, too, was David Block's fascinating *Baseball Before We Knew It: A Search for the Roots of the Game* (Lincoln: University of Nebraska Press, 2005). James L. Terry's *Long Before the Dodgers: Baseball in Brooklyn, 1855–1884* (Jefferson, N.C.: McFarland, 2002) will help those searching for their Brooklyn roots.

1900–1920

New York

Mike Wallace's *Greater Gotham: A History of New York City from 1898 to 1919* (New York: Oxford University Press, 2017) is a heroic work, while Clifton Hood's *722 Miles: The Building of the Subways and How They Transformed New York* (New York: Simon & Schuster, 1993) is a good guide to how the coming of the subway transformed New York baseball as well.

On the progress of the Machine, I turned, of course, to William L. Riordon's classic, *Plunkitt of Tammany Hall* (New York: E. P. Dutton, 1963). Richard Welch's groundbreaking *King of the Bowery: Big Tim Sullivan, Tammany Hall, and New York City from the Gilded Age to the Progressive Era* (Teaneck, N.J.: Fairleigh Dickinson University Press, 2008) is a terrific piece of work.

Moving to entertainments of the day (besides baseball), there are important works by Kathy Peiss, *Cheap Amusements: Working Women and Leisure in Turn-of-the-Century New York* (Philadelphia: Temple University Press, 1986) and M. H. Dunlop, *Gilded City: Scandal and Sensation in Turn-of-the-Century New York* (New York: William Morrow, 2000).

The best work on the defining event of the era in New York is easily David Von Drehle's *Triangle: The Fire That Changed America* (New York: Atlantic Monthly Press, 2003). Leon Stein broke the ground with his elegiac *The Triangle Fire* (Philadelphia: J. B. Lippincott, 1962).

Andy Logan's reporting broke open the murder of Beansy Rosenthal, *Against the Evidence: The Becker-Rosenthal Affair* (London: Weidenfeld & Nicolson, 1971)—nearly sixty years after the fact. Mike Dash's *Satan's Circus: Murder, Vice, Police Corruption, and New York's Trial of the Century* (New York: Crown, 2007) is also a very good account of this crime that even made it into the pages of *The Great Gatsby.* And speaking of great crimes, Lorraine B. Diehl's mesmerizing, illustrated history, *The Late, Great Pennsylvania Station* (New York: Four Walls Eight Windows, 1996), shows us just what we lost when one of the greatest architectural achievements of our nation was erased.

Baseball

Lawrence Ritter's *Glory of Their Times* (New York: Perennial, 2002) was a book I first read when it was being published in excerpts in *The Sporting News* in 1967 and have cherished ever since. Frank Deford's masterful *The Old Ball Game: How John McGraw, Christy Mathewson, and the New York Giants Created Modern Baseball* (New York: Atlantic Monthly Press, 2005) and Charles C. Alexander's poignant *John McGraw* (New York: Viking, 1988) provide everything you need to know about Muggsy.

Donald Dewey and Nicholas Acocella's incredible, stranger-than-fiction biography of Hal Chase, *The Black Prince of Baseball* (Wilmington, Del.: Sports Media Publishing, 2004), was a lifesaver. And to get a glimpse of the Big Six himself, readers should dig up Christy Mathewson's *Pitching in a Pinch: Baseball from the Inside* (the 2013

Penguin Books edition, with a foreword by Chad Harbach, preface by John N. Wheeler—and an afterword by Red Smith, from the 1977 Stein and Day edition).

Very useful was also G. H. Fleming's tale of the 1908 National League campaign as told through collected newspaper clippings, *The Unforgettable Season* (New York: Holt, Rinehart and Winston, 1981).

Eliot Asinof's indelible *Eight Men Out: The Black Sox and the 1919 World Series* (New York: Holt, Rinehart and Winston, 1963) was the first comprehensive retelling of the scandal that almost destroyed the game—and commenced on Manhattan's Upper West Side. (It was also the inspiration for one of John Sayles's finest films.) While David Pietrusza's *Rothstein: The Life, Times, and Murder of the Criminal Genius Who Fixed the 1919 World Series* (New York: Basic Books, 2011) does the very best job of figuring out what really happened—and why.

1920–1929
New York City

Robert Caro's *Power Broker: Robert Moses and the Fall of New York* (New York: Alfred A. Knopf, 1974) is simply the best book ever written about American urban politics. Donald L. Miller's *Supreme City: How Jazz Age Manhattan Gave Birth to Modern America* (New York: Simon & Schuster, 2014) and Bill Bryson's *One Summer: America, 1927* (New York: Doubleday, 2013) are highly enjoyable, eye-opening reads. George Walsh's *Gentleman Jimmy Walker: Mayor of the Jazz Age* (New York: Praeger, 1974) is well written and includes, remarkably, a foreword by Robert Moses.

Baseball

My take on Babe Ruth begins with Leigh Montville's splendid *The Big Bam: The Life and Times of Babe Ruth* (New York: Doubleday, 2006). I have read Montville since I was a boy, during his first days as a sports columnist for *The Boston Globe.* He only got better.

But then there is, appropriately, so much outstanding writing on the Babe, including Jane Leavy's *Big Fella: Babe Ruth and the World He Created* (New York: HarperCollins, 2018); my friend Ernestine

Gichner Miller's wonderful compendium, *The Babe Book: Baseball's Greatest Legend Remembered* (Guilford, Conn.: Lyons Press, 2000); and Bill Jenkinson's beautifully obsessive, meticulous, riveting *The Year Babe Ruth Hit 104 Home Runs* (New York: Carroll and Graf, 2007).

Of great use were also Daniel R. Levitt's *Ed Barrow: The Bulldog Who Built the Yankees' First Dynasty* (Lincoln: University of Nebraska Press, 2008); Robert Weintraub's *House That Ruth Built* (New York: Little, Brown, 2011); G. H. Fleming's *Murderers' Row: The 1927 New York Yankees* (New York: William Morrow, 1985); Steve Steinberg and Lyle Spatz's *Colonel and Hug: The Partnership That Transformed the New York Yankees* (Lincoln: University of Nebraska Press, 2015); and Steinberg's elegiac *Urban Shocker: Silent Hero of Baseball's Golden Age* (Lincoln: University of Nebraska Press, 2017). Mike Sowell's *Pitch That Killed* (New York: Macmillan, 1989) is the terribly sad story, terribly well told, of the death of Ray Chapman.

1929–1945
New York

So much of this era in the city can be told through the many outstanding biographies of its iconic mayor, beginning with Thomas Kessner's *Fiorello H. La Guardia and the Making of Modern New York* (New York: McGraw-Hill, 1989) and Mason B. Williams's superb *City of Ambition: FDR, La Guardia, and the Making of Modern New York* (New York: W. W. Norton, 2013). Other serious contenders include Alyn Brodsky's *Great Mayor: Fiorello La Guardia and the Making of the City of New York* (New York: Truman Talley Books, 2003); Lawrence Elliott's *Little Flower: The Life and Times of Fiorello La Guardia* (New York: William Morrow, 1983); and H. Paul Jeffers's *Napoleon of New York: Mayor Fiorello La Guardia* (New York: Wiley, 2002).

In tracing Harlem's sad but proud Great Depression, I relied on *A Renaissance in Harlem: Lost Essays of the WPA, by Ralph Ellison, Dorothy West, and Other Voices of a Generation,* ed. by Lionel C. Bascom (New York: Amistad, 1999).

Lorraine B. Diehl's *Over Here! New York City During World War II* (New York: Smithsonian Books, 2010) was simply terrific, as is everything she writes.

Baseball

Speaking of writing an era through biography, we are blessed with two about the great, enigmatic ballplayer of the period, Jonathan Eig's terrific *Luckiest Man: The Death and Life of Lou Gehrig* (New York: Simon & Schuster, 2005) and Ray Robinson's fine *Iron Horse: Lou Gehrig in His Time* (New York: HarperPerennial, 1991). On a harder note falls Richard Ben Cramer's painstakingly researched *Joe DiMaggio: The Hero's Life* (New York: Simon & Schuster, 2000). Michael Seidel's *Streak: Joe DiMaggio and the Summer of '41* (New York: McGraw-Hill, 1988) is atmospheric and a fine reference.

Ronald A. Mayer's *1937 Newark Bears: A Baseball Legend* (East Hanover, N.J.: Vintage Press, 1985) tells the story of this unique minor-league club, while Richard J. Tofel's terrifically engaging *A Legend in the Making: The New York Yankees in 1939* (Chicago: Ivan R. Dee, 2002) tells us what it all amounted to—another of the greatest teams ever.

Bums (New York: Pocket Books, 1984) may well be the finest of Peter Golenbock's many riveting oral histories—in this case the revival of the Brooklyn Dodgers, beginning in 1939 (albeit with a few explanatory pages of background about how this remarkable team could've come to exist in the first place). It makes excellent use of the voices of the Flock's incomparable fans.

When Baseball Went to War, ed. Todd Anton and Bill Newlin (Chicago: Triumph Books, 2008), is a good source for what the war years were like for baseball everywhere in the United States.

Finally, there is the very first baseball book I ever owned, one that my father bought me in 1966, in Tenafly, New Jersey. It was by John M. Rosenburg, "a Random House book for young people," and it was titled *The Story of Baseball: A Completely Illustrated and Exciting History of America's National Game.* It sure was.

Index

Illustration Credits

1 New York Knickerbockers baseball club: Corey Shanus
2 Christy Mathewson: Library of Congress
3 John Montgomery Ward: Library of Congress
3 Luther Taylor: Library of Congress
3 "Turkey Mike" Donlin: Library of Congress
3 John T. Brush: Library of Congress
4 Guy Zinn: Library of Congress
4 Jack Chesbro: Library of Congress
4 Hal Chase: Library of Congress
5 Five American League club presidents: Library of Congress
5 "Dead-heads" on Coogan's Bluff: John Thorn
6 Angry Giants fans: John Thorn
6 Hank O'Day: Library of Congress
6 Johnny "Crab" Evers: Library of Congress
7 Fred Merkle: Library of Congress
7 Bat Masterson: Library of Congress
7 Presidential golf outing: Library of Congress
8 Opening day, April 10, 1915, Washington Park: Library of Congress, Bain Collection
9 Wa-Tho-Tuk (Jim Thorpe): Library of Congress
9 Carl Mays: Library of Congress
9 Opening day, 1923, Yankee Stadium: Library of Congress
10 The Babe: Library of Congress
11 Wilbert Robinson: Library of Congress
11 Alex Pompez: RMY Auctions
12 Dyckman Oval: New York Public Library
14 Mayor Fiorello La Guardia: New York City Municipal Archives
16 Joe DiMaggio: Library of Congress

A Note About the Author

Kevin Baker is a novelist, historian, and journalist who lives in New York City with his wife, the playwright Ellen Abrams. He has been going out to the ball game since 1967, when he saw Mickey Mantle, Willie Mays, and Tom Seaver play in the same week, and has been writing about sports professionally since he was thirteen years old.

A Note on the Type

This book was set in Adobe Garamond. Designed for the Adobe Corporation by Robert Slimbach, the fonts are based on types first cut by Claude Garamond (ca. 1480–1561).

Composed by North Market Street Graphics
Lancaster, Pennsylvania

Printed and bound by Berryville Graphics
Berryville, Virginia

Designed by Michael Collica